T5-BZF-336

YALE CO-OP

4-50 2

$ 1.98

THE ROMAN ELEGIAC POETS

THE ROMAN
ELEGIAC POETS

EDITED, WITH INTRODUCTION
AND NOTES, BY

KARL POMEROY HARRINGTON

NORMAN : UNIVERSITY OF OKLAHOMA PRESS

Standard Book Number: 8061–0783–9

Library of Congress Catalog Card Number: 68–15669

Copyright 1968 by the University of Oklahoma Press, Publishing Division of the University. New edition manufactured and published at Norman, Oklahoma, U.S.A., from the original edition, copyright 1914 by Karl Pomeroy Harrington, published by the American Book Company.

PATRIS · MEMORIAE · QUI · INCEPIT · IDEMQUE
MENTEM · MEAM · AD · OPUS · PERSEQUENDUM
EXCITAVIT

PREFACE

THE need of a college textbook containing a judicious selection from the whole field of Roman elegy with suitable introductory matter and English comments has long been evidenced by the announcements of various publishers that such books were in preparation. The present edition was undertaken many years ago by my father, the plan as then conceived being somewhat less comprehensive than that which has now been worked out. At the time of his death he had already written some notes on Propertius for the contemplated book, the last words appearing in his manuscript, penned amid increasing feebleness, being, by a touching coincidence, one of his happy English versions, reading, 'Ah me! that the strain should be so feeble in my mouth!' (4, 1, 58). Such of those first-draft notes as were available have been included in this edition under the signature "(C. S.)."

The magnitude of the task has grown with the years, as the vast amount of material published in connection with the four authors from which these selections are taken has increased. Moreover, the classes in which a book of this kind will be used require in many cases a relatively advanced grade of comment; yet the linguistic basis for higher scholarship is too often in America sadly wanting, and, incongruous as it may appear, the somewhat elementary note seems to be required, side by side with one that stimulates to original research. It is with a full appreciation of the impossibility of meeting equally well all the possible varieties of demands made by the different users of the book that the editor ventures at length to give it to the public.

The arrangement of both the commentary and a carefully selected conspectus of variant textual readings on the same page with the text will, in practice, commend itself as the most practical one for the kind of classes for which the book is intended. Special effort has been made by running analysis to make the outline of the elegy clear to the student.

The text of the elegiac poets has been severely handled by editors, new and old, suffering with the ancient Athenian lust for " some new thing." To reconstruct a text to-day which should take seriously all the transpositions, divisions, combinations and smart conjectures of the German, English, and American " Athenians " of this, and the preceding, generation, would be a task from which even a modern Hercules might well shrink. Propertius, in particular, is a battle ground for the critics, and it is too much to hope that any text accepted and any views adopted about Propertius will receive unanimous approval. In advance of the complete publication of the Codex Romanus of Catullus, Professor Hale has kindly given me several important readings from his collation, and desires me in publishing them to call attention to their importance in establishing the character of R, and the age in general of such variants in G and R as were written by the first corrector of each. It has also been my privilege to make a personal examination of R and of several other important Mss. of the various authors represented in this volume. The text as now presented will show that, while conservative, it has been given the benefit of the results of recent critical ˜esearch.

By confining the selections strictly to poems written in the elegiac measure, by the choice of elegies, and by many cross-references to the four authors included, I have hoped to assist the student to obtain a general acquaintance with the development of this type of poetry at Rome. In citations from elegies printed in some part of this book, it has been thought best to refer to the passage without quoting in full.

I desire to make grateful acknowledgments to the various friends that have so kindly assisted my labors, especially to my colleague, Professor Joseph W. Hewitt, for his invaluable aid and suggestions in reading a large part of the manuscript before publication.

KARL POMEROY HARRINGTON.

WESLEYAN UNIVERSITY.

CONTENTS

8 CONTENTS

SEXTI PROPERTI ELEGIAE

BIBLIOGRAPHY

OF WORKS FREQUENTLY CITED, ARRANGED ALPHABETICALLY BY ABBREVIATIONS

A. = Allen and Greenough, New Latin Grammar, Boston, 1903.

AJA. = American Journal of Archaeology.

AJP. = American Journal of Philology.

Ald. = Catullus, et in eum commentarius M. Antonii Mureti. Ab eodem correcti, et scholiis illustrati, Tibullus, et Propertius. Venice, 1562.

Baehrens = Baehrens, Aemilius: Albii Tibulli Elegiarum Libri Duo. Accedunt Pseudo-Tibulliana, Leipzig, 1878.

Baehrens Cat. = Catulli Veronensis Liber. Recensuit Aemilius Baehrens. Vol. I, Leipzig, 1876; Vol. II, Commentarium continens, 1885; Nova editio a K. P. Schulze curata, 1893.

Baehrens PLM. = Poetae Latini Minores. Recensuit et emendavit Aemilius Baehrens, Leipzig, 1879–1883.

Baehrens Prop. = Sex. Propertii Elegiarum Libri IV. Recensuit Aemilius Baehrens, Leipzig, 1880.

Baehrens Tib. Bl. = Baehrens, Emil: Tibullische Blätter, Jena, 1876.

Baum. Denk. = Baumeister, A.: Denkmäler des klassischen Altertums, Munich and Leipzig, 1887.

Bell. = Belling, H.: Albius Tibullus, Untersuchung und Text, Berlin, 1897.

Bell. Prol. = Belling, H.: Kritische Prolegomena zu Tibull, Berlin, 1893.

B.G. = Becker, W. A.: Gallus, or Roman Scenes of the Time of Augustus, translated by Frederick Metcalfe. 7th ed., London, 1882.

BPW. = Berliner Philologische Wochenschrift.

Brandt = P. Ovidi Nasonis Amorum Libri Tres erklärt von Paul Brandt, Leipzig, 1911.

Burn, RL. and RA. = Burn, Robert: Roman Literature in Relation to Roman Art, London, 1888.

Bursian's JB. = Jahresbericht über die Fortschritte der klassischen Altertumswissenschaft, begründet von Conrad Bursian, Leipzig.

Butler = Sexti Properti Opera Omnia, with a Commentary, by H. E. Butler, London, 1905.

Cartault = Cartault, A.: Tibulle et les Auteurs du Corpus Tibullianum, Paris, 1909.

Cart. Corp. Tib. = Cartault, A.: Apropos du Corpus Tibullianum, un Siècle de Philologie Latine Classique, Paris, 1906.

Cart. Dist. El. = Cartault, A.: Le Distique Élégiaque chez Tibulle, Sulpicia, Lygdamus, Paris, 1911.

Carter = Carter, Jesse Benedict: Selections from the Roman Elegiac Poets, with Introduction and Notes, New York, 1900.

Champney = Champney, Elizabeth W.: Romance of Imperial Rome, New York, 1910.

Cranst. = Cranstoun, James: The Elegies of Albius Tibullus, translated into English verse, London, 1872.

Deutsch = Deutsch, Monroe E.: Notes on the Text of the Corpus Tibullianum, Berkeley, 1912.

Dissen = Dissennus, Ludolphus: Albii Tibulli Carmina ex recensione Car. Lachmanni passim mutata, Göttingen, 1835.

Draeger = Draeger, A.: Historische Syntax der Lateinischen Sprache, 2d ed., Leipzig, 1878.

Duff = Duff, J. W.: A Literary History of Rome, London, 1909.

Ellis, Com. = Commentary on Catullus, by Robinson Ellis, Oxford, 1876 (2d ed., 1889).

Ellis, Text = Catulli Carmina recognovit Robinson Ellis, Oxford, 1904.

Ellis, Trans. = Ellis, Robinson: The Poems and Fragments of Catullus translated in the Metres of the Original, London, 1871.

Enc. Brit. = The Encyclopaedia Britannica, 11th ed., Cambridge, 1911.

Enk = P. J. Enk: Ad Propertii Carmina Commentarius Criticus, Zutphen, 1911.

Fowler, Rom. Fest. = Fowler, W. Warde: The Roman Festivals of the Period of the Republic, London, 1899.

Friedrich = Catulli Veronensis Liber, erklärt von Gustav Friedrich, Leipzig and Berlin, 1908.

G. = Gildersleeve's Latin Grammar, 3d ed., by B. L. Gildersleeve and Gonzalez Lodge, New York, 1894.

Geikie = Geikie, Archibald: The Love of Nature among the Romans, etc., London, 1912.

Gruppe = Gruppe, Otto F.: Die römische Elegie, Leipzig, 1838.

H. = Harkness, Albert: A Complete Latin Grammar, New York, 1898.

H. & T. = Harrington, K. P., and Tolman, H. C.: Greek and Roman Mythology, Boston, 1897.

Hansen = Hansen, Marx: De Tropis et Figuris apud Tibullum, Kiel, 1881.

Haupt, Op. = Haupt, Moritz: Opuscula, edidit U. v. Wilamowitz-Moellendorff, Leipzig, 1875.

Hertzberg = Sex. Aurelii Propertii Elegiarum Libri Quattuor. Illustravit Guil. Ad. B. Hertzberg, Halle, 1843–1845.

Heyne-Wunderlich = Albii Tibulli Carmina 'Libri Tres cum libro quarto Sulpiciae et aliorum. Chr. G. Heynii editio quarta nunc aucta notis et observationibus Ern. Car. Frid. Wunderlichii, Leipzig, 1817.

Hiller = Hiller, Eduardus: Albii Tibulli Elegiae cum Carminibus Pseudo-Tibullianis, Leipzig, 1885.

Hosius = Sex. Propertii Elegiarum Libri IV. Recensuit Carolus Hosius, Leipzig, 1911.

Howe = Howe, George: Nature Similes in Catullus, in Vol. VII of Studies in Philology, Chapel Hill, N. C., 1911.

H.-V. = Catulli Tibulli Propertii Carmina a Mauricio Hauptio recognita. Editio Septima ab Iohanne Vahleno curata et a Rudolfo Helmio edita, Leipzig, 1912.

Jacoby = Jacoby, Karl: Anthologie aus den Elegikern der Römer, für den Schulgebrauch erklärt, Leipzig.

L. = Lane, G. M.: A Latin Grammar, rev. by M. H. Morgan, New York, 1903.

Lachmann = Sex. Aurelii Propertii Carmina emendavit et annotavit Carolus Lachmannus, Leipzig, 1816.

Lachmann, Cat. = Q. Valerii Catulli Veronensis Liber ex recensione Caroli Lachmanni, Berlin, 1829.

Lachmann, Prop. = Sex. Aurelii Propertii Elegiae ex recognitione Caroli Lachmanni, Berlin, 1829.

Lachmann, Tib. = Albii Tibulli Libri Quattuor ex recensione Caroli Lachmanni, Berlin, 1829.

Lamarre = Lamarre, Clovis: Histoire de la Littérature Latine, Paris, 1901.

Leo = Leo, F.: Ueber einigen Elegien Tibulls: Philologische Untersuchungen, 2tes Heft, Berlin, 1881.

LSHLG = Lindsay, W. M.: A Short Historical Latin Grammar, Oxford, 1895.

Madv. = Madvig, J. N.: A Latin Grammar for the Use of Schools, translated by Rev. George Woods. Edited by Thomas A. Thacher, Boston, 1880.

Martinengo = Martinengo-Cesaresco, Evelyn: The Outdoor Life in Greek and Roman Poets, London, 1911.

Merrill = Catullus, edited by Elmer Truesdell Merrill, Boston, 1893.

Monatsber. = Monatsberichte der Königlichen Preussischen Akademie der Wissenschaften, Berlin, 1881.

Munro = Munro, H. A. J.: Criticisms and Elucidations of Catullus, Cambridge, 1878.

Nageotte = Nageotte, E.: Histoire de la Poésie Lyrique, Paris, 1888.

Némethy = Albii Tibulli Carmina, accedunt Sulpiciae Elegidia, edidit, etc., Geyza Némethy, Budapest, 1905.

Némethy, Lyg. = Némethy, Geyza : Lygdami Carmina, Budapest, 1906.

Neue = Neue, Friedrich : Formenlehre der Lateinischen Sprache, 3te Aufl. von C. Wagener, Berlin, 1892.

Palmer = P. Ovidi Nasonis Heroides, edited by Arthur Palmer, Oxford, 1898.

PAPA. = Proceedings of the American Philological Association.

Phillimore = Sexti Properti Carmina recognovit Ioannes S. Phillimore, Oxford, 1901.

Phill. Ind. V. = Index Verborum Propertianus. Fecit Ioannes S. Phillimore, Oxford, 1905.

Pichon = Pichon, René : De Sermone Amatorio apud Latinos Elegiarum Scriptores, Paris, 1902.

Platner = Platner, Samuel Ball : The Topography and Monuments of Ancient Rome, Boston, 1904 (2d ed., 1911).

Plessis = Plessis, Frédéric : Études critiques sur Properce et ses élégies, Paris, 1884.

Plessis, Calvus = Calvus, Édition Complète des Fragments, etc., par F. Plessis, Paris, 1896.

Postgate = Postgate, J. P. : Tibulli Aliorumque Carminum libri tres, Oxford, 1905.

Postgate, Prop. = Select Elegies of Propertius, edited by J. P. Postgate, London, 1881.

Postgate, Sel. = Selections from Tibullus and others, edited by J. P. Postgate, London, 1903.

Preller³ = Preller, L. : Römische Mythologie, Dritter Auflage von H. Jordan, Berlin, 1881.

P. W. = Pauly, A. F. : Real-Encyclopaedie d. klass. Altertumswissenschaft, rev. by G. Wissowa, Stuttgart, 1894.

R. = Roby, Henry John : A Grammar of the Latin Language from Plautus to Suetonius, London, 1871–73.

Ramsay = Selections from Tibullus and Propertius, edited by George G. Ramsay, Oxford, 1900.

Riese = Die Gedichte des Catullus, herausgegeben u. erklärt von Alexander Riese, Leipzig, 1884.

Rothstein = Die Elegien des Sextus Propertius erklärt von Max Rothstein, Berlin, 1898.

Sandys = Sandys, John Edwin : A Companion to Latin Studies, Cambridge, 1910.

Schanz = Schanz, Martin : Geschichte der Römischen Litteratur, Munich, 1890–1913.

Schulze = Schulze, K. P. : Römische Elegiker : eine Auswahl aus Catull, Tibull, Properz und Ovid, für den Schulgebrauch bearbeitet, 5te Auflage, Berlin, 1910.

Schwabe = Catulli Veronensis Liber. Ludovicus Schwabius recognovit, Berlin, 1886.

Sellar = Sellar, W. Y. : Horace and the Elegiac Poets, Oxford, 1892.

Sellar³, Rep. = Sellar, W. Y. : The Roman Poets of the Republic, 3d ed., Oxford, 1905.

Shuckburgh = P. Ovidii Nasonis Heroidum Epistulae XIII, edited with notes and indices by Evelyn S. Shuckburgh, London, 1879 (2d edition reprinted, 1896).

Simpson = Select Poems of Catullus, ed. by Francis P. Simpson, London, 1879.

Sitzungsber. = Sitzungsberichte der Königlichen Preussischen Akademie der Wissenschaften zu Berlin.

Smith = The Elegies of Albius Tibullus, edited by Kirby Flower Smith, New York, 1913.

Stolz-Schmalz = Stolz, Friedrich, und Schmalz, J. H. : Lateinische Grammatik (Müller's Handbuch der klassischen Altertumswissenschaft, II, 2), 3te Aufl., Munich, 1900.

TAPA. = Transactions of the American Philological Association.

Teuffel⁵ = Teuffel, W. S. : History of Roman Literature, 5th ed., trans. by G. C. W. Warr, London, 1900.

Uhlmann = Uhlmann, Guilelmus : De Sex. Properti Genere Dicendi, Borna, 1909.

Ullman = Ullman, B. L. : The Manuscripts of Propertius, Class. Phil. VI, 3, 282–301.

Von Sybel = Von Sybel, L. : Weltgeschichte d. Kunst, Marburg, 1888.

Williams = Williams, Theodore C. : The Elegies of Tibullus, done in English Verse, Boston, 1905.

Wiss. = Wissowa, Georg : Religion und Kultus der Römer, Munich, 1902.

Wolff, de Enunt. Int. = Wolff, Oscar : De Enuntiatis Interrogativis apud Catullum, Tibullum, Propertium, Leipzig, 1886.

INTRODUCTION

ELEGY

1. In the broad sense Latin Elegy may be said to include everything in Latin written in the elegiac distich, which was a popular metrical form from the days of the Roman republic down to the later medieval epoch. But Roman elegy, in the more restricted and commonly accepted use of the term, refers to the elegiac verse of a noteworthy group of poets whose literary activity belongs chiefly to that most interesting half century of Rome preceding the Christian era, when the Republic fell and the Empire was built upon its ruins. The works of at least two or three of these elegiac poets have almost entirely disappeared. Posterity, however, has been more kind to four of them, Catullus, Tibullus, Propertius, and Ovidius (Ovid). The first and last of these did not confine their literary composition to the elegiac distich, as in all probability the second and third of the group did; but it is with elegy only that we are now concerned.

Pre-Roman Elegy

2. Like most other forms of Roman literature, elegy is deeply indebted to Greece for both its form and its content, though the origin of this type of poetry is beyond the reach of the literary historian, and most of its Greek masterpieces during the centuries succeeding such origin have long since vanished. Horace (*A. P.* 75–78) wrote : —

> *versibus impariter iunctis querimonia primum,*
> *post etiam inclusa est voti sententia compos ;*
> *quis tamen exiguos elegos emiserit auctor,*
> *grammatici certant, et adhuc sub iudice lis est.*

This case is still on the calendar, and doubtless many courts will adjourn *sine die* before an ultimate decision is rendered. Perhaps of barbarian origin, the rhythm of the pentameter was certainly used in early Ionian Asia in dirges or other songs of mournful remembrance, before the advent of the earliest writers of the elegy as a literary type. The regular accompaniment to these early songs was the flute. Possibly two parts of the verse were sung responsively by a double chorus.[1] The original names for this mournful pentameter, ἐλεγεῖον (ἔπος), ἐλεγεῖα (ἔπη), have been variously explained as derived from ἒ λέγε ἒ λέγε ἒ = 'Woe! Woe! cry woe!' (Suidas) or ἒ ἒ λέγ' ἒ ἒ λέγε (Wilamowitz); but from the beginning it was probably associated with the hexameter, either as an occasional verse after a group of hexameters, or in the form of a couplet, and the terms were in early times used also to designate this couplet, or distich. The form ἐλεγεία (ποίησις or ᾠδή) was favored later, and the Hellenistic Greeks and the Romans preferred the words ἔλεγοι and *elegi* for poems in this measure. (The form *elogium*, which appeared quite early in Latin, was reserved more especially for the sepulchral inscription or the epigram.)

3. The elegiac distich, apparently the first epodic Greek measure, became the vehicle of expression for a wide variety of poetic sentiments, varying from funeral song to erotic ecstasy. As compared with the hexameter the pentameter was considered weak (*mollis* was the Latin epithet), and the combination of the two seemed to lend itself more easily to the various emotions of the human heart, leading as an intermediate step to the more highly developed forms of lyric poetry. Archilochus (*floruit c.* 650 B.C.), to whom is attributed the invention of other poetic forms, used elegiac verse not only for funeral songs, but also to treat of warlike themes, of travel, and of the philosophy of life. The Ephesian Callinus, an older contemporary of Archilochus, employed the same metrical form for patriotic war songs. He was long credited with having invented the measure itself.

[1] Cf. P. W. 5, 2260 sqq.

Tyrtaeus likewise sang in the elegiac measure war songs to inspire the Lacedaemonians in the second Messenian war. Simonides (or Semonides) of Amorgos wrote elegies besides his iambic poems.

4. With Mimnermus of Colophon, towards the end of the seventh century B.C., an important innovation appeared. He produced not only war songs, like his predecessors, but also a book, or books, of erotic elegies, celebrating his love for a beautiful flute-playing girl named Nanno. Himself a flute player too, he expresses subjectively the sympathetic passion of the lover, and mourns over the swift passing of youth and its ardent feelings. That this book, which he called *Nanno* after his darling, occupied a prominent place as a prototype of Roman elegy in general, and of Propertius and his Cynthia book in particular, cannot be doubted.[1]

5. From this time to the end of the great period of Greek literature elegy was popular and treated a great variety of topics. Many leaders in public life as well as in literature wrote elegy. Solon, the famous lawgiver of Athens (*c.* 638–559), wrote of political and ethical subjects, as well as of youthful joys and loves. Demosthenes in his speech on the false embassy had part of an elegy of Solon read to the court in support of his plea. This ethical, or gnomic, elegy is represented also by the rivals, Phocylides of Miletus and Demodocus of Leros, in the sixth century, and by Theognis of Megara, the only one of all these early Greek elegists whose works have survived to our time in anything like completeness. Theognis belonged to the latter half of this century, and suffered many political vicissitudes. There was an elegy of his (not extant) upon the citizens of Syracuse who were saved in the siege ; and we have, attributed to him, a collection of wise sayings in two books, including many elegies addressed to special friends, such as Simonides, Clearistus, and Damocles, and especially to his dear young friend

[1] Cf. Prop. I, 9, 11; Wilamowitz in *Sitzungsberichte d. Kgl. Pr. Akad. d. Wiss.* 1912, pp. 100 sqq. (reprint with additions in *Sappho u. Simonides*, Berlin, 1913).

ROM. EL. POETS — 2

Cyrnus. In many cases at least they appear to have been first intended to be sung at banquets, and were only later prepared for the reading public without musical accompaniment. Antimachus, Dionysius Chalcus, two elegists named Euenus, of Paros, and Critias, one of the thirty tyrants, are among the many names of elegists during this period, while Plato and Aristotle dabbled in elegy much as Cicero did in hexameters, and Pliny in erotic verse.

6. Simonides of Ceos (556–468 B.C.), the gifted poet whose talent expressed itself in so many forms, did not neglect the patriotic idea, composing elegiac verses on the victories of Marathon, Salamis, and Plataea. But by his excellence in threnetic elegy, including certain famous epigrams, he did much to recall the original mournful character of the measure and thus to maintain the tradition concerning its nature which has survived to modern times in the significance of the term " elegy."[1] Finally, Antimachus of Colophon, who flourished about 400 B.C., paved the way for the Alexandrian school of elegy by his learned manner. This appeared indeed in his epic *Thebais*, but was especially noteworthy in the elaborate elegy in which he undertook to console himself for the death of his darling Lyde by telling in rather wearisome detail of the unhappy loves of mythology, thus creating the objective erotic type, as contrasted with the subjective type introduced by Mimnermus.

7. Among the famous group of scholars and men of letters who flourished in the Alexandrian epoch elegy and elegiac epigram were the most highly favored and developed forms of poetry. The prevalent type was erotic. Learning, elaboration, and technique, rather than invention or emotion, characterized the Alexandrian school, thus determining to an important degree elements that were to be prominent in the Roman elegy, whose immediate model it was to become. The two names that stand

[1] Cf. Hor. *Car.* 2, 1, 38: *Ceae retractes munera neniae*; Cat. 38, 8: *maestius lacrimis Simonideis*; though both these citations probably refer more especially to the lyric threnodies of Simonides. Cf. Nageotte, Vol. 2, p. 132.

out as foremost, at least in the esteem of posterity, among the Alexandrians are Callimachus and Philetas.[1] It is clear, however, that several other representatives of the Alexandrian school had a direct and important influence upon Roman elegy.

8. It was Philetas of Cos, the renowned teacher of Ptolemy II, as well as of Theocritus and Zenodotus, of whom it was told that in his devotion to study he became so thin that he was obliged to wear lead in his shoes to prevent the wind from blowing him away! Yet he found time to compose merry erotic elegies (παίγνια) and thus to immortalize the name of his wife, or mistress, Bittis.[2] Hermesianax of Colophon, pupil and friend of Philetas, wrote three books of elegies, chiefly about his darling Leontion. Phanocles handled the theme of love for beautiful boys, illustrating from the legends of gods and heroes. Euphorion, born in Euboean Chalcis (*c.* 275 B.C.), and after living long at Athens transplanted to Alexandria to care for the famous library, although a peculiarly ugly personality in character as well as in figure, wrote voluminously in elegy as well as in other fields of poetry. It was he whose elegies Gallus translated into Latin.

9. Callimachus (*c.* 310–240 B.C.), the most celebrated name in the Alexandrian group, came from the Dorian colony of Cyrene, and after studying at Athens and teaching grammar at Eleusis, a suburb of Alexandria, was put in charge of the great library of the Ptolemies. He is said to have left behind him eight hundred books to testify of his learning and his poetic skill. His elegies are the most famous of the poetical works, and the most noted of them was the *Aitia*, in four books, dealing with the origins of cities, games, religious forms, and other phenomena. The extant fragments of his works include some

[1] Or Philitas, cf. Crönert in *Hermes*, 37 (1902), p. 212; Bechtel in *Genethliakon C. Robert Ueberreicht*, p. 73; Wilamowitz in *Sitzungsberichte d. Kgl. Pr. Akad. d. Wiss.* 1912, p. 110. Cf. Quint. 10, 1, 58: *cuius [elegiae] princeps habetur Callimachus, secundas confessione plurimorum Philetas occupavit;* Prop. 3, 1, 1; Ovid, *A.A.* 3, 329: *sit tibi Callimachi, sit Coi nota poetae,* etc.

[2] Ovid, *Trist.* 1, 6, 1: *nec tantum Clario Lyde dilecta poetae, nec tantum Coo Bittis amata suo est ; Ex P.* 3, 1, 57: *non inferius Coa Bittide nomen habes.*

excellent epigrams and hymns. The character of the satirical poem *Ibis* is revealed in Ovid's imitation; and the *Berenice's Hair* is known to us through the translation of Catullus (No. 66). The *Aitia* furnished the model for the aetiological elegies of Propertius, who was otherwise deeply indebted to him, and often refers to him as his direct pattern.[1] As a fine example of the *doctus poeta*, Callimachus was duly appreciated even by his Roman imitators.[2]

10. Among the many other Alexandrian elegists may be mentioned Alexander the Aetolian, Poseidippus, and numerous epigrammatists, including Theocritus, some of whose epigrams have survived to our day. Of peculiar interest is Parthenius of Nicaea, brought to Rome in B.C. 73 as a prisoner taken in the war with Mithridates. That he had been a close student of the Alexandrian poets is evidenced by his frequent references to them as his authorities. For his friend the promising elegist Cornelius Gallus he collected Ἐρωτικὰ Παθήματα (*The Misfortunes of Love*) in prose. This tendency towards the tragic thus appearing even in erotic literature is seen also in the threnetic elegy which he seems especially to have affected. In Naples he was the teacher of Vergil, and the pseudo-Vergilian *Moretum* was an imitation of his Μυττωτός, as the *Ciris* was of one of his *Metamorphoses*.

Roman Elegy

11. Incalculable as is the debt of Roman elegy to Greek elegy, especially that of the Alexandrian school, as well as to Greek comedy and other forms of Greek literature, it must not be supposed that the Roman elegists were merely slavish imitators, lacking individual genius and invention. Rather must it be acknowledged by candid critics that Roman elegy developed into an independent product, covering its own field in its own way, and becoming one of the most successful and justly ap-

---

[1] *E. g.* 3, 1, 1; 9, 43; 4, 1, 64: *Umbria Romani patria Callimachi.*
[2] Cf. Ovid, *Am.* 1, 15, 14: *quamvis ingenio non valet, arte valet.*

preciated varieties of Roman literature. That this was not as
well appreciated by contemporary Romans themselves as by
posterity is not a unique literary phenomenon. We must beware
of accepting as the sober judgment of to-day the derogatory
remarks of the Romans about their own literature, or the scoffs
that authors then threw at their rivals. Cicero may, indeed,
when it happens to suit his argument, say, *doctrina Graecia nos et
omni litterarum genere superabat.*[1] Vergil may in his great epic
conciliate all literary parties by giving them severally their meed
of praise.[2] Horace may sneer at the Roman disregard of poetic
form and charge his own generation with prefering money to
culture. But similar pessimism is familiar in every day. What
poets and novelists have been rightly valued in their own time?
Who recognized Shakespeare as the dramatist of the world
while Shakespeare was still treading the boards? Who, when
Milton was alive, believed *Paradise Lost* to be our great English
epic? How many of the contemporaries of Dante supposed that
his name would be that around which would circle the whole
idea of Italian literature? Who listened to Edmund Burke's
speeches? Circumstances were unfavorable to the normal
development of originality in Roman literature; but in satire,
in the epistle, in didactic poetry, and in other branches of
literature the Romans worked out matchless types of their own.
In elegy, too, theirs was a master product, which surpassed its
pattern and achieved a style and beauty all its own. The
subjectivity of genuine personal feeling is ultimately happily
wedded to the objective learning of Alexandria, and the Roman
atmosphere pervades the whole. As Wilamowitz[3] says: ' The
Roman poets of the brief golden age . . . sucked the finest
education of taste from the greatest variety of flowers; but what
they produced was a honey of their own. . . . So Propertius
and Tibullus became creators of a new elegy.' By the end of
the first Christian century this began to be realized even at

---

[1] *Tusc. Disp.* I, I, I.   [2] *Aen.* 6, 847 sqq.
[3] *Sitzungsberichte d. Kgl. Pr. Akad. d. Wiss.* 1912, p. 122.

Rome, as is tersely stated by the foremost critic of the age, Quintilian: *Elegia quoque Graecos provocamus.*[1]

12. It is more than probable that Ennius, whose place as the father of Roman poetry has not been disputed for two millenniums, was responsible for the introduction into Latin of the elegiac distich as well as the heroic hexameter. The three well-known epigrams included among the fragments of his poetry, however, are the only indications left to us of his activity in the field of elegy; and it may be assumed that with elegy of the Alexandrian type he did not concern himself. Lucilius used the elegiac distich in some of his satires. There are also traces of the growth in popularity of the erotic epigram of Alexandrian form, with which such well-known men as Valerius Aedituus, Porcius Licinus, and Q. Lutatius Catulus amused themselves.[2] Had we, further, the erotic poems of Quinctius Atta, Laevius, Valerius Cato, and Ticidas, we might discover in them a very considerable body of relatively early attempts in elegiac form, whereas at present we know little of the metrical form in which their merry trifling was cast. How pervasive was the tradition that serious minds might well relax in this manner is curiously shown by Pliny the younger in his apology for his own course,[3] where he quotes as his examples many eminent names from Cicero to Verginius Rufus and the Caesars. And though Catullus is the oldest Roman elegiac writer whose works have survived, there was a very interesting group of poets of his own generation who tried their hand at this literary novelty, the loss of whose elegies we must deeply regret as depriving us of important evidence with regard to the rise and development of this type of poetry at Rome. Varro Atacinus (82–37 B.C.), whose tastes seem to have been well fitted for his

---

[1] *Inst. Or.* 10, 1, 93.

[2] Gell. 19, 9, 10 : *versus cecinit Valeri Aeditui veteris poetae, item Porcii Licini et Q. Catuli quibus mundius, venustius, limatius, tersius, Graecum Latinumve nihil quicquam reperiri puto.*

[3] *Ep.* 5, 3, 5.

tasks, adapted a number of the learned epic and didactic poems of the Alexandrian school, and also elegies of the erotic type.[1]

C. Licinius Macer Calvus (82–47 B.C.), the intimate friend of Catullus, excelled as orator and poet, and the playful rivalry of the two boon companions in composing light poetry has been celebrated by Catullus himself (No. 50). Yet through the pranks of fortune his verses have been reduced practically to the vanishing point. For the fragments see Plessis, *Calvus*. Like Catullus, he wrote erotic elegies, epigrams, and at least one famous lament, on the death of his wife, or mistress, Quintilia.[2] C. Valgius Rufus (consul suffectus, 12 B.C.), the friend of Horace, bewailed, presumably in elegiac form, the death of his favorite slave boy Mystes.[3]

More important than all of these was C. Cornelius Gallus (69–26 B.C.), recognized by the other elegists and by other literary critics as properly belonging to the small group of leading writers in this field.[4] Born in Gallia Narbonensis, at Forum Iulii (*Frejus*), he achieved at a comparatively early age an enviable position in the military and social life of Rome

[1] Quint. 10, 1, 87: *Atacinus Varro in iis per quae nomen est assecutus interpres operis alieni non spernendus quidem;* Ovid, *Trist.* 2, 439: *is quoque Phasiacas Argon qui duxit in undas, non potuit Veneris furta tacere suae;* Prop. 2, 34, 85: *haec quoque perfecto ludebat Iasone Varro.*

[2] Ovid, *Trist.* 2, 431: *par fuit exigui similisque licentia Calvi, detexit variis qui sua furta modis;* Prop. 2, 34, 89: *haec etiam docti confessa est pagina Calvi, cum caneret miserae funera Quintiliae;* 2, 25, 3: *ista meis fiet notissima forma libellis, Calve tua venia, pace Catullus tua;* Suet. *Iulius Caesar*, 73; Cat. 96; 14.

[3] Hor. *Car.* 2, 9, 9: *tu semper urges flebilibus modis Mysten ademptum;* cf. Tib. 4, 1, 179: *est tibi, qui possit magnis se accingere rebus, Valgius: aeterno propior non alter Homero;* Serv. on Verg. *Ec.* 7, 22: *ut Valgius in elegiis suis refert.*

[4] Ovid, *Trist.* 4, 10, 53: *successor fuit hic tibi, Galle, Propertius illi; quartus uò his serie temporis ipse fui;* 5, 1, 17: *aptior huic Gallus blandique Propertius oris aptior, ingenium mite, Tibullus erit;* *A. A.* 3, 333: *et teneri possis carmen legisse Properti, sive aliquid Galli, sive, Tibulle, tuum;* *Am.* 3, 9, 63; Quint. 10, 1, 93: *Elegia quoque Graecos provocamus, cuius mihi tersus atque elegans maxime videtur auctor Tibullus; sunt qui Propertium malint. Ovidius utroque lascivior, sicut durior Gallus.* That this epithet must refer to verse construction rather than lack of sentiment is clear from Ovid, *Rem. Am.* 765: *quis poterit lecto durus discedere Gallo?*

through his abilities and his personal qualities as a friend.
Under the favor of Augustus he was appointed the first prefect
of Egypt in 30 B.C. Besides the intimacy with the emperor
he enjoyed also that with other leaders in the literary life of
his day, like Asinius Pollio and Vergil, whose tenth Eclogue
is a condolence with Gallus for his unhappy love affairs.[1]
Tradition also has it — though its authenticity is seriously
questioned — that the fourth Georgic originally ended with a
glorification of the services of Gallus in Egypt, which
Vergil felt obliged to remove after the fall of the brilliant prefect, and then substituted the less relevant story of Aristaeus.
Too great prosperity apparently turned the head of Gallus, and
led him to such presumption that the growing disfavor of
Augustus, fostered probably by jealous rivals, was followed by a
decree of banishment. Gallus, unable to endure the disgrace,
promptly committed suicide. Besides certain translations from
Euphorion he wrote four books of elegies on Lycoris, a pseudonym, after the manner of the age, for his beloved Cytheris, a
celebrated actress whose name was coupled also with that of Mark
Antony.[2] To what extent, if any, the "*durior*" style of his
elegies may have contributed to their total loss it is impossible
for us to surmise. The direct influence of Greek elegy upon
his work, through the friendship of Parthenius, has been mentioned already (§ 10). For the various other names connected
more or less closely with elegy, see the works on Roman literature by Teuffel, Schanz, Duff, etc. The prevailing character of
all this body of literature is indicated by the expression of Tacitus,[3]
elegorum lascivias.

[1] Cf. *Ec.* 6, 64.

[2] Ovid, *Trist.* 2, 445: *non fuit opprobrio celebrasse Lycorida Gallo, sed linguam
nimio non tenuisse mero ; A. A.* 3, 536: *nomen habet Nemesis, Cynthia nomen habet:
vesper et eoae novere Lycorida terrae;* Prop. 2, 34, 91: *et modo formosa quam
multa Lycoride Gallus mortuus inferna vulnera lavit aqua !* The fascinating story
of Becker's *Gallus* is based throughout on classical authority, and is unsurpassed
as giving a word picture of life at Rome in this circle of society under Augustus.

[3] *Dial.* 10, 5.

CATULLUS

13. The first Roman elegist whose works have endured to our own time was C. Valerius Catullus, a member of the new group of poets who were doing so much to establish an Alexandrian school of poetry at Rome. He was born at Verona, the unsatisfactory evidence leaving it uncertain whether the date was 87 or 84 B.C. As there are no indications that any of his poems were written later than 54 B.C., and all signs point to his early death, this date is commonly assumed as correct for that event. His family and circumstances were such that his father entertained Julius Caesar, the governor of the province, and he himself possessed country estates at Sirmio on the shores of the Lacus Benacus, and at or near Tibur, the most aristocratic of Rome's suburban resorts.[1] He was able, after enjoying in boyhood such educational privileges as Verona afforded, to seek as a youth in Rome a wider acquaintance with the rather giddy life of the metropolis in that period of political and social unrest and extravagance, which bred a Caesar, a Catiline, and a Mamurra. His studies and tastes were fostered under the instruction of the well-known grammarian Valerius Cato (cf. § 12), where he became associated with the literary group comprising Helvius Cinna, Licinius Calvus, Furius Bibaculus, Ticidas, and other well-known poets representing the newer tendencies of the day. With an ardent and impulsive nature and the enthusiasm of young manhood he threw himself impetuously into his poetic studies and his social privileges alike. " The giddy round of his life is reflected in the constantly altering atmosphere of his poems. Whispered scandals, nameless vices, the gay girls of Pompey's portico, Caesar's minions, Egnatius, like Dickens's Mr. Carker showing his white teeth in everlasting smiles, the Roman cockney so suitably named Arrius to admit of his superfluous aspirates, doltish husbands with pretty wives, pilfering

1 *Carmina*, 31 and 44.

guests, faithful and faithless friends, make a vivid register of human nature in the great capital."[1]

14. It was in this gay complex of life at Rome that he met his fate in the person who was within a few brief years largely to ruin his life and happiness and to win him undying fame through the verses she drove him to write. There is no longer any question that this wonderful woman — amazing in her powers for both good and ill — for whom the poet's significant pseudonym is Lesbia, was the famous and unscrupulous belle of Rome in her day, Clodia, sister of P. Clodius Pulcher, and wife of Q. Metellus Celer.[2] The number and rank of her lovers (Catullus in a moment of petulance calls them 'three hundred!') and the epithets *Medea Palatina*, βοῶπις, and *quadrantaria*, as well as the terrible implication of Catullus's own epigram,[3] when taken together with the revelation of her as a captivating charmer and well-educated lady of high birth which is seen in the poems of her young poet adorer, show how appropriate the name Lesbia was for such an embodiment of luxuriant physical and intellectual development. With a poetic appreciation worthy of the Lesbian Sappho, she was naturally flattered by the devotion of the brilliant and passionate young poet, and with her greater sophistication led him for a time to believe that he was her only idol.[4] The process of disillusioning which must needs soon begin was a bitter one, and the successive phases of his love, suspicion, jealousy, hatred, and ultimate disgust, are perfectly mirrored in the frank utterances of this most transparent of poets.[5]

15. Desire to escape from an almost intolerable situation and

---

[1] Duff, p. 313.

[2] Ovid, *Trist.* 2, 427: *sic sua lascivo cantata est saepe Catullo femina, cui falsum Lesbia nomen erat;* Apul. *Apol.* 10: *accusent C. Catullum, quod Lesbiam pro Clodia nominarit, et Ticidam similiter, quod, quae Metella erat, Perillam scripserit, et Propertium, qui Cynthiam dicat, Hostiam dissimulet et Tibullum, quod ei sit Plania in animo, Delia in versu.*

[3] 79, 1: *Lesbius est pulcher: quid ni? quem Lesbia malit quam te cum tota gente, Catulle, tua.*

[4] Cf. No. 72.   [5] Cf. Sellar[3], *Rep.*, pp. 413 sq.

a wish to offer the last tokens of respect and affection at the tomb of his brother, who had died and been buried in the Troad, were among the motives that led Catullus to seek recreation and other scenes by joining Cinna as a member of the staff of C. Memmius,[1] who in 57 B.C. went to Bithynia as propraetor. Restive and sad as he was, we cannot think that he waited a whole year more to perform the mournful rites at his brother's grave, but must believe that he visited this spot and took his farewell of it on the outward journey to Bithynia. Even if we discount the violent expressions of disgust for his chief, found in Nos. 10 and 28 of the Catullus collection, it is clear that Memmius was no help or inspiration to Catullus. Yet the year's travel and novel experiences, including some contact with Greek, as well as even more eastern civilization, did not fail to leave its mark upon the impressionable poet: his " Peleus and Thetis " and his remarkable " Attis," *e.g.*, probably owe much local color, and perhaps even their very existence, to this sojourn.

The two years, more or less, that remained for Catullus after his joyous home-coming were spent partly in Verona and his favorite Sirmio, and partly in Rome. They were years of storm and stress. There were new alliances with men and women ; old hatreds were reopened. The growing power of Caesar and his favorites was attacked with intense bitterness ; but a reconciliation with Caesar as the friend of Catullus's father was not long in forthcoming. Clodia thought it worth her while to make advances toward a renewal of relations with one whose fortunes seemed in the ascendant, but the heart of the poet was utterly steeled against her forever. Very soon the career, all too short, of one for whom the best in life seemed perhaps just about to open, came to an end, with only a verse or two to indicate final weakness and gathering gloom before the lamp went out.

[1] Probably the same Memmius to whom Lucretius, the other great poet of this age, dedicated his *De Rerum Natura ;* cf. Lucr. 1, 26 and 42.

16. Although Ovid does not include Catullus in his well-known canon of the Roman elegists,[1] he elsewhere recognizes him as belonging to the same group[2] and Propertius[3] names as his series of erotic elegists, Varro Atacinus, Catullus, Calvus, Gallus, and himself.[4] If there was any reason why his contemporaries should omit Catullus from any list of the leading Roman elegists, it was doubtless because even thus early it was realized that it was the rest of his poems rather than his elegies that formed his surest title to immortality.   But the evidence is clearly ample that even then he belonged to the group in which the logic of fate has confirmed his membership, and that not mere accident has from the time of the renaissance produced successive editions of Catullus, Tibullus, and Propertius.   If in the more exact use of terms Catullus is a greater lyric than elegiac poet, nevertheless the elegies that he has left us form an invaluable link between the poetry of Alexandria and that of Tibullus and Propertius.   Something of the debt owed him directly by his successors in the field of elegy will be seen from a study of the selections in this book.   The genius of Horace led him mostly in other lines, so that his literary connection with Catullus is relatively slight.   Vergil, on the other hand, had evidently been a careful student of Catullus, as is clear not merely from those disputed poems of the so-called *Appendix Vergiliana*, but from many parallels in his certainly authentic works.[5]   And in Martial reminiscences of Catullus abound.

On the other hand, the influence of the Alexandrian school is

[1] *Successor fuit hic* [*Tibullus*] *tibi, Galle, Propertius illi ; quartus ab his serie temporis ipse fui.* — *Trist.* 4, 10, 53.

[2] E.g. *Am.* 3, 9, 59–65; *Trist.* 2, 427 sqq.

[3] 2, 34, 85 sqq.

[4] Propertius nowhere names Tibullus, though he surely owed much to him.   Cf. also Mart. 8, 73, 8, where Catullus is grouped with Gallus, Tibullus, Propertius, and Ovid.

[5] Cf. E. K. Rand, in *Harvard Stud. in Class. Phil.*, Vol. 17 (1906), pp. 15 sqq. For a list of real or assumed parallel passages in the Augustan poets cf. Simpson, pp. xxxvii sqq.   For a list of authors that mention or cite Catullus, cf. Schwabe, pp. vii sqq.

nowhere so definite and obvious in Roman poetry as in Catullus. The mere fact that of the 116 poems in the extant Catullus collection, nearly one half (Nos. 65–116) are in the elegiac meter is unique in a poet of essentially lyric tastes and genius. The forms of his measure constantly betray Alexandrian influence (cf. §§ 42, 43). Not merely the considerable proportion of epigrams and the subjects of various elegies but also the wealth of mythological learning displayed in such poems as No. 68 show that even in treating a matter of deep personal interest he at that period of his work believed it necessary to assume the Alexandrian manner. And finally the translation of the *Coma Berenices* of Callimachus (No. 66) brings us straight back to Alexandria as no other existing poem in Latin does. In some of those elegies we have a young poet trying his hand at the new style of verse just imported; while in the later elegists, even in Propertius, the influence of their models is much more artfully concealed, if indeed it is ever as direct. This is not the place to discuss the first 60 (shorter) poems of the Catullus collection, in various meters, or the group of four longer poems (61–64) — the two epithalamia, the " Attis " and the epyllion of Peleus and Thetis, which precede the elegies in the existing collection.

17. " Other Roman poets have produced works of more elaborate composition, and have shown themselves greater interpreters of nature and of human life: none have expressed so directly and truthfully the great elemental affections, or have uttered with such vital sincerity the happiness or the pain of the passing hour." [1] The fire of youth burned into furious love or furious hate, according to the fuel of the hour. Whether he admires a beautiful lake or a beautiful woman, or hates a vulgar society villain, the language of Catullus is that of absolute frankness — a frankness sometimes too complete for our tastes, yet compelling by its perfect revelation of every mood and tense of the writer. It is therefore natural that in the instrument of

1 Sellar [3], *Rep.*, p. 436.

such expression we find less artificial refinement in versification, a closer approximation to the language of everyday life, and a simplicity of expression that makes his language usually as transparent as his thought. The diction of Catullus has been analyzed by Simpson,[1] who shows the prominent elements in it to be the language of everyday life and of society, a well-developed lover's vocabulary, a remarkable mastery over diminutives with their varying shades of meaning,[2] some archaisms and contracted forms, some new descriptive terms coined with a poet's facility, and an abundance of inceptive, frequentative, and prepositionally-compounded verbs.[3] Some of these features are, however, better illustrated elsewhere than in the elegies.[4] While most of the familiar grammatical and rhetorical figures are amply illustrated in Catullus, his skill in the employment of simile, metaphor, and metonymy is especially noteworthy.[5]

18. Since Lachmann in 1829 brought out his epoch-making edition of Catullus, basing it upon two Berlin Mss., the Datanus (D) and the Laurentianus (L), both of the fifteenth century, great progress has been made in establishing the text of this author. In 1830 the Sangermanensis (G), No. 14137 of the National Library at Paris, written at Verona in 1375, was described by J. Sillig;[6] and in 1867 Robinson Ellis published the Oxoniensis (O), No. 30 of the Canonici Latin Mss. of the Bodleian Library. In 1896 W. G. Hale discovered the Romanus (R) in the Vatican (Cod. Ottob. 1829), a Ms. which he believes to be of about the same age as G and O, viz., the latter part of the fourteenth century.[7] A complete collation of R has not yet been published. Meanwhile the controversy that has arisen over the relative value of these various important Mss. and their relation to a lost archetype and to the host of

---

[1] Pp. 180 sqq.   [2] Cf. Platner in *AJP.*, Vol. 16 (1895), p. 186.
[3] *Index verborum* in Schwabe.   [4] Cf. Riese, pp. xxiv sqq.
[5] Cf. *e.g.* No. 68, vv. 53, 57, 63, 73, 109, 119, 125.
[6] *Jahrb. f. Phil.*, Vol. 13 (1830), pp. 261 sqq.
[7] Cf. *PAPA.*, Vol. 28 (1897), p. liii; *Class. Rev.*, Vol. 20 (1906), p. 160; Magnus in *BPW.*, Vol. 30 (1910), p. 780; etc.

later copies from one source or another, has resulted in more diligent search for Catullus Mss.[1]

The result up to the present appears to be that our text must be constituted chiefly on the three Mss., O G R, which are all derived from a lost Ms., V (Veronensis), which was seen by Petrarch and other scholars of his day; and that all the other existing Mss. were derived from these. O may have been a direct copy of V; G and R were copied probably from an intervening copy of V.

19. Besides the editions of Lachmann (1829) and Ellis (1867 and 1878) before mentioned, the most important editions in modern times have been those of Haupt (1853) (published with Tibullus and Propertius, and several times revised by Vahlen — 7th ed., 1912), Schwabe (1866 and 1886), Baehrens (1876; revised by K. P. Schulze, 1893), Riese (1884), Merrill (1893), the large commentary of Ellis (1876) and his later Oxford text (1904), and Friedrich (1908). The editions of Baehrens, Schulze, Riese, Merrill, and Friedrich have full exegetical commentaries. Several of the most important elegies are annotated in the selections made by Simpson, Jacoby, Schulze, and others; and the critical and epexegetical activity still centered upon Catullus remains unabated. The translations by Martin (1861), Ellis (1871), and Cornish (1912) deserve mention.

TIBULLUS

20. Although at first sight it would seem that we have a considerable body of valuable data for the life of Tibullus, careful sifting of the authorities makes these sources appear rather sterile. At the end of the Mss. is a brief epigram attributed to Domitius Marsus, as follows : —

> *Te quoque Vergilio comitem non aequa, Tibulle,*
> *mors iuvenem campos misit ad Elysios,*
> *ne foret, aut elegis molles qui fleret amores*
> *aut caneret forti regia bella pede.*

[1] Cf *Class. Phil.*, Vol. 3 (1908), p 233.

The Mss. also include a short *vita*, which has been uncon-
vincingly attributed to Suetonius.[1] The text of this *vita* is
plainly corrupt,[2] and some of its statements are hardly intel-
ligible (e.g. *eques regalis*), and others quite unsatisfactory
(e.g. *militaribus donis donatus est*, which is out of harmony
with the character of the poet, so far as revealed in his
elegies). Perhaps some of the statements were invented from
the elegies.[3] Both the epigram and the *vita* are believed
to have been in the archetype of our Mss.[4] A longer *vita*[5] is
evidently the work of a comparatively late hand and has little
worth. The testimony of classical writers, especially Ovid, to
certain features of the life, work, and character of Tibullus, is
important so far as it goes.[6] Even more valuable than all these
are the few allusions to his life found in the poet's own writings.

21. From a judicious use of this material it is safe to draw
the following conclusions. The poet's name was Albius Tibullus,
no praenomen being known.[7] The end of his life came at about
the same time as that of Vergil, who died, we know, September
21, 19 B.C.[8] As the only definite statement that could be used to
determine the date of his birth (3, 5, 17) evidently applies not to
Tibullus himself, but to Lygdamus (cf. § 25), we are forced to
resort to conjecture, which has commonly accepted 54 B.C. as a
probable approximation to the truth. The editor's reasons for
believing this too early (as given in *PAPA.*, Vol. 32 (1901),
pp. cxxxvii–cxxxviii) are that it would make Tibullus relatively
too old a man while he was engaged in writing elegies; that he
would have been likely to go on an expedition like the Aquitanian campaign (31 B.C.) soon after assuming the manly toga,

1 Baehrens, *Tib. Bl.*, p. 6.

2 For two forms of it cf. Baehrens, *Tib. Bl.*, p. 5, and Hiller, p. 60.

3 Cf. Magnus in Bursian's *JB.*, Vol. 51 (1887), p. 340.

4 Cf. Hiller in *Hermes*, Vol. 18 (1883), pp. 349 sqq.

5 Cf. Dissen, Vol. 1, p. x.

6 The references are collected in Hiller, pp. xx–xxiv.

7 He never speaks of himself by any other name than Tibullus; cf. 1, 3, 55;
1, 9, 83 ; 4, 13, 13.

8 Cf. the epigram of Marsus, and Ovid, *Trist.* 4, 10, 51.

i.e. at about seventeen years of age, according to Roman custom; that the smallness of the amount of his poetry would be difficult to explain if he died at the age of thirty-five; and that his being confused with Lygdamus would have been more natural if he were himself more nearly of the age of Lygdamus (b. 43 B.C.). In view of these considerations 48 B.C. seems a not unreasonable conjectural date to assign for the birth of Tibullus.

22. Whether or not the statement that he was of equestrian rank is founded on fact, it is clear from various passages in his elegies that he was of respectable family, and comfortably endowed, although he had lost part of his ancestral estates, perhaps through confiscations similar to those suffered by Vergil.[1] Horace, in Epistle 1, 4, which, there seems no good reason to doubt, refers to this Albius,[2] says that the gods had blessed Tibullus with wealth, beauty, and the art of enjoying life, and indicates that his home was in the district of Pedum, which was in Latium, not very far from Praeneste. The indications also are that he lost his father quite early but was survived by his mother and a sister.[3] Much weight in determining the poet's character and station must be given to the long intimacy between Tibullus and Messalla, the orator, statesman, warrior, litterateur, and trusted councilor of Augustus. It is not clear just when Messalla began to realize the qualities of the poet and foster an acquaintance that made Tibullus the central figure of the literary group that gathered around this accomplished patron of polite letters. It is not improbable that the tastes of Tibullus led him while getting an education at Rome into close touch with Horace, among others, that the older poet introduced him to Messalla not long before the battle of Actium, and that the last elegy of the first book was written about this time. Vergil must at least have been known and admired by Tibullus.[4]

---

[1] Cf. 1, 1, 19, 41, and 77; 2, 4, 53, etc.

[2] Cf. Ullman in *AJP.*, Vol. 33 (1912), pp. 149 sqq., and the rejoinders, pp. 450 sqq.

[3] Cf. 1, 3, 5; Ovid, *Am.* 3, 9, 50.   [4] Cf. Tib. 2, 5, 39 sqq.

23. At any rate, when after Actium Messalla was sent to Aquitania by Augustus, the young poet went with him to get his first taste of military life.[1] After that brief campaign he started with Messalla for the east, but, seized with a serious illness, was necessarily left behind on the island of Corcyra, his life trembling in the balance. These circumstances furnish the occasion of the earliest elegy which we can date with any certainty (1, 3), which was accordingly written in 30 B.C., perhaps in the latter part of the summer. This ended the military experiences of the poet,[2] who returned, as soon as health permitted, to his estate in the country, there to spend, apparently, most of the rest of his life. Certainly we have no indications that he took any prominent part in public affairs, although he was doubtless ever and anon in the city on occasions of special interest.[3] His tastes were gentle, he preferred the quiet of the fields to the excitement of the city; and for the remaining ten years of his life we can easily picture him enjoying the *regio Pedana*, surrounded by a small circle of close friends, and frequently visiting his patron, Messalla, in town, where he was welcomed as the most gifted member of Messalla's select coterie.[4]

24. Prominent members of this circle of friends were Sulpicia,[5] probably a niece of Messalla and daughter of Servius Sulpicius Rufus, Cornutus, probably another member of the same Sulpician family,[6] and Macer,[7] all of whom were destined to play a part in the collection of elegies bearing the name of Tibullus. But a far more important influence in determining the character of his poetry was exerted by the several persons, probably all of a lower rank, for whom he formed successive

---

[1] There is still controversy over the date of the Aquitanian Expedition; for a review of the case cf. Hiller in *BPW.*, Vol. 8 (1888), Sp. 808; R. Schultz, *Quaestiones in Tibulli Librum I.Chronologicae*, pp. 7 sqq.

[2] For another view cf. Bell., pp. 181 sqq.

[3] Cf. 1, 7; 2, 5.

[4] For charming fancy pictures of his home life at Pedum, cf. Martinengo, pp. 144 sqq.; Champney, Chap. I.

[5] Cf. 4, 2.   [6] Cf. 2, 2, Intr.   [7] Cf. 2, 6, 1, n.

attachments. The first of these, upon whom he lavished his fresh poetic vows of undying affection, was a lady named Plania (cf. § 14), whom Tibullus called Delia, doubtless because δῆλος = *planus*, and at the same time suggests her qualities as an inspirer of poetry, from the divine pair born at Delos. Delia's standing is somewhat obscure. She was hardly a patrician, although the suggestion has been made that she was identical with Sulpicia.[1] Neither is it clear that she was a *libertina*. Probably a plebeian, she seems to have occupied a dubious position. She had a mother living.[2] Either this mother or some other chaperon is characterized as *anus*[3] and again as *lena*.[4] We hear also of a *coniunx*,[5] but in exactly what sense the word is used is not easy to decide. For several years, beginning about the time when he first went away to the wars, Tibullus was her devoted, but not very successful, lover; and her figure dominates the first book of the elegies. To divert his attention from her fickleness the poet was for a short period deeply interested in a pretty boy whom he calls Marathus, and who corresponds to the Juventius whom Catullus has made famous. A second lady love was called by the significant name of Nemesis, though in exactly what sense she was to Tibullus as an avenging goddess is open to question. Certain it is that his passionate love for her met with but a poor response. Moreover, she was avaricious, and another *lena* appears as her guardian.[6] This attachment did not last as long as that to Delia, and the poet probably lived to publish his second book, of which she is the central theme, before his sorrows and his frail constitution brought him to an early death. The Glycera mentioned by Horace (*Car.* 1, 33) as faithless to Albius may be set down as another flame of Tibullus, as she cannot be identified with either Delia or Nemesis.

25. Besides the Delia book and the Nemesis book, the Tibullus collection as it has been handed down to us contains,

[1] Champney, Chap. I.
[2] 1, 6, 57.
[3] 1, 3, 84.
[4] 1, 5, 48.
[5] 1, 2, 41.
[6] Cf. 2, 6, 44.

in addition to a hexameter panegyric on Messalla, a number of other elegies, some of which are evidently not the work of Tibullus, while controversy as to the authorship of the rest has not ceased to rage.   For convenience this group of poems has long since been divided into a third and fourth book of the Tibullus collection, an arrangement which practical considerations have led the present editor to maintain.   The third book is evidently the work of an unknown poet who calls himself Lygdamus, and who sings especially of his love for a Neaera. While critics are pretty generally agreed[1] that the work of Lygdamus is in manner, meter, and thought inferior to the genuine work of Tibullus,[2] a wide diversity of views has been expressed with regard to the personality of the author.   Plessis thinks he was the older brother of Ovid, while their somewhat trifling and cold-blooded manner suggests even the possibility that these poems might have been a youthful work of Ovid himself.   The many parallels between Lygdamus and Ovid in language might be taken in confirmation of this hypothesis,[3] and especially the identity of statement as regards the birth of the two occurring in Tib. 3, 5, 18, and Ovid, *Trist.* 4, 10, 6 : *cum cecidit fato consul uterque pari*, referring to the death of both Hirtius and Pansa in battle in 43 B.C.[4]   But Propertius also has many parallels with both Tibullus and Ovid,[5] and this line of argument is inconclusive.   Lygdamus may have imitated Ovid, or Ovid have copied Lygdamus, or both have used a common original.   Several other interesting identifications have been suggested.[6]   The question as to whether Lygdamus lived

---

[1] Cf. Dissen, Vol. 2, p. 324 ; Postgate, *Sel.*, pp. xliii sqq.

[2] For a contrary view cf. Cranstoun, p. xxi.

[3] Cf. Hiller in *Hermes*, Vol. 18 (1883), p. 356, who believes Lygdamus to have been a contemporary of Ovid and to have added 3, 5, 15–20 at a later time to his own elegy.

[4] Cf. Gruppe, pp. 127–143; Kleemann: *De libri tertii carminibus quae Tibulli nomine circumferuntur.*

[5] Cf. Bürger in *Hermes*, Vol. 40 (1905), pp. 321 sqq.

[6] Cf. Magnus in Bursian's *JB.*, Vol. 51 (1887), p. 340; Lamarre, Vol. 2, pp. 482-483.

before Ovid or after him is still unsettled.[1] So is the problem
as to whether his name is a real one or a pseudonym referring
to the first name of Tibullus,[2] cunningly devised to lend countenance to the place of these elegies in the Tibullus collection.
But a most reasonable explanation of the existing Tibullus collection would appear to be that all of the poems in it were writ
ten by members of the Messalla circle, and were sooner or later
published together on that account. One theory is that Lygdamus may have been the editor. Certain indications of language
and style argue that he was not a native Roman, and may have
been a learned freedman.[3]

26. The fourth book opens with a panegyric on Messalla,
which is so crude that it is generally agreed that, whatever ad-
herent of that munificent patron was guilty of its composition,
we must not lay it to the charge of Tibullus. (Némethy thinks
it a youthful effusion of Propertius !) The next five poems are
short elegies dealing with the love of Sulpicia and one Cerinthus.[4]
In spite of all arguments to the contrary [5] no adequate considerations seem to have been advanced to remove them from the list
of Tibullus's own composition, and the parallels with his other
writings (cf. Némethy, pp. 334–335) and general tone of these
little elegies make strongly for their genuineness. They are
sometimes spoken of as the " Garland of Sulpicia." The following six little elegies (4, 7 to 4, 12, inclusive [6]), sometimes called
Elegidia like the preceding group, are evidently the work of
Sulpicia herself, and are very interesting and unique in Roman
literature as the work of a woman. They betray a warmth of

[1] Marx in P. W., I, 1327, dates the origin of the Tibullus collection between
Tiberius and Domitian.

[2] Cf. λύγδος and *albus*.

[3] But cf. Némethy, *Lyg.*, p. 29 ; Marx in P. W., I, 1325.

[4] Cf. 4, 2, Intr.

[5] *E.g.* Bürger in *Hermes*, Vol. 40 (1905), p. 333; Postgate in *Class. Rev.*, Vol. 9
(1895), p. 77.

[6] But cf. Magnus in Bursian's *JB.*, Vol. 51 (1887), pp. 262–263, for the view that
No. 7 belongs to the preceding " Garland."

feeling and a certain disregard of conventionalities that are noteworthy, and probably significant of the social tendencies of the
day. The last two poems of the collection (4, 13 and 14) are
of indeterminate authorship, but may be ascribed to Tibullus.[1]
A couple of Priapea ascribed to Tibullus are of doubtful authenticity.[2]

27. Tibullus, the country gentleman, was a gentle man.
Even in his bitterest disappointment as a lover he could sing:[3]—

> ' Thy sorrows let me not unseal!
> I am not worth that thou shouldst lose a smile,
> Nor that th' expressive light thine eyes reveal
> A single bitter tear-drop should defile.'   (Williams.)

The subjective value of love he could try to reveal to heartless
Nemesis thus:[4]—

> ' This whole year have I lain
> Wounded to death, yet cherishing the pain,
> And counting my delicious anguish gain.'   (Ibid.)

And even for the sister of his cruel mistress — that sister who had
come so sadly to an early grave — he wept affection's tears:[5]—

> ' and, as my sorrow flows,
> Unto that voiceless dust my grief confide.'   (Ibid.)

Not that he habitually sits beneath the cypress! His sympathetic nature leads him to join enthusiastically in the joy of
his friends, whether at some special occasion like the triumph of
Messalla (1, 7) or the installation of Messalinus into the college
of the Quindecimviri (2, 5), or at one of the regularly recurring
festivals like the Ambarvalia (2, 1). He shares in the simple
pleasures of the home-born slaves (2, 1, 23), encourages the
merry games of the rustics (2, 5, 83 sqq.), and has a word of indulgence for the swain who goes home " right mellow," not for-

---

[1] Postgate (Sel., pp. 191–199) makes an elaborate argument against the genuineness of the former.

[2] Cf. Hiller in Hermes, Vol. 18 (1885), pp. 343 sqq.; Teuffel[5], 254, 5.

[3] 2, 6, 41.   [4] 2, 5, 109.   [5] 2, 6, 33.

getting to plead for gentleness towards the fair ones who might suffer rudeness from such a lover (1, 10, 51 sqq.). And while the course of his own love fails to run smoothly, he can express a generous wish for better luck to his more fortunate friends (2, 2).

More than this, Tibullus prefers the quiet and gentle life and loves the peaceful world of nature best. " No other poet, with the exception of Vergil, is so possessed by the spirit of Italy, the love of the country and of the labor of the fields, and the piety associated with that sentiment." [1] It is natural, therefore, for him to express these primitive sentiments of love of home and friends and native land, of reverence for his gods and devotion to the scenes where these rustic divinities especially held sway, with a simplicity and directness that are worthy of his themes. That he was master of his art, to be sure, has come to be generally recognized ; and this was the same art that had produced the Alexandrian elegy. But no poet has succeeded better in exemplifying the dictum that the highest art consists in the concealment of art. He never obtrudes his learning upon the reader, as Propertius did, and in spite of many attempts to show a highly artificial structure in his elegies, the most patent fact about them is their utterly natural flow of a perfectly simple thought, oft-repeated, after the manner of one absorbed in the genuineness of his feeling.[2] The deliberate estimate of the master Quintilian (10, 1, 93), *mihi tersus atque elegans maxime videtur auctor Tibullus*, is confirmed by the sober judgment of the present day.[3] The relative merit of good poets is like that of oysters, a matter of taste. If one is bent on a fat capon, nothing else suits him. Within his field it is rash to assert that Tibullus is a second-rate poet, who just missed greatness. His wonderfully pure Latinity, in the Augustan age, his perfection in handling the elegiac distich, and his success in

---

[1] Sellar, p. 239. For Tibullus as a poet of nature cf. K. P. H. in *PAPA.*, Vol. 31 (1900), pp. xxxiv-xxxix; Geikie, pp. 85-86, *et passim*.

[2] Cf. *PAPA.*, Vol. 26 (1895), pp v-viii.

[3] Cf. Kirby F. Smith in Johns Hopkins Univ. Circular No. 6 (1910), pp. 26-31.

touching the human heart with a gentle sympathy place him among the masters of his art.

28. The means by which Tibullus achieved this result seem to have been relatively simple and direct; but no poet has been more successful in clearing away the rubbish of his workshop, so that we cannot be sure that we are entirely acquainted with his methods. That he had studied the earlier Greek, as well as the Alexandrian, models we cannot doubt. While we are not warranted in pressing too far our zeal to discover traces of elaborate symmetry in the composition of the elegies, traces of such symmetry appear.[1] Though it is impossible to discover all of the intimate connections with the Greek comedy, the earlier elegy, the pastoral of Theocritus, the leading Alexandrian elegists, and the lost elegies of Gallus, the debt of Tibullus to these predecessors was certainly a heavy one. Neither is it possible to estimate accurately the mutual indebtedness of the practically contemporary poets, Tibullus, Propertius, and Ovid.[2] But whatever the sources of Tibullus may have been, he used them so as to manifest a simple diction, a syntax essentially without individuality, a modest use of figurative language, and in the choice of expressions a taste that almost uniformly attains the elegant.[3] His tendency to repeat words and expressions, to postpone an epithet and to postpone -*que*, his scrupulous preference for the forms *at, seu, neu, nec*, for *sic* rather than *ita, nam* rather than *enim*, his care in the forms of declension, his avoidance of forms belonging properly to the *sermo cottidianus*, his slight use of diminutives, and his skill in placing words are among the palpable qualities of his style.[4] Such poems as 2, 5 illustrate the

[1] Cf. Bell., p. 293; P. W., Vol. 5, pp. 2291 sqq.; Bubendey, *Die Symmetrie der römischen Elegie*.

[2] Cf. Hiller in *Rh. Mus.*, Vol. 60 (1905), pp. 38–105; Skutsch, *Aus Vergils Frühzeit*, passim; Cartault, Chap. IV; Jacoby in *BPW.*, Vol. 29 (1909), Sp. 1464; Richard Bürger in Bursian's *JB.*, Vol. 153 (1911), pp. 135–144.

[3] *Index verborum* in Hiller.

[4] Cf. Postgate, *Sel.*, pp. 27 sqq.; Hansen, *De tropis et figuris apud Tibullum;* Sellar, pp. 245 sqq.; Richard Bürger, *Beiträge zur Elegantia Tibulls*, in Χάριτες

" national and historical tendency " of literature in the Augustan age.[1] Especially noticeable is the great advance in the technical refinement of the handling of the elegiac verse seen in Tibullus ; for some details cf. § 42.

29. The best Tibullus Mss. known to us are the Ambrosianus (A), written in 1374, discovered by Baehrens in the Ambrosian library at Milan in 1876, comparatively free from interpolations ; and the Vaticanus (V), discovered in the Vatican library by Gustav Loewe at the suggestion of Baehrens, a Ms. agreeing remarkably with A, and thus having less independent value, written probably at the end of the fourteenth, or the beginning of the fifteenth century. These two Mss. coming from a common archetype, their *consensus* furnishes the most reliable authority. A third Ms., the Guelferbytanus (G), found by Baehrens in the ducal library at Wolfenbüttel, was probably overestimated by him when he believed it to be derived from a different archetype. It is apparently somewhat interpolated. Its date, according to Baehrens, is about 1425 A.D. Lachmann had also, in the preparation of his edition of 1829, knowledge of the Parisinus (B), written in 1423, somewhat interpolated, and of little independent value ; Eboracensis (Y), now lost, and used only in part and at second hand ; and the *consensus* of three younger and inferior Mss. (C), viz., the Wittianus (c), the Datanus (d), and the Askewianus (e). All the Mss. thus far mentioned are believed to come from a common archetype. Besides these complete Mss. the Fragmentum Cuiacianum (F) was an important, older Ms., which began with 3, 4, 65, known by Scaliger, and collated by him on the margin of a Plantinian edition of 1569. This collation, which was known to Lachmann only at second hand, was long lost, but is now in the University library at Leyden ; F itself has been lost for centuries. There are also two series of excerpts which contain Tibullus passages. The Excerpta

F. Leo . . . dargebracht, pp. 371-394; Linke, *Tibullus quantum in poesi elegiaca profecerit comparato Catullo,* 1877.

[1] Cf. Burn, *KL and KA.,* p. 79.

Parisina (P) were made by some unknown monk, perhaps about
1000 A.D., with an evident purpose to emphasize certain moral
precepts or to cull passages of special beauty. The Codex
Thuaneus copy of these excerpts contains 266 vv. from the
Tibullus collection, about 100 of which differ materially from
the form in which they appear in the complete Mss. The
readings of P were copied by Scaliger, whose copy was copied
by Heinsius. Lachmann used the copy of Heinsius. The
Excerpta Frisingensia (M) were not seen by Lachmann till after
his edition was completed. They are in a Ms. which goes back
to the eleventh century and are apparently copied from a
purer original than the archetype of the complete Mss. Moreover, the purposes in the mind of the excerptor were not apparently such as to lead him to make arbitrary alterations in the
text. F and M therefore may be regarded as of considerable
value in correcting the readings of A and V.[1]

30. Combined editions of Catullus, Tibullus, and Propertius
have been common for centuries, such as the Aldine edition of
1562 with learned comments by Muretus; the Paris edition by
Scaliger in 1577; the Bonn edition of 1680 edited by Graevius
and containing notes by many famous scholars; and the Haupt-
Vahlen text edition (see § 19). The fourth edition of Heyne
(improved by Wunderlich, 1817) contains much exegetical
material. The first critical edition was that of Lachmann in
1829. This was followed by Dissen in 1835, with elaborate
introduction and commentary. After the discovery of the Mss.
A, V, and G, Baehrens brought out his text in 1878. E. Hiller
produced a good text with *index verborum* in 1885. Belling's
Untersuchung und Text appeared in 1897, Postgate's selections
in 1903, and his Oxford text edition in 1905 (much more conservative than that of 1903). Némethy's edition of Tibullus
and Sulpicia in 1905 was followed by a separate edition of

---

[1] Cf. Rothstein, *De Tibulli Codicibus*, Berlin, 1880; Protzen, *De Excerptis Tibul-
lianis*, Greifswald, 1869; Magnus in Bursian's *JB.*, Vol. 51 (1887), pp. 311 sqq.;
Postgate, *Sel.*, pp. 200–208.

Lygdamus in 1906, the latter with an *index verborum*. Like
Belling, he has attempted to rearrange the elegies in chronological order.[1] After completing his important review of the
work done on Tibullus during the last century (Cartault, *Corp.
Tib.*), A. Cartault in 1909 published an edition of his author
(or authors) with introduction and a conservative text.[2] The
edition by Kirby Flower Smith (1913) includes an introduction
and full commentary on Books 1, 2, and 4, 2–14. For editions of
selections by Jacoby and Schulze see § 19. Cranstoun's translation is perhaps the best. A more recent one by Williams omits
most of Book 4. The latest is Postgate's, in the Loeb library.

PROPERTIUS

31. Our information concerning the life of Propertius must be
drawn almost entirely from his own elegies, especially 1, 22, and
4, 1. Such knowledge is but limited, not including, *e.g.*, even his
full name. Donatus in his life of Vergil calls him Sextus Propertius, and the use of the same praenomen in the Codex Sal-
masianus of the Latin *Anthology* is probably derived from the
same source. Some of the Mss. have Aurelius Propertius Nauta,
plainly the product of pedantry. "Aurelius" may have been
accepted from a confusion with the name of Prudentius; while
"Nauta" has been explained as derived from the Mss. reading
navita of 2, 24, 38.[3]

From these passages, 1, 22, 9–10 ; 4, 1, 63–66 and 121–126, it is
certain that Propertius was born in Umbria, but whether at As-
sisium, Hispellum, Mevania, or at some other neighboring place
has been the subject of much discussion. The first of these, the
Assisi of to-day, or at least its vicinity, is now generally accepted

---

[1] Cf. Jacoby in *BPW.*, Vol. 26 (1906), Sp. 141.

[2] Cf. *Ibid.*, Vol. 29 (1909), Sp. 1460, for a detailed statement of its weaknesses.

[3] The inscription in honor of Sextus Aurelius Propertius, said to have been discovered at Hispellum (*Spello*), reproduced on p. 3 of Burmann's edition of Propertius, is clearly one of many similar forgeries.

as best entitled to the honor.[1] His father died while the
poet was still young,[2] and his mother brought him up and intended him for a public career.[3] He had no special ground for
pride in his family,[4] and whatever landed possessions he may
have inherited suffered the common fate of large confiscations,
as in the case of Vergil and Tibullus.[5] The confiscation probably was in connection with the allotment of lands to the veterans
of Octavian in 41 B.C., just before the Perusine war. At the
time of this war, then, Propertius, who lost a relative at that
time (cf. 1, 22, 7), was a boy whose father had recently died. If
we compare the youth of the poet at this date with the statements of Ovid (*Trist.* 4, 10, 41–54; 2, 463–468) that Propertius
was older than himself, though in some sense a successor of
Tibullus, we find ground for conjecture that Propertius was born
not before 48 B.C., perhaps a little later. As no reference to
a date later than 16 B.C. can be discovered in the elegies, it is
believed that he died not later than the year 15, perhaps after
attending himself to the publication of the last book. Many
hints in his poems would incline us to imagine him as having a
rather frail constitution, and we can picture him as pale and
thin, if we are to take seriously his expressions, *meo palleat ore* (1,
1, 22), *si exiles videor tenuatus in artus* (2, 22, 21), and *pallorem
totiens mirabere nostrum* (1, 5, 21). But he was particular about
his personal appearance.[6]

32. It is easy to see that such a temperament did not promise
much success in the prosaic profession of the law. Though well
educated under his mother's direction, whose remaining fortune

[1] Cf. 4, 1, 125; Sellar, pp. 268–276; Plin. *Ep.* 6, 15, 1, and the Assisi inscription
in honor of C. Passennus Sergius Paulus Propertius Blaesus.

[2] 4, 1, 127.

[3] 4, 1, 131 sqq.

[4] *Nullus et antiquo Marte triumphus avi* (2, 34, 56); *quamvis nec sanguine avito
nobilis* (2, 24, 37).

[5] 4, 1, 129–130; 2, 24, 38: *quamvis haud ita dives eras;* 2, 34, 55: *cui parva
domi fortuna relictast.*

[6] Cf. 2, 4, 5: *nequiquam perfusa meis unguenta capillis, ibat et expenso planta
morata gradu.*

was still ample, evidently, to provide for all the boy's needs, he early discovered his poetic gift, and turned his back on a Forum which seemed to him a madman's paradise (4, 1, 133–134). But he was no recluse. He loved good-fellowship, and was ambitious to rise into the highest literary circles. Among his best friends were Tullus, a nephew of the consul of 33 B.C.,[1] Ponticus (1, 7), and Bassus (1, 4). Lynceus (2, 34) may be a pseudonym for some tragic writer. Of the better known literary men, Ovid and Vergil were certainly included in his circle of friends. Tibullus and Propertius do not mention each other; but evidently they were well acquainted each with the work of the other. The relation of Propertius to Horace has been a subject for interesting discussions. There is no sign that they were friends, although belonging to the same literary circle, that of Maecenas. More than that, quite a case can be made out for thinking that Horace turned up his nose at the poetic aspirations as well as the personality of the ambitious young elegist. Postgate (*Prop.*, p. 33) has an elaborate argument for identifying the passage in Horace's *Epistles*, 2, 2, 87 sqq., as a direct attack upon Propertius. It was probably the publication of Book 1 of the elegies that won recognition and friendship from Maecenas, and placed Propertius in the most coveted position in Rome. Elegies 2, 1, and 3, 9 are addressed to Maecenas.[2] The friendship of Maecenas implied more or less direct relations with Augustus. The emperor is duly praised in various places.[3] Propertius seems to have lived a social life at Rome, seldom leaving it, and always anxious to return, when away. He was able to live on the Esquiline,[4] and occasionally we find him at Tibur, or back in Umbria for a brief sojourn.

33. But as with Catullus, the career of Propertius, as well as

[1] Cf. 1, 1; 1, 6; 1, 14; 1, 22; 3, 22.

[2] For a fascinating fancy sketch of the poet's relations to this group of men of letters cf. Anne C. E. Allinson, "A Poet's Toll," *Atlantic Monthly*, Vol. 106 (1910), pp. 774–784.

[3] 3, 4, 1; 11, 66; 4, 6, 14; 11, 60.

[4] 3, 23, 24.

his failure to realize all his possibilities, is largely due to one woman. True, his ardent nature led him when but a slip of a boy into an attachment to one Lycinna.[1] Who she was we can hardly guess; but when he protested to his jealous mistress later (v. 43) that Lycinna had been but a passing fancy of two or three early years (vv. 7–10) and added, *cuncta tuus sepelivit amor*, we may believe that he spoke as near the truth as forgetful lovers ever can. For when Cynthia dawned upon his life he became for the time being essentially a man of one idea. Her real name was Hostia,[2] the pseudonym suggesting not merely the qualities of an ordinary lover's "divinity," but more especially her function as an inspirer of his poetry; for she was not only herself a *docta puella*, but came of literary ancestry, her grandfather Hostius having written, it is believed, a poem on the Illyrian war.[3] Her fine literary tastes and elegant accomplishments were enhanced by all the feminine arts and graces and by a beauty which made the susceptible young poet her willing slave. Her birthplace was at Tibur, where she seems to have lived at times, while commonly maintaining a considerable establishment at Rome. It was she who made the first advances, partly, perhaps, because she admired the gifts of the young student of poetic promise. Indeed, she may have been more or less responsible for his forsaking the Forum and frequenting the salon. Immediately the Alexandrian impetus which is seen in his earliest work was concentrated on this absorbing affection and its object, and he tells the world of her golden hair, her taper fingers, her sparkling black eyes, and her stately carriage.[4]

But Cynthia was older than Propertius [5] and more artful. As a *meretrix* she could not contract a legal marriage; and there were other lovers to whom at times she gave more attention

---

[1] 3, 15, 3–6.   [2] Cf. § 14.
[3] *Splendidaque a docto fama refulget avo* (3, 20, 8).
[4] 2, 2, 5; 2, 3, 9 sqq.; 2, 12, 23–24.
[5] Cf. 2, 18, 19.

than the ardent poet lover could well endure.[1] There were quarrels and reconciliations. For some fault he was banished for a whole year from her presence[2]; yet much later, in his bitter leave-taking[3] he reminds her that he had been her devoted slave for five years.[4] The chronology of the poems appears to agree with this five-year period; for none of those referring to Cynthia appears to have been written earlier than 28 or later than 23 B.C. Yet the question of the relative order of the elegies and the determination of the exact years included in the five are unsolved problems. When the year of separation occurred, and whether the five years were interrupted or not, are moot questions.[5] The publication of the poet's first book of elegies,[6] probably in the year 25, dealing almost exclusively with his love, must have flattered the lady and cemented their affection for the time. But its genius won for Propertius also a place in the friendship of Maecenas, prince of patrons, and opened the way for the development of other interests and for increasing ambition to write on other themes. While about two thirds of all the elegies are connected in some way with Cynthia, there may be noted an increasing restlessness on the part of the poet, a sense of dissatisfaction that his work is confined within so narrow a circle, which feeling was probably fostered by his friends, who saw higher possibilities in him. He defends himself from time to time for not launching out on a broader sea, and tries his hand a little on a certain patriotic type of poetry. Meanwhile his *liaison* was running the natural course of all such attachments. The lover became tired of the imperiousness and the fickleness of the beloved; love was supplanted by disgust,

---

[1] Cf. 1, 8.   [2] 3, 16, 9.   [3] 3, 25, 3.

[4] Cf. 2, 8, 13: *ergo iam multos nimium temerarius annos, inproba, qui tulerim teque tuamque domum, ecquandone tibi liber sum visus?*

[5] Cf. Schanz, 287; Plessis, pp. 210 sqq.; Postgate, *Prop.*, pp. xxi sqq.; Ramsay p. xlvi; Otto, "Die Reihenfolge der Gedichte des Properz," in *Hermes*, Vol. 20 (1885), pp. 552-572.

[6] The *Cynthia Monobiblos* of Martial's epigram 14, 189: *Cynthia, facundi carmen iuvenale Properti, accepit famam, nec minus ipsa dedit.*

and, probably in the year 23, Propertius renounced his mistress
in two bitter elegies (3, 24 and 25), in which his hatred seems
as intense as his earlier love had been.   Whether there was any
sort of a reconciliation before her death (which may be put not
later than the year 18) seems very doubtful.[1]   It is not impossible that in conformity with the wishes of Augustus the poet may
have married some time before his death and become the
father of offspring.[2]

34. That the Cynthia book was published first, and as a
whole, is clear.[3]   Book 2 is somewhat larger, with thirty-four
elegies ; but they are still mostly on the same subject, and the
first and last poems are well adapted to open and close respectively such a book.   Lachmann, however, introduced apparently endless confusion into Propertius texts by deciding that a
third book begins with 2, 10.   His argument is based chiefly on
an assumed *lacuna* before 2, 10 ; on the apparent fitness of this
elegy to open a new book dedicated to Augustus ; and on the
use of the expression *tres libelli* in 2, 13, 25.[4]   On the other
hand, it may be urged (1) that it is not certain that 2, 10 is incomplete, or is preceded by any important omission.   (2) This
poem is not very suitable as an introduction to a book containing little but love elegies.   (3) *Libellus* does not necessarily
mean a 'book' of poems at all.[5]   Propertius in the passage in
question[6] does not appear to be thinking of near approaching
death, and might easily have been expecting to complete other
books of elegies before that should occur.   Perhaps a conventional number is suggested by the fact that Horace published

[1] But cf. Postgate's elaborate argument in his *Selections*, pp. xxiv–xxvii.

[2] Cf. Plin. *Ep.* 6, 15: *Passennus Paulus . . . scribit elegos. Gentilicium hoc illi : est enim municeps Properti atque etiam inter maiores suos Propertium numerat.*

[3] Cf. 2, 3, 3–4: *vix unum potes, infelix, requiescere mensem, et turpis de te iam liber alter erit ;* 2, 24, 1–2 : *cum sis iam noto fabula libro et tua sit toto Cynthia lecta foro.*

[4] Cf. Lachmann, pp. xx sqq.

[5] Cf. for its use as referring to a single poem, 1, 11, 19; 2, 25, 3; 3, 9, 43.

[6] 2, 13, 25.

three books of odes just about this time.[1]   Although there are ·
still found scholars to defend the theory of Lachmann, the growing disposition seems to be to return to the Ms. division into four
books.[2]   Book 2 was probably published about 24 B.C.,[3] but
some of its elegies were written at least several years earlier.[4]
The third book is still on the whole largely concerned with
Cynthia.   There are, however, in this book a number of more
general love poems,[5] and a third group, including the first five
elegies, in which he only starts with love, if love figures at
all in these, and branches off into other subjects.   The book
must have been published as late as, or later than, 23 B.C., as is
evidenced by 3, 18, on the death of Marcellus.   In fact, 3, 4
seems to be of the year 22.   In the fourth book elegies Nos. 7
and 8 at least refer to Cynthia.   Nos. 3 and 11 are of the type of
the *Heroides* of Ovid, while the others are of the aetiological
type which Propertius, following in the wake of Callimachus,
was evidently ambitiously planning to develop.[6]   The last
elegy of the collection was written in the year 16, and was
probably the last one he penned.   There is no cogent reason
for doubting that he attended himself to the publication of all
these books.

35. 'Propertius is the greater genius, Tibullus the greater
artist.'[7]   There are many points of similarity between Propertius
and Catullus.   Both undertook to follow the Alexandrian school
of elegy.   Both were gifted with the genuine poetic fire.[8]   Each
in the years of youthfully exuberant passions fell under the spell
of a somewhat older, yet commanding belle, who knew how

---

[1] For still other possibilities cf. Lachmann himself, *l.c.*, p. xxii.

[2] For the view that Book 1 was long lost and that the grammarians were wont
to cite from an edition of Books 2-4, cf. Ullman in *Class. Phil.*, Vol. 4 (1909), pp.
45–51, and Birt in *Rh. Mus.*, Vol. 64 (1909), pp. 393 sqq.

[3] Cf. 2, 10, Intr.   [4] *E.g.* 2, 31, which belongs to the year 28.

[5] *E.g.* 11 and 13.   [6] Cf. 4, 1, Intr.

[7] Leo, in *Die Kultur der Gegenwart*, "Die Römische Literatur," p. 350.

[8] For Propertius as a poet of nature cf. K. P. H. in *PAPA.*, Vol. 32 (1901),
pp. xx–xxii; Geikie, pp. 96–97, *et passim.*

to enthrall her lover and practically drove any more serious career for the time from his life. Both died prematurely, before the work that might have been expected in their maturity could materialize. But Propertius confined himself entirely to elegy and in that field not merely produced a remarkable group of erotic poems revealing the passion of his life, but worked out the beginnings, so far as Roman literature is concerned, of two new types which were to be developed more elaborately by his successor Ovid, the amatory epistle and the aetiological poem. The intensity of Propertius goes far to explain his work and its manner. When love holds him he forgets everything else, and pictures for the reader every changing mood and fortune of his passion. When ambition rules, he hesitates at no literary device to win and keep the attention and admiration of his audience. He believed thoroughly in the merits of the Alexandrian manner, and therefore almost outdid the Alexandrians themselves. This unrestrained temper as a poet brings about the strange juxtaposition of simple human passion and pedantic learning. It also leads the poet to an extreme recklessness of the conventionalities of the Latin language. He does not care to speak by the book, but uses often an idiom all his own. His desire to be considered the Roman Callimachus was doubtless responsible for much of the abstruse mythological lore that burdens his pages ; but his poetic imagination enabled him in spite of this pedantry to be a great poet. He carries the reader with him as he breaks abruptly in upon his own course of thought to ejaculate a question, or utter a reproach, or enunciate a principle. We follow him into the contagious gladness of love's heyday, and the next moment share his despair and forecast of death. Yet there are many indications that he studied carefully many models, not merely those of the Alexandrian epoch, but throughout the broader field of classic Greek. Modern scholarship has not yet fully worked out the intricate relations of Roman elegy. But among the interesting questions discussed in recent times are those of the amatory epistle as an intermediate type leading up to subjective

erotic elegy, the part played by the epigram as a seed thought
for such elegy, and the whole matter of the actual existence in the
Alexandrian epoch of anything corresponding to the Roman
subjective-erotic elegy as we know it in Propertius. Doubtless
the elements that Propertius combined in his effective product
were gathered from many sources; but there is little proof that
anything closely resembling these elegies ever existed in Alexandria.[1] Attention should also be called to the skillful arrangement of two or more elegies of Propertius in various instances.[2]
In his use of the elegiac distich Propertius manifests both the
skill and the freedom characterizing his work in other respects.
A growing care in its treatment is seen in the frequency of his
rimes and dissyllabic pentameter endings, and his treatment of
the pentameter in general was epoch-making.[3]

The language and style of Propertius furnish a subject worthy
of most careful investigation and analysis. Considering his
devotion to Greek models, his diction is notably free from Gre-
cisms.[4] The large freedom of treatment of many familiar words
like *cogo, venio, duco,* and the poetic abandon with which he
ranges through the language for unexpected expressions for
such familiar ideas as death, for example, have been carefully
investigated, as well as his unusual handling of various classes
of words.[5] The syntax of Propertius is remarkable for its reck-

[1] Cf. Jacoby in *Rh. Mus.*, Vol. 60 (1905), pp. 38–105; 64 (1909), pp. 601 sqq.;
65 (1910), pp. 22 sqq.; and in *BPW.*, Vol. 31 (1911), Sp. 169 sqq.; Heinemann,
Epistulae Amatoriae quo modo cohaereant cum elegiis Alexandrinis (1910); Reitzenstein in P.W., article *Epigramm;* Crusius in P.W., article *Elegie;* Bürger in Bursian's *JB.*, Vol. 153, pp 135–145; Hermann Peter, *Der Brief in der römischen
Litteratur*, pp. 188 sqq.; Fridericus Mallet, *Quaestiones Propertianae*, Göttingen,
1882; Maas, "Untersuchungen zu Properz und seinen Griechischen Vorbildern,"
in *Hermes*, Vol. 31 (1896), pp. 375 sqq.

[2] Cf. Ites, *De Propertii Elegiis inter se conexis*, Göttingen, 1908.

[3] Cf. Sellar, pp. 306–310; Foster in *TAPA.*, Vol. 40 (1909), pp. 31–62; Ramsay,
p. xlvii.

[4] J. S. Phillimore has published an *Index Verborum Propertianus*, Oxford, 1905.

[5] Cf. Uhlmann, pp. 83–88; Frahnert, *Zum Sprachgebrauch des Properz*, Halle,
1874; Kuttner, *De Propertii Elocutione Quaestiones*, Halle, 1878; Postgate, *Prop.*,
pp. xxxviii–xl.

lessness, vagueness, looseness, sometimes its intricacy, and often its obscurity.   No better instance can be cited than his omnibus use of the Ablative, which, however, only exaggerates in characteristic manner a tendency long dormant in the language.[1]   With the inconsistency of a lover, brevity wrestles with a fondness for periphrasis; *e.g.* in infinitive expressions.[2]   What Postgate[3] acutely calls the "polarization of an idea" so as to treat it immediately from another standpoint, may be compared with his "love of symmetry and correspondence" in arrangement.[4] If his metaphors are often far-fetched, they are nevertheless telling.   In short, the poetry of Propertius is the work of a brilliant young man, hardly more than a boy, unrestrained, unpruned, full of the marks of genius, and overcrowded with much as yet unassimilated learning.   His "faculty of evoking a dim consciousness of awe in lines which present an indefinable stimulus to the imagination"[5] is doubtless partly due to what Sellar calls his "desperate sincerity," and partly to an imagination that in its sweep leaves most Latin poets out of the race.

36.   The history of Propertian text criticism has been, and still is, a stormy one; and probably no important Latin author still labors under so much uncertainty as to what he actually wrote, or is so overburdened with the learned attempts of scholars in many lands to suggest what they surmise he may have written. The areas of arid wastes abandoned to Propertius text conjectures in the various periodicals in the field of classical philology are growing with alarming rapidity, and it will not be long, apparently, before an attempt to enumerate the suggested changes in a page of the text will occupy more space than the text itself.

Lachmann correctly decided that the Codex Neapolitanus (N), written about 1200 A.D. in the vicinity of Metz, now at Wolfen-

---

[1] Cf. Wagner, *De Syntaxi Propertiana*, Passau, 1888; Hoerle, *De Casuum usu Propertiano*, Halle, 1887; Postgate, *Prop.*, Intr., pp. lvii sqq.; the *Index Grammaticus* in Hosius; and the recent comprehensive study of Uhlmann.

[2] Cf. Postgate, *Prop.*, p. xlii; Uhlmann, p. 94.

[3] *L.c.*, p. lxvii.   [4] Postgate, *Prop.*, p. lxxi.   [5] Duff, p. 578.

büttel, was the most nearly correct and trustworthy of all the Propertius Mss. known in his day, although he overestimated sadly another Ms., now generally considered as of little worth (Groninganus, fifteenth century). After a half century of controversy over the relative merits of N, Baehrens in 1880 preferred to base his edition chiefly on four other Mss. belonging to two different families. These were the Vossianus (A) of Leyden, probably written in France in the latter part of the thirteenth or early part of the fourteenth century; the Laurentianus (F), a Milan Ms. of the fourteenth century, evidently of the same family and even believed by Ullman[1] to be "a granddaughter of A," the Ottobonianus Vaticanus 1514 (V), written in the fourteenth or fifteenth century; and the Daventriensis (D), of the same family as the last, written in the fifteenth century. More recent scholarship has rejected Baehrens's judgment and confirmed Lachmann's view that N is far the best of known Propertius Mss. Propertian criticism, however, is apparently ever increasingly active. The history of the Mss. already mentioned, and their relation to each other and to many others, mostly apparently inferior Mss., are the subject of vigorous discussion. New Mss. have been discovered, like the Codex Holkhamicus (L), written in Italy in 1421, and belonging to the same general class as the preferred Mss. of Baehrens, and several other Italian Mss., including the Codex Lusaticus (L), written in 1469 at Padua, which Paul Köhler[2] attempted to exalt to an important place beside N. But Postgate[3] has argued convincingly to show this last to have little independent value. O. L. Richmond[4] has in connection with a review of the known Mss. of Propertius compared five fifteenth century Mss. that appear to come from a common origin, which he denominates C, and thinks may have been written by an Irish scholar, and that it presented

---

[1] *Class. Phil.*, Vol. 6 (1911), p. 288.

[2] *Philologus*, Vol. 64 (1905), pp. 414–437.

[3] *Class. Rev.*, Vol. 20 (1906), pp. 349–352.

[4] *Jour. of Phil.*, Vol. 31 (1908–1910), pp. 162–196.

a " corrupt, but ancient tradition " of much importance, and was probably written earlier than any other of our Mss. This view, however, is not shared by B. L. Ullman,[1] who in discussing the Mss. of Propertius finds after examining as many as a hundred Mss. that none are earlier than the fifteenth century except N, A, and F, and gives an interesting chain of evidence to show that all our Mss. come from A and N, that a famous lost Ms. of Petrarch was copied from A, and that this lost Ms. was the archetype of F. Among the most prolific inventors of emendations to the text has been A. E. Housman.[2]

37. The first edition of Lachmann in 1816, with introduction and critical notes, was followed in 1829 by his text edition, in which he receded from his positions in many instances, but gave no explanation of the changes. Hertzberg's edition of 1843–1845 contains a wealth of material in the introductory *Quaestiones* and the elaborate commentary. Baehrens's text in 1880 was characteristically marred by the liberties he took with its traditional form. In 1898 Rothstein produced a masterly commentary, with up-to-date introduction and various happy textual emendations. Butler's edition with English commentary (1905) is somewhat disputatious and perhaps reactionary, but offers many valuable suggestions. The latest text editions are the Oxford text of Phillimore (1901) and the Teubner text of Hosius (1911).[3] Postgate's *Select Elegies* has a very useful introduction and analysis of Propertius's style, and a commentary rich in its illustrative material and its literary appreciation. Besides the Haupt-Vahlen text with Catullus and Tibullus, the elegiac selections of Ramsay, Schulze, Jacoby, and Carter should be noted (cf. § 19). Cranstoun's metrical translation in 1876 has been followed by Phillimore's prose version, after thirty years. Still more recent is Butler's, in the Loeb library.

[1] *Class. Phil.*, Vol. 6 (1911), pp. 282–301.

[2] Cf. Heydenreich in Bursian's *JB.*, Vol. 55 (1888), pp. 144–152. A good detailed description of the most important Mss. is found in Ramsay's introduction, pp. l–lvii; cf. Plessis, pp. 1–4; Housman in *Class. Rev.*, Vol. 9 (1895), pp. 19–29.

[3] Cf. Foster in *AJP.*, Vol. 33 (1912), pp. 330–342.

OVID

38. The wealth of material left us in the works of Ovid makes it possible to write his biography and estimate the value of his literary product with more ease and greater completeness than is the case with either of the other elegiac writers, his *Tristia* in particular furnishing us detailed information about his life.

Publius Ovidius Naso was born at Sulmo (*Solmona*) on March 20, 43 B.C.,[1] the second son of a noble equestrian father. He repeatedly refers to his native place and evidently appreciated the natural beauties and advantages of the well-watered valley.[2] As his family was in comfortable circumstances, all the educational advantages of the day were given him, including extensive privileges of travel, according to the growing tendency under the empire. With various embellishments we have essentially in Ovid a repetition of the early years of the other elegiac poets, so far as we know them, only with more detailed knowledge. He enjoyed the companionship and tutelage of the best rhetoricians of his day, especially Arellius Fuscus and Porcius Latro. He studied in Athens and extended his travels to the East and to Sicily. He, too, was intended for a lawyer and the public career open to an equestrian. He, too, was of an easygoing disposition and preferred poetry to official humdrum. He, too, liked gay society and knew the town as other young men with well-lined purses knew it. He filled one or two minor offices, and cared little for such duties. But his native poetic ability was even more remarkable than that of any of his predecessors. He must indeed have " lisped in numbers." We cannot imagine that Ovid ever had to labor to write poetry. Such genius could not fail of recognition ; and even as a young man he began to know and associate with Propertius, Horace, Ponticus, Bassus, Macer, and other less known poets, and was

---

1 *Trist.* 4, 10, 5–6.
2 Ct. *Am.* 2, 16, 1 sqq.; *Trist.* 4, 10, 3 ; Martinengo, p. 163.

even in a fair way to have an intimate acquaintance with Vergil and Tibullus, had not too early death removed them from the brilliant literary set that graced the court of Augustus.

Welcomed thus in young manhood as a brilliant and companionable acquisition to the best society of Rome, he lived till past fifty as its idol, and produced a large body of verse especially adapted to the temper of the writer and to the time and manners of which he was so prominent a part. Twice married and divorced in young manhood, he was happily married later to a lady of the Fabian family, and had a daughter. Suddenly and without warning, probably in the year 8 A.D., while Ovid was away from Rome at Elba, an imperial decree of *relegatio* required him to take up his residence at Tomi on the Black Sea. Speculation has never been able to arrive at a certain solution of the riddle of this banishment. Ovid himself mentions *carmen et error*[1] as explanations. We are certain that the *Ars Amatoria* was the 'poem'; but that alone, and years after its composition, could hardly have been a sufficient reason. What 'mistake' Ovid made we shall never know. He was not a political intriguer, nor, at this time in his life at least, can we believe him to have been a party of the first part in any scandal. His family acquaintance with the two Julias, the daughter and the granddaughter of the emperor, has led to various guesses, one of the least unlikely of which is that Ovid knew about the younger Julia's adulterous relation with Silanus.[2] What it meant for this favorite ornament of metropolitan society to be compelled thus to hurry home, take leave of his devoted family, and hasten to the provincial and bleak northwestern frontier of the empire can hardly be imagined. No wonder that he spent most of his time during the next ten years in writing mournful elegies to persuade Augustus to take pity on him by a recall, and that he died a broken-hearted man in the year 18.

39. The literary activity of Ovid began probably with the *Amores*, mostly erotic elegies dealing with the love relations

---

[1] *Trist.* 2, 207.   [2] Cf. *Schanz,* § 291.

between Ovid and Corinna (probably a type rather than a real person), which were published in an edition of five books but later pruned to three books. Meanwhile some of the Epistles (*Heroides*) of fair heroines of the mythical world to the corresponding heroes had been produced, and a group of them was probably published before the second edition of the *Amores* appeared. To whatever the original idea of the *Heroides* is to be traced,[1] they at least are modeled to a considerable degree on the only parallel that preceded them in Roman literature, viz. the elegy of Propertius (4, 3) written in the form of a love letter of Arethusa to Lycotas.[2] Much controversy has raged over the genuineness of some of the twenty-one extant epistles, and the question is hardly yet settled.

In the *Ars Amatoria*, in three books, published 2, or 1, B.C., Ovid still keeps the elegiac verse, but assumes a didactic tone, though often plainly ironical, as he gives advice to lovers how to win and retain affection. This advice is addressed to men in Books 1–2, to women in Book 3. The *Remedia Amoris*, in one book, counsels those who would rid themselves of love. The *Medicamina Faciei*, addressed to the ladies who would possess the fairest complexions, is incomplete, and was apparently written before the publication of the *Ars Amatoria*.

The *Fasti*, a poetic elaboration of the Roman calendar, especially of the festivals, was to have contained twelve books, one for every month. Of them six had been written at the time of his *relegatio* and the work had been dedicated to Augustus. The other six were never written. After the death of Augustus the poet re-dedicated the work to Germanicus and began a revision of it which affected little except the first book. The *Fasti* are a systematic treatment based on a similar idea to that of the aetiological elegies of the fourth book of Propertius, for which, of course, there were interesting Alexandrian models. Ovid also had the important calendar of Verrius Flaccus as a model, which he seems to have followed quite closely in places.

[1] Cf. § 35. [2] Cf. Rohde, *Der Griechische Roman*, p. 112, n. 4.

An even more fascinating field for Ovid's story-telling art was afforded by his master work, the *Metamorphoses*, written in hexameters, in fifteen books, in which with consummate skill he weaves together in continuous narrative a large part of the tales of classical mythology, emphasizing particularly the marvelous transformations which were so common in that mythology. Although on the eve of his departure for Tomi he consigned his copy of this work to the flames, it was already known in other copies and thus spared to posterity.

The five books of *Tristia* and the four following (*Epistulae*) *Ex Ponto*, written during his exile, were addressed to his wife, to Augustus, to various friends, and in many cases to nobody in particular, uttering his complaints upon his sad lot, his petitions for its alleviation, his flattery of the emperor. Naturally the variations on this theme grow increasingly feeble towards the end of the long series. These are written in elegiac verse, as is the *Ibis*, an attack upon some enemy, modeled after the similar poem of Callimachus addressed to Apollonius. There is also a fragment in hexameter called *Halieutica*, dealing with the fishes of the Euxine. Besides this large amount of the extant literary product of Ovid's genius, he wrote a tragedy under the title *Medea*, an epithalamium for Fabius Maximus, an elegy on the death of Messalla, an astronomical work called *Phaenomena*, certain epigrams, a cento on bad poets, and some other occasional poems. Still other poems were falsely attributed to him, particularly an elegy entitled *Nux* and a *Consolatio ad Liviam*.

40. We see already in Ovid traces of a tendency in Roman elegy to recur from the subjective-erotic to the objective-erotic elegy. The poet is too facile to be sincere. The *Amores* have, to be sure, the form of personal experience, and undoubtedly they represent a composite of many personal experiences, as well as the knowledge and imagination of many others such as Ovid's world could furnish. Corinna, too, is apparently but a composite photograph of many brilliant and fascinating Roman girls. A theory that Corinna was only another name for the

imperial Julia was long since exploded. In the *Heroides* and the *Ars Amatoria* the feeling becomes, of course, quite objective, although Ovid betrays constantly his intimate and discerning knowledge of the feminine nature. The *Fasti* are the elaboration of the aetiological elegy. The fatal facility of Ovid is a sign of a rather shallow nature, or at any rate of one whose genuine qualities were polished off in the easy society of the capital into monotonous smoothness. Nowhere does this appear more conclusively than in relation to the ethical significance of his work. It is not probable that his personal character was any more degraded than that of the other poets of this brilliant group of elegiac writers. But his lack of sincerity leads him to deal with questionable themes in so cold-blooded and intimate a way as to shock even those who would not be accused of prudish sentiments. The *Ars Amatoria* has been bluntly described as a manual of seduction, and estimated as the most immoral book ever written; and even if we grant that it is not so unfair a mirror of the society that called it forth and that read it with avidity, we cannot pardon its author for the lightness with which he could project such a weapon for evil into a world of unknown dimensions. Occasionally we get what seem to be touches of genuine feeling, and such elegies as that on the death of Tibullus are among the world's treasures. It is form, however, rather than substance that is ever before Ovid's mind. He dresses up his thought in immaculate Latin, and writes without apparent effort a perfected form of the elegiac distich which is faulty only in exhibiting too obviously an unusual refinement. As a student in the rhetorical schools he had been fond of the *Suasoriae;* in his poetry he elaborates these in impeccable metrical form. A rare gift of imagination and a love for everything beautiful made it possible for him to describe the beautiful in nature in the most telling way, and to people the natural world with all sorts of fairy and mythical beings in fascinating pictures in a perfect setting.[1] Not only are all the arts of the

[1] Cf. Martinengo, Chap. IX.

rhetorician at his command, but he also has the benefit of all
that has preceded him in Roman literature, as well as in that of
Greece, and makes good use of it.[1] No Latin author probably
has borrowed as freely and extensively from his contemporaries
and immediate predecessors.[2] But Ovid does not lack the
genuine poetic power of coining new words to meet his necessi-
ties. Something like half a thousand of these we probably owe
to his invention.[3] No noteworthy syntactical peculiarities worry
the student of Ovid. His style is perfectly transparent, and as
a rule the thought of each distich is complete in itself.

But his even regularity was fatal to the life of elegy. " Tibullus had written naturally and feelingly on love, old age, and
the country. But themes which had been by him treated simply
soon became fixed conventions. Ovid, despite his clearness, contributed to the progress of artificiality. The loss of the true
Tibullian simplicity in theme and the loss of the true Ovidian
ease in movement are evident many generations before the
elegies, at once sensuous and frigid, which were written by
Maximianus in the sixth century."[4]

41. This is not the place to discuss the Mss. and editions of all
of Ovid's works in detail. The Mss. of the *Amores* and *Heroides*
are somewhat fragmentary. The Codex Parisinus (Puteanus)
8242 (P), of the eleventh (or ninth ?) century, contains most of the
Amores and the larger part of the *Heroides*. The Parisinus Regius
7311 (R), of the tenth century, has, besides several others of the
erotic works, *Amor.* 1, 1, 3 – 2, 49. The Sangallensis 864 (S), of
the eleventh century, contains the *Amores* as far as 3, 9, 10, with
the omission of 1, 6, 46–8, 74. The Guelferbytanus (G), of
the twelfth century, much corrected by a later hand (thirteenth

---

[1] Cf. Zielinski in *Philologus*, Vol. 64 (1905), p. 16.

[2] Cf. E. K. Rand in *TAPA.*, Vol. 35 (1904), pp. 143 sqq.; Gansemüller in
Philologus, Vol. 70 (1911), pp. 274-311 and 397-437.

[3] Linse, *De P. Ovidio Nasone, Vocabulorum Inventore*, allows him 487 ; Schütte.
in *BPW.*, Vol. 12 (1892), Sp. 12, thinks the number may be increased to 514.

[4] Duff, p. 611.

century) contains the *Heroides*. An Eton fragment (E) of the eleventh century contains the *Heroides* up to 7, 157 only. Other excerpts or fragments may be passed over at this time except the Schedae Vindobonenses (V), beginning at 10, 14. For the *Tristia* and *Ex Ponto*, the chief Mss. besides the corrupt Laurentianus (L), eleventh century, are the Guelferbytanus (G), thirteenth century, Holkhamicus (H), thirteenth century, Palatinus (P), fifteenth century, and Vaticanus (V), thirteenth century, besides a lost Marcianus Politiani (A).[1]

The chief text editions of all of Ovid's works are those of Riese (2d ed.,1889 sqq.), Ehwald-Merkel (4th ed., 1888 sqq.), and Postgate's *Corpus Poetarum Latinorum*. The *Amores* have been edited in German with valuable introduction, commentary, and appendices (including useful bibliography) by P. Brandt. The editions of Palmer (1898) and Sedlmayer (1886) are most important for the *Heroides*. Thirteen *Heroides* are in the convenient English edition of Shuckburgh, with introduction and commentary. For the *Tristia* Owen's edition (1889) is valuable. The Epistles *Ex Ponto* are in a critical edition by Korn[2] (1868). Ovid's works have metrical English versions by Dryden and other poets.

THE ELEGIAC DISTICH

42. The laws governing the relatively simple metrical form composed of a single dactylic hexameter followed by a single dactylic pentameter — so-called — are but few; and at first sight it would seem as if there were only a narrow margin for the exercise of originality in treatment. In the hexameter there are certain positions between which the writer must choose for his verse caesura; he is expected to employ a fair proportion of dactyls, one being regularly found in the fifth foot; the verse

---

[1] Cf. Postgate's *Corpus Poetarum Latinorum*, Ehwald's *Praefatio*, Shuckburgh's *Introduction;* Owen's edition.

[2] Cf. *BPW.*, Vol. 16 (1896), Sp. 1163 sqq.

should end preferably with a word of either two or three syl lables; harsh elisions should be avoided. In the pentameter the end of a word should always coincide with the end of the first half of the verse; the last half of the verse must always consist of two dactyls followed by a single syllable; elisions should be sparingly employed, and at any rate harsh ones avoided.

But besides such few simple principles for the government of the meter, we find that in practice there grew up various other rules, and many refinements came into vogue, so that we can trace a very interesting progress in the mode of the verse from Catullus to Ovid and can see many indications of individuality in its treatment by the various authors. The subject is too large to be discussed exhaustively here; but the student may be referred to a large body of studies, which is constantly growing, with reference to it, and encouraged to pursue his own investiga tions along this line.

The growth of new conventional usages in this verse is seen especially in the endings of the hexameter and of the pentameter, the treatment of the verse caesura, the relative proportion of dactyls and spondees and their arrangement, in care in avoiding harsh elisions, especially those of a long vowel before a short one,[1] middle and end rime in both hexameter and pentameter, in alliteration, repeated sounds and syllables, and other euphonic embellishments,[2] and in the tendency, culminating in Ovid, to make each distich a complete thought in itself. Some of the results of studies along some of these various lines are given below, virtually in the form in which they were published in *PAPA.*, Vol. 34 (1903), pp. xxviii–xxx.

---

[1] Cf. the exhaustive studies in Hosius, p. 180. Ovid avoids eliding monosylla bles almost entirely; cf. Winboldt, *Latin Hexameter Verse*, p. 177.

[2] Cf. the richly illustrated article of B. O. Foster "On Certain Euphonic Em bellishments in the Verse of Propertius" in *TAPA.*, Vol. 40 (1909), pp. 31–62.

I HEXAMETERS

(1) Monosyllabic endings: Catullus and Propertius employ them frequently; Tibullus and Ovid, very rarely.

(*a*) Catullus has 13 examples, including pronouns, forms of *esse*, and forms of *res*. Four times his verse ends in two monosyllables.

(*b*) Of the 31 cases in Propertius, 20 are a singular form of the first or second personal pronoun, 5 are forms of *qui;* 4, forms of *esse; fles* occurs once, and *iam* once.

(*c*) Ovid in the *Amores* (which are used for these tests) has 4 cases, viz. a form of *esse*, and *me*, twice each.

(*d*) Tibullus (Bks. 1 and 2, which are the only safe ground for an investigation of his usage) has *sint* once. No instance occurs in the book of Lygdamus.

(2) Polysyllabic endings. These are more rare. They are occasional in Catullus; twice Ovid uses a quadrisyllabic proper name; Propertius has similar instances; Tibullus has none.

(3) Spondees still play an important part in the hexameters of Catullus, whose taste is like that of Ennius. This appears most strikingly at the end of the verse. He has 13 spondaic verses out of 322; of these one ends in a monosyllable, one in a trisyllable, the other 11 in words of not less than four syllables. 68, 87 has 5 spondees; 116, 3 is worthy of Ennius himself, being composed entirely of spondees.

In the other elegists, however, the proportion of dactyls and spondees is not unlike that of the other Augustan writers.

Tibullus employs the dactylic beginning of the hexameter in the proportion of about four of these to one beginning with a spondee.[1]

(4) Rime. A species of middle, or Leonine, rime begins to be noted in Catullus, and continues throughout the whole group of writers, being apparently an extension, or an echo, of the very common similar rime in the pentameter. In the hexameter this rime occurs between the last syllable of the verse and that pre-

[1] Cf. Hennig, *Untersuchungen zu Tibull* (1905), p. 19.

ceding the verse caesura, *i.e.* between the endings of the two
parts of the verse. Not less than 41 examples of this may be
found even in Catullus, *e.g.* 96, 1 : *Si quicquam mutis ‖ gratum
acceptumve sepulcris.* The percentage of such cases increases in
Tibullus, reaches a maximum in Propertius, and decreases again
in Ovid.

When this is combined with the common pentameter middle
rime, and is at the same time an end rime, we have a still greater
refinement, as in Tibullus, 1, 9, 25–26 : —

> *ipse deus tacito*
> *permisit lingua ministro*
> *ederet ut multo*
> *libera verba mero.*[1]

In many cases, though the rime is imperfect, the similarity of
sounds, as of a long vowel to a diphthong, or of one vowel followed by *s* to another vowel and *s*, produces a pleasing effect,
which was frequently sought by these poets, *e.g.* Tibullus, 2, 5,
69–70 : —

> *quasque Aniena sacras*
> *Tiburs per flumina sortes*
> *portarit sicco*
> *pertuleritque sinu.*

The variety of these effects is countless.

(5) Verse caesura. This depends, of course, upon the individual taste of the different authors.

(*a*) Catullus is fairly orthodox, with 267 out of 318 hexameters
exhibiting the pènthemimeral caesura, 30 the hephthemimeral,
16 the feminine caesura in the third foot, and 5 the so-called
"bucolic" diaeresis. One or two verses have no verse caesura
at all.

(*b*) But Tibullus, with nearly double the number of verses,
shows his fondness for the hephthemimeral caesura by using it
five times as often, 152 times in all, 32 times without the customary accompanying trithemimeral. A frequent added refine

---

[1] Cf. Ovid, *Am.* 3, 2, 17–18; Prop. 1, 6, 17–18.

ment is a rime subsisting between the syllables preceding the
two caesuras; *e.g.* 1, 1, 47 : —

> *aut, gelidas*
> *hibernus aquas*
> *cum fuderit auster.*

In still other cases there is a similar sound, but not a perfect
rime.

Tibullus employs an even smaller proportion of feminine caesuras, 19 in all, but has also 19 bucolic diaereses, which looks
as if he did not regard these as blemishes.

(*c*) Lygdamus is so orthodox as to be positively dull, having
but 10 of his 145 hexameters that are not of the penthemimeral
type. Of these, 7 are perfect trithemimeral-hephthemimeral
cases, 1 is a feminine, and 3 are bucolics.

II. PENTAMETERS

All the elegists show in these rather more care than in the
hexameters.

(1) Monosyllabic endings. Catullus has one instance; Tibullus, Lygdamus, and Ovid, none; Propertius, with characteristic independence, 4, all being of the same form, viz. *sat est.*

(2) Verse endings longer than a dissyllable. Catullus has 83
trisyllabic endings, Tibullus but 22 out of twice as many verses,
Lygdamus but 3. Of polysyllabic endings Catullus has 92 (18
pentasyllabic, and 1 heptasyllabic), Tibullus 23, Lygdamus but
7. Indeed, Lygdamus in such matters of formal comparison
usually more than holds his own. In Ovid the law of a uniformly dissyllabic ending is thoroughly established.

(3) Endings of first half of pentameter. The tendency toward
the dissyllable here is not so completely followed. Catullus has
36 monosyllabic endings, Tibullus 7. Almost as many trisyl-
lables as dissyllables appear in Tibullus ; but Ovid holds closely
to the dissyllable.

(4) The separation of the two halves of the pentameter becomes increasingly careful.   In Catullus there are 18 cases where they are run together by elision ; *e.g.* 67, 44 : —

> *speraret nec linguam esse nec auriculam.*

(5) The preference for dactyls or spondees in the first half varies. Catullus seems slightly to prefer verses of the form, dactyl, spondee, long syllable ; but the form, spondee, spondee, long syllable (*i.e.* 5 successive long syllables) is a close second, which can hardly be true of any of his successors. Next comes the form, spondee, dactyl, long syllable ; last, dactyl, dactyl, long syllable.

In Tibullus, however, there is an overwhelming preference for opening the verse with a dactyl.

(6) Middle rime.   22 per cent of the pentameters of Catullus exhibit this, and 17 per cent have similar endings.   In the later writers the proportion frequently far exceeds this.   Often, too, this rime is combined with the same phenomenon in adjacent hexameters, to a noteworthy extent.   In Propertius, 2, 34 (a poem of 94 vv.), there are 38 instances of the middle rime, and the 6 consecutive vv., 85–90, have it throughout.

(7) End rime.   There are over 200 cases in Catullus, Tibullus, and Lygdamus, fewest of all in Lygdamus.   Propertius has 1 in every 14 verses.   Sometimes they occur in triplets.   Propertius has one quadruplet rime.

43. The studies of Haupt, a half century ago, showed that Catullus was relatively careless in allowing the elision of a long syllable before a short one.[1]   The recent elaborate studies of Siedow [2] show that Ovid was more careful than either of the other three elegists in avoiding elision, as well as in avoiding a plurality of elisions in a single verse and the elision of long syllables or diphthongs ; that Catullus is most free of them all in

---

[1] Cf. Haupt, *Opuscula*, Vol. 1, pp. 88 sqq.

[2] *De elisionis aphaeresis hiatus usu in hexametris Latinis ab Ennii usque ad Ovidii tempora*, 1911, with valuable bibliography and tabular statements.

eliding monosyllables; and that Lygdamus leads in avoiding hiatus, not exhibiting a single instance of that phenomenon.[1] Similarly interesting studies can be made with reference to the arrangement of words in the verse as a whole, or in different parts of the verse.[2] Diaeresis is particularly common in *solvo* and its compounds.

In other matters, *e.g.* prosody, progress will be noted after Catullus. Lengthening the final short syllable in the thesis occurs rarely in Tibullus.[3] Shortening final *-o* in verbs is the opposite phenomenon. In the treatment of quantities before a mute and liquid Tibullus is quite orthodox.[4]

[1] Cf., on the hiatus in Catullus, Friedrich's note on *Cat.* 3, 16. Cartault thinks Tibullus shows greater looseness in elision in Book 2 than in Book 1 as well as in other metrical matters; but Hörschelmann undertakes to show a distinct advance in these respects in Book 2 (cf. elision tables in Hosius, p. 180).

[2] Cf. Braum, *De Monosyllabis ante caesuras hexametri Latini collocatis*, Marburg, 1906; Isidor Hilberg, *Die Gesetze der Wortstellung im Pentameter des Ovid;* Hornstein, *Die Wortstellung im Pentameter des Tibull und Ps.-Tibull*, Czernovitch, 1909; Petrus Rasi, *De Elegiae Latinae Compositione et Forma*, Padua, 1894; Smith, pp. 103 sqq.

[3] For the instances of the same in Propertius cf. Hosius, p. 184.

[4] Cf. Rasi, *de positione debili*, etc.; Brenner, *Die prosodischen Funktionen inlautender muta cum liquida im Hexameter und Pentameter des Catull, Tibull, und Properz;* Winbolt, *Latin Hexameter Verse*, 1903.

CATULLUS MSS. SIGNS

V = Codex " Veronensis " = the consensus of **O** and **G**.

O = Codex Oxoniensis.

G = Codex Sangermanensis.

R = Codex Romanus.

M = Codex Venetus.

D = Codex Datanus.

ω = late or inferior Mss., or corrections.

CATVLLI CARMINA

65

Etsi me adsiduo confectum cura dolore
   sevocat a doctis, Ortale, virginibus,
nec potis est dulcis musarum expromere fetus
   mens animi: tantis fluctuat ipsa malis:

65. 1. confectum G defectu O.

65

The Ortalus to whom this elegy is addressed was probably the celebrated orator, Quintus Hortensius (H)Ortalus, the friend and rival of Cicero. It was written to accompany some other poem or poems, particularly, as seems most likely, No. 66. Written about 60 B.C. For Hortensius as a poet cf. 95, 3 (written at a later period); Gell. 19, 9, 7; Ovid, *Trist.* 2, 441; Plin. *Ep.* 5, 3, 5.

The elegy is in one long paragraph, with parenthetical address to his brother, who has lately died. Catullus is in no mood to write in his usual vein, he says; but, that Ortalus may not think him forgetful of his request, he sends the accompanying translation from Callimachus.

1. Etsi: the apodosis begins at v. 15; cf. *Ciris*, 1–11.

2. doctis . . . virginibus: the Muses; cf. 35, 16: *Sapphica puella musa doctior*; Tib. 3, 4, 45; Ovid, *Am.* 3, 9, 62; Mart. 1, 61, 1. At this (Alexandrian) period of his poetry Catullus with special fitness calls his muse "*doctus*"; cf. Intr. § 16.

3. potis est: for other examples of the uncontracted form of *potest* cf. 76, 24; Lachmann's Lucr. 5, 880. — **fetus**: for the same idea of literary creations cf. Quint. 10, 4, 2: *scripta nostra tamquam recentes fetus*.

4. mens animi: cf. Lucr. 3, 615; Cic. *De Fin.* 5, 36: *animi partis, quae princeps est, quaeque mens nominatur*. —On the form of this verse and v. 8 note Intr. § 42, II (6).

69

5   namque mei nuper Lethaeo gurgite fratris
         pallidulum manans adluit unda pedem,
     Troia Rhoeteo quem subter litore tellus
         ereptum nostris obterit ex oculis.
     adloquar, audiero numquam tua facta loquentem,
10   numquam ego te, vita frater amabilior,
     adspiciam posthac. at certe semper amabo,
         semper maesta tua carmina morte canam,
     qualia sub densis ramorum concinit umbris

   9. *omitted in* **VR** adloquar audiero numquam tua loquentem **Dω** *the lacuna
between* tua *and* loquentem *variously supplied as* facta (**D** *man. sec.*), verba,
fata **ω**. *Lachmann, followed by Haupt- Vahlen, believed there was a lacuna in*
V *of seven verses after 8, and supplied before 9 six verses from 68, 20–24, and
92–96.*   11. at **D** aut **V**.   12. canam *or* legam **ω** tegam **VR** (*in* **R** *the verse
reads:* semp mesta tua carmine morte tegam).

5. **Lethaeo gurgite**: best taken
as abl. of source; cf. v. 6, n.
This seems to be the first reference
to the Lethe myth in Roman
poetry; cf. Tib. 3, 3, 10. —**fratris**:
probably an older brother. He
died in the Troad, and was buried
there; cf. 68, 90–100; 101.

6. **pallidulum**: a pathetic diminutive, implying fond tender-
ness; probably either coined by
Catullus or borrowed from the
speech of everyday life; not used
elsewhere before the silver Latin
period; cf. Intr § 17; Juv. 10,
82; Platner, *Dimin. in Catull.*
—**manans**: Catullus's conceptions
of underworld geography were
probably at least as hazy as those
of all the Roman poets with regard to terrestrial geography (cf.
66, 12, n). He may have pictured
his brother as fording Lethe, or
being ferried over in a skiff

(Charon's); but the emphasis of
manans adluit is best preserved
if we assume that he meant that,
escaping from its ordinary bounds,
the flood of Lethe, this stray wave
had borne the innocent youth all
too early to the waters of ob-
livion.

7. **Rhoeteo**: celebrated also as
the site of the grave of Ajax. — **subter**: the use of this preposition with
the abl. is very rare, hardly occurring elsewhere except in Vergil;
cf. Verg. *Aen.* 9, 514.

9. **audiero**: sometimes a fut.
perf. is used with no appreciable
difference in meaning from that
of the fut.; cf. Prop. 2, 5, 22;
Plaut. *Most.* 526; Tib. 1, 1, 29, n.

10. **numquam** belongs to both
adloquar and *audiero*.

11. **posthac** seems to indicate
that his brother's death was quite
recent.

Daulias absumpti fata gemens Ityli:
15   sed tamen in tantis maeroribus, Ortale, mitto
       haec expressa tibi carmina Battiadae,
     ne tua dicta vagis nequiquam credita ventis
       effluxisse meo forte putes animo,
     ut missum sponsi furtivo munere malum
20   procurrit casto virginis e gremio,
     quod miserae oblitae molli sub veste locatum,
       dum adventu matris prosilit, excutitur:

14. Daulias = Procne, or, according to another myth, Philomela, from Daulis, the scene of the Tereus myth. — **Ityli**: according to a Homeric myth, Itylus, son of Zethus and Aëdon, was killed by his mother by mistake, and she became a nightingale. When the Tereus myth was developed, the name of the boy was given as Itys. As the two myths are essentially one, it is not strange that the name of the former should be transferred to the latter, perhaps under the idea that it was a diminutive of Itys; cf. German *Willychen*, etc.

15. sed tamen: the conclusion of the periodic sentence begun in v. 1. — **in tantis maeroribus**: note the concessive force of the construction. The plural expresses mere poetic intensity.

16. expressa: 'translated.' — **carmina**: 'verses': a single couplet may be a *carmen*; cf. 64, 383; Ovid, *Sapph.* 6; Prop. 2, 13, 25, n. on *tres . . . libelli*. At any rate we have no translation of

Callimachus in this collection except No. 66. — **Battiadae**: the celebrated elegiac poet Callimachus, who claimed to be a descendant of Battus, the founder of Cyrene. It was certainly true in a general sense, as Callimachus was a native of Cyrene; cf. 116, 2.

17. tua dicta: implies a previous request on the part of Ortalus for some poem, whether a translation from Callimachus or something else. — **nequiquam**: best taken with *credita*; cf. 30, 10; the usual medium of communication by sound is "*ventis*."

19. malum: the most common gift of lovers; cf. Verg. *Ec.* 3, 64: *malo me Galatea petit*; 71: *aurea mala decem misi*; Prop. 1, 3, 24: *furtiva cavis poma dabam manibus*; the myth of the apple of discord, etc.

20. Cf. the Latin proverb quoted by Festus, p. 165: *nec mulieri nec gremio credi oportet*; *quod plerumque*, he adds, *in gremio posito, cum in oblivionem venerunt propere exsurgentium, procidunt*.

atque illud prono praeceps agitur decursu,
huic manat tristi conscius ore rubor.

66

Omnia qui magni dispexit lumina mundi,
qui stellarum ortus comperit atque obitus,

66. 1. dispexit ω despexit **V**.   2. obitus ω habitus **V**.

23. The rhythm, including the
alliteration, *prono praeceps*, and
the spondaic ending of the verse,
is admirably adapted to express
the bounce of the apple and the
astonishment and confusion of the
girl. Cf. 68, 59.

24. **huic**: contrasted with *illud*
(v. 23). — **tristi**: 'rueful.'

66

There is little doubt that this
is the poem referred to in No. 65,
viz. the translation from Callimachus sent to Ortalus. The meager fragments of the original
Βερενίκης Πλόκιμος of Callimachus indicate that this elegy of
Catullus was not a literal translation, though it was a work of
little originality. All the characteristic vices of the Alexandrian
type of elegy are here illustrated
better, perhaps, than in any other
existing Latin poem, — the artificiality of tone, the far-fetched,
and often obscure, allusions, the
adulation of the court, the general

air of superior learning appropriate to the "*doctus poeta*." Its
interest is accordingly greater
from the standpoint of literary
history than *per se*. Cf. Lamarre,
Vol. 2, p. 560.

The legend upon which the
elegy is based is referred to by
Hyginus, *Astr.* 2, 24 : *vovisse
Berenicen, si victor Ptolomaeus
redisset, se crinem detonsuram,
quo voto damnatam crinem in
Veneris Arsinoes Zephyritidis po-
suisse templo eumque postero die
non comparuisse. Quod factum
cum rex aegre ferret, Conon
mathematicus, ut ante diximus,
cupiens inire gratiam regis crinem
inter sidera videri conlocatum et
quasdam vacuas a figura septem
stellas ostendit quas esse fingeret
crinem.*

Ptolemy Euergetes (king of
Egypt, 247–222 B.C.), soon after
his marriage to Berenice II, was
compelled to go on an expedition
against Seleucus II of Syria. To
insure the safe return of her hus-

flammeus ut rapidi solis nitor obscuretur,
ut cedant certis sidera temporibus,

band the young bride vowed to
the gods a part of her fine head of
hair. Upon the return of Ptolemy
the vow was duly performed, and
the hair was placed in the temple
of Arsinoë on the promontory of
Zephyrion, not far from Alexandria. When it was discovered, next
morning, that the hair had disappeared from the temple, the
royal astronomer Conon seized
the opportunity to declare that he
had already discovered it in the
heavens as a constellation ; and
to this day the group of stars is
known under the appellation *Coma
Berenices.*

The elegy is spoken by the
hair itself in the first person, and
is sometimes playful, sometimes
petulant, sometimes gently ironical
in its tone : 1–8 : 'In the heavens
Conon discovered me, Berenice's
hair ; 9–14 : which she vowed to
the gods when as a bride she
was obliged to let her husband go
off to war. 15–20 : Despite the
tears of brides, they really love
their husbands dearly. 21–32 :
Was it a separation from a
brother merely that you so
dreaded ? What then became
so suddenly of your well-known
courage ? Was it not rather the
anguish of a lover at the thought
of parting ? 33–38 : Then you
vowed me to the gods on behalf
of his safe return ; and here I am
among the immortals paying your

vow. 39–50 : It grieved me sorely
to leave your head ; but how could
I resist the power of steel ? That
power has even leveled mountains.
Cursed be the inventors of steel !
51–56 : It was a sad day for my
sister locks when the winged horse
of Arsinoë came to bear me away
to the goddess his mistress. 57–
68 : She sent him after me that
I might honor her as a new constellation like that made from
Ariadne's golden tresses, and
might be beside Virgo, Leo, Callisto and Boötes. 69–78 : But,
no matter how ungrateful I may
appear, I cannot feel as much joy
at my new honors as sorrow at
being torn from the head of my
mistress, and from all the royal
perfumes there enjoyed. 79–88 :
In compensation, ye brides, offer
unguents to me on your wedding
days, ye who are worthy, and may
love ever abide with you ! 89–92 :
As to you, my queen, when you
propitiate Venus on holidays, do
not forget me. 93–94 : But what
are stars to me ? Would that I
were back upon thy head !'

1. **qui** : the antecedent is *ille
Conon* (v. 7).— **dispexit** : ' distinguished '; cf. v. 7, n.

3. Conon is said to have
brought together the earlier Egyptian records of eclipses.

4. This verse refers to the annual disappearance of certain constellations at fixed times. Cf.

5   ut Triviam furtim sub Latmia saxa relegans
        dulcis amor gyro devocet aerio,
     idem me ille Conon caelesti in lumine vidit
        e Bereniceo vertice caesariem
     fulgentem clare, quam multis illa dearum
10   levia protendens bracchia pollicitast,
     qua rex tempestate novo auctus hymenaeo
        vastatum finis iverat Assyrios,

5. relegans ω religans **V**.   7. in lumine *Voss* celesti numine **V**.
9. multis illa dearum **VR** cunctis illa deorum *Haupt*.

Hor. *Car*. 3, 1, 27; and Verg.
Aen. 3, 516, where *pluviasque
Hyadas* refers to the usual bad
weather at the season of the year
when the Hyades are in a certain
position.

5. **Triviam**: the goddess of the
crossroads, the Latin name for
the Greek Hecate, *i.e.* the moon
as goddess of the night. — **Latmia
saxa**: the grotto on Mt. Latmus
in Caria, where Selene used to
meet her loved Endymion. For
the significance of the myth cf.
H. and T. § 61.

7. **Conon**: a native of Samos;
astronomer of the court of Ptolemy; friend of Archimedes; reputed author of several astronomical works, which are not extant.
The rather fulsome flattery of the
court poet is responsible, however,
for so many things being attributed to him in vv. 1–6. As a
matter of fact, he was of minor
importance as an astronomer,
compared with such famous
Alexandrians as Aristarchus and

Hipparchus. Cf. Verg. *Ec*. 3,
40–42: *in medio duo signa, Conon
et — quis fuit alter, descripsit
radio totum qui gentibus orbem,
tempora quae messor, quae curvus
arator haberet ?*

8. **e . . . vertice**: sc. *detonsum*.

9. **multis . . . dearum**: cf. v.
33; it was the custom for women
to offer their hair to certain goddesses; then in making the vow all
the divinities would be included;
so there is no contradiction between the two verses; cf. Serv.
Georg. 1, 21 : *more pontificum
. . . post speciales deos . . .
generaliter omnia numina invoca-
bantur*. Cf. Friedrich's note on
this passage.

10. **protendens bracchia**: for
the position see that of the
'praying boy' in the Berlin Museum ; cf. Von Sybel, p. 297.

11. **novo | auctūs hymenaeo**:
cf. Intr. § 43.

12. **Assyrios** = *Syrios*; cf. the
introduction to this elegy ; also v.
36 ; Tib. 1, 3, 7, n.

dulcia nocturnae portans vestigia rixae
    quam de virgineis gesserat exuviis.
15   estne novis nuptis odio Venus? anne parentum
    frustrantur falsis gaudia lacrimulis,
ubertim thalami quas intra limina fundunt?
    non, ita me divi, vera gemunt, iuerint.
id mea me multis docuit regina querellis
20   invisente novo proelia torva viro.
at tu non orbum luxti deserta cubile,
    sed fratris cari flebile discidium?
quam penitus maestas exedit cura medullas!
    ut tibi tum toto pectore sollicitae
25   sensibus ereptis mens excidit! at te ego certe
    cognoram a parva virgine magnanimam.
anne bonum oblita es facinus quo regium adepta's

25. te *Avantius ; omitted in* **V**.   26. magnanimam D magnanima **V**.

14. de: 'for.'

16. frustrantur: sc. *nuptae.* — **lacrimulis**: the contemptuous diminutive: 'crocodile tears.'

17. ubertim: the stock adverb with verbs of weeping.

18. ita . . . iüerint: cf. Tib. 2, 5, 63, n. Propertius has the same shortened form of this verb in 2, 23, 22 ; cf. L. 891.

20. invisente: he 'saw' the struggle as we say a soldier 'saw service.'

21. at tu: 'Do you say?' — **luxti** = *luxisti* ; similar shortened forms in Catullus are *tristi* (v. 30), *duxti* (91, 9), *promisti* (110, 3), etc.

22. fratris cari: a bantering reference to the custom whereby

the Egyptian kings sometimes married their sisters. As a matter of fact, Berenice and her husband were cousins. Cf. P.W. 284.

23. The reply to the preceding question extends through v. 32 ; it was not sisterly, but conjugal love. — **cura**: 'love' (for thy husband). — **medullas**: cf. 35, 15 : *ignes interiorem edunt medullam* ; 45, 16 : *ignis mollibus ardet in medullis* ; Verg. *Aen.* 4, 66 : *est mollis flamma medullas.*

26. a parva virgine: 'from girlhood'; cf. Ter. *Andr.* 35 : *a parvolo.* — **magnanimam**: 'courageous.'

27. facinus: the story is found in Justinus 26, 3, 2 : Apama, the mother of Berenice, wished to

> coniugium, quod non fortior ausit alis?
> sed tum maesta virum mittens quae verba locuta's!
30 Iuppiter, ut tristi lumina saepe manu!
> quis te mutavit tantus deus? an quod amantes
> non longe a caro corpore abesse volunt?
> atque ibi me cunctis pro dulci coniuge divis
> non sine taurino sanguine pollicita's,
35 si reditum tetulisset. is haut in tempore longo
> captam Asiam Aegypti finibus addiderat.
> quis ego pro factis caelesti reddita coetu
> pristina vota novo munere dissoluo.

28. quod non fortior **VR** quo **D** fortius *Muretus.*

marry her to Demetrius, a brother of king Antigonus of Macedonia, instead of regarding her previous betrothal to Ptolemy. But soon after the arrival of Demetrius at Cyrene he became the paramour of the mother, furnishing Berenice an opportunity to head a band of soldiers who took the life of her would-be husband, and so left her free to marry Ptolemy. Apama was probably spared.

28. quod . . . alis: 'which many another better adapted for deeds of manly prowess would not venture.' — **fortior** is essentially a word of masculine hardihood, and is here contrasted with *magnanimam* (v. 26). — **alis** = *alius:* the form occurs only here in classical literature; *alid* (29, 15) is quite common in Lucretius.

30. Iuppiter: cf. v. 48; 1, 7; Hor. *Sat.* 2, 1, 43. — **tristi** = *tristi;* cf. v. 21, n.

31. an: the first part of the

question is omitted, as commonly: 'Was it indeed any god at all, or rather the fact that,' etc. ?

33. ibi: temporal, taking up the thread of the story broken off with v. 14. — **cunctis . . . divis**: cf. v. 9, n.

34. taurino sanguine: probably a part of the promise.

35. tetulisset: the usual early Latin form for *tulisset;* cf. LSHLG, p. 99; *reditum tetulisset = rediisset.* — **in tempore longo**: A. 256, *a.*

36. Asiam: with the notorious geographical vagueness of the Roman poets. The famous inscription discovered at the Ethiopian city Adule states that not only Asia Minor, but also other parts of the continent, even beyond the Euphrates, were subdued.

37. coetu: dat.; a form found only here and in 64, 385.

38. dissolŭo: cf. *evoluam,* v. 74; Intr. § 43.

invita, o regina, tuo de vertice cessi,
40   invita: adiuro teque tuumque caput,
digna ferat quod siquis inaniter adiurarit:
        sed qui se ferro postulet esse parem?
ille quoque eversus mons est quem maximum in orbe
        progenies Thiae clara supervehitur,
45 cum Medi peperere novum mare cumque iuventus
        per medium classi barbara navit Athon.
quid facient crines, cum ferro talia cedant?
        Iuppiter, ut Chalybon omne genus pereat,
et qui principio sub terra quaerere venas
50   institit ac ferri frangere duritiem!

---

39. Cf. Verg. *Aen.* 6, 460: *invitus, regina, tuo de litore cessi.*

40. adiuro . . . caput: the fragment of Callimachus (35 *b*, Schneider), σήν τε καρὴν ὤμοσα σόν τε βίον, shows how closely Catullus here followed his original, preserving the acc. with *adiuro*, a construction that does not appear again before Vergil (*Aen.* 12, 816: *adiuro Stygii caput implacabile fontis*).

41. Note the inverted order. — **digna** (acc.): *i.e. poenam.*

42. qui: for the regular substantive form *quis.* — **ferro:** referring to the shears that clipped the lock.

43. ille . . . mons: 'that famous mountain,' Athos. — **quoque:** *i.e.* as well as I, a hapless lock of hair. — **eversus:** sc. *ferro.* The hyperboles in this sentence are uttered naïvely by the lock.

44. progenies Thiae: Helios.

45. Medi: the hosts of Xerxes. — **novum mare:** the canal cut through the isthmus of Athos at the time of the invasion of Greece.

46. navit: cf. 64, 1: *pinus dicuntur liquidas Neptuni nasse per undas.*

47. That the mood in such questions depends on the feeling of the writer is shown clearly by a comparison of Verg. *Ec.* 3, 16: *quid domini faciant, audent cum talia fures?* Livy, 21, 10, 11: *dedemus ergo Hannibalem? dicet aliquis.*

48. Iuppiter: cf. v. 30, n.; Hor. *Sat.* 2, 1, 42: *o pater et rex Iuppiter, ut pereat positum robigine telum.* — **Chalybon:** a people of Pontus, celebrated for their skill in mining and iron-working.

50. ferri . . . duritiem: = *ferrum durum*; cf. Lucr. 5, 1241: *aes atque aurum ferrumque repertumst et simul argenti pondus;*

abiunctae paullo ante comae mea fata sorores
   lugebant, cum se Memnonis Aethiopis
unigena inpellens nictantibus aera pennis
   obtulit Arsinoes Locridos ales equus,
55   isque per aetherias me tollens avolat umbras
   et Veneris casto collocat in gremio.
   ipsa suum Zephyritis eo famulum legarat,

---

53. nictantibus *Bentley* nutantibus **V** mutantibus **M** mitantibus, motantibus, natantibus, *various minor authorities.* 54. Locridos *Bentley* elocridicos **VR** Cypridos *Bergk.* ales **D** alis **VR**.

2, 449 : *validi silices ac duri robora ferri aeraque.*

51. paullo ante : to be taken with *abiunctae* (sc. *a me*). The bereavement had but just occurred, that very day. For the meter see Intr. § 42, I (5) (*b*).

52. Aethiopis : the epithet may have significance as referring to the dark color of Memnon's brother, the *ales equus* of v. 54. Cf. also *umbras* (v. 55).

53. unigena : ' own brother,' *i.e.* Emathion, who, like Memnon, was a son of Eos and Tithonus ; cf. 64, 300. The rendering, ' only-begotten' does not agree with Ovid, *Met.* 13, 608–609 : *pariter sonuere sorores innumerae.* — **nictantibus** : the imagery has a rare charm.

54. Arsinoes : Arsinoë II, daughter of Ptolemy I ; wife first of Lysimachus, king of Thrace, later of her brother, Ptolemy Philadelphus (cf. v. 22, n.). Among other honors, she was identified with Venus, and a temple was erected in her name on the prom-

ontory of Zephyrion, near Alexandria, whence is derived also the name Zephyritis (v. 57). — **Locridos** : it is possible that the appearance of this obscure epithet here may be due to confusion or comparison of this particular Zephyrion with the more famous Italian promontory of the same name in Bruttii, which from early times was settled by the Locrians. The term *Cypridos*, if it can be justified critically as the correct reading here, is more appropriate and more accurate historically. Cf. P. W. 2, 1286. — **ales equus** : probably the ostrich, here identified with Emathion (cf. n. on v. 52) ; Pausanias (9, 31, 1) describes the service rendered to Arsinoë by an ostrich : τὴν δὲ Ἀρσινόην στρουθὸς φέρει χαλκῆ τῶν ἀπτήνων. Others understand the phrase to refer to Zephyrus.

57. Zephyritis : cf. n. on v. 54. — **famulum** : *i.e.* the *ales equus* of v. 54, the ostrich. Cf. Ovid, *Met.* 3, 229, where Actaeon's hounds are his *famuli* ; and Manil. 4, 760,

Graia Canopiis incola litoribus.
hic iuveni Ismario ne solum in lumine caeli
60   ex Ariadneis aurea temporibus
fixa corona foret, sed nos quoque fulgeremus
devotae flavi verticis exuviae,
uvidulam a fletu cedentem ad templa deum me
sidus in antiquis diva novum posuit:
65   virginis et saevi contingens namque leonis

---

59. hic iuveni Ismario *Ellis* hi dii ven ibi vario **V** hi dij venibi (*or* ven ibi) vario **R** arduei ibi *Haupt* invida enim *Vahlen* numen ibi *Ritschl* hic liquidi *Friedrich*. lumine *or* limine ω mumine **R** numine **V**.

---

where the *famulus* of Cybele is the lion.

58. Graia: referring to the Greek ancestry of Arsinoë as compared to her ultimate home in Egypt (*Canopiis*). This Greek woman took precedence of all the members of the royal house of Egypt in becoming the first of the Ptolemies to be deified. The Alexandrian obscurity of this whole passage may easily have been enhanced by the poet's ignorance of Egyptian conditions.

59. hic: temporal. — **iuveni Ismario:** Bacchus, whose vine was abundant on Ismarus; cf. Verg. *Georg.* 2, 37: *iuvat Ismara Baccho conserere.*

60. ex Ariadneis . . . corona: at the marriage of Ariadne to Bacchus, after her desertion by Theseus, Venus gave her as a bridal gift a magnificent crown of gold and precious gems (made by Vulcan). Its metamorphosis into a constellation ('the northern

crown') at the translation of Ariadne to heaven is a theme of frequent recurrence in the poets: Ovid, *Fast.* 3, 459–516; 5, 345: *Baccho placuisse coronam ex Ariadneo sidere nosse potes; Met.* 8, 177–182; Manil. 5, 21: *Ariadneae caelestia dona coronae;* Prop. 3, 17, 7: *testatur in astris lyncibus ad caelum vecta Ariadna tuis.*

62. flavi: the Homeric ideal; so Ariadne's hair is described by the same epithet in 64, 63: *flavo . . . vertice.*

63. uvidulam: a characteristic Catullus diminutive. — **fletu:** due to its compulsory condition as *exuviae.* — **templa:** cf. Enn. *Ann.* 1, 49 (Vahlen): *ad caeli caerula templa;* Lucr. 1, 1014: *nec mare nec tellus neque caeli lucida templa.*

65. virginis: the constellation Virgo was variously identified with Dike-Astraea, Isis, Tyche, Erigone, etc. Cf. *Class. Dict.* — **namque:** on the position cf.

79

lumina, Callisto iuncta Lycaoniae,
vertor in occasum, tardum dux ante Booten,
qui vix sero alto mergitur Oceano.
sed quamquam me nocte premunt vestigia divum,
70   lux autem canae Tethyi restituit :
pace tua fari hic liceat, Rhamnusia virgo :
namque ego non ullo vera timore tegam,
nec si me infestis discerpent sidera dictis,

Draeger, 2, p. 162 ; Tib. 1, 7, 12, n.
— leonis : Zeus was responsible
for the metamorphosis of the
famous Nemean lion, slain by
Hercules, into the constellation
Leo, the fifth sign of the zodiac.
66. Callisto : dat. ; but one of
several irregular forms in the decl.
of this word. Her history is variously told, the adj. **Lycaoniae** here
having patronymic force. As attendant of Artemis in Arcadia she
became by Zeus mother of Arcas,
was changed into a bear, and later,
either after death, or to escape
death, into a constellation, this
being one of the many identifications explanatory of the origin of
Ursa Major. — **iuncta** : ' next to.'
67. dux ante : a touch of pride
that she should show the way to
the ' oxen-driver,' or charioteer,
Boötes. — **Booten** : the constel-
lated Arcas, son of Callisto ; or
Lycaon ; or Icarius.
68. vix sero . . . mergitur : a
characteristic noticed by Homer,
Od. 5, 272 : ὀψὲ δύοντα βοώτην,
and explained by Sir G. C. Lewis
(*Astronomy of the Ancients*, p. 59)
on the ground that its setting,

" inasmuch as the constellation is
in a perpendicular position, occu-
pies some time, whereas his rising
is rapid, being effected in a hori-
zontal position."
69. quamquam belongs to *restituit* as well as to *premunt* ; the
principal clause begins at v. 75. —
premunt vestigia divum : cf. Arat.
359 : θεῶν ὑπὸ ποσσὶ φορεῖται ;
Manil. (1, 803) adopts this phrase.
70. Tethyi : to whom, rather
than to her husband Oceanus (cf.
v. 68), the maidenly modesty of
the *Coma* prefers to represent herself as surrendered for the passage
by day (*lux*) back around the
earth to her next rising. Cf. Tib.
2, 5, 59–60.
71–74. Parenthetical.
71. Rhamnusia virgo : Nemesis,
so called from her temple at Rhamnus in Attica, whose province it
was to punish presumptuous words.
Cf. 68, 77 ; 50, 20 : *ne poenas
Nemesis reposcat a te.*
73. nec : sc. *tegam.* Only if
tum, or some other emphatic word,
were expressed, should we think
nec=ne . . . quidem. This verse
is an emphatic reiteration of the

condita quin veri pectoris evoluam :

75   non his tam laetor rebus, quam me afore semper,
     afore me a dominae vertice discrucior,
     quicum ego, dum virgo quondam fuit omnibus expers
     unguentis, una milia multa bibi.
     nunc, vos optato quom iunxit lumine taeda,
80   non prius unanimis corpora coniugibus
     tradite nudantes reiecta veste papillas,
     quam iucunda mihi munera libet onyx,

---

77. expers **V** expersa *Heinsius* expressa *Statius* ex pars *Munro*.   78. un-
guentis **V** unguenti si *Lachmann* unguenti surii *Auratus*.   79. quom *Haupt*
quem **V** quas **ω**.   80. prius **ω** post **G**.   82. quam **V** quin *Lachmann*.

previous one. — **si** = *etiamsi.* —
discerpent : probably the word is
more literal than figurative in the
mind of the poet ; but as a metaphor it must be regarded as a *ἅπαξ*
λεγόμενον. Cf. Cic. *Ad Att.* 2,
19, 3 : *qua dominus qua advocati*
sibilis conscissi. The tense signifies the probability of the fate. —
dictis : instr.

74. **quin** indicates that *tegam*
was used as a verb of ' hindering.'
— **evolŭam** ; cf. Intr. § 43.

75. **his** . . . **rebus** : *i.e.* the
great honors recently described.

76. **afore me** : emphatic and
artistic inversion, forming a chias-
mus with the expression in v. 75.

77. **expers** : in the active sense,
and with concessive force, ' though
caring little for.' Cf. Plaut. *Amph.*
713 : *eo more expertem te* ; Ovid,
Met. 1, 479 ; Hor. *Car.* 3, 11, 11.
Cf. also K. P. H. in *BPW.*, Vol.
30, Sp. 285.

78. **una** : to be taken with
quicum.

79. **nunc** = *νῦν δέ* = *ut nunc est.*
— " Blessings brighten as they
take their flight," and under the
changed conditions, the lock eagerly demands in its translated
state offerings of the choicest perfumes from newly wedded brides,
who by the act will remind her of
her lost home and her beloved
mistress.—**lumine** = *die*, as in v. 90.

80. **unanimis** : ' in mutual affection.'

82. **onyx** : an ointment vase
made of onyx. They were even
more common, especially in Egypt,
of alabaster (*alabastron*). For
typical shapes v. Dennis, *Cities*
and Cemeteries of Etruria, p. cxxv,
ill. 77 and 78. Cf. Hor. *Car.* 4, 12,
17 : *nardi parvus onyx eliciat*
cadum ; Prop. 2, 13, 30 ; St. Mark
14, 3 : " alabaster box (R.V.
" cruse ") of ointment."

vester onyx, casto petitis quae iura cubili.
　　sed quae se inpuro dedit adulterio,
85　illius ah mala dona levis bibat inrita pulvis:
　　namque ego ab indignis praemia nulla peto.
　　sed magis, o nuptae, semper concordia vestras,
　　　semper amor sedes incolat adsiduus.
　　tu vero, regina, tuens cum sidera divam·
90　　placabis festis luminibus Venerem,
　　unguinis expertem non siris esse tuam me,
　　　sed potius largis adfice muneribus.
　　sidera corruerint utinam! coma regia fiam:
　　proximus hydrochoi fulgeret Oarion.

91. unguinis *Bentley* sanguinis **V.**　non siris *Lachmann* ne siveris *Scaliger*
non vestris **V.**　tuam *Avantius* tuum **V.**

83. vester : emphatic, 'only yours,' and containing the implied antecedent of *quae*. — **iura** : *i.e.* those of a *iustum matrimonium*.

87. sed magis : 'but rather,' *i.e.* than experience in any unholy union the shame and disappointments just referred to. For this essentially adversative use of *magis* cf. 68, 30. Cf. also v. 92.

91. unguinis=*unguenti*, a comparatively rare equivalent. — **expertem** : here in the passive sense, 'lacking in.' — **non** : cf. v. 80 ; Ovid, *A. A.* 1, 389: *aut non temptaris aut perfice*. — **siris** = *siveris*. — **tuam** : cf. Hor. *Car.* 1, 25, 7 : *me tuo longas pereunte noctes, Lydia, dormis*.

93. Throwing off the grand tone of the previous verses, the lock bursts forth once more at the close with an ejaculation of its real feelings.

94. In the illogical petulance of youth it forgets that it has just wished the destruction of the whole stellar system, and gayly imagines a complete confusion of the established order in the sky. — **proximus** : though the distance between the two constellations Aquarius and Orion is now at least 90°. — **hydrochoi** : dat. — **Oarion**: the Greek form Ὠαρίων was not only the sign of the *doctus poeta*, but was preferred here, as undoubtedly in the original, for metrical reasons.

68

Quod mihi fortuna casuque oppressus acerbo
conscriptum hoc lacrimis mittis epistolium,

68. *Title* Ad Mallium **RM** Ad Mallium, Malium, Manlium **ω**.

68

Many editors have believed this elegy made up of two or more separate poems, and it appears accordingly in various editions as 68ᵃ(vv. 1–40), 68ᵇ(41–160), or 68ᵇ(41–148), and 68ᶜ(149–160). The arguments for such mutilation are shrewdly stated by Riese in his annotated edition of 1884, and by Merrill (1893). For the defense of the poem's unity, however, see Magnus, in Bursian's *JB*., Vol. 87 (1887), pp. 151 sqq., and Vol. 126 (1906), pp. 139 sqq., and *Jahrbücher f. Phil. u. Päd.*, Vol. 3 (1875), pp. 849 sqq. ; Kiessling, *Analecta Catulliana* (Greifswald Program, 1877); Harnecker, *Das 68 Gedicht des Catullus* (Friedeberg Program, 1881); Friedrich (who, however, puts the worst construction upon it) ; Schanz, and his bibliography ; etc. The difficulties of interpretation do not seem to be removed, but rather enhanced, by the proposed division ; and the elegy is best considered as one, a carefully evolved and acutely involved product of the poet's Alexandrian period.

The hopeless confusion, in the Mss., of the name of the person may be most simply explained by adopting Lachmann's conjecture that he was M'. Allius. It is then very easy to see how the title *Ad Mallium*, and the various readings in vv. 11, 30, 41, 66, arose. For an acute discussion of the origin of these variants, cf. Friedrich, pp. 44 sqq. No editor has ventured to follow the Mss. implicitly in this matter. In the main part of the elegy (vv. 41–148) Allius is spoken of in the third person as the subject of the eulogy which is pronounced upon him for his friendly services ; in the introduction (vv. 1–40) it is not unnatural, but in harmony with the direct (second personal) address of the epistolary style employed, that the more familiar praenomen Manius should be used. But in v. 150 of the epilogistic close (vv. 148–160) the same name would naturally be employed as that to which reference is made in the same sentence by the word *nomen* (v. 151).

From the passage beginning at v. 27 it is seen that Catullus was at Verona, while Allius was doubtless at Rome, as was also Lesbia. It can scarcely be doubted that the poet expected, nay, probably in-

> naufragum ut eiectum spumantibus aequoris undis
> sublevem et a mortis limine restituam,
> 5   quem neque sancta Venus molli requiescere somno

tended, the elegy to come to
the attention of his mistress;
and it should be read with this in
mind.

Briefly, the argument of the
poem is developed as follows:
1–10: 'You write that you have
neither love nor poetry which
soothes your sorrowing heart, and
ask for both these sources of comfort from me; 11–32: but you do
not know that my brother's death
has plunged me into such grief
that I am in no mood to write of
love's dalliance, and my sadness is
enhanced by what you write of my
mistress's faithlessness; 33–40:
neither can I send you any other
poems, for they are all at Rome;
you must not blame me then for
not doing what I cannot. 41–69:
I must not, however, let the opportunity pass to hand down to eternal
fame the name of such a friend as
Allius, and his kind offices in opening to Lesbia and me a home for
our lover's meetings; 70–130:
thither came my mistress, aflame
with a love like that of Laodamia
for her bridegroom when that
short-lived home was established
upon which the Fates had already
caused to fall the blighting spell
of Troy, accursed Troy, which has
taken from me too all joy, as it did
from her, whose love was deeper
than the storied abyss by Pheneus,

more joyous than the grandsire's
on the birth of his anxiously
awaited heir, fonder than a dove's
for her mate; 131–148: thus came
Lesbia; and if sometimes she has
wavered in her devotion, I will
bear it as Juno does the fickleness
of Jove, and will remember the
wondrous joys of those golden
days. 149–160: Such is the gift of
poetic praise which I could offer,
my friend; may the gods bless
thee too, and thine, and mine, who
is still the light of my life!'

1. **Quod . . . mittis**: this prosaic epistolary form occurs thrice
in this part of the poem, appearing
again in vv. 27 and 33. — **casu . . .
acerbo**: speculation has been rife
as to its nature, whether political
or domestic: cf. v. 6, n.

2. **lacrimis**: instrumental. The
hyperbole may be considered as
quoted from the letter of Allius to
Catullus. — **epistolium**: this Gk.
diminutive occurs nowhere else in
Lat. before Apuleius.

3. **naufragum**: shipwreck as a
figure of ruined fortunes is a literary
commonplace.

4. Cf. Plin. *N. H.* 7, 44, 143:
a limine ipso mortis revocatus;
Culex, 224: *restitui superis leti
iam limine ab ipso.*

5–8. These verses evidently are
the reasons given by Allius for his
request.

desertum in lecto caelibe perpetitur,
nec veterum dulci scriptorum carmine musae
    oblectant, cum mens anxia pervigilat,
id gratum est mihi, me quoniam tibi dicis amicum,
10   muneraque et musarum hinc petis et Veneris :
sed tibi ne mea sint ignota incommoda, Mani,
    neu me odisse putes hospitis officium,
accipe, quis merser fortunae fluctibus ipse,
    ne amplius a misero dona beata petas.
15   tempore quo primum vestis mihi tradita purast,
    iucundum cum aetas florida ver ageret,
multa satis lusi : non est dea nescia nostri

---

11. incommoda **Dω** commoda **VM** comoda **R**. Mani *Lachmann* mali **VRM** al' mauli *sec. man. in* **M** *margin of* **R** mauli *or* malli **Dω**.

---

6. desertum in lecto caelibe: of the various theories advanced to explain the sadness of Allius, *e.g.* that he had quarreled with his wife or with his mistress, that one or the other of them was seriously ill, or separated from him suddenly for some other reason, or had recently died, only the last is irreconcilable with v. 155. A reminiscence of the phrase is found in Ovid's *Laodamia* epistle (*Her.* 13, 107).

7. veterum . . . scriptorum: either Greek or Roman.

8. cum: temporal.

10. muneraque . . . musarum: poems to serve in place of those of the *veterum scriptorum* of v. 7. — **hinc:** 'from me.' — [**munera**] **Veneris:** erotic poetry (cf. *lusi*, v. 17), referring back to vv. 5 and 6. The last request is answered first,

in vv. 11–32; the first one, last, in vv. 33–36.

12. hospitis officium: *i.e.* gratitude. Allius had indeed proved himself a genuine old Roman *hospes*, as is evidenced by vv. 67–72, and 156. If, however, *hospitis* = 'host,' we must suppose that Allius means by *munera . . . Veneris* (v. 10) that Catullus should open his house as a lover's rendezvous.

13. quis: abl.

14. dona beata = *dona beati.*

15. tempore: abl. of source. — **vestis . . . pura** = *toga pura, toga libera, toga virilis,* the assumption of which marked the beginning of young manhood.

16. The conditions under which erotic poetry thrives.

17. lusi: *i.e.* especially in writing love poems. Cf. 50, 2 : *multum*

quae dulcem curis miscet amaritiem :
sed totum hoc studium luctu fraterna mihi mors
20   abstulit. o misero frater adempte mihi,
tu mea tu moriens fregisti commoda, frater,
tecum una tota est nostra sepulta domus,
omnia tecum una perierunt gaudia nostra,
quae tuus in vita dulcis alebat amor.
25   cuius ego interitu tota de mente fugavi
haec studia atque omnis delicias animi.
quare, quod scribis Veronae turpe Catullo

27. Catullo **Dω** Catulle **VR**.

lusimus; 61, 232 : *lusimus satis ;*
Hor. *Car.* 1, 32, 1 : *Si quid vacui
sub umbra lusimus tecum.* — **dea** :
Venus.

18. dulcem . . . amaritiem : an
oxymoron familiar to all literature,
as to all human experience ; cf.
64, 95 : *sancte puer, curis hominum
qui gaudia misces ;* Sappho, *Frag.*
40 : γλυκύπικρον ἀμάχανον ὄρπετον ;
Plaut. *Cist.* 1, 1, 69 : *ecastor amor
et melle et fellest fecundissumus :
gustu dat dulce, amarum ad
satietatem usque oggerit ;* Ben Jon-
son, *Sad Shepherd,* 1, 2 : "I have
known some few, And read of
more, who have had their dose, and
deep, Of these sharp bitter-sweets."
This parallel archaic form of the
noun (**amaritiem**), though of a
common type, occurs nowhere else.

19. totum hoc studium : *i.e.*
both love's dalliance and the poetry
that accompanies it, including both
ideas expressed in v. 26. — **fraterna . . . mors** : cf. 65, 5, n. ; 101.

21. moriens : instrumental.

22. tota . . . sepulta domus :
to be understood in no literal sense,
but as the natural extravagant expression of poignant grief. The
next verse repeats the thought in
different form.

26. haec studia : the writing
of love poetry. — **omnis delicias
animi** : the joys of love itself.
This phrase reminds Catullus of a
remark in the letter of Allius, to
which he replies parenthetically
in vv. 27–30, resuming the main
argument in v. 31.

27. Veronae : the quotation
from the letter of Allius begins
here and includes the next two
verses, quoting, as is common in
literature, not the whole sentence
of Allius, but the important part,
something like *est,* or *credo esse,*
evidently being omitted. Catullus
after his brother's death is tarry-
ing at his old home in Verona,
while (so Allius writes) Lesbia's
lovers are taking advantage of him
in his absence from Rome.

esse, quod hic quisquis de meliore nota
frigida deserto tepefactat membra cubili,
30   id, Mani, non est turpe, magis miserumst.
ignosces igitur, si, quae mihi luctus ademit,
    haec tibi non tribuo munera, cum nequeo.
nam quod scriptorum non magna est copia apud me,
    hoc fit quod Romae vivimus : illa domus,
35   illa mihi sedes, illic mea carpitur aetas :
    huc una ex multis capsula me sequitur.
quod cum ita sit, nolim statuas nos mente maligna

---

28. quisquis **V** quivis *Lachmann.*   29. tepefactat *altered from* tepefacit
RM tepefacit **V** tepefaxit *Lachmann* tepefactet *Bergk.*   30. Mani *Lachmann*
mali **VRM** mauli *or* malli **Dω.**

---

28. hic: *i.e.* Rome, whence
Allius wrote. — **quisquis**: apparently used for *quisque* without *est*;
cf. Cic. *Ad Fam.* 6, 1, 1 : *quocumque in loco quisquis est*; *Tusc.
Disp.* 5, 34, 98 ; also the legal
phrase, *quod quemquam hac lege
profiterei oportebit*, which Lachmann quotes on Lucr. 5, 264, from
the *Lex Iulia Municipalis*, 13. —
meliore nota: Clodia and her
various paramours belonged to an
aristocratic circle of society.

29. deserto: *i.e.* by Catullus
when he went to Verona. — **tepefactat**: this expressive frequentative form is a ἅπαξ λεγόμενον,
as is one other of the two dozen
frequentatives used by Catullus,
trusantem (56, 6). But the present instance, it should be noted,
is a quotation from Allius.

30. magis: cf. 66, 87, n. —
miserumst: *i.e.* a reason to pity
me, a further cause for such sorrow

as to prevent me from complying
with your request.

31. ignosces: mild command.

32. haec . . . munera: the love
poetry. — **cum** : a good illustration
of the narrow line dividing the
temporal from the causal. Perhaps both ideas were in the mind
of the poet.

33. nam anticipates the question why Catullus cannot comply
with the first part of the request
in v. 10, *i.e.* send him some books
of poetry (*scriptorum*), not necessarily erotic ; perhaps translations
from Callimachus, like No. 66,
perhaps of a different character.

34. vivimus: here in Verona I
am merely temporarily managing
to exist; real life, with all that
makes it worth living, is only at
Rome, for me.

36. huc: to Verona.—**capsula** :
for books. — **sequitur** = *secuta est.*

37. statuas : 'conclude.'

id facere aut animo non satis ingenuo,
quod tibi non utriusque petenti copia postast:
40   ultro ego deferrem, copia siqua foret.
non possum reticere, deae, qua me Allius in re
iuverit aut quantis iuverit officiis,
ne fugiens saeclis obliviscentibus aetas
illius hoc caeca nocte tegat studium,
45   sed dicam vobis, vos porro dicite multis
milibus et facite haec charta loquatur anus

*   *   *   *   *   *   *

notescatque magis mortuus atque magis,
nec tenuem texens sublimis aranea telam

39. posta **VRM** facta **Dω**.   41. *No gap before this v. in* **VRM**.   qua me
Allius *Scaliger* quam fallius **VRM**.

39. non utriusque = *neutrius*, referring to the two requests of v.
10. — **postast**: although the only
example of this verb with *copia*,
it seems (to say nothing of its
Ms. authority) to express better
than the more usual *facta* the
thought of offering, or setting before Allius, a choice of what was
desirable; and the origin of *posta*
as a false reading is very hard to
explain.

41. non possum: cf. *nequeo*
(v. 32); though he cannot accede
to either request of Allius formally, he cannot refrain from writing the praises of Allius himself.
Conventionalities prevent certain
things for people in mourning;
but the phenomenon of eluding
these restrictions and allowing
Nature to assert herself under other
forms is a familiar one in all times,
as in this poem, where Catullus
really sings of the former delights
of his association with Lesbia,
partly in direct manner, and partly
by indirection through the parallel of Laodamia. — **deae** = *Musae.*

42. iuverit . . . iuverit: note
the emphatic repetition.

43. obliviscentibus: poetically
used with causative force.

44. caeca: active. — **nocte** =
caligine.

45. porro: 'in turn.'

46. anus: 'when old' (and
presumably garrulous, a quality
which may have been further
elaborated in the following missing verse). With this adjectival
use cf. 77, 10: *qui sis fama loque-
tur anus;* 9,4: *anumque matrem;*
Mart. 12, 4, 4: *chartaque dicet anus.*

48. notescat: one of several
inceptives that appear first in Cat.

50   in deserto Alli nomine opus faciat.
nam mihi quam dederit duplex Amathusia curam
    scitis, et in quo me corruerit genere,
cum tantum arderem quantum Trinacria rupes
    lymphaque in Oetaeis Malia Thermopylis,
55   maesta neque adsiduo tabescere lumina fletu
    cessarent tristique imbre madere genae,
qualis in aerii perlucens vertice montis
    rivus muscoso prosilit e lapide,
qui cum de prona praeceps est valle volutus,
60   per medium densi transit iter populi,
dulce viatori lasso in sudore levamen,

---

50. Alli **O** ali **GR** alii **M.**   54. Malia **ω** Maulia **VRM** Manlia **D.**

The subj., of course, is Allius. —
magis . . . atque magis: Catullus
employs also the shorter *magis
magis* in 38, 3 and 64, 274.

50. deserto . . . nomine: the
picture is that of an inscription
neglected and forgotten. Ellis
cites Shakespeare, *Sonnets*, 55, 4:
"unswept stone, besmear'd with
sluttish time."

51. duplex Amathusia: 'the
two-phased goddess of Amathus';
cf. v. 18. At Amathus was one
of the celebrated Cyprian temples
of Aphrodite. The supposed reference here to a Hermaphroditic
statue of the goddess is probably
due to the learned imagination of
the commentators.

52. genere : 'manner.'

53. Trinacria rupes: Aetna, the
ever-active volcano.

54. lympha: the hot springs
at Thermopylae, on one side of

which is Mt. Oeta, and on the
other, the Malian gulf.

56. imbre: 'flood' of tears.

57. qualis: points of likeness
in the simile are the high, clear,
and beautiful source of the stream,
its crystal purity, and its sudden
burst into full flow. To these we
may possibly add the relief afforded
by it to the wayfarer through the
weary wastes of burning passion;
but vv. 59–62 seem rather the
mere natural rounding out of a
beautiful description of natural
scenery without special significance, the poet being himself
carried on by the force of his own
rhetoric, like his mountain brook-
let. Cf. also Howe, p. 12.

58. muscoso: this descriptive
word goes further to paint the
picture than any other. Cf. Verg.
Ec. 7, 45: *muscosi fontes*.

59. prona praeceps: cf. 65, 23, n.

cum gravis exustos aestus hiulcat agros.

hic, velut in nigro iactatis turbine nautis

    lenius adspirans aura secunda venit

65   iam prece Pollucis, iam Castoris inplorata,

    tale fuit nobis Allius auxilium.

is clausum lato patefecit limite campum,

    isque domum nobis, isque dedit dominam,

ad quam communes exerceremus amores.

70   quo mea se molli candida diva pede

intulit et trito fulgentem in limine plantam

    innixa arguta constituit solea,

---

66. Allius (*in the margin* Manllius) **O** Manlius **GRM** Mallius *altered from* Manlius **D** Manius *lachmann.*   67. clausum **O** classum **GM** claussum ω. 68. dominam **VM** dominae *Froelich.*

---

62. Cf. Sall. *Iug.* 19, 6 : *loca exusta solis ardoribus.*

63. **hic** refers back to the *cum* of v. 53.

65. Pollucis . . . Castoris : obj. gen., like the more natural *precationibus deorum dearumque* (Livy, 1, *Praef.* 13); Prop. 4, 1, 101. — **inplorata** agrees, probably, with *aura.* Cf. Prop. 1, 17, 18, n.

66. nobis = *mihi* ; so also in v. 68.

67. limite : the means by which Catullus gained access to his love ; a kind of 'cross-lots' route, upon which might well have been inscribed, " private way, dangerous passing."

68. dominam : 'the lady of the house,' who would supposably act as chaperon and lend the air of propriety to the meeting. What house and what lady, whether Allius's wife or not, we are not informed.

69. ad = *apud.*—**quam** : i.e. *domum,* the previous clause being parenthetical.— **communes** : 'mutual' ; cf. Lucr. 4, 1195 : *communia . . . gaudia* ; 1208 : *est communi' voluptas.* —**exerceremus** : 'enjoy.'

70. diva : cf. Shak. *T. G. of Ver.* 2, 4, 147 : —

    " She is an earthly paragon, —
      Call her divine."

Mids. Night's Dream, 3, 2, 226 : —
    "To call me goddess, nymph, divine and rare,
      Precious, celestial."

71. trito : cf. v. 115. — **fulgentem** : the hyperbole of enthusiasm, instead of *nitidus*, which is the usual equivalent of the Homeric epithet λιπαροὶ (πόδες) ; cf. *Il.* 2, 44.

72. arguta . . . solea : the modern poet would be more likely to apply the epithet to a silk skirt worn by his divinity.

coniugis ut quondam flagrans advenit amore
    Protesilaeam Laodamia domum
75 inceptam frustra, nondum cum sanguine sacro
    hostia caelestis pacificasset eros.
nil mihi tam valde placeat, Rhamnusia virgo,
    quod temere invitis suscipiatur eris.
quam ieiuna pium desideret ara cruorem,
80 docta est amisso Laodamia viro,
coniugis ante coacta novi dimittere collum,
    quam veniens una atque altera rursus hiems
noctibus in longis avidum saturasset amorem,
    posset ut abrupto vivere coniugio,
85 quod scibant Parcae non longo tempore abisse,

85. scibant **VM** sceibant **D** scibat *Lachmann* scirant *Lucian Mueller.*

74. Laodamia: in extent and detail this episode is worthy of the poet's Alexandrian models, and is paralleled in Catullus only by the Ariadne episode in No. 64. Laodamia is a type of intense and constant conjugal affection. When her newly wedded spouse, Protesilaus, the first of the Greeks to perish on the plain of Troy, was permitted to return for three brief hours to earth, she committed suicide that she might accompany him on his final journey to the lower world. For various forms and details of the myth cf. Hom. *Il.* 2, 695–710 ; Eurip. *Protesilaus*; Hygin. *Fab.* 103 ; Ovid, *Her.* 13.

75. inceptam frustra: because never finished, either literally or figuratively; cf. *Il.* 2, 701: καὶ δόμος ἡμιτελής.

76. hostia ··· pacificasset: just what sacrifice was omitted is not clear; but it seems to have been one that should have preceded the beginning of a new house by Protesilaus, an important undertaking which should not have lacked preliminary divine approval. — **eros**: this unusual designation for the gods is repeated in v. 78.

77. Rhamnusia virgo: cf. 66, 71, n.

78. quod = *ut id.* — **invitis . . . eris**: cf. 76, 12.

79. ieiuna: cf. Prop. 3, 15, 18: *vilem ieiunae saepe negavit aquam.*

82. Cf. Intr. § 42, I (5) (*a*).

84. vivere: 'bear to live.'

85. quod: *coniugio.* — **scibant**: the regular early form in this conjugation, but later supplanted by

si miles muros isset ad Iliacos :
nam tum Helenae raptu primores Argivorum
    coeperat ad sese Troia ciere viros,
Troia (nefas) commune sepulcrum Asiae Europaeque,
90   Troia virum et virtutum omnium acerba cinis.
quaene etiam nostro letum miserabile fratri
    attulit ?   hei misero frater adempte mihi,
hei misero fratri iucundum lumen ademptum,

---

91. quaene etiam *Heinsius* que vetet id **VM** qualiter et *Ellis* quandoquidem
et *F. W. Shipley PAPA. 35, vii* quae vae, vae, et *Scaliger* quae taetre id
Munro.

---

the forms in *-iebam*, etc., after the
analogy of the 3d conjugation.
Cf. LSHLG, p. 94. Cf. 84, 8. —
tempore : the abl. of time within
which is accurately used with
abisse; within a comparatively
short time this wedlock would be
a thing of the past. — **abisse** : the
use of this perfect for the fut. perf.
idea enforces the certainty of fulfillment of the decree. For the
syntax cf. Livy, 21, 8, 8 : *Poeno
cepisse iam se urbem, si paulum
adnitatur, credente.*

87. Cf. Intr. § 42, I (3) ; also
vv. 89, 109 ; 76, 15 ; etc.

89. The mention of the hateful name of Troy distracts the
poet for a time into a passionate
outburst of fresh grief over his
brother's death, from which he
does not return to Laodamia until
v. 101. — **nefas** : 'unspeakable,'
an ejaculation of concentrated
hatred. Cf. Verg. *Aen.* 8, 688 : *se-
quiturque (nefas) Aegyptia coniunx.* — **commune sepulcrum** : *e.g.*
of the unnumbered victims of the

ten years' war who sank to earth
in both armies.

90. Cf. Verg. *Aen.* 1, 565 : *quis
Troiae nesciat urbem virtutesque
virosque aut tanti incendia belli?* —
acerba : the quality of fruit plucked
before its time ; hence the meaning 'untimely' ; cf. Verg. *Aen.* 6,
427–429 : *infantumque . . . quos
. . . ab ubere raptos . . . funere
mersit acerbo.* — **cinis** : here used
of the place of reduction to ashes,
'pyre': 'Troy, the pyre where
heroes and heroism all met an
untimely death.'

91. quaene = *nonne ea enim ;*
originally rhetorically interrogative, such forms acquired sometimes asseverative or causal force.
Here, however, the exclamatory
question is in harmony with the
tone of the passage.

92–96. Cf. 20–24. The repetition argues for the unity of the
poem. The phrase *frater adempte
mihi* recurs in 101, 6.

93. Cf. Verg. *Aen.* 3, 658, for a
reminiscence of form.

    tecum una tota est nostra sepulta domus,
95 omnia tecum una perierunt gaudia nostra,
    quae tuus in vita dulcis alebat amor.
    quem nunc tam longe non inter nota sepulcra
    nec prope cognatos conpositum cineres,
    sed Troia obscena, Troia infelice sepultum
100   detinet extremo terra aliena solo.
    ad quam tum properans fertur simul undique pubes
    Graeca penetralis deseruisse focos,
    ne Paris abducta gavisus libera moecha
    otia pacato degeret in thalamo.
105 quo tibi tum casu, pulcherrima Laodamia,
    ereptum est vita dulcius atque anima
    coniugium : tanto te absorbens vertice amoris
    aestus in abruptum detulerat barathrum,

---

98. conpositum: 'laid to rest'; cf. Tib. 3, 2, 26.

99. obscena and **infelice** here are synonyms. — **infelice**: the form is metrically more convenient to this verse than the orthodox abl. in *ī*, which Catullus elsewhere employs. Cf. 62, 30.

100. extremo: 'far away'; cf. Hor. *Ep.* 1, 1, 45 : *extremos curris mercator ad Indos.*

102. penetralis: where were the shrines of the household gods, the most sacred, and so the dearest spot of home.

103. moecha: Catullus refers to Helen with characteristic bluntness, the more remarkable when we consider Lesbia's own character and vv. 135–148. But only a Catullus, love-blinded, could write

this elaborate parallel between the constant Laodamia and the inconstant Lesbia.

105. casu: the chronological coincidence of the expedition against Troy with the marriage of Protesilaus and Laodamia.

107. tanto, etc. : in confirmation of the preceding comparison. — **absorbens vertice . . . aestus** : the imagery suggests an irresistible force, combining the undertow of ebb-tide with the concentration of the whirlpool's vortex. Cf. Cic. *Brut.* 81, 282 : *hunc quoque absorbuit aestus . . . gloriae ;* Verg. *Aen.* 3, 421 : *vastos sorbet in abruptum fluctus.*

108. barathrum : this Greek word is especially applicable to an underground channel.

quale ferunt Grai Pheneum prope Cylleneum
110   siccare emulsa pingue palude solum,
quod quondam caesis montis fodisse medullis
audit falsiparens Amphitryoniades,
tempore quo certa Stymphalia monstra sagitta
perculit imperio deterioris eri,
115   pluribus ut caeli tereretur ianua divis,
Hebe nec longa virginitate foret.
sed tuus altus amor barathro fuit altior illo,
qui durum domitam ferre iugum docuit.

118. durum domitam *Lachmann* tuum domitum **VM** tantum indomitam
Statius tunc indomitam *Conr. de Allio* tamen indomitam *Heyse* tum te indomitam *Riese* actutum domitum *Ellis* te tum domitam *Macnaghten* tum te domitam *Friedrich.*

109. **Pheneum**: an Arcadian town near the base of Mt. Cyllene, in a plain which was sometimes so inundated as to become a troublesome lake.

110. **pingue**: 'heavy,' because saturated and enriched by the abundant moisture.

111. **quod** refers to *barathrum.*

112. **audit** = *dicitur* ; cf. Hor. *Ep.* 1, 16, 17: *tu recte vivis, si curas esse quod audis.* The construction is like the similar use of *clueo* and ἀκούω, but this is the only case extant where *audio* is so used with an infinitive. — **falsiparens Amphitryoniades**: Heracles, really the son of Juppiter, was reputed to be the son of Amphitruo.

113. Several other feats of Heracles belonging to this time and region are by nature closely

allied to this story of the draining of the plain of Pheneos : the tale of the Stymphalian birds, also that of the Hydra, the Erymanthian boar, and the stables of Augeas. Cf. H. & T. §§ 138–140.

114. **deterioris eri**: Eurystheus.

115. **pluribus . . . divis** : their number being increased by the addition of Heracles. The action of the verb being involuntary (and even unconscious) rather than voluntary, *divis* is best considered an instrumental abl. ; a less convincing instance is Hor. *Sat.* 1, 6, 116: *cena ministratur pueris tribus.*

116. **Hebe**: the bride of the deified Heracles. Her Roman name was Iuventas.

117. Even this comparison does not duly represent the intensity of Laodamia's affection.

118. **durum**: *i.e.* for maidenly

nam nec tam carum confecto aetate parenti
120   una caput seri nata nepotis alit,
       qui, cum divitiis vix tandem inventus avitis
          nomen testatas intulit in tabulas,
       inpia derisi gentilis gaudia tollens
          suscitat a cano volturium capiti :
125 nec tantum niveo gavisa est ulla columbo
       conpar, quae multo dicitur inprobius

modesty to assume. This idea, which is emphasized to prove the truth of *amor . . . altior*, appears prominently in both of the epithalamia of Catullus; cf. 61, 81, 83, 95 ; 62, 20–24 ; also Hor. *Car.* 3, 9, 17 : *redit Venus, diductosque iugo cogit aeneo.* — iugum : cf. 61, 45 : *coniugator amoris.*

119–124. A second parallel to the intensity of Laodamia's love is found in that of an old man for his long-hoped-for grandson. — carum . . . caput . . . alit = *carum est caput seri nepotis quod nata alit.*

120. caput : 'life.' Cf. Prop. 4, 11, 10, n. — seri : and therefore long-expected.

121. qui refers to *nepotis.* — inventus : the heir so long awaited, when at length he arrives, is said to have been 'found,' as if the object of careful search.

122. testatas . . . tabulas : the last will and testament of the grandfather. The participle is best regarded as from the active form of the verb, and so used here in the passive sense, *i.e.* the will is duly signed and witnessed.

123. inpia : because *pietas* especially implies loyalty to the highest interests and wishes of the older members of one's family, in the broad or narrow sense of the word family ; and here a more distant relative had selfishly and greedily hoped for disappointment of the grandsire's fondest hopes. — derisi gentilis : now in turn mocked by the rotation of Fortune's wheel. The Laws of the XII Tables provided : *si paterfamilias intestato moritur, familia pecuniaque eius agnatum gentiliumque esto* (Cic. *De Inv.* 2,50).

124. volturium : the *gentilis.* Cf. Sen. *Ep.* 95, 43 : *amico aegro aliquis adsidet* ; *probamus* : *at hoc si hereditatis causa facit, voltur est, cadaver exspectat* ; Plaut. *Trin.* 101 : *sunt alii qui te volturium vocant.* — capiti :' an abl. form unparalleled in the classical period, and exceedingly rare even in the postclassical period. Cf. Neue, Vol. 1, p. 366.

125–128. A third comparison is found in the proverbial fondness of a dove for its mate.

126. conpar : 'mate.'

oscula mordenti semper decerpere rostro
    quam quae praecipue multivola est mulier :
sed tu horum magnos vicisti sola furores,
130   ut semel es flavo conciliata viro.
aut nihil aut paullo cui tum concedere digna
    lux mea se nostrum contulit in gremium,
quam circumcursans hinc illinc saepe Cupido
    fulgebat crocina candidus in tunica.
135 quae tamen etsi uno non est contenta Catullo,
    rara verecundae furta feremus erae,
ne nimium simus stultorum more molesti.
    saepe etiam Iuno, maxima caelicolum,

127. **mordenti**: cf. 2, 2–4; *cui primum digitum adpetenti et acris solet incitare morsus*; Plaut. *Men.* 195.

128. **multivola**: ἅπαξ λεγ. in classical Latin. The *multa* forming the first part of the compound refers to *oscula*.

129. **tu**: Laodamia. — **furores**: cf. 2, 8: *uti gravis acquiescat ardor*; Verg. *Aen.* 4, 101: *ardet amans Dido traxitque per ossa furorem*; Prop. 1, 13, 20: *tantus erat demens inter utrosque furor*.

130. **flavo**: of a typical ancient hero.

131. Reverting to the comparison in vv. 70–74, Catullus takes up again the theme of Lesbia's love and entrancing loveliness.

132. **lux mea**: cf. v. 160; Tib. 4. 3, 15: *tum placeant silvae, si, lux mea, tecum arguar*; Prop. 2, 14, 29: *nunc ad te, mea lux, veniat mea litore navis*.

133. Lesbia seems a very Venus to her enthralled lover; cf. vv. 70–72; Hor. *Car.* 1, 2, 33: *Erycina . . . quam . . . circum volat et Cupido*.

134. **crocina**: the same color as the bridal veil; so Hymen is represented in this color in 61, 8: *flammeum cape*, etc.

135. Catullus has heard enough of Lesbia's frailties to disturb his peace of mind; but, in no mood yet to cast her off, would excuse her as even in this respect also like the immortals.

136. **verecundae**: that Lesbia did not reveal her amours to the world is considered an extenuating circumstance. — **furta**: see Lex. Cf. v. 145; Prov. 9, 17: "Stolen waters are sweet." — **erae**: used also by Ovid in *Her.* 9, 78, for the more usual *domina*.

137. **molesti**: *i.e.* jealous.

coniugis in culpa flagrantem concoquit iram,
140   noscens omnivoli plurima furta Iovis.
atqui nec divis homines conponier aequumst:
    ingratum tremuli tolle parentis onus.
nec tamen illa mihi dextra deducta paterna
    fragrantem Assyrio venit odore domum,
145 sed furtiva dedit mira munuscula nocte,
    ipsius ex ipso dempta viri gremio.
quare illud satis est, si nobis is datur unis

---

139. concoquit *Lachmann* cotidiana O quotidiana GM contudit *Hertzberg*
concipit *Baehrens* continet *Santen.* 140. furta ω facta VM. 141. atqui
ω atque VM at quia D. *There is no gap in the Mss. after this verse.*

---

139. in: 'in cases of.' — concoquit: cf. the slang phrase, "sim-
mer down."

140. omnivoli: another ἅπαξ
λεγ. of the same pattern as *multivola* (v. 128); but the first part
of the compound in this instance
refers to persons (*puellas ?*); and
an important part of classical mythology deals with their history.

141. conponier: the three other
instances of the archaic infin. ending in Catullus are all in No. 61
(vv. 42, 65, 68).

142. 'Have done with the se-
nile vexatiousness of over-jealousy'
(Ellis). As men and gods are
incomparable, a comedy scene is
suggested as a parallel, the irritable
old man enraged at the amorous
escapades of a son. The thought
essentially repeats that of v. 137,
and is addressed to himself, like
Prop. 2, 5, 14: *subtrahe colla iugo*,
without any expressed vocative.

143. nec tamen: 'And, after all,
she was not,' etc. Cf. Prop. 3, 16,
11 ; Munro on Lucr. 5, 1177. —
deducta: in the wedding procession. — paterna: in a figurative
sense only, referring to the fact
that the father gave away the
bride *in manus* of the bridegroom.

145. Cf. v. 136, n. — dedit:
Lesbia gave the voluntary offering
of passionate affection, as contrasted with the reluctance of the
bride whose father had arranged a
marriage, perhaps without consulting her wishes. The moral for
Catullus seems to be, "You
shouldn't look a gift horse in the
mouth," but be judiciously blind
to some failings.

147. is: the antecedent *diem*
is incorporated in the following
relative clause. — unis: 'only';
Catullus is most favored, of all the
lovers of Lesbia.

quem lapide illa diem candidiore notet.

hoc tibi quod potui confectum carmine munus

150   pro multis, Alli, redditur officiis,

ne vestrum scabra tangat robigine nomen

haec atque illa dies atque alia atque alia.

huc addent divi quam plurima, quae Themis olim

antiquis solita est munera ferre piis.

155 sitis felices et tu simul et tua vita,

et domus ipsa in qua lusimus, et domina,

† et qui principio nobis terram dedit aufert,

a quo sunt primo omnia nata bona,

148. notet **D** notat **V**.   150. Alli *Scaliger* aliis **VM** alys **R** Manli **ω**.
157. terram **VRM** teneram *Statius* te et eram *Munro*.   aufert **VRM** Anser
Heyse Afer *Munro* audens *Friedrich*.   158. bona **ω** bono **VM**.

**148. lapide . . . diem candidi-
ore**: corresponding to our phrase,
' a red-letter day.' The custom
was said to be a Cretan one, to
count prosperous days by white
pebbles. Cf. 107, 6; Plin. *Ep.* 6,
11, 3 : *o diem . . . laetum notan-
dumque mihi candidissimo calculo !*
Hor. *Car.* 1, 36, 10 : *Cressa ne
careat pulchra dies nota* ; Pers. 2,
1 : *diem numera meliore lapillo.*

149. The panegyric now completed, Catullus turns in personal
address to his friend with the final
words of goodwill ; cf. Intr. to the
poem.

151. vestrum : *i.e.* the family
name. — **scabra . . . robigine** : cf.
Latimer, *Misc.:* " a new canker to
rust and corrupt the old truth."

152. The flight of time ; cf. 64,
16.

153. huc : *i.e.* to this *munus*
which I have offered. — **Themis** :

the divinity that represented
" law." Her attributes were the
horn of plenty, symbolizing bless-
ing, and the balance, indicating
exact justice.

155. vita = *domina,* but
whether a parallel to Lesbia or a
lawful wife it is impossible to determine.

156. domus : cf. v. 68. — **domina** is the same person as *dominam* in v. 68. — *sit felix* is to be
supplied several times in vv. 156–
157, and in v. 160.

157–158. These verses are still
an unsolved puzzle for commentators. Perhaps they refer to a
third person who assisted in the
merry plot, *terram* being taken in
the sense of a basis of undertaking,
a footing from which to carry on
the intrigue, a *terra firma* of refuge after being tossed on the
waves of doubt, and *omnia* refer-

et longe ante omnes mihi quae me carior ipsost,
160   lux mea, qua viva vivere dulce mihist.

70

Nulli se dicit mulier mea nubere malle
    quam mihi, non si se Iuppiter ipse petat.
dicit: sed mulier cupido quod dicit amanti,
    in vento et rapida scribere oportet aqua.

72

Dicebas quondam solum te nosse Catullum,
    Lesbia, nec prae me velle tenere Iovem.

ring to the love affair as a whole.
Vahlen's proposition to change *et*
at the beginning of v. 157 to *dum*
and understand both verses to refer
to Jove has met with little favor.
— **primo | omnia** : cf. Intr. § 43.
    160. lux = Lesbia.

70

The first of the shorter, epigram-
matic poems which end the
Catullus collection. Probably addressed to Lesbia. A comparison
with 72, 2 suggests that Catullus
had already begun to have sus-
picions of Lesbia, and that this
was intended as a playful warning
to her.
    1. mulier mea : a lover's term,
found only here in the elegists, in
this sense, though *puella* is often
so used; but cf. Hor. *Epod.* 12,
23 : *magis quem diligeret mulier
sua quam te.* — **nubere** = *tenere*
in 72, 2. Cf. Plaut. *Cist.* 43 :

*haec quidem ecastor cottidie viro
nubit.*
    2. Iuppiter : cf. 72, 2. — **petat** :
' come to woo.'
    3. dicit : the repetition of this
word suggests epigram 25 of Callimachus as a probable model : —
Ὤμοσε Καλλίγνωτος Ἰωνίδι, μή-
    ποτ᾽ ἐκείνης
ἕξειν μήτε φίλον κρέσσονα, μήτε
    φίλην.
ὤμοσεν. ἀλλὰ λέγουσιν ἀληθέα,
    τοὺς ἐν ἔρωτι
ὅρκους μὴ δύνειν οὔατ᾽ ἐς ἀθα-
    νάτων; etc.—**cupido**: cf. 107, 1.
    4. Cf. Tib. 4, 4, 8; Prop. 2,
28, 8.

72

Catullus is now well aware of
Lesbia's true character; and,
though his passion is not quenched,
he cannot longer respect her. Cf.
Nos. 73 and 85.
    1. Dicebas . . . Iovem : cf. *di-
cit . . . Iuppiter*, 70, 1. — **nosse** :

dilexi tum te non tantum ut vulgus amicam,
    sed pater ut gnatos diligit et generos.
5   nunc te cognovi: quare etsi inpensius uror,
    multo mi tamen es vilior et levior.
qui potis est? inquis.   quod amantem iniuria talis
    cogit amare magis, sed bene velle minus.

73

Desine de quoquam quicquam bene velle mereri
    aut aliquem fieri posse putare pium.

73. 1. quicquam **D** quisquam **VM**.

i.e. as an accepted lover; the history of Lesbia's career before this makes it impossible to believe that Catullus ever understood her to use the word in *sensu venerio.* Cf. such expressions as "this one thing I do," "I am resolved to know only," etc.

2. **tenere:** cf. 11, 18: *conplexa tenet*; 64, 28.

3. **dilexi:** love mingled with esteem is meant, as compared with the merely sensual *amare.* Cf. *bene velle,* v. 8.

4. **gnatos ... generos:** by way of contrast to *amicam,* those in the family circle toward whom there is the least element of that *amor* here in mind; and so a more emphatic expression than even *uxorem* or *filiam* would be.

5. **inpensius uror:** the flames of passion are all the hotter, though my esteem is gone. Cf. Ter. *Eun.* 72: *et taedet et amore ardeo.*

7. **qui:** cf. 67, 17: *qui possum.* — **potis est** = *potest.* Cf. 76, 24, 16; *potis* early became common in gender, and its perfect composition with *esse* was but slowly accomplished; cf. the following passages in Lucr. 3, 1079 (*pote*); 1, 452 (*potis est*); 1, 665 (*potesse*); 5, 881 (*potissit*); 1, 652 (*posse*); 1, 546 (*possint*); etc.

8. **bene velle:** cf. 75, 3.

73

An outburst of bitterness against the ingratitude of a friend, possibly the Alphenus of No. 30, or the Rufus of No. 77.

1. **quicquàm:** adverbial acc. with *bene mereri.* — **velle:** to be taken with *desine.*

2. **aliquem:** for *quemquam.* — The alliteration expresses the passionate disappointment of Catullus. — **pium:** 'appreciative.'

omnia sunt ingrata, nihil fecisse benigne:
  immo etiam taedet, taedet obestque magis,
5 ut mihi, quem nemo gravius nec acerbius urget
    quam modo qui me unum atque unicum amicum
    habuit.

75

Huc est mens deducta tua, mea Lesbia, culpa,
  atque ita se officio perdidit ipsa suo,
ut iam nec bene velle queat tibi, si optima fias,
  nec desistere amare, omnia si facias.

---

73. 3. benigne **V** *Friedrich adds* est.   4. *Guyetus prefixed* prodest *to the verse.*   taedet, taedet *Avantius* taedet obestque magisque magis **V** taedet, si fit *Lachmann.*

75. 1. huc **VRM** nunc *Codex Cuiacianus, accepted by Scaliger, who transposed the poem and joined it to* **87.**   deducta **VRM** diducta *Lachmann.*

---

3. **ingrata**: 'unthanked'; for a similar use in the passive sense cf. 76, 6; Plaut. *Truc.* 535: *ingratum donum.* — **nihil fecisse benigne**: sc. *est*; 'to have done a favor counts for naught.' Cf. Plaut. *Capt.* 344: *at nil est ignotum ad illum mittere.*

4. **taedet**: ''tis a bore.'—**magis** = *potius.*

5. **mihi**: sc. *obest.*

6. The unusual phraseology and the recklessness in regard to elision suggest that perhaps Catullus is quoting the very expression of his friend. Cf. Intr. § 43; Gell. 18, 4, 2: *se unum et unicum lectorem esse.* — **habuit**: *i.e.* professed to feel so.

75

A poem of similar tone to that of No. 72.

1. **huc . . . deducta**: 'has reached such a point.' — **mea**: this sign of affection helps illustrate the state of Catullus's feelings.

2. **officio**: 'the bonds of devotion.'

3. **bene velle**: contrasted with *amare* in v. 4; cf. 72, 8.

4. **omnia**: *i.e.* any imaginable kind of excess.

76

Siqua recordanti benefacta priora voluptas
    est homini, cum se cogitat esse pium,
nec sanctam violasse fidem nec foedere in ullo
    divum ad fallendos numine abusum homines,
5   multa parata manent in longa aetate, Catulle,
    ex hoc ingrato gaudia amore tibi.
nam quaecumque homines bene cuiquam aut dicere
    possunt
    aut facere, haec a te dictaque factaque sunt.

76. *Follows* **75** *in the Mss. immediately, and was therefore also transposed after* **87–75** *by Lachmann.*   3. in ullo **ω** nullo **VRM.**

76

Realizing thoroughly the entire unworthiness of Lesbia and bitterly conscious of the faithlessness with which she has rewarded his constant devotion, Catullus has resolved to cure himself of his love. But, finding reason powerless to cope with passion, he summons the aid of the gods to rid him of his infatuation.

  1. benefacta: cf. vv. 7, 8.

  2. pium: 'conscientious'; explained by the next two verses. Several such expressions in this elegy are to be explained only from the point of view of the poet consumed by the one thought already stated in the introduction to the poem.

  3. fidem: to men, as contrasted with that obligation towards the gods which is referred to in the following clause.

  4. divum . . . numine: 'an oath in the name of the gods'; cf. 64, 134: *neglecto numine divum*; Ovid, *Met.* 10, 430: *promissaque numine firmat.*

  5. longa aetate: 'during a long life'; *i.e.* he has enough memories of this kind (cf. *multa*) to last him a lifetime.

  6. ingrato: cf. 73, 3, n.

  7. cuiquam: this indefinite, more common in universal negatives, is sometimes employed also in universal affirmatives, usually in expressed, or implied, conditions; cf. Cic. *Ad Fam.* 6, 14, 1: *si quisquam est timidus . . . is ego sum.*

omnia quae ingratae perierunt credita menti.
10   quare cur te iam amplius excrucies?
quin tu animo offirmas atque istinc teque reducis,
    et dis invitis desinis esse miser?
difficile est longum subito deponere amorem.
    difficile est, verum hoc qua lubet efficias:
15 una salus haec est, hoc est tibi pervincendum:
    hoc facias, sive id non pote sive pote.
o di, si vestrum est misereri, aut si quibus umquam
    extremam iam ipsa morte tulistis opem,
me miserum adspicite et, si vitam puriter egi,
20   eripite hanc pestem perniciemque mihi.

---

10. cur te iam **VM** iam te cur **Dω** cur tu te iam *Schoell.*   11. istinc teque
Heinsius instincteque **O** instinctoque **GM** istinc te ipsa *Ellis.*

---

9. ingratae: here in the act.
sense, 'thankless.' — perierunt:
'have been wasted.'

11. offirmas: for a similar in-
trans. use of this verb cf. Plaut.
Stich. 68: *offirmabit pater advor-
sum nos.* — istinc: a scornful expression: 'from that unworthy
love.'

12. dis invitis: best taken in
the causal sense with *desinis*. Cf.
68, 78. — esse miser: 'to make
yourself unhappy.'

13. Catullus the lover makes
answer to Catullus the reasoner.
— longum: not absolutely long
was the period covered by the love
of Catullus for Lesbia, but relatively long, as it absorbed the best
years of his life.

14. Reason again gets the
upper hand. Cf. the struggle of
Propertius, 3, 21, 5.

15. haec refers to the same
thing as *hoc* in vv. 14, 15, 16; the
gender here conforms to that of
salus.

16. pote: sc. *est.* Cf. v. 24;
72, 7, n.; Prop. 3, 7, 10; Pers. 1,
56: *qui pote?*

18. extremam iam ipsa morte:
'in the last article of death.' Catullus feels that his is a desperate,
life-and-death struggle.

19. puriter: in the sense elaborated in the opening verses of this
elegy. The form is one of the
poet's archaisms; cf. 39, 14; Cato,
R. R. 23, 2.

20. pestem perniciemque: this
expression, found in various other
writers, was doubtless considered
especially emphatic from its alliteration and assonance. Cf.
"beastly bore," "plaguey particular," and the like.

hei mihi, subrepens imos ut torpor in artus
　　expulit ex omni pectore laetitias!
non iam illud quaero, contra ut me diligat illa,
　　aut, quod non potis est, esse pudica velit:
25　ipse valere opto et taetrum hunc deponere morbum.
　　o di, reddite mi hoc pro pietate mea.

82

Quinti, si tibi vis oculos debere Catullum
　　aut aliud siquid carius est oculis,
eripere ei noli, multo quod carius illi
　　est oculis seu quid carius est oculis.

21. hei *Lachmann* seu **VM** sei *Ellis*.

22. **ex omni pectore laetitias**:
'every joyful feeling from my
heart.'

23. **contra . . . me diligat**: 're-
ciprocate my love'; *diligere* stands
here for a higher type of affection
than *amare*, as usual. Cf. 72, 3, n.

24. **potis est**: cf. 72, 7, n.

25. **ipse**: 'it is for myself that
I pray.' The emphasis is by con-
trast with *illa* (v. 23). A. 195, b;
L. 2376.

26. **pietate**: cf. v. 2, n.

82

Catullus beseeches Quintius
(probably the same person mentioned in 100, 1) not to wrest from
him his greatest treasure (presumably Lesbia). If this is the correct

interpretation, it must have been
written at an earlier period than
Nos. 72 and 76, while the poet
still felt that Lesbia was his to
lose, and still experienced the
pangs of jealousy at the mention
of other lovers.

2. **carius . . . oculis**: cf. 104,
2: *ambobus mihi quae carior est
oculis*; 3, 5: *quem plus illa oculis,
suis amabat*.

3. **ei**: synizesis.

4. **seu quid . . . oculis**: the
phrase takes the place of another
substantive in the same construction as the preceding *oculis*. Cf. 13,
9: *sed contra accipies meros amores
seu quid suavius elegantiusve est*;
23, 12: *corpora sicciora cornu aut
siquid magis aridum est*.

83

Lesbia mi praesente viro mala plurima dicit:
  hoc illi fatuo maxima laetitiast.
mule, nihil sentis. si nostri oblita taceret,
  sana esset: nunc quod gannit et obloquitur,
5   non solum meminit, sed, quae multo acrior est res,
  irata est, hoc est, uritur et coquitur.

84

Chommoda dicebat, si quando commoda vellet
  dicere, et insidias Arrius hinsidias,

83. 6. coquitur *Lipsius* loquitur **VRM.**

83

" The lady doth protest too much, methinks." Cf. No. 92. Written not later than 59 B.C., the year in which Lesbia's husband, Q. Caecilius Metellus Celer, died.

1. **praesente** : Catullus, however, seems not himself to have been there on the occasion referred to, as is indicated by *oblita* (v. 3), *meminit* (v. 5).

2. **fatuo** : the derivation of the word (*fari*) makes it peculiarly appropriate to one expressing ill-grounded boasts.

3. **mule** : much less frequent as a term of abuse than *asinus*.

4. **sana** : *i.e.* not wounded by Cupid's darts. Cf. Tib. 4, 6, 18.

5. **acrior** : ' more important,' because to the possessor of subtle

discernment it implies much more.

6. **irata** : cf. Ter. *Andr.* 555 : *amantium irae amoris integratiost.* — **uritur** : *i.e.* with love. Cf. Verg. *Aen.* 4, 68 : *uritur infelix Dido*; Tib. 2, 6, 5 ; 4, 6, 17. — **coquitur** : ' is tormented,' *i.e* by her passion.

84

The use of the aspirate was much restricted in early Latin ; but by the beginning of the first century B.C. the increasing frequency of Greek loan-words led to a tendency to go to the other extreme and apply the aspirate to both vowels and consonants where it had no etymological justification. Cf. Quint. 1, 5, 20 ; Cic. *De Orat.* 160. Devotion to such a

et tum mirifice sperabat se esse locutum,
   cum quantum poterat dixerat hinsidias.
5   credo, sic mater, sic liber avunculus eius,
   sic maternus avus dixerat atque avia.
hoc misso in Syriam requierant omnibus aures:
   audibant eadem haec leniter et leviter,
nec sibi postilla metuebant talia verba,
10   cum subito adfertur nuntius horribilis,
Ionios fluctus, postquam illuc Arrius isset,
   iam non Ionios esse, sed Hionios.

84. *3 and 4, which stand as 9 and 10 in the Mss., were transposed by Politianus.*

fad became especially ridiculous when found in a parvenu of meager education. Such a person apparently was the Arrius of this witty epigram (cf. vv. 5, 6), who seems to have been as extravagant with his *h*'s as a modern cockney. It has been conjectured, but without other than circumstantial evidence, that he may have been the Q. Arrius whom Cicero (*Brut.* 242) mentions as a worthless orator, without ability or noble birth, who had gained some prominence by political methods.

1. **Chommoda :** ' whages.' — **vellet :** this is perhaps the earliest example of the Subjunct. of Indef. Frequency, a construction appearing about this time in isolated instances (*e.g.* Caes. *B.C.* 3, 110, 4), but increasingly common in imperial times.

2. **hinsidias :** ' hambuscade.'

4. **quantum poterat :** ' with as much emphasis as possible.'

5. **credo :** ' no doubt.' — **liber :** the implication plainly is that either this uncle or some other uncle of his had not been free, and thus that Arrius was at least connected with a family of *libertini*, apparently on his mother's side, from comparison of the list of relatives mentioned here. It is certain that ignorance of the proper use of the aspirate was especially common among the lower classes. Cf. Gell. 13, 6, 3 : *rusticus fit sermo, inquit, si adspires per-peram.*

7. **misso in Syriam :** if the above identification of Arrius be correct, this mission to Syria was doubtless with his friend Crassus (Cic. *Brut.* 242), *i.e.* in 55 B.C., and this would give an approximate date to the epigram.

8. **audibant :** cf. 68, 85, n.

9. **postilla :** the anteclassical equivalent of *postea;* another of the many archaisms of Catullus.

85

Odi et amo.   quare id faciam, fortasse requiris.
nescio, sed fieri sentio et excrucior.

86

Quintia formosa est multis, mihi candida, longa,
   recta est.   haec ego sic singula confiteor,
totum illud "formosa" nego : nam nulla venustas,
   nulla in tam magno est corpore mica salis.
5   Lesbia formosa est, quae cum pulcherrima totast,
   tum omnibus una omnes surripuit Veneres.

85

A brief and emphatic statement of the same theme as that of Nos. 72 and 75.

1. **Odi et amo** : cf. the imitation in Ovid, *Am.* 2, 4, 5 : *odi nec possum cupiens non esse, quod odi.*

2. **nescio . . . sentio** : the fact is determined not by the intellect, but by the emotions.

86

The superiority of Lesbia's charms to those of an unknown beauty named Quintia. In No. 43 Catullus expressed his impatience of another such comparison.

1. **candida, longa, recta** : that these qualities were considered essential elements of female beauty is evident from such passages as the following : 13, 4 : *cenam non sine candida puella* ; Hor. *Sat.* 1, 2, 123 : *candida rectaque sit* ;

munda hactenus ut neque longa nec magis alba velit, quam dat natura, videri ; Ovid, *Am.* 2, 4, 33 : *quia tam longa es, veteres heroidas aequas.*

2. **sic** : *i.e.* as in vv. 1 and 2.

3. **totum illud "formosa"** : *i.e.* the expression "*formosa*," with all that the term properly implies.

4. **nulla . . . mica salis** : 'not a particle of wit' (sparkling fascination, *urbanitas*) ; cf. Mart. 7, 25, 3 : *nullaque mica salis nec amari fellis in illis gutta.*

5. **pulcherrima** : 'very pretty'; of mere physical faultlessness, which might be true of a doll-like "putty-face," such as Quintia appears to be in the eyes of Catullus, without including at all the intellectual and emotional fascinations of an ideal "*formosa.*"

6. **omnes . . . Veneres** : 'every charm,' *i.e.* all Venus's gifts and graces. Cf. Quint. 10, 1, 79 : *omnes dicendi Veneres sectatus est.*

87

Nulla potest mulier tantum se dicere amatam
vere, quantum a me Lesbia amata mea es.
nulla fides ullo fuit umquam foedere tanta,
quanta in amore tuo ex parte reperta meast.

92

Lesbia mi dicit semper male nec tacet umquam
de me : Lesbia me dispeream nisi amat.
quo signo? quia sunt totidem mea : deprecor illam
adsidue, verum dispeream nisi amo.

87. 2. es *Scaliger* est **VM**.   3. ullo **VM** nullo ω.

87

Perhaps a fragment, though not necessarily incomplete. The supposition of Scaliger and other editors that No. 75 should be used to complete it is entirely gratuitous. More in sorrow than in reproach, Catullus reminds his Lesbia of the singleness and intensity of his love, which he apparently now realizes has been trifled with.

1. Cf. 8, 5: *amata nobis quantum amabitur nulla*; 37, 12; 58, 2: *illa Lesbia quam Catullus unam plus quam se atque suos amavit omnes.*

3. **foedere**: a common term for mutual plighted faith in the lover's vocabulary; cf. Prop. 4, 3, 69; Pichon, *s.v.*

4. **amore tuo ex parte reperta meast**: 'the love that I have bestowed upon thee.' — **tuo**: objective; similarly, 64, 253. — **mea**: emphatic by contrast with that of the other lovers of Lesbia.

92

The theme is the same as that of No. 83.

2. **dispeream nisi**: cf. Prop. 2, 21, 9: *dispeream, si quicquam aliud quam gloria de te quaeritur.*

3. **quo signo**: sc. *hoc concludo*; cf. Plaut. *Mil. Gl.* 1001: *quo argumento.* — **sunt totidem mea**: 'I have exactly the same two experiences,' viz. (1) curse her; (2) love her. — **deprecor**: 'denounce.' For this unusual sense of the word, see the discussion of this passage in Gell. 7 (6), 16.

93

Nil nimium studeo, Caesar, tibi velle placere,
nec scire utrum sis albus an ater homo.

95

Zmyrna mei Cinnae nonam post denique messem
quam coepta est nonamque edita post hiemem,

93

Catullus does not care to be on good terms with Caesar. The same hatred towards the great "Imperator" appears in Nos. 29, 54, 57, where the connection has given rise to Baehrens's conjecture that this passage and the others mentioned were written soon after the arrival of Caesar with his retinue at Verona after the campaign of 55 B.C., when the military licentiousness which naturally prevailed crossed the path of the poet's own private life at some point, perhaps in the pursuit of Ameana by the notorious Mamurra.

1. **Nil nimium studeo**: 'I am not particularly anxious.' Somebody has apparently tried to reconcile Catullus to Caesar. A similar use of *nimis* is a favorite with Catullus; cf. *e.g.* 64, 22: *o nimis optato saeclorum tempore nati heroes*; cf. also Mart. 9, 81, 3: *non nimium curo*. — **velle** is superfluous, as in Cic. *Mur.* 25, 50: *nolite a me commoneri velle.*

2. **scire utrum sis albus an ater**: a proverbial phrase; cf. Cic. *Phil.* 2, 41: *vide quam te amarit is, qui albus aterne fuerit ignoras*; Apul. *Apol.* 16: *libenter te . . . albus an ater esses, ignoravi*; cf. also Quint. 11, 1, 38.

95

On the appearance of the *Zmyrna*, a carefully elaborated poem by his friend C. Helvius Cinna, Catullus compares this work favorably with the attempts of three inferior poets. There is no need of separating vv. 9-10 from the rest of the poem.

1. **Zmyrna**: another name for Myrrha, whose unnatural love for her father, Cinyras, was the theme of the poem and gave it its name. The story is related in Ovid, *Met.* 19, 298 sqq. The inconsiderable fragments are collected in Baehrens's *Frag. Poet. Rom.*, p. 324. — **nonam**: cf. Quint. 10, 4, 4: *Cinnae Zmyrnam novem annis accepimus scriptam.* Horace is very likely alluding to this case when he rec-

milia cum interea quingenta Hortensius uno

*   *   *   *   *   *   *

5   Zmyrna cavas Satrachi penitus mittetur ad undas,
    Zmyrnam cana diu saecula pervoluent.
    at Volusi annales Paduam morientur ad ipsam
    et laxas scombris saepe dabunt tunicas.

ommends that a book (*A. P.*, v. 388) *nonumque prematur in annum*. Such exhaustive carefulness was more a proof of the erudition to be expected from its Alexandrian tone than of great poetic power; and we are not surprised to learn that the poem was so obscure even at the time of its appearance that scholars wrote learned commentaries to explain its meaning. For the construction, see A. 424 f.

2. **edita**: sc. *est.*

3. **milia . . . quingenta**: a mere hyperbole for an indefinitely large number. Cf. 9, 1: *Verani, omnibus e meis amicis antistans mihi milibus trecentis.* — **Hortensius**: cf. Intr. to No. 65. What caused Catullus to feel so differently towards him at this time can only be conjectured. It may be remarked, however, in general, that to criticize the work of another poet is quite another thing from being invited to contribute one's own poetic effusions. — **uno**: *anno, mense,* and *die* have been suggested by different editors as probable nouns in the missing v. 4, which may be variously supplied. In any case, the idea must have been an unfavorable con-

trast between the rapid work of Hortensius and the carefully finished *Zmyrna.* Cf. Hor. *Sat.* 1, 4, 9–16.

5. **cavas**: 'deep'; cf. 17, 4: *cavaque in palude*; Luc. 1, 396: *cavo tentoria fixa Lemanno.* — **Satrachi**: the Satrachus was an obscure inland stream in Cyprus. It was in this region that the story of Zmyrna was located. — **penitus**: 'far inland.'

6. **cana**: 'hoary'; cf. Mart. 8, 80, 2: *nec pateris, Caesar, saecula cana mori.* — **pervolŭent**: cf. Intr. § 43.

7. **Volusi**: the same tiresome versifier is referred to in No. 36. For an elaborate argument to identify him with Tanusius Geminus see Friedrich on this passage. — **ipsam**: the emphasis thus put upon Padua indicates this place as the home of Volusius, whose prosy verses will never travel farther than their birthplace, as contrasted with the imaginative work of Cinna, which is to penetrate to the remotest parts of the earth.

8. **laxas**: because the material is abundant. — **tunicas**: *i.e.* wrapping paper. The idea is borrowed by Martial (4, 86, 8): *nec scombris tunicas dabis molestas.*

parva mei mihi sint cordi monumenta sodalis:
10   at populus tumido gaudeat Antimacho.

96

Si quicquam mutis gratum acceptumve sepulcris
    accidere a nostro, Calve, dolore potest,
quo desiderio veteres renovamus amores
    atque olim missas flemus amicitias,

---

95. 9. sodalis *written by a 15th cent. hand at end of verse* in **R** *omitted in* **V**.

---

9. **parva**: the *Zmyrna* was but a short poem. — **sodalis**: cf. 10, 29: *meus sodalis Cinna est Gaius*.

10. **populus**: 'the multitude,' who, of course, lack literary appreciation of the best. — **tumido**: 'wordy.' — **Antimacho**: a voluminous epic and elegiac poet of Colophon, who lived about 400 B.C., and in popular esteem was adjudged one of the greatest of Greek poets. Cf. Intr. § 6; Cic. *Brut.* 191; Quint. 10, 1, 53: *ei secundas fere grammaticorum consensus deferat*.

96

The brevity and delicacy of this little elegy to his dear friend Calvus on the death of his beloved Quintilia prove Catullus a true poet and master of the art of consolation. To the genuine comradeship of these two early Roman

elegiac writers such poems as Nos. 14, 50, and 53 bear ample testimony. We see from Prop. 2, 34, 89, that Calvus himself wrote of his lost Quintilia.

1. **Si quicquam**: this conditional statement of immortality is paralleled often in Roman literature and inscriptions. Cf. Ovid, *Am.* 3, 9, 59; Cic. *Ad Fam.* 4, 5, 6; Tac. *Agr.* 46, 1; *CIL.* 10, 8131, 14: *si sapiunt aliquid post funera Manes*; *CIL.* 6, 6250: *bene adquiescas, Hilara, si quid sapiunt inferi*; also K. P. H. on "Conceptions of Death and Immortality in Roman Sepulchral Inscriptions," *PAPA.*, Vol. 30, pp. xxviii–xxxi.

2. **nostro**: *i.e.* of the living in general.

3. **desiderio**: in apposition with *dolore*.

4. **missas**: 'lost,' *i.e.* relinquished of necessity.

5   certe non tanto mors inmatura dolori est
     Quintiliae, quantum gaudet amore tuo.

99

     Surripui tibi, dum ludis, mellite Iuventi,
       saviolum dulci dulcius ambrosia.
     verum id non inpune tuli : namque amplius horam
       suffixum in summa me memini esse cruce,
5   dum tibi me purgo nec possum fletibus ullis
       tantillum vestrae demere saevitiae.

96. 5. dolori est D dolore est ω dolor est **VM** dolorist *Haupt* doloreist *Ellis.*

---

6. quantum : *i.e. gaudium.*

99

Catullus protests against the torture inflicted upon him by Juventius in punishment for a stolen kiss. The series of poems connected with the fondness of Catullus for the pretty boy Juventius includes among others Nos. 15, 24, 48, 81. Some editors have argued that Juventius, as well as Marathus, the boy favorite of Tibullus, are mere literary fictions. It seems more probable that Juventius, at any rate, was a real person, who afforded some diversion for the poet's affections after he had finally cast off Lesbia as unworthy.

1. **mellite** : cf. 48, 1–3 : *mellitos oculos tuos, Iuventi, siquis me sinat usque basiare, usque ad milia basiem trecenta.*

2. **saviolum** : a rare example of Catullus's favorite diminutive formation ; cf. v. 14 ; perhaps only in these two instances. — **dulci dulcius** : cf. v. 14 ; also 22, 14 : *infaceto est infacetior rure* ; etc.

3. **namque . . . memini** : 'I guess I didn't ! For I haven't forgotten how,' etc.

4. **summa** . . . **cruce** : cf. Eng. 'on the hatchel.' The kind of crucifixion involving impalement brought the greatest torture to the victim ; cf. Sen. *Ad Marciam de Cons.* 20, 3 : *cruces non unius quidem generis, . . . alii per obscena stipitem egerunt* ; *Ep.* 101, 12 : *suffigas licet et acutam sessuro crucem subdas.*

5. **tibi** : 'in your eyes.'—**purgo** : used with conative force ; A. 467.

6. **tantillum** : 'a particle' ; cf. the slang expression, 'not a little bit.' — **vestrae** : referring not to the individual, but to the class to which Juventius belonged.

nam simul id factum est, multis diluta labella
    guttis abstersisti omnibus articulis,
ne quicquam nostro contractum ex ore maneret,
10   tamquam conmictae spurca saliva lupae.
praeterea infesto miserum me tradere Amori
    non cessasti omnique excruciare modo,
ut mi ex ambrosia mutatum iam foret illud
    saviolum tristi tristius helleboro.
15   quam quoniam poenam misero proponis amori,
    numquam iam posthac basia surripiam.

101

Multas per gentes et multa per aequora vectus
    advenio has miseras, frater, ad inferias,

99. 8. abstersisti ω abstersti O astersi **GM.**

7. **id:** the stealing of the kiss.

8. **guttis:** *i.e.* of water. — **articulis:** 'fingers'; cf. Prop. 2, 34, 80: *Cynthius inpositis temperat articulis.*

9. **contractum:** cf. the Eng. 'contract a disease'; Plin. *N.H.* 36, 27, 69: *pestilentiae quae obscuratione solis contrahitur.*

10. Cf. 78, 8: *savia conminxit spurca saliva tua.*

11. **Amori:** *i.e.* as to an executioner. The offishness of Juventius made the flames of Catullus's love burn all the hotter.

14. **tristi tristius:** cf. v. 2, n.

15. Catullus shows philosophic insight into the boyish contrariness of Juventius, and meeting him on his own ground is likely to win the day.

101

Written on visiting his brother's tomb at Rhoeteum, and probably used as an epitaph there. This visit must have been made on his way to Bithynia with Memmius in 57 B.C., rather than on the return journey, and was indeed one of the principal motives that prompted him to go to the East at that time. Cf. 65, 5–11; 68, 19–24, 89–100; also Tennyson's familiar poem.

1. **per gentes:** *i.e.* past their shores, while **multa per aequora** means 'over' many seas. Some of the seas were doubtless the Ionian, the Sicilian, the Cretan, the Myrtoan, the Aegean. To a landsman who had traveled little by either land or sea, this

ut te postremo donarem munere mortis
	et mutam nequiquam adloquerer cinerem,
5	quandoquidem fortuna mihi tete abstulit ipsum,
	heu miser indigne frater adempte mihi.
nunc tamen interea haec prisco quae more parentum
	tradita sunt tristis munera ad inferias
accipe fraterno multum manantia fletu,
10		atque in perpetuum, frater, ave atque vale.

verse must have seemed literally true. Cf. Verg. *Aen.* 6, 692: *quas ego te terras et quanta per aequora vectum accipio.* — **vectus** is to be taken closely with **advenio**, so that the expression = *iam diu vehor et nunc adveni*; hence the tense of **donarem** in v. 3.

2. **inferias**: as his brother is already buried, and no other members of the family are present, the funeral rites are necessarily much abridged in this case, and perhaps consist essentially only in the placing of this epitaph and the final adieu, spoken in v. 10, without the garlands, perfumes, and other features of more elaborate ceremonies.

5. **fortuna**: 'misfortune,' as in 64, 218. — **tete**: cf. 30, 7: *certe tute iubebas.*

6. Cf. 68, 20 and 92; Ovid, *Fast.* 4, 852: *atque ait 'invito frater adempte, vale!'*

7. **nunc**: 'even as it is.' — **interea** merely intensifies **tamen**, without any distinct notion of time. Cf. *Ciris*, 44: *haec tamen interea . . . accipe dona* (an imitation of

this passage); Lucr. 5, 83: *si tamen interea mirantur.* — **more parentum**: cf. *CIL.* 9, 4508, 1: *frater, post tempora nostra maiorum ut faceres more suprema mihi.*

8. **ad inferias**: purpose acc.

9. **fraterno multum manantia fletu**: cf. Mart. 6, 85, 11: *accipe cum fletu maesti breve carmen amici atque haec absentis tura fuisse puta.*

10. **in perpetuum**: this common phrase does not refer to the mortality of the soul, but merely to the irrevocable fact of death; cf. the Christian inscriptions, Buecheler, *Car. Lat. Epig.* 734, 10: *Paula soror tumulum dedit et solacia magni parva tulit luctus, tristique heu pectore 'salve perpetuomque vale frater carissime' dixit*; 737, 10: *iam vale perpetuo dulcis et in pace quiesce.* — **ave atque vale**: such *novissima verba* were regularly employed at the close of funeral rites; cf. Verg. *Aen.* 6, 231: *lustravitque viros dixitque novissima verba*; 11, 97: *salve aeternum mihi, maxime Palla, aeternumque vale.*

102

Si quicquam tacito commissum est fido ab amico,
　　cuius sit penitus nota fides animi,
meque esse invenies illorum iure sacratum,
　　Corneli, et factum me esse puta Harpocratem.

107

Si quoi quid cupido optantique obtigit umquam
　　insperanti, hoc est gratum animo proprie.
quare hoc est gratum nobis quoque, carius auro,
　　quod te restituis, Lesbia, mi cupido,
5　restituis cupido atque insperanti, ipsa refers te
　　nobis. o lucem candidiore nota!

107. 1. quoi quid *Ribbeck* quicquid **GM** quid quid **O** quicquam **D**.

102

An unknown Cornelius is assured that Catullus can keep a secret.

1. tacito: *i.e.* to one that knows how to hold his tongue.

2. cuius: the antecedent is *tacito*. — **animi**: for the pleonasm cf. 68, 26; Lucr. 1, 307: *umor aquai*.

3. meque = *me quoque*; cf. 31, 13: *gaudete vosque*; Prop. 3, 1, 35. — **illorum**: such as the previous verses have described. — **iure**: 'oath.'

4. Harpocratem: the Greek name of the younger Egyptian divinity Horus, who came to be regarded as the god of silence.

107

The joy of Catullus on the unexpected return of Lesbia after an estrangement. Evidently written before any serious rupture in their intimacy occurred. The repetitions in the phraseology (see vv. 1 and 4, 2 and 3, 4 and 5) are noteworthy as an indication of his rapturous excitement.

1. cupido: cf. 68, 158, n.

2. hoc: used of the general proposition, while in v. 3 it refers to this particular case as stated in v. 4.

3. nobis: cf. 116, 3, n. — **carius auro**: cf. Tib. 1, 8, 31: *carior est auro iuvenis*.

5. ipsa: 'of your own accord.'

6. candidiore nota: lucky or happy days were marked with a

quis me uno vivit felicior, aut magis hac rem
    optandam in vita dicere quis poterit ?

108

Si, Comini, populi arbitrio tua cana senectus
    spurcata inpuris moribus intereat,
non equidem dubito quin primum inimica bonorum
    lingua execta avido sit data vulturio,

---

107. 7. hac rem *Postgate* hac ē **O** me est **GM** hac res *Lachmann*.   8. op-
tandam in *Postgate* optandus **VM** optandas *Lachmann* magi' mi esse optan-
dum in *Statius.*

108. 1. Si, Comini, *Guarinus* sic homini **VM**. populi arbitrio *Statius*
populari arbitrio **VM**.   4. execta ω exercta **O** exerta **GM** excerpta *Ellis.*

---

white chalk mark or by a white
stone; cf. 68, 148, n.
    8. in vita: cf. Prop. 2, 9, 43:
*te nihil in vita nobis acceptius
umquam.*

108

The subject of this lampoon
was probably one of two brothers
Cominius of Spoletium, who played
a prominent part as prosecutors,
an especially unpopular case being
their prosecution of C. Cornelius
in 66 B.C., and the following
year, when he was defended by
Cicero.
    1. cana senectus: cf. 61, 162:
cana . . . anilitas.
    3. inimica bonorum: perhaps
some of the special friends of Catullus had been attacked; at any
rate, remembering the poet's im-

pulsiveness and extravagance in
his expressions, we need not at
once convict Cominius of being
such a monster of iniquity as he
is here described.
    4. execta = *exsecta.* — sit data :
it is doubtful whether the tense
has any special significance here,
any more than the rather frequent
active forms in tenses of completed action found in the elegiac
writers, where tenses of incomplete
action would be expected.   Cf.
Tib. 1, 1, 29, n.— vulturio : all the
creatures enumerated here are of
the sort that viciously peck or
snap at other flesh, so that the
comparison in each case is appropriate ; cf. Ovid, *Ibis*, 169-172 :
*unguibus et rostro crudus trahet
ilia vultur, et scindent avidi perfida
corda canes, deque tuo fiet — licet*

5   effossos oculos voret atro gutture corvus,
       intestina canes, cetera membra lupi.

109

Iucundum, mea vita, mihi proponis amorem
    hunc nostrum inter nos perpetuumque fore.
di magni, facite ut vere promittere possit
    atque id sincere dicat et ex animo,
5   ut liceat nobis tota perducere vita
       aeternum hoc sanctae foedus amicitiae.

109. 5. perducere **VRM** producere ω.

hac sis laude superbus — insatia-
bilibus corpore rixa lupis.

  5. effossos . . . voret: 'peck
and devour.' Cf. Vulg. *Prov.* 30,
17 : *oculum . . . effodiant eum
corvi.* — **atro** : 'ugly,' not merely
black ; cf. Tib. 1, 3, 4.

109

  A prayer that Lesbia's hope for
future unalloyed affection between
herself and her lover may be realized. It is clear, however, that
past experience has already given
ground for anxiety on the part of
the poet, so that he lacks absolute
confidence.
  1. **mea vita**: cf. 68, 155. —
proponis amorem hunc . . . fore:
'declare that this love of ours shall
be.' That Catullus regards this
declaration as a promise is seen
in *promittere* (v. 3). Merrill cites

Caes. *B.G.* 5, 58, 5 : *magna
proponit iis qui occiderint praemia.*
  3. **di magni** : here not an idle
exclamation, but a genuine address. — **possit** : Catullus perhaps
had reason to mistrust Lesbia's
capability to be ingenuous. Here
he is probably secretly wondering
whether she can be sufficiently
freed from other attachments to
make her promise an honest
one.
  4. Cf. Ter. *Eun.* 175 : *utinam
istuc verbum ex animo ac vere di-
ceres.*
  5. **perducere** : cf. Lucr. 5, 1027 :
*nec potuisset adhuc perducere sae-
cla propago.*
  6. **aeternum** : 'lasting'; cf.
Cic. *In Cat.* 4, 22 : *quare mihi
cum perditis civibus aeternum
bellum susceptum esse video.*

116

Saepe tibi studioso animo venante requirens
　　carmina uti possem mittere Battiadae,
qui te lenirem nobis, neu conarere
　　telis infestum mittere in usque caput,
5　　hunc video mihi nunc frustra sumptum esse laborem,
　　Gelli, nec nostras hic valuisse preces.
contra nos tela ista tua evitamus amictu:
　　at fixus nostris tu dabi' supplicium.

116

On the failure of the poet's attempts to conciliate Gellius; cf. Nos. 74, 80, 88, 90, 91, for the virulent attacks which doubtless prevented any further friendship between their object and their author.

1. **studioso**: dat. As a 'learned' man he would be more apt to appreciate the poetry of the 'doctus' Callimachus.

2. **carmina**: sc. *expressa*. — **Battiadae**: cf. 65, 16, n.

3. **qui** = *quibus*. — **nobis** = *mihi*, although it stands so close to *lenirem*; cf. vv. 5–8; 107, 3–6. — This verse is composed entirely of spondees. Cf. Intr. § 42, I (3).

4. **in usque** = *usque in*: 'at my very head.'

6. **hic**: 'in this respect.'

7. **contra**: adv.: my tactics are now changed, and I am prepared to defend myself and to strike home at your weak points. — **amictu**: *i.e.* the fold of the toga around the left arm is sufficient for defense, because your weapons are so harmless. Cf. Pacuv. 186: *clamide contorta astu clupeat braccium*; Petron. 80: *intorto circa brachium pallio conposui ad proeliandum gradum*.

8. **dabi'**: the archaic elision of final *s*, which occurs frequently in Lucretius and in Cicero's early poetic attempts, occurs only here in their contemporary Catullus. Cicero already counsels its avoidance in *Orat.* 161. Cf. LSHLG, p. 36, n. 2.

TIBULLUS MSS. SIGNS

A = Codex Ambrosianus.
V = Codex Vaticanus.
G = Codex Guelferbytanus.
O = Consensus of **AVG**.
Y = Codex Eboracensis.
P = Excerpta Parisina.
M = Excerpta Frisingensia.
F = Fragmentum Cuiacianum.
ω = late or inferior Mss., or corrections.

ALBII TIBVLLI ELEGIARVM

LIBER PRIMVS

I

Divitias alius fulvo sibi congerat auro
et teneat culti iugera multa soli,

1.   2. multa **GPM** magna **AVY.**

I, 1

Written probably in the early part of B.C. 29 (cf. Intr. § 23), perhaps on his country estate at Pedum. This elegy stands at the head of the collection, not chronologically, but as a typical representative of the work of Tibullus, setting forth his tastes and ideals, and serving as a kind of a dedication of Book 1 to Delia, who is here brought forward as the center of his hopes and joys. The poet signifies his preference for living in peaceful retirement on his family estates, enjoying the delights and freedom of rural life rather than encountering the hardships and perils of a soldier, even for the wealth that might be thus acquired. The acme of his hopes, however, is to be found in the continuance of the favor of his beloved Delia till his dying day.

Haase, Ribbeck, Baehrens, and others, by their transposition of verses, have wrought havoc with the gentle ebb and flow of the poetic thought so characteristic of Tibullus, which is illustrated in this poem as well as in any. The theme, briefly stated in vv. 1–14, is twice repeated in reverse order (15–36, 37–50), and the third time (51–78) the erotic element in his longing for a quiet stay-at-home life is expanded to the end of the elegy. Cf. Vahlen, *Monatsber. d. Ber. Akad.* 1878, pp. 343 sqq.; Leo, pp. 28 sqq. For a more artificial analysis cf. K. P. H. in *PAPA.*, Vol. 26 (1895), p. viii. For an appreciation of the genuineness of its feeling, cf. Reitzenstein in *Hermes* 47 (1912), pp. 60–116.

1–14: 'Let another endure the hardships and risks of a soldier's life for the wealth that he may thus gain: but let me rather pass my days in the quiet, humble

quem labor adsiduus vicino terreat hoste,
Martia cui somnos classica pulsa fugent:

country life of my own little farm,
thanking the gods for a modest
competence.' 15–36: (The previous thought in reverse order),
'To you, rustic divinities of my
now humble possessions, will I
offer appropriate sacrifices, if only
you will let me enjoy them in
peace, be my own gardener, my
own shepherd, and be undisturbed
by either thieves or wolves.' 37–
50: The same thought expressed
for the third time, in the same
order as in the previous section.
In v. 46 the erotic element is introduced, to be expanded in the
last division of the elegy. 51–78:
'Yes, Messalla and his legions
shall win their trophies on land
and sea; but as for me, let me enjoy my Delia's unfailing love while
life endures, and live contented
with my little store.'

1. fulvo: cf. 2, 1, 88. — congerat: hort. subj. — auro: abl.
instr.

2. culti . . . soli: the well-tilled
farms of other owners were often
confiscated and allotted by victorious generals to their soldiers, as
by Augustus more than once.
The story of the loss and recovery
of Vergil's estates near Mantua is
well known; it is not impossible
that Tibullus may have had some
similar experience, to which reference is made in the various passages suggesting that his wealth
had been seriously diminished,

such as vv. 5, 19–20, 37, 41. Gold
and lands were the two sources of
wealth for which Roman soldiers
followed their profession. Ullman, however, argues (*AJP.*, Vol.
33 (1912), pp. 160 sqq.) that the
property of Tibullus had been reduced from its ancestral proportions more probably by extravagance on the part of his father;
cf. Hor. *Sat.* 1, 4, 28: *stupet
Albius aere.* — iugera multa: cf.
2, 3, 42: *ut multa innumera
iugera pascat ove*; 3, 3, 5; Ovid,
Fast. 3, 192: *iugeraque . . . pauca
tenere soli*; K. P. H. in *Class.
Rev.*, Vol. 9 (1895), p. 108. For
indications that his *iugera* were
not now *multa*, see previous note.

3. quem . . . terreat: best regarded as subj. of characteristic,
like *fugent* in the next verse. —
labor adsiduus: the various routine
duties of a Roman soldier's life in
camp, including foraging amid the
peril of an attack, which naturally
terreat.

4. somnos: the plural refers
to the repeated instances of the
experience which this verse describes. Cf. v. 27, n. — classica:
for the evolution of the word's
meaning cf. R. 1097. From the
idea of being a means of distinguishing or summoning the *classes*
it came to refer to the thing so
used, *i.e.* the trumpet. — pulsa:
an expression transferred from
stringed to wind instruments.

5   me mea paupertas vita traducat inerti,
     dum meus adsiduo luceat igne focus.
     ipse seram teneras maturo tempore vites
     rusticus et facili grandia poma manu:
     nec Spes destituat, sed frugum semper acervos

5. vita **PM** vite (= vitae) **A**.

5. me: for the liberal use of
personal pronouns cf. vv. 35, 41,
49, 53, 55, 57, 75, 77; 3, 3; etc.
— **paupertas**: not to be interpreted
too literally, but rather as a playful
comparison with the *divitias* of
the professional soldier. So Horace in *Sat.* 1, 6, 71 speaks of his
father as *macro pauper agello*, yet
proceeds to tell how this same
father was able to give him at
Rome an education as good as the
sons of rich men enjoyed, and
adds: *vestem servosque sequentes,
in magno ut populo, si qui vidisset,
avita ex re praeberi sumptus mihi
crederet illos.* And Horace says
of Tibullus (*Ep.* 1, 4, 7): *di tibi
divitias dederunt artemque fru-
endi.* — **vita**: abl. of the way by
which: cf. Hirt. *B.G.* 8, 27: *nisi
flumine Ligeri . . . copias tra-
duxisset.* For a different construction cf. *CIL*, 6, 12072, 11:
*ut longum vitae liceat transducere
tempus.* — **traducat**: *i.e.* through
life. — **inerti**: cf. vv. 58, 71. It
was on account of the prominence
of this thought in this poem (the
word does not occur in any other
elegy of Tibullus) that Vahlen proposed to read *iam modo iners* in
v. 25.

6. adsiduo . . . igne: 'with
steady glow'; cf. v. 3. Such repetitions of a word are common
enough in Tibullus (cf. previous
note). — **focus**: the hearth fire was
essential to every Roman house;
indeed, the name for the hearth is
often used by metonymy for the
home; Ter. *Eun.* 815: *domi foci-
que fac vicissim ut memineris*;
Hor. *Ep.* 1, 14, 1: *agelli, quem tu
fastidis, habitatum quinque focis.*
The depth of poverty associated
with the extinguished hearth fire is
indicated in Cat. 23, 1–2: *Furi, cui
neque servus neque arca nec cimex
neque araneus neque ignis*; cf. 2,
1, 22; Verg. *Ec.* 5, 70; Mart. 10,
47, 4; *et passim*.

7. ipse: 'with my own hand.'
— **seram**: like *traducat* (v. 5),
opt. subj.

8. rusticus belongs to the
predicate. — **facili**: due to experience. — **grandia**: 'sturdy,' as
contrasted with *teneras* (v. 7). —
poma = *pomos*; cf. Verg. *Georg.*
2, 426; but in v. 13 it is used in
the ordinary sense; the regular
pomus occurs in 2, 1, 43.

9. Spes: 'Hope,' the goddess
of the sower and the gardener.
Very appropriately she had a tem-

10   praebeat et pleno pinguia musta lacu.
      nam veneror, seu stipes habet desertus in agris
         seu vetus in trivio florida serta lapis :
      et quodcumque mihi pomum novus educat annus,
         libatum agricolae ponitur ante deo.
15   flava Ceres, tibi sit nostro de rure corona

12. florida O florea ω.

ple in the Forum Holitorium at Rome; cf. Preller[3], Vol. 2, p. 253. Cf. also 2, 6, 21. — **destituat**: used absolutely here. — **frugum**: the product of the *grandia poma*, as *musta* is that of the *tenerae vites*.

10. **pinguia**: 'rich'; cf. Hor. *Sat.* 2, 4, 65: *pingui mero.* — **lacu**: the trough-like wine vat into which the juice of the grape ran when first pressed out. Cf. 2, 5, 86.

11. **nam**: 'and I have good reason to hope, for' I am faithful in my worship of all the rustic divinities, even the humblest. For this elliptical use of *nam*, cf. Ter. *Ad.* 190. — **stipes . . . lapis**: old tree trunks, stakes, and stones, either plain, or rudely carved, often represented divinities to the Romans, and were worshiped, whether standing by themselves in the fields, or set up at the crossroads. Boundary stones furnish an excellent illustration; for as representatives of the god Terminus they were honored with garlands hung upon them at certain times. Cf. Ovid, *Fast.* 2, 641 sqq.: *Termine, sive lapis, sive es defossus in agro stipes, ab antiquis tu quoque numen habes.*

te duo diversa domini de parte coronant binaque serta tibi binaque liba ferunt; Prop. 1, 4, 24; Lucr. 5, 1199, and Munro's note on the passage; Lucian, *Alex.* 30; Champney, p. 4. — **desertus**: 'standing alone,' contrasted with *trivio* (v. 12).

12. **florida**: for the more exact *florea*; cf. 1, 2, 14; on the other hand Vergil, *Aen.* 1, 430, uses *florea* for *florida*.

13. **novus . . . annus**: a newly recurring harvest time.

14. **libatum**: 'as a consecrated offering.'—**ante**: adverbial.—**deo**: in the collective sense, including Spes, as well as Vertumnus, Pomona, or Silvanus. Cf. 1, 5, 27.

15. **flava**: the usual epithet, transferred to the goddess from the ripened grain which she represents. Cf. Servius on Verg. *Georg.* 1, 96: *flava dicitur propter ar tarum colorem in maturitate*; Ovid, *Fast.* 4, 424. — **corona spicea**: the most appropriate offering; cf. 2, 1, 4; 1, 10, 22; Hor. *Car. Saec.* 29-30: *fertilis frugum pecorisque Tellus spicea donet Cererem corona*; Ovid, *Am.* 3, 10, 3; Baum. *Denk.* p. 417.

spicea, quae templi pendeat ante fores,
pomosisque ruber custos ponatur in hortis,
    terreat ut saeva falce Priapus aves :
vos quoque, felicis quondam, nunc pauperis agri
20   custodes, fertis munera vestra, lares :
tum vitula innumeros lustrabat caesa iuvencos,
    nunc agna exigui est hostia parva soli :
agna cadet vobis, quam circum rustica pubes
    clamet 'io messes et bona vina date' :
25   iam modo iam possim contentus vivere parvo

25. iam modo iam possim **M** iam modo non possum **O** quippe ego iam possum **P** iam modo nunc possum **ω** iam modo si possum *Lachmann* iam modo iners possim *Vahlen* iam mihi, iam possim *Schneidewin* dum modo iam possim *Baehrens.*

16. ante fores: cf. Prop. 4, 3, 17.

17. ruber custos: wooden figures of Priapus were commonly painted with vermilion and placed in gardens, where they served as the prototype of the scarecrow of to-day. Cf. Ovid, *Fast.* 1, 415: *at ruber, hortorum decus et tutela, Priapus*; Verg. *Georg.* 4, 110: *et custos furum atque avium cum falce saligna Hellespontiaci servet tutela Priapi*; Hor. *Sat.* 1, 8, 3–8.

18. falce: 'pruninghook,' the gardener's weapon. — **Priapus**: a god of fruitfulness in both plants and animals; his worship was not indigenous in Italy, but imported from the Asian shores of the Hellespont. Translate in apposition with *ruber custos*.

19. felicis quondam: cf. v. 2, n. ; Verg. *Ec.* 1, 75: *ite meae felix quondam pecus ite capellae.*

20. fertis: the present of customary action. — **munera vestra**:

i.e. those usually offered as most appropriate ; cf. Hor. *Sat.* 2, 5, 12: *dulcia poma et quoscumque feret cultus tibi fundus honores, ante larem gustet venerabilior lare dives.* — **lares**: here the *lares rurales*; for their nature see H. and T. § 189. At the festival of Ambarvalia (cf. 2, 1) they were honored with the other rural divinities.

21. tum: in the times referred to in *felicis quondam* (v. 19). — **lustrabat**: cf. 2, 1, 1 ; there were several festivals of purification, such as the Ambarvalia (2, 1), the Palilia (2, 5, 85 sqq.), and the Feriae Sementivae (Ovid, *Fast.* 1, 658) ; at any of these the customs described in vv. 21–24 might be witnessed annually.

25. iam . . . iam: 'henceforth'; the repetition emphasizes the idea of the actual completion of his military experiences and of

nec semper longae deditus esse viae,
sed canis aestivos ortus vitare sub umbra
    arboris ad rivos praetereuntis aquae.
nec tamen interdum pudeat tenuisse bidentes
30   aut stimulo tardos increpuisse boves,
non agnamve sinu pigeat fetumve capellae
    desertum oblita matre referre domum.
at vos exiguo pecori, furesque lupique,
    parcite : de magno est praeda petenda grege.
35 hic ego pastoremque meum lustrare quot annis

his having obtained from now on,
without interruption, that quiet
life which he desires. For the
repetition, with inserted word, cf.
Verg. *Aen.* 12, 179. — **modo** =
dummodo. — **possim** = *mihi liceat.*
— **vivere** = *vitam degere.* — **parvo** :
'my modest competence.'

26. nec : 'without being.' —
semper implies the rather impatient memory of several expeditions already engaged in. — **viae** :
'marches.'

27. canis : *i.e.* the dog star,
Sirius. The climax of summer
heat is usually coincident with the
days following the star's appearance in July, and the ancients regarded it as a cause ; cf. the modern
expression, "dog days"; cf. I, 4,
6 : *aestivi tempora sicca canis* ; I,
7, 21. — **ortus** : plural, referring to
the daily rising of the sun (and the
heat) during the period after the
canis has appeared. Cf. Hor. *Car.*
4. 15, 15 ; I, 17, 17. — **sub umbra** :
cf. Verg. *Ec.* I, I, I ; Hor. *Car.* I,
1, 21 ; *Epod.* 2, 23 ; Lucr. 2,
30.

28. ad rivos : cf. Ovid, *Rem.
Am.* 194 : *ipse potes rivos ducere
lenis aquae*; Hor. *Epod.* 2, 25 :
labuntur altis interim ripis aquae;
Lucr. 2, 29–30 : *prostrati in
gramine molli propter aquae rivum
sub ramis arboris altae.*

29. tenuisse : there is no appreciable difference in meaning between the perfect tense here, and
in v. 30, and the present, in *referre*
(v. 32). The perfect forms were
sometimes more convenient metrically. Cf. vv. 46 and 74 ; also I,
10, 61–63 ; Prop. I, I, 15 ; 17, I.
— **bidentes** : a common garden
implement.

31. agnamve sinu: cf. Isaiah,
40, 11 : "He shall gather the
lambs with his arm, and carry
them in his bosom."

32. oblita matre : abl. abs.

35. hic : on my little farm, in
contrast to the preceding verse.—
-**que . . . et** : cf. I, 3, 25. — **lustrare** : the annual purification here
referred to took place at the Palilia
(or Parilia) on April 21 ; cf. nn.
on 2, 5, 87, and 90.

et placidam soleo spargere lacte Palem.
adsitis, divi, nec vos e paupere mensa
   dona nec e puris spernite fictilibus.
fictilia antiquus primum sibi fecit agrestis
40   pocula, de facili conposuitque luto.
non ego divitias patrum fructusque requiro
   quos tulit antiquo condita messis avo :
parva seges satis est, satis est, requiescere lecto
   si licet et solito membra levare toro.
45   quam iuvat inmites ventos audire cubantem
   et dominam tenero continuisse sinu

---

46. continuisse **O** detinuisse **Y** tum tenuisse *Baehrens.*

---

36. placidam : used prolepti-
cally.

37. paupere mensa : in contrast to the expensive tables of
the rich, a kind of extravagance
which was a special fad at Rome ;
cf. B. *G.*, pp. 294–296.

38. fictilibus : although Tibullus appears to be pleading his
poverty as an excuse for using
earthenware dishes instead of vessels of silver and gold in sacrific-
ing to the gods, as a matter of
fact it was the well-known con-
servatism always attaching to religious rites which required that
the old-fashioned sacrificial vessels
of pottery should be retained even
long after this time. Cf. Lanciani,
*Anc. Rome in the Light of Mod.
Disc.*, p. 43 ; Pliny, *N. H.* 35, 46 :
*in sacris quidem etiam inter has
opes hodie non murrinis crystal-
linisve, sed fictilibus prolibatur ;*

Juv. 6, 342–345. With the general
idea of vv. 38–39 cf. 1, 10, 17–18.

40. facili : in the passive sense,
'plastic.' — For the position of **ego**
cf. *BPW.*, Vol. 18 (1898), Sp. 213 ;
for -**que** before a dissyllable ending
a pentameter cf. v. 78 ; Intr. § 28.

42. condita : 'ingathered.'

43. satis est : for similar repetitions, which are quite in the manner of Tibullus, cf. 1, 3, 4–5 ; 1, 2,
29–30 ; 1, 5, 61–65 ; 2, 5, 100 ;
Prop. 2, 13, 25.

44. solito : cf. Ovid, *Trist.* 3, 3,
39. — **toro :** properly the bedding
or covering, the part upon which
the body lies, as distinguished
from *lectus* as a whole.

45. iuvat : with the thought
cf. Lucr. 2, 1–2 : *suave, mari
magno turbantibus aequora ventis,
e terra magnum alterius spectare
laborem.* — **cubantem :** sc. *aliquem.*

aut, gelidas hibernus aquas cum fuderit auster,
   securum somnos imbre iuvante sequi !
hoc mihi contingat : sit dives iure, furorem
50   qui maris et tristes ferre potest pluvias.
o quantum est auri pereat potiusque smaragdi,
   quam fleat ob nostras ulla puella vias.
te bellare decet terra, Messalla, marique,
   ut domus hostiles praeferat exuvias :
55   me retinent vinctum formosae vincla puellae,

47. For the rime cf. Intr.
§ 42, I (5)(*b*).

48. imbre iuvante : cf. Hor.
Epod. 2, 28.

51. potius : belongs to both
clauses. On the arrangement of
words (synchysis) cf. I, 3, 56 ;
Hansen, p. 36.—**smaragdi** : 'gems' ;
for tne collective use cf. Prop. 1,
14, 12 ; Ovid, *Am.* 3, 13, 25 : *vir-
ginei crines auro gemmaque pre-
muntur*.

52. Cf. Prop. 3, 20, 4 : *tantine,
ut lacrimes, Africa tota fuit ?*

53. terra . . . marique : cf. 1,
3, 56. Messalla is still away at war.
— **Messalla** : Marcus Valerius Messalla Corvinus, b. 64 B.C., d. *c.*
8 A.D., the patron of Tibullus,
distinguished in public life and
literary circles at Rome. In the
civil wars he was successively
allied with the fortunes of Brutus,
Antony, and Octavian, and rendered the latter excellent service
in the final struggle at Actium for
the mastery of the Roman world.
After this he was intrusted with
several important military commis-
sions by Augustus, among them
the Aquitanian expedition, probably in 31 B.C., and the ordering of
affairs in various eastern provinces
immediately thereafter (see Intr.
to I, 3). He was the first to hold
the office of Praefectus Urbi, which
he soon resigned as inconsistent
with his political opinions. As an
orator he achieved much fame and
earned the praise of Cicero. He
wrote also poetry and historical
works. The literary coterie of
which he was the center included
particularly Tibullus, Lygdamus,
Sulpicia, and other minor poets ;
and he was also the friend of
Horace, Asinius Pollio, and Ovid ;
cf. 1, 3, 1 ; 5, 31 ; 7, 7, *et passim* ;
2, 1, 31–34 ; 5, 119.

54. praeferat : it was the custom to hang at the entrance of
houses and temples the trophies
won from vanquished enemies.
Cf. Verg. *Aen.* 7, 183 sqq. : *multaque praeterea sacris in postibus
arma, captivi pendent currus cur-
vaeque secures et cristae capitum
et portarum ingentia claustra spe-
culaque clipeique ereptaque rostra
carinis* ; Prop. 3, 9, 26.

et sedeo duras ianitor ante fores.
non ego laudari curo, mea Delia: tecum
 dum modo sim, quaeso segnis inersque vocer.
te spectem, suprema mihi cum venerit hora,
60 te teneam moriens deficiente manu.
flebis et arsuro positum me, Delia, lecto,
 tristibus et lacrimis oscula mixta dabis.
flebis: non tua sunt duro praecordia ferro
 vincta, neque in tenero stat tibi corde silex.
65 illo non iuvenis poterit de funere quisquam
 lumina, non virgo, sicca referre domum.
tu manes ne laede meos, sed parce solutis
 crinibus et teneris, Delia, parce genis.
interea, dum fata sinunt, iungamus amores:
70 iam veniet tenebris Mors adoperta caput,

---

56. duras: as if the doors were to blame for shutting him out. — **ianitor**: doorkeepers were often kept chained to their positions at the entrance (cf. *vinctum*).

57. laudari: of military honors; cf. Prop. 1, 6, 29. "Here is the same 'linked sweetness long drawn out,' which gives such a charm to Gray's *Elegy*" (Cruttwell, *Hist. Rom. Lit.*, p. 301). — **curo**: 'take pains.'

60. Ovid in his beautiful elegy on the death of Tibullus (*Am.* 3, 9, 58) expresses historically the same idea that Tibullus here utters as prophetic longing. Cf. Shakespeare, *Son.* 92: "O what a happy title do I find, Happy to have thy love, happy to die!"

61. flebis et . . . et . . . dabis: the fut. of confident expectation. —

lecto: 'my bier,' which would be placed upon the funeral pyre and consumed with it. Cf. Prop. 4, 11, 10.

63–64. Cf. 1, 10, 59; Ovid, *Am.* 3, 6, 59: *ille habet et silices et vivum in pectore ferrum.*

67. tu: cf. 1, 4, 39; Prop. 1, 7, 25. — **manes ne laede**: the spirit of the departed is represented as being pained by too great grief on the part of loved ones left behind; cf. Prop. 4, 11, 1.

69. dum . . . sinunt: cf. Prop. 1, 19, 25; 2, 15, 23: *dum nos fata sinunt, oculos satiemus amore.* — **iungamus amores**: cf. Cat. 64, 372: *quare agite optatos animi coniungite amores.*

70. iam: for this use of the word cf. *Lex.* s.v. C. 3; cf. 2, 5, 56. — **Mors**: the abstract idea is

iam subrepet iners aetas, neque amare decebit,
　dicere nec cano blanditias capite.
nunc levis est tractanda Venus, dum frangere postes
　non pudet et rixas inseruisse iuvat.
75　hic ego dux milesque bonus: vos, signa tubaeque,
　ite procul, cupidis vulnera ferte viris.
ferte et opes: ego conposito securus acervo
　despiciam dites despiciamque famem.

3

Ibitis Aegaeas sine me, Messalla, per undas,
　o utinam memores ipse cohorsque mei:

72. capite **OP** capiti **ω**.

here personified according to Roman habit; but the picture of the
goddess thus formed in the imagination of the poet does not correspond at all to the Greek god
Thanatos, commonly represented
as a youth sinking down in sleep,
with a reversed torch. The idea
of such a being was too indistinct
at Rome to be represented in any
regular Roman type. Horace
(*Sat.* 2, 1, 58) may be intending to
liken Mors to an evil bird of prey:
Mors atris circumvolat alis. Perhaps the picture here painted by
Tibullus takes its main characteristic of a veiled countenance from
the Roman custom of concealing
the face when applying the torch
to a funeral pyre, or from the dim
uncertainty shrouding the real
nature of death and the future life.
Cf. 1, 10, 34.

71. **aetas** = *senectus*.

72. **cano . . . capite**: abl.
abs.; cf. for the construction 2, 6,
18; and for a similar idea, 1, 2,
90–92. — **blanditias**: 'soft noth-
ings.'

74. **rixas**: quarrels of rival
lovers. — **inseruisse**: 'engage in.'

75. **hic**: 'in this field'; cf. the
opening verses of the elegy with
these closing ones. On the ellipsis of *sum* cf. Deutsch, pp. 180–
181.

76. **cupidis**: *i.e.* for the *opes* of
v. 77, viz. the same as described
in vv. 1–2.

78. Cf. Hor. *Car.* 2, 10, 5–8.

1, 3

After the Aquitanian expedition
(probably of 31 B.C.) Messalla
was sent by Augustus to the East
to settle affairs in Cilicia, Syria,
and other districts. Tibullus, who
had been in his retinue in Aqui-

me tenet ignotis aegrum Phaeacia terris :
abstineas avidas, Mors precor atra, manus.

3. 4. Mors precor atra **Yω** Mors modo nigra **O** Mors violenta *Codex Wittianus.*

tania, decided to accompany him thither also. But before he had proceeded far on his journey, the poet fell sick and Messalla was obliged to leave him behind on the island of Corcyra. This elegy must have been written there some time during the year 30 B.C., perhaps in the late summer or the fall, and is the earliest of the collection to which a definite date can be assigned.

Sick and lonesome, Tibullus in characteristic fashion at one moment fears imminent death, and the next hopes for a joyful return to his home and his Delia. Three times do gloomy forebodings give way to hope, in each case the ground of his pleasant anticipations being a different one, approached in a very skillful manner.

1–34. 'Alas! I am left alone, with none to perform the last offices at my grave; how much better it would have been, had I heeded the omens and forebodings which we both had before my departure ! How faithful was Delia to thy service, O Isis ! Surely thou wilt save me for her sake. 35–52 : How much pleasanter it would have been to live in the golden age, when I should not have tempted Providence by sailing the sea, — before, under Jove's

rule, war, the messenger of death, had been invented ! But thou, Juppiter, shouldst save me, a religious man. 53–94 : But if I must die, let me be duly honored, and let my spirit fly to Elysium. If any have taken advantage of my absence from my love, let his abode be amidst the horrors of Tartarus. But do thou, Delia, remain true to me : and oh ! after all, may I live to return unexpectedly and find you waiting for me in your chaste home.'

1. **Ibitis** : although Messalla, his patron, stands alone for emphasis at the beginning of the elegy, the verb is in the plural referring to the idea of *ipse cohorsque* in the next verse; cf. Hor. *Epod.* I, 1.

2. **memores** : sc. *sitis*, or *vivatis ;* cf. 3, 5, 31. Such an omission is unusual, but begins to be more common in Tacitus. — **cohors:** 'retinue,' composed of not only the necessary officials, but also usually, in such a case, of many young men of rank, just getting thus their first taste of military life ; cf. Intr. §§ 21 and 23.

3. **Phaeacia** : this mythical isle of Homer's *Odyssey* was identified by later writers with Corcyra. It was a *terra incognita* to the poet's friends ; cf. Ovid, *Am.* 3, 9, 47.

4. **Mors . . . atra** : cf. 1, 10, 33.

5   abstineas, Mors atra, precor : non hic mihi mater
      quae legat in maestos ossa perusta sinus,
    non soror, Assyrios cineri quae dedat odores
      et fleat effusis ante sepulcra comis,
    Delia non usquam ; quae me cum mitteret urbe,
10   dicitur ante omnes consuluisse deos.
    illa sacras pueri sortes ter sustulit, illi
      rettulit e trinis omina certa puer.
    cuncta dabant reditus : tamen est deterrita numquam,

---

12. trinis *Muretus* triviis **O**. omina *over an erasure* **A** omnia **Y**, *apparently* **V**.

---

5. For the repetition cf. 1, 1, 43, n. Similar chiastic repetition in Ovid, *Ex P*. 1, 2, 58. — **non hic** : cf. Ovid, *Trist*. 1, 2, 53 : *est aliquid . . . mandare suis aliqua et sperare sepulcrum.*

6. For the details of the *ossilegium*, which it was the duty of the nearest relative to perform, cf. 3, 2, 9–26 and nn.

7. **Assyrios** = *Syrios*, by a common confusion due partly to the similarity in sound, and partly to the haziness of geographical knowledge at Rome. All the products of the East were frequently called *Syrios*, because shipped to Rome from Antioch, or other Syrian ports. So "Port" wine from Oporto ; see Taylor, *Words and Places*, p. 282 ; cf. Cat. 68, 144 ; Prop. 2, 13, 30. — **dedat** : 'devote.'

8. **sepulcra** : poetic plural.

9. **cum mitteret** : with conative force : 'when she was trying to make up her mind to let me go.'

11. **pueri sortes** : little tablets of wood or bronze which would be managed by a *puer sortilegus* ; they were inscribed with some sentiment and drawn one at a time, as a method of divination. All sorts of fortune tellers, astrologers, and soothsayers flourished at Rome, plying their trade especially in certain quarters of the city ; cf. Hor. *Sat*. 1, 6, 113 : *fallacem circum vespertinumque pererro saepe forum ; adsisto divinis* ; Cic. *De Div*. 2, 41. — **ter** : to make the matter sure.

12. **rettulit** : ' interpreted.' — **trinis** : referring to *ter* in v. 11 ; the word is not a distributive here.

13. **cuncta** : referring not only to *omina* in the preceding verse, but also to the *omina* implied in v. 10. — **dabant** : 'foretold.' — **reditus** : the plural refers to the repeated instances where a safe return was prophesied ; cf. 1, 1, 4, n ; Ovid, *Fast*. 1, 279 : *ut populo reditus pateant ad bella profecto.*

> quin fleret nostras respiceretque vias.
> 15   ipse ego solator, cum iam mandata dedissem,
>   quaerebam tardas anxius usque moras;
> aut ego sum causatus aves aut omina dira,
>   Saturnive sacram me tenuisse diem.
> o quotiens ingressus iter mihi tristia dixi
> 20   offensum in porta signa dedisse pedem!
> audeat invito nequis discedere Amore,
>   aut sciat egressum se prohibente deo.
> quid tua nunc Isis mihi, Delia, quid mihi prosunt

---

14. respiceretque O respueretque ω despueretque *Haupt.* **17.** aves aut ω aves dant O. **18.** Saturnive *accepted by Broukhusius from a certain scholar* Saturni O. **22.** sciat O sciet *Doering.*

15. solator: the appositive is here equivalent to a concessive clause: 'though I tried to console her'; cf. Madv. 220. — **mandata:** 'parting injunctions'; cf. Ovid, *Trist.* 1, 3, 59.

16. tardas: in the active sense; cf. Hor. *Sat.* 1, 9, 32: *tarda podagra.*

17. Cf. Ovid, *Her.* 5, 49–52; *Met.* 9, 767; Ter. *Phorm.* 705 sqq.

18. Saturnive . . . diem: subject of *tenuisse.* The Jewish Sabbath (the seventh day of the week) was known to the Romans as Saturn's day (Saturday). Of this use of the term in literature this is one of the earliest instances, perhaps the earliest. Many passages show that Jewish customs had their share of respectful observance at Rome along with the host of foreign superstitions by this time introduced into Roman life; cf. Edwin Post in *Meth. Rev.*,

Vol. 79 (1897), p. 81; Ovid, *A. A.* 1, 415: *quaque die redeunt rebus minus apta gerendis culta Palaestino septima festa Syro*; *Rem. Am.* 219; Hor. *Sat.* 1, 9, 69. — **săcram:** Tibullus's rule in regard to this word's quantity seems to be that when one syllable is long the other is short; cf. *e.g. sācra* in v. 25. But cf. *BPW.*, Vol. 32 (1912), Sp. 394.

22. sciat: *i.e.* 'let him learn' from sad experience like my own. — **deo** = *Amore: i.e.* even if the gods seem propitious, here is a really opposing divinity.

23. tua . . . Isis: the worship of the Egyptian goddess Isis had become common at Rome, and was especially popular among women. As the patroness of navigation there would have been particular appropriateness in her being besought by Delia to give Tibullus a safe return.

illa tua totiens aera repulsa manu,

25   quidve, pie dum sacra colis, pureque lavari
      te (memini) et puro secubuisse toro?

nunc, dea, nunc succurre mihi (nam posse mederi
      picta docet templis multa tabella tuis),

ut mea votivas persolvens Delia voces

30   ante sacras lino tecta fores sedeat

bisque die resoluta comas tibi dicere laudes
      insignis turba debeat in Pharia,

24. aera: the *sistrum*, a rattle composed commonly of several pieces of metal (hence the plural), the usual accompaniment of Isis-worship; cf. Ovid, *A. A.* 3, 635.

25. dum sacra colis: especially at the two more important annual festivals of the goddess. — **pureque lavari . . . et . . . secubuisse**: sc. *prosunt*; the two principal requirements of the devotees of Isis at these festivals; cf. Prop. 2, 33, 1–4; also Tib. 2, 1, 11; Ovid, *Am.* 3, 9, 33.

27. posse mederi: sc. *te*. Cf. Stolz-Schmalz, 162, 2; Draeger, 454; Ter. *Phorm.* 610: *venire salvom volup est.*

28. picta . . . tabella: the custom of placing a votive picture in the temple of a deity after escape from sickness, shipwreck, or other danger, was a common one, especially in temples of Isis; cf. Juv. 12, 27: *votiva testantur fana tabella plurima; pictores quis nescit ab Iside pasci*; Hor. *Car.* 1, 5, 13; *Sat.* 2, 1, 33. The custom still persists in some churches in Italy.

29. votivas . . . voces = *vota*, *i.e.* those of Tibullus himself, viz. vv. 30–32.

30. lino tecta: 'clothed in linen.' The priests and devotees of Isis wore linen so much as to have the standing epithet *liniger*, like the goddess herself; cf. Ovid, *Met.* 1, 747: *linigera . . . turba*; *Ex P.* 1, 1, 51: *linigerae . . . Isidis.* Linen raiment was worn also by those consulting the subterranean oracle of Trophonius (Paus. 9, 39, 8), in the cult of earth gods (Dieterich, *Abraxas* 158 A), in magic rites (ib. 179, 9, etc.), and in incubation (Deubner, *De Incubat.* p. 25). — **sedeat**: cf. Prop. 2, 28, 45.

31. bisque die: in the early morning, before sunrise, and towards evening. — **resoluta comas**: cf. 2, 5, 66, where the Sibyl is likewise engaged in serving a deity.

32. insignis: *i.e.* for her unusual beauty. — **Pharia** = *Aegyptia*; Pharos was the island on which stood the famous lighthouse at the entrance to the harbor of Alexandria.

at mihi contingat patrios celebrare penates
    reddereque antiquo menstrua tura lari.
35   quam bene Saturno vivebant rege, prius quam
    tellus in longas est patefacta vias !
nondum caeruleas pinus contempserat undas,
    effusum ventis praebueratque sinum,
nec vagus ignotis repetens conpendia terris
40   presserat externa navita merce ratem.
illo non validus subiit iuga tempore taurus,
    non domito frenos ore momordit equus,
non domus ulla fores habuit, non fixus in agris,
    qui regeret certis finibus arva, lapis.
45   ipsae mella dabant quercus, ultroque ferebant

33. contingat: like *sedeat* (v. 30), and *debeat* (v. 32), introduced by *ut* (v. 29). — **celebrare penates**: the usual custom on returning from a journey; cf. Ter. *Phorm.* 311.

34. antiquo: in comparison with such new-fangled cults as that of Isis. — **menstrua**: the *lar* was worshiped especially on the Calends, as well as the Ides, the Nones, and festival occasions. — **lari**: up to the time of Augustus the *lar familiaris* was spoken of properly only in the singular, indicating the protector of the *familia* as a whole ; cf. Wissowa, *Rel. u. Kult. d. Römer*, p. 149.

35. The following description of "the good old days" of the "golden age" under Saturn's rule is worthy to be compared with the many similar passages in the Roman poets, such as Ovid, *Met.* 1,

89–112; *Am.* 3, 8, 35-44; *Fast.* 2, 289–298; Hor. *Epod.* 16, 41–66; Verg. *Ec.* 4, 9 sqq.; *Georg.* 1, 125 sqq. Like Vergil, Tibullus distinguishes but two ages; Horace and Aratus have three; Ovid, four; Hesiod, five. The golden age was already recognized as a trite theme in the *Aetna*, vv. 9–15.

36. longas . . . vias: cf. 1, 1, 26. Acc. of purpose.

37. contempserat : cf. Hor. *Car.* 1, 3, 21–24; Tibullus is wishing that he had never set sail on this expedition; the idea of 'spurning the billows' has become a commonplace even among English poets.

38. On the position of *-que* cf. 2, 5, 72, n.

45. ipsae . . . quercus: 'the very oaks'; the emphasis is on *quercus*, a kind of tree which does not ordinarily give honey, but was be-

obvia securis ubera lactis oves.

non acies, non ira fuit, non bella, nec ensem
    inmiti saevus duxerat arte faber.

nunc Iove sub domino caedes et vulnera semper,
50   nunc mare, nunc leti mille repente viae.

parce, pater.   timidum non me periuria terrent,
    non dicta in sanctos inpia verba deos.

quod si fatales iam nunc explevimus annos,
    fac lapis inscriptis stet super ossa notis:

55 'hic iacet inmiti consumptus morte Tibullus,
    Messallam terra dum sequiturque mari.'

sed me, quod facilis tenero sum semper Amori,
    ipsa Venus campos ducet in Elysios.

hic choreae cantusque vigent, passimque vagantes

---

50. repente **G** reperte **AV** multa reperta via ω.

lieved to have done so in this fabulous age; cf. Verg. *Ec.* 4, 29–30:
*incultisque rubens pendebit senti-
bus uva, et durae quercus suda-
bunt roscida mella*; Ovid, *Met.* 1,
111–112: *flumina iam lactis, iam
flumina nectaris ibant, flavaque
de viridi stillabant ilice mella*;
also the Israelitish "land flowing
with milk and honey."

46. securis: sc. *dominis*. They
were free even from the ordinary
care of providing themselves daily
food.

48. duxerat: *i.e.* on the anvil;
cf. Eng. "ductile"; Verg. *Aen.*
7, 633.

50. repente: with adjectival
force; cf. A. 321, d.; *mare* is one
of these new ways of sudden death;
cf. Prop. 3, 7, 31, n.

51. pater: Juppiter. — **timidum**: a predicate adjective here;
cf. the English "strike him dead."

52. Clearly Tibullus does not
consider the sentiment of v. 49
any sacrilege.

53. fatales: which fate has allotted.

54. notis: sc. *litterarum*.

55. Cf. 3, 2, 29; Prop. 2, 13, 35.

56. Note favorite position of
the *-que*; cf. 1, 1, 51, n.

57. me: in contrast to *lapis*
(v. 54).

58. Cf. Ovid, *Am.* 3, 9, 60. —
ipsa Venus: this function was
usually ascribed to Mercury.

59. For the description cf.
Verg. *Aen.* 6, 637 sqq. — **choreae**:
instead of the usual *chorēae*; cf.
Prop. 2, 19, 15.

60   dulce sonant tenui gutture carmen aves,
       fert casiam non culta seges, totosque per agros
       floret odoratis terra benigna rosis :
       at iuvenum series teneris inmixta puellis
       ludit, et adsidue proelia miscet Amor.
65   illic est, cuicumque rapax mors venit amanti,
       et gerit insigni myrtea serta coma.
       at scelerata iacet sedes in nocte profunda
       abdita, quam circum flumina nigra sonant :
       Tisiphoneque inpexa feros pro crinibus angues

61. casiam : not the common *casia* of Italy referred to in Verg. *Ec.* 2, 49; but the imported product, corresponding to our common cinnamon bark. — **non culta :** A. 496, note 3 ; H. 636, 3. — **seges :** for a similar use of the word cf. 4, 2, 18.

63. at : used often by Tibullus without any adversative force ; cf. v. 87, n. ; also 1, 7, 7 ; 10, 41 ; in 2, 5, 7 *sed* is used in the same sense.

64. proelia : cf. 1, 10, 53 ; Hor. *Car.* 1, 6, 17 : *proelia virginum.* With these military terms in connection with lovers cf. the English " conquest," " win," " lay siege," etc. The idea here is not that of a falling out.

65. cuicumque : the antecedent is *amanti* (= *amatori*).

66. insigni belongs to the predicate. — **myrtea :** cf. Verg. *Ec.* 7, 61 : *gratissima . . . formosae myrtus Veneri.*

67. at : here used with its regular adversative force. — **scelerata**

= *sceleratorum* ; cf. Verg. *Aen.* 6, 543 : *inpia Tartara ;* Ovid, *Met.* 4, 456 sqq.

68. circum : this preposition is always postpositive in Tibullus ; cf. 1, 1, 23. — **flumina nigra :** the rivers that may properly be said to surround Tartarus are Phlegethon and Pyriphlegethon, the rivers of fire ; cf. Verg. *Aen.* 6, 550–551 : *quae rapidus flammis ambit torrentibus amnis, Tartareus Phlegethon, torquetque sonantia saxa.* The poets' conceptions of the details of the lower world were naturally vague and differed widely. Cf. Cat. 65, 6, n.

69. Tisiphone, with her wriggling locks of serpents, is a familiar figure in descriptions of the horrors of Tartarus ; cf. Prop. 3, 5, 40 ; Verg. *Aen.* 6, 570–572 ; Ovid, *Met.* 4, 474–475 ; Hor. *Car.* 2, 13, 35– 36. The expression **pro crinibus** is a modifier of *angues,* equivalent to a relative clause. — **angues :** for the construction cf. *capillos,* v. 91. Serpents are particularly connected

70   saevit, et huc illuc inpia turba fugit :
        tum niger in porta serpentum Cerberus ore
          stridet, et aeratas excubat ante fores.
        illic Iunonem temptare Ixionis ausi
          versantur celeri noxia membra rota,
75   porrectusque novem Tityos per iugera terrae
          adsiduas atro viscere pascit aves.
        Tantalus est illic, et circum stagna, sed acrem
          iam iam poturi deserit unda sitim :

with earth gods and beings of the
lower world, *e g.* Furies, Giants,
and Cerberus.   Souls of the dead
were often represented as serpents.

  70. Cf. *Culex*, 219.

  71. **tum**: cf. Verg. *Aen.* 4, 250,
for similar use of the conj. to add
another detail. — **in porta**: of
Tartarus, as in Verg. *Georg.* 4,
483 ; but Cerberus is usually the
keeper of the entrance to the lower
world as a whole ; cf. Verg. *Aen.*
6, 417. — **serpentum . . . ore stri-
det**: 'visage of hissing serpents';
cf. Ovid, *Met.* 11, 597 : *non vigil
ales ibi cristati cantibus oris evocat
Auroram* ; Plin. *N. H.* 10, 56, 77 :
ore rubicundo (of a hen) ; the expression gives us no definite information as to whether Tibullus
conceived Cerberus as with one
head or more, or with the snakes
on his head (Hor. *Car.* 3, 11, 18),
around his neck (*Culex*, 221), or
composing his head, or heads.
For the idea that Cerberus really
was a snake cf. Paus. 3, 25, 5.
Honey cakes were thrown to the
snakes of Trophonius in Boeotia,

as to Cerberus.   Hence the varying conceptions, perhaps.

  73. **illic** belongs to the next
distich as well as to this one ; similarly the force of *illic* in v. 77 extends as far as v. 80. So the
examples of condemned wretches
in Tartarus are arranged in pairs.
The first two, Ixion and Tityos,
were guilty of unbridled lust, and
Tibullus wishes vv. 71–82 to be
taken as a parallel to these. Tantalus and the Danaides were punished for presumptuous ingratitude
and lack of appreciation of the
good gifts of the gods, which in
the latter case were represented
by good husbands ; these examples are quoted rather as a warning to Delia herself, and are to be
compared with vv. 83–84.

  77. **circum**: adverb ; sc. *sunt* ;
cf. Caes. *B. C.* 2, 10 : *ubi ex ea turri
quae circum essent opera tueri se
posse sunt confisi.*

  78. **iam iam**: the repetition
makes more vivid the picture of
the sufferer's palpitating hope ever
just on the verge of realization.
Cf. Verg. *Aen.* 6, 602.

et Danai proles, Veneris quod numina laesit,
80   in cava Lethaeas dolia portat aquas.
illic sit quicumque meos violavit amores,
    optavit lentas et mihi militias.
at tu casta precor maneas, sanctique pudoris
    adsideat custos sedula semper anus.
85   haec tibi fabellas referat positaque lucerna
    deducat plena stamina longa colu.
at circa gravibus pensis adfixa puella
    paullatim somno fessa remittat opus.
tunc veniam subito, nec quisquam nuntiet ante,
90   sed videar caelo missus adesse tibi.
tunc mihi, qualis eris, longos turbata capillos,
    obvia nudato, Delia, curre pede.

86. colu **M** colo **OP.**   87. at **P** ac **O.**   89. tunc **O** tum **ω.**   91. tunc **GV** nunc **A.**

80. cava = *cavata* = 'perforated'; cf. Ovid, *A. A.* 1, 432: *elapsusque cava fingitur aure lapis*; *Met.* 12, 130: *parmam gladio galeamque cavari cernit.*

81. quicumque: a comprehensive term for potential or actual rivals.

83. tu: the same as *meos amores* in v. 81, *i.e.* Delia.

84. anus: either Delia's mother (cf. 1, 6, 57-66) or nurse (cf. Prop. 4, 3, 41). For the picture cf. Ter. *Haut.* 275 sqq.

85. fabellas referat: the older woman is to 'spin yarns' to the maidens while they all spin yarn, — their evening's task. Cf. the story of Lucretia's occupation in Livy, 1, 57, 9. — **lucerna**: the fact that lights were necessary so early

indicates perhaps that this elegy was written in the fall of the year.

87. at = *ac.* Tibullus is particular not to use *ac* before a palatal; cf. Haupt, *Opusc.* 1, 109; cf. v. 63, n. — **puella**: the collective use for *puellae*; cf. Lachmann on Prop. 3, 3, 29.

90. caelo: Tibullus uses the preposition in a similar phrase in 4, 13, 13.

92. nudato: Delia, surprised at her quiet evening's work, not only will leave her hair unconfined, but also will not even stop to put on her sandals as she runs to meet her lover. It is clear from this idyllic picture of Delia's modest home life that she was not a married woman.

hoc precor, hunc illum nobis Aurora nitentem
　　Luciferum roseis candida portet equis.

7

Hunc cecinere diem Parcae fatalia nentes
　　stamina non ulli dissoluenda deo;

93. hunc: 'such as this.' —
illum . . . Luciferum: 'that happy
day.'

I, 7

After Messalla's brief but victorious campaign in Aquitania,
probably in B.C. 31, he was sum-
moned by Augustus to help settle
affairs in the East (cf. 1, 3, Intr.),
and his triumph over the Aquitani
was therefore delayed until his
return to Rome in B.C. 27, when
it was celebrated on Sept. 25.
His birthday occurring a few days
thereafter, he received from Tibullus for the occasion this con-
gratulatory poem. Belling (*Untersuchung*, pp. 174–175) has
collected an interesting series of
parallelisms from Vergil's *Georgics*.
1–12: 'The Fates decreed that
this should be the birthday of one
who should subdue proud Aquitania. That has come true, Messalla; the Romans have seen thy
triumph; I was a witness of thy
glorious deeds, as were the ocean,
strange rivers, and people. 13–
22: Witnesses, too, of thy victorious progress are such eastern
lands as Cilicia, Syria, and Egypt.

23–42: Egypt! 'Tis to thee,
father Nile, and to thee, great
Osiris, that she owes her preëmi-
nence in agriculture, especially in
the fruit of the vine, which gladdens
the heart of man and drives dull
care away. 43–54: Yea, Osiris,
thou lovest the festal day, with
dance and song and beauty.
Come then, and join in the celebration of this glad natal day!
Come thou, Genius of the day,
and let me offer thee appropriate
offerings! 55–64: And, Messalla,
may thy sons live to emulate thy
deeds and bring honor to thy
declining years! Let not men
forget thy blessings conferred upon
them! And may this day many
times return, with ever-increasing
joy!'

1. Hunc . . . diem: Messalla's
birthday. — **Parcae:** the three sisters, Clotho ('spinner'), Lachesis
('allotter'), and Atropos ('inevitable'). — **nentes:** so the fates
sang as they spun before the birth
of Pollio's son in Verg. *Ec.* 4, 46–
47: '*talia saecla,' suis dixerunt,
'currite' fusis concordes stabili
fatorum numine Parcae.* In Cat.
64, 323 sqq the prophecy is uttered

hunc fore, Aquitanas posset qui fundere gentes,
　quem tremeret forti milite victus Atax.
5　evenere: novos pubes Romana triumphos
　vidit et evinctos bracchia capta duces:
at te victrices lauros, Messalla, gerentem
　portabat niveis currus eburnus equis.
non sine me est tibi partus honos: Tarbella Pyrene

7. 8. niveis ω nitidis **O**.　9. Tarbella *Scaliger* tua bella **O**.

at the wedding of the father and
mother, with the oft-recurring refrain, '*currite ducentes subtegmina,
currite, fusi.*' In Tib. 4, 5, 3, the
Parcae are represented as singing
the fates at the time of birth: *te
nascente novum Parcae cecinere
puellis servitium*. In this case
the time is undefined. Ovid
seems to have had this passage in
mind when he wrote (*Trist*. 5, 3,
25), *scilicet hanc legem nentes fatalia Parcae stamina bis genito bis
cecinere tibi.*

2. dissolŭenda: cf. v. 40; Cat.
66, 38, n. — **deo**: emphatic; not
even the gods can escape the de-
crees of fate.

3. hunc: best taken as referring
to Messalla himself: for a similar ambiguity in pronouns cf.
tibi (vv. 53 and 55) referring to
different persons, and *haec* (Prop.
1, 13, 9, 11, 13); Prop. 3, 11, 37,
n.

4. milite: instrumental.—**Atax**:
this river (the modern Aude) was
in Gallia Narbonensis; but Roman
geography was notoriously in-
exact; moreover vv. 9–12 show
that the poet is not confining the

account of the victorious progress
of Messalla to the limits of Aquitania proper. As the Atax was
directly in the line of march from
the 'Province' to Aquitania, very
likely it was the scene of the first
conflict between the armies.

5. evenere: *i.e.* the predictions
of the preceding verses. — tri-
umphos: like *lauros* (v. 7), merely
a poetic plural. Cf. 2, 5, 117.

6. capta: by hypallage for *cap-
tos*. — **duces**: among the features
of Roman triumphal processions
was a selection of the noblest captives led, bound, to death (commonly inflicted at the Tullianum);
cf. Ovid, *A. A.* 1, 215: *ibunt
ante duces onerati colla catenis.*

8. portabat: descriptive imperfect. — **niveis**: cf. Ovid, *A. A.* 1,
214: *quattuor in niveis aureus
ibis equis!* — **currus eburnus**: the
triumphal car was richly adorned
with gold and ivory, and drawn by
four horses, often, but not always,
white. For details of the Roman
triumph see Pohlmey's *Der römische Triumph*. Cf. 2, 5, 120.

9. non sine me: *i.e.* Tibullus
was present in the Aquitanian cam-

10   testis et Oceani litora Santonici,
        testis Arar Rhodanusque celer magnusque Garumna,
        Carnuti et flavi caerula lympha Liger.
        an te, Cydne, canam, tacitis qui leniter undis
        caeruleus placidis per vada serpis aquis,
15   quantus et aetherio contingens vertice nubes
        frigidus intonsos Taurus alat Cilicas?

12. Carnuti ω Carnoti O Carnutis M.   13. an ω at O.

paign. — **Tarbella Pўrēnē**: the *Tarbelli* were an Aquitanian tribe living close up under the Pyrenees, near the ocean.

10. Santonici: the *Santones* occupied the territory on the coast just north of the river Garonne.

11. Arar: the modern Saône.

12. Carnuti . . . flavi: gen. sing. used in the collective sense: ' of the fair-haired Carnute.' The *Carnuti* lived between the Seine and the Loire. — **et**: the trajection of this copula occurs more often in this elegy than in any other of Tibullus; cf. vv. 15, 21, 38, 39, 54. Propertius is equally free in this respect; Ovid, more cautious; no example occurs in Catullus. Cf. Haupt, *Opusc.* 1, p. 122. — **caerula lympha**: in apposition with *Liger*: the epithet must refer to the bay at the mouth of the river, if it has any meaning.

13. an . . . canam: the missing first member of this double question might be supplied thus: *utrum taceam quod non ipse vidi.* — **Cydne**: though not the largest river of Cilicia, the Cydnus was important because Tarsus was situ-

ated upon it, and interesting because of the peculiarity possibly referred to in these verses and described by Strabo, viz. that before actually reaching the sea it flows into a kind of lake (ῥῆγμα).

14. placidis: ' Thy placid stream, thine azure gleam, and thy wavelet's noiseless flow' (Cranstoun). Such tautologies are not uncommon in the poets; cf. *aestiva* in v. 22 following the same idea in v. 21; Sen. *Herc. Fur.* 680: *placido quieta labitur Lethe vado.* — **vada**: ' course.'

15. quantus . . . contingens . . . Taurus alat = *quantus sit Taurus qui contingit et alit*; cf. *qualis . . . abundet* (vv. 21–22). The Taurus furnished support to the Cilicians by its cultivated slopes and its grazing grounds.

16. intonsos: here a sign of rude barbarity: cf. Liv. 21, 32, 7: *homines intonsi et inculti*; Ovid, *Ex P.* 4, 2, 2: *intonsis . . . Getis.* But the early Romans had not been so particular; barbers first came to Rome in the year 300 B C.; cf. F. W. Nicolson's discussion of Greek and Roman Barbers in *Harvard*

quid referam, ut volitet crebras intacta per urbes
  alba Palaestino sancta columba Syro,
utque maris vastum prospectet turribus aequor
20 prima ratem ventis credere docta Tyros,
qualis et, arentes cum findit Sirius agros,
  fertilis aestiva Nilus abundet aqua?
Nile pater, quanam possim te dicere causa
  aut quibus in terris occuluisse caput?
25 te propter nullos tellus tua postulat imbres,
  arida nec pluvio supplicat herba Iovi.
te canit atque suum pubes miratur Osirim

Stud. in Class. Philology, Vol. 2, pp. 41 sqq.; Varro, *R. R.* 2, 11, 10.

18. Palaestino: an adjective, used with no well-defined meaning by Tibullus. Palestine was a part of Syria, to be sure; but the fact referred to here was no more characteristic of Palestine than of other parts of the general region. — **sancta**: because the dove was sacred to Astarte, as well as to her Greek counterpart, Aphrodite. — **Syro**: dat. of ref.: 'in the eyes of the Syrian.'

19. turribus: 'lofty palaces'; a vague word; cf. Prop. 3, 21, 15. The modern term is "skyscraper," at least in American cities.

21. qualis, etc.: cf. note on v. 15. — **Sirius**: cf. 1, 1, 27, n.

22. fertilis: active, 'fertilizing.' — **abundet**: the annual overflow of the Nile begins about the time of the rising of Sirius.

23. pater: cf. Ennius, *Ann.* (Vahlen) 1, 54: *teque pater Tiberine tuo cum flumine sancto.* The

epithet is particularly appropriate to the Nile, without which Egypt would not exist except as a part of the desert; it befits a Roman poet well, too, for Egypt was one of the principal granaries of Rome. No doubt Tibullus was well acquainted with the beautiful statue of father Nile, the type of which was imitated in representations of the Tiber; cf. Baum. *Denk.*, p. 1028. — **causa**: the question is answered by Ovid, *Met.* 2, 254–255: *Nilus in extremum fugit perterritus orbem occuluitque caput, quod adhuc latet.*

24. occuluisse caput: only in recent times has the source been discovered. The Nile problem was discussed by Herodotus in Bk. 2, by Seneca, *Nat. Quaest.* 4, 1 sqq. and elsewhere.

26. pluvio . . . Iovi: cf. H. & T. § 207.

27. Osirim: as the greatest male divinity of the Egyptians, Osiris, the representative of the

barbara, Memphiten plangere docta bovem.
primus aratra manu sollerti fecit Osiris
30   et teneram ferro sollicitavit humum,
primus inexpertae commisit semina terrae
pomaque non notis legit ab arboribus.
hic docuit teneram palis adiungere vitem,
hic viridem dura caedere falce comam :
35   illi iucundos primum matura sapores
expressa incultis uva dedit pedibus.
ille liquor docuit voces inflectere cantu,
movit et ad certos nescia membra modos,
Bacchus et agricolae magno confecta labore

principle of fructification, was supposed to be responsible for the
annual overflow of the Nile, and
so his worship is here coupled appropriately with that of father
Nile ; cf. Fraser, *Adonis, Attis,
and Osiris.*

28. Memphiten . . . bovem: the
sacred bull, Apis, the incarnation
of Osiris, kept at Memphis. —
plangere : the method of mourning,
used for the general idea of mourning for one ; rare with an object.
On the death of Apis the whole
people went into mourning until a
new bull was found to take his
place ; cf. Plin. *N. H.* 8, 46 ;
Cumont, *Oriental Relig. in Roman
Paganism,* pp. 97 sqq.

29. aratra : Osiris, in many respects the counterpart of the
Greek Dionysus, was credited also
with the invention of the plow,
and of the culture of various fruits
besides that of the vine. The invention of the plow was usually

attributed to Ceres.   For another
point of view, cf. 1, 10, 45.

30. teneram : by way of contrast to *ferro sollicitavit.* — **sollicitavit** : cf. Ovid, *Fast.* 4, 396 : *quas
tellus nullo sollicitante dabat ;*
Verg. *Georg.* 2, 418 : *sollicitanda
tamen tellus pulvisque movendus.*

32. non notis : *i.e.* those with
the edible qualities of whose fruit
men were as yet unacquainted.

33. teneram : cf. 1, 1, 7 ; Cic.
Cat. Mai. 15, 52 : *vitis . . .
nisi fulta est, fertur ad terram.* —
palis adiungere : the so-called *al-
ligatio* and *amputatio* referred to
in these two verses were the most
important arts in connection with
viticulture.

35. illi : Osiris. — **sapores** : cf.
v. 5, n.

36. incultis : 'inexperienced.'

37. ille : adjectival, 'such.'

38. certos : 'regular.' — **nescia** :
'unaccustomed.'

39. Bacchus = *vinum.*

40   pectora tristitiae dissoluenda dedit.
      Bacchus et adflictis requiem mortalibus adfert,
      crura licet dura compede pulsa sonent.
      non tibi sunt tristes curae nec luctus, Osiri,
      sed chorus et cantus et levis aptus amor,
45   sed varii flores et frons redimita corymbis,
      fusa sed ad teneros lutea palla pedes
      et Tyriae vestes et dulcis tibia cantu
      et levis occultis conscia cista sacris.
      huc ades et genium ludo geniumque choreis

49. genium ludo *Heyne* centum ludos O ludis ω.

40. tristitiae: the gen. after the analogy of the Greek, instead of the regular abl. Cf. Hor. *Car.* 3, 17, 16: *cum famulis operum solutis;* Plaut. *Rud.* 247: *me omnium iam laborum levas.* A regular epithet of Bacchus is *Lyaeus* ('freer' from care). — **dissŏlŭenda dedit** = *fecit ut dissolverentur;* cf. also v. 2, n.

42. compede: the idea of a 'chain gang' of workers is not modern; cf. 2, 6, 25-26.

43. sunt: sc. *apti;* as the adjective is expressed only in v. 44, it agrees with the nearest noun.

45. corymbis: usually, as here, of a cluster of ivy berries, the ivy being especially sacred to Bacchus and to Osiris; cf. Ovid, *Fast.* 1, 393: *festa corymbiferi celebrabas Graecia Bacchi;* Fraser, *Adonis, Attis, and Osiris,* p. 279; Creuzer, *Symbolik u. Mythologie,* Vol. 4, pp. 10 sqq.

46. sed: for the position cf. v. 12, n. — **lutea palla**: a long

saffron robe was appropriate to Bacchus — the woman's garment being suggestive of his almost feminine beauty, and the color being suitable for festive occasions; cf. Prop. 3, 17, 32: *et feries nudos veste fluente pedes;* Sen. *Oed.* 422: *lutea vestem retinente zona.* The combination of such an effeminate garment with the insignia of Hercules is ridiculed in the *Frogs* of Aristophanes, v. 46.

47. Tyriae vestes: a cloak of Tyrian purple.

48. cista: the box containing the mystic emblems of the god, which was carried in the processions of the festivals of Bacchus; cf. Cat. 64, 259: *cavis celebrabant orgia cistis.*

49. huc ades: with consummate skill the thought has been developed from the Aquitanian triumph to this summons to Osiris to be present on this festal day as the wine god whose worship (in a

50   concelebra et multo tempora funde mero:
        illius et nitido stillent unguenta capillo,
           et capite et collo mollia serta gerat.
        sic venias hodierne: tibi dem turis honores,
           liba et Mopsopio dulcia melle feram.
55   at tibi succrescat proles, quae facta parentis
           augeat et circa stet veneranda senem.
        nec taceat monumenta viae, quem Tuscula tellus

---

54. liba **AV** libem **G.**   melle **ω** mella **O.**   feram **AV** favo **G.**

---

figurative sense) will necessarily
be prominent. — **genium** : *i.e.* Messalla's.   The Genius was the individual man's tutelary divinity (corresponding to the Juno of each
woman; cf. H. & T. § 188), pre-
siding over his life from birth to
death (cf. *gigno*).   Each man had
his own Genius, who was worshiped, especially on his birthday,
with offerings of wine, cakes, perfumes, and garlands; cf. 2, 2, 1,
sqq.; B. *G.*, p. 78, n. 15.   For
the form of the verse cf. 1, 10,
28.

50. Cf. 1, 2, 3 : *neu quisquam
multo percussum tempora Baccho
excitet.*

51. **illius** : *i.e. Genii.*   It was
appropriate on such occasions to
decorate the image of the divinity
honored.   In this case, however,
we must not forget that the Genius
is closely identified with the man
himself.   Evidently the poet is
here not thinking of the serpent
form of Genius representations. —
stillent : cf. 2, 2, 7.

53. **hodierne** : sc. *deus; i.e.*
the Genius, who was the particular divinity of a birthday, and to
whom the next word refers; cf. 2,
2, 5 ; 5, 5 ; 4, 5, 9.

54. **Mopsopio** : honey from Mt.
Hymettus.   Mopsopus was a myth-
ical king of Attica, in which
Hymettus stands.

55. **tibi** : Messalla ; for the sudden change in meaning from the
tibi in v. 53 cf. v. 3, n. — **proles** :
Messalla had two sons and a
daughter.   Cf. 2, 5.

56. **augeat** : cf. 2, 5, 115–120,
and especially v. 119, n. — **veneranda** : 'worthy of honor.' —
senem : sc. *te.*

57. **taceat** : sc. *ille* from the
following relative clause. — **monumenta** : 'monumental work.' —
viae : the Via Latina, which Messalla had repaired, paying the
expense from the spoils of war according to the command of Augustus.   Citizens of Tusculum and Alba
would reach Rome by this road.
Cf. Burn, *RL. and RA.*, p. 252.

candidaque antiquo detinet Alba lare.
namque opibus congesta tuis hic glarea dura
60   sternitur, hic apta iungitur arte silex.
te canit agricola, e magna cum venerit urbe
serus inoffensum rettuleritque pedem.
at tu, natalis multos celebrande per annos,
candidior semper candidiorque veni.

I O

Quis fuit, horrendos primus qui protulit enses?
quam ferus et vere ferreus ille fuit!

58. candida: the reference is to the same appearance in the limestone rock which had originally given the name Alba. Cf. Taylor, *Words and Places*, pp. 141–142.—**lare**: 'home.'

59. glarea: the broken rock and gravel used for foundation, while the *silex* was the polygonal flint (*selce*) regularly used for the surface, as still to-day in many Italian cities.

60. apta . . . arte: how neat the joints were can still be seen from many extant examples on various ancient Roman roads, *e.g.* the Via Praenestina.

62. serus: 'though late,' and therefore presumably rather mellow. Cf. Cic. *Ad Fam.* 7, 22: *bene potus seroque redieram.*—**inoffensum**: 'without stumbling.'

63. natalis: sc. *dies*.

64. candidior semper candidiorque: 'more and more joyous.' Cf. I, 10, 45; Ovid, *Trist.* 5, 5, 13:

optime Natalis . . . candidus huc venias.

I, 10

This is generally considered the earliest of Tibullus's elegies. 1. It contains no definite hints at any relations between the poet and either his patron, Messalla, or his mistress, Delia, with both of whom they were established by the latter part of the year 31 B.C. 2. The reference to war in vv. 13 and 14 can hardly be to any war later than the Aquitanian expedition in 31 B C., and therefore, if not to an earlier one, expresses a vague premonition of the approaching conflict of which the events of 31 B.C. were a part. 3. The simplicity of the form of composition, and the frequent recurrence of similar thoughts in different connections, while belonging to the genuine manner of Tibullus, are so marked here as

tum caedes hominum generi, tum proelia nata,
    tum brevior dirae mortis aperta viast.
5   an nihil ille miser meruit, nos ad mala nostra

10. 5. an **AV** at **G** forsan et ille nihil **P.**

to suggest early work. Belling,
through a series of parallel passages in other elegies of this first
book, has sought to show that this
was written last, as a climax (Bell.
p. 244 sqq.); but the examples
may as easily be considered imitations of this, as imitated by this
elegy. The early part of B.C. 31,
or possibly the end of B.C. 32,
is, therefore, the most probable
date when the poet fears that he
will be drawn into the impending
conflict. If the expectation is
based on his liability to serve the
usual campaign as a young man of
seventeen years, this may be an
important poem in determining
the date of the author's birth.
Cf. Intr. § 21. The elegy forms a
fitting close to Bk. 1, from its
striking similarity in theme and
many points of treatment to the
opening poem of the book.

1–14: 'War is a hateful thing,
a child of avarice; the good old
days knew it not. It would have
been pleasanter to live then ! 15–
32 : Preserve me, Lares, as you
did in my childhood; things were
better in the days of simplicity
which you represent; spare me,
and I will render you your due.
Let another be a doughty warrior !
33–44: What madness to covet a
violent death on the battlefield !

All is gloom in Acheron; how
much better to lead a humble,
peaceful life on a little farm ! 45–
68 : Let peace hold sway, under
whose rule happy home life flourishes, and there are no battles
save those of love, and even these
but playful contests! Come, Peace,
and bless us!'

1. enses : the words lead up to
the idea of *ferreus*, 'iron-hearted.'

2. ferus . . . ferreus : alliteration and assonance, which played
an important rôle in early Latin
poetry, survived in the classical
period mainly in certain formulas
or stereotyped expressions. This
one, for example, occurs in Cic.
Ad Q. Fr. 1, 3, 3; *quem ego ferus
ac ferreus e complexu*; cf. Cat.
76, 20. The same process has
been gone through in other lan-
guages; cf. Eng. "weal and woe,"
"slow and sure," "fun and frolic,"
etc. Other instances of *ferreus*
in this sense in Tibullus may be
seen : 1, 2, 65 : *ferreus ille fuit*;
2, 3, 2 ; 3, 2, 2.

4. mortis . . . via: cf. 1, 3, 50;
Ovid, *Met.* 11, 792 : *letique viam
sine fine retemptat*; Prop. 3, 7, 2 ;
Hor. *Car.* 1, 3, 32 : *tarda necessitas
leti corripuit gradum.*

5. miser : 'unfortunate' in being blamed rather than really responsible. Note the asyndeton

vertimus in saevas quod dedit ille feras?
divitis hoc vitium est auri, nec bella fuerunt,
   faginus adstabat cum scyphus ante dapes.
non arces, non vallus erat, somnumque petebat
10   securus varias dux gregis inter oves.
tunc mihi vita foret, vulgi nec tristia nossem
   arma nec audissem corde micante tubam:
nunc ad bella trahor, et iam quis forsitan hostis

11. vulgi **O** dulcis *Heinsius.*

in the contrast with the emphatic *nos.*

6. in . . . feras: the preposition here expresses purpose; cf. Prop. 1, 7, 6, n.

7. divitis: 'precious'; cf. 1, 9, 31: *non ullo divitis auri pondere*; 3, 3, 11: *nam grave quid prodest pondus mihi divitis auri*; Prop. 3, 5, 4. — **vitium est auri:** cf. 1, 1, 1; Prop. 3, 7, 1–2.

8. faginus: a token of primitive simplicity in Rome, before the advent of cups made of silver and gold, or precious stones; cf. Prop. 3, 5, 4; Plin. *N. H.* 16, 38: *Manius Curius iuravit se nihil ex praeda attigisse praeter guttum faginum quo sacrificaret*; Ovid, *Met.* 8, 669; *Fast.* 5, 522: *pocula fagus erant*; Verg. *Ec.* 3, 36. The same general idea is brought out in Tib. 1, 1, 37–40, where the *fictilia pocula* (of common pottery) are praised; cf. 1, 1, 38, n. — **scyphus:** cf. Varro, *apud Gell.* 3, 14, 3.

9. vallus: the rarer masc. form for the sake of the meter.

10. varias: no effort was made to separate sheep of different colors, but all were allowed to run in the same flock. — **dux gregis** = 'the shepherd'; but in 2, 1, 58, *dux pecoris* = 'the ram'; cf. Ovid, *Am.* 3, 13, 17: *duxque gregis cornu per tempora dura recurvo.*

11. foret: for the more exact *fuisset,* i.e. *o si tum vixissem!* The tense makes the picture more vivid. An unfulfilled wish in this form is rare; cf. G. 261, N. 2. — **vulgi:** it is an everyday passion, fit for the rabble, to fight and win sordid gain; Tibullus thinks his tastes purer and higher.

13. nunc = νῦν δέ, 'as it is,' referring to the actual state of affairs by way of contrast to the previous condition contrary to fact. — **trahōr:** the syllable is lengthened in this thesis before the following caesura. Cf. Intr. § 43; Verg. *Aen.* 11, 323: *considant si tantus amŏr, et moenia condant.* — **quis:** for the more usual *aliquis,* because taken closely with *forsitan,* a compound of *an.*

haesura in nostro tela gerit latere.

15   sed patrii servate lares : aluistis et idem,
      cursarem vestros cum tener ante pedes.

    neu pudeat prisco vos esse e stipite factos :
      sic veteris sedes incoluistis avi.

    tunc melius tenuere fidem, cum paupere cultu
20   stabat in exigua ligneus aede deus.

    hic placatus erat, seu quis libaverat uvam
      seu dederat sanctae spicea serta comae :

    atque aliquis voti compos liba ipse ferebat
      postque comes purum filia parva favum.

14. haesura : 'destined to rankle.'

15. servate : *i.e. from* war, not *in* war. — **et idem :** pleonastic.

16. tener : 'in tender youth.' — **ante pedes :** because the little images of the Lares used to stand in a shrine called the *Lararium* over the hearth ; cf. 2, 2, 22.

17. neu pudeat : cf. 1, 1, 38. — **prisco :** 'old-fashioned'; cf. v. 15 ; 1, 3, 34 ; 2, 1, 60 : 1, 7, 58. The frequent use of such epithets for the Lares implies a consciousness that they no longer enjoyed the universal veneration of former days. — **stipite :** in early times the images of the Lares were made of wood ; later, of stone or metal, often of silver. See Preller[3], 2, p. 108 ; Baum. *Denk.*, Vol. 2, p. 810 ; 1, p. 77, fig. 79.

18. sic : *i.e.* when your images were fashioned of such humble material as wood.

19. tenuere : sc. *homines.* — **paupere cultu :** 'slight adornment.'

20. exigua . . . aede : 'humble shrine,' as contrasted with the more elaborate *Lararia* of later times. — **deus :** the reference is here apparently to the Lares ; but a similar simplicity prevailed in early times in the form of other images of divinities ; cf. Ovid, *Fast.* 1, 201–202 : *Iuppiter angusῑ ɩ vix totus stabat in aede inque Iovis dextra fictile fulmen erat ;* Verg. *Aen.* 7, 177 sqq.: *veterum effigies ex ordine avorum antiqua e cedro, Italusque paterque Sabinus . . . vestibulo adstabant.*

21. placatus : 'gracious.' — **uvam** = *vinum.*

22. spicea serta : cf. 1, 1, 15.

23. aliquis = *si quis erat.*

24. filia parva : cf. Ovid, *Fast.* 2, 652 : *porrigit incisos filia parva favos.* On the propitiatory power of honey, especially for the souls of the dead, cf. Porph. *De Ant. Nymph.* 16 and 28 Wissowa (*Rel. u. Kult. d. Römer.*, p. 153) considers the Lares to be the souls of the dead.

25   at nobis aerata, lares, depellite tela,
       hostiaque e plena rustica porcus hara.
     hanc pura cum veste sequar myrtoque canistra
       vincta geram, myrto vinctus et ipse caput.
     sic placeam vobis: alius sit fortis in armis,
30   sternat et adversos Marte favente duces,
     ut mihi potanti possit sua dicere facta
       miles et in mensa pingere castra mero.
     quis furor est atram bellis arcessere mortem?
       inminet et tacito clam venit illa pede.
35   non seges est infra, non vinea culta, sed audax
       Cerberus et Stygiae navita turpis aquae:
     illic percussisque genis ustoque capillo

---

26. *Pontanus conjectured a lacuna before this, and supplied 4 vv.*
hostiaque e **O** hostia erit **ω**.   37. percussisque **O** perscissisque **P** pertusisque
Livineius rescissisque *Lachmann* (parce!) ustisque *Deutsch.*

---

25. nobis: emphatic; 'but in my case' the petition is, "*depellite tela!*"

26. porcus: and so an extraordinary thankoffering is promised instead of the usual trifling gifts mentioned in vv. 21–24. Sc. *erit.* For similar omissions of the copula cf. I, 3, 49, 50; Prop. 3, 16, 8. This verse is practically the conclusion of the condition implied in the impv. *depellite*; for the thought cf. I, I, 22.

27. myrtoque: cf. Hor. *Car.* 3, 23, 16. — **canistra**: these contained sacrificial utensils and offerings.

29. sic: by such offerings. — **alius**: cf. I, I, I.

32. pingere … mero: cf. Ovid, *Her.* I, 31–32: *atque aliquis po-sita monstrat fera proelia mensa pingit et exiguo Pergama tota mero.*

34. inminet: note the contrast to *arcessere.* — **tacito … pede**: cf. Ovid, *A. A.* 3, 712: *ipsa nemus tacito clam pede fortis init.*

35. non seges … culta: cf. I, 3, 61. The whole description of the lower world following I, 3, 61 is to be compared with this passage.

36. navita turpis: Charon: cf. Verg. *Aen.* 6, 315: *navita sed tristis*; 299: *terribili squalore Charon*; Prop. 3, 18, 24.

37. percussisque genis: the imagination of the ancients pictured the dead as continuing in the same state as that in which they were last seen in the flesh, *i.e.* on the

errat ad obscuros pallida turba lacus.

quam potius laudandus hic est quem prole parata

40 occupat in parva pigra senecta casa!

ipse suas sectatur oves, at filius agnos,

et calidam fesso conparat uxor aquam.

sic ego sim, liceatque caput candescere canis,

temporis et prisci facta referre senem.

45 interea Pax arva colat. Pax candida primum

duxit araturos sub iuga curva boves,

Pax aluit vites et sucos condidit uvae,

funderet ut nato testa paterna merum:

pace bidens vomerque nitent — at tristia duri

50 militis in tenebris occupat arma situs —

---

39. quam **GP** quin **AV**. 40. occupat **O** occulit **P**. 46. curva **AV**
panda **P**. 49. bidens **PV** nitens **A**. vomerque **PV** vomer **A**. nitent *Guyetus*
nitet **P** vident **A** viderit **V** vigent *sec. man.* **V** ω.

funeral pyre. Cf. 2, 6, 39-40.
Hence the idea of shades 'with
smitten cheeks and singed locks'
('sunken chaps,'—Cranst.).

38. lacus: the rivers of the
lower world are continually represented as sluggish, like standing
water; cf. 3, 5, 24; Prop. 4, 11,
15; Verg. *Aen.* 6, 323: *Cocyti
stagna alta vides Stygiamque paludem.*

39. laudandus: 'to be deemed
happy.'—**hĭc**: rare quantity.

40. occupat: 'overtakes.' —
pigra: cf. 1, 1, 58.

42. aquam: for bathing. Cf.
Hor. *Epod.* 2, 43 : *exstruat lignis
focum lassi sub adventum viri.*

43. sic ego sim: cf. the close
of the previous paragraph, v. 29;

the poet recurs to the main wish,
viz. to avoid war and enjoy peace.
— **candescere**: cf. Prop. 2, 18, 5 :
*quid mea si canis aetas candesceret
annis.* — **canis**: sc. *capillis.*

44. temporis ... prisci: cf. Hor.
Ep. 2, 3, 173 : *laudator temporis
acti,* a tendency characteristic of
old age.

45. interea: *i.e.* till I reach old
age. Cf. 1, 1, 69.

46. araturos: A. 499, 2. Cf. 1,
7, 29. — **curva**: cf. Ovid, *Ex P.*
1, 8, 54 : *ducam ruricolas sub iuga
curva boves.*

48. testa: *i.e. amphora*; cf.
note on 2, 5, 85. — **merum**: see
B. *G.*, p. 128, n. 7.

49. nitent: cf. Ovid, *Fast.* 4,
927 : *sarcula nunc durusque bidens*

rusticus e lucoque vehit, male sobrius ipse,
　　uxorem plaustro progeniemque domum.
sed Veneris tum bella calent, scissosque capillos
　　femina perfractas conqueriturque fores :
55　flet teneras subtusa genas, sed victor et ipse
　　flet sibi dementes tam valuisse manus.
at lascivus Amor rixae mala verba ministrat,
　　inter et iratum lentus utrumque sedet.
ah lapis est ferrumque, suam quicumque puellam
60　　verberat : e caelo deripit ille deos.
sit satis e membris tenuem rescindere vestem,
　　sit satis ornatus dissoluisse comae,
sit lacrimas movisse satis : quater ille beatus

---

51. *Haupt conjectured the loss of a distich before this v.*　55. subtusa
O obtusa *Némethy.*　61. rescindere ω perscindere **AV.**

---

et vomer aduncus, ruris opes, ni-
teant ; inquinet arma situs.

51. lucoque : the sacred grove
where the religious rites of a rural
holiday would be celebrated, followed by the festive amusements
of the day. Cf. Prop. 4, 6, 71 ;
Ovid, *Fast.* 3, 525 sqq. ; Hor. *Ep.*
2, 1, 140–144. For the position of
the *-que*, cf. Intr. § 28 ; Munro's
note on Lucr. 2, 1050 ; Ovid, *Fast.*
2, 177, etc. — **male** = *non ;* cf.
Ovid, *Fast.* 6, 785 : *ecce suburbana*
rediens male sobrius aede ; Her.
7, 27 : *ille quidem male gratus ;*
Verg. *Aen.* 2, 23 : *statio male fida*
carinis. — **ipse :** as distinguished
from the wife and children. Cf.
for the customary indulgence 2,
1, 29.

52. Cf. Livy, 5, 40, 10.

53. scissosque capillos : with
this passage cf. Prop. 2, 5, 21 sqq.;
Hor. *Car.* 1, 17, 26–28.

56. flet : cf. 2, 5, 103.

58. iratum . . . utrumque : ' the
angry pair ' (Cranst.). — **lentus :**
' calmly '; cf. Ovid, *Am.* 3, 6, 59–
60 : *ille habet et silices et vivum*
in pectore ferrum, qui tenero lacri-
mas lentus in ore videt.

59. Cf. v. 2 ; 1, 1, 63.

60. deripit : cf. 1, 2, 82 : *ser-*
taque de sanctis deripuisse focis.
The idea here is borrowed from
the attack of the Giants upon
heaven.

62. sit satis : cf. the repetition
in 1, 1, 43. — **dissolüisse :** for the
tense cf. 1, 1, 46, n.

63. For another point of view
see 1, 1, 51. — **quater :** a variation

> quo tenera irato flere puella potest.
65 sed manibus qui saevus erit, scutumque sudemque
> is gerat et miti sit procul a Venere.
> at nobis, Pax alma, veni spicamque teneto,
> perfluat et pomis candidus ante sinus.

LIBER SECVNDVS

I

Quisquis adest, faveat: fruges lustramus et agros,
ritus ut a prisco traditus extat avo.

68. perfluat ω prefluat **AV** profluat **G**.

on the common formula, *terque quaterque*; cf. 3, 3, 26; Verg. *Aen.* 1, 94.

65. scutumque . . . gerat: *i.e.* let him rather than me go to war.

67. Representations of Pax (found mostly on coins) commonly have not only an olive branch and a cornucopia, but also a bundle of ears of corn in one hand. — **teneto:** the colloquial impv. in *-to* without special fut. force. Cf. *PAPA.*, Vol. 26 (1895), p. lxi.

68. ante: adv. of place.

2, 1

As different Roman festivals had certain features in common, it is not always easy to decide positively which occasion may be in the mind of a poet like Vergil or Tibullus. Some of the features in the following description have led editors to suppose the poet to refer to the Sementivae, or Paganalia, celebrated in January; cf. Ovid, *Fast.* 1, 657–680; Fowler, *Rom. Fest.*, pp. 294 sqq. But the poet is more commonly supposed to be describing the Ambarvalia. Cf. Fowler, *Rom. Fest.*, pp. 124 sqq. Cf. also Fowler, *Class. Rev.*, Vol. 22 (1908), pp. 37–40. Besides the public festival of the Ambarvalia, celebrated annually in May, every Roman possessor of a farm used to perform similar rites of purification for his own fields and crops about the last of April or first of May. The name of the festival is derived from the custom of leading thrice around the estate (*arva* and *ambire*) the sacrificial victim or victims before slaying them. At the greater celebration the victims were a boar, a ram, and a bull (*suovetaurilia*); but private citi-

Bacche, veni, dulcisque tuis e cornibus uva
   pendeat, et spicis tempora cinge, Ceres.
5 luce sacra requiescat humus, requiescat arator,
   et grave suspenso vomere cesset opus.

zens might employ the lesser *suo-vetaurilia* (pig, lamb, calf), or offer only one of these. The divinities especially worshiped were Mars (in early times), Ceres, and Bacchus. This description of the Ambarvalia must have been written after 27 B.C. (cf. v. 33), perhaps the next spring. Another picture of the same festival may be seen in Verg. *Georg.* 1, 338 sqq. For a modern description see Walter Pater's *Marius the Epicurean*, pp. 3 sqq.

1–14: Invitation to the feast: 'Keep silence all! Come, Bacchus! Come, Ceres! This is a sacred day, a day of rest for man and beast. Come purified to the sacred altars! 15–26: The solemn procession advances. Gods of my father, accept this offering, defend field and flock, and grant prosperity to my estate. Lo! the prayer is heard. 27–36: Now let us enjoy the festal banquet, and drink our fill; and while each pledges thy health, Messalla, come thyself and inspire my song of praise. 37–66: My theme is agriculture and its gods. They taught men to lead a civilized life. How delightful is rustic life, with its plenty and its joys! Hence came the drama, the forms of worship, and the art of weaving. 67–90:

Cupid, too, they say, is a child of the fields. How skillful and bold he has grown ! Neither old man, youth, nor maid is safe from his darts. Yet happy he who wins his favor ! Come then, Cupid, to the feast, but leave thy quiver behind. Invoke, friends, the favor of this God for the flocks; for yourself too, if you will. Make merry ! for night comes on apace.'

1. faveat: sc. *lingua*, *i.e.* let no inauspicious word fall. Cf. 2, 2, 1 ; Hor. *Car.* 3, 1, 2 : *favete linguis.* — **fruges lustramus:** *i.e.* by anticipation.

3. cornibus: Bacchus was sometimes represented with horns, as an emblem of power and abundance (cf. cornucopia) ; cf. Baum. *Denk.*, p. 435 ; Prop. 3, 17, 19 : *per te et tua cornua, vivam* ; Hor. *Car.* 2, 19, 29 : *te vidit insons Cerberus aureo cornu decorum* ; K. P. H. in *AJA.*, Vol. 5 (1901), p. 7.

4. spicis . . . cinge: the wreath of ears of corn was a stated attribute of Ceres ; cf. 1, 1, 15 ; 1, 10, 22 ; Hor. *Car. Saec.* 30 : *spicea donet Cererem corona.* Baum. *Denk.*, p. 417.

5. luce = *die.* — **5 sqq.:** cf. Ovid, *Fast.* 1, 663–665.

6. suspenso: so slight and simple an affair was the ancient plow

solvite vincla iugis: nunc ad praesepia debent
   plena coronato stare boves capite.
omnia sint operata deo: non audeat ulla
10   lanificam pensis inposuisse manum.
vos quoque abesse procul iubeo, discedat ab aris,
   cui tulit hesterna gaudia nocte Venus.
casta placent superis: pura cum veste venite
   et manibus puris sumite fontis aquam.
15 cernite, fulgentes ut eat sacer agnus ad aras
   vinctaque post olea candida turba comas.
di patrii, purgamus agros, purgamus agrestes:

(for a description see Verg. *Georg.*
1, 169–175) that this word is literally correct. The plow was often
hung on a limb in the same position as that of a scythe to-day.

7. **iugis**: 'the team,' just as we
say, "a yoke of oxen." Best considered as a dat.; for the connection shows that everything is to
be done on this occasion for the
comfort and well-being of the
cattle, as well as that of their
owners. This does not prevent
the emphasizing of the idea of
separation in translation. Cf. A.
229; H. 427.

8. Wreathing of cattle was
practiced not merely when the
animals were to be sacrificed.
One of the most familiar decorative features in art is garlanded
ox skulls.

9. **operata**: 'be performed in
honor of,' *i.e.* 'praise'; cf. v. 65;
2, 5, 95; Prop. 2, 28, 45; Verg.
Georg. 1, 339. — **non**: instead of
the regular *ne*, because it belongs

to *ulla*; *nullus* is quite often divided in poetry. — **ulla**: sc. *puella*;
cf. 1, 3, 87. Woman's work is to
stop, as well as man's.

10. **lanificam**: a poetic adjective, perhaps first found in this
passage.

11. **vos**: explained by the following clause, where the construction changes; for a similar change
from plural to singular, cf. 1, 6,
39: *tum procul absitis, quisquis
colit arte capillos.*

14. **fontis**: only living water
would do for purposes of purification.

15. **agnus**: the victim had been
led three times around the farm,
and is now about to be sacrificed.

16. **candida**: cf. 1, 10, 27. —
turba: the whole *familia, agrestes*,
etc.

17. **di patrii**: an indefinite
term, including doubtless Mars,
Bacchus, and Ceres, and all others
under whose protection the ancestral estate had hitherto thrived.

vos mala de nostris pellite limitibus,
neu seges eludat messem fallacibus herbis,
20   neu timeat celeres tardior agna lupos.
tum nitidus plenis confisus rusticus agris
      ingeret ardenti grandia ligna foco,
turbaque vernarum, saturi bona signa coloni,
      ludet et ex virgis extruet ante casas.
25   eventura precor : viden ut felicibus extis
      significet placidos nuntia fibra deos ?
nunc mihi fumosos veteris proferte Falernos

---

18. pellite : 'avert': used instead of the obsolete *averruncare* of the ancient formula.

19. eludat : originally a gladiatorial term, to 'parry' an enemy's thrust ; hence to 'disappoint.' We should have expected *messorem* ; but the 'crop' is represented as disappointed because it cannot fulfill its promise. — **herbis** : the green blades which make only a fair show.

21. tum : 'in that case,' *i.e.* if my prayers are granted. — **nitidus** : 'trim.'

22. Cf. Hor. *Epod.* 2, 43 : *sacrum vetustis exstruat lignis focum.*

24. ante : adverb, sc. *fores.* — **casas** : leafy bowers such as were often woven together on festal occasions, in which to enjoy the luxuries of idleness and wine-drinking. Cf. 2, 5, 97 ; *Pervigilium Ven.* 6–7 : *inter umbras arborum inplicat casas virentis de flagello myrteo ; Copa* 8 : *et triclia umbrosis frigida harundin-*

ibus ; Ovid, *Fast.* 3, 528 : *e ramis frondea facta casa est ; Class. Rev.*, Vol. 22 (1908), p. 39.

25. extis : including theoretically the liver, heart, lungs, gall, and caul of the victims ; but we need not suppose that a minute examination was made, if there were signs of a propitious omen.

26. fibra : here in the proper signification of the filament terminating the *exta* ; often by synecdoche for *exta* itself, as in 1, 8, 3 : *nec mihi sunt sortes nec conscia fibra deorum.*

27. fumosos : wine was commonly left in a *fumarium*, or smoke-chamber, where it gathered a flavor much relished by the ancients ; cf. Ovid, *Fast.* 5, 518 : *fumoso condita vina cado.* B. *G.*, p. 489. — **Falernos** : sc. *cados.* Falernian and Chian wines are types of the choicest vintages, native and foreign. As the former was acid and the latter sweet, they were favorites for mixing. Cf. Intr. § 42, I (4).

consulis et Chio solvite vincla cado.
vina diem celebrent: non festa luce madere
30   est rubor, errantes et male ferre pedes.
sed 'bene Messallam' sua quisque ad pocula dicat,
nomen et absentis singula verba sonent.
gentis Aquitanae celeber Messalla triumphis
et magna intonsis gloria victor avis,
35   huc ades adspiraque mihi, dum carmine nostro
redditur agricolis gratia caelitibus.
rura cano rurisque deos.   his vita magistris
desuevit querna pellere glande famem:

1. 29. celebrent **AV** celebrant **P.**   38. glande **GP** grande **AV.**

28. consulis: the age of the wine was indicated by the name, on the jar or the tag attached to it, of the consul under whom it was made. Good Falernian, according to Plin. *N. H.* 23, 34, should be not less than 15 years old. — **vincla**: both the stopper and the gypsum or pitch with which it was sealed.

29. madere: sc. *vino.* Cf. 2, 2, 8; 5, 87; Plaut. *Most.* 319: *ecquid tibi videor ma-ma-madere?*

30. errantes: 'unsteady.'

31. bene Messallam: sc. *valere iubeo;* cf. our own abbreviated form of toasts, " Here's to," etc. Cf. Ovid, *Fast.* 2, 637: '*bene vos, bene te, patriae pater, optime Caesar!*'

32. absentis: sc. *Messallae;* the participle has concessive force. — **singula**: a hyperbole: let his name recur at almost every word

spoken, *i.e.* be constantly on the lips of the banqueters!

33. celeber: this may be the first instance of the use of the word in the sense of 'famous.' — **triumphis**: for the plural cf. 1, 7, 5; the occasion is the same there referred to.

34. intonsis: a common epithet of the Romans of early times, before the tonsorial art was in vogue. Cf. Hor. *Car.* 1, 12, 41: *intonsis Curium capillis.* Cf. 1, 7, 16, n.

35. ades adspiraque: Messalla is invoked, as if he were one of the Muses. So Vergil called upon Maecenas in *Georg.* 2, 39: *tuque ades, inceptumque una decurre laborem, o decus . . . Maecenas.*

36. agricolis: 'patrons of husbandry.'

38. glande: for acorns as a staple of food in the Golden Age, cf. Ovid, *Met.* 1, 106; *Am.* 3, 10, 9; *Fast.* 1, 676; Tib. 2, 3, 68:

illi conpositis primum docuere tigillis
40   exiguam viridi fronde operire domum,
illi etiam tauros primi docuisse feruntur
        servitium et plaustro supposuisse rotam.
tum victus abiere feri, tum consita pomus,
        tum bibit inriguas fertilis hortus aquas,
45 aurea tum pressos pedibus dedit uva liquores
        mixtaque securo est sobria lympha mero.
rure terunt messes, calidi cum sideris aestu
        deponit flavas annua terra comas.
rure levis verno flores apis ingerit alveo,
50   conpleat ut dulci sedula melle favos.
agricola adsiduo primum satiatus aratro
        cantavit certo rustica verba pede

43. tum consita **AG** tunc consita **V** tunc insita **ω**.

glans alat, et prisco more bibantur aquae. glans aluit veteres.

41. Ovid, *Am.* 3, 10, 13 : *prima iugis tauros supponere colla coegit et veterem curvo dente revellit humum.* — illī : for the elision cf. Intr. § 42.

44. inriguas : in the active sense, as in Ovid, *Am.* 2, 16, 2 : *inriguis ora salubris aquis.*

46. securo : another poetical active instead of the ordinary passive use ; cf. Verg. *Aen.* 6, 715 : *securos latices et longa oblivia potant.*

47. rure : abl. without a preposition for the more usual locative *ruri.* — terunt : the subject is indefinite = *agricolae.* — sideris : according to the usage of the Roman poets Tibullus can scarcely escape here the charge of ambiguity, as

sidus might refer either to the sun, or to Sirius ; most editors refer this passage to the sun, but without any very good reason think Horace is referring to the dog star in *Epod.* 1, 27 : *ante sidus fervidum.* So Ovid, *Met.* 1, 424, *aetherioque recens exarsit sidere limus,* is quoted as referring to the sun ; but Tibullus, 1, 7, 21, attributes the same result to Sirius as Vergil does in *Aen.* 3, 141 : *tum steriles exurere Sirius agros.*

48. annua = *quotannis*, an odd adverbial use, with such a noun as *terra.* — comas : here used of the grain itself.

49. verno : agreeing with *alveo*, but used in the adverbial sense. — alveo : synizesis.

52. certo . . . pede : 'regular rhythm.'

et satur arenti primum est modulatus avena
    carmen, ut ornatos diceret ante deos,
55   agricola et minio suffusus, Bacche, rubenti
    primus inexperta duxit ab arte choros.
huic datus a pleno, memorabile munus, ovili
    dux pecoris curtas auxerat hircus opes.
rure puer verno primum de flore coronam
60   fecit et antiquis inposuit laribus.
rure etiam teneris curam exhibitura puellis
    molle gerit tergo lucida vellus ovis.
hinc et femineus labor est, hinc pensa colusque,
    fusus et adposito pollice versat opus:

---

58. curtas auxerat hircus opes *Waardenburg* yrcus hauxerat yrcus oves **A**
hauserat **VG** hirtas duxerat hircus oves *Heinsius.*

---

53. **satur**: 'after eating his fill.'
—**avena**: for a similar scene cf.
Verg. *Ec.* 1, 1–2.

54. **ornatos**: with wreaths.

55. **minio**: originally, doubtless, made of the lees of wine, the
most convenient substance on such
occasions. Cf. Hor. Ep. 2, 3, 277 :
*quae canerent agerentque peruncti
faecibus ora.* Later a prepared
vermilion was used for both man
and god; cf. 1, 1, 17. From this
custom masks came to be used in
the dramatic representations origi-
nating in the same rustic festivals.
—**Bacche**: it was at the festivals
of Dionysus that the Greek drama
began, just as such native Italian
dramatic forms as the Fescenninae
and Saturae came from similar
celebrations in Etruria.

56. **ab**: used to make it clear
that the idea is one of source here.
Cf. Prop. 2, 27, 11, n.

57. **huic**: *i.e. agricolae*, in recognition of his skill as leader of
the chorus. — **ovili**: we might
have expected *caprili*; but this
word seems to have been little
used and *ovile* elsewhere does
duty for both sheep and goats ;
cf. Ovid, *Met.* 13, 828: *aliis
in ovilibus haedi.* Cf. Bentley,
Horace, Vol. 2, p. 33.

58. **auxerat**: for the tense cf.
Prop. 1, 12, 11 ; 2, 13, 38, n ; Ovid,
Trist. 3, 11, 25 : *non sum ego quod
fueram.*

62. **lucida** : an unusual adjective
in the sense of 'white,' indicating
a glistening effect, and corresponding to our familiar expression, 'as
white as snow,' used of wool.

63. **hinc** refers to the wool.

64. **pollice** : the thumb of the
right hand, while the left hand
holds the distaff ; Cat. 64, 313 :
tum prono in pollice torquens

65 atque aliqua adsiduae textrix operata Minervae
        cantat, et adplauso tela sonat latere.
    ipse quoque inter agros interque armenta Cupido
        natus et indomitas dicitur inter equas.
    illic indocto primum se exercuit arcu :
70   hei mihi, quam doctas nunc habet ille manus !
    nec pecudes, velut ante, petit : fixisse puellas
        gestit et audaces perdomuisse viros.
    hic iuveni detraxit opes, hic dicere iussit
        limen ad iratae verba pudenda senem :
75 hoc duce custodes furtim transgressa iacentes
        ad iuvenem tenebris sola puella venit
    et pedibus praetemptat iter suspensa timore,
        explorat caecas cui manus ante vias.
    ah miseri, quos hic graviter deus urget ! at ille
80   felix, cui placidus leniter adflat Amor.

---

67. quoque inter agros **A** quoque inter greges **V** interque greges **G** apros
R. Klotz.

*libratum tereti versabat turbine
fusum;* Ovid, *Met.* 6, 22 : *sive
levi teretem versabat pollice fusum.*
  65. aliqua : *i.e.* here and there
one. — **operata** : ' engaged in the
service of'; cf. note on v. 9. —
Minervae : the patroness of weaving ; cf. H. & T. § 39. This is best
considered *not* a case of metonymy.
  66. latere : used collectively,
referring to the pieces of brick by
which the threads of the warp were
weighted to keep them taut, and
which would often strike together
as the web was moved back and
forth for the passage of the shuttle ;
' rings the web beneath the driven
/ay ' (Cranst.).

  67. Cf. *Pervigilium Ven.* **77** :
*ipse Amor puer Dionae rure natus
dicitur.* Tibullus is fond of using
ipse with the name of a divinity ;
cf. *e.g.* 1, 3, 58 ; 2, 2, 5 ; 1, 8, 5.
  73. The perfect tenses express
customary action.
  74. iratae : sc. *puellae.*
  76. iuvenem : ' her lover.'
  77. pedibus praetemptat iter :
' her way on tiptoe feels '
(Cranst.).
  78. ante : adverb.
  80. adflat : cf. 2, 4, 57 : *ubi
indomitis gregibus Venus adflat
amores.* — **Amor** : the more common name of this god in Tibullus.

sancte, veni dapibus festis, sed pone sagittas
   et procul ardentes hinc precor abde faces.
vos celebrem cantate deum pecorique vocate
   voce: palam pecori, clam sibi quisque vocet.
85 aut etiam sibi quisque palam: nam turba iocosa
   obstrepit et Phrygio tibia curva sono.
ludite: iam Nox iungit equos, currumque sequuntur
   matris lascivo sidera fulva choro,
postque venit tacitus furvis circumdatus alis
90   Somnus et incerto Somnia nigra pede.

81. sancte: cf. Cat. 64, 95: *sancte puer, curis hominum qui gaudia misces.* — **veni:** followed by the dat., as if it were *ades.*

83. celebrem: 'to whom many resort'; cf. 4, 4, 23; Hor. *Car.* 2, 12, 20: *Dianae celebris die.*

86. obstrepit: *i.e.* the noise is so great that there is no danger of being overheard. — **tibia curva:** the Phrygian pipe was bent only at its mouth, where it terminated in a broadening curve. Cf. Rich's Dict. *s.v. tibia,* 6; Howard in *Harv. Stud.* 10, 19. As it was associated with the worship of Cybele, the playing is here referred to as wild and noisy, such as to drown other sounds. Cf. Cat. 63, 22: *tibicen ubi canit Phryx curvo grave calamo.*

87. Nox: among the Greeks and Romans night was not regarded as a negative idea, but was as definitely conceived of as moving through the heavens once every twenty-four hours as was day. So, as the sun drove his chariot, and the moon rode backward on her

steed, the personified Night is spoken of as driving over the heavenly course a chariot, sometimes with two horses, as in Verg. *Aen.* 5, 721: *et Nox atra polum bigis subvecta tenebat;* at others, with four horses, as in Tib. 3, 4, 17: *iam Nox aetherium nigris emensa quadrigis.*

88. matris: the idea that the stars are children of night is several times expressed by the Greek poets, *e.g. Orph. Hymn.* 7, 3: ἀστέρες οὐράνιοι, Νυκτὸς φίλα τέκνα μελαίνης; but of the Romans Tibullus alone seems to have imitated the figure.

89. circumdatus alis: Tibullus evidently has in mind the conception of the god of sleep most common in the art of his own time, viz. that of a bearded man with large wings on the shoulders, and others on the head, which together seem almost to envelop the rest of the figure. Cf. Baum. *Denk.,* p. 707.

90. Dreams may be regarded as the children of Sleep. — **nigra** · 'gloom-wrapt' (Cranst.).

2

Dicamus bona verba : venit Natalis ad aras :
   quisquis ades, lingua, vir mulierque, fave.
urantur pia tura focis, urantur odores
   quos tener e terra divite mittit Arabs.
5   ipse suos Genius adsit visurus honores,

2. 5. Genius adsit **O** adsit Genius **ω.**

2, 2

To his friend Cornutus, whose
first birthday since his marriage is
being celebrated, Tibullus sends
this dainty poem, with good wishes
appropriate to the occasion. Cornutus is, perhaps, the M. Caecilius
Cornutus who became a member
of the Arval College about 20 B.C.,
and may be identical with the
Cerinthus of Bk. 4, the latter name
being then a poetic pseudonym.
His bride in that case is Sulpicia.
Cf. Intr. § 26 ; Bell. *U.*, pp. 292,
297 sqq.

1–10 : ' While all keep a propitious silence, let acceptable offerings be made to your Genius, and
let him graciously draw nigh to
enjoy your worship and listen to
your petitions. Lo ! Our prayer
is granted. Make known your request. 11–22 : My guess is that
you will ask for the unchanging
love of your beloved wife, which is
better than all other earthly wealth.
Your wish is fulfilled.   Now let
Amor seal the bond, never to be
broken, and thus, in your old age,

may a numerous progeny gladden
the hearts of their grandparents.'

1. **bona** : ' of good omen ' ; cf.
Ovid, *Fast.* 2, 638 : *suffuso per
bona verba mero.* — **Natalis** =
Genius ; cf. 4, 5, 19 : *at tu, Natalis,
quoniam deus omnia sentis, adnue*;
Ovid, *Trist.* 5, 5, 13 : *optime
Natalis . . . opto candidus huc
venias.* — **ad** : ' before.'

2. **fave** : cf. 2, 1, 1 ; Ovid,
Trist. 5, 5, 5 : *lingua favens adsit,
. . . quae, puto, dedidicit iam bona
verba loqui.*

3. **pia** : adverbial, ' duly.'

4. **tener** : ' effeminate ' ; cf.
Verg. *Georg.* 1, 57 : *India mittit
ebur, molles sua tura Sabaei* ; by
the Romans this character was
attributed to the people of the
East (not very logically) because
they produced the things that women and fops admired. — **terra
divite** : Arabia Felix, the country
of the Sabaeans ; cf. 4, 2, 18.

5. **Geniūs** : cf. 1, 7, 49, n. For
the quantity cf. Intr. § 43. — **visurus** expresses pure purpose. —
honores : such as have been already described, 1, 7, 49 sqq., and

cui decorent sanctas mollia serta comas.

illius puro destillent tempora nardo,

    atque satur libo sit madeatque mero,

  adnuat et, Cornute, tibi, quodcumque rogabis.

10   en age, quid cessas? adnuit ille: roga.

auguror, uxoris fidos optabis amores:

    iam reor hoc ipsos edidicisse deos.

nec tibi malueris, totum quaecumque per orbem

    fortis arat valido rusticus arva bove,

15 nec tibi, gemmarum quidquid felicibus Indis

    nascitur, eoi qua maris unda rubet.

vota cadunt: utinam strepitantibus advolet alis

    flavaque coniugio vincula portet Amor,

vincula, quae maneant semper, dum tarda senectus

17. utinam **O** viden ut *Guyetus* ut iam *Baehrens*.

are here referred to in the following verses.

7. puro: the costly nard oil of Arabia was commonly diluted, but is to be used 'unmixed' in the worship of the Genius.

8. libo: cf. 1, 7, 54. — **madeat**: not in the sense of 2, 1, 29; but the word corresponds for potables to the use of *satur* for edibles.

12. edidicisse: because they have heard this same prayer so often.

14. fortis: ' honest '; cf. French *brave*; and the obsolete English vague use of "brave": *e.g.* "It being a brave day, I walked to Whitehall" (Pepys).

15. gemmarum: 'pearls'; cf. 4, 2, 19; Prop. 1, 14, 12.

16. eoi: the Indian Ocean is vaguely referred to, although its richness in abundance of pearls was doubtless exaggerated in the imagination of classical writers; cf. Curtius, 8, 9, 19 : *gemmas margaritasque mare litoribus infundit.* — **rubet**: the characteristic hues of the Red Sea proper are extended to the whole Erythraean Sea, or Indian Ocean; they were largely due to coral formations; cf. 4, 2, 19.

17. cadunt: 'are fulfilled'; cf. Eng. "fall to the lot of." — **strepitantibus**: 'rustling.'

18. flava: 'flame-colored,' the color of the bridal veil, in token of the kindling ardor of love's passion. Cf. Cat. 61, 121 : *tollite, o pueri, faces: flammeum video venire* — **vincula**: the god is not besought to grant prayers already answered, but to confirm the

20 inducat rugas inficiatque comas.
   hic veniat Natalis avis prolemque ministret,
   ludat et ante tuos turba novella pedes.

5

  Phoebe, fave : novus ingreditur tua templa sacerdos :
   huc age cum cithara carminibusque veni.

21. hic **A** hec **V** haec **G** hac *Heinsius* sic *Belling.* Natalis **O** genialis *Baeh-rens.* avis **O** avi *Heinsius.* prolemque **O** prolesque *Baehrens.* 22. et **O** ut **ω**.

answer by personally sealing the bond of passionate marital affection.

21. hic = *talis, i.e.* may he continue to come attended by Amor, as the years pass. — **prolemque** : the noun is collective. Cf. 1, 7, 55. For the position of the copula, cf. 1, 10, 51, n.

2, 5

Written in honor of the installation of Messalla's elder son, M. Valerius Corvinus Messalla Messalinus, as a member of the sacred college of Sibylline priests (*quin-decimviri sacris faciundis et sibyllinis libris inspiciendis*). For further information about this man cf. Tac. *Ann.* 3, 34 ; 1, 8 ; Teuffel, § 267, 6.

The number of priests, originally two, was later increased to ten, and, probably in Sulla's time, to fifteen. Under the Caesars the number was indefinitely enlarged, though the appellation *Quinde-cimviri* was not again changed. The addition of Messalinus at this time brought the number up to twenty-one. The honor of becoming a member of this priestly college was much sought by noble Roman youth. The Valerian *gens* prided itself on its prominence in the Roman religion ; cf. Preller[3], Vol. 2, p. 86. In the inscription commemorating the Secular Games in 17 B.C. (*Eph. Epig.* 1891, pp. 222, 274) the name of Messalinus occurs last in the list of members of the college. Cf. Lanciani, *Pagan and Christian Rome*, Appendix.

For the legend concerning the origin of the Sibylline books, cf. Gell. 1, 19 ; Preller[3], Vol. 1, pp. 299 sqq. ; Diels, *Die Sibyllinische Blätter.* For their subsequent history, cf. Lanciani in *Atlantic Monthly*, Vol. 69, p. 150 (cf. his *Pagan and Christian Rome*, p. 75) ; Preller[3], Vol. 1, pp. 306-312, *passim* ; Lact. *Inst.* 1, 6 ; and the bibliography in M. S. Terry's *The Sibylline Oracles.* Mommsen fixes the date of this poem as 19 B.C. (cf. *Eph. Epig.* 8, 2, 241).

TIBVLLI

nunc te vocales inpellere pollice chordas,
nunc precor ad laudes flectere verba meas.

5. 4. meas O tuas ω mea *Lachmann* novas *Vahlen.*

1-18: 'Apollo, accept the new priest who to-day enters thy shrine, and show thine approval by thy presence, decked in festal attire. 19-66: It was this Sibyl, who to Aeneas, on his arrival in Italy, when naught but rural simplicity reigned where now is great Rome, prophesied the city's future greatness and his own deification. 67-82: All these things are accomplished; likewise the greater prodigies prophesied by other Sibyls. But, Apollo, let dreadful portents now cease; and give us a favorable omen for the future. 83-104: If the omen is propitious, let rustic merriment abound, and all its simple and unconstrained joys, even to the petty quarrel of the "lover and his lass." 105-122: But perish Cupid's darts! And may my Nemesis spare me till the joyous day when I can sing the praises of Messalinus celebrating a proud triumph over conquered cities!' (For a more artificial analysis, cf. *PAPA.*, Vol. 26 (1895), p. vii.)

1. **Phoebe**: Apollo apparently is addressed under the form in which he appeared in the famous statue by Scopas, the Apollo Citharoedus, imported by Augustus from Rhamnus expressly for the temple of Apollo which he built on the Palatine (cf. vv. 2, 5, 7, 8). Rep-

resentations of this statue are found on coins of Augustus, and a very similar type on some of Nero, to which corresponds the well-known statue in the Vatican, found at Tivoli. Cf. 3, 4, 23-40; Prop. 2, 31, 15-16; Ovid, *Met.* 11, 165; *Fast.* 2, 106; *Am.* 1, 8, 59; Baum. *Denk.*, Vol. 1, p. 99; von Sybel, p. 236. Friedländer, *Das Kgl. Münz Kabinet*, No. 992; K. P. H. in *AJA.*, Vol. 5 (1901), p. 7. — **templa**: although we have no record of the transfer of the Sibylline books to the Palatine temple of Apollo earlier than 12 B.C. (Suet. *Oct.* 31), it is probable that they were deposited there much earlier; certainly the only appropriate place accordant with the picture here presented would be that temple. Built by Augustus in honor of his special protecting deity at the battle of Actium, it was dedicated in B.C. 28, and with its surrounding porticoes and adjacent library was one of the most noted specimens of temple magnificence. Cf. Prop. 4, 6; 2, 31; Hor. *Car.* 1, 31; Suet. *Oct.* 29; Preller³, Vol. 1, pp. 309-310; Lanciani, *Ancient Rome*, pp. 109-115. The books were deposited in the basis on which stood the statue.

3. **te**: emphatic. Apollo is besought himself to supply the

5   ipse triumphali devinctus tempora lauro,
      dum cumulant aras, ad tua sacra veni.
    sed nitidus pulcherque veni : nunc indue vestem
      sepositam, longas nunc bene pecte comas,
    qualem te memorant Saturno rege fugato
10   victori laudes concinuisse Iovi.
    tu procul eventura vides, tibi deditus augur
      scit bene quid fati provida cantet avis,
    tuque regis sortes, per te praesentit aruspex,
      lubrica signavit cum deus exta notis :
15   te duce Romanos numquam frustrata Sibylla,

poet with the prelude to the main part of the song sung by the poet (*meas*), cf. 3, 4, 39-42 : *hanc primum veniens plectro modulatus eburno felices cantus ore sonante dedit: sed postquam fuerant digiti cum voce locuti, edidit haec dulci tristia verba modo;* cf. Bell. *U.*, p. 163, Anm. — **vocales . . . chordas** : 'eloquent strains.' — **inpellere** : the inf. with *precor* is found nowhere else in Tibullus except here (and in the next verse — *flectere*) though it occasionally occurs in Ovid.

4. flectere verba : 'sing in well-modulated tones.'

5. triumphali : Apollo would appropriately wear the emblems of his own triumphs (cf. vv. 9-10, n.) when assisting in honoring the son of Messalla. For the father's triumph, cf. 1, 7 ; for the son's, yet to come, cf. vv. 115 sqq. — **devinctus** : cf. v. 117.

7. sed . . . veni : 'not only come, but come in festal attire';

cf. 1, 3, 63, n. — **nitidus pulcherque** : 'in all thy radiant beauty.'

8. sepositam : kept laid aside for special occasions, and so = 'sumptuous.' — **longas . . . comas** : cf. Ovid, *Am.* I, I, 11.

9-10 : explanatory of *triumphali* in v. 5 ; the reference is to Apollo's triumphant strains on the occasion of Juppiter's vanquishing the Titans. Cf. Sen. *Agam.* 332 ; Verg. *Aen.* 8, 319.

11. tu : Apollo's personal control is affirmed over each of the four well-known methods of seeking prophetic knowledge : (1) the characteristic Roman augury by the flight of birds ; (2) *sortes*, 'lots'; cf. 1, 3, 11 ; (3) the Etruscan method of divination by examining the entrails of newly slain animals ; (4) the Sibylline books.

15. Sibylla : the Cumaean Sibyl, the prophetess from whom, according to the tradition, came the Sibylline books themselves.

abdita quae senis fata canit pedibus.

Phoebe, sacras Messalinum sine tangere chartas

    vatis, et ipse precor quid canat illa doce.

haec dedit Aeneae sortes, postquam ille parentem

20   dicitur et raptos sustinuisse lares.

nec fore credebat Romam, cum maestus ab alto

    Ilion ardentes respiceretque deos.

Romulus aeternae nondum firmaverat urbis

    moenia, consorti non habitanda Remo,

25   sed tum pascebant herbosa Palatia vaccae

    et stabant humiles in Iovis arce casae.

lacte madens illic suberat Pan ilicis umbrae

    et facta agresti lignea falce Pales,

pendebatque vagi pastoris in arbore votum,

30   garrula silvestri fistula sacra deo,

fistula, cui semper decrescit arundinis ordo:

---

16. senis . . . pedibus: dactylic hexameters in which the oracles were expressed.

18. illa = *Sibylla vates*.

20. Cf. Verg. *Aen.* 1, 378.

22. ardentes: 'in flames,' applies to both *Ilion* and *deos* (*i.e.* the images of the gods).

23. Cf. Verg. *Aen.* 1, 278: *his ego nec metas rerum nec tempora pono, imperium sine fine dedi.* — **aeternae . . . urbis**: 'the eternal city' is no modern name for Rome: cf. F. G. Moore in *TAPA.*, Vol. 25 (1894), pp. 34–60. — **firmaverat**: cf. Prop. 3, 9, 50. With the description of Rome's site in prehistoric times (a favorite subject for Roman poets) cf. Prop. 4, 1; Verg. *Aen.* 8, 313–368; Ovid,

Fast. 1, 509 sqq., 243; *A. A.* 3, 119.

27. Cf. 1, 1, 36. — **Pan**: corresponding in many ways to the Italian Faunus. Cf. Hor. *Car.* 1, 17.

28. Cf. 1, 1, 18; 1, 10, 20.

29. votum: a votive offering, the *fistula* of v. 30.

30. silvestri . . . deo = Silvanus, who was identified with Pan.

31. fistula: the pandean pipe composed of several (usually 7–9) reeds of carefully graded lengths, a prototype of the organ, common among shepherds. Cf. Ovid, *Met.* 2, 682. For its Greek name (*syrinx*) and origin, cf. Ovid, *Met.* 1, 705–712. For its form see Rich's *Dict.* s.v. *arundo*.

nam calamus cera iungitur usque minor.
at qua Velabri regio patet, ire solebat
exiguus pulsa per vada linter aqua.
35 illa saepe gregis diti placitura magistro
ad iuvenem festa est vecta puella die,
cum qua fecundi redierunt munera ruris,
caseus et niveae candidus agnus ovis.
'inpiger Aenea, volitantis frater Amoris,
40 Troica qui profugis sacra vehis ratibus,
iam tibi Laurentes adsignat Iuppiter agros,
iam vocat errantes hospita terra lares.

It is described by Ovid, *Met.* 8, 189–195. Cf. Verg. *Ec.* 2, 36: *disparibus septem conpacta cicutis fistula*; Hor. *Car.* 4, 12, 10.

32. usque minor: 'constantly decreasing.'

33. at: cf. 1, 3, 63, n.—**Velabri**: the low, swampy valley between the Capitoline, Palatine, and Aventine hills, bordering on the Tiber, which was continually overflowing into it. One of the first great engineering enterprises at Rome was the draining of this valley, including the Forum Romanum site, farther back from the river. This was accomplished by an early sewer along the general line of the present Cloaca Maxima, which still performs its ancient functions and can be inspected at several points. See Lanciani, *Ancient Rome*, p. 54; cf. Prop. 4, 9, 5–6: *qua Velabra suo stagnabant flumine quaque nauta per urbanas velificabat aquas*; Ovid, *Fast.* 6, 405–406.

34. pulsa . . . aqua: cf. Cat. 64, 58: *iuvenis . . . pellit vada remis*; Prop. 4, 2, 8: *remorum auditos per vada pulsa sonos.*

35. illa: *i.e. aqua* (= *via.*)— **placitura**: 'to delight'; cf. R. 1115, (3).

36. iuvenem = *gregis . . . magistro* of the preceding verse. — **festa . . . die**: probably the Palilia (April 21); cf. v. 87.

39. The speech of the Sibyl here takes up the thread of thought broken off at v. 20.— **frater Amoris**: Venus was the mother of Aeneas by Anchises, and of Cupid by Ares (as is usually assumed); cf. Verg. *Aen.* 1, 667: *frater ut Aeneas.*

40. Troica . . . sacra: the Penates; cf. Verg. *Aen.* 1, 68: *portans victosque Penates.*

41. Aeneas landed near Laurentum, the ancient city near the mouth of the Tiber, where he was hospitably received by Latinus.

illic sanctus eris, cum te veneranda Numici
    unda deum caelo miserit indigetem.
45 ecce super fessas volitat Victoria puppes ;
    tandem ad Troianos diva superba venit.
ecce mihi lucent Rutulis incendia castris :
    iam tibi praedico, barbare Turne, necem.
ante oculos Laurens castrum murusque Lavinist
50 Albaque ab Ascanio condita longa duce.
te quoque iam video, Marti placitura sacerdos
    Ilia, Vestales deseruisse focos,

43-44: The Numicius (or Numicus) was the little stream (perhaps the modern *Rio Torto*) near Lavinium, on whose banks Aeneas was victorious over the Rutuli and their allies. The legend was that he immediately thereafter disappeared in its waters, and was then deified as Juppiter Indiges, as Romulus afterwards similarly became Quirinus. The local *genii* of places seem to have been recognized originally as their Indigetes *(indu + gigno)*. So the Pater Indiges or Deus Indiges of this spot became identified with Aeneas. Cf. Preller [3], pp. 91–94. For the story cf. Ovid, *Met*. 14, 581–608 ; Liv. 1, 2. 6. Vergil's version of the legend is different.

44. caelo : Madv. § 251. Cf. Verg. *Aen.* 9, 785 : *tot miserit Orco*.

45. fessas : cf. *Aen.* 1, 168 : *fessas non vincula naves ulla tenent*.

— **Victoria :** referring to the conquest of the Rutuli. The goddess Victoria (Gr. Nike) was a favorite at Rome, and often represented in art. The most celebrated of all her statues was the Nike of Samothrace, which stood on a ship's bow. Perhaps this familiar conception suggests to the poet this expression, as if the goddess were now at length hovering above the ship of Aeneas and about to alight on the prow and guide it into a haven of victory. Cf. Baum. *Denk*., pp. 1019–1023.

48. Turnus, his great enemy, was finally overcome by Aeneas in mortal combat.

49. The first home of the Trojan exiles in Italy was a permanent camp near Laurentum ; then Aeneas founded Lavinium ; Alba Longa was built years later by Ascanius.

52. Ilia : mother of Romulus and Remus by Mars ; daughter of Aeneas and Lavinia according to the older tradition ; later, in order to weave in the Alban legends, said to be the daughter of Numitor, the Alban king, and, as such, a vestal virgin, usually called Rea Silvia.

.oncubitusque tuos furtim vittasque iacentes
    et cupidi ad ripas arma relicta dei.
55 carpite nunc, tauri, de septem montibus herbas,
    dum licet : hic magnae iam locus urbis erit.
Roma, tuum nomen terris fatale regendis,
    qua sua de caelo prospicit arva Ceres,
quaque patent ortus et qua fluitantibus undis
60   Solis anhelantes abluit amnis equos.
Troia quidem tum se mirabitur et sibi dicet
    vos bene tam longa consuluisse via.
vera cano : sic usque sacras innoxia laurus

53. furtim modifies the implied participle agreeing with *concubitus* (Heyne suggests *peractos*). The motive was a favorite one in Roman art, and has survived in various mural paintings and bas-reliefs. See Preller³, Vol. 2, p. 347 ; Friedrichs-Wolters, *Antike Bildwerke*, No. 2141 ; Baum. *Denk.*, p. 886 ; Ovid, *Fast.* 3, 11 sqq.

55. septem montibus : rather a conventional than an exact description of the site of Rome. The seven principal elevations now reckoned in the list do not coincide with those of the original "Septimontium," some of which were "hills" scarcely now distinguishable as such. Cf. Richter², *Topog. von Rom.*, pp. 36–38 ; *Enc. Brit.*, Vol. 23, p. 589 ; Sandys, p. 35 ; Platner, pp. 39 sqq.

56. iam : cf. 1, 1, 70, n.

57. nomen : whatever be its true origin, the name *Roma* had certainly long before this become identified in the minds of Greek and Roman writers with the Greek Ῥώμη (= 'strength '), and was therefore in itself *fatale*, 'portentous.' — **terris . . . regendis** : cf. Madv. § 415.

58. Cf. Ovid, *Fast.* 1, 85–86 ; *Iuppiter arce sua totum cum spectet in orbem, nil nisi Romanum, quod tueatur, habet.*

59. quaque . . . et qua : 'both where . . . and where.'

60. amnis = *Oceanus*, which, according to the generally accepted notion, was a stream whose current never ceased to move around the earth. Cf. 3, 4, 17–18 : *iam Nox aetherium nigris emensa quadrigis mundum caeruleo laverat amne rotas :* Hom. *Il.* 14, 245. The river motion is implied also in Cat. 66, 69–70.

61. se : *i.e.* at her new and greater self, reproduced in mightier Rome.

63. vera cano : sic : to make the form of the adjuration complete an *ut* should be supplied at

5, 64]

TIBVLLI

vescar, et aeternum sit mihi virginitas.'
65   haec cecinit vates et te sibi, Phoebe, vocavit,
iactavit fusas et caput ante comas.
quidquid Amalthea, quidquid Marpesia dixit
Herophile, Phyto Graia quod admonuit,
quasque Aniena sacras Tiburs per flumina sortes

68. Phyto *Huschke* Phebo **A** Phoebo **V** Phoeto *Lachmann*.   Graia *Lach-mann* grata **O**.   quod admonuit **O** grataque quod monuit **ω**.   69. quasque **ω** quodque **AV** quaeque *Belling*.

the beginning to correspond with the *sic*. Cf. Ter. *Haut.* 463 ; Prop. I, 18, 11. But when the first part of the expression is of an imperative or optative nature, *sic* is equivalent to *si* with that verb idea repeated in a different form; *e.g.* in v. 121 : *adnue: sic tibi sint = si adnues, tibi sint.* Such expressions are very common in the poets of this period. Cf. 2, 6, 30 ; Prop. 3, 15, 1 ; Verg. *Ec.* 9, 30 ; Hor. *Car.* 1, 3, 1 ; Ovid, *Her.* 3, 135. The fundamental idea of the Roman religion was that of a bargain between men and the gods. A trace of it still survives in our own form of oath, " So help me God." — **innoxia** : in the passive sense. Cf. Lucr. 6, 394 : *volvitur in flammis innoxius.* — **laurus** : Tibullus uses this noun in the acc. pl. twice elsewhere, but each time in the 2d declension form (v. 117 and 1, 7, 7).

64. vescar, like the other deponent verbs commonly used with the ablative, sometimes governs the accusative in early Latin, and this is occasionally imitated by writers in all periods. Cf. Tac. *Agr.* 28. The prophets chewed the laurel leaves, sacred to Apollo, for the sake of inspiration.

66. caput ante : *i.e.* 'before her forehead.'

67. Amalthēā : (quantity the same in Ovid, *Fast.* 5, 115) best understood as the Cumaean Sibyl herself, following whom three other celebrated Sibyls are mentioned. Certainly the name of the woman who brought the Sibylline books to Tarquin was Amalthea. Cf. Lact. 1, 6 ; Serv. on Verg. *Aen.* 6, 72. — **Marpesia . . . Herophile :** the Erythraean Sibyl, who dwelt at Marpesus, on Mt. Ida, near Troy.

68. Phyto Graia : the Sibyl of Samos, called Greek by contrast with the last mentioned.

69. Tiburs : the famous Sibyl of Tibur, whose name was Albunea ; cf. Hor. *Car.* 1, 7, 12. The little church of S. Giorgio at Tivoli, perched on the edge of the precipice above the Anio ravine, is thought to be the temple of Albunea.

172

70   portarit sicco pertuleritque sinu
      (hae fore dixerunt belli mala signa cometen,
         multus ut in terras deplueretque lapis :
      atque tubas atque arma ferunt strepitantia caelo
         audita et lucos praecinuisse fugam,
75   ipsum etiam Solem defectum lumine vidit
         iungere pallentes nubilus annus equos
      et simulacra deum lacrimas fudisse tepentes
         fataque vocales praemonuisse boves),
      haec fuerunt olim : sed tu iam mitis, Apollo,
80   prodigia indomitis merge sub aequoribus,
      et succensa sacris crepitet bene laurea flammis,

---

70. portarit **O** portarat *Belling.* pertuleritque **ω** perlueritque **O** pertulerat-
que *Belling.*   71. hae **ω** hec **AV.**   72. ut **G** et **AV.** deplueretque **ω** deplue-
ritque **AG** depuleritque **V.**   79. fuerunt *or* fuerint **ω** fuerant **O.**

70. **portarit** : note the change
to the indirect question. — **sicco** :
Albunea was said to carry her
prophecies through the waters of
the Anio, and yet keep them dry.

71. The list of portents mentioned here seems to refer especially to those connected with the
assassination of Julius Caesar. Cf.
Verg. *Georg.* 1, 463–492 ; Ovid,
Met. 15, 783 sqq. ; Luc. 1, 524
sqq. ; Pliny, *N. H.* 2, 98.

72. Note position of *-que* (after
5th word). Cf vv. 22, 70, 86, 90 ;
employing this favorite position
at the end of the fifth foot becomes a mannerism in Tibullus.
Cf. Postgate, *Sel.*, p. xxix.

76. This year of feebler power
of the sun, mentioned also by
Pliny and Plutarch, seems to be
attributable to sun spots. Similar

phenomena have been observed in
other and more recent years ; cf.
the Lemaire edition of Pliny, Vol.
1, p. 306.

78. **vocales** : speaking with a
human voice.

79. **fuĕrunt** : cf. L. 857.

80. Even to-day the power of
the sea to receive and render
harmless and pure all the filth of
the world remains a wonder. The
poet here is applying this old
truth to more abstract pollutions.
Cf. 4, 4, 7–8.

81. Not only was the sacred
laurel of Apollo supposed to supply inspiration to those chewing it
(cf. v. 63), but the crackling noise
it made in burning was the source
of a popular divination, good fortune being apparently indicated in
proportion to the amount of crack-

omine quo felix et sacer annus erit.

laurus ubi bona signa dedit, gaudete coloni:

distendet spicis horrea plena Ceres,

85   oblitus et musto feriet pede rusticus uvas,

dolia dum magni deficiantque lacus.

at madidus Baccho sua festa Palilia pastor

concinet (a stabulis tum procul este lupi):

ille levis stipulae solemnis potus acervos

90   accendet, flammas transilietque sacras.

et fetus matrona dabit, natusque parenti

87. at ω ac **O.**

ling ; cf. Verg. *Ec.* 8, 82 ; *fragiles incende bitumine laurus* ; Prop. 2, 28, 36.

83. dedit : for tense cf. A. 520, 2.

85. oblĭtus . . . musto : before the invention of masks the lees of wine were daubed on the faces at rustic festivals. — **feriet pede** : the wine-making process included (1) pressing out the juice of the grape by treading on the fruit with the bare feet, the juice running into the vats (*lacus*) ; (2) turning it into large, wide-mouthed jars (*dolia*) to settle and ferment ; (3) drawing it off into storage jars (*amphorae*) after a time ; (4) putting away whatever was not used at once to gather age and flavor in the storeroom (*apotheca*) ; cf. I, I, 10 ; Cato, *R. R.* 113.

86. deficiantque : for position of *-que*, cf. v. 72, n.

87. madidus : cf. *lacte madens* (v. 27) ; 2, 1, 29. — **Palilia** (sometimes written *Parilia*) : the feast

in honor of Pales, the patron goddess of the shepherds, was celebrated annually on the 21st of April, the traditional birthday of Rome. A comparison of *pasco*, *pabulum*, *Pales*, *Palatium* (= a fortified fold for the shepherds and their flocks), may serve to indicate the connection between the goddess and this merry day, which is still kept as a festival in the eternal city. For a fuller description of the customs of the feast, cf. I, I, 35 ; Ovid, *Fast.* 4, 721 sqq. ; Preller³, I, pp. 413 sqq. ; Prop. 4, 4, 73 sqq. ; 4, 1, 19 ; Scholia to Pers. I, 72.

88. concinet : cf. v. 10.

90. No other peculiarity of the *Palilia* seems to be as often mentioned as this custom of leaping over blazing piles of hay or stubble. Cf. Ovid, *Fast.* 4, 781 sqq. ; Prop. 4, 4, 77 ; Pers. I, 72 ; Fowler, *Rom. Fest.*, p. 83.

91. fetus : there shall be fruitfulness in the family as well as in

174

oscula conprensis auribus eripiet,
nec taedebit avum parvo advigilare nepoti
balbaque cum puero dicere verba senem.
95   tunc operata deo pubes discumbet in herba,
arboris antiquae qua levis umbra cadit,
aut e veste sua tendent umbracula sertis
vincta, coronatus stabit et ante calix.
at sibi quisque dapes et festas extruet alte
100   caespitibus mensas caespitibusque torum.
ingeret hic potus iuvenis maledicta puellae,
post modo quae votis inrita facta velit:
nam ferus ille suae plorabit sobrius idem
et se iurabit mente fuisse mala.

98. ante ω ipse O.

the flock, and a simple, happy home life.

92. conprensis auribus: this particular manner of kissing, in which the ears of the one kissed were held like the two handles of an *amphora*, was called the "pitcher kiss," and is still sometimes called the "sailor kiss." For a similar scene cf. Verg. *Georg.* 2, 523.

94. balba: an onomatopoetic word (akin to *barbarus*) representing originally the unintelligible prattle of an infant.

95. operata deo: cf. 2, 1, 9, 65. — discumbet: the regular word for reclining at a banquet.

96. levis: cf. Prop. 1, 18, 21.

98. coronatus: for the Roman custom of wreathing mixing bowls and cups on festal occasions, cf. Verg. *Aen.* 1, 724; 3, 525; 7,

147; Stat. Silv. 3, 76. — et: for the position cf. 1, 10, 51, n.

99. at: cf. 1, 3, 63. — dapes: a sacrificial feast for the gods; cf. 2, 1, 81; 1, 5, 28.

102. post modo: we see here in *modo* almost its original force as an abl. of degree of difference; literally, 'afterwards by a measured (or limited, *i.e.* moderate) amount,' = shortly afterwards, pretty soon, presently. — votis . . . velit: emphatic redundancy.

103. ferus ille suae plorabit: 'he that was so cruel will beg forgiveness before his darling.' Cf. Prop. 1, 12, 15, n.

104. mente . . . mala: *i e. mente male sana*. The expression was commonly used in begging pardon for an injury done. Cf. Sen. *De Ben.* 3, 27: *cum malam mentem habuisse se pridie iurasset*, etc.

105 pace tua pereant arcus pereantque sagittae,
    Phoebe, modo in terris erret inermis Amor.
ars bona : sed postquam sumpsit sibi tela Cupido,
    heu heu quam multis ars dedit illa malum!
et mihi praecipue.   iaceo cum saucius annum
110 et faveo morbo, cum iuvat ipse dolor,
usque cano Nemesim, sine qua versus mihi nullus
    verba potest iustos aut reperire pedes.
at tu (nam divum servat tutela poetas),
    praemoneo, vati parce, puella, sacro,
115 ut Messalinum celebrem, cum praemia belli
    ante suos currus oppida victa feret,
ipse gerens lauros, lauro devinctus agresti

109. iaceo ω taceo O. cum O qui ω iam *Wisser*.   110. cum O tam ω
quin *Leo*.   111. usque O vixque ω.

105. The lover's quarrels just described remind the poet of his own trials at the hands of Cupid. — **pace tua** : A. 420, 4. Apollo and Diana were the typical archers.

107. **ars bona** : *i.e.* archery.

108. **dedit . . . malum** : 'played the mischief with.' The expression is a common formula, which is seen as early as in the famous old Saturnian verse, *dabunt malum Metelli Naevio poetae.*

109. **et mihi** : sc. *dedit.* — **cum** : temporal (= *dum*). — **annum** seems to indicate that a year had elapsed since the beginning of his passion for Nemesis.

110. **faveo morbo** : 'nurse my complaint.' — **cum** here approximates the causal force so common in early Latin. Cf. H. 599.

111. **Nemesim** : who succeeded Delia as mistress of Tibullus's heart. See Intr. § 24. — **mihi** : H. 432. Note the unusual form of caesura, in the 5th foot ; cf. Intr. § 42, I (5) (b).

112. **iustos** belongs to both *verba* and *pedes* in thought.

115. **celebrem** : *i.e.* in the future, whenever the opportunity occurs, as he had done for his father Messalla in 1, 7.

116. **oppida victa** : pictures and models of conquered countries, cities, and fortresses were carried in the triumphal processions ; cf. Prop. 3, 4, 16 ; Ovid, *A. A.* 1, 219. In addition to the customs here referred to, cf. 1, 7, 5–8.

117. **ipse** : *i.e.* Messalinus. — **devinctus** : cf. v. 5. — **agresti** : 'wild.'

miles ' io ' magna voce ' triumphe ' canet.
tum Messalla meus pia det spectacula turbae
120   et plaudat curru praetereunte pater.
adnue : sic tibi sint intonsi, Phoebe, capilli,
sic tua perpetuo sit tibi casta soror.

6

Castra Macer sequitur : tenero quid fiet Amori?
sit comes et collo fortiter arma gerat?

118. miles : collective.

119. Neither Messalla nor Tibullus lived to see the triumph of Messalinus, which is said to have been actually celebrated in 11 A.D. with Tiberius, on account of the campaign in Illyria. Cf. Ovid, *Ex Ponto*, 2, 2, 75–88. — **pia det spectacula** : exhibit his affection in the manner indicated by the following verse.

121. sic : cf. v. 63, n. — **intonsi . . . capilli** : cf. 1, 4, 37–38 ; 4, 4, 2 ; Hor. *Car.* 1, 21, 2 ; *Epod.* 15, 9.

It is hard to understand why any one familiar with the artless art of Tibullus should argue against the genuineness of this poem on the ground that it is incomplete !

2, 6

This, perhaps the last elegy composed by Tibullus, has a peculiar simplicity of beauty, and illustrates excellently the poet's gentle nature and tender heart.

His resolve to drown the sorrows of unsatisfied love in the sterner scenes of war is soon broken, and after confessing how a groundless hope had so often disappointed him, and after appealing once more to his Nemesis, by her love for her lost sister, to look upon him in pity, he closes by affirming repeatedly that after all his beloved is not herself hard-hearted, and that he does not wish to cause her a moment's pain.

1–14 : 'Macer is going to war ; why not I, too? Yes! I will bid farewell to love, and be a warrior. Empty words ! How often I have sworn to go, but all in vain! 15–28 : Cruel Cupid! Perish thy darts! I am tormented continually and should have perished long since but for the kind goddess Hope. Do not try to thwart her, my beloved! 29–40 : Be merciful, I beg, by the memory of thy unhappy sister, the favor of whose shade I shall seek in my behalf ! 41–54 : After all, I would not

et seu longa virum terrae via seu vaga ducent
    aequora, cum telis ad latus ire volet?
5   ure, puer, quaeso, tua qui ferus otia liquit,
    atque iterum erronem sub tua signa voca.
quod si militibus parces, erit hic quoque miles,
    ipse levem galea qui sibi portet aquam.
castra peto, valeatque Venus valeantque puellae:
10   et mihi sunt vires, et mihi facta tubast.
magna loquor, sed magnifice mihi magna locuto
    excutiunt clausae fortia verba fores.

6. 8. levem **AV** levi **G.**   10. facta **O** flata *Cornelissen* laeta *Postgate.*

cause my mistress pain. It is not
she, but the old hag that guards
her, who grieves me. Curses upon
the wretch!'

1. **Macer**: probably Aemilius
Macer of Verona, who, as a friend
and contemporary of Vergil, would
have been also a friend of Tibullus.
He wrote poems on various subjects connected with natural
history.

2. **sit**: G. 259; R. 1610. The
answer expected is, of course, a
negative one. Cf. Wolff, *De
Enuntiatis Interrogativis*, p. 26.

3. **vaga**: 'inconstant.' Cf. 2,
3, 39: *praeda vago iussit geminare
pericula ponto.*

4. **latus**: *i.e.* Macer's. — **volet**:
the mood changes to correspond
with the verb of the protasis, *ducent*, which expresses a probability.

5. **ure**: the allusion is to the
custom of branding runaway
slaves, with all the torture thus
implied. — **puer**: Amor.

7. **hic** = *ego*. Cf. Plaut. *Trin.*
1115: *hic homost omnium homi-*

num praecipuos; also ὅδε in Greek
drama, and Eng. slang, "You
don't catch this chicken," etc.

8. **ipse**: Tibullus proposes to
enlist merely as a private, and
would perform every service, however menial, for himself. — **levem**:
in the same sense in which the
word is used of food, *i.e.* 'easy to
digest'; so the plain, hard fare of
a soldier's life is thought of. Cf.
Hor. *Od.* 1, 31, 16; *cichorea le-
vesque malvae.* — **galea**: the handi-
est cup a soldier had; cf. Prop.
3, 12, 8: *potabis galea fessus
Araxis aquam.*

10. **facta tubast**: *i.e.* not
only have I strength in general,
but an especial opportunity now
open, to go.

11. **magna**: cf. Ovid, *Met.* 1,
751: *quem quondam magna loquentem*; 6, 151: *cedere caelitibus,
verbisque minoribus uti.*

12. **fores**: *i.e.* of the house of
Nemesis; to find her door closed
against him takes all the starch
out of his brave resolve.

iuravi quotiens rediturum ad limina numquam!
    cum bene iuravi, pes tamen ipse redit.
15 acer Amor, fractas utinam tua tela sagittas,
    si licet, extinctas adspiciamque faces!
tu miserum torques, tu me mihi dira precari
    cogis et insana mente nefanda loqui.
iam mala finissem leto, sed credula vitam
20 Spes fovet et fore cras semper ait melius.
Spes alit agricolas, Spes sulcis credit aratis
    semina, quae magno fenore reddat ager:
haec laqueo volucres, haec captat arundine pisces,
    cum tenues hamos abdidit ante cibus:
25 Spes etiam valida solatur compede vinctum
    (crura sonant ferro, sed canit inter opus):

14. bene: 'finely,' *i.e.* with great apparent bravado. Cf. Plaut. *Pers.* 495: *bene dictis tuis bene facta aures meae auxilium exposcunt.* — **iuravi**: H. 599, 1. — **pes . . . ipse**: for the reverse idea cf. Prop. 2, 25, 20: *invitis ipse redit pedibus.*

15. acer Amor: cf. 4, 2, 6. — **sagittas . . . faces**: H. & T. § 111.

16. adspiciamque: on the position of the copula cf. 2, 5, 72, n.

18. nefanda: not merely such as have just been spoken (vv. 15–16), but more serious blasphemies. Cf. 3, 5, 14; 4, 16.

19. finissem: we should expect *nisi Spes vitam foveret*; but the apodosis becomes an indicative clause, to state the fact more emphatically. Cf. Ovid, *A. A.* 3, 43: *nunc quoque nescirent! sed me Cytherea docere iussit.*

20. cras: a scrawler on the walls of the basilica at Pompeii evidently had this verse in mind when he wrote (*CIL.* 4, 1837): *cur gaudia differs spemque foves et cras usque redire iubes.*

22. magno fenore: this modal ablative is really more exact than the corresponding abl. of accomp. in Ovid, *Rem. Am.* 173: *semina . . . quae tibi cum multo faenore reddat ager;* for the original seed is not itself returned to the sower with others at all, but comes back to him only by the 'increase.' Cf. 1 Ep. to the Corinthians 15, 36–38.

24. tenues: 'slender,' *i.e.* in comparison to the creatures which are caught on them.

26. crura sonant ferro: the subject is different in English: 'the iron fetters clank upon his legs.'

Spes facilem Nemesim spondet mihi, sed negat illa.
hei mihi, ne vincas, dura puella, deam.
parce, per inmatura tuae precor ossa sororis:
30   sic bene sub tenera parva quiescat humo.
illa mihi sancta est, illius dona sepulcro
et madefacta meis serta feram lacrimis,
illius ad tumulum fugiam supplexque sedebo
et mea cum muto fata querar cinere.
35   non feret usque suum te propter flere clientem:
illius ut verbis, sis mihi lenta veto,
ne tibi neglecti mittant mala somnia manes,

—canit: the subject is violently changed to a personal one easily imagined from the context (*vinctum*).

27. Nemesim: see Intr. § 24.

28. deam: Spes.

29. inmatura: ' not yet due to death,' so ' untimely.' — ossa: by metonomy for *mors*. Cf. Prop. I, 19, 1, n. — sororis: this rather shadowy person is nameless, but from the definiteness of the details given below seems to be real rather than fictitious.

30. sic . . . quiescat: cf. 2, 5, 63, n. — sub tenera . . . humo: the petition will be that the ground shall rest tenderly upon the ashes of her dead sister as if it had consciousness to appreciate the conventional request, *sit tibi terra levis*. The belief that the soul of the dead rested eternally in the grave, while by no means universal among the Romans, is clearly indicated in many epitaphs. Cf.

K.P.H. in *PAPA.*, Vol. 30 (1899), p. xxx.

31. dona: besides garlands, these included offerings of blood, oil, milk, honey, and perfumes. B.*G.*, p. 521 ; H. & T. § 3. — sepulcro: not a terminal dat. ; ' in honor of her tomb.'

34. cum: the word implies the poet's expectation of finding sympathy with him in his woes. — muto: equivalent to a concessive clause.

35. clientem: he claims her as a patroness, just as in v. 33 he has played the part of a fugitive slave seeking refuge at her tomb.

36. illius ut verbis: ' as if I were using her own words.' — sis: the rare subjv. instead of the regular inf. with *veto.* H. 642, 5. — lenta: ' indifferent.'

37. Cf. H. & T. § 3 ; Verg. *Aen.* 6, 896 ; and J. W. Hewitt in *Harvard Studies*, 19, 92, n. 6. The Manes might also send good

maestaque sopitae stet soror ante torum,
    qualis ab excelsa praeceps delapsa fenestra
40   venit ad infernos sanguinolenta lacus.
desino, ne dominae luctus renoventur acerbi :
    non ego sum tanti, ploret ut illa semel.
nec lacrimis oculos digna est foedare loquaces :
    lena nocet nobis, ipsa puella bonast.
45   lena necat miserum Phryne furtimque tabellas
    occulto portans itque reditque sinu :
saepe, ego cum dominae dulces a limine duro
    agnosco voces, haec negat esse domi :
saepe, ubi nox promissa mihi est, languere puellam
50   nuntiat aut aliquas extimuisse minas.
tum morior curis, tum mens mihi perdita fingit,

---

45. necat **G** vetat **AV** vocat *Lachmann suggests.*

dreams. 'Her sweet forgotten shade' (Williams).

39. qualis: cf. I, 10, 37, n.

40. lacus: cf. Verg. *Aen.* 6, 134 : *bis Stygios innare lacus.*

41. desinŏ: the only instance of the short final syllable in this word. Tibullus has also *nesciŏ.* Similar shortenings are rare up to the time of Ovid. Cf. L. 2443. — **luctus:** over her sister's untimely death.

42. Cf. I, I, 51, 52. The standpoint of I, 10, 63–64 is a different one. Cf. also Ovid, *Trist.* 2, 209 : *nam non sum tanti, renovem ut tua vulnera.*

43. digna est: 'it is not meet that she.' — **foedare loquaces:** cf. Cat. 3, 17 : *tua nunc opera meae*

puellae flendo turgiduli rubent ocelli.

44. lena: 'her old hag of a guardian.' Tibullus feels obliged to vent his feelings upon somebody.

45. tabellas: 'billets-doux.'

47. cum: concessive, with ind. Cf. note on Cat. 68, 32. — **duro:** it is called hard-hearted because it will not let him pass to his lady love.

48. haec: *lena.* Cf. the story of Nasica and Ennius, Cic. *De Orat.* 2, ch. 68.

49. 'Often when a meeting has been arranged.'

50. aliquas: made by some unnamed rival perhaps.

51. perdita: 'desperately jealous.'

quisve meam teneat, quot teneatve modis.
tum tibi, lena, precor diras : satis anxia vivas,
moverit e votis pars quotacumque deos.

LIBER TERTIVS

2

Qui primus caram iuveni carumque puellae
  eripuit iuvenem, ferreus ille fuit.
durus et ille fuit, qui tantum ferre dolorem,
  vivere et erepta coniuge qui potuit.
5 non ego firmus in hoc, non haec patientia nostro
  ingenio : frangit fortia corda dolor :
nec mihi vera loqui pudor est vitaeque fateri
  tot mala perpessae taedia nata meae.

---

52. meam teneat : 'is caressing my darling.'

53. satis : sarcastically ; cf. Eng., 'You'll get all you want of it.' — **vivas** = *sis*.

54. 'Should even the least little bit of my prayers be answered.' A. 519.

3, 2

On the authorship and poetic merit of Book 3, cf. Intr. § 25.

1–8 : 'A heartless wretch has stolen my promised bride ; I no longer care to live ; 9–30 : my wish is that Neaera and her mother may duly perform for me all the last sad offices.'

2. ferreus ille fuit : cf. 1, 10, 2. Similar imitations of the genuine work of Tibullus are frequent in this book.

4. coniuge : 'betrothed' ; probably a *coniunx* by anticipation only ; cf. Verg. *Aen.* 3, 330 : *ereptae magno flammatus amore coniugis* ; *2, 344 : gener auxilium Priamo . . . ferebat.* — **qui :** of the same antecedent as the *qui* in v. 3 ; cf. Cat. 64, 96 : *quaeque regis Golgos quaeque Idalium frondosum.*

5. in hoc = *usque adeo* ; 'to this extent.'

6. For a similarly sententious verse, cf. 3, 4, 76 : *vincuntur molli pectora dura prece.*

ergo cum tenuem fuero mutatus in umbram
10   candidaque ossa super nigra favilla teget,
ante meum veniat longos incompta capillos
    et fleat ante meum maesta Neaera rogum.
sed veniat carae matris comitata dolore:
    maereat haec genero, maereat illa viro.
15   praefatae ante meos manes animamque precatae
    perfusaeque pias ante liquore manus,
pars quae sola mei superabit corporis, ossa
    incinctae nigra candida veste legent,
et primum annoso spargent collecta Lyaeo,
20   mox etiam niveo fundere lacte parent,
post haec carbaseis umorem tollere velis

2. 15. precatae ω rogate **A** rogatae **V** recentem *Postgate.*

9. **ergo**: cf. Prop. 2, 13, 17. —
tenuem . . . in umbram: cf. Verg.
Aen. 4, 278: *in tenuem ex oculis
evanuit auram.*

10. The details of the Roman
burial customs here following are
given with varying degrees of
completeness in several other noteworthy passages ; *e.g.* Prop. 2, 13 ;
1, 17, 19–24 ; 4, 1, 127 ; Ovid,
Trist. 3, 3 ; Verg. *Aen.* 6, 202–
235. See B. *G. Excursus*, Scene
12 ; Guhl und Koner[6], p. 857. —
super . . . teget: tmesis.

12. **fleat**: of the lament just as
the pyre was lighted. — **Neaera**:
cf. Intr. § 25 ; also 1, 1, 61 sqq.

13. **matris . . . dolore** = *a
matre dolente ;* cf. Cat. 66, 50, n.

14. **genero . . . viro**: dat.; cf.
v. 4, n.

15. **sqq.**: cf. B.*G.* 519. — **praefatae ante**: pleonastic.

16. **liquore**: *i.e. aqua.*

18. **incinctae**: 'enveloped' (in
the black mourning robe). — **nigra
candida**: the juxtaposition of the
words is intended to heighten the
effect of the contrast. — **veste**: instrumental abl.; the ashes are
gathered into the robe itself. —
legent, like *spargent* in v. 19, expresses greater confidence than
the following optative subjunctives.

20. **fundere**: cf. 1, 7, 50. —
lacte: for its appropriateness as an
offering to earth powers, cf. Fowler,
Roman Festivals, p. 103 ; cf. its
use in incantations, *e.g.* 1, 2, 48.

21. **carbaseis . . . velis**: 'a linen
cloth' upon which the ashes were
dried. For the plural see Lex.
s.v. Cf. Cic. *In Ver.* 5, 12, § 30:
*tabernacula carbaseis intenta velis
conlocabat.*

atque in marmorea ponere sicca domo.
illic quas mittit dives Panchaia merces
    eoique Arabes, pinguis et Assyria,
25 et nostri memores lacrimae fundantur eodem :
    sic ego conponi versus in ossa velim.
sed tristem mortis demonstret littera causam
    atque haec in celebri carmina fronte notet.
'Lygdamus hic situs est : dolor huic et cura Neaerae,
30   coniugis ereptae, causa perire fuit.'

24. pinguis ω dives O.

22. **marmorea . . . domo**: *i.e.* *sepulcro*; cf. the epitaph in Buecheler's *Car. Epig.* 434, v. 15 : *haec domus aeterna est, hic sum situs, hic ero semper*; also *PAPA.*, Vol. 30, p. xxx; Prop. 2, 13, 32, n. — **sicca**: 'when dry.'— Only one in every three pentameters in this Elegy opens with a spondee ; and one in every three contains only dactyls, *e.g.* v. 2. Cf. Intr. § 42, II (5).

23. **Panchaia**: a fabulous island supposed to be in the Erythraean Sea. — **merces**: perfumes. Cf. Ovid, *Fast.* 3, 561 : *mixta bibunt molles lacrimis unguenta favillae*.

24. **Assyria**: on the form of the verse cf. Intr. § 42, II (2).

25. **lacrimae**: cf. 1, 3, 8.

26. **sic**: *i.e.* as just described. — **conponi**: 'to be consigned to the tomb'; cf. Prop. 2, 24, 35 : *tu mea conpones et dices, 'ossa, Properti, haec tua sunt.'* — **versus in**

ossa : 'when I have become "dust to dust."'

27. **littera**: 'inscription'; cf. Ovid, *Met.* 11, 705 : *inque sepulcro si non urna, tamen iunget nos littera*.

28. **celebri**: 'upon the thronged highway.' This is exactly the situation that Propertius (3, 16, 25) prays his tomb may not have.

29. **Lygdamus**: the word occurs nowhere else in the book. A comparison of the Greek λύγδος suggests the probability that it was formed to furnish an equivalent for Albius (Tibullus).

30. **perire**: poetic with *causa* ; cf. Verg. *Aen.* 10, 90 : *quae causa fuit, consurgere in arma*. As other commentators have remarked, this was about the last reason Neaera would have assigned in an epitaph upon a rejected lover or husband ! Tibullus would hardly have been so absurd.

3

Quid prodest caelum votis inplesse, Neaera,
    blandaque cum multa tura dedisse prece,
non ut marmorei prodirem e limine tecti,
    insignis clara conspicuusque domo,
5 aut ut multa mei renovarent iugera tauri
    et magnas messes terra benigna daret,
sed tecum ut longae sociarem gaudia vitae
    inque tuo caderet nostra senecta sinu
tum cum permenso defunctus tempore lucis
10   nudus Lethaea cogerer ire rate ?
nam grave quid prodest pondus mihi divitis auri,
    arvaque si findant pinguia mille boves ?
quidve domus prodest Phrygiis innixa columnis,
    Taenare sive tuis, sive Caryste tuis,

3, 3

1–26: 'Alas! Neaera, what does it profit that I pray continually — not for wealth, for that were idle — but for thy return to me, even though poverty be our lot ? 27–38: Without thee not all the riches of the world can satisfy me. Let me have my beloved, or let me die!'

2. blandaque . . . tura: cf. Prop. 4, 6, 5.

3. prodirem: *i.e.* as the owner.

5. multa: cf. 1, 1, 2. — **renovarent:** *i.e.* by plowing; cf. Ovid, *Trist.* 5, 12, 23: *assiduo si non renovatur aratro.*

8. caderet nostra senecta = *ego senex occiderem.*

10. nudus: cf. Job 1, 21; Prop. 3, 5, 14. — **Lethaea:** cf. 3, 5, 24. We might have expected *Stygia ;* but the poets are not particular to distinguish the infernal streams. Mention of the river Lethe does not appear till after the classical Greek period.

12. Sc. *quid prosit.*

13. Phrygiis: a popular marble at Rome; white with purple streaks.

14. Taenare: the marble quarried on this promontory was black. — **Caryste:** in Euboea; here a marble combining white and green tints was obtained. The remains of ancient structures in Rome abound in fragments of rare marbles, and the interior of such a

15   et nemora in domibus sacros imitantia lucos
        aurataeque trabes marmoreumque solum ?
    quidve in Erythraeo legitur quae litore concha
        tinctaque Sidonio murice lana iuvat,
    et quae praeterea populus miratur ? in illis
20   invidia est : falso plurima vulgus amat.
    non opibus mentes hominum curaeque levantur :
        nam Fortuna sua tempora lege regit.
    sit mihi paupertas tecum iucunda, Neaera :
        at sine te regum munera nulla volo.
25   o niveam, quae te poterit mihi reddere, lucem !
        o mihi felicem terque quaterque diem !
    at si, pro dulci reditu quaecumque voventur,
        audiat aversa non meus aure deus,
    nec me regna iuvant nec Lydius aurifer amnis
30   nec quas terrarum sustinet orbis opes.
    haec alii cupiant, liceat mihi paupere cultu

building as the basilica of *S. Paolo Fuori le Mura* gives us a slight hint as to the magnificence in that respect that must have been common in Rome's best days. The poets frequently refer to this; cf. Hor. *Car.* 2, 18, 3–5 ; 2, 15, 20 ; Statius Silv. 1, 5, 34 sqq. ; Prop. 3, 2, 9.

15. nemora : in the peristyles of luxurious houses, and the great villas of the wealthy.

16. aurataeque : cf. Hor. *Car.* 2, 18, 1 : *Non ebur neque aureum mea renidet in domo lacunar.*

17. concha : by metonomy for the pearl within the *concha.* Cf. 2, 4, 30 : *e rubro lucida concha mari.*

20. invidia : *i.e. causa invidiae.* — **falso :** ' without reason.'

21. levantur : a zeugma ; the minds are not ' relieved,' and cares are not ' removed.'

23. Cf. 1, 1, 57–58. — **tecum :** *i.e. dummodo tecum sim.*

25. niveam : cf. Cat. 107, 6, n. This is, however, an unusual adjective. Cf. the current slang, " Treated him white." The opposite is *atra* (or *nigra*) *dies* ; cf. 3, 5, 5, n. ; Ovid, *A. A.* 1, 418.

28. non meus : ' unfriendly.'

29. Lydius aurifer amnis : the Pactolus. Cf. Prop. 1, 14, 11.

30. quas = *quascumque.*

31. Cf. 1, 1, *passim.* — **paupere cultu :** cf. 1, 10, 19.

securo cara coniuge posse frui.

adsis et timidis faveas, Saturnia, votis,

et faveas concha, Cypria, vecta tua.

35   aut si fata negant reditum tristesque sorores

stamina quae ducunt quaeque futura neunt,

me vocet in vastos amnes nigramque paludem

dives in ignava luridus Orcus aqua.

5

Vos tenet Etruscis manat quae fontibus unda,

unda sub aestivum non adeunda canem,

3. 36. neunt **O** canunt *Heinsius* regunt *Dissen.*   38. dives in **O** Ditis et ω.

---

33. **Saturnia**: Juno, the patroness of wedlock.

34. **concha**: cf. Baum. *Denk.*, p. 94. — **Cypria**: Venus, who might aid the poet's suit for a return of Neaera's favor.

35. **sorores** = *Parcae.*

36. Cf. 1, 7, 1. — **quaeque**: for the repetition cf. 3, 2, 4. — **neunt** = *nent*; the form occurs only here; cf. L. 837.

37. **vastos**: 'desolate.'

38. **dives**: the Latinized epithet of the Greek Hades (Plouton) is here applied to the more vague equivalent, *Orcus*; H. & T. § 101. Translate in this order: *dives Orcus, luridus in ignava aqua.*

3, 5

1–20: 'While you, my friends, are seeking health at the Etruscan springs, I am languishing at home, near death. Spare me, Persephone! I have done no crime, nor committed sacrilege, and I am still a young man. 21–34: Spare me, all ye gods of the nether world, till old age shall ripen me for death! I hope my fears are groundless; but, friends, while you enjoy yourselves at the springs, do not forget to offer sacrifices for my recovery.'

1. **Vos**: we have no clue to the names of his friends here addressed. — **Etruscis . . . fontibus**: there are said to have been hot springs of a considerable reputation at various places in Etruria, *e.g.* Caere, Pisae, and Centumcellae. — **unda** = *aqua.*

2. **non adeunda**: on account of the unhealthy climate, which is still notorious all along this coast.

nunc autem sacris Baiarum proxima lymphis,
cum se purpureo vere remittit humus:
5   at mihi Persephone nigram denuntiat horam:
inmerito iuveni parce nocere, dea.
non ego temptavi nulli temeranda virorum
audax laudandae sacra docere deae,
nec mea mortiferis infecit pocula sucis
10   dextera nec cuiquam trita venena dedit,
nec nos sacrilegos templis admovimus ignes,
nec cor sollicitant facta nefanda meum,
nec nos insanae meditantes iurgia mentis
inpia in adversos solvimus ora deos:
15   et nondum cani nigros laesere capillos,
nec venit tardo curva senecta pede.
natalem primo nostrum videre parentes,

5. 7. virorum ω deorum O piorum *Itali.*   11. sacrilegos **G** sacrilegis **AV** sacrilegi ω.   12. facta O furta *Baehrens.*   16. tardo O tacito **P.**

3. **nunc**: at this time of year. — **autem**: the word is not used by Tibullus, and occurs only here in the whole Tibullus collection. — **proxima**: in popularity.

4. **remittit**: *i.e.* from the frosts of winter.

5. **nigram . . . horam**: *i.e.* of death; cf. 1, 3, 4–5; 3, 3, 25, n.; Prop. 2, 24, 34: *non niger ille dies.*

7. **virorum**: the presence of any of the male sex at the rites of the Bona Dea was strictly forbidden. Cf. 1, 6, 22: *sacra bonae maribus non adeunda deae*; Ovid, *A. A.* 3, 637; *Fast.* 5, 153; Plut. *Cic.* 19; Macr. 1, 12, 26; Prop. 4, 9, 25; Paus. 8, 31, 8. Men were excluded from the temples of 'great goddesses.'

8. **laudandae**: *i.e. bonae.* — **docere**: 'to divulge.'

10. **dextera . . . dedit**: mixing poison, and offering it to anybody, are distinguished. Both were far too common in this age. Cf. Aristoph. *Frogs,* 123 sqq.

15. **cani**: cf. 1, 8, 42: *cum vetus infecit cana senecta caput*; Prop. 3, 5, 24. For the close parallels, to this and the following vv., in Ovid cf. *A. A.* 2, 669; *Trist.* 4, 10, 5; *Am.* 2, 14, 23. For theories in explanation cf. Intr. § 25.

16. **tardo . . . pede**: to be taken with *senecta.* Cf. Ovid, *A. A.* 2, 670: *iam veniet tacito curva senecta pede.*

cum cecidit fato consul uterque pari.
quid fraudare iuvat vitem crescentibus uvis
20 et modo nata mala vellere poma manu ?
parcite, pallentes undas quicumque tenetis
duraque sortiti tertia regna dei.
Elysios olim liceat cognoscere campos
Lethaeamque ratem Cimmeriosque lacus,
25 cum mea rugosa pallebunt ora senecta
et referam pueris tempora prisca senex.
atque utinam vano nequiquam terrear aestu !
languent ter quinos sed mea membra dies.
at vobis Tuscae celebrantur numina lymphae
30 et facilis lenta pellitur unda manu.
vivite felices, memores et vivite nostri,
sive erimus seu nos fata fuisse velint.

---

18. consul uterque: the consuls Hirtius and Pansa both fell in battle at Mutina, B.C. 43. This verse occurs again in Ovid, *Trist*. 4, 10, 6. For a discussion of the chronological and other difficulties which thus arise cf. Intr. §§ 21, 25.

19. Cf. Ovid, *Am*. 2, 14, 23.

21. pallentes: cf. 3, 1, 28: *pallida Ditis aqua*.

22. duraque: the use of the two adjectives with *regna* is permissible in view of the fact that *tertia regna* is practically equivalent to *Orcum*. The three kingdoms were those of the three brothers, Zeus, Poseidon, and Hades.

23. olim: 'at some future time.'

24. Lethaeamque: cf. 3, 3, 10, n. — **Cimmeriosque lacus**: cf. 1, 10. 38, n. The Cimmerii were a fabulous people whom Homer located only vaguely in the far west, where they were supposed to live in the midst of perpetual clouds and darkness. But later writers endeavored to localize them more definitely in different places, among others, in caves near Cumae, where they dwelt in perpetual darkness: cf. 4, 1, 64; Cic. *Acad.* 2, 19, 61. Hence 'Cimmerian' darkness became proverbial, and the epithet was easily applied to the regions (here, *lacus*) of the lower world.

27. aestu = *febri*.

30. manu: *i.e.* of the swimmers.

32. fuisse: the well-known euphemism for death. Cf. Verg. *Aen.* 2, 325 : *fuimus Troes, fuit Ilium*.

189

interea nigras pecudes promittite Diti
et nivei lactis pocula mixta mero.

LIBER QVARTVS

2

Sulpicia est tibi culta tuis, Mars magne, kalendis:
  spectatum e caelo, si sapis, ipse veni.
hoc Venus ignoscet; at tu, violente, caveto

33. **nigras:** as the most appropriate sacrifices to the gods of the lower world, to whom (*e.g.* Dis, Vejovis, and Manes) black sheep were offered. The same idea appears in the folklore of other nations.

34. **lactis:** cf. 3, 2, 20, n.

4, 2

On the authorship of Book 4, see Intr. § 26.

The old Roman year began on March 1, on which day it was customary to give presents, even after the reformation of the calendar in 46 B.C. by Julius Caesar, which established Jan. 1 as New Year's day. As March 1 was the festival of the Matronalia (the *femineae kalendae* of Juv. 9, 53), it was especially appropriate for husbands to give presents to their wives. This poem seems to have been written to accompany such a gift made by Cerinthus to Sulpicia, — a lover to a prospective wife, — which may have been, as Belling

believes it was (Bell. *U.*, p. 3), the following group of poems (4, 3-6), or they may have accompanied other gifts. On the personality of Cerinthus (whose name does not, indeed, appear in this elegy) and of Sulpicia, cf. Intr. § 24, and 2, 2, Intr.

1-14: 'On thy festal day, great Mars, Sulpicia's native beauty is so heightened by her adornment as to make her fit to be compared with the divine Vertumnus. 15-24: She is the only maiden worthy to receive all costly gifts. Therefore, ye Muses, sing of her your choicest praises.'

1. **tibi culta:** 'arrayed in thine honor.'

2. **ipse veni:** cf. 2, 5, 5.

3. **Venus:** the beloved of Mars. — **ignoscet:** on account of Sulpicia's remarkable beauty. Cf. Prop. 2, 28, 33. For the quantity of the last syllable cf. 1, 10, 13, n. — **caveto:** the tense implies the usual colloquial familiarity: "You'd better look out." Cf. *PAPA.*, Vol. 26 (1895), p. lxi.

ne tibi miranti turpiter arma cadant.

5   illius ex oculis, cum vult exurere divos,

accendit geminas lampadas acer Amor.

illam, quidquid agit, quoquo vestigia movit,

conponit furtim subsequiturque Decor.

seu solvit crines, fusis decet esse capillis ;

10   seu compsit, comptis est veneranda comis.

urit, seu Tyria voluit procedere palla ;

urit, seu nivea candida veste venit.

talis in aeterno felix Vertumnus Olympo

mille habet ornatus, mille decenter habet.

15   sola puellarum digna est, cui mollia caris

vellera det sucis bis madefacta Tyros,

---

4. **miranti**: 'as you gaze in admiration.' — **arma cadant**: several ancient works of art represent Mars thus forgetful of all but the amorous intentions of the moment. Cf. Baum. *Denk.*, p. 886.

5. **oculis**: cf. Propertius, of Cynthia (2, 3, 14) : *oculi, geminae, sidera nostra, faces*.

6. **geminas lampadas**: cf. 2, 6, 16 ; Prop. 3, 16, 16.

8. **conponit** = *ornat*.

9. **solvit crines**: as was often the case in the retirement of the home; cf. 1, 3, 91 ; Prop 2, 1, 7 : *vidi ad frontem sparsos errare capillos*; Ter. *Haut.* 288 sq. : *ornatam ita uti quae ornantur sibi, nulla mala re os expolitam muliebri.*

10. **compsit**: as was more appropriate when she appeared in public places. — **veneranda** : 'adorable,' in the slang use of the word.

11. **Tyria** : for outdoor wear.

12. **candida** : for indoor use.

13. **Vertumnus** : the changing (*vertere*) god of gardens and fruits exhibited varying phases of beauty as the seasons advanced. Cf. Prop. 4, 2, a poem devoted to this god, his origin, name, and statue.

14. Cf. Prop. 4, 2, 22 : *in quamcumque voles verte, decorus ero* ; Ovid, *Am.* 2, 5, 43 : *spectabat terram : terram spectare decebat ; maesta erat in vultu : maesta decenter erat.*

16. **sucis bis madefacta** : 'double-dyed.' The most costly Tyrian purple was thus prepared (*dibapha*), first with scarlet, then with the *purpura*. Cf. Hor. *Car.* 2, 16, 35 : *te bis Afro murice tinctae vestiunt lanae* ; Pliny, *N. H.* 9, 39, 137 : *dibapha tunc dicebatur quae bis tincta esset.*

possideatque, metit quidquid bene olentibus arvis
   cultor odoratae dives Arabs segetis
et quascumque niger rubro de litore gemmas
20   proximus eois colligit Indus aquis.
hanc vos, Pierides, festis cantate kalendis,
   et testudinea Phoebe superbe lyra.
hoc solemne sacrum multos haec sumet in annos:
   dignior est vestro nulla puella choro.

4

Huc ades et tenerae morbos expelle puellae,
   huc ades, intonsa Phoebe superbe coma.
crede mihi, propera, nec te iam, Phoebe, pigebit
   formosae medicas adplicuisse manus.

2. 23. haec sumet **F** hoc sumet **O** sumat **ω**. 24. vestro **O** festo *Cartault*. choro **ω** toro **G** thoro **AV**.

17. Cf. 2, 2, 3–4; 3, 2, 23–24.

19. Cf. 2, 2, 15–16, n. — **niger**: cf. 2, 3, 55: *sint comites fusci, quos India torret.*

21. **Pierides**: 'daughters of Pieria' = Muses.

22. Cf. 4, 4, 2. — **testudinea . . . lyra**: which Hermes invented and presented to Phoebus; cf. Prop. 4, 6, 32.

23. **sacrum**: that performed by women in honor of Juno, the mother of Mars, on the feast of the Matronalia, March 1, his birthday. — **haec**: Sulpicia. — **sumet**: 'shall undertake.'

4, 4

Consolation to Cerinthus, during Sulpicia's illness.

1–14: 'Help, Phoebus! Lay healing hands upon Sulpicia, and restore her to her anxious lover. 15–20: Cerinthus, your fears are groundless. 21–26: Hear my prayer, Phoebus: and you shall win surpassing praise.'

1. **Huc ades**: cf. 1, 7, 49.

2. **intonsa**: *i.e.* ever youthful; cf. 2, 5, 121; 1, 4, 37: *solis aeterna est Baccho Phoeboque iuventas: nam decet intonsus crinis utrumque deum.* — **Phoebe superbe**: cf. 4, 2, 22.

3. **propera**: the imperative, as commonly, stands in the relation of protasis to the following verb (*pigebit*).

4. **medicas . . . manus**: naturally the god who sends disease can ward it off. Cf. H. & T. § 51.

5   effice ne macies pallentes occupet artus,
      neu notet informis candida membra color,
    et quodcumque malist et quidquid triste timemus,
      in pelagus rapidis evehat amnis aquis.
    sancte, veni, tecumque feras, quicumque sapores
10   quicumque et cantus corpora fessa levant :
    neu iuvenem torque, metuit qui fata puellae
      votaque pro domina vix numeranda facit.
    interdum vovet, interdum, quod langueat illa,
      dicit in aeternos aspera verba deos.
15 pone metum, Cerinthe : deus non laedit amantes.
      tu modo semper ama : salva puella tibist.
21 nil opus est fletu : lacrimis erit aptius uti,
      si quando fuerit tristior illa tibi.
17 at nunc tota tua est, te solum candida secum
      cogitat, et frustra credula turba sedet.
    Phoebe, fave : laus magna tibi tribuetur in uno
20   corpore servato restituisse duos.
23 iam celeber, iam laetus eris, cum debita reddet
      certatim sanctis laetus uterque focis.
25 tum te felicem dicet pia turba deorum,
      optabunt artes et sibi quisque tuas.

4. 5. pallentes **O** tabentes *Heinsius*.   6. candida **ω** pallida **O** languida *Rigler*.   23. laetus **O** lautus *Haupt* gratus *Martignon* lotus *Broukhusius*.

8. **in pelagus**: cf. 2, 5, 80, n.
9. **sapores** : 'medicines.'
10. **cantus** : 'incantations.'
14. **aspera verba** : cf. 1, 3, 52.
15. Cf. Prop. 3, 16, 11.
21–22. This distich has clearly been misplaced in the Mss.
22. **tristior** : cf. Prop. 1, 6, 10.
17. **candida** : *i.e.* in heart, 'sincere.'

18. **turba** : of suitors.
20. **corpore** : 'life.'—**restituisse duos** : cf. Prop. 2, 28, 41 ; Ovid, *Am.* 2, 13, 15 : *huc adhibe vultus, et in una parce duobus.*
23. **celeber . . . eris** : 'thy temple shall be thronged,' and therefore, as a derived meaning, 'thou shalt be renowned'; cf. 2, 1, 83 ; 3, 2, 28.

6

Natalis Iuno, sanctos cape turis acervos,
  quos tibi dat tenera docta puella manu.
tota tibi est hodie, tibi se laetissima compsit,
  staret ut ante tuos conspicienda focos.
5   illa quidem ornandi causas tibi, diva, relegat:
  est tamen, occulte cui placuisse velit.
at tu, sancta, fave, neu quis divellat amantes,
  sed iuveni quaeso mutua vincla para.
sic bene conpones: ullae non ille puellae
10   servire aut cuiquam dignior illa viro.
nec possit cupidos vigilans deprendere custos,
  fallendique vias mille ministret Amor.
adnue purpureaque veni perlucida palla:

6. 3. tota O lota ω.

4, 6

On Sulpicia's birthday the poet
wishes for her the fulfillment of her
greatest desire.

1–4: 'Juno of Sulpicia, may
she and her offerings be acceptable to thee this day! 5–20: She
has adorned herself ostensibly
for thee, but really to please her
lover; Juno, they are both worthy;
assist her, that their love may be
mutual and may triumph over
every obstacle.'

1. **Natalis Iuno**: the tutelary
spirit of each woman, corresponding to the Genius of each man,
worshiped especially on birthdays.
Cf. 1, 7, 49; H. & T. § 188. —

sanctos: the adjective really belongs with *turis*.

2. **docta**: cf. note on Prop.
1, 7, 11; 2, 13, 11; Ovid, *Trist*.
3, 7, 31; etc.

5. **relegat**: 'ascribes,' a poetic
meaning.

6. **cui**: *i.e.* Cerinthus.

8. **vincla**: sc. *Amoris*.

9. **sic**: 'by so doing,' refers to
the previous verse. — **ullae** = *ulli*:
the only instance of this form; cf.
Prop. 1, 20, 35: *nullae pendebant
debita curae . . . poma*; 3, 11, 57:
toto . . . urbi.

11. **nec**: correlative with **-que**
in v. 12. — **possit**: optative.

13. The vagueness of the line
of demarcation between the lady

ter tibi fit libo, ter, dea casta, mero;
15   praecipit et natae mater studiosa quod optat:
illa aliud tacita, iam sua, mente rogat.
uritur, ut celeres urunt altaria flammae,
nec, liceat quamvis, sana fuisse velit.
sit iuveni grata, et veniet cum proximus annus,
20   hic idem votis iam vetus adsit amor.

8

Invisus natalis adest, qui rure molesto
et sine Cerintho tristis agendus erit.
dulcius urbe quid est? an villa sit apta puellae
atque Arretino frigidus amnis agro?
5   iam, nimium Messalla mei studiose, quiescas,

15. praecipit et O praecipit en *Heinsius.*   optat O optet ω.   19. sit iuveni
ω si iuveni O sis iuveni F sis, Iuno, *Gruppe.*   grata et ω grata O gratae *Lachmann* grata ut *Eberz* gratum *Rigler.*   veniet O adveniet ω vertet *Baehrens.*
20. votis O vobis *Cartault.*   adsit ω esset O exstet *Cartault (suggested by
Baehrens).*

and her Juno is here well illustrated. — **perlucida**: the famous
diaphanous garments of Coan silk,
which served to drape rather than
to conceal a graceful form and fair
skin.

14. **fit**: *i.e.* sacrifice is offered.

15. **praecipit**: perhaps a whispered suggestion. — **optat**: sc.
mater. She may have picked out
a rich lover, or may prefer some
one else for an unknown reason.

16. **sua**: nom.; 'independently,' 'according to her own
choice.'

18. **liceat**: sc. *sana fuisse.*

20. **iam vetus**:   and so,
stronger.

4, 8

For the authorship of this and
the two following elegies, see Intr.
§ 26.   In a poetic billet-doux
Sulpicia protests against a proposed journey with Messalla which
will take her away from Rome on
the birthday of her lover Cerinthus, very possibly the same day
referred to in 4, 5.

1. **molesto**: 'tiresome.'

3. Cf. Cic. *Ad Att.* 5, 11, 1. —
an . . . sit: cf. 2, 6, 2, n.

5. **studiose**: Messalla was probably her uncle, and may well have
been her guardian since the death
of her father.

non tempestivae saepe propinque viae.
hic animum sensusque meos abducta relinquo,
    arbitrio quamvis non sinis esse meo.

9

Scis iter ex animo sublatum triste puellae?
natali Romae iam licet esse tuo.
omnibus ille dies nobis natalis agatur,
    qui nec opinanti nunc tibi forte venit.

I I

Estne tibi, Cerinthe, tuae pia cura puellae,
    quod mea nunc vexat corpora fessa calor?

8. 6. non ω neu O seu *Cartault.* saepe O saeve *Unger* perge monere *adopted from Baehrens by Hiller* tempestivast sive *Cartault.* 8. quamvis **AV** quoniam G quam vis *Statius.* sinis O sinit *Statius.*

9. 2. tuo **OF** suo ω meo *Huschke.* 3. natalis O genialis ω tam laetus *Baehrens.* 4. qui O quam *Baehrens* quod *Drenckhahn.*

6. **non tempestivae**: 'inopportune'; from the standpoint of the young lady. — **saepe propinque**: 'prone to undertake'; an odd expression, in which editors discover a feminine style.
7. **hic**: at Rome. — **abducta**: with concessive force.
8. **quamvis**: a characteristically feminine petulance.

4, 9

The journey is called off, she writes, and they can celebrate at home after all.
1. **Scis**: cf. L. 1502. — **ex animo**: *i.e.* it has ceased to be a cause for anxiety.

3. **omnibus**: in youthful exuberance of spirits she plans a family celebration.
4. **qui**: *i.e.* in its present phase, with the unexpected presence of Sulpicia, and a general merrymaking, it will be almost a surprise party for Cerinthus.

4, 11

Sulpicia is ill and lonely. In a fit of the blues she tells Cerinthus that if he doesn't care about her suffering, she doesn't care to recover. Cf. Cat. 38.
1. **Estne**: Sulpicia really hopes for an affirmative answer. Cf. L. 1504.

ah ego non aliter tristes evincere morbos
   optarim, quam te si quoque velle putem.
5   at mihi quid prosit morbos evincere, si tu
   nostra potes lento pectore ferre mala?

13

Nulla tuum nobis subducet femina lectum :
   hoc primum iuncta est foedere nostra Venus.

11. 5. at **F** Ha **A** Ah **V** an *Cartault* cum **ω**.   quid **A** quod **ω**.   si **ω**.

2. **quod . . . vexat**: the reason is Sulpicia's; perhaps Cerinthus does not know the situation. — **calor**: 'fever.'

3. **non aliter**: 'under no other conditions.'

4. **optarim . . . putem**: a mere possibility. — **te . . . velle**: note the emphatic position of the subject.

6. **lento**: cf. 2, 6, 36, n. He would surely be a lover 'slow of heart' that would not be moved by such an appeal as this!

4, 13

Addressed to an unknown lady, possibly the 'Glycera' mentioned by Horace, *Car.* 1, 33, 1–3: *Albi, ne doleas plus nimio memor in mitis Glycerae, neu miserabilis decantes elegos.* The perfection of form, the characteristic mannerisms and sentiments, and the beautiful simplicity and intensity of its spirit of devotion, mark it as a certainly genuine poem of Tibullus. (Cf. Magnus in Bursian's *JB.*, Vol. 51 (1887), p. 359. For the opposite view cf. Postgate, *Sel.*, Appendix C.) The composite character and authorship of this fourth book of the Tibullus collection permits us only to conjecture to what original series of elegies this gem may have belonged.

1–4: 'Thou only in my eyes art fair. 5–16: May thy beauty not appeal to others; my love needs not the stimulus of envy; thou art my all in all — so swear I by great Juno. 17–24: Foolish oath! Henceforth I'm at thy mercy. Yet will I ever faithful be, and pray for Venus's favor.'

1. **subducet**: 'steal away.' — **lectum**: *i.e. amorem.* Cf. the similar use of λέχος and λέκτρον by the Greeks for 'wife'; this same form of usage occurs, *e.g.* 29 times in the *Helena* of Euripides.

2. **iuncta est**: cf. 1, 1, 69.

tu mihi sola places, nec iam te praeter in urbe
　　formosa est oculis ulla puella meis.
5　atque utinam posses uni mihi bella videri!
　　displiceas aliis: sic ego tutus ero.
nil opus invidia est, procul absit gloria vulgi:
　　qui sapit, in tacito gaudeat ille sinu.
sic ego secretis possum bene vivere silvis,
10　qua nulla humano sit via trita pede.
tu mihi curarum requies, tu nocte vel atra
　　lumen, et in solis tu mihi turba locis.
nunc licet e caelo mittatur amica Tibullo,
　　mittetur frustra, deficietque Venus.

13. 8. ille ω ipse O.

3. Cf. Prop. 2, 7, 19: *tu mihi
sola places: placeam tibi, Cynthia,
solus*; Ovid, *A. A.* 1, 42: *elige cui
dicas 'tu mihi sola places.'*
4. **formosa**: cf. Cat. 86.
6. **sic**: 'only in that case.' —
ero: the rapid increase of hope, as
Tibullus dwells on the thought,
is expressed by the changing
tenses and moods: *posses* (impossible), *displiceas* (possible), *ero*
(probable, taken for granted).
7. **opus**: sc. *mihi*. — **gloria**:
sc. *tua*.
8. Cf. Prop. 2, 25, 30: *in tacito
cohibe gaudia clausa sinu*; Némethy, pp. 297, 339.
9. **sic**: *i.e.* if safe in the pos-
session of thy love.
11. Cf. Prop. 1, 11, 23–24;
Hom. *Il.* 6, 429–430:

Ἕκτορ, ἀτὰρ σύ μοί ἐσσι πατὴρ καὶ
πότνια μήτηρ,

ἠδὲ κασίγνητος, σὺ δέ μοι θαλερὸς
παρακοίτης·

A similar mood appears in
Shakespeare, *Sonnets*, 91: "Thy
love is better than high birth to
me, Richer than wealth, prouder
than garments' cost, Of more delight than hawks or horses be; And
having thee, of all men's pride I
boast." 43: "All days are nights
to see till I see thee, And nights
bright days when dreams do show
thee me." 112: "You are my all
the world."

13. **e caelo**: *i.e.* even a goddess. — **Tibullo**: the use of his
own name emphasizes the contrast between his humble self
(poor Tibullus) and the divine
mistress from the skies. Cf. Hor.
Sat. 2, 1, 18: *Flacci verba per
attentam non ibunt Caesaris
aurem.*

15   hoc tibi sancta tuae Iunonis numina iuro,
         quae sola ante alios est mihi magna deos.
      quid facio demens? heu heu mea pignora cedo.
         iuravi stulte: proderat iste timor.
      nunc tu fortis eris, nunc tu me audacius ures:
20   hoc peperit misero garrula lingua malum.
      iam faciam quodcumque voles, tuus usque manebo,
         nec fugiam notae servitium dominae,
      sed Veneris sanctae considam vinctus ad aras.
         haec notat iniustos supplicibusque favet.

15. hoc **A** hec **V**.

15. Iunonis: cf. 4, 6, 1, n. —
numina: the omission of *per*
occurs mostly in the poets.
    17. pignora: *i.e. iste timor* of
v. 18 ('that anxiety of yours'
for fear of losing my affection),
which acts as a safeguard to your
constancy.

    19. nunc: 'now' that I have
declared myself thus.
    23. vinctus: as a willing slave.
    24. notat: cf. 1, 8, 5: *ipsa
Venus magico religatum bracchia
nodo perdocuit multis non sine
verberibus*.

PROPERTIUS MSS. SIGNS

N = Codex Neapolitanus (or Guelferbytanus).
A = Codex Vossianus (ends with 2, 1, 63).
F = Codex Laurentianus (or Florentinus).
L = Codex Holkhamicus (begins with 2, 21, 3).
D = Codex Daventriensis (begins with 1, 2, 14).
V = Codex Ottoboniano-Vaticanus.
O = consensus of the foregoing, as a rule, of all, so far as extant.

N₁, N₂, N₃, N₄, A₁, A₂, etc., = the 1st, 2d, 3d, etc., hands in the respec‐tive Mss.

ω = late or inferior Mss., or corrections.

SEXTI PROPERTI

ELEGIARVM

LIBER PRIMVS

I

Cynthia prima suis miserum me cepit ocellis,
  contactum nullis ante cupidinibus.
tum mihi constantis deiecit lumina fastus

Apparently written as an introduction to this "Cynthia Monobiblos."

1–8: 'Cynthia was the first
woman to bring me to her feet.
9–18: Milanion won Atalanta by
persistence and by enduring hardships for her sake; but Cupid has
failed to teach me to succeed.
19–28: I would resort to anything to rid myself of my anguish,
magic rites to win the affections
of my mistress, or heroic treatment to be free from her power.
29–38: Bear me away, friends,
where no woman can ever come;
remain, you who are well matched,
but see that you escape the torture
under which I suffer, or you will
wish you had heeded my warn-
ings!'

Note the riming endings of

the two halves of vv. 1, 6, 7,
8, 12, etc.; for other metrical
features cf. Intr. § 42.

1. **Cynthia**: cf. Intr. § 33.
This first word furnishes a correct
keynote to the whole book. —
prima: only in the usual sense
of lover's protestations; cf. 3, 15,
3–6. Propertius, however, doubtless never had been so completely
enthralled by any other mistress.
— ocellis = *oculis*; not at all a
fond lover's diminutive; Propertius is not in a flattering mood.

2. **ante**: used as an adjective.
Cf. 1, 22, 2, n.

3–4: Cupid is represented as
engaging in an actual struggle
with the poet, as in an arena,
wherein the victor's success is
marked by the actions indicated
by *deiecit* and *pressit*. — **constantis**
. . . **fastus**: gen. of description;
his former pride is now broken.

et caput inpositis pressit Amor pedibus,
5 donec me docuit castas odisse puellas
  inprobus et nullo vivere consilio:
et mihi iam toto furor hic non deficit anno,
  cum tamen adversos cogor habere deos.
Milanion nullos fugiendo, Tulle, labores
10 saevitiam durae contudit Iasidos.
nam modo Partheniis amens errabat in antris,
  ibat et hirsutas ille videre feras:
ille etiam Hylaei percussus vulnere rami
  saucius Arcadiis rupibus ingemuit.
15 ergo velocem potuit domuisse puellam:
  tantum in amore preces et benefacta valent.
in me tardus Amor non ullas cogitat artes,
  nec meminit notas, ut prius, ire vias.

---

6. inprobus: 'the naughty wretch.' — **nullo vivere consilio:** *i.e.* a reckless life of wantonness.

7. mihi: emphatic; the case may be different with Cynthia. — **anno:** this is apparently written at the end of a year of enforced separation from Cynthia, perhaps that referred to in 3, 16, 9.

8. cum: concessive, with the indicative mood; cf. H. 599, 1.

9. Tulle: cf. 1, 6, Intr.

10. Iasidos: Atalanta of Arcadia (not to be confused with the Boeotian heroine of the same name), whose suitor was Milanion.

11. modo: we should expect a corresponding *modo* in v. 13, where *etiam* is substituted. — **Partheniis:** the slopes of Mt. Parthe-nium (or Parthenius) were on the border between Arcadia and Argolis. — **antris:** a popular word with Propertius, with rather vague signification; cf. 1, 2, 11; 4, 4, 3; not found in Tibullus.

12. videre: purpose inf.; cf. 1, 6, 33.

13. Hylaei: probably an adjective. Hylaeus was a centaur. — **rami:** centaurs are represented as using rude clubs for weapons; the more hasty their preparation, the more nearly would these clubs approximate the unformed branch of a tree.

15. domuisse: cf. Tib. 1, 1, 29, n.

17. in me: 'in my case.' — **tardus:** belongs closely with *cogitat*; 'is slow to think of.'

at vos, deductae quibus est fallacia lunae
20   et labor in magicis sacra piare focis,
en agedum dominae mentem convertite nostrae,
        et facite illa meo palleat ore magis.
tunc ego crediderim vobis et sidera et amnes
        posse Cytaeines ducere carminibus.
25   aut vos, qui sero lapsum revocatis, amici,
        quaerite non sani pectoris auxilia.
fortiter et ferrum, saevos patiemur et ignes,
        sit modo libertas quae velit ira loqui.
ferte per extremas gentes et ferte per undas,
30   qua non ulla meum femina norit iter.
vos remanete, quibus facili deus adnuit aure,
        sitis et in tuto semper amore pares.
in me nostra Venus noctes exercet amaras,
        et nullo vacuus tempore defit amor.
35   hoc, moneo, vitate malum : sua quemque moretur

1. 24. Cytaeines *or* Cytaines *Hertzberg* Cytaeinis ω Cythalinis **N** Cytalinis
V Citalinis **F** Cythainis **N**₂ Cytaeaeis *Guyetus.*   25. aut *Hemsterhusius* at **F**₂
et **O**.   33. noctes **O** voces *Postgate.*

19. **fallacia**: ' the pretense ' ; a
common one ; cf. 2, 28, 37 ; Hor.
Epod. 5, 45 ; Verg. *Ec.* 8, 69 :
carmina vel caelo possunt de-
ducere Lunam.
22. **palleat**: a common token
of being in love. The masks in
ancient comedy are said to have
represented lovers thus.
23. **tunc** = *si id feceritis.*
24. **posse**: the expected subject, *vos*, is found in the dative
with *crediderim.* — **Cytaeines** =
Medea, who was born at Cytae; she
is the typical witch. The form is
a patronymic.

25. **lapsum:** ' a ruined man.'
26. **non:** ' no longer.' — **au-**
xilia: ' remedy.'
27. **ferrum ... ignes:** the sur-
geon's knife, or the physician's
cauterization.
28. **loqui:** for the inf. with
libertas, cf. 3, 15, 4 : *data libertas*
noscere amoris iter.
32. **tuto:** ' faithful ' ; cf. Hor.
Car. 1, 27, 18 : *depone tutis auri-*
bus. — **pares:** ' well-mated.'
33. **in me:** cf. v. 17. — **nostra :**
cf. *nobis,* 1, 12, 2. — **exercet :**
' makes restless.'
34. **vacuus :** ' unsatisfied.'

cura, neque adsueto mutet amore locum.
quod siquis monitis tardas adverterit aures,
heu referet quanto verba dolore mea !

2

Quid iuvat ornato procedere, vita, capillo
et tenues Coa veste movere sinus,
aut quid Orontea crines perfundere murra,
teque peregrinis vendere muneribus,
5   naturaeque decus mercato perdere cultu,
nec sinere in propriis membra nitere bonis ?

---

36. cura = *amica*; frequently so; cf. Verg. *Ec.* 10, 22 : *tua cura Lycoris*; Ovid, *Am.* 3, 9, 32; Pichon *s.v.*

38. referet: 'recall.'

1, 2

1–6: 'Why prefer borrowed finery to your native beauty, Cynthia? **7–24**: Neither Cupid himself, nor the flowers and birds, nor the heroines of the olden days have ever done so. **25–32**: Surely you do not think me less worthy than the lovers of those days; if you are perfect in one lover's eyes, it is enough; of course you are; for have you not all the gifts bestowed by Phoebus, Venus, and Minerva?'

1. ornato . . . capillo: for the highly artificial methods of wearing and adorning the hair at Rome,

cf. B. *G.*, p. 739; Baum., pp. 619, 792. — **procedere**: 'appear,' *i.e.* to "show off"; cf. Tib. 4, 2, 11; Hor. *Epod.* 4, 7–8. — **vita**: cf. Cat. 109, 1.

2. Coa . . . sinus: 'rustle the delicate folds of your Coan robe' (C. S.). These notorious gauzy silken fabrics were adopted to reveal rather than conceal the person of their wearer. Cf. 2, 1, 5–6; Tib. 2, 3, 53.

3. Orontea: *i.e.* from Antioch on the Orontes, an important center of this trade.

4. te: the emphasis is on this word: 'to sell (exchange) your own sweet *self* for foreign-bought adornments.' The idea is repeated under different forms in vv. 5 and 6.

5. mercato: L. 1492.

6. propriis . . . bonis: 'natural charms.'

crede mihi, non ulla tuae est medicina figurae:
nudus Amor formae non amat artificem.

adspice quos submittat humus formosa colores,
10   ut veniant hederae sponte sua melius,
surgat et in solis formosius arbutus antris,
et sciat indociles currere lympha vias.
litora nativis persuadent picta lapillis,
et volucres nulla dulcius arte canunt.
15   non sic Leucippis succendit Castora Phoebe,
Pollucem cultu non Hilaira soror,
non Idae et cupido quondam discordia Phoebo

---

2. 7. tuae est **DV** tua est (= tuaest?) **AFN.**   9. quos **O** quot **ω** quo *Lachmann.*   10. ut *Itali* et **O.**   13. persuadent **O** persudant **V₂** collucent **ω** praefulgent *Baehrens* praelucent *Hertzberg.*

---

7. **medicina figurae:** *i.e.* it cannot be improved upon.

8. **nudus Amor:** the highest type of beauty, and therefore in need of no artificial adornment.

9. Cf. Matt. 6, 28–29: "Consider the lilies," etc.

10. **veniant:** 'come,' in the sense of 'shoot,' or 'grow,' is good English; cf. *Cent. Dict. s.v.* 4; Verg. *Georg.* 2, 11; 1, 54.

11. **antris:** here nearly equal to *convallibus* (C. S.); cf. 1, 1, 11, n. Did Gray have this in mind in the *Elegy*, 54: "The dark, unfathom'd caves of ocean bear: Full many a flower is born to blush unseen," etc?

12. **indociles:** antithetic with *sciat* (C. S.); it here = *non doctas*, a ἅπαξ λεγόμενον. Cf. Cic. *Acad.* 2, 1, 2.

13. **persuadent:** used absolutely; 'allure,' it may be to wander along the beach, it may be to slumber; cf. Hor. *Epod.* 2, 25–28. Note the admirable onomatopoetic alliteration of the verse. Cf. Ovid, *Am.* 2, 11, 13: *nec medius tenuis conchas pictosque lapillos pontus habet: bibuli litoris illa morast.*

14. **nulla . . arte:** 'because art is lacking' (C. S.). The abl. abs. expresses the cause.

15. **sic:** explained by the epexegetical *cultu* in v. 16. — The two daughters of Leucippus, Phoebe and Hilaïra, having been betrothed to Lynceus and Idas, were carried off by Castor and Pollux (C. S.).

17. **non:** *i.e. non sic.* — **discordia.** See Harper's *Lex. s.v.* B. 1.

Eueni patriis filia litoribus,
nec Phrygium falso traxit candore maritum
20   avecta externis Hippodamia rotis :
sed facies aderat nullis obnoxia gemmis,
qualis Apelleis est color in tabulis.
non illis studium vulgo conquirere amantes :
illis ampla satis forma pudicitia.
25   non ego nunc vereor ne sim tibi vilior istis :

18. Eueni . . . filia: Marpessa, the most beautiful of all the women of her age, was the wife of Idas. Apollo seized and carried her off. Idas pursued him, and Zeus sent Hermes to settle the quarrel. He gave Marpessa her choice between the rivals, and she chose Idas. Her father, disconsolate from her loss, threw himself into the Lycormas River, which thenceforth took his name (C. S.).

19. Phrygium . . . maritum: Pelops, see H. & T. § 130. — **falso**: 'artificial' (C. S.). — **traxit**: see Lex. *s.v.* 2, A. 1.

20. avecta: *i.e.* carried back home to Pisa to be the bride of Pelops. -- **externis**: 'a stranger's,' *i.e.* Pelops's. Cf. 2, 32, 31 : *Tyndaris externo patriam mutavit amore*. Ovid, in his imitative passage (*A. A.* 2, 8), uses an epithet less harsh: *vecta peregrinis Hippodamia rotis*.

21. facies: 'beauty'; cf. Ovid, *A. A.* 3, 105 : *cura dabit faciem*. — **obnoxia**: 'indebted' (C. S.).

22. Apelleis . . . tabulis: the subjects of Apelles's paintings were usually nude. The natural richness of the complexion (*color*) was brought out in his portraits, hence the force of the comparison. Aphrodite coming forth from the sea was his masterpiece, and the admiration of all antiquity. Cf. 3, 9, 11.

23. non illis studium (sc. *erat*): the reason follows in v. 24.

24. forma = *facies* in v. 21. — With this whole passage cf. Sen. *Cons. ad Helviam*, chap. 16, a passage which was evidently an outgrowth of this poem : *non te maximum saeculi malum, inpudicitia, in numerum plurium adduxit : non gemmae te, non margaritae flexerunt. . . . non faciem coloribus ac lenociniis polluisti : numquam tibi placuit vestis, quae nihil amplius nudaret, cum poneretur ; unicum tibi ornamentum pulcherrima et nulli obnoxia aetati forma, maximum decus visa est pudicitia.*

25. non ego nunc vereor: cf. 1, 6, 1 ; 1, 19, 1. — **tibi**: 'in your eyes.' Cf. 1, 8, 2. — **istis** refers to *amantes* (v. 23), for whom those heroines disdained to prink.

uni siqua placet, culta puella sat est;
cum tibi praesertim Phoebus sua carmina donet
    Aoniamque libens Calliopea lyram,
unica nec desit iucundis gratia verbis,
    omnia quaeque Venus quaeque Minerva probat.
his tu semper eris nostrae gratissima vitae,
    taedia dum miserae sint tibi luxuriae.

6

Non ego nunc Hadriae vereor mare noscere tecum,
    Tulle, neque Aegaeo ducere vela salo,

26. *I.e.* let this rather be your conviction.

27. cum tibi praesertim : 'and this is especially true in your case, for,' etc. — **carmina** : 'power of song.' Cf. Pott's *Lat. Prose Comp.*, p. 32 (C. S.).

28. Aoniam : *i.e.* Boeotian, of the land of Helicon and the Muses, among whom Calliope holds the first place. Cf. Milton's *Par. Lost*, I, 14 : "to soar above the Aonian mount." — **Calliopea** : this form occurs in Vergil and Ovid; also, cf. 3, 3, 38, n.

29. verbis : sc. *tuis*. Propertius often refers to the fact that Cynthia was a *docta puella*. Cf. I, 7, 11, n.

30. Sc. *adsint*; cf. 4, 1, 17–19. There are several examples of this sort of brachyology in Propertius. — **Minerva** : in her capacity as patroness of feminine handiwork.

31. nostrae . . . vitae : more emphatic than *nobis* would be. Cf. Plaut. *Men.* 675 : *aetati tuae*.

I, 6

The reason why Propertius cannot accept the invitation of Tullus to accompany him to the East. The same Tullus, to whom this first book of Propertius is dedicated, and who appears to have been a most intimate friend, is addressed also in I, I, 9; 14, 20; 22, I ; 3, 22, 2. He is believed to have been a nephew of L. Volcatius Tullus, and had doubtless asked Propertius to go with him to Asia in his uncle's train. As the latter was consul in 33 B.C. and, according to the *Lex Pompeia de iure magistratuum*, a provincial command could not be assumed till five years after the end of the year of office, the date of his departure for the East, and of this poem, was probably about 27 B.C.

The obvious similarity of the theme to that of Tibullus I, I, serves to emphasize the differences between the poets and their loves.

cum quo Rhipaeos possim conscendere montes,
   ulteriusque domos vadere Memnonias:
5 sed me conplexae remorantur verba puellae,
   mutatoque graves saepe colore preces.
illa mihi totis argutat noctibus ignes,

Tibullus does not wish to leave home and Delia; Propertius, with a sigh, admits that he dare not meet the tirade of reproaches with which Cynthia would inevitably receive the announcement of such a purpose. These early poems of the Cynthia book suffice to show that Propertius already felt the attachment often a grievous burden, yet one which he could not bring himself to lay down; a situation in many respects similar to that existing between Catullus and Lesbia.

1–6: 'Not the dangers of the deep, but the words of my mistress hold me back, Tullus, from sailing with you. 7–18: Her complaints are unendurable; I would rather give up seeing the wonders of the world than risk them. 19–24: Go! win your spurs; for Cupid has not yet aimed his shafts at you. 25–30: But I am not for deeds of glory. 31–36: Where'er you go, forget not my unlucky star!'

1. **vereor**: of the awesome respect of the Romans often expressed for the sea. Cf. Hor. *Car.* 1, 3; Luc. 3, 193 sqq.; Petron. (Baehrens *PLM.*, Vol. 4, p. 94).

2. **ducere vela** = *navigare.* — **salo**: a favorite word with Proper-

tius; cf. 1, 15, 12; 3, 13, 6; 3, 7, 40. Poetic abl. of place.

3. **cum quo . . . possim**: 'for with thee I could.'— **Rhipaeos**: the mention of the extreme regions of cold and heat is frequently paralleled in the poets of this age, *e.g.* Hor. *Car.* 1, 22, 17–24. Cf. Cat. 11. 1–14.

4. **ulterius**: the narrowness of the line distinguishing adverb and preposition is well illustrated in this use of the comp. adv. for the positive *ultra* as a preposition with acc. — **domos . . . Memnonias**: *i.e.* Aethiopia.

5. Cf. Tib. 1, 1, 55.

6. **mutato . . . colore**: perhaps the best commentary is 1, 15, 39: *quis te cogebat multos pallere colores*, referring to alternating blushes and pallor. Cf. 1, 18, 17. — **saepe** belongs to *mutato.*

7. **illa**: note the eager repetition of the pronoun, in contrast with the personal pronouns with which this short poem abounds. — **totis . . . noctibus**: duration of time. — **argutat**: an impatient and not very gallant term. The verb is usually deponent and intransitive, but here has *ignes* (*i.e. amorem*) as an object. Cf. Verg. *Aen.* 4, 2; Ovid, *Trist.* 4, 10, 45: *saepe suos solitus recitare Proper-*

et queritur nullos esse relicta deos :
illa meam mihi iam se denegat : illa minatur,
10   quae solet ingrato tristis amica viro.
his ego non horam possum durare querellis :
ah pereat, siquis lentus amare potest !
an mihi sit tanti doctas cognoscere Athenas
atque Asiae veteres cernere divitias,
15   ut mihi deducta faciat convicia puppi
Cynthia et insanis ora notet manibus,
osculaque opposito dicat sibi debita vento,
et nihil infido durius esse viro ?
tu patrui meritas conare anteire secures,
20   et vetera oblitis iura refer sociis :

---

6. 10. ingrato *Itali* irato **O.**

---

tius ignes; Novius, *Exodio apud Non.* (Mueller, p. 376): *totum diem argutatus quasi cicada.*

8. Cf. 3, 7, 18.

11. his . . . querellis : dat. with *durare* (= *durus esse*), 'be insensible to.'

12. lentus : 'unresponsive.' Cf. Ovid, *Her.* 15, 169: *amor tetigit lentissima Pyrrhae pectora.* This verse gives the key to the career of Propertius.

13. doctas : a natural epithet; cf. 3, 21, 1.

15. deducta : the ships were drawn up on the shore in winter, and launched again when a journey was to begin. Cf. Hor. *Car.* 1, 4, 2 : *trahuntque siccas machinae carinas.*

16. ora notet manibus : cf. Tib. 1, 1, 68 ; 10, 37.

17. opposito : *i e.* she may tell her grievance to the wind that blows in her face, perhaps as she gazes after the vanishing ship that bears away her lover. — **debita** : still ' due ' from her lover.

19. tu, like the *tua* in v. 21 and the *tibi* in v. 23, serves to emphasize the contrast with *me* in v. 25. Cf. the thought with Tib. 1, 1, 53–55. — **patrui** : see introduction to this poem. — **meritas** : a complimentary epithet. — **anteire** : 'surpass.'—**secures** : *i.e.* the greatness which the official axes symbolized.

20. vetera . . . iura : many Asiatic peoples had formerly been true to their Roman allies, before the political anarchy which for a time intervened during the civil wars.

nam tua non aetas umquam cessavit amori,
    semper at armatae cura fuit patriae,
et tibi non umquam nostros puer iste labores
    adferat et lacrimis omnia nota meis.
25   me sine, quem semper voluit Fortuna iacere,
    hanc animam extremae reddere nequitiae.
multi longinquo periere in amore libenter,
    in quorum numero me quoque terra tegat.
non ego sum laudi, non natus idoneus armis:
30   hanc me militiam fata subire volunt.
at tu seu mollis qua tendit Ionia seu qua
    Lydia Pactoli tingit arata liquor,
seu pedibus terras seu pontum carpere remis
    ibis, et accepti pars eris imperii,

22. at O et ω.

21. **aetas** = *vita*. — **cessavit**: 'has had leisure for.'

22. **at**: for the position cf. 3, 5, 14; Verg. *Ec.* 7, 67: *saepius at.* — **cura**: sc. *tua* or *tibi*; the State had been his mistress. Cf. Tac. *Ann.* 4, 8, 4: *e complexu rei publicae.*

23. **puer**: Amor. — **iste** is more expressive than translatable.

25. **iacere**: 'take life easy.' Cf. Cic. *Phil.* 10, 7, 14: *in pace iacere quam in bello vigere maluit. quamquam ille quidem numquam iacuit.*

26. **hanc animam**: 'this life of mine.' — **nequitiae**: 'wanton worthlessness.'

29. Cf. Tib. 1, 1, 57. — **laudi**: *i.e.* military glory.

30. **hanc . . . militiam**: *i.e.* the service of my mistress. Cf. Tib. 1, 1, 75.

31. **mollis . . . Ionia**: cf. Verg. *Georg.* 1, 57: *molles sua tura Sabaei.*

32. **Pactoli**: the proverbial river which contributed so greatly in legend to the fabulous riches of Lydia. Cf. the modern verse: "Where Afric's sunny fountains roll down their golden sands." — **arata** (sc. *loca*) = *arva*. — **liquor**: cf. 3, 18, 28.

33. **carpere**: cf. 1, 1, 12, n.

34. **accepti**: *i.e.* by the peoples who soon would be under *pax Romana* in Asia. — **pars**: Tullus would naturally hold some office under his uncle's control.

35 tum tibi siqua mei veniet non inmemor hora,
    vivere me duro sidere certus eris.

7

Dum tibi Cadmeae dicuntur, Pontice, Thebae
  armaque fraternae tristia militiae,
atque, ita sim felix, primo contendis Homero,
  sint modo fata tuis mollia carminibus,
5 nos, ut consuemus, nostros agitamus amores,

---

36. duro sidere: cf. 4, 1, 150;
Ovid, *Trist.* 5, 10, 45: *tam grave
sidus.* Astrology and its language
were at this time much in vogue.
We still exclaim: "My lucky
stars!"

1, 7

1–14: 'You are writing great
epics, Ponticus, while I am busy
only with my love, and from thence
must hope for inspiration and
future fame. 15–26: But if per-
chance Cupid should turn his bow
upon you, how you would envy
me, in vain, and wish, too late,
to write elegy also! So, beware!'

1. Cf. Ovid, *Am.* 2, 18, 1–4;
Anacreontea, 23, 1: θέλω λέγειν
'Ατρείδας, θέλω δὲ Κάδμον ᾄδειν,
ἁ βάρβιτος δὲ χορδαῖς Ἔρωτα
μοῦνον ἠχεῖ.— **tibi**: poetic dat. for
abl. of agent. — **Cadmeae**: Cadmus was the legendary founder of
Thebes. — **dicuntur**: cf. Tib. 1, 3,

31. — **Pontice**: Ponticus was one
of the few literary friends whom
Propertius felt free to address
familiarly. His fame as an epic
poet rests mainly upon this passage
and 1, 9, 9, together with Ovid,
Trist. 4, 10, 47: *Ponticus heroo,
Bassus quoque clarus iambis.* —
Thebae: many a "Thebais" was
attempted by the Roman poets;
only that of Statius has survived.

2. fraternae: *i.e.* of Eteocles
and Polynices. Cf. H. & T.
§ 171.

3. ita sim felix: cf. Tib. 2, 5,
63, n. — **primo**: so acknowledged
now nearly three millenniums! —
Homero: the rare poetic dat. with
contendo occurs also in 1, 14, 7.

5. consuēmus = *consuevimus:*
the other syncopated forms of the
perf. are more common. Cf., as
other examples of this tendency in
Propertius, 2, 7, 2: *flemus = flevi-
mus;* 2, 15, 3: *narramus = nar-
ravimus;* 9: *mutamus = muta-*

atque aliquid duram quaerimus in dominam:
nec tantum ingenio quantum servire dolori
   cogor et aetatis tempora dura queri.
hic mihi conteritur vitae modus, haec mea famast,
10   hinc cupio nomen carminis ire mei.
me laudent doctae solum placuisse puellae,
   Pontice, et iniustas saepe tulisse minas:
me legat adsidue post haec neglectus amator,
   et prosint illi cognita nostra mala.
15 te quoque si certo puer hic concusserit arcu,

vimus. — amores: the plural emphasizes the varying phases of his passion.

6. aliquid: *i.e.* some poetic appeal to her fancy. — duram: cf. the preceding elegy. — in dominam: the preposition implies purpose. This use with both *in* and *ad* is unusually common in Propertius, there being all together some 40 cases, of which more than half are with *in*, which is elsewhere rare in this signification. For a complete list of the examples cf. the editor's collection in *PAPA.*, Vol. 28 (1897), p. xxiii.

7. ingenio: an implication that his own taste might lead him to greater themes, were he not absorbed in his passion. Such a claim is justified by Book 4.

9. hic . . . haec . . . hinc: emphatic repetition of the subject of his poetry, viz. his love.

10. nomen: 'glory.' The wish has been fulfilled; cf. the phrase "Cynthia Monobiblos."

11. laudent: the subject is indefinite. — doctae . . . puellae: the same epithet is applied to Cynthia in 2, 11, 6 and 2, 13, 11, doubtless because she herself wrote poetry; cf. 1, 2, 27-28. Catullus (65, 2) uses the term of the Muses themselves. — solum: so far as his poetic offerings were concerned, Propertius surely could win over all rivals for Cynthia's favor; but the poet hopes for a unique affection also. Cf. 2, 7, 19: *tu mihi sola places: placeam tibi, Cynthia, solus.*

12. iniustas . . . minas: cf. Intr. to 1, 6, *ad fin.*

14. cognita nostra mala: cf. previous note.

15. te: by attraction for the emphatic *tu* which we should expect here as the subject of *flebis.* — certo: cf. 2, 12, 9-12; Ovid, *Am.* 1, 1, 25. — puer hic: cf. 1, 6, 23, n.; 3, 10, 28: *quem gravibus pennis verberet ille puer*; in this case the pronoun is determined by the contrast between the experience of the speaker and his friend.

quod nolim nostros eviolasse deos,
  longe castra tibi, longe miser agmina septem
flebis in aeterno surda iacere situ,
  et frustra cupies mollem conponere versum,

20   nec tibi subiciet carmina serus Amor.
tum me non humilem mirabere saepe poetam:
  tunc ego Romanis praeferar ingeniis,
nec poterunt iuvenes nostro reticere sepulcro
  'ardoris nostri magne poeta, iaces.'

25   tu cave nostra tuo contemnas carmina fastu:
  saepe venit magno fenore tardus Amor.

---

7. 16. quod **O** quo *Codex Barberinus.* eviolasse **O** evoluisse *or* te violasse *Itali* evoluisse *Canter* quam nolis . . . heu violasse *Heinsius* quam nolim . . . te violasse . . . ! *Rothstein.*

16. 'Though I should be sorry to have my patron divinities do such a dastardly deed.' — **quod**: poetic cognate acc. — **nostros**: Venus and Amor. — **eviolasse**: intensive compound. The variant reading *evoluisse* would be properly used only of the Parcae.

17. **longe**: 'sorely.' — **castra . . . agmina**: cf. vv. 1–2.

19. **mollem**: a common epithet of elegiac verse as distinguished from heroic measures. Cf. Intr. § 3. Perhaps both the metrical weakening (shortening) of the alternate verse and the character of the subject matter are implied in the term. Cf. 2, 1, 19–20; 2, 1, 2; 2, 34, 43–44; Dom. Marsus,

Ep.: ne foret, aut elegis molles qui fleret amores aut caneret forti regia bella pede.

20. **subiciet**: 'suggest'; cf. Livy, 3, 48, 8: *clamitant matronae . . . cetera, quae . . . dolor . . . subicit.* — **serus**: the reason.

21. **non humilem**: *i.e.* the relative situation of Ponticus and Propertius will be reversed.

22. **ingeniis**: 'men of genius'; cf. English, 'a genius.' Rare in this concrete sense.

23. **reticere**: 'keep from exclaiming.'

26. **fenore tardus**: cf. Ovid, *Her.* 4, 19: *venit Amor gravius, quo serius.*

213

8

Tune igitur demens, nec te mea cura moratur?
  an tibi sum gelida vilior Illyria,
et tibi iam tanti, quicumque est, iste videtur,
  ut sine me vento quolibet ire velis?
5   tune audire potes vesani murmura ponti
  fortis, et in dura nave iacere potes?
tu pedibus teneris positas fulcire pruinas,
  tu potes insolitas, Cynthia, ferre nives?

1, 8

1-8: 'Are you beside yourself, Cynthia, to abandon me for such a fellow, and with him to brave wind and weather? 9-16: May the tempests of winter prevent your sailing and my grieving. 17-26: But if you go, may safety attend you; for I shall ever be faithful, and know that you are still destined for me.' Cf. Vahlen, "Ueber zwei Elegien des Propertius," in *Sitz. d. Kgl. Pr. Akad. d. Wiss.* 1882, pp. 262-280.

1. igitur: we are introduced to the situation not at the beginning, but toward the conclusion of the poet's meditations. Cf. 3, 7, 1. — mea: better taken in the objective sense. Cf. 1, 15, 31: *tua sub nostro . . . pectore cura.*

2. tibi: 'in your eyes.' — gelida: a stock epithet of depreciation; cf. Hor. *Car.* 4, 5, 25: *quis Parthum paveat, quis gelidum Scythen.* Propertius naturally desires to exaggerate the severity of the climate as he does further in

vv. 7-9. — Illyria: poetic tor *Illyrico.*

3. iam: implying a sudden development of the passion. — quicumque est, iste: an assumption of contemptuous ignorance. Of course the person is the "praetor." Cf. 2, 16, 1.

4. vento quolibet: the abandon of the lover.

5. tune: the emphatic pronoun used here and repeatedly in the following verses calls attention to the absurdity of the idea that so luxurious a lady as Cynthia should plan so rough an experience.

6. dura: Propertius seems to be thinking of the planks as the only bed on shipboard. But the sailors' comforts would contrast sharply with the pampered life of Cynthia. Cf. Hor. *Car.* 2, 13, 27: *dura navis, dura fugae mala, dura belli.*

7. pedibus teneris: cf. Verg. *Ec.* 10, 49: *ah, tibi ne teneras glacies secet aspera plantas!* — positas . . . pruinas: the fallen snow, as distinguished from the

o utinam hibernae duplicentur tempora brumae,
10   et sit iners tardis navita vergiliis,
nec tibi Tyrrhena solvatur funis harena,
    neve inimica meas elevet aura preces,
atque ego non videam tales subsidere ventos,
    cum tibi provectas auferet unda rates,
15   ut me defixum vacua patiatur in ora
    crudelem infesta saepe vocare manu.
sed quocumque modo de me, periura, mereris,

8. 15. ut *Hemsterhusius* et **O.**

falling snow (*nives*) in the next
verse. — **fulcire**: 'tread firmly.'
For an attempted justification of
this unique usage see Postgate,
Prop., Appendix B.

9. hibernae: 'stormy'; cf.
Verg. *Aen.* 5, 126; *hiberni con-*
dunt ubi sidera Cori; Hor. *Epod.*
15, 8: *turbaret hibernum mare.*

10. tardis . . . vergiliis: causal;
the adjective has a predicate force.
The rising of the Pleiades was the
signal for the safe opening of the
navigation season.

11. Tyrrhena: the praetor, a
Roman official, would be more apt
to sail from the station of the
Roman fleet at Ostia, than from
Brindisi. — For the meter, cf. Intr.
§ 42, I (4). In imagination the
poet sees the whole picture of the
proposed departure, and utters a
succession of wishes that the various details of it one by one may
not be realized in fact.

12. inimica: used as a part of
the predicate. — **elevet**: 'mock'
(make light of).

13. ego . . . videam: if it must
happen, may *I* never live to see
the day. — **tales**: *i.e.* such as are
described or implied in the preceding verses.

14. This verse is equivalent to
a coördinate clause with the preceding.

15. defixum: petrified with
grief and despair, as he watches
the receding fleet. — **patiatur**: *i.e.*
be obliged to hear (sc. *unda*); cf.
Vahlen, *l. c.*, pp. 263 sqq.

16. crudelem probably refers
to *undam* to be supplied. It is
out of harmony with the general
absence of reproaches throughout
the poem that it should refer to a
te. Cf. Verg. *Ec.* 5, 23: *deos*
atque astra vocat crudelia mater.
— **infesta . . . manu**: the angry
shaking of the fist would have no
place here, if it referred to Cynthia
instead of the waves.

17. Under no conditions will a
like feeling of enmity (*infesta*) be
treasured against his darling, no
matter how he hates the cruel sea.

sit Galatea tuae non aliena viae,
 ut te, felici praevecta Ceraunia remo,
20 accipiat placidis Oricos aequoribus.
nam me non ullae poterunt corrumpere de te,
 quin ego, vita, tuo limine verba querar :
nec me deficiet nautas rogitare citatos
 'dicite, quo portu clausa puella meast ?'
25 et dicam ' licet Atraciis considat in oris,
 et licet Hylleis : illa futura meast.'

19. ut te **NAFV**₂ utere **DV**. 21. de te **O** taedae **ω**.

— **periura** : with concessive force :
'though you go back on all your
protestations.'

18. **Galatea** : a friendly sea
divinity, as were all the Nereids,
appropriately invoked as a type
of female beauty, and so presumably especially interested in
Cynthia. Cf. H. & T. 70 ; Ovid,
Am. 2, 11, 34 (this whole poem is
strongly imitative).

19. **praevecta** : voc. for acc.,
an extreme example of Propertius's
fondness for the vocative. Possibly *confisa* is a parallel, in 1, 11,
9. Cf. also 3, 22, 30 : *nec tremis
Ausonias, Phoebe fugate, dapes.*
Cf. Vahlen, *l. c.*, pp. 266 sqq. —
Ceraunia : the dangerous promontory Acroceraunia, behind which
lay the haven of Oricos (Ori-
cus, Oricum). Cf. Hor. *Car.*
I, 3, 20 : *infamis scopulos, Acroceraunia.*

21. **non ullae** : sc. *feminae* ; a
unique use of the fem. plur. ; but
cf. 4, 11, 50. — **corrumpere de te** :
cf. Plaut. *As.* 883 : *me ex amore
huius corruptum oppido.*

22. **verba querar** : cf. Ovid,
Met. 9, 303 : *moturaque duros
verba queror silices.*

23. **deficiet** with subject inf.
clause is a poet's way of saying
'I shall not fail to,' etc., a lover's
hyperbole. — **citatos** : 'hurrying' ;
cf. Sen. *Herc. Fur.* 178 : *properat
cursu vita citato* ; *Phaedra*, 1049 :
*pistrix citatas sorbet aut frangit
rates.*

25. **dicam** : *i.e.* in reply to the
answer of the sailors, whatever it
may be. — **Atraciis** : the only Atrax
historically known was in central
Thessaly. Either Propertius is
implying that it makes no difference whether Cynthia is in Illyria
or elsewhere, or in poetic hyperbole, or the usual geographical in-
exactness, he is stretching the
limits of Illyria as far eastward as
possible for the effect desired in
this contrast.

26. **Hylleis** : the name of a not
definitely located Illyrian tribe,
who traced their descent from
Hyllus, a son of Heracles by the
water nymph Melite. Cf. Apollon.

8b

Hic erit, hic iurata manet. rumpantur iniqui!
  vicimus : adsiduas non tulit illa preces
falsa licet cupidus deponat gaudia livor :
30   destitit ire novas Cynthia nostra vias.
illi carus ego et per me carissima Roma
  dicitur, et sine me dulcia regna negat.
illa vel angusto mecum requiescere lecto

27. *Divided from the foregoing by Lipsius. No break in* O.

Rhod. 4, 535–539 : ἀμφὶ πόλιν ἀγανὴν Ὑλληίδα . . . Ὕλλον, ὃν ἐνειδὴς Μελίτη τέκεν Ἡρακλῆι δήμῳ Φαιήκων. — illa futura meast : 'she is destined for me.'

1, 8 b

The sequel to the preceding poem, written as soon as Propertius learns the successful result of his petitions. 27–38 : 'Victory! Cynthia stays, and says she prefers me to all that kings could give. 39–42 : It was not by such offers that she was won, but by my potent verse. 43–46 : Now she is mine so long as life shall last.'

27. Hic . . . hic : the emphasis in the first overjoyed exclamations of delight is upon the thought that instead of wandering in the remote and vague regions just mentioned in the preceding poem, she is to be 'here.' **iurata** : 'she has taken her oath to.' Cf. v. 17 for the unrealized fear. — **rumpantur** :

cf. Hor. *Sat.* 1, 3, 135 : *miserque rumperis.*
28. adsiduas : 'importunate.' — **non tulit** : since they were irresistible.
29. falsa : 'groundless,' because based on a fear which is now not to become fact. — **gaudia** : jealousy dotes on every opportunity to gratify its passion. — **livor** : Propertius gloats over the *livor*, as if it had a personal and separate existence.
30. destitit : 'has given up her purpose.' — **nostra** : emphatic.
31. ego : sc. *dicor :* note the triumphant repetitions of the personal pronoun in these three verses.
32. sine me : cf. v. 4. — **dulcia** : sc. *esse.*
33. angusto : it is the slenderness of the circumstances of the owner that the poet means to imply. Cf. Sen. *Thyestes,* 452 : *scelera non intrant casas, tutusque mensa capitur angusta cibus.*

et quocumque modo maluit esse mea,
35   quam sibi dotatae regnum vetus Hippodamiae,
et quas Elis opes ante pararat equis.
quamvis magna daret, quamvis maiora daturus,
non tamen illa meos fugit avara sinus.
hanc ego non auro, non Indis flectere conchis,
40   sed potui blandi carminis obsequio.
sunt igitur musae, neque amanti tardus Apollo;
quis ego fretus amo : Cynthia rara meast.
nunc mihi summa licet contingere sidera plantis :

---

34. quocumque modo: cf. the phraseology of the marriage ritual : "for better, for worse, for richer, for poorer." Observe the triple rime; cf. Cholmeley, *Theocritus*, pp. 44 sq.

35. sibi: the force of the *esse* in the preceding verse is continued here.— **dotatae**: her *dos* was the *regnum* of her father, Oenomaus.

36. et: 'namely'; the verse explains further the meaning of *dotatae*. Cf. for this *et* 3, 7, 29. — **ante pararat**: 'has ever won.' Cf. 3, 11, 65 for the tense. — **equis**: as if Pelops and the other kir.gs of Elis had owned all the horses which during the centuries won the Olympian prizes!

37. daret: the rival. — **daturus**: sc. *esset;* 'would probably have given,' perhaps even 'promised to give.'

38. avara belongs to the predicate.

39. conchis: by metonymy for the pearl within. Cf. 3, 13, 6 : *et venit e rubro concha Erythraea*

salo; Tib. 3, 3, 17; 2, 4, 30 : *e rubro lucida concha mari;* Ovid, *Am.* 2, 11, 13.

40. blandi carminis: the previous poem answers the description, in its remarkable self-restraint and irresistible attraction. But Propertius may not refer to this poem alone. — **obsequio**: 'through obedience to the compelling power!' It is not the poet, but his mistress, that has obeyed.

41. sunt igitur musae: cf. 4, 7, 1 : *Sunt aliquid manes.*

42. quis = *quibus*. — **rara**: cf. 1, 17, 16.

43. summa: for there is nothing higher to mortal vision, or mortal ken. — **contingere sidera plantis**: Propertius outdoes his predecessors and his successors. We are content to be "on the mountain top." Horace's phrase for his hoped-for triumph is only *sublimi feriam sidera vertice* (*Car.* 1, 1, 36). But Propertius, the favored lover, is among the immortals, and, like theirs, his celes-

sive dies seu nox venerit, illa meast,
45   nec mihi rivalis certos subducit amores.
ista meam norit gloria canitiem.

9

Dicebam tibi venturos, inrisor, amores,
   nec tibi perpetuo libera verba fore:
ecce iaces supplexque venis ad iura puellae,
   et tibi nunc quaevis imperat empta modo.

9. 4. quaevis **O** quovis **V₂** quidvis *Postgate.*

tial steps are planted on the stars;
cf. Cat. 66, 69.

46. ista: the scornful pronoun
refers to the praetor's failure to
accomplish exactly what Propertius
had achieved: that glory which
my rival hoped for, viz. *subducere
amores*, is to be mine forever, in
having won it away from him for
all time.

I, 9

The sequel to I, 7. Ponticus
has indeed succumbed to Amor,
and Propertius prescribes elegiac
composition as likely to offer
relief. 1–8: 'I told you so;
you're dead in love, and all too
well I know what that means.
9–16: Of what avail are now your
epics? turn to elegy, for which,
fortunately, you are well equipped.
17–22: Your troubles are but just
begun. 23–32: Don't imagine
that you are master of the situation; Cupid is all-powerful, and
can do with you as he will.
33–34: So speak your woes in
verse.'

1. Dicebam: in I, 7. The formula for recalling a warning.
Cf. Ovid, *Am.* I, 14, 1: *Dicebam
'medicare tuos desiste capillos';*
Plaut. *As.* 938: *dicebam, pater,
tibi ne matri consuleres male.*

2. libera: *i.e.* because not re-
strained from scoffing by any
consciousness of being himself
vulnerable to a like attack.

3. iaces: 'are humbled.'—
venis ad iura: a legal formula,
of 'coming to court' (the pun is
English only), indicating, with
supplex, a complete dependence
upon the decision (or sentence?)
of the fair judge.

4. quaevis: Propertian ambiguity; best taken as acc. plur.—
modo: 'but yesterday'; *i.e.* the
girl is a *libertina*, or possibly still
even a slave.

5   non me Chaoniae vincant in amore columbae
        dicere quos iuvenes quaeque puella domet.
    me dolor et lacrimae merito fecere peritum :
        atque utinam posito dicar amore rudis !
    quid tibi nunc misero prodest grave dicere carmen
10   aut Amphioniae moenia flere lyrae?
    plus in amore valet Mimnermi versus Homero :
        carmina mansuetus lenia quaerit Amor.
    i quaeso et tristis istos conpone libellos,
        et cane quod quaevis nosse puella velit.

12. lenia ω levia O.

5. **me** : emphatic. — **Chaoniae** = *Epiroticae*. At Dodona in Epirus was a very celebrated ancient oracle of Zeus, to whom doves were originally sacred ; cf. *Jour. Hellen. Stud.*, Vol. 21 (1901), p. 105. — **vincant** : 'excel'; potential. — **columbae** : as sacred to Venus these oracular birds would be especially sure to hit the truth in matters of love.

6. **dicere** : poetic construction with *vincant* : cf. Sil. Ital. 6, 141 : *non ullo Libycis in finibus amne victus limosas extendere latius undas*.

7. **merito** : *i.e.* I have nobody to blame but myself.

8. **atque** : adversative. — **rudis** : cf. 2, 34, 82 : *sive in amore rudis sive peritus erit*.

9. **grave** : *i.e.* an epic.

10. Cf. 1, 7, 1, n. Amphion, one of the twin kings of Thebes, played so skillfully on the lyre given him by Hermes that the huge stones arranged themselves to form the city wall. — **flere** : cf. 3, 9, 37 ; Hor. *Epod.* 14, 11 : *cava testudine flevit amorem*.

11. **Mimnermi** : a venerable figure in the field of elegy, and the elegist who originated the erotic type. Cf. Intr. § 4. For his relation to Propertius cf. Wilamowitz in the *Sitz. d. Kgl. Pr. Akad. d. Wiss.* 1912, pp. 100 sqq. — **versus Homero** : the juxtaposition heightens the contrast between the single verse of the master of love elegies and Homer, epics and all !

13. **tristis** : cf. *flere*, v. 10. — **istos** : those worthless for the purpose to which you have been devoting yourself. — **conpone** : *i.e.* roll together and put away in their case. Cf. Hor. *Car.* 4, 14, 51 : *Sygambri conpositis venerantur armis* ; Cic. *Ad Fam.* 16, 20 : *libros conpone*. This verse, however, affords an elegant example of the characteristic ambiguity of our poet ; in another interpretation

15 quid si non esset facilis tibi copia? nunc tu
    insanus medio flumine quaeris aquam.
necdum etiam palles, vero nec tangeris igni:
    haec est venturi prima favilla mali.
tùm magis Armenias cupies accedere tigres
20   et magis infernae vincula nosse rotae,
quam pueri totiens arcum sentire medullis
    et nihil iratae posse negare tuae.
nullus Amor cuiquam facilis ita praebuit alas,
    ut non alterna presserit ille manu.

---

conpone = 'write,' cf. 1, 7, 19; then with **tristis** cf. Hor. *Car.* 1, 33, 2: *miserabiles elegos*; and **istos** = 'those which you have scorned.' — **libellos**: more common of a short poem. Cf. 2, 13, 25, n.

15. In such a case you would have more excuse for hesitation. — **copia**: *i.e.* 'facility' in composition.

16. The familiar fable of the thirsty sailors at the mouth of the Amazon is but a later adaptation of a classical commonplace. Cf. Ovid, *Trist.* 5, 4, 9: *nec frondem in silvis, nec aperto mollia prato gramina, nec pleno flumine cernit aquam.*

17. palles: cf. 1, 1, 22, n. — **igni**: of love.

18. prima favilla mali: the expression would well suit the usual phenomenon of a preliminary shower of ashes before a great volcanic eruption, familiar to the Romans of this period from frequent instances at Aetna and Stromboli. But probably Propertius is thinking only of the apparently lifeless ashes under which still lie dangerous fires, which may burn the curious meddler.

19. Armenias: a stock epithet to indicate ferocity. Cf. Tib. 3, 6, 15: Verg. *Ec.* 5, 29: Ovid, *Met.* 8, 121: *Armeniae tigres austroque agitata Charybdis.*

20. vincula: the brazen band with which Ixion was bound to the wheel. — **nosse**: *i.e.* experience.

21. pueri: Cupid.

22. iratae: *i.e.* whenever you are out of favor.

23. nullus: 'in no case.' — **facilis . . . alas**: the successful lover proverbially "treads on air." It is unnecessary to look for a reference to Cupid's own wings.

24. alterna (not *altera*): 'in turn.' The 'ups and downs' of love are equally certain. One moment the lover soars above the heads of ordinary mortals; the next, he falls to the ground in hu-

25   nec te decipiat, quod sit satis illa parata:
         acrius illa subit, Pontice, siqua tuast;
      quippe ubi non liceat vacuos seducere ocellos,
         nec vigilare alio nomine cedat Amor,
      qui non ante patet, donec manus attigit ossa.
30   quisquis es, adsiduas ah fuge blanditias.
      illis et silices possunt et cedere quercus;
         nedum tu possis, spiritus iste levis.
      quare, si pudor est, quam primum errata fatere:
         dicere, quo pereas, saepe in amore levat.

31. possunt et ω et possunt **DV** et possint **NAF**.

miliation and dejection. Which-
ever one of the figures suggested
by various commentators Propertius had in mind, the parallel
quoted from Shak. *Rom. and Jul.*
2, 2, 177 is interesting: "I would
have thee gone: And yet no
further than a wanton's bird; Who
lets it hop a little from her hand,
Like a poor prisoner in his twisted
gyves, And with a silk thread
plucks it back again, So loving-
jealous of his liberty."

25. quod sit: 'the idea that
she is.'—**parata**: 'responsive.'

26. acrius . . . subit refers to
soul-suffering.

27. quippe ubi: 'for this is a
case where.'—**vacuos**: 'to relieve
the tension'; the word belongs
to the predicate by a proleptic use.

28. vigilare: 'keep love's vigil';
the object of *cedat*: *i.e.* to suffer
the anxieties of a lover.—**alio
nomine**: 'for the sake of any
other loved one.'

29. The correlation **ante . . .
donec** is unique.

30. adsiduas: like those just
described.

31. An ancient proverbial
thought; cf. Ovid, *Am.* 3, 7, 57:
*illa graves potuit quercus adaman-
taque durum surdaque blanditiis
saxa movere suis*; Plaut. *Poen.*
290: *illa mulier lapidem silicem
subigere, ut se amet, potest.*

32. Note the subtle sarcasm
in *possis.*—**iste**: 'such as thou
art.'

33. quare: not found in Tib.;
used six times in Prop.—**pudor**:
the sense of shame is due to
having boasted (but idly) to Propertius that he was immune from
love.

34. quo pereas: 'for whom
thou languishest.' The gender of
the pronoun is purposely indefinite.
Cf. Hor. *Car.* 1, 27, 10: *dicat
. . . quo beatus volnere, qua
pereat sagitta.*

I 2

Quid mihi desidiae non cessas fingere crimen,
    quod faciat nobis conscia Roma moram ?
tam multa illa meo divisa est milia lecto,
    quantum Hypanis Veneto dissidet Eridano,
5 nec mihi consuetos amplexu nutrit amores,
    Cynthia nec nostra dulcis in aure sonat.
olim gratus eram : non illo tempore cuiquam
    contigit ut simili posset amare fide.
invidiae fuimus : num me deus obruit ? an quae

12. 9. num **DV** non **NAF** nunc ω.

I, 12

To the reproaches of an unknown friend for his spiritless life,
— especially, it would seem, his
lack of interest in an invitation to
travel, — Propertius replies (1–6)
that it is not Cynthia who re-
strains him, for she is estranged ;
7–14 : once a favored lover, he is
now for some unknown reason
cast off, and lonely in his bitter
sorrow ; 15–20 : though unable to
touch her heart with sympathy, or
to transfer his affection to another,
he can at least be faithful to her
unto death.

1. **mihi:** cf. 3, 11, 3.

2. **conscia:** 'which knows the
secret of my love.' Cf. 2, 13, 42.
— **Roma:** *i.e.* Rome and its fascination, including Cynthia.

3. **tam multa . . . milia:** that
there was a literal separation at
this time may be indicated by the

preceding poem, in which **Cynthia**
is amusing herself in the gay life
of Baiae. But the comparison in
v. 4 shows that it is of the spiritual
separation that the poet is especially thinking. — **illa:** for Propertius there was but one 'she,'
and he is unconscious of any ambiguity.

4. Cf. "as far as the east is
from the west." It may be
doubted whether Propertius had
any clear idea of the location of
the Hypanis, and authorities are
divided as to its location. If there
was one in India, it would suit the
context best.

6. **Cynthia:** *i.e.* the name. Cf.
1, 18, 22.

7. Cf. Cat. 87.

9. **invidiae:** pred. dat.: 'an
object of envy '; *i.e.* on account
of his good fortune in possessing
the favor of Cynthia. — **num:**
the poet cannot believe his enemy

10   lecta Prometheis dividit herba iugis?
        non sum ego qui fueram : mutat via longa puellas :
          quantus in exiguo tempore fugit amor!
        nunc primum longas solus cognoscere noctes
          cogor et ipse meis auribus esse gravis.
15   felix qui potuit praesenti flere puellae :
          non nihil adspersis gaudet Amor lacrimis ;
        aut si despectus potuit mutare calores :
          sunt quoque translato gaudia servitio.
        mi neque amare aliam neque ab hac discedere fas est :
20   Cynthia prima fuit, Cynthia finis erit.

14

Tu licet abiectus Tiberina molliter unda
Lesbia Mentoreo vina bibas opere,

has been a god; rather the witch-craft or magic potions of a human rival. — quae : indef.

10. Prometheis . . . iugis : Prometheus was bound on the Caucasus. — dividit : sc. *me ab illa.* — herba : apparently the φάρμακον Προμήθειον, said to have sprung from the blood of Prometheus and to have an unenviable efficacy in magic potions. Cf. Apollon. Rhod. 3, 845; Val. Flac. 7, 356–7 : *Prometheae florem de sanguine fibrae Caucaseum promit nutritaque gramina ponti.*

11. Cf. Hor. *Car.* 4, 1, 3 : *non sum qualis eram bonae sub regno Cinarae.* For the tense cf. 2, 13, 38, n.

13. solus : to be taken with *cognoscere.*

14. meis : instead of those of his *puella* (v. 15).

15. puellae : for the dat. cf. Tib. 2, 5, 103.

17. Sc. *felix qui.* — calores : *i.e.* the person exciting the passion.

19. neque . . . fas : wrong in the sight of the powers that be, perhaps especially Venus and Cupid.

I, 14

The joys of love are far superior to those of luxurious wealth (C.S.).   The third in the group of elegies dealing intimately with the experiences and feelings of the

et modo tam celeres mireris currere lintres
    et modo tam tardas funibus ire rates,
5   et nemus omne satas intendat vertice silvas,
    urgetur quantis Caucasus arboribus:

---

14. 5. omne **O** unde *Lachmann* utque nemus tantas *Kuehlewein.* intendat **O** ut tendat *Rothstein* ut nemus amne satas incingat *Fonteinius.*

---

lover is addressed to his friend Tullus.

1–14: 'All your luxury is no match for that love which makes me a Croesus and a king. 15–24 : Venus is the mistress of every heart. Without her possessions are futile ; with her I can disdain them.'

1. **Tu** : the name of Tullus does not occur till v. 20. — **abiectus . . . molliter** : 'having thrown yourself down in the abandon of easy luxury, on the banks of Tiber's stream.' It is an elegant expression for utter freedom from care and restraint (C. S.). — **unda** : this locative abl. seems to be a mixture of the ideas, *ripa* and *ad undam*, either of which would have been more exact. Tullus probably owned a suburban villa on the Tiber below Rome. Cf. Mart. 4, 64.

2. **Lesbia . . . vina** : the Lesbian was one of the best of the Aegean wines, noted for its sweetness and harmlessness. It could be drunk freely without intoxication. Hence Hor. *Car.* 1, 17, 21 : *hic innocentis pocula Lesbii duces sub umbra.* It was sometimes called Methymnaean from a city of

Lesbos (C. S.). — **Mentoreo . . . opere** : Mentor was the most celebrated silver-chaser among the Greeks. None of his larger works were extant in Pliny's time, but smaller cups existed and were very costly (C. S.). Cf. 3, 9, 13.

3. **mireris** : 'see with admiration.' — **lintres** : passenger boats, probably, the swiftest known then, corresponding to our best motor boats to-day.

4. **rates** is contrasted with *lintres.* The allusion is to the heavily laden canal boats or the raft-like vessels called *caudicariae.* These boats were towed from Ostia to Rome by means of oxen. They brought to the two principal docks of Rome, the Marmorata and the Emporium, vast quantities of merchandise, corn, and building materials (C. S.). Cf. Lanciani, *Anc. Rome in the Light of Mod. Disc.,* p. 236.

5. **nemus omne**, etc. : 'a whole grove spreads out its planted shade trees with top as high as the trees with which Caucasus is clothed.' The courts of the Roman villas were often planted with shrubbery and watered with fountains on a magnificent scale

non tamen ista meo valeant contendere amori :
nescit Amor magnis cedere divitiis.

nam sive optatam mecum trahit illa quietem,
10   seu facili totum ducit amore diem,
tum mihi Pactoli veniunt sub tecta liquores,
et legitur rubris gemma sub aequoribus :
tum mihi cessuros spondent mea gaudia reges :
quae maneant, dum me fata perire volent.
15   nam quis divitiis adverso gaudet Amore ?
nulla mihi tristi praemia sint Venere !
illa potest magnas heroum infringere vires,
illa etiam duris mentibus esse dolor :
illa neque Arabium metuit transcendere limen,
20   nec timet ostrino, Tulle, subire toro,

(C. S.).   Cf. Tib. 3, 3, 15. — intendat goes with *licet*, v. 1. —
vertice : instrumental, referring to
nemus. The editors abound in
other explanations such as : abl.
of source with *satas*, loc. abl.,
dat. (= *caelo*, *i.e.* the zenith)
(Rothstein).

7. ista refers to *Tu* in v. 1 and
to the following description. —
contendere : *i.e.* 'to vie with.' —
amori : cf. 1, 7, 3, n.

9. trahit : 'prolongs' (C. S.).
— illa : cf. 1, 12, 3, n.

10. facili : 'willing,' *i.e.* mutual.
— ducit : 'spends' (C. S.).

11. Pactoli : cf. 1, 6, 32, n.

12. Cf. Tib. 2, 2, 15–16, nn.

13. cessuros : sc. *esse.* — spondent : 'assure' (C. S.).

14. dum . . . volent : the fut.
with *dum* in the sense of 'until' is

very rare in the classical period.
L. 1996.

15–16. The sentiment is as old
as Mimnermus (*Frag.* 1) : τίς δὲ
βίος, τί δὲ τερπνὸν ἄτερ χρυσέης
Ἀφροδίτης ; Cf. Hor. *Ep.* 1, 6,
65 : *si, Mimnermus uti censet, sine
amore iocisque nil est iucundum*
(C. S.).

19. The allusion seems to be to
some of the beautiful stones of the
east, sometimes used for the posts
and thresholds of houses. Alabaster and onyx were so used in
the dwellings of the wealthy ; cf.
Pliny, *N. H.* 36, 3, 7 (C. S.).
Cf. Tib. 3, 3, 14–16. — Ārabium :
similar quantity may be observed
in 2, 10, 16, *et passim.*

20. subire : 'to steal into.' —
toro : poetic dat. Cf. Ovid,
Ex P. 4, 15, 30 : *ne subeant*

et miserum toto iuvenem versare cubili :
  quid relevant variis serica textilibus ?
quae mihi dum placata aderit, non ulla verebor
  regna vel Alcinoi munera despicere.

17

Et merito, quoniam potui fugisse puellam !
  nunc ego desertas adloquor alcyonas.

24. vel **0** nec **ω** aut *Mueller.*

animo taedia iusta tuo. Perhaps this construction may here be partly due to the influence of *ostrino*, which refers, of course, to the covering, as *toro* does principally to the cushion. Love steals under the gorgeous couch and cover, and the youth suddenly finds that even there he is not safe from such attacks.

21. versare : 'to make him toss'; cf. 2, 22, 47 : *quanta illum toto versant suspiria lecto.*

22. quid relevant : cf. Lucr. 2, 34 : *nec calidae citius decedunt corpore febres textilibus si in picturis ostroque rubenti iacteris.* — variis . . . **textilibus** : abl. of quality, to be rendered as one phrase with *serica* : 'variety of silken fabrics.' — **serica** : the Seres, the modern Chinese, furnished textile fabrics in large variety : garments, tapestries, bedspreads, and even carpets. Several words in this elegy indicate the wide range of Roman commerce in search of rich and rare luxuries (C. S.). The

material used by the Seres gave the generic name, 'silks.'

24. vel : we should expect *nec ;* but we have such sequences as *nec . . . vel, e.g.* in Tib. 1, 9, 59. — **Alcinoi** : the king of the Phaeacians, who gave such liberal gifts (*munera*) to Odysseus (C. S.) ; 'gifts like those of Alcinous.'

I, 17

In the perils of a storm at sea Propertius bewails his folly and fate and contrasts his death with what it would have been had he died at Rome amid the lamentations of his mistress (C. S.). Whether the scene was real or imaginary we have no means of knowing. If it was real the anxieties caused by the perils of the sea were unnecessary, as the trip did not terminate fatally. The poet seems in 3, 21, to be really planning flight over the sea to Athens ; but the situation here cannot be identified with one at that late

nec mihi Cassiope solito visura carinam,
  omniaque ingrato litore vota cadunt.
5 quin etiam absenti prosunt tibi, Cynthia, venti :
  adspice, quam saevas increpat aura minas.

17. 3. solito O solo *Palmer.*

stage of the progress of his relations with Cynthia. In his loneli-
ness, his hatred of the sea, his
longing for his loved one, as well
as in the geographical situation,
he is like Tibullus in 1, 3.

1–4: 'I deserve it all, for having
forsaken my darling. 5–12: The
storm does your will, Cynthia,
upon me; can you not relent?
Can you really bear that I should
perish thus? 13–18: Cursed be
he who first learned to sail the
sea! Better anything than its
cruel pitilessness! 19–24: Had I
only stayed at home, even to die,
my love would have shown her
heart in the last sad offices. 25–
28: Yet, daughters of the sea,
come to my help, and spare me!'

1. **Et merito:** Propertius usually plunges *in medias res* at once
in his elegies, several times, as here,
apparently presupposing a considerable process of thought; cf.
1, 9; 2, 10; 3, 7; 3, 23; 4, 7.
This habit may serve to justify the
divisions of the poems in some
cases. Cf. *e.g.* 1, 8 *b.* — **fugisse:**
cf. Tib. 1, 1, 29, n.

2. **desertas:** 'lonely' (C. S.).
— **alcyonas:** 'sea birds'; strictly,
kingfishers. There was a fancy
that they were connected with the

sea, ἅλς : hence, *halcedo*, 'halcyon.'
The "halcyon days" were the
fourteen days of the bird's incubation, during which the sea was
supposed to be more calm and
navigable (C. S.); cf. 3, 10, 9:
*alcyonum positis requiescant ora
querellis.*

3. **Cassiope:** a port on the
northern end of the island of
Corcyra, the first made on the
regular course from Brundusium
to Greece, and the last at which
navigators called on the return
voyage. Cf. Cic. *Ad Fam.* 16, 9, 1 ;
Gell. 19, 1, 1 ; Suet. *Nero*, 22 ;
Pliny, *N. H.* 4, 12, 52. — **solito:**
'as usual' (C. S.). This absolute
use of the participle is an easy extension of the more common one
after comparatives, *e.g.* Livy, 24, 9:
plus solito. — **visura:** sc. *est.*

4. **cadunt:** 'fall unnoticed,' *i.e.*
fail. Cf. the modern colloquial
"fall down."

5. **prosunt:** 'take your part'
(C. S.).

6. **increpat:** the indicative is
used because the dependent clause
has more the nature of an exclamation than of an indirect question.
Such constructions are found even
in Cicero, and quite often in the
poets, both early and classical.

nullane placatae veniet fortuna procellae?
  haecine parva meum funus arena teget?
tu tamen in melius saevas converte querellas:
10   sat tibi sit poenae nox et iniqua vada.
an poteris siccis mea fata reponere ocellis,
  ossaque nulla tuo nostra tenere sinu?
ah pereat, quicumque rates et vela paravit
  primus et invito gurgite fecit iter.
15   nonne fuit levius dominae pervincere mores

---

11. reponere **O** opponere **ω** reposcere *Baehrens.*

They follow especially verbs of seeing and saying. Cf. Draeger, 155 (C. S.).

7. placatae . . . procellae: epexegetical gen. with *fortuna.*

8. haecine: cf. LSHLG., p. 80. — **funus:** the vocabulary of death is rich in Propertius, and the variations in usage manifold. This word here means 'dead body,' as in 4, 11, 3 (but body and soul are there identified), and as *fata* does in v. 11. Cf. Verg. *Aen.* 9, 491: *funus lacerum tellus habet.*

9. Unless Cynthia's curses cease soon Propertius believes his doom will be certain death.

10. nox: 'the blackness of the tempest' (C. S.).

11. fata: cf. v. 8, n. — **reponere:** 'lay away' *i.e.* in the tomb; but here in the more general sense (cf. 'consign to earth'), as the place and circumstances are thought of as beyond the ken of Cynthia. Propertius means to say, 'Could you bear to have me die where you couldn't bury me?'

12. ossaque . . . tenere: 'and yet not be able to clasp to your bosom.' — **sinu:** for the burial custom in this particular see B. *G. Exc.* 12, p. 519 (C. S.); cf. Tib. 1, 3, 6.

13. pereat, quicumque: navigation was an exceedingly perilous business in those days, and Roman poetry abounds in curses on the folly of tempting Providence by venturing off the land. *E.g.* Tib. 1, 3, 50; Prop. 3, 7, 29-32; Hor. *Car.* 1, 3, 9 sqq.: *illi robur . . . erat, qui . . . commisit pelago ratem.*

14. primus: the invention of ships and the beginnings of navigation are variously ascribed to Jason, Semiramis, Danaus, Erythras. The Phoenicians are thought to be the first nation that engaged extensively in commerce. But cf. Tib. 1, 7, 20 (C. S.).

15. Cf. Verg. *Ec.* 2, 14: *nonne fuit satius, tristes Amaryllidis iras atque superba pati fastidia?* For *fuit* cf. Madv. 348, *c.*

229

(quamvis dura, tamen rara puella fuit),
  quam sic ignotis circumdata litora silvis
    cernere et optatos quaerere Tyndaridas?
  illic siqua meum sepelissent fata dolorem,
20   ultimus et posito staret amore lapis,
  illa meo caros donasset funere crines,

---

16. rara: cf. 1, 8, 42.

18. optatos . . . Tyndaridas: Castor and Pollux, whose favor as bringing fair weather was constantly sought by sailors; cf. *BPW*., Vol. 30 (1910), Sp. 517. Perhaps the origin of the idea is to be traced to the convenience of their constellation, Gemini, as a guide for pilots, which would require fair weather, of course, to be useful, and the desire for this would cause petitions to the deified twins. But besides this the phenomenon known as St. Elmo's fire, at the masthead, was early recognized as an indication of the favor of Castor and Pollux. Cf. Pliny, *N. H.* 2, 37, 101; Hor. *Car.* 1, 3, 2; 1, 12, 27; 4, 8, 31; Cat. 68, 65; Geikie, p. 341. The mother of the twins was Leda, wife of Tyndareus; but legend and literature more often regard Juppiter as their father.

19. illic: at Rome, which now seems so remote as to suggest this adverb. There, moreover, 'she' (*illa*, v. 21) is, the poet is thinking; cf. 1, 12, 3, n.

20. amore may be taken as practically equivalent to *amatore* ('her dead lover'); cf. 2, 28, 39.

n. — lapis: the sepulchral stone (C. S.).

21. meo . . . funere: with characteristic vagueness in both words and syntax, as again in *extremo . . . pulvere* in v. 23, Propertius leaves us in doubt whether he refers especially to time or to place. Fortunately for poets, they are not required to parse what they write; we may render the expressions respectively, 'would have presented her dead lover,' and 'would have called my name aloud when life had forever left this clay.' — **crines**: the friends of the dead often cut off their hair and laid it sometimes on the breast and sometimes on the tomb of the deceased. Cf. Ovid, *Met.* 3, 505: *planxere sorores Naides et sectos fratri posuere capillos*. Several of the burial customs of the Romans are indicated in this and the following lines. To decorate the graves of the dead with flowers seems to be a natural expression of the heart in all ages, but probably has some significance of a magic or mystical character also. Cf. Siebourg in *Archiv. f. Religionswissenschaft*, Vol. 8, pp. 390, sqq. To call upon

molliter et tenera poneret ossa rosa:
illa meum extremo clamasset pulvere nomen,
ut mihi non ullo pondere terra foret.
25   at vos aequoreae formosa Doride natae,
candida felici solvite vela choro:
si quando vestras labens Amor attigit undas,
mansuetis socio parcite litoribus.

18

Haec certe deserta loca et taciturna querenti,
et vacuum zephyri possidet aura nemus:

the name of the deceased was
usual among the Romans. S· T·
T· L (*sit tibi terra levis*) was
often inscribed on the tomb as
well as uttered among the last
farewells. See B. *G. Exc.* 12
(C. S.). The *conclamatio*, or custom of having all present shout
loudly the name of the deceased
as soon as death appears to have
taken place, is still practiced on
the death of a Pope of Rome.

25. Doride natae: Doris was
the daughter of Oceanus and
Tethys. She married Nereus and
was the mother of Nereids. Propertius appeals to them by the
fellowship of love to spare him
and give him tranquil waters
(C. S.).

28. mansuetis . . . litoribus:
instrumental. — **socio**: *i.e.* because
they could then have a fellow-feel-
ing for his distress.

I, 18

In the silent solitude of the for-
est Propertius bitterly laments the
hardheartedness of Cynthia.

1–8: 'Here at least I may utter
my complaint; but where shall
I begin to rehearse my sad estate? 9–16: What have I done to
merit thy disdain? Have I been
unfaithful? I swear I have not,
richly as thou deservest to be forsaken. 17–22: Or do I not protest
enough? the very trees shall witness my devotion. 23–26: Or
have I revealed thy infidelities? I
have borne all in silence. 27–32
And for all this my only reward is
to wander lonely in the wildwood
and make it vocal with the echoes
of thy name?'

1. Haec certe: the poet has
been almost bursting with grief,
and only here at last does he find

hic licet occultos proferre inpune dolores,
   si modo sola queant saxa tenere fidem.
5 unde tuos primum repetam, mea Cynthia, fastus?
   quod mihi das flendi, Cynthia, principium?
   qui modo felices inter numerabar amantes,
   nunc in amore tuo cogor habere notam.
   quid tantum merui? quae te mihi crimina mutant?
10   an nova tristitiae causa puella tuae?
   sic mihi te referas, levis, ut non altera nostro
   limine formosos intulit ulla pedes.
   quamvis multa tibi dolor hic meus aspera debet,
   non ita saeva tamen venerit ira mea

18. 9. crimina ω carmina O.

relief in voicing his feelings. —
querenti: dat. of ref.

2. Cf. Martial 6, 76, 6: *et
famulum victrix possidet umbra
nemus.*

3. **occultos:** *i.e.* up to this time.
— **inpunĕ:** note the shortening of
the final vowel.

4. Perhaps the poet recalls the
legend of King Midas and his servant, whose secret was not safe
even when confided only to a
hole in the ground. Cf. Pers. 1,
119.

5. 'At what point shall I begin
to rehearse the long story of thy
proud disdain?'

7. **modo:** 'but yesterday,' it
seemed to Propertius, as he re-
called the heyday of his love.

8. **in:** cf. 3, 2, 2, n. — **notam:**
known to the world as Cynthia's
discarded love, he looks upon this
knowledge as a stigma, like the
mark of disgrace affixed by the
censors to a citizen degraded
from his former rank.

9. **crimina:** 'charges' brought
by Cynthia herself.

10. **an:** A, 335, *b.* — **tristitiae:** 'coldness.'

11. **sic . . . ut:** cf. Tib. 2, 5,
63, n. — **levis:** 'O madam light-
of-love' (Phillimore).

12. Cf. Cat. 68, 70–72. — **limine** is best considered instrumental, but rendered 'over my
threshold.'

13. **aspera:** substantive use:
'bitter experiences' (cf. colloquial
'bad quarter of an hour'). —
debet: poetic indic. with *quamvis*; cf. L. 1906; H. 586, 2, 2;
A. 527, *e.*

14. **venerit:** *venio* and *eo* are
not infrequent equivalents of *sum*
in Propertius; cf. 1, 15, 4: *in
nostro lenta timore venis*; 1, 4,
10: *inferior duro iudice turpis
eat.*

15 ut tibi sim merito semper furor et tua flendo
        lumina deiectis turpia sint lacrimis.
    an quia parva damus mutato signa colore
        et non ulla meo clamat in ore fides ?
    vos eritis testes, siquos habet arbor amores,
20   fagus et Arcadio pinus amica deo.
    ah quotiens teneras resonant mea verba sub umbras,
        scribitur et vestris Cynthia corticibus !
    an tua quod peperit nobis iniuria curas,

17. colore O calore V₂.

15. furor: cf. Harper's *Lex.
s.v.* 2 ; Pichon *s.v.* at the end.
    16. Cf. Tib. 1, 1, 51–52 ; 2, 6,
41–43 ; Ovid, *Am.* 3, 6, 57–60 :
*quid fles et madidos lacrimis cor-
rumpis ocellos pectoraque insana
plangis aperta manu ? ille habet
et silices et vivum in pectore ferrum, qui tenero lacrimas lentus in
ore videt.*
    17. The second possible charge
against the poet-lover,—here again,
as in the previous instance, in the
form of an indignant question, implying a negative answer, — is that
he gives little external manifesta-
tion of his passion, such as young
and ardent lovers usually exhibit,
viz. in countenance and in words.
— **mutato . . . colore:** cf. 1, 6, 6,
n. Probably both the temporary
change of the occasional blush,
and the more permanent change
from normal color to the habitual
paleness traditionally ascribed to
lovers are in the mind of the poet.

18. in ore fides: 'pledge on
my lips'; cf. Ovid, *Her.* 2, 31:
*iura, fides ubi nunc commissaque
dextera dextrae, quique erat in
falso plurimus ore deus ?*
    19. Propertius answers that
much more enduring signs are on
the trees, and that the woods are
vocal with his protestations of
fidelity.
    20. fagus: the tree that still
serves best for the carving of
sweethearts' names. — **pinus amica
deo:** Pitys, a nymph beloved by
Pan, was changed into a pine.
This tree would thus easily be
thought of as especially sympathetic with lovers' confidences.
    23. The third possible charge.
— **peperit:** 'brought forth' = 'revealed.' — **iniuria:** 'the wrongs
you have done me' ; a regular
word for infidelity in the elegiac
writers ; cf. 3, 25, 7 ; Cat. 72, 7. —
curas: the bitterness of heart that
lovers know.

> quae solum tacitis cognita sunt foribus?
25 omnia consuevi timidus perferre superbae
> iussa, neque arguto facta dolore queri.
> pro quo divini fontes et frigida rupes
> et datur inculto tramite dura quies:
> et quodcumque meae possunt narrare querellae,
30 cogor ad argutas dicere solus aves.
> sed qualiscumque es, resonent mihi 'Cynthia' silvae
> nec deserta tuo nomine saxa vacent.

---

27. divini fontes O dumosi montes *Heinsius* mi duri montes *Enk suggests.*

---

24. quae: the gender may be explained by noting that it refers here not so much to *curas* (its apparent antecedent) as to the expression of them, which would be in *verba*. — **solum . . . cognita sunt:** *i.e.* hitherto have been; Cynthia fears now that in desperation they may have been uttered. — **foribus:** the doors of his mistress's house have told no tales of what had happened there, — all too well known to Propertius, shut out while others were admitted.

25. perferre: 'to endure in silence.' — **superbae:** cf. 3, 24, 2, *et passim.*

26. arguto: 'loud-mouthed,' 'blabbing.'

27. quo: refers to the whole patient and discreet conduct of the poet as described above. — **divini:** a mere variation from the more common epithet, *sacri:* cf. Verg. *Ec.* 1, 52: *hic inter flumina nota et fontes sacros frigus captabis opacum;* Hor. *Car.* 1, 1, 22: *ad aquae lene caput sacrae;* Milton, *Ode on the Morning of Christ's Nativity:* "The lonely mountains o'er, And the resounding shore, A voice of weeping heard, and loud lament; From haunted spring, and dale, Edg'd with poplar pale."

30. Cf. 1, 17, 2.

31. qualiscumque: though the poet was rash enough, in this temporary estrangement in the earlier period of his passion, to risk such a universal declaration, we see from 3, 24, 18, and other passages in that and the following poem that his eyes were entirely opened, and a complete revulsion of sentiment took place. — **Cynthia:** voc. This is the cry uttered repeatedly by the poet, as he wanders to and fro, and as such is used without change of form, in apposition to an implied *verbum.* Cf. Verg. *Aen.* 4, 383: *nomine Dido saepe vocaturum.*

19

Non ego nunc tristes vereor, mea Cynthia, manes,
    nec moror extremo debita fata rogo:
sed ne forte tuo careat mihi funus amore,
    hic timor est ipsis durior exequiis.

5 non adeo leviter nostris puer haesit ocellis,
    ut meus oblito pulvis amore vacet.
illic Phylacides iucundae coniugis heros

I, 19

With a lover's forebodings, Propertius anticipates an early death, but dreads only the possibility that Cynthia's love will then die too.

1–4: 'I fear not death, only that you will cease to love me when I am in the tomb; 5–10: for my own love defies death, like the love of Protesilaus, 11–18: and will remain absolutely true to you in the spirit-world. 19–24: O that you may be conscious of this fidelity! that I may be spared my fear that your love will be stolen away from me. 25–26: Then let us love here while we may!'

1. **nunc** seems to imply a reconciliation with Cynthia. — **manes**: the development of the meaning is: 'spirits of the dead,' then 'association with these spirits,' therefore 'condition of death.' In nothing does Propertius show a wider imagination than in his treatment of the idea of death, for which his metonymic expressions in this poem alone include, besides this word, *fata* (2), *funus* (3), *exequiis* (4), *fati* (12), *favilla* (19). Only at length in v. 20 does the poet reach the point of speaking plainly the ill-omened word *mors*. Cf. also *pulvis* (6), and *pulvere* (22), and *ossa* (18).

2. **moror**: see Lex. *s.v.* 2, B.

2. — **fata**: the word includes the ideas of necessity, death, and burning (C. S.).

5. **puer**: Cupid. — **haesit**: cf. 2, 12, 13–15. — **ocellis**: where love first enters.

6. **meus . . . pulvis**: 'even when I am but dust and ashes.' — **oblito**: pass. — **vacet**: the antithesis of *haesit*: 'forget my love and again be unpossessed.'

7. **illic**: the unseen world suggested by *pulvis*, and further specified in the next verse. — **Phylacides**: Protesilaus; cf. Cat. 68, 74, n.

non potuit caecis inmemor esse locis,
  sed cupidus falsis attingere gaudia palmis
10   Thessalis antiquam venerat umbra domum.
illic quidquid ero, semper tua dicar imago :
  traicit et fati litora magnus amor.
illic formosae veniant chorus heroinae,
  quas dedit Argivis Dardana praeda viris ;
15 quarum nulla tua fuerit mihi, Cynthia, forma
  gratior, et (Tellus hoc ita iusta sinat)
quamvis te longae remorentur fata senectae,
  cara tamen lacrimis ossa futura meis.

19. 10. Thessalis **DV** Thessalus **NAF.**

9. **falsis . . . palmis** : 'with his
mere semblances of hands'; cf.
Verg. *Aen.* 6, 292 : *tenues sine
corpore vitas.* — **gaudia** : 'his darling'; cf. Cat. 2, 5 : *desiderio
meo nitenti* (C. S.).

10. **Thessalis . . . umbra** : 'a
mere ghost of a Thessalian,'
predicate use.

11. At first sight the certainty
of the second part of the verse
seems inconsistent with the in-
definiteness of the first. But the
poet means to doubt only with
reference to the conditions of existence in the world of shades ;
that he as a shade will still be
known to all as her lover he cannot doubt.

12. A noble line, where the
longing for immortality defies the
narrow confines of the senses.

13. **chorus** : in apposition with
heroinae : 'the band of beautiful
heroines,' Helen, Andromache,

Cassandra, Briseis, Tecmessa, etc.
(C. S.).

15. **fuerit** : the poet uses the
most positive mood and tense
(fut. perf.) possible, regardless
of the form of the implied condition in v. 13.

16. **Tellus** : as goddess of the
underworld. Cf. H. & T. § 213. —
hoc : the long life for Cynthia
referred to in the next verse, here
unselfishly asked of the goddess
who sooner or later claims all for
her own. To refer *hoc* to the
same confident assurance of eternal
fidelity already expressed in the
previous verses would be bathos. —
ita = *hac condicione* and belongs
to *iusta* ; *i.e.* Tellus would be just
only in case she grants this per-
mission.

18. Cf. 1, 6, 24. — **ossa** : sc. *tua.*
Propertius asserts again that no
matter how long it may be before
Cynthia's bones shall lie beside

quae tu viva mea possis sentire favilla!
20   tum mihi non ullo mors sit amara loco.
quam vereor ne te contempto, Cynthia, busto
     abstrahat a nostro pulvere iniquus Amor,
cogat et invitam lacrimas siccare cadentes!
flectitur adsiduis certa puella minis.
25   quare, dum licet, inter nos laetemur amantes:
non satis est ullo tempore longus amor.

2 2

Qualis et unde genus, qui sint mihi, Tulle, penates,
     quaeris pro nostra semper amicitia.

his own in the common receptacle of all mankind, he shall ever remain faithful to her, and this verse seems vaguely to foreshadow an affectionate reunion. There was no general uniformity of belief among the Romans as to the future state. Cf. H. & T. § 9; Cat. 96, 1, n.

19. mea . . . favilla: 'when I am already but dust and ashes.' The expression is one of the extreme liberties which Propertius takes with the language. Cf. 1, 17, 21, n.

21. contempto: *i e.* by you.

24. certa: 'however constant' (C. S.). The poet courteously forgets his past experiences with his inconstant mistress.

25. dum licet . . . laetemur amantes: cf. Tib. 1, 1, 69 sqq.; Cat. 5, 1: *Vivamus, mea Lesbia, atque amemus.*

26. *non est ullum tempus ubi dicas, amor est satis longus.*

1, 22

Following the fashion of Augustan poets (cf. Verg. *Georg.* 4, 559–566; Hor. *Ep.* 1, 20, 19–28; Ovid, *Amor.* 3, 15, and *Trist.* 4, 10) Propertius closes this first book, which was independently published, with an autobiographical statement, a statement chiefly remarkable for its vagueness. For the author gives the public (for whom, of course, the poem was really intended) no definite information as to his name or his birthplace, and very little as to his family.

1–10: 'Tullus, as a friend you ask me of my origin. If you know accursed Perugia, you know the neighboring part of Umbria, my birthplace.'

1. Qualis: of what general stock, *e.g.* whether Campanian, Etruscan, Latin, or Umbrian. —

si Perusina tibi patriae sunt nota sepulcra,
    Italiae duris funera temporibus,
5   cum Romana suos egit discordia cives
    (sic, mihi praecipue, pulvis Etrusca, dolor,
tu proiecta mei perpessa es membra propinqui,
    tu nullo miseri contegis ossa solo),
proxima supposito contingens Umbria campo
10   me genuit terris fertilis uberibus.

unde: referring to birthplace. — **genus**: acc. of specification belonging to both *qualis* and *unde*, sc. *sim* from the *sint*; cf. for similar omission of the subjunctive 1, 8, 37. — **Tulle**: the book suitably closes with an envoy addressed to the same friend to whom he speaks in the opening poem. Cf. Intr. § 32. — **penates**: the gods of the household store evidently here connote the circumstances, social rank, etc., of the family. The poet reserves his answer to this question altogether for the present, to be given in 4, 1, 129–134 in connection with more exact information as to his birthplace.

2. semper: an adverb with adjectival force is not an uncommon phenomenon in good prose as well as poetry, being especially frequent in Livy; cf. 1, 1, 2; Livy, 21, 8, 5: *tres deinceps turres*; Ter. *Andr.* 175; *eri semper lenitas*: Cic. *De N. D.* 2, 66, 166: *deorum saepe praesentiae*.

3. si . . . sunt nota: the apodosis is in the ellipsis to be supplied in connection with vv.

9–10. — Perusina . . . sepulcra: the gruesome mortality of the civil conflict known as the *bellum Perusinum* (41–40 B.C.) impressed the Romans unusually. Cf. **Cat.** 68, 89–90.

4. Italiae: best taken with *funera*, which unmodified would seem vague.

5. Romana: the identity of meaning between this word, *patriae* (v. 3), and *Italiae* (v. 4) at this period is noteworthy. — **egit**: 'pursued,' as in Hor. *Epod.* 7, 17 : *acerba fata Romanos agunt*.

6. sic: 'hence,' *i.e.* due to the *discordia.*—**pulvis Etrusca**: for the gender cf. 2, 13, 35.

7. proiecta: *i.e.* rather than *conposita*, as they would naturally be. — **propinqui**: very likely the Gallus of the preceding elegy.

9. supposito . . . campo: dat. with *proxima*; *supposito* refers to the hilltop of Perugia. — **contingens**: adjective: 'the neighboring part of Umbria, adjacent to the plain at the foot of Perugia's hill.' This makes Assisi possible, or any other of the proposed sites.

LIBER SECVNDVS

I O

Sed tempus lustrare aliis Helicona choreis,
　　et campum Haemonio iam dare tempus equo.
iam libet et fortes memorare ad proelia turmas,
　　et Romana mei dicere castra ducis.

2, 10

The poet, possibly inspired by a hint from court, tries to raise himself to the epic level and sing of the contemporary triumphs of Roman arms, but finding the task beyond his strength, falls back upon his familiar erotic verse. Cf. 3, 3, Intr.

1–12: 'It is time to try my hand at celebrating military triumphs; 13–18: and the glory of Caesar's arms furnishes abundant material. 19–26: Some day! — My humble Muse dares not yet essay so lofty themes.'

It was this poem that Lachmann, on insufficient grounds, thought began a new (third) book. See Intr. § 34.

From the various historical references in vv. 13–18 it appears that the elegy must have been written after the Indian envoys came to Augustus in 26 or 25 B.C., but not later than the early part of 24 B.C., in the latter part

of which year the Arabian expedition came to grief.

1. **Sed**: cf. 1, 17, 1, n. There is no need of assuming a preceding *lacuna* in the Mss. — **choreis**: the poet elsewhere also imagines himself joining in the round dance of the inspiring Muses at their favorite haunts; cf. 3, 1, 4.

2. **campum**: *i.e.* free scope. From the association with the following words we can readily conjure up the long line of events worthy of epic treatment associated by the poets with the plains of Thessaly, from the battles of gods and giants, Centaurs, and Lapithae to the critical day of Pharsalus. — **Haemonio . . . equo**: the famous horses of Thessaly were adapted for battle, or for the chariot-race deeds of glory.

3. **fortes . . . ad**: cf. Ovid, *Fast.* 2, 688: *fortis ad arma.*

4. **Romana**: the glory of Rome is the first consideration. — **mei . . . ducis**: the glorification of Augustus is inseparably joined to the prosperity of the empire.

5   quod si deficiant vires, audacia certe
         laus erit: in magnis et voluisse sat est.
     aetas prima canat Veneres, extrema tumultus:
         bella canam, quando scripta puella meast.
     nunc volo subducto gravior procedere vultu,
10   nunc aliam citharam me mea musa docet.
     surge, anima, ex humili iam carmine: sumite vires,
         Pierides: magni nunc erit oris opus.
     iam negat Euphrates equitem post terga tueri
         Parthorum, et Crassos se tenuisse dolet:
15   India quin, Auguste, tuo dat colla triumpho,

5. audacia: 'courage,' a relatively rare usage. With these two verses cf. Tib. 4, 1, 3–7: *a meritis si carmina laudes, deficiant . . . est nobis voluisse satis.*

6. laus: 'a ground for praise'; 'praiseworthy.'

7. extrema: a poetic hyperbole, as Propertius was still a young man of less than thirty years.

8. quando: causal, a Ciceronian, yet comparatively rare use.—**scripta puella**: as a matter of fact, however, practically the whole of this book is as completely devoted to Cynthia and the theme of love, as is the preceding book.

9. subducto . . . vultu probably refers to elevating the eyebrows, in scornful disdain of the erotic follies of youth; 'with frowning visage.'

10. aliam citharam: 'different strains,' *i.e.* poetry in a loftier style.

12. magni . . . oris: 'sonorous tone'; cf. Verg. *Georg.* 3, 294:

magno nunc ore sonandum. For the case cf. Livy, 22, 51, 3: *ad consilium pensandum temporis opus esse.*—**nunc**: *i.e.* from now on.

13. Euphrates: practically the western boundary of the Parthian sway in its period of greatest extent. — **post terga tueri**: the characteristic strategy of the Parthians. Cf. 3, 9, 54.

14. Parthorum: this elegy was written about the time of that contest for the Parthian throne between Phraates and Tiridates which gave Augustus opportunity for effective diplomacy in dealing with this people. Cf. Hor. *Car.* 1, 26, 5: *quid Tiridaten terreat.*—**Crassos . . . tenuisse**: both father and son lost their lives through Parthian treachery in 53 B.C., and neither their ashes nor their standards had yet been restored. The latter were finally recovered in 20 B.C.

15. India: an embassy from India is said to have found Augus-

et domus intactae te tremit Arabiae:
et siqua extremis tellus se subtrahit oris,
   sentiat illa tuas post modo capta manus.
haec ego castra sequar.   vates tua castra canendo
20   magnus ero.   servent hunc mihi fata diem !
ut caput in magnis ubi non est tangere signis,
   ponitur hic imos ante corona pedes,
sic nos nunc, inopes laudis conscendere culmen,
   pauperibus sacris vilia tura damus.
25   nondum etiam Ascraeos norunt mea carmina fontes,
   sed modo Permessi flumine lavit Amor.

10.   22. hic **DV** hac **NF**.   23. culmen **ω** carmen **O** currum *Markland*.

tus in Spain in 26–25 B.C.; but
the last part of this verse must be
set down as pure adulation.

16. Arabiae: the march of
Aelius Gallus into this land of
fabulous wealth in 24 B.C. was immediately followed by an igno-
minious retreat before the heat and
pestilence which were rapidly
eating up his army. Cf. 1, 14,
19, n.

17. When Augustus set out for
Gaul in 27 B.C., it was understood
that one of his objects was a campaign of conquest in Britain.
This, however, never materialized.

18. post modo: Propertius hints
that the plan may be renewed
under more favorable conditions.

19. haec: *i.e.* rather than the
camp of Love. Cf. 4, 1, 135;
Tib. 1, 1, 75.

20. servent . . . diem: *i.e.* till
I am ready for it; an inverted
manner of saying, 'let me live to
see it.'

21. in: 'in the case of.'

22. hic: from the standpoint of
one standing at the base.

23. nunc: as contrasted with
the *diem* of v. 20. — **inopes**: 'too
weak'; the only case where this
word is followed by the epexegetical infinitive.

24. The use of incense alone
became more and more restricted
to the simple household sacrifices
or preliminary offerings in public
sacrifices; those who were able
offered more costly, bloody sacrifices; cf. *CIL.* 6, 2065; Suet. *Tib.*
70; Livy, 10, 23, 1; 43, 13, 8.

25. Ascraeos . . . fontes: Aganippe and Hippocrene, the famous
haunts of the Muses and supposed
sources of poetic inspiration.   The
tradition was fostered by the fact
that Hesiod may have been born
at Ascra, and certainly lived there.

26. Permessi: a little stream
which included among its sources
one or both of the storied springs

II

Scribant de te alii vel sis ignota, licebit:
　　laudet, qui sterili semina ponit humo.
omnia, crede mihi, tecum uno munera lecto
　　auferet extremi funeris atra dies:
5　　et tua transibit contemnens ossa viator,
　　nec dicet 'cinis hic docta puella fuit.

11. 3. tecum O secum ω.

referred to in the previous verse. Propertius does not venture yet to drink from the fountain-head of poetry, but has only dipped into the stream of inspiration that is derived thence. Cf. 2, 13, 4–6. Perhaps in both passages he was thinking of the phrase in Verg. *Ec.* 6, 64: *errantem Permessi ad flumina Gallum*.

2, 11

Having now deliberately decided to stick to erotic poetry for the present, Propertius warns Cynthia that unless his services are appreciated her name will perish at her death. There is no reason to consider the poem other than complete as it stands. 1–6: 'Whether you find others or not to celebrate your claims, they will perish with you.'

1. **te**: the poet feels it unnecessary to name Cynthia.

2. **laudet**: as subject, we are to understand any of the *alii* of the

preceding verse; as object, the *munera* of v. 3, which would be the natural theme of any new adorer of Cynthia. This is the beginning of a new tone, which reveals a different attitude toward Cynthia. — **sterili semina ponit humo**: proverbial, indicating wasted labor. Cf. Sen. *De Ben.* 1, 1, 2: *semina in solum effetum et sterile non spargimus*.

3. **omnia**: cf. Lucian, *Dial. Mort.* 18, 1 sqq.; 24, 2; Shak. *Hamlet*, 5, 1: "to this favour she must come." — **crede mihi**: Propertius finds Cynthia an unwilling listener. — **munera**: 'gifts and graces.' Cf. 1, 2, *passim*; 2, 12, 23–24; 3, 20, 7. These *munera* are both physical and mental. — **lecto**: 'bier.'

4. **extremi**: 'which ends all.' — **atra**: cf. Tib. 1, 3, 4; Verg. *Aen.* 6, 429: *abstulit atra dies et funere mersit acerbo*.

6. **docta puella**: cf. 1, 7, 11, n.; 2, 13, 11, n.

242

I 2

Quicumque ille fuit puerum qui pinxit Amorem,
  nonne putas miras hunc habuisse manus?
is primum vidit sine sensu vivere amantes
  et levibus curis magna perire bona.
5 idem non frustra ventosas addidit alas,

12. 3. is **NDV** hic **F.**

2, 12

The genius of the inventor of a familiar art type of Eros, the usual one from the Hellenistic period; cf. Gardner, *Greek Sculpt.*, p. 364. Propertius appears to be speaking of a painting or paintings quite well known to his readers, perhaps wall frescoes in Rome. The thought is not original. For parallels cf. *e.g.* Moschus, *Id.* I, 16 sqq.; *Meleager, passim*; Quint. 2, 4, 26.

I–12: 'It was a clever conception to paint Cupid as a thoughtless, winged boy, with quiver full of barbed arrows, flitting about from heart to heart, and swiftly wounding his victims. 13–16: The picture is true to life in my case, except that the wings are apparently lacking, and the god remains, in incessant warfare against my peace. 17–24: Why, Cupid, not try your weapons on another? I am reduced already to a mere shadow of myself. If you destroy me utterly, who will sing the claims of my lady?'

1. **puerum**: 'as a boy.' — **qui**: sc. *primus*.

2. **miras**: in imagination more than technique; a transfer of the work of the brain to the hands.

3. **primum . . . sine sensu**: referring to the quality of *puerilitas* implied in v. I. Cupid has the boyish lack of wisdom in estimating values (as well as a disregard of the suffering of others), a motive that predominates in classical comedy — " Love is blind." Cf. Shak. *Mids. Night's Dream*, I 1, 236–239: "Nor hath Love's mind of any judgment taste; Wings and no eyes figure unheedy haste: And therefore is Love said to be a child, Because in choice he is so oft beguiled."

4. **curis**: *i.e. amoribus.* Cf. 3, 21, 3. — **bona**: *e.g.* wealth, social connections, etc.

5. **ventosas**: 'like those of the wind.' Vergil (*Aen.* 12, 848) uses exactly the same phrase of the Furies: *ventosasque addidit alas.* Swiftness and fickleness are both in the mind of the poet.

243

fecit et humano corde volare deum;
scilicet altẹrna quoniam iactamur in unda,
nostraque non ullis permanet aura locis.
et merito hamatis manus est armata sagittis
10   et pharetra ex umero Gnosia utroque iacet;
ante ferit quoniam, tuti quam cernimus hostem,
nec quisquam ex illo vulnere sanus abit.
in me tela manent, manet et puerilis imago:
sed certe pennas perdidit ille suas,
15   evolat heu nostro quoniam de pectore nusquam,
adsiduusque meo sanguine bella gerit.

15. heu *Muretus* é **N** e **DFV**.

Cf. Ovid, *Am.* 2, 9, 49: *tu levis es multoque tuis ventosior alis.*

6. fecit: 'represented.' — humano corde volare deum: 'the god as flying from a human heart.' This is the picture. Cupid has just shot his arrow and is flying away to a new victim. To interpret *corde* as a locative is not only artistically unlikely, but robs the whole poem of its point, as brought out in vv. 14–18. Cf. also Moschus, 2, 16: καὶ πτερόεις ὡς ὄρνις ἐφίπταται ἄλλον ἐπ' ἄλλῳ, ἀνέρας ἠδὲ γυναῖκας.

7. alterna . . . unda: up and down, like the crests and troughs of alternate waves. The change of figure would seem harsh but for *aura*, of the following verse, which is naturally suggested by *ventosas*. Love's boat rises and sinks before a fitful breeze like a bird on the wing (C. S.).

8. nostra: 'fair.'

9. merito: cf. *non frustra*, v. 5. — hamatis: 'barbed.'

10. Gnosia: because the Cretans were renowned archers (C. S.). The expression comes from the important town on the north coast now famous for archaeological discoveries. — utroque: the god is in flight; and his quiver is naturally in the position where generally carried when not in use. Cf. Hom. *Il.* 1, 45: τόξ' ὤμοισιν ἔχων ἀμφηρεφέα τε φαρέτρην.

11. tuti: 'in our (false) security.'

12. sanus abit: 'escapes unscathed.'

13. in me: 'in my own case.' — manent, manet: the poet's passion is no passing whim.

16. meo sanguine: 'at the cost of my blood' (C. S.), a good example of the characteristic Propertian vagueness in the use of the abl. Various grammatical cate-

quid tibi iucundum est siccis habitare medullis?

     si pudor est, alio traice tela tua.

intactos isto satius temptare veneno:

20   non ego, sed tenuis vapulat umbra mea.

quam si perdideris, quis erit qui talia cantet

     (haec mea musa levis gloria magna tuast),

qui caput et digitos et lumina nigra puellae

     et canat ut soleant molliter ire pedes?

---

18. pudor V₂ puer O.   alio O animo *Phillimore.*   tela tua ω puella tuo O (quod superest alio tramite pelle sitim *Phillimore in Class. Phil. Vol. 4, pp. 315-317!*).

gories may be suggested for the classification of this case; *e.g.* price, cause, manner, abl. abs.; but it must be strongly suspected that this is one of those instances where the poet spoke in disdainful disregard of grammar. Cf. I, 17, 21; I, 19, 19, nn.

17. siccis . . . medullis: 'a bloodless heart,' its vitality having been drained in so many struggles and wounds. Cf. Theoc. 2, 55: αἰαῖ Ἔρως ἀνιαρέ, τί μευ μέλαν ἐκ χροὸς αἷμα ἐμφὺς ὡς λιμνᾶτις ἅπαν ἐκ βδέλλα πέπωκας; cf. also with this verse, and the following, Ovid, *Am.* 2, 9, 13-16: *quid iuvat in nudis hamata retundere tela ossibus? ossa mihi nuda relinquit amor. tot sine amore viri, tot sunt*

sine amore puellae: hinc tibi cum magna laude triumphus eat.

18. alio: 'elsewhere'; *i.e.* to some other heart.

20. vapulat: a word common in comedy. — umbra mea: 'my ghost'; this playful statement is in harmony with the spirit of the word *vapulat.* That the hyperbole is not intended to be taken seriously is clear from *quam si perdideris* in v. 21.

21. talia: such songs as mine; *i.e.* dwelling on such themes, the glory of his playful (*levis*) muse, as are mentioned below, vv. 23-24 (C. S.). These features of Cynthia's beauty are dwelt upon in various passages; *e.g.* I, I, I; 2, I, 9; 2, 2, 5 sqq.; 2, 3, 9 sqq. Cf. Cat. 68, 70-72.

13

Non tot Achaemeniis armantur Susa sagittis,
spicula quot nostro pectore fixit Amor.
hic me tam graciles vetuit contemnere musas,

13. **1.** Susa ω etrusca O Itura *Pontanus* Atusa *Ellis* Erythra *Housman*.

2, 13

Propertius explains that it is his all-mastering passion for Cynthia that inspires whatever poetry he may yet live to write, and foreseeing an early death, expresses his wishes with regard to his obsequies, adding the hesitating hope that she will mourn for her devoted lover. It seems incomprehensible that editors have so often insisted on the division of this beautiful elegy into two or three *membra disiecta*, "XIII–*b*" and "XIII–*c*" being supposed to begin respectively at vv. 17 and 43.

1–16: 'Cupid has wounded me sorely and forced me to write only elegies to please Cynthia. 17–26: So when death shall come, let elegies compose my funeral train; 27–30: but follow thou too, my love, and perform the last sad offices; 31–38: let all due rites be observed, including an epitaph that shall pay tribute to my passion, an epitaph destined to be read as often as that of Achilles; 39–42: when at length thou, too, must die, may thy tomb

be near mine; but meanwhile neglect not my ashes; 43–50: O that I had not lived so long, to know such sadness! 51–56: Yet thou wilt weep for me; even gods weep for mortals; 57–58: but it will be too late: my ashes can write no more elegies then.'

1. Achaemeniis : 'Persian,' *i.e.* Parthian. Achaemenes, the ancestor of the Persian kings, was proverbial for wealth and power, so that his descendants were known as Achaemenidae. Persian and Parthian were essentially identical to the poetic imagination. The well-known Parthian skill in archery made a most effective illustration at this time, when that people was occupying so prominent a place in Roman thought.— **Susa** : the ancient winter capital of the Persian kings.

2. Cf. the previous elegy, vv. 13, 16, 17, *et passim*.

3. graciles . . . musas : such simple poetry as elegies (C. S.). The contrast with epic poetry, to which reference follows in vv. 5–6, is in mind. Cf. Ovid, *Ex. P.* 2, 5, 26; *materiae gracili sufficit ingenium.*

iussit et Ascraeum sic habitare nemus,
5   non ut Pieriae quercus mea verba sequantur,
    aut possim Ismaria ducere valle feras,
    sed magis ut nostro stupefiat Cynthia versu :
    tunc ego sim Inachio notior arte Lino.
    non ego sum formae tantum mirator honestae,
10   nec siqua inlustres femina iactat avos :
    me iuvet in gremio doctae legisse puellae,
    auribus et puris scripta probasse mea.

---

4. Ascraeum . . . habitare nemus: *i.e.* to practice the poet's art ; cf. 2, 10, 25, n.

5. Pieriae: the Thracian Pieria was probably originally referred to, as that belongs to the same general region as *Ismaria valle* (v. 6). Perhaps Propertius did not know the difference between this district and the more famous Macedonian district of the same name near Mt. Olympus, which was especially associated with the Muses. On poetic geography cf. v. 1, n ; Tib. 1, 3, 7, n. — **sequantur**: the legendary effect of the playing and singing of Orpheus. Cf. *ducere . . . feras* (v. 6). Propertius is not seeking a large following, only Cynthia.

6. Ismaria: cf. Verg. *Ec.* 6, 30 : *nec tantum Rhodope miratur et Ismarus Orphea.*

7. magis = *potius*, as several times in Propertius, *e.g.* 2, 3, 53. — **stupefiat** : 'be fascinated.'

8. tunc : 'in that case.' — **Inachio** = *Argivo :* Inachus was the mythical first king of Argos, really

a mere personification of a type. — **Lino** : a famous legendary singer of Argos, said to have taught Orpheus, and to have perished in a musical contest with Apollo himself.

9. tantum = *tam :* instead of the expected correlative *quantum* at the beginning of v. 11, the poet permits himself an emphatic anacoluthon. — **mirator**: cf. 3, 1, 33, n. — **honestae** : 'noble.'

10. femina : the incorporated antecedent of *siqua.*

11. doctae : cf. 1, 7, 11, n. That Cynthia possessed all three of the attractions enumerated in vv. 9–11, beauty, rank, and education, we are abundantly assured in other passages. Cf. 3, 20, 7–8 : *est tibi forma potens, sunt castae Palladis artes, splendidaque a docto fama refulget avo.* — **legisse** : cf. *probasse* (v. 12), *tenuisse,* Tib. 1, 1, 29, n. The object to be supplied is *scripta . . . mea* in the next verse, and Propertius is thinking of reading aloud.

12. puris : of literary taste : uncorrupted, undefiled by any un-

haec ubi contigerint, populi confusa valeto
    fabula: nam domina iudice tutus ero.
15 quae si forte bonas ad pacem verterit aures,
    possum inimicitias tunc ego ferre Iovis.
    quandocumque igitur nostros mors claudet ocellos,
    accipe quae serves funeris acta mei.
    nec mea tum longa spatietur imagine pompa,
20   nec tuba sit fati vana querella mei,
    nec mihi tum fulcro sternatur lectus eburno,
    nec sit in Attalico mors mea nixa toro.

worthy models of style, unlike the
ears of the *populus* of v. 13.

14. fabula: ' babble,' *i.e.* ' talk
of the town '; cf. Hor. *Epod.* 11,
8 : *fabula quanta fui!* The personality of Propertius and the
peculiarities of his style doubtless
aroused contemporary criticism.

15. bonas: ' kindly ' (C. S.). —
ad pacem: ' with favor '; (C. S.) ;
purpose acc. ; sc. *meam*.

16. tunc: cf. v. 8, n.

18. accipe : the change from
the 3d to the 2d person, henceforth
maintained throughout the elegy,
is an instance of a very common
phenomenon in Propertius. Cf.
e.g. 1, 3, vv. 8 and 22 ; Hertzberg,
pp. 115, 116. — **acta** : like the English " programme." A somewhat
peculiar use of the past participle
for what would be, more accurately, *agenda* (C. S.).

19. mea : ' for me.' — **longa** . . .
imagine : collective use for *longa
serie hominum imagines geren-
tium*. — **spatietur** : men wearing
the wax masks of the ancestors in

noble families, and dressed otherwise to represent them, with their
insignia, preceded the bier of a
member of such a family. Cf.
B. *G. Exc.* 12, p. 512.

20. tuba : the Twelve Tables
permitted as many as ten *tubicines*
at funerals. Cf. Hor. *Sat.* 1, 6, 42 :
*hic, si plostra ducenta concur-
rantque foro tria funera magna,
sonabit cornua quod vincatque
tubas.* For details of funeral customs see Tib. 3, 2, 10, n. ; Prop.
1, 17, 21, n.

21. fulcro . . . eburno : the rich
coverings of the *lectus funebris*
hid a large part of it from view,
and the legs, being thus the most
prominent part of it, were sometimes made of ivory.

22. Attalico : not merely was
the name of the Attalidae, kings
of Pergamum, proverbial for magnificence, but in particular Attalus
III is said by Pliny the elder (*N. H.*
8, 74, 196) to have invented a new
luxury in fabrics, by interweaving
threads of gold. Cf. 2, 32, 12 :

desit odoriferis ordo mihi lancibus, adsint
   plebei parvae funeris exequiae.
25   sat mea sat magna est si tres sint pompa libelli,
   quos ego Persephonae maxima dona feram.

25. sat magna est ω sit magna O sic magnast *Baehrens* sit magno *Philli-more* sed magna est *Otto*.

porticus, aulaeis nobilis Attalicis.
— **mors mea** = *ego mortuus, i.e.* as
cadaver. Cf. 1, 19, 19, n. Cic.
Pro Milone, 32, 86: *mortem eius lacerari.*

   23. odoriferis . . . lancibus:
abl. with *ordo*, a Propertian
phrase. Cf. 2, 32, 13: *platanis creber pariter surgentibus ordo.*
The reference is probably to in-
cense, which was burned in the
atrium beside the body lying in
state, and during the procession.
Strangely enough, only here in
the three authors, Catullus, Tibullus, and Propertius does the word
odorifer occur. — **mihi,** midway
between *desit* and the strongly
contrasted *adsint*, belongs to both.

   24. plebei . . . funeris: the
exequiae, or funeral rites, of a poor
man were conducted in the night,
without parade, by persons hired
for the purpose (C. S.). Cf. Mar-
quardt u. Mommsen, Vol. 7, p. 343.
— **parvae . . . exequiae**: 'humble
ceremonies'; *exequiae* primarily
refers to the procession (*exsequor*),
and that this is especially in the
poet's mind may be seen from the
following verses.

   25. sat mea sat: cf. Tib. 1,
1, 43, n. — **tres . . . libelli**: the

perverted wisdom of scholars has
based partly upon these words
the confusion still existing in
the numbering of the poems in the
Propertius collection. For the
various interpretations that may
be put upon this expression see
Intr. § 34. It is sufficient here
to remark that the question
whether *libellus* be taken in the
sense of a poem or a book of
poems makes no difficulty. The
poet is not looking for immediate
dissolution, and if at this time he
had not completed three books of
collected poems, he might thus
express his hope to do so. The
lover's despondency in this elegy
must be compared with his ela-
tion in the next one to show that
it is rather moods than mathe-
matics with which we are dealing
here.

   26. Persephonae . . . dona:
Postgate suggests that Propertius
may have in mind Aeneas and the
golden branch, Verg. *Aen.* 6, 142.
— **maxima**: elegies excel all other
gifts in the honor they carry, as
well to the queen of the underworld as to the queen of the poet's
heart. Literary modesty does not
characterize Propertius.

tu vero nudum pectus lacerata sequeris,
    nec fueris nomen lassa vocare meum,
osculaque in gelidis pones suprema labellis,
30   cum dabitur Syrio munere plenus onyx.
deinde, ubi suppositus cinerem me fecerit ardor,
    accipiat manes parvula testa meos,
et sit in exiguo laurus super addita busto,
    quae tegat extincti funeris umbra locum.
35 et duo sint versus, 'qui nunc iacet horrida pulvis,
    unius hic quondam servus Amoris erat.'

27. tu vero: instead of the stately procession referred to in vv. 19 sqq., Propertius expects Cynthia; and that will be a greater joy to him. — **nudum . . . lacerata**: one of the many forms of outward mourning; cf. Tib. 1, 1, 67–68, n. Tibullus thinks less of self and more of his ladylove.

28. fueris: fut. perf., to correspond with *sequeris*, expressing confident expectation. — **vocare**: the infinitive with *lassus* is entirely Propertian. See Draeger, 434, *d*. It is found here and in 2, 15, 46; 2, 33, 26. The gerund would be the more natural construction (C. S.). For the practice cf. 1, 17, 23; Tib. 1, 1, 61 sqq.; 3, 2, 10–12, nn.

30. Syrio . . . onyx: cf. Cat. 66, 82, n. The perfumes used for anointing the body before burning would naturally have come from Antioch, in Syria, the chief eastern mart for this trade.

32. manes = *cineres*: the identification of the physical and the

spiritual is common in Roman epitaphs, *e.g. CIL.* 6, 10969: *sede sub hac parva titulo parvoque tenetur parva anima*; cf. Tib. 3, 2, 22, n.; Verg. *Aen.* 4, 427: *nec patris Anchisae cineres manesve revelli.*

33. laurus: not the funereal cypress which Horace speaks of, *Car.* 2, 14, 23 (*praeter invisas cupressos*), but the poet's badge of immortality (C. S.). On the "ecstatic and maddening power" of laurel, cf. Farnell, *Cults of the Greek States*, Vol. 4, p. 188, *a*. — **busto**: 'tomb.'

34. extincti funeris: cf. Serv. on *Aen*. 2, 539: *funeris est iam ardens cadaver.* — **umbra**: epexegetical with *quae*, which is practically rendered equivalent to *cuius*.

35. duo . . . versus: incomplete, and so better fitted for this passage than to stand alone as an epitaph.

36. unius . . . Amoris: but cf. 1, 1, n.

nec minus haec nostri notescet fama sepulcri,
    quam fuerant Phthii busta cruenta viri.
tu quoque si quando venies ad fata, memento,
40   hoc iter ad lapides cana veni memores.
interea cave sis nos adspernata sepultos :
    non nihil ad verum conscia terra sapit.
atque utinam primis animam me ponere cunis
    iussisset quaevis de tribus una soror !
45 nam quo tam dubiae servetur spiritus horae ?
    Nestoris est visus post tria saecla cinis.

37. haec . . . fama: *i.e.* the fame that shall rise from my unique devotion to Cynthia.

38. fuerant: sc. *nota* from *notescet.* The plup. for the imp. is a favorite use of Propertius. Cf. 1, 12, 11 ; the *nota* to be supplied does not check Propertius from indulging his mannerism. — **Phthii . . . viri:** Achilles. — **cruenta:** referring to the death of Polyxena, beloved of Achilles, at his tomb. It would help the comparison here to assume that the poet is thinking of the version of the story in which Polyxena committed suicide at the grave of her lover ; then the emphasis will fall on the fact that his constancy to Cynthia, though expressed only in elegies, will make him as famous as Polyxena became by giving her life in a more spectacular way for her lover.

39. si quando : the poet gallantly puts off the evil day to a remote future.

40. hoc iter : Propertius hopes Cynthia's tomb will be near his own. — **cana :** 'in hoary age.' — **memores :** 'that ever call to mind' ; probably the poet is thinking both of the ordinary function of a tombstone and of the undying memory of Cynthia connected with his own.

41. sis . . . adspernata: the present tense is the usual construction ; but for the poet's fondness for tenses of completed action, cf. v. 38, n. ; 1, 17, 1, n. — **sepultos :** the ashes may be said to be 'buried' in the tomb.

42. 'Not all unconscious is the clay ; it has some notion of the truth.' — **verum :** the end toward which the dull earth is groping.

43. atque : adversative. — **ponere** = *deponere.*

44. tribus : sc. *Parcis.*

45. quo : 'to what end?' — **horae :** 'duration ;' genitive.

46. Nestoris : the proverbial old man of wisdom and experience ; yet even he would better have died earlier. — **tria saecla :** cf. Hom. *Il.* 1, 250 sqq

quis tam longaevae minuisset fata senectae
Gallicus Iliacis miles in aggeribus !
non ille Antilochi vidisset corpus humari,
50   diceret aut 'o mors, cur mihi sera venis?'
tu tamen amisso non numquam flebis amico :
fas est praeteritos semper amare viros.
testis, cui niveum quondam percussit Adonem
venantem Idalio vertice durus aper :

---

47. quis tam longaevae O cui si tam longae *Livineius* quoi stamen longae
renuisset *Baehrens.*   53. cui *Huschke* qui O.

---

47. **quis** : interrogative used in
exclamation ; *i.e.* 'how mar y a
soldier might have cut short his
career!'
48. **Gallicus** = *Troianus ;* perhaps from Gallus, a river of Phrygia
in the vicinity of Troy (C. S.) ; a
contemptuous term.
49. **Antilochi** : son of Nestor,
killed in the Trojan War. Cf. Juv.
10, 250 sqq. for a similar reference
(C. S.) ; also Hor. *Car.* 2, 9, 13 :
*at non ter aevo functus amabilem
ploravit omnis Antilochum senex
annos ;* Hom. *Od.* 3, 111 sqq.
50. **diceret** : the tense represents vividly the ever-sounding
wail of Nestor. — **aut** : for the position, cf. 3, 21, 27. The sequence
non . . . aut is rare and poetic ;
cf. 2, 1, 19 sqq. for the recklessness of Propertius in such
matters.
51. **tu tamen** : after the anxiety expressed in vv. 41–42 has
prompted the fit of despair in
which the poet wishes he had

never been born, he reverts again
to the hope of vv. 27–30. The
transition is not abrupt from Nestor
bemoaning his son to Cynthia
weeping for her lover.
52. **praeteritos** = *mortuos*, like
the idiomatic use of οἰχομένους. —
viros : in the sense of 'lovers,'
common in the elegiac writers.
Cf. Pichon, *s.v.*
53. **testis** : sc. *est ea, i.e.*
Venus. — **niveum** : of ideal beauty.
Cf. 1, 2, 19 ; Bion, *Epit. Adon.* 7
sqq. : κεῖται καλὸς Ἄδωνις ἐν
ὤρεσι μηρὸν ὀδόντι, λευκὸν μηρὸν
ὀδόντι τυπείς. — **Adonem** : the familiar story is told at length in
Ovid, *Met.* Bk. 10.
54. **Idalio vertice** : Cyprus in
general, and the town of Idalium
in particular, were favorite abodes
of Venus ; but *vertice* seems a
mere poetic vagueness, especially
when taken with *paludibus* in
v. 55. Some other writers who
venture to localize the tragedy
place it in Syria.

55   illis formosum iacuisse paludibus, illuc
        diceris effusa tu Venus isse coma.
      sed frustra mutos revocabis, Cynthia, manes:
      nam mea quid poterunt ossa minuta loqui?

26

Vidi te in somnis fracta, mea vita, carina
    Ionio lassas ducere rore manus,

55. formosum O formosus *Postgate*. iacuisse O lavisse *or* flevisse ω.   58. quid
FDV qui **N**.

55. illis = *illius regionis:* cf.
Hertzberg, Vol. I, p. 144. — for-
mosum : sc. *dicunt* from *diceris*
(v. 56); a Propertian harshness.
   56. **effusa . . . coma**: cf. Tib.
3, 2, 11.

2, 26

The poet probably tells a real
dream, and takes the opportunity
to prove his devotion to Cynthia
by expressing his willingness to
share the danger of a real voyage
and lose his own life, if need be, in
saving hers (C. S.). There seems
to be no valid reason for beginning
a new poem, as some editors do,
at v. 21. Hertzberg rightly says
that it would be absurd to have
the story of the dream lead up to
nothing.

   1–10: 'I dreamed you were
shipwrecked, darling, and nearly
exhausted with swimming. How
I prayed for your rescue! 11–20:
You called me to help; had the
sea divinities spied you, you would
have been included in their company; but, while I was struggling
to plunge to your relief, a dolphin
rushed to your aid. 21–28: Now
isn't it plain why my mistress
clings to me? No wealth could
draw her from her poet-lover; lav-
ish gifts do not imply constancy
in love. 29-44: I will follow my
mistress through every peril of the
sea, even to death — will even relinquish my own happiness in a
future life for hers. 45–58: But
neither sea, nor sky, gods would
harm lovers, witness many an
example! Yet if I can but die for
thee, it will be a glorious death.'

   1. **Vidi**: of belief, not actual
sight; hence the following infini-
tives, instead of participles. — **mea
vita**: cf. 2, 20, 11; Cat. 104, 1;
without *mea*, 1, 2, 1, *et passim*;
the latter form is the more common
in Propertius. — **carina**: a favorite synecdoche of Propertius, who
employs it about a dozen times.

et quaecumque in me fueras mentita fateri,
   nec iam umore graves tollere posse comas,
5   qualem purpureis agitatam fluctibus Hellen,
   aurea quam molli tergore vexit ovis.
quam timui ne forte tuum mare nomen haberet
   atque tua labens navita fleret aqua!
quae tum ego Neptuno, quae tum cum Castore fratri,
10   quaeque tibi excepi, iam dea Leucothoe!

2. **Ionio**: perhaps because it was by this route that Cynthia had planned to leave Propertius (1, 8). —**ducere**: the motion of swimming; cf. Ovid, *Met.* 4, 353: *alternaque bracchia ducens in liquidis translucet aquis.*—**rore**: cf. Lucr. 4, 438; *quaecumque supra rorem salis edita pars est remorum, recta est.*

3. **in me**: 'against me.' —**fueras mentita**: cf. 2, 13, 38, n.

5. **qualem . . . agitatam . . . Hellen**: after the analogy of the Greek, the participle, which refers both to *te* (v. 1) and to *Hellen*, is used here only, and, like *qualem* and *Hellen*, attracted into the case of *te*. For the myth, cf. H. & T. § 163. — **purpureis** = the Homeric epithet πορφύρεος (*e.g. Il.* 16, 391); cf. Verg. *Georg.* 4, 373; Cic. *Ac. Pr.* 2, 105. In the last passage its comparison with other phases of the sea expressed by the words *caeruleum, ravum,* etc., indicates the appearance of the water when dark and rough from the wind, evidently the poet's thought in this verse.

6. **tergore**: poetic for the more usual neuter form *tergo.*

7. **quam timui**: the exclamation contains a most delicate compliment as well as a strong expression of his love. Her loss would be unbearable even though she were immortalized by a *mare Cynthiacum* (C. S.). —**tuum . . . nomen**: *i.e.* as the Hellespont bore that of Helle. A similar derivation of 'Aegean' from the drowning of Aegeus, father of Theseus, was current. Cf. also *mare Icarium.*

8. **labens**: 'gliding along'; cf. 1, 20, 19: *labentem . . . Mysorum scopulis adplicuisse ratem*; 4, 6, 48.—**fleret**: at the memory of her fate.

9. **quae**: sc. *vota.* —**cum Castore fratri** = *Castori fratrique.* Cf. 1, 17, 18, n.

10. **excepi**: for the more usual *suscepi.* — **iam dea**: Leucothoë had been changed from a mortal to a goddess under similar circumstances, and could sympathize (C. S.). Cf. 2, 28, 19, n. — **Leucothoe**: the variation in form (cf. also 2, 28, 20) from the etymologically correct Leucothea (Λευκοθέα = 'white goddess'), may be due

at tu vix primas extollens gurgite palmas
    saepe meum nomen iam peritura vocas.
quod si forte tuos vidisset Glaucus ocellos,
    esses Ionii facta puella maris
15 et tibi ob invidiam Nereides increpitarent,
    candida Nesaee, caerula Cymothoe,
sed tibi subsidio delphinum currere vidi,
    qui, puto, Arioniam vexerat ante lyram.
iamque ego conabar summo me mittere saxo,

to the analogy of the group of names represented by *Cymothoe* (v. 16); cf. H. & T. § 70.

11. primas . . . palmas: 'thy finger tips'; cf. Cat. 2, 3; *primum digitum dare;* Cynthia is apparently doomed to drown.

12. saepe: 'again and again.' — **meum nomen . . . vocas**: less for succor than in remorse; cf. Verg. *Aen.* 4, 382 sqq.: *spero . . . supplicia hausurum scopulis et nomine Dido saepe vocaturum.*

13. Glaucus: 'the glittering' sea god; cf. H. & T. § 69. — **ocellos**: 'dear eyes.'

14. puella: 'mistress,' the *puella* of this sea.

15. invidiam: caused particularly by the beauty of Cynthia, which would rival even that of immortals.

16. The two Nereids mentioned are typical beauties whose particular charms to the eye are indicated by the epithets *candida* and *caerula*, referring to familiar phases of marine loveliness.

17. Greek and Roman literature are full of myths and tales of the friendliness of the dolphin to gods and men. Cf. P. W., *s.v.* Indeed, the dolphin was said to be a metamorphosed man. It was a devotee of Aphrodite, and as such was said to have brought her first to land after her birth from the sea foam. Its association with Eros was familiar in legend and in art (cf. the Augustus of Primaporta). It is therefore most appropriate that a dolphin should rescue Cynthia in her lover's dream, as told in an ideal erotic elegy, by one inspired by Apollo, to whom likewise the dolphin was sacred.

18. puto: not to be taken too seriously, but more like the Yankee 'guess.' — **Arioniam . . . lyram** = *Arionem lyramque eius.* For the familiar myth see *Class. Dict.*

19. iamque . . . conabar: *i.e.* 'for some time I had been trying,' as is usual in a nightmare. — **me mittere saxo**: Propertius may be thinking of the tale told by Plutarch (*Mor.* 984, E.) of the lover Enalos, who actually threw himself

20   cum mihi discussit talia visa metus.
        nunc admirentur quod tam mihi pulchra puella
        serviat et tota dicar in urbe potens.
        non, si Cambysae redeant et flumina Croesi,
        dicat ' de nostro surge, poeta, toro.'
25   nam mea cum recitat, dicit se odisse beatos :
        carmina tam sancte nulla puella colit.
        multum in amore fides, multum constantia prodest :
        qui dare multa potest, multa et amare potest.
        seu mare per longum mea cogitet ire puella,

---

into the sea to save his sweet-
heart, and was himself rescued by
a dolphin.

20. discussit : a strong word,
as if the mirror were shattered in
which the vision was seen (C. S.).
The growing intensity of the
experience finally wakens the
dreamer with a start

21. nunc : emphatic ; *i.e.* now
that I have related such a dream
as that. Two elements must be
noted in the transition to the
second part of the poem : 1. The
fidelity of the lover in his dream.
2. His poetic skill in describing
it. 'Can anybody wonder any
longer,' he cries, 'that a lover who
loves thus unto death and can tell
his love with such inspiration
should be preferred to all others ? '
Upon these two thoughts are built
the remainder of the argument. —
admirentur : the subject is indefinite, referring to his rivals and
detractors.

23. Cambysae . . . flumina :

plurals expressing a type ; kings
as wealthy as Cambyses, and rivers of gold like the Pactolus, which
made Croesus a proverb of wealth.
— **redeant :** those kings of fabulous wealth were gone long before
this.

24. poeta : who had just presented her with so elegant a sam-
ple of his art and proof of his
devotion, and is therefore preferred to the most boundless
wealth.

25. beatòs : ' rich lovers.'

28. qui : *e.g.* the praetor of 2,
16. — **multa et amare :** concentration of affection on the one
object cannot be expected under
these circumstances ; and the
multa doubtless includes the idea
of *multas.*

29. seu : something of emphasis is added to the correlative from
the omission of the first *seu :*
'even if' (C. S.). — **mare per
longum :** 'a long voyage over the
sea ' (C. S.).

30   hanc sequar, et fidos una aget aura duos.
      unum litus erit sopitis unaque tecto
         arbor, et ex una saepe bibemus aqua,
      et tabula una duos poterit conponere amantes,
         prora cubile mihi seu mihi puppis erit.
35   omnia perpetiar : saevus licet urgeat eurus,
         velaque in incertum frigidus auster agat,
      quicumque et venti miserum vexastis Ulixen
         et Danaum Euboico litore mille rates,
      et qui movistis duo litora, cum rudis Argus

26. 39. rudis **F₂** ratis **O**. Argus **ω** Argo **O**.

30. hanc: emphatic pronoun. excluding all other loves. — **sequar**: probably, like *aget*, future ; more positive than the pres. subj. would have been.

33. conponere: 'nestle' (Phillimore).

36. frigidus auster: *auster* is normally a hot wind ; but the poets enjoy much freedom of imagination in applying epithets to winds, which are indeed variable in temperature as well as in direction. Cf. 2, 9, 34: *nec folia hiberno tam tremefacta noto* ; 4, 3, 48 ; Verg. *Georg.* 4, 261 : *frigidus ut quondam silvis immurmurat Auster* ; J. E. Church in *Univ. of Nev. Studies* 2, 4, pp. 92–98.

38. Euboico litore: *i.e.* on the promontory of Caphareus, where the Grecian fleet was shipwrecked on the return from Troy. Cf. 3, 7, 39 ; 4, 1, 114 ; Verg. *Aen.* 11, 260 : *Euboicae cautes ultorque Caphareus.* — **mille**: not literally a thousand ; cf. H. 163, 2 ; though

Homer says there were 1186 Grecian ships in the expedition against Troy, Dares, the impostor, says 1140 ; Dio, 1200 ; the Scholiast of Euripides, 1170 (C. S.). Whatever the original number, it was doubtless reduced on the return. Cf. *Class. Jour.*, Vol. 4 (1909), p. 165.

39. duo litora: the Symplegades, the two notorious rocky islands near the entrance to the Bosporus, which were reputed to float hither and thither and to crush unlucky vessels between them. Cf. Apollon. Rhod. 2, 317 sqq. For an explanation of the phenomenon see Smith, *Dict. Geog.*, article " Bosporus." — **cum rudis Argus**: cf. 3, 22, 13 : *qua rudis Argoa natat inter saxa columba* ; Luc. 3, 193 : *inde lacessitum primo mare, cum rudis Argo.* By being first sent through the perilous passage the dove became the pathfinder of the ship. Cf. the dove sent by Noah.

40   dux erat ignoto missa columba mari.

illa meis tantum non umquam desit ocellis,
        incendat navem Iuppiter ipse licet.

certe isdem nudi pariter iactabimur oris:
        me licet unda ferat, te modo terra tegat.

45 sed non Neptunus tanto crudelis amori,
        Neptunus fratri par in amore Iovi.

testis Amymone, latices cum ferret, in Argis
        conpressa, et Lernae pulsa tridente palus.

iam deus amplexu votum persolvit: at illi
50   aurea divinas urna profudit aquas.

crudelem et Boream rapta Orithyia negavit:
        hic deus et terras et maria alta domat.

crede mihi, nobis mitescet Scylla nec umquam

---

47. Argis ω arvis O.

41. illa: the only "she" for Propertius.

42. Cf. Hom. *Od.* 12, 415.

43. nudi: 'stripped' of our all.

44. The poet is willing to risk wandering unburied this side of paradise, if Cynthia's body can only be saved and duly buried.

45 sqq. "All the world loves a lover." Cf. 3, 16, 11 sqq.

46. Iovi: Jove was the divine lover *par excellence*; yet Neptune here is his equal, says Propertius.

47. Amymone, sent by her father Danaus to find water in time of drought, was ravished by Neptune, who with his trident produced the spring of Lerna, or *Amymone Lernae palus*, as her reward for yielding to his em-

brace. — **ferret** may have conative force.

49. iam . . . amplexu: 'even while in her embrace.' — **votum**: a preliminary promise to fulfill her chief desire is assumed for Neptune. What ardent lover ever failed to give it? What god would break it? — **illi**: Amymone; corresponding to *deus*; she returned full-handed to her father.

51. Orithyia: daughter of Erechtheus; as she strayed from home in play, she was carried away by Boreas and became the mother of a famous progeny.

52. Boreas represented wild stormy weather, to the people of southern climes especially.

53. nec umquam = *et numquam.*

alternante vacans vasta Charybdis aqua,
55 ipsaque sidera erunt nullis obscura tenebris,
purus et Orion, purus et haedus erit.
quod mihi si ponenda tuo sit corpore vita,
exitus hic nobis non inhonestus erit.

27

At vos incertam, mortales, funeris horam
quaeritis, et qua sit mors aditura via,
quaeritis et caelo Phoenicum inventa sereno,
quae sit stella homini commoda quaeque mala,

57. quod **FLV₂** quid **NDV**.

27. 1. At **O** et **ω**.

54. **alternante . . . aqua**: 'the water's ebb and flow.'

56. **Orion . . . haedus**: both constellations rise at a stormy time of year, and were commonly regarded as the cause of bad weather. Cf. Verg. *Aen.* 4, 52: *dum pelago desaevit hiems et aquosus Orion*; 9, 668: *veniens pluvialibus Haedis verberat imber humum.* Haedi is a double star in Auriga, and the name is usually in the plural.

57. **tuo . . . corpore**: 'for thy body'; *i.e.* if my life must be lost in saving thine (C. S.).

58. **erit**: another example of the change from possibility in protasis to probability in apodosis.

2, 27

1–10: 'O fellow men, ye anxiously seek to know the time and the manner of your death; 11–16: but only the lover knows his fate; if his mistress call, he would even return to her from the jaws of hell.'

Rothstein on insufficient grounds joins this to the preceding elegy.

1. **funeris** = *mortis*: cf. 1, 17, 8, n.

3. **Phoenicum**: the Roman's indistinct knowledge of eastern affairs appears here again: the Chaldaeans were the inventors of astrology, probably; the Phoenicians were good astronomers certainly, so far as the art of navigation was concerned, and doubtless practiced astrology like other eastern nations. — **inventa**: to be taken in apposition with v. 4. Cf. Job 38, 33: "Knowest thou the ordinances of heaven?"

5   seu pedibus Parthos sequitur seu classe Britannos,
        et maris et terrae caeca pericla viae,
    rursus et obiectum fletis capiti esse tumultum,
        cum Mavors dubias miscet utrimque manus,
    praeterea domibus flammam domibusque ruinas,
10   neu subeant labris pocula nigra tuis.
    solus amans novit quando periturus et a qua
        morte, neque hic boreae flabra neque arma timet.
    iam licet et Stygia sedeat sub arundine remex,

---

5. sequitur ω sequimur O. 7. fletis ω fletus N flemus FLDV fles tu *Housman*. capiti LDVF₂ caput NF. tumultum O tumultu ω. 10. labris . . . tuis O suis *Broukhusius* vestris . . . labris *Foster*.

---

5. **Parthos . . . Britannos**: the two widely remote objects of the ambition of Augustus, constantly reappearing in the literature of the period. — **sequitur**: the subject is supplied from *homini*.

6. Epexegetical of v. 5; *maris et terrae* modify *viae*.

7. **fletis**: here followed by three different constructions: acc. and inf. (v. 7), acc. alone (v. 9), and subj. with *ne* (v. 10). In the last two instances the idea of fear is the prominent one in *fletis*.

8. **Mavors**: this longer and perhaps more impressive, because more sonorous, form occurs only here in Propertius, though he uses the shorter usual form six times.

9. Cf. Juv. 3, 190–202.

10. **nigra**: 'deadly'; cf. Verg. *Aen.* 4, 514: *nigri cum lacte veneni*. — **tuis**: for a similar example of the individualizing singular instead of the expected general plural cf. 2, 25, 41–47: *vidistis . . . tuis . . . ocellis*.

11. **periturus**: sc. *sit*: cf. 1, 8, 37. — **a qua**: cf. for the use of the preposition, 3, 2, 25; 4, 3, 39; Tib. 2, 1, 56; Uhlmann, p. 40.

12. **morte**: *i.e.* the disfavor of his darling.

13. **sub**: cf. 3, 9, 36. — **arundine**: characteristic of the banks of sluggish streams like those in the infernal world; cf. Verg. *Georg.* 4, 478: *quos circum limus niger et deformis arundo Cocyti tardaque palus inamabilis unda alligat, et noviens Styx interfuso coercet*. — **remex**: Aristophanes (*Frogs*, 197 sqq.) represents the dead as paddling their own canoe; and Vergil (*Aen.* 6, 320: *illae remis vada livida verrunt*) probably implies the same.

cernat et infernae tristia vela ratis :
15   si modo clamantis revocaverit aura puellae,
concessum nulla lege redibit iter.

28

Iuppiter, adfectae tandem miserere puellae :
tam formosa tuum mortua crimen erit.

15. clamantis **O** damnatis **V**₂ damnatum **ω**.

14. tristia vela ratis : the phantom ferryboat of Charon appears to be equipped not merely with oars but also with sails to catch any shadow of a breeze that may stir in that calm locality !

15. clamantis : it might be at the *conclamatio* just after death, at the funeral pyre, or perhaps at the tomb. — **aura** : the faintest whisper only might reach the Styx, indeed only the breath of the voice might fan the ghostly cheeks of the lover.

16. Cf. 4, 11, 4.

2, 28

Cynthia is dangerously ill. Propertius utters fervent, and ultimately effectual, prayers for her recovery. The arguments advanced by different editors for dividing this elegy variously into two or three separate poems seem insufficient. The natural vacillations of anxiety, despair, hope, and ultimate confidence pass swiftly before the sympathies of the reader. For various parallels, cf. Ovid, *Am.* 2, 13.

1-4 : 'Juppiter, show pity in my darling's hour of need ; 5-14 : true, she may have brought her affliction upon herself by offending some divinity, perhaps through perjury or overweening pride. 15-24 : Yet, like other famous beauties who had offended some divinity, you too, Cynthia, may ultimately triumph over your difficulties ; 25-30 : but if you must die, glory and fame will be yours in death ; 31-34 : humble yourself, however, before the gods ; and hesitate not, Jove, to grant our petition. 35-46 : All the omens and incantations fail to give us any encouragement ; my life is bound up in hers ; pity us both, and both of us will pay thee our vows ; 47-58 : Persephone and Pluto, confirm my hope ; already fair ones enough are in your realms, and sooner or later must we all come to you. 59-62 : And, light of my life, forget not to pay

venit enim tempus quo torridus aestuat aer,
　　incipit et sicco fervere terra cane.
5　sed non tam ardoris culpa est neque crimina caeli
　　quam totiens sanctos non habuisse deos.
　hoc perdit miseras, hoc perdidit ante, puellas:
　　quidquid iurarunt, ventus et unda rapit.
　num sibi collatam doluit Venus? illa peraeque
10　prae se formosis invidiosa deast.
　an contempta tibi Iunonis templa Pelasgae,
　　Palladis aut oculos ausa negare bonos?
　semper, formosae, non nostis parcere verbis:
　　hoc tibi lingua nocens, hoc tibi forma dedit.
15　sed tibi vexatae per multa pericula vitae

28. 9. num **DFL** nun **V** non **N.**

your vows.' (Cf. 2, 9, 25: *haec
mihi vota tuam propter suscepta
salutem*, etc., for an interesting
"parallel column.")

　2. formosa . . . mortua = *for-
mosam mortuam esse*; see Hertzberg 1, p. 155; cf. Ovid's imitation
(*Am.* 2, 11, 35): *vestrum crimen
erit talis iactura puellae.*

　3. Summer and early fall were
the dangerous months at Rome,
although the ancients knew but
vaguely the causes of the diseases
here attributed to *torridus aer*.

　4. Cf. Tib. 1, 7, 21. — **fervĕre**:
the same quantity occurs, 2, 8, 32,
the only other place in Propertius
where this verb is used.

　8. Cf. Cat. 70, 3–4; Tib. 4, 4,
8; Ovid, *Am.* 2, 16, 45.

　9. num: the poet hesitates to
suggest the thought that Cynthia

had ventured such a comparison.
— **peraeque**: to be taken with
invidiosa.

　11. This is no occasion for
offending any divinity; and Propertius hastens to add the names of
the other two fair goddesses whom
Paris had slighted in his famous
decision. — **Pelasgae**: as a favorer
of Greeks, here in contrast especially to the Trojans.

　12. oculos: the special physical
feature of Athena, referred to in
the stock epithet γλαυκῶπις. Yet
this feature seems to have been
the object of ridicule on the part
of her rival goddesses and criticism by others; cf. Hygin. 165;
*Iuno et Venus cum eam irriderent,
quod et caesia erat et buccas in-
flaret . . . vidit se merito irrisam.*
— **ausa**: sc. *es.*

extremo veniet mollior hora die.

Io versa caput primos mugiverat annos :

nunc dea, quae Nili flumina vacca bibit.

Ino etiam prima terris aetate vagatast :

20   hanc miser inplorat navita Leucothoen.

Andromede monstris fuerat devota marinis :

haec eadem Persei nobilis uxor erat.

Callisto Arcadios erraverat ursa per agros :

haec nocturna suo sidere vela regit.

25   quod si forte tibi properarint fata quietem,

---

16.   veniet **V**₂ veniat ω venit **O**.

---

16. extremo : 'ultimately' ; cf. 2, 10, 7, n.

17. Io versa : on account of the jealousy of Hera. — **caput** : Propertius is following two types of her representation in the same sentence ; she was frequently represented as a beautiful woman with only the horns of a heifer to call attention to the myth ; but both Greek and Egyptian art also represented her as a heifer throughout. A type representing her as a cow-headed maiden was, perhaps, invented to identify Io with Isis. Cf. *Harv. Stud.*, Vol. 12, pp. 335 sqq.

18. dea : Isis, with whom Io was ultimately identified. — **bibit** : perfect tense.

19. Ino : daughter of Cadmus. When pursued by her insane husband Athamas, she leaped into the sea, and becoming a marine divinity was known as Leucothea (Leucothoë in v. 20 and in

2, 26, 10, *q.v.*). — **terris** : as contrasted with her later home in the sea.

21. Andromede : daughter of Cassiope (or Iope) and Cepheus. Her mother's proud boast of being more beautiful than the sea nymphs brought upon the unhappy girl the fate of being exposed on the shore to a sea monster. Cf. v. 51, n. — **monstris** : poetic plural.

22. Persei : Perseus rescued the maiden and became her husband. Ultimately she found a place among the stars.

23. Callisto : daughter of Lycaon, the Arcadian king ; an attendant of Artemis ; beloved of Zeus ; changed by Artemis or Hera in anger into a bear ; translated by Zeus to the skies as Ursa Maior ; mother of Arcas and the Arcadian race.

25. properarint : 'prove to have decreed a premature (death).' — **quietem** : cf. Verg. *Aen.* 10, 745 :

illa sepulturae fata beata tuae.

narrabis Semelae, quo sit formosa periclo :

    credet et illa, suo docta puella malo :

et tibi Maeonias inter heroidas omnis

30   primus erit nulla non tribuente locus.

nunc, utcumque potes, fato gere saucia morem :

    et deus et durus vertitur ipse dies.

hoc tibi vel poterit, coniunx, ignoscere Iuno :

    frangitur et Iuno, siqua puella perit.

35   deficiunt magico torti sub carmine rhombi,

    et iacet extincto laurus adusta foco,

et iam Luna negat totiens descendere caelo,

    nigraque funestum concinit omen avis.

---

olli dura quies oculos et ferreus urget somnus, in aeternam clauduntur lumina noctem.

26. illa . . . fata : in apposition with *fata* (v. 25). — **beata :** anticipating the description in the following verses.

27. formosa : substantive : 'the perils of a beauty.' — **periclo :** abl. of quality.

28. suo . . . malo : Semele, beloved of Zeus, was nevertheless destroyed by his lightning. when she craved his companionship as the sky god.

29. Maeonias = H o m e r i c, as Maeonia was an old name for Lydia, the birthplace of Homer. — **inter :** for the poetic lengthening of the final syllable as the ictus syllable where the following word begins with *h*, cf. 2, 8, 8 : *vinceres aut vincis, haec in amore rotast.*

31. nunc : imagination gives place to fact ; dreams to the needs of the present moment.

33. tibi : Juppiter, addressed in *coniunx.* — **ignoscere :** cf. Tib. 4, 2, 3.

34. Cf. Tib. 4, 4, 15.

35. rhombi : a magic wheel, apparently used in different ways for purposes of divination. Cf. 3, 6, 26 : *staminea rhombi ducitur ille rota* ; Tib. 1, 3, 11, n.

36. adusta : 'but singed,' instead of entirely consumed : a bad sign. Cf. Tib. 2, 5, 81, n. The sharp crackle of the burning laurel was considered a good omen.

37. descendere : cf. 1, 1, 19, n.

38. nigra : 'ill-omened.' — **avis :** the owl. Cf. Ovid, *Am.* 3, 12, 2 : *omina non albae concinuistis aves* ; Verg. *Aen.* 4, 462 : *solaque culminibus ferali carmine bubo ;* Hor. *Sat.* 1, 9, 73.

una ratis fati nostros portabit amores
40   caerula ad infernos velificata lacus.
si non unius, quaeso, miserere duorum.
    vivam, si vivet : si cadet illa, cadam.
pro quibus optatis sacro me carmine damno :
    scribam ego ' per magnum salva puella Iovem,'
45   ante tuosque pedes illa ipsa operata sedebit,
    narrabitque sedens longa pericla sua.
haec tua, Persephone, maneat clementia, nec tu,
    Persephones coniunx, saevior esse velis.
sunt apud infernos tot milia formosarum :
50   pulchra sit in superis, si licet, una locis.

41. si FLDV set N.

39. ratis fati : Charon's skiff. —
nostros . . . amores = *nos amantes* ; cf. 4, 4, 37, n.

40. caerula : cf. Verg. *Aen.* 6,
410 : *caeruleam advertit puppim* ;
but in v. 303 the *cymba* is "*ferru-
ginea.*"

41. Cf. Tib. 4, 4, 19 ; Ovid,
Am. 2, 13, 15 : *in una parce
duobus.*

43. carmine : cf. 2, 13, 35, n.

44. This may be the abstract
of a prepared poem or hymn ; cf.
Tib. 1, 3, 31.

45. tuosque : here it is Juppiter, in v. 60 it is Diana, and in
v. 61 it is Isis, to whom special
thanksgiving is paid, although it is
Persephone by whose favor the
sick one is represented (vv. 47,
sqq.) as being relieved from her
dangerous position. The poet
does not find it necessary to give
us all the intermediate steps of his
thought. — **operata :** cf. Tib. 2, 1,

9, n. — **sedebit :** for the custom
cf. Tib. 1, 3, 30.

47. After the encouraging vision
of vv. 45-46 the poet turns hope-
fully to Jove's brother, Pluto, to
whom all must ultimately come
(v. 58), and to his fair bride Persephone, to whom the youth and
beauty of Cynthia should especially
appeal, and realizing that the very
lingering of the sick one on this
side the grave implies *clementia*
on their part, urges that this mercy
be continued for the present, since
they do not need another beauty
in the lower world. There is no
confidence expressed till v. 59. —
tu : Pluto.

49. For **inferni** = *inferi* in
Prop. cf. *BPW.*, Vol. 28 (1908),
Sp. 541. — **fōrmōsārūm :** cf. Intr.
§ 42, I (3).

50. superis . . . locis : *i.e.* on
earth, as contrasted with *inferis
locis,* the underworld.

265

vobiscum est Iope, vobiscum candida Tyro,
  vobiscum Europe, nec proba Pasiphae,
et quot Troia tulit vetus et quot Achaia formas,
  et Phoebi et Priami diruta regna senis :
55 et quaecumque erat in numero Romana puella,
  occidit : has omnis ignis avarus habet.
nec forma aeternum aut cuiquam est fortuna per-
    ennis :
  longius aut propius mors sua quemque manet.
tu quoniam es, mea lux, magno dimissa periclo,
60   munera Dianae debita redde choros,

54. Phoebi **O** Thebae *Scaliger.*

51. Iope : sometimes identified with Cassiepeia (Cassiope), daughter of Aeolus. It was from her that the city of Joppa was supposed to have been named. A famous mythological beauty, whom (as Cassiepeia) tradition placed ultimately among the stars, as it did her daughter Andromeda. Cf. v. 21, n. — **Tyro** : wife of Cretheus ; in love with the Thessalian river god Enipeus, and beloved by Poseidon. Odysseus held converse with her in the lower world ; cf. Hom. *Od.* 11, 235 sqq.

52. Europe : daughter of Phoenician Agenor ; Zeus in the form of a white bull carried her off to Crete to woo her. — **nec proba** = *et inproba*. — **Pasiphae** : wife of Minos, and mother of the Minotaur.

54. Phoebi : Phoebus and Poseidon helped Laomedon build the walls of Troy. Hesione, daughter of Laomedon, was given by Heracles to Telamon as the prize for

help in the sack of this city. — **Priami** : the later city of Priam was taken by the Greeks in the famous ten years' war, and the fair Helen was then the chief prize. — **regna** : in apposition only with *Troia*, if the text is correct ; for the awkward arrangement cf. Cat. 68, 68-69.

55. in numero : 'worth mentioning' (*i.e.* in this list).

56. ignis : *i.e.* of the funeral pyre.

58. Cf. Hor. *Car.* 2, 3, 25 : *omnes eodem cogimur, omnium versatur urna serius ocius.*

59. If this elegy was written after Cynthia's recovery, this verse represents the actual condition of things at the time of composition ; if it was penned during the progress of the disease, it expresses a more or less well-grounded faith that his prayers are heard. But cf. v. 47, n.

60. munera . . . debita : thank-offerings to the deity ; for proces-

redde etiam excubias divae nunc, ante iuvencae,
 votivas noctes et mihi solve decem.

31

Quaeris, cur veniam tibi tardior.   aurea Phoebi
 porticus a magno Caesare aperta fuit.

sions as thank-offerings cf. Arr. *Anab.* 2, 24, 6. — **choros**: perhaps Propertius refers to the torchlight processions at the temple of Diana Nemorensis, near Aricia, in which a woman whose prayer had been granted would be especially likely to join; see Preller³, Vol. 1, p. 317; cf. Ovid, *Fast.* 3, 269: *saepe potens voti, frontem redimita coronis, femina lucentes portat ab urbe faces.* That Cynthia was accustomed to take part in these rites is seen from 2, 32, 9: *accensis devotam currere taedis in nemus et Triviae lumina ferre deae.* Moreover the chief annual occasion of this practice was on the Ides of August; cf. vv. 3–4. But if *choros* means merely 'dances,' cf. Tib. 1, 3, 31.

61. **excubias**: cf. 2, 33, 1–2; Tib. 1, 3, 25, n. — **divae . . . iuvencae**: cf. vv. 17, 18, nn.

62. **decem**: the same number as ritual prescribed for the goddess. Cf. Cumont, *Oriental Relig. in Rom. Paganism*, p. 90.

2, 31

Propertius apologizes for his tardiness in meeting an engagement (presumably with Cynthia) with the excuse that the fascination of the newly opened temple of Apollo on the Palatine, including the sacred inclosure and its surrounding *porticus*, had detained him. Beginning with the *porticus* and its decorations he describes what he had seen in proceeding even to the image of the god in the *cella* of the temple itself. The brevity of this description may be explained by the facts that in excusing tardiness prolixity is out of place, and that up to this period in the poet's compositions this was an unusual type of subject, which he might attack with some hesitation. The impression made upon him by the whole architectural and decorative scheme is clearly that produced by a novelty, and we must date the poem on the day of opening the temple, Oct. 9, 28 B.C.

The work of building had commenced soon after the return of Augustus from the defeat of Sextus Pompey in 36 B.C. But the temple was known as that of Apollo Actius through whose favor Octavian in 31 B.C. had won his final victory

tota erat in speciem Poenis digesta columnis,
inter quas Danai femina turba senis.
5 hic equidem Phoebo visus mihi pulchrior ipso
marmoreus tacita carmen hiare lyra,
atque aram circum steterant armenta Myronis,

31. 3. tota ω tanta O.

over all rivals. It was the most
magnificent thing of its kind that
Rome had ever seen, situated on
the northeast corner of the Palatine hill, adjacent to the Domus
Augustana. The Sibylline books
were transferred hither at an uncertain date. Cf. Tib. 2, 5, 1, n.;
Jordan, *Top.* 1, 3, pp. 66 sqq.;
Platner, *Top.* p. 142.

1. **tibi**: "ethical" dative. —
aurea: because made of the
golden yellow Numidian marble
now called *giallo antico* (cf. v. 3).

2. **aperta fuit**: this form combines the thoughts of *aperta erat*
(plup.) and *aperta erat* (adj. and
imp.). 'The opening had just occurred, and there it stood open to
invite me in as I passed.' Cf. G.
250, R. 1. Note the following
series of descriptive secondary
tenses.

3. **in speciem**: purpose acc.;
i.e. to make an especially fine appearance. Cf. *PAPA.*, Vol. 28
(1897), p. xxiv.

4. **femina**: used here as an
adj. — **turba**: the fifty Danaides,
whose statues stood in the inter-
columnar spaces. Cf. Ovid, *A. A.*
1, 73: *quaque parare necem mi-
seris patruelibus ausae Belides et*

stricto stat ferus ense pater.
Acron, quoted by the Scholiast at
Persius 1, 56, states that (bronze)
equestrian statues of their ill-fated
husbands stood in front of them
in the open space of the sacred
inclosure.

5. **hic**: adv. Propertius unconsciously assumes that the
reader has followed him through
the colonnade and out into the
area where stood this famous
statue of Apollo near the altar in
front of the temple. — **equidem**:
emphasizes *mihi*. — **pulchrior ipso**:
cf. the slang phrase, "as big as
life and twice as natural."

6. **marmoreus**: sc. *Phoebus.* —
tacita . . . lyra: with concessive
force. — **hiare**: active; 'to be
opening his lips in song.' The
type of this Apollo has not been
certainly identified.

7. **steterant**: had taken their
stand, and so 'were standing.' —
armenta Myronis: Myron, a
sculptor contemporary with Poly-
clitus and Phidias, worked mostly
in bronze, and achieved special
distinction for his realistic representations of animals as well as human figures. Cf. Gardner, *Hand-
book of Greek Sculpture*, p. 287.

quattuor artifices, vivida signa, boves.

tum medium claro surgebat marmore templum,

10   et patria Phoebo carius Ortygia.

in quo Solis erat supra fastigia currus,

et valvae, Libyci nobile dentis opus,

altera deiectos Parnasi vertice Gallos,

altera maerebat funera Tantalidos.

15   deinde inter matrem deus ipse interque sororem

Pythius in longa carmina veste sonat.

8. **vivida signa**: probably bronze. Cf. 3, 9, 9.

9. **claro . . . marmore**: white Luna (Carrara) marble was the material; cf. Verg. *Aen.* 8, 720: *niveo candentis limine Phoebi.*

10. **Ortygia**: the one identified with Delos, the birthplace of Phoebus.

11. **Solis . . . currus**: as an acroterium ornament at the apex of the pediment. How many others were on this roof is unknown; Pliny (*N. H.* 36, 5, 13) states that there were at any rate statues of Bupalus and Athenis. This kind of architectural adornment grew in popularity. In a corresponding position on the temple of the Capitoline Juppiter, which Octavian restored in this same year, stood a statue of Jove in a quadriga. On the next Capitoline-Juppiter temple, built after the fire of 69 A.D., stood not only a similar statue, but also two other chariots, two eagles, and statues of the Capitoline trinity of gods, Juppiter, Juno, and Minerva; cf. Platner, p. 283.

12. **dentis**: 'ivory.'

13. **altera**: in partitive apposition with *valvae*: sc. *maerebat* from v. 14. The Gauls under Brennus attacked Delphi in 279 B.C., but were routed through the interposition of Apollo himself. Cf. 3, 13, 51: *torrida sacrilegum testantur limina Brennum, dum petit intonsi Pythia regna dei*; Paus. 1, 4, 4.

14. **maerebat**: 'pictured the pitiful story of.' — **funera Tantalidos**: the death of the children of Niobe, whom Apollo and his sister Artemis punished for her presumptuous pride in them.

15. **deinde**: *i.e.* leaving the outside of the temple, and entering the ivory-carven doors, we are face to face with the object of supreme interest, the famous statue of Apollo Citharoedus by Scopas. — **matrem**: the statue of Leto was by the younger Cephisodotus; cf. Pliny, *N. H.* 36, 5, 24. — **sororem**: the Artemis was a work of Timotheus; cf. Pliny, *N. H.* 36, 5, 32.

16. Cf. Tib. 2, 5, 1, n.

LIBER TERTIVS

I

Callimachi manes et Coi sacra Philetae,
in vestrum, quaeso, me sinite ire nemus.
primus ego ingredior puro de fonte sacerdos

1. 1. Philetae **N** Philitae **FLDV.**

3, 1 (and 2)

At the beginning of Book 3 the poet magnifies his office, and defines its scope. In the Mss. a new poem begins with v. 39; but it is probably best to regard the two elegies as originally a unit, since neither seems quite complete without the other.

1–6: 'Callimachus and Philetas, let me be your representative successor as the Roman elegist, and reveal to me the sources of your inspiration; 7–20: already in my chosen field I am leaving far behind those who essay epic strains; so, Muses, wreath me with your own garlands; 21–38: what care I for the envious detractor of to-day? I foresee that after death I shall be to elegy as Homer is to the epic art; 1–10: so let me return to my own sphere, that many a fair lady may dote upon my verses — what wonder if they do, when we remember Orpheus, Amphion, and Galatea! 11–16: For I must win my friends not by wealth, but by

the aid of the Muses; 17–26: and so, fortunate indeed is she who gains a name through my pen! The splendors of the external world will perish by fire and flood, but the glory of genius dieth not.'

1. **Callimachi**: the two great Alexandrian elegists are named in the order of their importance; cf. Intr. §§ 7–9. — **manes ... sacra**: both words are to be taken with both genitives. Propertius asks to enter the sacred grove (*nemus*, v. 2) where as the accepted priest he can perform the sacred rites in honor of the souls of his great models.

3. **primus**: the claim is that he is the first to measure up to the standards of the Alexandrian tradition; Propertius has not already forgotten the list of his predecessors in Roman elegy with which the previous poem in the collection closes; but his temper here is essentially that of 4, 1, 64. In this sort of self-conceit Propertius is perhaps *primus inter pares* among the Romans; but cf. Hor. *Car.* 3, 30, 13: *princeps*

Itala per Graios orgia ferre choros.

5   dicite, quo pariter carmen tenuastis in antro?
        quove pede ingressi? quamve bibistis aquam?
     ah valeat, Phoebum quicumque moratur in armis!
        exactus tenui pumice versus eat.
     quo me Fama levat terra sublimis, et a me
10   nata coronatis musa triumphat equis,
     et mecum in curru parvi vectantur Amores,
        scriptorumque meas turba secuta rotas.
     quid frustra missis in me certatis habenis?
        non datur ad musas currere lata via.
15   multi, Roma, tuas laudes annalibus addent,

Aeolium carmen ad Italos deduxisse modos; Foster in *Matzke Memorial Vol.* pp. 104 sqq. — **puro** = *integro*.

4. The figure of carrying Italian mysteries through the mazes of Greek dances means the treating of the secrets of love among the Italians in the Greek style. Cf. Cat. 64, 259: *obscura cavis celebrabant orgia cistis*; Sen. *Herc. Aet.* 594: *nos Cadmeis orgia ferre tecum solitae condita cistis*; Enk, *ad loc.*

5. pariter: of the two elegists in v. 1. — **carmen tenuastis**: 'spin your fine thread of song.'

6. pede: if this refers to meter at all, it is to refinement in treatment. The poet's questions have an eye to his initiation into the deeper mysteries of the elegiac art as practiced by Callimachus and Philetas.

7. valeat: Propertius will soon leave such a poet far behind. — **moratur**: 'tries to hold the attention of'; cf. Hor. *A. P.* 321: *valdius oblectat populum meliusque moratur*.

8. Polish, rather than a great theme, is his boast.

9. quo: *i.e.* such a *versus*.

10. coronatis . . . equis: cf. Ovid, *Trist.* 4, 2, 22: *ante coronatos ire videbit equos*.

11. Amores: as children of triumphing generals, who sometimes took their children with them, *e.g.* Germanicus; cf. Tac. *Ann.* 2, 41, 4: *currusque quinque liberis onustus*.

14. currere: purpose inf. = *ad currendum.* — **lata via**: where it is easy for a number to vie in reaching a goal. The particular Via Lata at Rome was identical with the modern *Corso*, whose name is significant in this connection.

qui finem imperii Bactra futura canent:
sed, quod pace legas, opus hoc de monte sororum
detulit intacta pagina nostra via.
mollia, Pegasides, date vestro serta poetae:
20   non faciet capiti dura corona meo.
at mihi quod vivo detraxerit invida turba,
post obitum duplici fenore reddet Honos.
omnia post obitum fingit maiora vetustas:
maius ab exequiis nomen in ora venit.
25 nam quis equo pulsas abiegno nosceret arces.
fluminaque Haemonio cominus isse viro,

---

23. omnia **FLDV** Famae **N**. vetustas **FLDV** vetustae **N** (*cf. Enk ad loc.*)

---

16. **Bactra**: on the outskirts of Roman geographical knowledge beyond Parthia. Cf. 2, 10, 13–16, nn.

17. **sororum** = *Musarum.*

18. Propertius affects for the moment an air of superiority as compared to the epic poets; but the real reason why he writes elegy appears shortly in v. 20; and we have only to compare 2, 10; 3, 3; and 3, 9 to realize that he would gladly have sung epic strains, had he not known himself unfit for the task.

19. **mollia**: cf. 4, 1, 61–62. — **Pegasides**: this name for the Muses is derived from the horse whose hoof stamped out their fountain Hippocrene. Cf. 3, 3, 2.

20. **non faciet** corresponds here exactly to the English idiom, 'will not do.' For a similar sense with the acc. cf. Ovid, *Her.* 15,

190: *ad talem formam non facit iste locus.*

21. Cf. Hor. *Car.* 2, 20, 4 sqq.: *invidiaque maior urbes relinquam . . . non ego . . . obibo nec Stygia cohibebor unda . . . me Colchus et, qui dissimulat metum Marsae cohortis, Dacus et ultimi noscent Geloni;* Ovid, *Am.* 1, 15, 39–40.

24. **ab**: 'from the time of.' Cf. Ovid, *Trist.* 4, 10, 121: *vivo sublime dedisti nomen, ab exequiis quod dare fama solet.*

25. **pulsas**: the walls of Troy were literally battered down to let in the wooden horse; but the broader, figurative sense is probably intended here.

26. **Haemonio . . . viro**: Achilles was the most famous Thessalian, for which Haemonia is a synonymous term. For the dat. with *isse*, cf. 4, 1, 148; Uhlmann, p 38.

Idaeum Simoenta Iovis cum prole Scamandro,
    Hectora per campos ter maculasse rotas ?
Deiphobumque Helenumque et Polydamanta et in
    armis
30   qualemcumque Parin vix sua nosset humus.
exiguo sermone fores nunc, Ilion et tu
    Troia bis Oetaei numine capta dei.
nec non ille tui casus memorator Homerus
    posteritate suum crescere sensit opus.

---

27. cum prole Scamandro *G. Wolff a lacuna in* **N** Iovis cunabula **parvi**
FLDV Idaeos montes Iovis incunabula *Palmer*.   29. Polydamanta *Lachmann*
Polydamantis *Phillimore* Polilidamantas *changed to* — es **N** (*unchanged in*
NFL).

27. Cf. Hom. *Il.* 21, 2 ; 223,
and the context. The attempts
to justify the Mss. reading here
can hardly be convincing, as the
sense is thus widely interrupted ;
and the silence of **N** is significant ;
cf. Butler and Enk, *ad loc.*

28. Cf. Verg. *Aen.* 1, 483 : *ter
circum Iliacos raptaverat Hectora
muros.*

29. Pōlydamanta : this group-
ing of Polydamas, son of Panthous,
with three famous sons of Priam
is justified by his close association
with leading Trojans in Homer
and in Latin poetry ; cf. 1, 14, 19,
n.; Ovid, *Met.* 12, 547.

30. qualemcumque : 'sorry warrior as he was.' — **vix** . . . **humus** :
cf. Ovid, *Trist.* 5, 5, 54 : *forsitan
Evadnen vix sua nosset humus.*

31. Ilion : Vergil similarly uses
this name several times in juxtaposition with *Troia, e.g. Aen.* 2,
625 : *Ilium et ex imo verti Nep-*

tunia Troia. What distinction,
if any, was intended by the poets,
is uncertain.

32. bis . . . **capta** : Heracles took
Troy in person in revenge for the
perjury of Laomedon ; and the
Greeks took it in the famous ten
years' war, but only, according to
prophecy, by using the arrows of
Heracles (which Philoctetes had
inherited) with which to kill Paris,
whose death indirectly caused the
fall of the city. — **Oetaei . . . dei** :
Heracles, who ascended from Mt.
Oeta to his place among the
gods.

33. memorator : Propertius is
fond of rare verbal nouns in *-tor* ;
cf. 2, 13, 9.

34. posteritate : one of the
poet's vague ablatives, apparently
expressing means ; cf. *vetustas*
(v. 23). — **sensit** : perf. def., implying the conscious existence of
the soul of Homer after death.

35   meque inter seros laudabit Roma nepotes:
     illum post cineres auguror ipse diem.
     ne mea contempto lapis indicet ossa sepulcro
     provisum est Lycio vota probante deo.

2

Carminis interea nostri redeamus in orbem :
     gaudeat in solito tacta puella sono.
Orphea detinuisse feras et concita dicunt
     flumina Threicia sustinuisse lyra:
5   saxa Cithaeronis Thebas agitata per artem
     sponte sua in muri membra coisse ferunt:
quin etiam, Polypheme, fera Galatea sub Aetna
     ad tua rorantes carmina flexit equos:

35. meque = *me quoque* ; cf. Cat. 102, 3.

37. Cf. 2, 13, 37.

38. Lycio . . . deo : famous oracles were given by Apollo at his temple at Patara in Lycia. The poet speaks as if this were one of them.

3, 2

1. Cf. 3, 3, 21.

2. gaudeat in : Propertius often uses a superfluous *in* with ablatives that are really causal; cf. 4, 8, 63 : *Cynthia gaudet in exuviis* ; 1, 18, 8 ; 3, 9, 11. — **puella** : collective ; cf. v. 10 *infra*.

3. Propertius enforces his argument by citing three famous instances of the marvelous power of a singer to draw after him inanimate nature, beasts, and even a

divine being like Galatea, and that too in spite of her great reluctance.

5. artem : that of Amphion.

6. membra : purpose acc.

7. quin etiam : introducing the most remarkable instance.

8. ad tua . . . carmina flexit : Propertius delights in the obscure version of a myth ; cf. 4, 4, Intr. According to the well-known idyls of Theocritus (6 and 11) and the metamorphoses of Ovid (13, 735 sqq.) Polyphemus was unsuccessful in his suit ; but that there was a version according to which his efforts were not in vain is evident from the Greek mythographer Nonnus, of the fifth century A.D. (*Dion.* 6, 300–324) ; cf. App. *Ill.* 1, 2, where Keltos, Illyrios, and Galas are referred to as sons of Polyphemus and Galatea. — **roran-**

miremur, nobis et Baccho et Apolline dextro

10   turba puellarum si mea verba colit?

quod non Taenariis domus est mihi fulta columnis,

nec camera auratas inter eburna trabes,

nec mea Phaeacas aequant pomaria silvas,

non operosa rigat Marcius antra liquor:

15   at Musae comites, et carmina grata legenti,

et defessa choris Calliopea meis.

fortunata, meo siqua est celebrata libello!

2. 17. est O es ω.

tes: dripping with brine as they showed themselves above the surface of the sea.

9. Baccho: Bacchus has already appeared as a patron of poets in Tib. 3, 4, 43: *casto nam rite poetae Phoebusque et Bacchus Pieridesque favent*; cf. also Prop. 2, 30, 38: *medius docta cuspide Bacchus*; E. Maass in *Hermes*, Vol. 31 (1896), pp. 375 sqq.; Farnell, *Greek Cults*, Vol. 5, pp. 114, 143, 148. — **dextro** = *fausto*; cf. 3, 18, 5.

11. Cf. Hor. *Car.* 2, 18, 1: *Non ebur neque aureum mea renidet in domo lacunar, non trabes Hymettiae premunt columnas ultima recisas.* — **Taenariis**: the marble from Taenarum was black, rare, and so a sign of wealth where used.

12. camera: a vaulted ceiling rather than the *lacunar* ('panel ceiling') referred to by Horace.

13. Phaeacas: the special feature of the wealth of King Alcinous was the magnificence of his orchards and gardens. Cf. Hom. *Od.* 7, 112; Verg. *Georg.* 2, 87: *pomaque et Alcinoi silvae.*

14. operosa: 'artfully constructed'; cf. 3, 3, 27. — **Marcius**: *i.e.* brought by the Aqua Marcia, whose water was justly celebrated in ancient times, and is still in use at Rome; built by A. Marcius Rex in 144 B.C., and restored by Agrippa; cf. 3, 22, 24: *aeternum Marcius umor opus*; Tib. 3, 6, 58: *temperet annosum Marcia lympha merum*; Pliny, *N. H.* 31, 24, 41: *clarissima aquarum omnium in toto orbe frigoris salubritatisque palma praeconio urbis Marcia est.*

16. Calliopea: Propertius makes no more attempt here to differentiate the functions of individual Muses than Horace does in addressing at different times Euterpe, Polyhymnia, Clio, and Melpomene. Indeed Calliope is the only Muse whom Propertius ever mentions; cf. 3, 3, 38, n.

17. libello: 'my verse'; a noncommittal word; cf. 2, 13, 25, n.

carmina erunt formae tot monimenta tuae.
nam neque pyramidum sumptus ad sidera ducti
20   nec Iovis Elei caelum imitata domus
nec Mausolei dives fortuna sepulcri
mortis ab extrema condicione vacant.
aut illis flamma aut imber subducet honores,
annorum aut ictu pondere victa ruent.
25   at non ingenio quaesitum nomen ab aevo
excidet: ingenio stat sine morte decus.

3

Visus eram molli recubans Heliconis in umbra,
Bellerophontei qua fluit umor equi,

24. pondere **NDVL** pondera **F.**

19-24. Cf. Hor. *Car*. 3, 30, 1–
5: *Exegi monumentum aere per-
ennius regalique situ pyramidum
altius, quod non imber edax, non
Aquilo impotens possit diruere
aut innumerabilis annorum series
et fuga temporum.*

**19. pyramidum sumptus . . .
ducti**: poetic for *pyramides sump-
tuosae ductae.*

20. The Zeus-temple at Olympia
had no roof over the *cella*, which
was itself of large proportions; so
Zeus might seem to the worshiper
literally enthroned in the sky.

21. For the construction cf. v.
19, n. The tomb of King Mauso-
lus of Halicarnassus, built by his
wife, Artemisia, was of such size
and grandeur that it was consid-

ered one of the seven wonders of
the world, and has given the name
ever since to any tomb of unusual
size or beauty. Cf. Pliny, *N. H.*
36, 5, 30.

24. annorum . . . ictu: like the
steady stroke of the battering-ram.

25. ab aevo excidet: the cause
is represented under its original
guise of source. It may be
thought of as the agent, and the
verb rendered as a passive. L.
1318; A. & G. 404; 405, *a.*

3, 3

The idea of the previous elegy
that the poet is divinely called to
this field of his art rather than to
epic strains is here repeated in
the form of a dream. The fre-

reges, Alba, tuos et regum facta tuorum,
   tantum operis, nervis hiscere posse meis,
5 parvaque tam magnis admoram fontibus ora,
   unde pater sitiens Ennius ante bibit,

quent recurrence of a similar theme, *e.g.* in 2, 10; 3, 9; and his more elaborate apology in 3, 11, betray a restless longing on the part of Propertius to essay more serious writing, a consummation which he had already begun to reach in Book 4, and might well have fully realized, had he enjoyed long life.

1–12: 'Methought on Helicon I sang the glorious past of Rome; 13–24: but Phoebus chid me for wandering from my province; 25–36: and, leading me to the Muses' grot, showed me how they were busy each with her appointed function; 37–52: then one of them, — I think, Calliope, — appointed me my lot, to sing of love, and gave me an inspiring draught from the spring whence drank Philetas.'

1. **Visus eram**: the tense indicates that he had already entered upon the themes he mentions, when he was interrupted by Apollo, v. 13 (C. S.). Reference to the famous dream of Ennius on Helicon is a commonplace in Roman literature; cf. Pers. *Prol.* 1: *nec fonte labra prolui caballino, nec in bicipiti somniasse Parnaso memini*; Cic. *Som. Scip.* 1, 2: *pariant aliquid in somno tale quale de Homero scribit Ennius*;

Fronto, 4: *Ennium nostrum, quem tu ais ex somno et somnio initium sibi fecisse.* — **Heliconis**: the favorite haunt of the Muses; cf. 2, 10, 1; 3, 5, 19.

2. **Bellerophontei . . . umor equi**: Hippocrene. It is said to have been produced by the hoof of Pegasus, the horse which carried Bellerophon in the fight against Chimaera (C. S.).

4. **tantum operis**: for the expression cf. 3, 11, 70; for the syntax, an apposition with the rest of vv. 3 and 4, cf. L. 1081. Coming between the verb and its object, this expression serves somewhat to tone down the harshness of the construction. — **hiscere**: cf. 2, 31, 6; Browning, *The Glove*, 1: "'Heigho!' yawned one day King Francis, 'Distance all value enhances!'" Still better, in the sense of speaking in a braggart or presumptuous manner, cf. *Ayenbite of Inwyt*: "Yelpth other of his wyth, other of his kenne, other of his workes." Cf. also Walt Whitman, *Song of Myself*, 52: "I sound my barbaric yawp over the roofs of the world."

6. **pater**: Ennius is traditionally the 'father' of Roman poetry; cf. Hor. *Ep.* 1, 19, 7.

et cecini Curios fratres et Horatia pila,
  regiaque Aemilia vecta tropaea rate,
victricesque moras Fabii pugnamque sinistram
10   Cannensem et versos ad pia vota deos,
Hannibalemque lares Romana sede fugantes,
  anseris et tutum voce fuisse Iovem,
cum me Castalia speculans ex arbore Phoebus

3. 7. cecini ω cecinit O.

7. Curios = *Curiatios* ; for similar poetic shortenings in Propertius, besides *Horatia* and *Aemilia* in this passage, cf. *Baiae* (1, 11, 30), *Tatiae* (4, 4, 31), etc. This unusually violent abbreviation may have been supported in the mind of Propertius by the idea that the Roman Curii were descended from the Curiatii, there being some doubt in antiquity whether the latter were Alban or Roman champions. Cf. Livy, 1, 24, 1 (*nominum error manet*) at the beginning of the description of this famous combat. — **pila**: the spoils of the Curiatii taken by Horatius were probably placed upon a memorial column. At any rate there was a *pila Horatia* in the Forum at the corner of the Basilica Julia; cf. Platner, *Top.* p. 258. Cf. 3, 4, 6, n.

8. regia . . . tropaea: referring to the victory at Pydna over Perseus, King of Macedonia, by Aemilius Paulus in 168 B.C.

9 moras Fabii: the successful policy of Fabius Cunctator against Hannibal.

10. versos . . . deos: after the battle of Cannae the gods listened to the prayers of the Romans and became propitious (C. S.).

11. lares: the mysterious failure of Hannibal to take Rome in 211 B.C. was attributed to divine interposition; cf. Varro, *Sat. Men.* (*Herc. T. F.*): *noctu Hannibalis cum fugavi exercitum, Tutanus hoc Tutanum Romae nuncupor* ; and for another tradition, Paulus, *Epit. Festi*, p. 283; *Rediculi fanum extra portam Capenam fuit, quia accedens ad Urbem Hannibal ex eo loco redierit quibusdam perterritus visis.*

12. anseris . . . tutum voce refers to the historic (?) cackling which saved Jove's temple from the Gauls; cf. Livy, 5, 47.

13. Castalia: more poetic geography ! Cf. Tib. 1, 3, 7, n. Propertius speaks of a Pierian spring, a Castalian wood, or the shades of Helicon, in a conventional sense, much as we do to-day. Castalia is, of course, on Parnassus in Phocis, while the poet is supposed to be dreaming on Helicon in

sic ait, aurata nixus ad antra lyra,

15 'quid tibi cum tali, demens, est flumine? quis te
  carminis heroi tangere iussit opus?
  non hic ulla tibi speranda est fama, Properti:
  mollia sunt parvis prata terenda rotis,
  ut tuus in scamno iactetur saepe libellus,

20 quem legat expectans sola puella virum.
  cur tua praescripto sevecta est pagina gyro?
  non est ingenii cymba gravanda tui.
  alter remus aquas, alter tibi radat arenas:
  tutus eris: medio maxima turba marist.'

25 dixerat, et plectro sedem mihi monstrat eburno,
  qua nova muscoso semita facta solost.
  hic erat adfixis viridis spelunca lapillis,

Boeotia! — arbore: laurel; here used collectively.

15. flumine: *i.e. fontibus*, v. 5 (C. S.).

17. hic: 'in this field.'

18. 'Thy tiny wheels must press the velvet mead': a pretty metaphor for the simple prose, 'Elegy is your proper field'; yours are no chariot wheels to rut the battlefield (C. S.).

19. iactetur saepe: because of the impatient restlessness of the *puella* under these conditions. Postgate recalls Strato "addressing his book": πολλάκι φοιτήσεις ὑποκόλπιον ἢ παρὰ δίφροις βληθέν.

21. sevecta: ἅπαξ λεγ. — **gyro:** the elegiac routine (C. S.). Propertius uses the word again, in its literal sense, in 3, 14, 11: *gyrum pulsat equis.*

22. non ... gravanda: 'must not be overloaded.'

23. Cf. 3, 9, 35; Verg. *Aen.* 5, 163: *litus ama et laevas stringat sine palmula cautes; altum alii teneant.*

24. turba: 'turmoil'; hence danger to so slight a craft. The clash of conflicting armies, or other epic theme, is no suitable inspiration for the genius of Propertius.

25. dixerat: itself a reminiscence of the conventional epic manner.

27. adfixis ... lapillis: cf. the shell room in the 'New Palace' at Potsdam. Propertius had doubtless seen artificial grottoes corresponding to this description in the parks of well-to-do Romans. Pliny calls them by the significant name *musaea* (*N. H.* 36, 21,

pendebantque cavis tympana pumicibus,
orgia Musarum et Sileni patris imago
30   fictilis, et calami, Pan Tegeaee, tui,
et Veneris dominae volucres, mea turba, columbae
    tingunt Gorgoneo punica rostra lacu,
diversaeque novem sortitae rura puellae
    exercent teneras in sua dona manus.
35   haec hederas legit in thyrsos, haec carmina nervis
    aptat, at illa manu texit utraque rosam.
e quarum numero me contigit una dearum :

29. orgia *Heinsius* ergo **O** organa *Eldikius.*

154) ; cf. *operosa . . . antra* (3, 2, 14).

28. tympana : the tambourines especially dedicated to Cybele (C. S.), and used also in the service of Bacchus, who sometimes supplanted Apollo as the inspirer of poetry ; cf. 4, 1, 62 ; 3, 2, 9, n. ; 2, 30, 38 ; Tib. 1, 7, 37 ; Ovid, *Met.* 11, 17 : *tympanaque et plausus et Bacchei ululatus obstrepuere sono citharae.*

29. orgia : 'mystic instruments.'— **imago :** a terra cotta bust ; cf. E. Maass in *Hermes,* Vol. 31 (1896), p. 382.

30. Tegeaee : Tegea was a typical Arcadian town, and Arcadia was the home of Pan. For the special cult of Pan at Tegea, cf. Farnell, *Greek Cults,* Vol. 4, p. 433.

31. mea turba = *mea cura,* or *meae deliciae* (C. S.).— **columbae :** amorous birds, sacred to Venus ; cf. 4, 5, 63 ; Ovid, *Met.* 13, 674.

32. tingunt : 'moisten.'— **Gorgoneo . . . lacu :** Hippocrene, pro-

duced by the hoof of Pegasus ; and Pegasus sprang from the blood of the Gorgon Medusa, and is sometimes called *equus Medusaeus* (C. S.). Cf. v. 2, n. ; 3, 1, 19, n.— **punica :** 'purple-red,' the adjective referring more to their famous dye than to the people who produced it. Cf. Ovid, *Am.* 2, 6, 22 (of a parrot).

33. diversae : in different parts of the cave. The nine Muses are represented as each engaged in her allotted sphere (C. S.). But this does not necessarily refer to the stereotyped functions of later times.

35. in thyrsos : purpose acc. The Muse is given the function of a Bacchante, in harmony with the spirit of the passage. Cf. v. 28, n. ; 2, 30, 38 : *medius docta cuspide Bacchus erit* ; Lucr. 1, 922 : *acri percussit thyrso laudis spes magna meum cor et simul incussit suavem mi in pectus amorem Musarum.*

ut reor a facie, Calliopea fuit.

'contentus niveis semper vectabere cycnis,

40   nec te fortis equi ducet ad arma sonus.

nil tibi sit rauco praeconia classica cornu

flare, nec Aonium tinguere Marte nemus,

aut quibus in campis Mariano proelia signo

stent et Teutonicas Roma refringat opes,

45   barbarus aut Suevo perfusus sanguine Rhenus

saucia maerenti corpora vectet aqua.

quippe coronatos alienum ad limen amantes

nocturnaeque canes ebria signa fugae,

42. flare *Fruterius* flere O.

38. Calliopea: cf. 3, 2, 16, n. While Propertius uses this form in these two passages and in 1, 2, 28, he employs the shorter form in v. 51, and in two other passages: 2, 1, 3; 4, 6, 12.

39. vectabere cycnis: Propertius as an erotic poet fancies himself riding in the car of Venus herself as Ovid did, *A. A.* 3, 809: *cygnis descendere tempus, duxerunt collo qui iuga nostra suo.* Sometimes it is drawn by doves, and again by swans; cf. Hor. *Car.* 3, 28, 14: *Paphum iunctis visit oloribus.*

40. arma: *i.e.* epic poetry. Cf. 1, 7, 1, n.

41. 'Be it not yours to blare with hoarse trumpet the praise of naval fights' (C. S.). — **tibi**: *ad te* would be rather more regular, but the construction varies widely, and Propertius is fond of the dative; cf. Lucr. 3, 830: *nil igitur mors est ad nos*; Tib. 4, 3, 3: *nec tibi sit*

duros acuisse in proelia dentes; Plaut. *Stich.* 718: *haud tuom istuc est te vereri.*

42. Aonium . . . nemus: cf. 1, 2, 28, n.

43. The construction shifts from the infinitive clause to the substantive clause of ind. quest. — **quibus in campis**: Marius defeated the Teutons at Aquae Sextiae in 102 B.C., and the Cimbri near Vercellae, a year later. — **Mariano . . . signo**: Marius made the eagle the exclusive mark of the Roman legions. Wolves, minotaurs, horses, and boars had previously also been used (C. S.).

45. It is most natural to suppose that the poet refers to the victory of Caesar over Ariovistus in 58 B.C., cf. Caes. *B. G.* 1, 53.

47. coronatos: still wearing the garlands of this evening's revel. — **alienum**: cf. *viros* (v. 50).

48. ebria signa fugae: in humorous contrast with v. 43. We

ut per te clausas sciat excantare puellas,
50   qui volet austeros arte ferire viros.'
talia Calliope, lymphisque a fonte petitis
ora Philetaea nostra rigavit aqua.

4

Arma deus Caesar dites meditatur ad Indos,
et freta gemmiferi findere classe maris.

see here the picture of the torches borne with unsteady hand by the roisterers who disturb domestic peace, hurrying this way and that to escape just punishment for their insults. The adjective belongs more to *fugae* than to *signa*.

49–50. A task worthy of Ovid! Cf. also Tib. 1, 1, 73; 2, 1, 75–78.

50. ferire: 'to trick'; a slang use which reminds the reader of Plaut. *Trin.* 247: *ibi illa pendentem ferit;* also of our colloquial "strike the old man for fifty dollars"; cf. Ter. *Phorm.* 47, *ferietur alio munere.* — **viros:** 'husbands.'

52. Philetaea: cf. 3, 1, 1, n.

3, 4

Propertius expresses confidence that the projected expedition against the Parthians will achieve great success. In harmony with the spirit of the preceding elegy he disclaims any direct interest in the expected spoils of victory won by heroic deeds, but hopes as a lover to gaze with his lady upon the expected triumph of Augustus.

1–10: 'The expedition that Caesar is planning will surely bring victory, revenge, and rich booty; 11–22: ye gods, let me live to see with my darling the glorious triumph on his return.'

1. **deus:** starting with the worship of the city of Rome, which had begun here and there in the East in republican times, Augustus organized throughout the provinces of the empire a regular worship of *Roma et Augustus.* The direct worship of Augustus in his lifetime sprang up here and there in Italy where individuals or communities were under some special obligation to him, or for some similar reason. In Cumae a temple was erected to him. In the city of Rome itself he deemed it politic to permit only the indirect worship under the form of the *Lares Augusti* and the *Genius Caesaris.* The poets, however, do not hesitate to use the word *deus* of their patron. Cf. 4, 11, 60; Rushforth, *Latin Historical In-*

282

magna, viri, merces.   parat ultima terra triumphos :
  Tigris et Euphrates sub tua iura fluent :
5 sera, sed Ausoniis veniet provincia virgis :
  adsuescent Latio Partha tropaea Iovi.
ite agite, expertae bello date lintea prorae,
  et solitum armigeri ducite munus equi.
omina fausta cano.   Crassos clademque piate :

scriptions, pp. 44–46; Shuckburgh, *Augustus*, p. 196; Hor.
Car. 4, 5, 32–35; *Ep.* 2, 1, 16;
Verg. *Ec.* 1, 6. — **meditatur :**
Rome had long been restless to
recover from the Parthians its lost
military standards, and once for
all to settle the supremacy of
the East. In 22 B.C. Augustus
finally started with an army for
the East via Sicily. But the
victory was a bloodless one, for
in 20 B.C., the Parthian king
Phraates sent back the Roman
standards and such prisoners as
did not prefer to remain. — **Indos :**
poetic enthusiasm is largely responsible for the word here. The
Indians represent the far East, but
the Parthians were the real limit
of the martial plans of the hour.
Cf. 2, 10, 15, n.

  2. gemmiferi . . . maris : cf.
Tib. 2, 2, 15–16, nn.; 4, 2, 19–20.

  3. viri : those planning to accompany Augustus on the expedition; cf. v. 21. — **parat :** sc. *tibi*
(*i.e.* Augustus) from the *tua* in v. 4.

  4. Cf. Hor. *Car.* 2, 9, 21 :
*Medumque flumen gentibus ad-
ditum victis minores volvere
vertices.*

  5. provincia : *i.e.* the *ultima
terra* of v. 3. — **virgis :** dative ; the
fasces, an emblem of Roman
authority.

  6. Partha : it is common in
poetry to use the gentile name for
the adjective (here *Parthica*) ; cf.
3, 3, 7. — **tropaea :** the poet fore-
sees not merely the return of the
lost Roman standards, but also
the placing of Parthian emblems
in the temple of the Capitoline
Jove.

  7–8. While Propertius has laid
himself open to the charge of
ambiguity as to the syntax of
prorae and *equi*, it seems most
likely that he is intending to address *ite agite* to the *viri* of v.
3, and that the same vocative is
in mind in vv. 9 and 10 ; *prorae*
as dative is also more logical than
as a vocative ; while *ducite* is
natural for the rider, but not for
the horse. ' Guide the accustomed
task of the war horse ' is Propertian
for ' Guide the war horse to perform
his familiar function.'

  9. omina . . . cano : cf. Tib.
2, 1, 25. — **Crassos :** cf. 2, 10, 14,
n. While the great defeat at
Carrhae in 53 B.C. loomed largest

10   ite et Romanae consulite historiae.
      Mars pater et sacrae fatalia lumina Vestae,
        ante meos obitus sit, precor, illa dies
      qua videam spoliis oneratos Caesaris axes,
        ad vulgi plausus saepe resistere equos,
15   inque sinu carae nixus spectare puellae
        incipiam, et titulis oppida capta legam,
      tela fugacis equi et bracati militis arcus
        et subter captos arma sedere duces.

in Roman thought, the standards returned to Augustus included also those lost by Decidius Saxa in 40 B.C. and by Antony in 36 B.C.

11. Mars pater: Mars as the father of Romulus and Remus had a clear title to this designation, but he and Jove did not enjoy a monopoly of the distinction; cf. Lucil. 1, 9 (Mueller): *nemo ut sit nostrum, quin aut pater optumu' divom aut Neptunu' pater, Liber, Saturnu' pater, Mars, Iann', Quirinu' pater siet ac dicatur ad unum.* — **fatalia**: the Romans believed the destiny of Rome was closely linked with the life or extinction of the sacred fire of Vesta; cf. Livy, 26, 27, 14: *aeternos ignes, et conditum in penetrali fatale pignus imperii Romani.*

13. oneratos . . . axes: figuratively the triumphal car of the emperor would be loaded with spoils: literally they were carried before him in a long procession. See Pohlmey, *Der römische Triumph*, pp. 15 sqq., where the various features of the triumph referred to in the following verses are described.

14. ad . . . plausus: purpose acc. The triumphal car stopped ever and anon for the *triumphator* to receive and acknowledge the plaudits of the multitude; and the fine-spirited horses might seem themselves to share in this appreciation. Cf. Ovid, *Trist.* 4, 2, 53: *ipse sono plausuque simul fremituque canente quadriiugos cernes saepe resistere equos.*

16. titulis: the inscription upon the representations of conquered towns carried in the procession; cf. Tib. 2, 5, 116, n. — **oppida**: object of both *spectare* and *legam*, while in vv. 17–18 the force of *spectare* only is continued.

17. fugacis equi: referring to the Parthians' characteristic method of warfare. — **bracati**: a feature of Oriental dress; cf. Pers. 3, 53: *bracatis inlita Medis porticus.*

18. subter: with *arma*. It was beneath a trophy that the eminent captives would be sitting in chains.

ipsa tuam serva prolem, Venus : hoc sit in aevum,
20   cernis ab Aenea quod superesse caput.
praeda sit haec illis quorum meruere labores :
me sat erit sacra plaudere posse via.

5

Pacis Amor deus est, pacem veneramur amantes :
sat mihi cum domina proelia dura mea.
nec tantum inviso pectus mihi carpitur auro,

Cf. Ovid, *Ex P.* 3, 4, 104 : *stentque super victos trunca tropaea viros.*

19. prolem : Augustus, as the adopted son of Julius Caesar.

21. Cf. Tib. 1, 1, 1 ; 49–50 ; 75–77.

22. sacra . . . via : the regular route of a triumphal procession ; cf. 2, 1, 34 : *Actiaque in sacra currere rostra via.*

3, 5

The poet once again defines his mission and states his ambition. Though not, probably, as various eminent scholars have believed, one with the previous elegy, this may be regarded as a meditation suggested by the text found in the final couplet of 3, 4, and written shortly afterward. Indeed it forms the final poem of the closely connected group that opens this book, and that is also connected in thought with the end of Book 2. Cf. Ites, *De Properti Elegiis inter se Conexis*, pp. 51–56,

where a large number of parallels in this group is cited.

The thought is similar to that in Tib. 1, 1, and various passages in Horace, *e.g.* in *Epod.* 1, 1 ; *Car.* 2, 18 ; 2, 3 ; 1, 4 ; etc. With vv. 25–38, cf. *Aetna*, 219–251. Curiously at variance with modern ideas is the inclusion under scientific investigation of speculation with regard to the future life.

1–18 : ' As a poet of love, I prefer peace to war and all its prizes for which men struggle, only to leave them behind when death comes. 19–22 : In youth I have played the lover and sung the songs of love ; 23–46 : but when advancing age has cooled love's ardor, let it be my delight to delve into the secrets of nature and try to solve the problems of the afterworld. 47–48 : You who love war, bring home the standards of Crassus.'

1–2. Cf. Tib. 1, 10, 49–56 ; 1, 1, 73–76.

nec bibit e gemma divite nostra sitis,

5   nec mihi mille iugis Campania pinguis aratur,
     nec miser aera paro clade, Corinthe, tua.
     o prima infelix fingenti terra Prometheo!
     ille parum caute pectoris egit opus :
     corpora disponens mentem non vidit in arte.

10   recta animi primum debuit esse via.
     nunc maris in tantum vento iactamur, et hostem
        quaerimus, atque armis nectimus arma nova.
     haud ullas portabis opes Acherontis ad undas :

5. 8. caute **O** cauti **ω**.

4. **gemma**: cf. Verg. *Georg.* 2,
506: *ut gemma bibat* ; Cic. *In Ver.*
4, 62 : *erat etiam vas vinarium,
ex una gemma pergrandi trulla
excavata manubrio aureo.* — **nostra sitis**: the thing for the person ; cf. 3, 16, 17.

5. **Campania**: the most fertile
and valuable land in Italy was,
and still is, in this district. For the
thought, cf. Hor. *Sat.* 2, 6, 1 :
*Hoc erat in votis : modus agri
non ita magnus* ; 1, 6, 58 : *non ego
circum me Satureiano vectari rura
caballo . . . narro.*

6. **miser**: in his present temper
Propertius views the avaricious
man as a truly pitiable object ; cf.
Hor. *Sat.* 1, 1, 63 : *iubeas miserum
esse, libenter quatenus id facit.* —
aera . . . clade, Corinthe: the especially valuable alloy known as
Corinthian bronze was said to
have been accidentally produced
at the destruction of Corinth by
Mummius in 146 B.C. Cf. Pliny,
N. H. 34, 2, 6 ; *hoc casus miscuit*

Corintho, cum caperetur, incensa.
For the craze for the genuine article at Rome cf. Hor. *Sat.* 1, 4, 27 :
stupet Albius aere ; 2, 3, 20 : *quaerere amabam, quo vafer ille pedes
lavisset Sisyphus aere, quid sculp-
tum infabre, quid fusum durius
esset.*

7. **infelix**: *i.e.* because avarice
was one of the elements included
in the composition of man ; cf.
Hor. *Car.* 1, 16, 13 : *fertur Prometheus addere principi limo coactus
particulam undique.* — **Prometheo**: for representations of Prometheus creating man, cf. Baum.
Denk., p. 1413. For the synizesis, cf. Tib. 2, 1, 49.

8. **parum caute**: *i.e.* he ill deserved his name "Prometheus"
('man of forethought') = *provi-
dens* (cf. *non vidit*, v. 9). —
pectoris: 'the heart'; cf. vv. 9–10.

11. **nunc**: referring to the actual state of things in contrast
with what ought to have been
(*debuit*).

nudus at inferna, stulte, vehere rate.

15 victor cum victis pariter miscebitur umbris :
      consule cum Mario, capte Iugurtha, sedes.
    Lydus Dulichio non distat Croesus ab Iro.
      optima mors, parca quae venit acta die.
    me iuvat in prima coluisse Helicona iuventa,
20   musarumque choris inplicuisse manus :
    me iuvat et multo mentem vincire Lyaeo
      et caput in verna semper habere rosa.
    atque ubi iam Venerem gravis interceperit aetas,
      sparserit et nigras alba senecta comas,
25 tum mihi naturae libeat perdiscere mores,

---

14. at inferna . . . rate *Schrader* ad infernas . . . rates O ab . . . rate ω ad infernos . . . rate *Palmer*.   18. parca O Parcae *Lachmann* carpta *Baehrens.*   21. iuyat DV iuvet NFL.   24. sparserit et N sparserit DV sparsit et FL.   et nigras ω integras DV et integras NFL.

14. **nudus . . . stulte**: numerous parallels from Holy Scripture will occur to the reader, *e.g.* Job 1, 21: "naked shall I return thither"; Luke 12, 20: "Thou fool, . . . then whose shall those things be, which thou hast provided?" Lucian, *Dial. Mort.* 10.

16. **Iugurtha** and his captor, **Marius**, illustrate *victis* and *victor* of v. 15.

17. **Dulichio . . . Iro**: the famous beggar in the *Odyssey* (18 *init.*), a type of poverty, as the more famous Croesus is a type of wealth. For the thought, cf. Hor. *Car.* 2, 14, 9: *unda scilicet omnibus . . . enaviganda, sive reges sive inopes erimus coloni*; 1, 4, 13; 2, 18, 32.

18. **parca**: this word sums up the thought of the elegy thus far : the climax of the best life is that which comes in the natural course of human events to the man of humble means.

19. Cf. 4, 1, 131 sqq. — **Helicona**: cf. 3, 3, 1.

20. Cf. 3, 3, 37.

21. Cf. 2, 10, 7. — **vincire Lyaeo**: literally ' to bind with the loosener ' is an oxymoron indicating that Propertius realizes the real nature of the much-vaunted freedom that is given by wine. Cf. Verg. *Georg.* 2, 94 : *temptatura pedes olim vincturaque linguam.*

25. **mores** = *leges* ; cf. Verg. *Aen.* 1, 264 : *moresque viris et moenia ponet.*

quis deus hanc mundi temperet arte domum,
qua venit exoriens, qua deficit, unde coactis
cornibus in plenum menstrua luna redit,
unde salo superant venti, quid flamine captet
30   eurus, et in nubes unde perennis aqua,
sit ventura dies, mundi quae subruat arces,
purpureus pluvias cur bibit arcus aquas,
aut cur Perrhaebi tremuere cacumina Pindi,
solis et atratis luxerit orbis equis,
35   cur serus versare boves et plaustra Bootes,

26. deus . . . temperet: the Epicurean idea that it is necessary to eliminate the divine element from natural law is not followed by Propertius, any more than by Horace; cf. Hor. *Car.* 1, 12, 15: *qui mare et terras variisque mundum temperat horis*; but Horace leaves the gods out in *Ep.* 1, 12, 16 (*quid temperet annum*), where questions similar to those in this passage are suggested. Cf. also Ovid, *Met.* 15, 66 sqq. Vergil, on the other hand, does not raise the question of theism in his two well-known passages that suggest questions similar to those broached here, *Georg.* 2, 477 sqq., and *Aen.* 1, 742-746. — **temperet:** ' controls.'

27. venit: there is a characteristically Propertian disregard of mood throughout this series of a score of indirect questions, the indicatives somewhat outnumbering the subjunctives. — **coactis:** cf. Ovid, *Her.* 2, 3: *cornua cum lunae pleno semel orbe coissent;*

Met. 10, 295: *coactis cornibus in plenum.*

31. Cf. Lucr. 5, 95: *una dies dabit exitio*, quoted by Ovid, *Am.* 1, 15, 24. Indeed the inspiration given by Lucretius to his successors in similar queries is incalculable.

32. bibit: a common poetic conception; cf. Verg. *Georg.* 1, 380: *bibit ingens arcus.*

33. The origin of earthquakes is treated under a typical case, viz. that of the Pindus range between Thessaly and Epirus. Tribes called *Perrhaebi* were located on either side of this range.

34. luxerit: 'puts on mourning.'

35. serus: sc. *sit*. As a matter of fact Ursa Major does not set at all in the latitude of the Romans. Cf. Ovid, *Met.* 2, 528: *gurgite caeruleo Septem prohibete triones.* — **versare:** *i.e.* to set. Used with the adjective *serus.* — **boves et plaustra:** the constellation of the Wain, or wagon, *i.e.*

Pleiadum spisso cur coit igne chorus,
    curve suos fines altum non exeat aequor,
        plenus et in partes quattuor annus eat,
    sub terris sint iura deum et tormenta nocentum,
40   Tisiphones atro si furit angue caput,
    aut Alcmaeoniae furiae aut ieiunia Phinei,
        num rota, num scopuli, num sitis inter aquas,
    num tribus infernum custodit faucibus antrum
        Cerberus, et Tityo iugera pauca novem,
45   an ficta in miseras descendit fabula gentis,
    et timor haud ultra quam rogus esse potest.

---

39. nocentum *Haupt* Gigantum **FLDV** *omitted in* **N** reorum *Housman*.

Ursa Major, or the *Septemtriones*, the seven oxen. Cf. 2, 33, 24: *flectant Icarii sidera tarda boves.* — **Bootes**: the ox-driver, or plowman, whose constellation, otherwise known as Ursa Minor, is so situated that it seems to be driving the oxen in Ursa Major.

36. Cf. Germanicus, *Arat.* 256: *Pleiades suberunt brevis et locus occupat omnes, nec faciles cerni, nisi quod coeuntia plura sidera communem ostendunt ex omnibus ignem*; Hor. *Car.* 4, 14, 21: *Pleiadum choro scindente nubes.*

37. Cf. Hor. *Ep.* 1, 12, 16; Psalms 104, 9.

39. **nocentum**: it is the question of future punishment for guilty mortals that the poet is proposing to tackle, cf. Statius, *Silv.* 2, 7, 117: *nescis Tartaron et procul nocentum audis verbera.*

40. Cf. Tib. 1, 3, 69, n.

41. **furiae**: Alcmaeon was pursued by the furies for having slain his mother Eriphyle. — **ieiunia**: caused by the Harpies, who were sent to steal his food, after he had put out his sons' eyes. Neither of the punishments mentioned in this verse was ordinarily supposed to have been suffered after death.

42. **rota**: of Ixion. — **scopuli**: of Sisyphus. — **sitis**: of Tantalus.

44. **pauca**: 'scant.' — Propertius exaggerates the usual form of the myth willfully, showing that he has reached the *reductio ad absurdum* in his catalogue, and is ready for the probable alternative of the next verse. Cf. Tib. 1, 3, 75.

45. Read Lucr. 3, 978–1023 for the Epicurean explanation of all the foregoing myths.

46. We should have expected *ultra rogum* in place of this illogical statement.

exitus hic vitae superest mihi : vos, quibus arma
grata magis, Crassi signa referte domum.

7

Ergo sollicitae tu causa, pecunia, vitae,
per te inmaturum mortis adimus iter.

47. superest O superet ω.

7. 1. vitae NFL vitae es DVF₂.

47. exitus hic : *i.e.* one busy
with such discussions.

3, 7

The drowning of Paetus with
its sad lessons and reflections
(C. S.). It is not improbable
that this sympathetic elegy was
written to comfort the sorrowing
mother of the ill-fated youth, of
whose personality we know
nothing that is not contained in
the poem itself. Pedantic efforts
to rearrange, in what has seemed
to individual scholars a more
logical order, the spontaneous
expression of poetic feeling in this
typical elegy have been as futile
as unnecessary. Cf. Tib. 1, 1,
Intr. ; J. Vahlen (*Sitzungsber. d.
Kgl. Preuss. Akad. d. Wissenschaften,* 1883, pp. 69-90) has
made a careful, and in most respects, convincing study of the
development of the thought.

1–12: 'O money, source of
many woes, 'tis thou hast o'er-
whelmed Paetus in the waters,
and left to his sad mother not

even a corse to bury ! 13–28 :
Ye winds, ye waves, how could
you destroy so innocent, so con-
fiding a youth ? Alas! Agamemnon knew your ruthlessness too
well. And since you have the
life of Paetus, restore his body for
burial, that his tomb may warn
others against like rashness. 29–
42 : But nay! Foolish men will
not cease to venture on the deep,
though certain ruin awaits them,
as Ulysses learned. 43–66 : Paetus, too, had he not thirsted for
wealth, might now be alive.
How delicate a youth for so terrible a death ! So did he tell
the gods of wind and wave, as the
waters closed over him. 67–72 :
Why did you not save him,
Nereids, Thetis ? A lesson to me,
never to trust myself off the land !'

1. **Ergo:** cf. 1, 8, 1, n. — Note
the middle rime in this and many
other hexameter verses here.

2. **inmaturum:** hypallage; in
thought it belongs to *mortis.* —
The verse ends in a favorite
rhythm for Book 3; cf. vv. 10,

tu vitiis hominum crudelia pabula praebes:
    semina curarum de capite orta tuo.
5   tu Paetum ad Pharios tendentem lintea portus
    obruis insano terque quaterque mari.
nam dum te sequitur, primo miser excidit aevo,
    et nova longinquis piscibus esca natat:
et mater non iusta piae dare debita terrae,
10   nec pote cognatos inter humare rogos,
sed tua nunc volucres adstant super ossa marinae,
    nunc tibi pro tumulo Carpathium omne marest.
infelix Aquilo, raptae timor Orithyiae,
    quae spolia ex illo tanta fuere tibi?
15   aut quidnam fracta gaudes, Neptune, carina?
    portabat sanctos alveus ille viros.

22; see Kuttner, *De Propertii
Elocutione Quaestiones*, p. 42.

3. **crudelia**: *i.e.* in the result.

4. **de capite ... tuo** = *de te
capite*; cf. Cat. 55, 2: *ubi sint
tuae tenebrae*.

5. **Pharios ... portus**: cf.
Tib. 1, 3, 32, n.

6. **insano ... mari**: cf. 1, 8,
5; Verg. *Ec.* 9, 43: *insani feriant
sine litora fluctus.* — **terque quaterque**: a common expression for
an indefinitely large number.
Propertius is thinking of the body
of Paetus floating long in the sea.

7. **dum te sequitur**: Paetus
went on a commercial venture. —
primo ... aevo: temporal. — **excidit**: used absolutely, as in 3, 2. 26.

8. Ovid imitates (*Ibis*, 148)
thus: *nostraque longinquus viscera
piscis edet.* It rouses the poet's
wrath to think that fish in foreign

seas must have new delicacies
while thus the mother of Paetus
cannot bury her dead.

9. **piae ... terrae**: dative;
otherwise *debita* is superfluous;
'the earthly remains of her dutiful
son.' Cf. 2, 13, 42. Cf. English
"pious dust of the martyrs."

10. **pote**: cf. Cat. 72, 7, n.; 76,
16, n. — **cognatos ... rogos**: cf.
Cat. 68, 98.

11. Cf. Ovid, *Her.* 10, 123:
*ossa superstabunt volucres inhu-
mata marinae.*

12. **Carpathium**: Horatian par-
ticularity; cf. v. 57.

13. **infelix**: 'disastrous'
(C.S.); cf. Verg. *Aen.* 2, 245:
*monstrum infelix sacrata sistimus
arce.* — **timor**: 'terror' (C.S.). —
Orithyiae: cf. 2, 26, n.

16. **sanctos**: involves a protest
(C.S.); 'innocent'; akin to the

Paete, quid aetatem numeras? quid cara natanti
    mater in ore tibi est? non habet unda deos.
nam tibi nocturnis ad saxa ligata procellis
20   omnia detrito vincula fune cadunt.
sunt Agamemnonias testantia litora curas,
    quae notat Argynni poena minantis aquae.
hoc iuvene amisso classem non solvit Atrides,
    pro qua mactata est Iphigenia mora.
25   reddite corpus humo : posita est in gurgite vita :

---

22. quae **FV** qua **NLD**. notat **O** natat **F₂** nota **ω**. Argynni **V₂** Agynni **N**
Arginni **L** Argivum **DV** Argium **F** Argynnus *Waardenburg* Argynnum *Otto*.
poena minantis aquae **O** praeda morantis *Thompson* praeda minantis *Enk*
Athamantiadae *Hertzberg* Mimantis aquae *Ellis*.

"royal plural"; cf. 4, 9, 34: *pan-
dite defessis hospita fana viris*
(of Hercules), and Verg. *Aen.* 7,
98: *externi venient generi* (of
Aeneas).

17. **aetatem numeras**: 'plead
thy youth' (C. S.).

18. **non . . . deos**: *i.e.* Aquilo
and Neptunus, just addressed,
must be mere myths; the world is
too much out of joint to accept
theism. Cf. Ennius, *Telamo*, fr.
I, (Ribbeck): *nam si curent,
bene bonis sit, male malis, quod
nunc abest.* But cf. vv. 57 and 62.

19. **nam**: proof of the foregoing assertion; the poet thinks it
incredible that real gods should
violate the helpless trustfulness of
pious men. — **ad saxa ligata**: cf.
4, I, 110. But I, 20, 20 has
scopulis adplicuisse ratem.

20. **detrito . . . fune**: *i.e.* an
essential part of the *vincula* was

worn away by the storm during
the night.

21. **sunt**: emphatic. — **testantia**: 'that can call to witness,' *i.e.*
can witness to the treachery of
water, as expressed in v. 18. —
curas: 'grief.'

22. 'Which gained notoriety
through the penalty that Argynnus
paid to the threatening waters.'
The penalty was for the same
misplaced confidence that Paetus
had in the waters. The circumstances were different, for Argynnus, the youth beloved of
Agamemnon, was drowned in the
Cephisus River. Agamemnon was
said to have founded there a
temple in memory of the beautiful
youth. — **Argynni**: obj. gen. —
aquae: subj. gen.

24. Cf. 4, I, III–II2.

25. **reddite**: Propertius is addressing the waves, but does not

Paetum sponte tua, vilis arena, tegas :
et quotiens Paeti transibit nauta sepulcrum,
    dicat ' et audaci tu timor esse potes.'
ite, rates curvas et leti texite causas :
30   ista per humanas mors venit acta manus.
terra parum fuerat fatis : adiecimus undas,
    fortunae miseras auximus arte vias.
ancora te teneat, quem non tenuere penates ?
    quid meritum dicas, cui sua terra parumst ?
35   ventorum est quodcumque paras : haut ulla carina
    consenuit, fallit portus et ipse fidem.
natura insidians pontum substravit avaris :

29. curvas Passerat curvae O.

feel it necessary to specify them
to the reader ; cf. 2, 11, 1, n.

26. vilis : the poet does not
hesitate to address the sand by
this bitter expression of his feelings, because he does not think
it necessary to conciliate, but
assumes the service asked as
due.

28. timor : cf. v. 13.

29. ite . . . texite : here the
address is to the fatuous children
of men. Cf. 3, 18, 17. For the
rapid change of persons cf. Tib.
1, 7, 55, n. — **et** : cf. 1, 8, 36, n. —
leti . . . causas : *i.e. rates.*

31. Cf. Sen. *Q. N.* 5, 18, 8 :
*parum videlicet ad mortes nostras
terra late patet* ; Hor. *Car.* 1, 3,
21–26 ; Tib. 1, 3, 50.

32. fortunae : evil fortune, in
this case. She has been biased
to their harm by human folly

(C. S.). The expression is only
a variation on *mortis . . . iter* (v.
2) and *fatis* (v. 31).

33. te : the singular is used
merely to individualize the address. The poet is still speaking
to the foolish men who venture
upon the sea.

34. sua terra : cf. Ovid, *Am.* 2,
11, 30 : *et 'felix' dicas, 'quem sua
terra tenet!'*

35. haut ulla carina : not so
much of a hyperbole then as it
would be now. But commentators
recall the yacht of Catullus ; and
even Propertius himself draws the
picture he here refuses to recognize
in 2, 25, 7 : *putris et in vacua
requiescit navis arena.*

36. Cf. 2, 25, 23 : *an quisquam
in mediis persolvit vota procellis,
cum saepe in portu fracta carina
natet.*

293

ut tibi succedat, vix semel esse potest.

saxa triumphales fregere Capharea puppes,

40   naufraga cum vasto Graecia tracta salost.

paullatim socium iacturam flevit Ulixes,

in mare cui soliti non valuere doli.

quod si contentus patrio bove verteret agros,

verbaque duxisset pondus habere mea,

45   viveret ante suos dulcis conviva penates,

pauper, at in terra, nil ubi flere potest.

non tulit hic Paetus stridorem audire procellae

et duro teneras laedere fune manus,

---

42. soliti ω soli O solum ω.   46. flere O flare *Jacob*.   47. hic ω haec **N** hunc **DVL** hoc **F**.

38. One prosperous voyage is great good luck (C. S.).

39. **triumphales . . . puppes**: the Greek fleet on its return after the sack of Troy. — **Capharĕa**: the promontory of Caphareus, or Cephereus, on the southeast coast of Euboea, where Nauplius, father of Palamedes, set false signals in revenge for the loss of his son, and wrecked the fleet. Cf. 4, 1, 113–116.

40. **Graecia**: a strong expression for the catastrophe suffered by the fleet by whose loss Greece herself was overwhelmed in the briny waste (C. S.).

41. **paullatim**: to be taken with *iacturam* (C. S.). — **socium**: the short form of the genitive, found in many words, was regular for *socius* in the formula, *socium et nominis Latini*.

42. **in** here = 'against.' — **doli**: 'wiles.'

43. **contentus**: the subject in the Propertian manner abruptly returns to Paetus, the poet unconsciously assuming that the reader is following the intensity of his own thought.

45. **dulcis**: *i.e.* to the other *convivae*.

46. **pauper**: relatively, as compared with the wealth he hoped to achieve by his voyage. — **nil . . . potest**: the disastrous, sorrow-causing, heart-breaking sea is the theme, and the land, in comparison, can bring no tears (C. S.). Render, 'where one may live a tearless life,' *i.e.* relatively. None of the proposed emendations avoids hyperbole.

47. **hic**: so long as he remained on shore (C. S.).

sed Chio thalamo aut Oricia terebintho
50   et fultum pluma versicolore capùt.
huic fluctus vivo radicitus abstulit ungues,
    et miser invisam traxit hiatus aquam ;
hunc parvo ferri vidit nox inproba ligno :
    Paetus ut occideret, tot coiere mala.
55 flens tamen extremis dedit haec mandata querellis,
    cum moribunda niger clauderet ora liquor.
'di maris Aegaei quos sunt penes aequora, venti,
    et quaecumque meum degravat unda caput,
quo rapitis miseros primae lanuginis annos?

49. Chio **O** Thyio *Santen* Thyiae *Itali.*

49. A positive verb to correspond with the negative *non tulit* must be supplied, in the Propertian manner; the editors suggest *amabat.* Cf. 1, 2, 30, n. — **Chio . . . terebintho**: in a chamber finished in marble from Chios or turpentine-wood from Oricum; cf. "I dreamt I dwelt in marble halls." Propertius is again reckless of his syntax, and we can speculate as to whether *Oricia terebintho* is thought of as expressing material, quality, or place. Note the hiatus before the caesura; cf. Intr. § 43.

50. pluma versicolore: *i.e.* a feather pillow with a bright-colored cover.

51. huic: 'from so delicate a youth as this !'— **vivo**: to enhance the horror of the contrast, the poet imagines that instead of losing his nails from the disintegrating effect of the water after many days, he wears them down to the roots in the vain attempt to climb upon the wreck or up some sharp rock against which he is dashed by the waves. Cf. Hom. *Od.* 5, 432, sqq.

52. miser . . . hiatus = *huius miseri os hians.*

53. parvo . . . ligno: the poet imagines Paetus clinging to a fragment of the wreck.

54. Paetus: after the *huic* and *hunc* of the preceding verses the repetition of the name here achieves a climax of emphasis, in contrast to *tot coiere mala.* Only the delicate Paetus, and yet all the power of the cruel sea trained upon him!

55. mandata: these are found in vv. 63–64 after the *querellae* proper.

57. di: *i.e. venti.*

59. primae lanuginis: *i.e.* of my early youth (C. S.).

60   attulimus longas in freta vestra manus.
        ah miser alcyonum scopulis adfligar acutis :
        in me caeruleo fuscina sumpta deost.
        at saltem Italiae regionibus evehat aestus :
        hoc de me sat erit si modo matris erit.'
65   subtrahit haec fantem torta vertigine fluctus ;
        ultima quae Paeto voxque diesque fuit.
        o centum aequoreae Nereo genitore puellae,
        et tu materno tacta dolore Thetis,
        vos decuit lasso supponere bracchia mento :
70   non poterat vestras ille gravare manus.
        at tu, saeve Aquilo, numquam mea vela videbis :
        ante fores dominae condar oportet iners.

---

60. longas **O** sanctas *Waardenburg.*   61. adfligar **NFL** affligor **DV**
affigar **ω.**   63. evehat **O** advehat **ω.**   68. tacta **V₂** tracta **O** fracta *Heinsius.*

---

60. **longas**: a mark of beauty and gentility ; cf. 2, 2, 5 : *fulva coma est longaeque manus* ; Cat. 43, 3 : *longis digitis.*

61. **alcyonum**: *i.e.* the cliffs about which they fly. Cf. 1, 17, 2, n.

62. **caeruleo . . . deo**: Neptune ; cf. Ovid, *Trist.* 1, 2, 59 : *viridesque dei, quibus aequora curae.*

63. **evehat**: 'yield me up.' Cf. Ovid, *Her.* 18, 197 : *optabo tamen ut partis expellar in illas et teneant portus naufraga membra tuos.*

64. **hoc de me**: my corpse ; cf. 3, 12, 13 : *neve aliquid de te flendum referatur* ; Verg. *Aen.* 9, 491 : *hoc mihi de te, nate, refers? hoc sum terraque marique secuta?* —

sat: *i.e.* all that can be expected under the circumstances, and as such affording satisfaction to his mother. — **matris erit**: *i.e.* shall come into her hands.

67. **centum**: the orthodox number was fifty ; cf. Hygin. *Fab.*, where the names are given. But there are some variations ; cf. Ovid, *Fast.* 6, 499 : *Panope centumque sorores* ; Plato, *Critias*, 116 E.

68. **materno . . . dolore**: *i.e.* for Achilles.

69. **lasso . . . mento**: cf. Ovid, *Ex P.* 2, 3, 39 : *mitius est lasso digitum supponere mento.*

72. **iners**: even though it involve a life of inactivity (C. S.). Cf. Tib. 1, 1, 58.

9

Maecenas eques Etrusco de sanguine regum,
   intra fortunam qui cupis esse tuam,
quid me scribendi tam vastum mittis in aequor?
   non sunt apta meae grandia vela rati.
5 turpe est, quod nequeas, capiti committere pondus,
   et pressum inflexo mox dare terga genu.

3, 9

In reply to a request from
Maecenas to essay the grand style
of poetry, Propertius says that thus
far he has tried to imitate his
patron's modesty, and hints that
he must continue to do so until
Maecenas shows him the way to
heroic strains. That this is, however, only an *argumentum ad
hominem* is evident from a comparison of 3, 1, 7 and 9; 2, 1, and
various other elegies indicating
clearly the poet's own taste. Cf.
Mallet, *Quaestiones Propertianae*,
p. 11.

1–6: 'Noble, yet modest Maecenas, why do you urge me beyond my strength? 7–20: Men
differ in their gifts. *Non omnia
possumus omnes.* 21–34: I have
imitated your own modesty of
achievement. 35–46: Rather than
venture into the epic field, I have
been satisfied with the themes
of elegy; 47–60: but, if you will
set the pace, perhaps I may yet
relate great deeds.'

1. **eques ... regum**: Maecenas
voluntarily chose to remain in
the rank of the Equites rather
than undertake a senatorial career. Horace frequently refers to
this fact, and to the royal ancestry
of his patron, *e.g. Car.* 1, 20, 5:
care Maecenas eques; 1, 1, 1:
Maecenas atavis edite regibus;
Sat. 1, 6, 1–13; *Car.* 3, 16, 20;
29, 1.

2. Cf. Vell. Pat. 2, 88, 2: *C.
Maecenas equestri, sed splendido
genere natus ... nec minora con-
sequi potuit, sed non tam concu-
pivit*; Ovid, *Trist.* 3, 4, 25: *intra
fortunam debet quisque manere
suam.*

3. **scribendi ... aequor**: cf. 3,
3, 23. Commentators note that
the use of the gerund with *aequor*
is like a modern use of the verbal
noun.

5. **nequeas**: sc. *ferre*, implied
from the following clause. — **capiti**:
the ancient, as well as the modern,
place for bearing burdens, in Italy.

6. **pressum** agrees with *te* to
be supplied from *nequeas*. — **dare**

omnia non pariter rerum sunt omnibus apta,
    fama nec ex aequo ducitur ulla iugo.
gloria Lysippo est animosa effingere signa,
10   exactis Calamis se mihi iactat equis,
in Veneris tabula summum sibi poscit Apelles,
    Parrhasius parva vindicat arte locum,

9. 8. fama ω flamma O (flamina **LD**) (*cf. Enk*) palma *Itali.* ulla O una ω.
11. summum *Rothstein* suma **L** summam **NFDV.**

terga: Propertius mixes metaphors here; for this phrase belongs to military life.

7. omnia . . . rerum: stronger than *omnes res*, just as *opaca locorum* (Verg. *Aen.* 2, 725) is stronger than *opaca loca*, implying minuter detail. The idea of the verse is a commonplace.

8. The thought of this much-discussed verse (cf. B. O. Foster in *Matzke Memorial Volume*, pp. 103 sqq.) is closely connected by *nec* to that of the preceding verse. Men have their individual excellencies, and cannot excel if compelled to do exactly as their neighbors, *i.e.* to trot in pairs; for in a pair, team-work is desired, as in a single hitch individual superiority is striven for. — aequo may perhaps be rendered 'equalizing.'

9. Lysippo: his specialty was bronze statuary and his portrait work was so celebrated that Alexander the Great gave him the exclusive right to represent him in statuary; cf. Hor. *Ep.* 2, 1, 239: *edicto vetuit, ne quis se . . . alius Lysippo duceret aera*; Cic. *Ad Fam.* 5, 12, 7: *Alexander ille . . .*

potissimum . . . a Lysippo fingi volebat. — animosa . . . signa: cf. 2, 31, 8.

10. exactis: 'perfect.' — Calamis: a contemporary of Phidias. His subjects were general; but the same superiority in modeling horses that is here emphasized is suggested by other passages; cf. Ovid, *Ex P.* 4, 1, 33: *vindicat ut Calamis laudem, quos fecit, equorum.* — mihi: 'in my opinion.'

11. Veneris tabula: the celebrated painting of the Venus (Aphrodite) Anadyomene, often referred to in Roman literature, *e.g.* Ovid, *Ex P.* 4, 1, 29: *ut Venus artificis labor est et gloria Coi, aequoreo madidas quae premit imbre comas*; Pliny, *N. H.* 35, 91. — summum: sc. *locum* from.v.12. — Apelles: grouped with Lysippus in Cic. *Ad Fam.* 5, 12, 7 (cited at v. 9) as the only painter whom Alexander the Great would permit to paint his portrait. This portrait brought the sum of twenty talents, and was placed in the temple of Diana (Artemis) at Ephesus.

12. Parrhasius: a contemporary and rival of Zeuxis, who flourished

argumenta magis sunt Mentoris addita formae,
    at Myos exiguum flectit acanthus iter,
15 Phidiacus signo se Iuppiter ornat eburno,
    Praxitelen propria vindicat urbe lapis.
est quibus Eleae concurrit palma quadrigae,
    est quibus in celeres gloria nata pedes.
hic satus ad pacem, hic castrensibus utilis armis.

16. propria **O** Paria *Broukhusius* Parius **ω** patria *Hertzberg.*

---

about 400 B.C. — **parva . . . arte** : as
Parrhasius excelled in accurate
drawing, correct proportion, and
the representation of fine shades
of expression, it seems best to take
these words in the sense of 'his
skill in details,' or 'fine points of
excellence.'

13. After comparing two sculptors of differing tastes and two
painters, Propertius compares two
silver chasers. — **argumenta** : 'subjects'; *i.e.* the artistic conception
and arrangement of his groups or
scenes. Cf. Ovid, *Met.* 13, 683 :
*fabricaverat Alcon Hyleus, et
longo caelaverat argumento.* —
Mentoris : cf. 1, 14, 2, n. — **formae** :
'design.'

14. **Myos** : Mys, the other to-
reutic artist, did his greatest work
a generation after Phidias, when
he engraved on the inside of the
shield of Athene Promachos the
battle of the Centaurs after a design of Parrhasius (cf. v. 12) ; evidently he excelled in workmanship
and graceful finish. — **exiguum** :
probably the more slender, spiny
acanthus was used in such deco-

ration, cf. Verg. *Georg.* 4, 123 :
flexi tacuissem vimen acanthi.
— **iter** : a cognate acc.

15. **Phidiacus . . . Iuppiter** :
the most famous work of Phidias
was the chryselephantine statue
of Zeus made for the temple at
Olympia about 435 B.C. Render,
'at the bidding of Phidias, Juppiter,'
etc.

16. **Praxitelen** : one of the
greatest Greek sculptors, of the
later Attic school, who flourished
in the fourth century B.C. — **propria . . . urbe lapis** : Pentelic
marble, in which he worked rather
than in gold and ivory, and which
is abundant in Athens. With the
abl. of source some participle is
customary.

17. **est quibus** = ἔστιν οἷς, for
the regular Latin, *sunt quibus* ; cf.
Hor. *Car.* 1, 1, 3. — **Eleae . . .
quadrigae** : chariot racing was a
feature of the Olympic games after
680 B.C. — **concurrit** = *contingit.*

18. Propertius has turned the
thought inside out; he means :
'there are others whose swift feet
are destined for glory.'

20   naturae sequitur semina quisque suae.

at tua, Maecenas, vitae praecepta recepi,

cogor et exemplis te superare tuis.

cum tibi Romano dominas in honore secures

et liceat medio ponere iura foro,

25   vel tibi Medorum pugnaces ire per hastas

atque onerare tuam fixa per arma domum,

et tibi ad effectum vires det Caesar, et omni

tempore tam faciles insinuentur opes,

parcis, et in tenues humilem te colligis umbras,

30   velorum plenos subtrahis ipse sinus.

crede mihi, magnos aequabunt ista Camillos

iudicia, et venies tu quoque in ora virum,

Caesaris et famae vestigia iuncta tenebis:

Maecenatis erunt vera tropaea fides.

35   non ego velifera tumidum mare findo carina:

25. hastas *Markland* hostes **O** astus *Lachmann.*

21. recepi: 'I have adopted as my own.'

22. exemplis: Maecenas repeatedly declined honors. — **superare**: 'confute.'

23. dominas: here used adjectivally: 'emblems of power' = 'imperial.' — **honore**: 'official position.' — **secures**: those of the lictors.

24. ponere: used by zeugma. Hor. *Sat.* 1, 3, 105 uses the expression *ponere leges*, as in English we say "lay down the law," but *dare leges* is more usual.

26. Cf. Tib. 1, 1, 54. — **per arma**: poetic for *armis*: cf. Ovid, *Her.* 18, 7: *freta ventis turbida perque cavas vix adeunda rates.*

28. insinuentur = *in sinus cadant, i.e.* 'pour into your lap.'

29. parcis: the intransitive use is very rare. — **te colligis**: 'shrink.'

30. subtrahis: 'furl.' The more usual word is *contrahere*; cf. Hor. *Car.* 2, 10, 22: *sapienter idem contrahes vento nimium secundo turgida vela.*

31. Camillos: tradition attributed to the famous M. Furius Camillus a contentment which became proverbial. Cf. L. 1105.

32. iudicia: cf. L. 1110.

33. famae: dative with *iuncta.* — **tenebis** *i.e.* through all time.

34. fides: to friends, particularly to Augustus, next to his poetic protégés.

35. Cf. 3, 3, 23, n. — **findŏ** is one of the early examples of the shortening of the final *ō* which so

tuta sub exiguo flumine nostra morast.

non flebo in cineres arcem sedisse paternos

    Cadmi, nec septem proelia clade pari,

nec referam Scaeas et Pergama Apollinis arces,

40   et Danaum decimo vere redisse rates,

moenia cum Graio Neptunia pressit aratro

    victor Palladiae ligneus artis equus.

inter Callimachi sat erit placuisse libellos

    et cecinisse modis, Coe poeta, tuis.

45   haec urant pueros, haec urant scripta puellas,

    meque deum clament et mihi sacra ferant.

---

36. tuta ω tota **O**.   44. Coe *Beroaldus* dure **O** Dore *Scriverius* dare *Ayrmann* docte *Foster*. Philita *is accepted for* poeta *by Hosius from an anonymous source.*

soon became general in all verbs. Cf. Intr. § 43.

36. sub: 'under the protection of'; the poet is thinking of his surroundings in the imagined picture.

37. flebo: 'tell the harrowing tale'; cf. 1, 7, 18. — **arcem . . . Cadmi**: cf. 1, 7, 1, n. — **paternos**: Propertius is ambiguous, as often; he seems to be referring to the city-state of Thebes, the fatherland, and trying to indicate its complete destruction, in which the fall of the citadel involved the whole.

38. septem proelia: the warfare waged by the Seven against Thebes; cf. H. & T. § 171. — **clade pari**: all the heroes (except Adrastus) met the same fate. Many literary masterpieces were composed upon the legends of Thebes. As an epic theme it

attracted many; cf. 1, 7; H. & T. § 167; the only surviving work of this nature is the *Thebaid* of Statius.

39. The poet refers to the story of the *Iliad*. — **Scaeas**: sc. *portas*; the famous western gate of Troy, where Homer represents Helen coming to meet the oldest councilors of the city (*Il.* 3, 149). — **Apollinis**: Apollo and Neptune (Poseidon) built the walls (cf. *Neptunia*, v. 41).

41. pressit aratro: *i.e.* the ultimate result to which the ruse of the wooden horse led.

42. Palladiae . . . artis: 'contrived by Pallas'; gen. of the author.

43. Cf. 3, 1, 1.

46. Cf. Ovid, *Rem. Am.* 813: *postmodo reddetis sacro pia vota poetae.*

te duce vel Iovis arma canam caeloque minantem
   Coeum et Phlegraeis Oromedonta iugis,
celsaque Romanis decerpta Palatia tauris
50   ordiar et caeso moenia firma Remo,
eductosque pares silvestri ex ubere reges,
   crescet et ingenium sub tua iussa meum,
prosequar et currus utroque ab litore ovantes,
   Parthorum astutae tela remissa fugae,
55   castraque Pelusi Romano subruta ferro,
   Antonique graves in sua fata manus.
mollis tu coeptae fautor cape lora iuventae

48. Oromedonta **O** Eurymedonta *Huschke.*

47. te duce: the fair presumption is that Propertius suggests a more aggressive public career for his patron. — **Iovis arma**: the *Gigantomachia* is the first possible epic subject to be mentioned.

48. Coeum: a Titan: but the distinction between Giant and Titan is often overlooked. — **Phlegraeis . . . iugis**: the place where the mythical struggle occurred; it was localized sometimes in Thrace, sometimes in Campania. The most magnificent representation of the scene in art was that which has been found on the Zeus altar at Pergamon.

49. Cf. 4, 1, 1-4; Tib. 2, 5, 25.

50. firma = *firmata.* — **Remo**: the abl. abs. expresses means; probably there was some more occult meaning to the tradition, perhaps a connection with such human sacrifices as are believed to have been made in connection with bridge building.

51. pares . . . reges: Romulus and Remus. — **silvestri . . . ubere**: the famous bronze group in the Capitoline (Conservatori) Museum followed the tradition.

52. crescet . . . sub: 'shall come to measure up to.'

53. prosequar: *i.e.* metaphorically. — **utroque ab litore**: quoted from Verg. *Georg.* 3, 33. The reference is a hyperbolical one to the shores of the ocean at the east and west boundaries of the world.

54. Cf. 3, 4, 17, n.

55. Propertius is probably romancing here for effect. Pelusium surrendered to Octavian, according to the accepted version of history, promptly after the appearance of the hero of Actium in its harbor.

56. in sua fata: acc. of purpose: we should expect *in se.*

57. mollis: 'kindly.' — **coeptae . . . iuventae**: 'my youthful under-

dexteraque inmissis da mihi signa rotis.
hoc mihi, Maecenas, laudis concedis, et a test
60   quod ferar in partes ipse fuisse tuas.

I I

Quid mirare, meam si versat femina vitam
et trahit addictum sub sua iura virum,

takings.' — **fautor**: Maecenas is usually like the partisan at the races cheering on his favorite team. But here the poet suggests that he come for the nonce to the chariot itself, and guide it where it may undertake a new course.

58. inmissis . . . rotis: as an elegiac poet Propertius is already far on in the race. — **da . . . signa**: but as patron Maecenas will now give the starter's signal for a new course, *i.e.* in epic poetry, to which he must, however, have himself conducted the poet, as indicated in v. 57.

59. hoc . . . laudis: *i.e.* that I look to you for inspiration and suggestion.

60. in partes ipse fuisse tuas: 'that even I have belonged to thy followers,' *i.e.* those recognized by Maecenas. The acc. is due to the implied motion which must have preceded *fuisse*; cf. Plaut. *Amph.* 180: *mi in mentem fuit.*

3, 11

The good fortune of Rome in escaping from the power of a woman through the merit of Augustus.

An elegy beginning with the commonplace, for our poet, of the thralldom of woman's love, and ending with the glories of Rome and the Emperor, seems almost like a playful supplement to 3, 9, a hint of what Propertius might do under proper conditions, in the epic style.

1–8: 'Do you think it strange that I bow to a woman? Men learn by experience and so may you. 9–26: Remember the power of Medea, Penthesilea, Omphale, Semiramis! 27–49: Yea, come nearer home, and think of Cleopatra and how great was the danger that she would bring glorious Rome under the sway of shameless Egypt! 49–72: But, thanks to Augustus, Rome was spared such humiliation and the gods still smile upon us as of old. So let every sailor on the Ionian Sea give thanks to Augustus!'

1. versat: my life is 'at the beck and call' of a woman. Cf. Tib. 2, 1, 64. The verb has frequentative force.

2. addictum: an insolvent debtor was called *addictus* when

criminaque ignavi capitis mihi turpia fingis,
　　quod nequeam fracto rumpere vincla iugo?
5　venturam melius praesagit navita noctem,
　　vulneribus didicit miles habere metum.
ista ego praeterita iactavi verba iuventa:
　　tu nunc exemplo disce timere meo.
Colchis flagrantis adamantina sub iuga tauros
10　　egit et armigera proelia sevit humo,
custodisque feros clausit serpentis hiatus,
　　iret ut Aesonias aurea lana domos.
ausa ferox ab equo quondam oppugnare sagittis
　　Maeotis Danaum Penthesilea rates;
15　aurea cui postquam nudavit cassida frontem,
　　vicit victorem candida forma virum.

---

he was formally delivered by the praetor to his creditor (C. S.). Formal bondage, as compared with informal slavery of v. 1.

3. Cf. 1, 12, 1.

5. melius: the sailor foretells the promise of the coming night better than a landsman. The poet justifies his own judgment on love matters by a comparison with the sailor and soldier (C. S.).

7. ista: 'such as yours.'

9. Colchis: Propertius refers to Medea four times by this word. — **flagrantis**: 'fire-breathing.'

10. egit . . . sevit: *i.e.* she made it possible for Jason to accomplish these feats. — **armigera**: cf. H. & T. §§ 123, 166.

11. serpentis: the dragon.

12. lana: this less usual word for 'fleece' is used by Ovid also, *Her.* 12, 128; *Fast.* 3, 876.

13. ferox belongs to the predicate. — **ab equo**: like the Greek ἀφ' ἵππου.

14. Maeotis: unusual employment of the word to imply the region from which, *i.e.* the vicinity of Lake Maeotis, the modern sea of Azov. Other writers located the Amazons on the Thermodon, or more vaguely. — **Penthesilea**: the handsome daughter of Ares and queen of the Amazons, who was slain in battle by Achilles. Cf. Verg. *Aen.* 1, 491.

15. nudavit cassida: 'the removal of the helmet disclosed,' by a kind of brachyology (C. S.). Another instance of this rare by-form of the nom. occurs in Verg. *Aen.* 11, 775.

16. Cf. Horace's well-known expression: *Graecia capta ferum victorem cepit* (*Ep.* 2, 1, 156).

Omphale in tantum formae processit honorem,
  Lydia Gygaeo tincta puella lacu,
ut, qui pacato statuisset in orbe columnas,
20   tam dura traheret mollia pensa manu.
Persarum statuit Babylona Semiramis urbem,
  ut solidum cocto tolleret aggere opus,
et duo in adversum missi per moenia currus
  ne possent tacto stringere ab axe latus,
25 duxit et Euphratem medium, qua condidit arces,

11. **23.** missi O mitti *Tyrrell.*   **24.** ne **DV** nec **NFL.**

17. **Omphălĕ**: note quantity
and hiatus. Omphale was said to
be the queen of Lydia, and daughter of King Iardanus. Cf. H. &
T. § 145.

18. **Gygaeo . . . lacu**: near Sar-
dis, named after the well-known
Lydian king. — **tincta** = *lauta*,
with an increment of poetic imagination. Cf. Verg. *Aen.* 3,
665 : *fluctus latera ardua tinxit.*
Propertius means merely to indicate the region from which she
came. — **puella** : she was the young
widow of Tmolus.

19. **columnas**: 'the pillars of
Hercules,' on both sides the *fre-
tum Herculeum* ; Abyla in Africa,
and Calpe (Gibraltar) in Europe,
said to have been one mountain
till sundered by the power of
Hercules.

20. **traheret . . . pensa**: the
customary occupation of a female
slave. Cf. Tib. 1, 3, 85–88.

21. **Persarum** : from whom the

Parthians got their empire; but
Propertius neglects any reference
to the older empires under which
Babylon flourished. — **Semiramis** :
the Babylonian queen who was,
according to one prevalent tradition, the founder of the city. Cf.
Strabo, 16, 1, 2 ; Ovid, *Met.* 4, 58.

22. **cocto**: 'baked,' *i.e.* of brick.
— **tolleret**: consecutive.

23. Fabulous accounts of the
walls of Babylon have survived.
Herodotus (1, 178) says they were
337 feet high and 84 feet wide.

24. **ne**: instead of the expected
completion of his consecutive
phrase, Propertius loosely tries to
combine a purpose and a result
idea in the same clause. What
he means is that Semiramis had
in mind a wall so broad that two
chariots could pass without contact. Cf. A. & G. 537, 2, *a*, n. —
tacto . . . ab axe: 'through the
grazing of a hub' (C. S.) ; cf. 3,
2, 25, n.

iussit et imperio subdere Bactra caput.

nam quid ego heroas, quid raptem in crimina divos?

Iuppiter infamat seque suamque domum:

quid, modo quae nostris opprobria vexerit armis

30   et famulos inter femina trita suos

coniugis obsceni pretium Romana poposcit

moenia et addictos in sua regna patres?

noxia Alexandria, dolis aptissima tellus,

---

27. crimina **V**₂ crimine **0**.   31. coniugis **0** coniugii *Passerat.*

---

26. imperio subdere . . . caput: 'to bow its head to her sway.' While the poet in leading up to the power of Cleopatra apparently intends to neglect the erotic element in the case of Semiramis, we must assume that he probably knew, and expected his readers to know, the story of the personal charms of the queen, her earlier marriage to Ormes, a general of Ninus, and the infatuation of Ninus himself for her, which led to the death of Ormes.

27. nam quid: there is an ellipsis: ' Enough such examples. Why need I dwell on ancient heroes, or even gods, to illustrate love and crime? Juppiter himself might furnish an instance. But we have one bad enough right at home in Antony and Cleopatra' (C. S.).

29. quid . . . quae: *i.e. quid de ea dicam quae.* — **modo:** 'but yesterday.' — **opprobria;** because of the character of the woman, as well as the very fact that it was a woman with whom they were matched, it was an insult to the Roman army to engage in the fiasco at Actium.

30. et = *etiam.* — **femina:** scornful term. — **trita:** 'too familiar.' Propertius regards Cleopatra merely as an abandoned woman, distinguished from others of her class only in that she demanded the empire as her price (C. S.). He disdains to name her.

31. coniugis obsceni: subj. gen. Propertius, like Horace, is ashamed to mention the name of Antony. — **pretium:** cf. *Eleg. in Maec.* 1, 53: *hic modo miles erat, ne posset femina Romam dotalem stupri turpis habere sui.*

33. noxia Alexandria: the poet apostrophizes Egypt through her two chief cities, Memphis and Alexandria, as the bane of Rome, most apt in treachery, and source of bloodshed and disgrace (C. S.). — **dolis aptissima:** cf. Bell. *Alex.* 7, 3: *aptissimum esse hoc genus ad proditionem dubitare nemo potest.*

et totiens nostro Memphi cruenta malo,
35   tres ubi Pompeio detraxit harena triumphos!
tollet nulla dies hanc tibi, Roma, notam.
issent Phlegraeo melius tibi funera campo,
vel tua si socero colla daturus eras,
scilicet incesti meretrix regina Canopi,

34. **totiens**: in particular, in
the Alexandrian war of Caesar, the
various engagements during the
struggle of Octavian against
the power of Cleopatra, and the
event to which reference is made
in v. 35. — **nostro . . . malo**: one
of Propertius's vague ablatives:
'to our hurt.'

35. **tres . . . triumphos**: over
Numidia (80 B.C.), Spain (71
B.C.), and Mithridates (61 B.C.);
cf. Cic. *Pro Sest.* 61, 129: *vir is,
qui tripertitas orbis terrarum oras
atque regiones tribus triumphis
adiunctas huic imperio notavit.* —
ubi: used loosely of *tellus* in general. — **detraxit harena**: Pompey
was murdered in the little boat in
which he was proceeding to land,
and his corpse was left upon the
sandy beach, naked and headless.

37. **issent** = *fuissent*: cf. Juv.
7, 29: *dignus venias hederis*; German "*Wie geht's?*"—**Phlegraeo . . .
campo**: a willful or careless ambiguity. The expression may refer
to Campania, where Pompey was
dangerously ill at Naples. in 50 B.C.
(cf. Cic. *Tusc. Disp.* 1, 86); or to
Pharsalus, where he was finally
defeated by Caesar, in a battle
which might be poetically com-

pared to that of the Giants on the
neighboring Phlegraean plains of
Macedonia. The former interpretation seems to have been accepted
by Juvenal (10, 283 sqq.); the
latter, which suits better the development of the thought here,
was apparently in the mind of
Lucan (7, 144 sqq.; 8, 530, 531).
— **tibi**: Pompey, though there is
no new vocative to change the
person addressed from that in the
previous verse; cf. Tib. 1, 7, 3, n.

38. **vel . . . si**: 'even if' =
'even though,' if the second interpretation of v. 37 is accepted. —
socero: Julius Caesar, whose
daughter Julia became Pompey's
wife in 59 B.C. — **daturus eras**:
i.e. in losing in the battle of Pharsalus, if we accept the second interpretation of v. 37.

39. **scilicet**: a sarcastic introduction to a most bitterly scornful
passage. — **incesti . . . Canopi**:
Canopus, a notorious resort twelve
miles east of Alexandria, was reputed far to outdo the excesses of
Baiae; Juvenal, who knew Egypt
at first hand, speaks (15, 46) of
famoso . . . Canopo; and Κανω-
βίσμος became proverbial. —
meretrix regina: so also Pliny,

40   una Philippeo sanguine adusta nota,
        ausa Iovi nostro latrantem opponere Anubim,
        et Tiberim Nili cogere ferre minas,
        Romanamque tubam crepitanti pellere sistro,
        baridos et contis rostra Liburna sequi,
45   foedaque Tarpeio conopia tendere saxo,
        iura dare et statuas inter et arma Mari.

N. H. 9, 119. With fine irony Cleopatra is called queen of Canopus, rather than of Egypt.

40. una: the poet speaks relatively rather than absolutely. — **Philippeo sanguine**: source, the customary preposition being omitted. The Ptolemies claimed to trace their descent from Philip of Macedon. — **nota**: ablative. No infamy like Cleopatra's had ever overtaken the Ptolemies.

41. ausa: sc. *est*. — **latrantem**: the Egyptian god Anubis was represented with a jackal's, or dog's, head; Vergil (*Aen.* 8, 698) and Ovid (*Met.* 9, 690) use the expression *latrator Anubis*. The inferiority of Egypt to Rome is implied in the series of comparisons: (1) great gods; (2) local river gods; (3) army; (4) navy; (5) national character; (6) laws.

42. Cf. 2, 33, 20: *cum Tiberi Nilo gratia nulla fuit.*

43. crepitanti: 'jingling.' To rouse them to deeds of battle they must rely on the barbarian *sistrum*, a mere adjunct of their characteristic worship.

44. baridos: it was like matching our canal boat with the steam war vessel (C. S.). The βᾶρις was a clumsy river transport propelled by poles (*contis*). — **Liburna**: swiftly moving galleys like those used by the Illyrian pirates. They had played an important part in the victory of Actium.

45. Tarpeio . . . saxo: where the heroic Roman character had been so often exhibited, and death scorned. — **conopia**: to a Roman soldier mosquito netting would be the extreme of effeminacy. Cf. Hor. *Epod.* 9, 15: *interque signa turpe militaria sol adspicit conopium.*

46. iura dare: what a feminine regime like that of Cleopatra would be at Rome is hinted from the previous verse, and the effect of the imaginary picture is heightened by the contrast with the rule of the most virile heroes in Roman history, like Marius. — **statuas**: of the great gods of Rome and of famous Romans. They grew so numerous that they began to be removed by the State from the Capitol as early as 179 B.C., from the Forum in 158 B.C. — **arma Mari**: the trophies that Marius won from Jugurtha, and

quid nunc Tarquinii fractas iuvat esse secures,
   nomine quem simili vita superba notat,
si mulier patienda fuit ? cape, Roma, triumphum,
50   et longum Augusto salva precare diem.
fugisti tamen in timidi vaga flumina Nili :
   accepere tuae Romula vincla manus.
bracchia spectavi sacris admorsa colubris,
   et trahere occultum membra soporis iter.

51. vaga **DV** vada **NFL.**

from the Cimbri and Teutons, set
up on the Capitoline hill, were
torn down by Sulla, but restored
by Julius Caesar. Cf. Suet. *Iul.*
11.

47. quid : acc. of inner obj.
(cognate). — **nunc :** *i.e.* if such
conditions are to prevail ; referring
to the first clause in v. 49. —
Tarquinii : the last king of Rome.
— **iuvat :** sc. *Romam.* — **secures :**
the sign of absolute power, per-
petuated in the insignia of the
consuls, the *fasces*.

48. nomine : *i.e.* Tarquinius
Superbus.

49. cape : 'rejoice, O Rome,
in thy triumph ' (C. S.).

50. diem = *vitam.*

51. The subject is Cleopatra,
with another of Propertius's sudden transitions, and unannounced.
— **tamen :** *i.e.* in spite of the presumptuous pride voiced in vv.
39–46. — **timidi :** the epithet is
transferred from Cleopatra by
metaphor (C. S.). The fleeing
fleet is included also. — **vaga :**
'wandering' through various
mouths in its course to the sea.

52. accepere . . . manus : figuratively. — **Romula :** this adjective is used also in 4, 4, 26 ; the
usual prose form is *Romulea* =
Romana ; cf. Hor. *Carm. Saec.*
47 : *Romulae genti.*

53. bracchiă : cf. Intr. § 43. —
spectavi : Propertius doubtless
saw in the triumphal procession
an effigy of Cleopatra with the
asp that common tradition in literature and art has accepted as
the means of her death, though
here, as often, the tradition rests
on an uncertain basis. Cf. Hor.
Car. 1, 37, 26 ; Plut. *Ant.* 86. —
sacris : *i.e.* to Isis ; cf. Ovid,
Am. 2, 13, 13 : *pigraque dabatur
circa donaria serpens :* Juv. 6, 538 :
*et movisse caput visa est argentea
serpens.*

54. Propertius mixes his metaphors, the last sleep, and that
journey from which there is no return. The frame drinks in the
poison which causes the queen to
start on the journey to the world
of the dead. Only Propertius
would dare to speak of 'draining
a draught of journey !'

309

55 'non hoc, Roma, fui tanto tibi cive verenda'
        dixit 'et adsiduo lingua sepulta mero.'
    septem urbs alta iugis, toto quae praesidet orbi,
        femineas timuit territa Marte minas.
    Hannibalis spolia et victi monimenta Syphacis
60   et Pyrrhi ad nostros gloria fracta pedes!
    Curtius expletis statuit monimenta lacunis,
        at Decius misso proelia rupit equo,
    Coclitis abscissos testatur semita pontes,
        est cui cognomen corvus habere dedit.

                    55. fui ω fuit O.

55. hoc . . . tanto . . . cive:
Augustus is complimented by being
referred to under his favorite title
of *Princeps*.   The abl. abs. is
equivalent to a clause of proviso.
— **fui:** Cleopatra is speaking.

56. Sc. *non fuit verenda* with
lingua, referring to Antony.

57. toto: cf. 2, 1, 47 (*uno*);
Tib. 4, 6, 9, n.

58. Marte = *bello.*

59. The general sense of this
fine outburst is that in Augustus
Rome had a hero far greater than
in all her past history, and possessing him she scarcely need fear
Jove himself (C. S.), much less a
woman.   The glory of defeating
Hannibal, Syphax (a Numidian
king who helped Hannibal), and
Pyrrhus, as representing masculine
warriors from Greece and Africa,
the countries that Cleopatra represented, is appropriately contrasted
here with the terrorizing influence
she had over Rome, expressed in
v. 58.   The animadversions of

the critics and the transpositions
by the editors in the latter part of
this poem are incomprehensible.
Cf. Vahlen, *Ind. Lect.* 1886–87,
Berlin.

61. Here follow instances of
self-sacrificing heroism to save the
State in earlier days. — **Curtius:**
the story is told in Livy, 7, 6. —
monimenta: such word repetitions
are not uncommon in the Roman
elegy; cf. vv. 16, 17; 19, 21; 36,
40; Vahlen, *l.c.*

62. at: the method of Decius
was a different one; see Livy, 8, 9;
10, 28; Cic. *Tusc. Disp.* 1, 37, 89.

63. Coclitis: Horatius Cocles,
the hero of the bridge; cf. Livy, 2,
10. — **semita:** the location of the
street named after Horatius is not
known.

64. est cui: M. Valerius Corvus; see Livy, 7, 26. — **habere** =
habendam; cf. Verg. *Aen.* 5, 260:
*loricam quam Demoleo detraxerat
ipse victor . . . donat habere viro;*
R. 1363.

                    310

65 haec di condiderant, haec di quoque moenia servant:
  vix timeat salvo Caesare Roma Iovem.
 nunc ubi Scipiadae classes, ubi signa Camilli,
  aut modo Pompeia Bospore capta manu?
 Leucadius versas acies memorabit Apollo.
70 tantum operis belli sustulit una dies.
 at tu, sive petes portus seu, navita, linques,
  Caesaris in toto sis memor Ionio.

65. condiderant: even before these heroic deeds the gods had established Rome.

66. salvo Caesare: the construction is a repetition of *hoc tanto . . . cive* (v. 55). The thought of the verse is contrasted with that of v. 58.

67. nunc ubi: *i.e.* in comparison with the glorious victory of Augustus at Actium. — **Scipiadae:** the regular patronymic formation in this family. — **classes:** the famous fleet prepared in 45 days in 205 B.C. to bring the second Punic war to a close. The plural, like *pontes,* in v. 63, is purely rhetorical. Cf. L. 1110. — **signa Camilli:** taken from the Gauls in 390 B.C.; cf. Livy, 5, 49, 7: *dictator . . . triumphans in urbem rediit*; Verg. *Aen.* 6, 825: *referentem signa Camillum.*

68. modo: 'but recently,' contrasted with the other great Roman victories mentioned. — **Bospore:** vocative. It was from Panticapaeum on the Cimmerian Bosporus, which Pliny (*N. H.* 4, 78) calls the edge of Europe, that the body of the dead Mithridates was sent to Pompey at Amisus; but Propertius flatters the memory of Pompey by intimating that the latter conquered a region that he probably never saw.

69. Leucadius . . . Apollo: the celebrated temple of Apollo on the north promontory of the island of Leucas looked down upon the battle of Actium. The Leucadian Apollo was frequently invoked by sailors. — **versas acies:** cf. Hor. *Epod.* 9, 17–20.

70. tantum operis belli: *i.e.* the fleet of Cleopatra. — **una dies:** that of the battle of Actium.

72. Augustus has cleared the seas of all the enemies of Rome, including pirates. Cf. Hor. *Car.* 4, 5, 19: *pacatum volitant per mare navitae.*

16

Nox media, et dominae mihi venit epistula nostrae :
　　Tibure me missa iussit adesse mora,
candida qua geminas ostendunt culmina turres
　　et cadit in patulos lympha Aniena lacus.
5　quid faciam? obductis committam mene tenebris,
　　ut timeam audaces in mea membra manus?
at si distulero haec nostro mandata timore,
　　nocturno fletus saevior hoste mihi.
peccaram semel, et totum sum pulsus in annum :
10　in me mansuetas non habet illa manus.

16. 9. pulsus **FLDV** portus **N** postus *Phillimore* tortus *Gwynn.*

3, 16

1–10 : 'A summons from Cynthia at midnight to come to Tibur at once ! Which alternative is to be accepted — to risk the perils of the journey, or to risk her displeasure? 11–20 : But all the world loves a lover, and I shall be safe ; 21–30 : even if I die in the attempt, it will be worth while ; she will honor my tomb — and may it be "far from the madding crowd!"'

2. Tibure : locative. Cynthia probably spent a considerable part of her time in this beautiful and popular suburban resort (cf. 2, 32, 5), and was buried there (4, 7, 81–86). Cf. Lanciani, *Wanderings in the Roman Campagna*, pp. 88 sqq.

3. candida . . . culmina : hilltops on either side the Anio covered with villas and temples which would glisten in the moonlight as well as in the sunshine. — **geminas . . . turres** : high buildings on the two sides of the river. Cf. Tib. 1, 7, 19.

4. On these famous falls cf. Hor. *Car.* 1, 7, 12 : *domus Albuneae resonantis et praeceps Anio ac Tiburni lucus et uda mobilibus pomaria rivis.*

5. obductis : sc. *caelo* or *terrae.* — **mene** : for a similar position of the interrogative particle, cf. 3, 6, 12 : *ornabat niveas nullane gemma manus ?*

6. audaces in mea membra : for the dangers from highway robbers, cf. Juv. 3, 302–308 ; 10, 20–21.

9. Cf. Intr. § 33.

10. in me : cf. *in mea membra* (v. 6). — **mansuetas non . . . manus** : the phrase justifies the expression *pulsus* in v. 9.

nec tamen est quisquam, sacros qui laedat amantes :
   Scironis media sic licet ire via.
quisquis amator erit, Scythicis licet ambulet oris :
   nemo adeo ut noceat barbarus esse volet.
15 luna ministrat iter, demonstrant astra salebras,
   ipse Amor accensas percutit ante faces,
saeva canum rabies morsus avertit hiantis :
   huic generi quovis tempore tuta viast.
sanguine tam parvo quis enim spargatur amantis
20 inprobus ?   exclusis fit comes ipsa Venus.
quod si certa meos sequerentur funera casus,
   talis mors pretio vel sit emenda mihi.
adferet haec unguenta mihi sertisque sepulcrum

---

16. percutit O praecutit *Guyetus.*   22. talis O tali **V**₂.   23. haec *Guyetus* huc O.

---

11. **nec tamen est** : 'and, after all, there isn't.' For the sentiment, cf. 2, 26, 45 sqq.; Tib. I, 2, 27 : *quisquis amore tenetur, eat tutusque sacerque qualibet: insidias non timuisse decet.*

12. **Scironis** : Sciron was a famous robber who haunted the road leading from the isthmus into Megara and Attica. He was slain by Theseus (C. S).

13. This couplet, with unimportant variations, was found scratched upon the wall of the basilica in Pompeii; cf. *C I L.* 4, 1950.

16. **ipse Amor** : Cupid in person performs the duty of the slave that lights the way. — **accensas percutit** : 'kindles up and brandishes'; *percutit* is here an intensive form of *quatit.*

17. **saeva canum rabies . . . avertit** = *canes saevi rabiosique . . . avertunt.* — **morsus** : *i.e. os mordens.*

18. **huic generi** : lovers (C. S.).

19. The masks of lovers were conventionally pale, indicating a traditional belief that their blood was thin or scanty.

20. **exclusis . . . ipsa** : even when the lover is unlucky enough to be denied admission to his beloved, Venus watches over him ; much more, it is implied, when he is on his way to an expectant mistress.

23. **haec** : as usual, the one and only 'she' for Propertius. — **unguenta** : cf. 2, 13, 30. — **sertisque . . . ornabit** : cf. 1, 17, 22. There was a special day for such decoration, known as *rosales escae.*

ornabit custos ad mea busta sedens.

25 di faciant, mea ne terra locet ossa frequenti,

qua facit adsiduo tramite vulgus iter.

post mortem tumuli sic infamantur amantum.

me tegat arborea devia terra coma,

aut humer ignotae cumulis vallatus harenae.

30 non iuvat in media nomen habere via.

18

Clausus ab umbroso qua ludit pontus Averno,
fumida Baiarum stagna tepentis aquae,

18. 2. fumida *Scaliger* humida O.

25. Lygdamus's wish was just
the opposite : cf. Tib. 3, 2, 29, n.
And Cynthia's tomb is represented
as beside a road, the favorite custom in Roman sepulture.

28. arborea . . . coma can well
be taken as a descriptive ablative
with *terra :* cf. also 2, 13, 33.

29. Rather than lie in a public
place he would prefer to be cast
on an unknown shore, like Paetus
(3, 7, 26).

3, 18

The death of M. Claudius Marcellus, son of Octavia, the sister of
Augustus, at Baiae in 23 B.C., in
the twentieth year of his age, disappointed many hopes. By his
marriage in 25 B.C. to his cousin
Julia, the daughter of Augustus, he
had become the heir apparent, and
as such was very acceptable to the
Romans. Vergil immortalized his
memory in the famous verses *Aen.*

6, 860–886, at the recital of which
Octavia is said to have swooned.
Propertius, however, takes pains
not to mention the name of Marcellus anywhere. The elegy was
evidently written soon after the
event.

1–10 : 'In Baiae, home of myths
and marvels, he is dead. 11–16 :
Yes, dead ! in spite of all he had
to live for ; 17–30 : wealth and
fame save none from death — witness kings and heroes of old ;
31–34 : but while Marcellus "goes
the way of all the earth," it is for
him a gathering to the gods.'

1. Clausus : *i.e.* by the narrow
strip referred to in v. 4. —umbroso
. . . Averno : cf. Verg. *Aen.* 3,
442 : *divinosque lacus et Averna
sonantia silvis* ; 6, 136–139 ; 238–
242. — pontus : the bay of Baiae.

2. fumida . . . stagna : in apposition with *pontus.* — tepentis
aquae : the hot springs of this vol-

qua iacet et Troiae tubicen Misenus arena,
   et sonat Herculeo structa labore via,
5 hic ubi, mortales dexter cum quaereret urbes,
   cymbala Thebano concrepuere deo,
(at nunc, invisae magno cum crimine Baiae,
   quis deus in vestra constitit hostis aqua?)
his pressus Stygias vultum demisit in undas,

5. mortales **N** mortalis **FLDV**.   dexter **NFL** dextra **DV**.

canic region appear not only on land but also here and there in the bay.

3. **iacet . . . arena**: cf. Verg. *Aen.* 6, 162: *Misenum in litore sicco.* The remarkable promontory at the outer western limit of the bay of Baiae was traditionally the tomb of the drowned Misenus, and is still called by his name, *Capo di Miseno.*

4. **sonat**: *i.e.* from the surf. — **Herculeo structa labore via**: this was a narrow strip of sand just wide enough for a carriage road separating the bay from the Lucrine Lake. The myth attributed its construction to Hercules (C. S.). Cf. I, 11, 2: *qua iacet Herculeis semita litoribus.*

5. **hic**: adverb. — **mortales** perhaps merely = *mortalium* here by contrast to *deo* in the next verse; but it is possible that the poet meant to emphasize the perishable nature of the cities, as well as of their inhabitants in this vicinity; as this would be in harmony with the spirit of this passage, and with history both before and after he penned these words. For the

cities of these *campi phlegraei* had been devastated by early wars, and were ever in danger of earthquake or volcanic cataclysm. — **dexter . . . quaereret**: 'visited with beneficent intent,' *i.e.* in introducing the vine which flourishes especially in Campania. The western progress of Dionysus is less celebrated than that in the east; cf., however, Sil. Ital. 3, 101 : *tempore quo Bacchus populos domitabat Hiberos.*

6. **Thebano . . . deo**: Bacchus, who, according to the prevailing tradition, was born in Thebes; so, too, was Hercules. — **concrepuere**: cf. Lucian, *Bacch.* 4; Cat. 64, 262. Bacchus follows Hercules similarly in Verg. *Aen.* 6, 801–807.

7. **invisae . . . Baiae**: vocative. — **crimine**: the charge was that of responsibility for the death of Marcellus.

8. **hostis** belongs to the predicate, and is contrasted with the previously mentioned kindly visits of Hercules and Bacchus.

9. **his**: one of the vague ablatives of Propertius referring apparently to *Baiae* and its malign

10   errat et in vestro spiritus ille lacu.

quid genus aut virtus aut optima profuit illi
    mater, et amplexum Caesaris esse focos,
aut modo tam pleno fluitantia vela theatro,
    et per maternas omnia gesta manus ?

15 occidit, et misero steterat vigesimus annus :
    tot bona tam parvo clausit in orbe dies.

i nunc, tolle animos et tecum finge triumphos,

influence, yet possibly to *undas.* — **pressus**: 'overwhelmed.' The language of this verse would apply to drowning, malarial fever, sulphurous gases, or any other of the deadly ills which may have caused the demise of the young man. Perhaps Propertius is intentionally vague, in view of the conflicting rumors at that time as to the cause of his death.

10. errat . . . spiritus ille: 'he flits a spirit' (C. S.). This use of *spiritus* is very rare till later Latin. — **vestro**: *i.e.* of Baiae.

11. quid . . . profuit: cf. 4, 11, 11. — **genus**: for the fame of the Claudian family cf. v. 33.

12. mater: Octavia retired henceforth to private life. — **Caesaris . . . focos**: Marcellus became not only the son-in-law of Augustus, but his son by formal adoption.

13. modo: 'but yesterday.' — **vela**: the awnings stretched over the theater by Marcellus at the shows he gave as *Curule Aedile* in the year of his death. He even stretched awnings over the Forum.

Cf. Pliny, *N. H.* 19, 24. The word gives one illustration of the lavishness with which he performed his official duties. Cf. also 4, 1, 15.

14. omnia perhaps includes all that Octavia did for her son before and after his death. Plutarch says she built the library in the Porticus Octaviae as a memorial to him.

15. 'And for the unfortunate youth his twentieth year suddenly stood still' (C. S.); *i.e.* the passage of the year is thought of as like that of the sun or the moon, which should halt in the midst of its course. The tense is the familiar Propertian pluperfect.

16. dies: 'his brief day' (C. S.).

17. Cf. 3. 7, 29; Ovid, *Her.* 9, 105 : *i nunc, tolle animos et fortia gesta recense.* The pointing in this passage of the familiar moral that death is inevitable and impartial gives opportunity to compare the manner of Propertius with that of his contemporary Horace in such passages as *Car.* 1, 4, 13–20; 1, 28, 7–16; 4, 7, 14–28.

stantiaque in plausum tota theatra iuvent,
   Attalicas supera vestes, atque omnia magnis
20   gemmea sint ludis : ignibus ista dabis.
   sed tamen huc omnes, huc primus et ultimus ordo :
   est mala, sed cunctis ista terenda viast :
   exoranda canis tria sunt latrantia colla,
   scandenda est torvi publica cymba senis.
25 ille licet ferro cautus se condat et aere :
   mors tamen inclusum protrahit inde caput.
   Nirea non facies, non vis exemit Achillem,
   Croesum aut Pactoli quas parit umor opes.
   hic olim ignaros luctus populavit Achivos,
30   Atridae magno cum stetit alter amor.

21. huc . . . huc *Beroaldus* hoc . . . huc **O** hoc . . . hoc *Lachmann.*

18. Cf. Ovid, *Ex Pont.* 2, 6, 28 : *in quorum plausus tota theatra sonant.* For instances of such applause cf. Cic. *Ad Att.* 2, 19, 3 ; Hor. *Car.* 1, 20, 3–8.

19. **Attalicas** : cf. 2, 13, 22, n. — **magnis** : probably not to be taken in the technical sense (= *Romanis*), but in general.

20. **gemmea** : a mere hyperbole. — **ignibus** = *rogo.*

21. **huc** : sc. *tendimus* (C. S.). Cf. Ovid, *Met.* 10, 34 : *tendimus huc omnes, haec est domus ultima.*

22. Cf. 2, 30, 14 : *nos modo propositum, vita, teramus iter.*

23. **canis** : Cerberus is mentioned four times by Propertius ; cf. *e.g.* 4, 11, 25. Note the hypallage.

24. **publica** : 'that ferries all' (C. S.). — **senis** : Propertius does

not mention Charon by name ; cf. v. 31 ; 4, 11, 7.

25. **ille** : the man trying to escape death, referred to in the next verse under the term *inclusum caput.*

27. **Nirea** : the handsomest but one of all the Greeks at the siege of Troy. Cf. Hom. *Il.* 2, 673–674.

28. **Pactoli** . . . **umor** : cf. 1, 6, 32, nn.

29. **hic** . . . **luctus** : *i.e.* the sorrows of inevitable death (C. S.). — **ignaros** : 'unconscious of the cause of their trouble' (C. S.). Men are only in modern times beginning to understand the causes of pestilence ; the Greeks before Troy could only ascribe it to the wrath of Apollo.

30. An excellent example of Propertian ambiguity: *Atridae*

at tibi, nauta, pias hominum qui traicis umbras,
  huc animae portent corpus inane tuae:
qua Siculae victor telluris Claudius et qua
  Caesar, ab humana cessit in astra via.

2 I

Magnum iter ad doctas proficisci cogor Athenas,
  ut me longa gravi solvat amore via.

32. tuae O suae *Markland.*

may be either gen. or dat.; *magno,*
dat. or abl. (of price); *stetit* may
= *erat* or mean 'cost' (with
magno); and *alter amor* may
refer to Chryseis or Briseis, according as the *primus amor* is supposed to be Clytemnaestra, Argynnus, or Chryseis.

31. nauta: cf. v. 24, n.

32. huc: *i.e.* to the place of
entombment, which is at the same
time that of departure for the other
world. — animae ... corpus inane:
cf. Ovid, *Met.* 13, 488: *quae corpus conplexa animae tam fortis
inane.* — tuae: 'for which it is thy
special function to care'; usually;
in this case, the poet goes on to
explain, Charon has no duty to
perform, as the soul itself has been
translated among the celestials;
animae is thus gen. Those who
prefer to take *animae ... tuae*
as nom. explain the meaning
as = *flabra,* the unseen messen-
gers that waft the soul to Charon,
the word being used as in Hor.
Car. 4, 12, 2: *inpellunt animae*

lintea Thraciae. In this case
corpus = *manes* by a common
confusion in Propertius; cf. *e.g.*
2, 13, 32.

33. qua: of the route by which.
— Claudius: M. Claudius Marcellus, the most illustrious of his
direct ancestors, five times consul,
and the conqueror of Syracuse in
212 B.C. It would have been
highly inappropriate to deify Caesar and the young Marcellus, and
omit his famous progenitor!

34. Caesar: his grandfather by
adoption. — humana . . . via:
that *via leti,* which by all *calcanda
semel* (Hor. *Car.* 1, 28, 16).

3, 21

The poet, in desperate anxiety
to rid himself of his love for Cynthia, proposes to leave Rome and
take up his abode in Athens.
There is no proof that the plan
was ever carried out; cf. 1, 17,
Intr. Catullus, when in a similar state of mind (No. 76), proposes only to conquer his passion

crescit enim adsidue spectando cura puellae:
   ipse alimenta sibi maxima praebet amor.
5 omnia sunt temptata mihi, quacumque fugari
   possit: at ex omni me premit iste deus.
vix tamen aut semel admittit, cum saepe negarit:
   seu venit, extremo dormit amicta toro.
unum erit auxilium: mutatis Cynthia terris
10   quantum oculis, animo tam procul ibit amor.
nunc agite, o socii, propellite in aequora navem,
   remorumque pares ducite sorte vices,

---

21. 6. iste ω ille **DV** ipse **NFL**.   8. amicta *Scaliger* amica **O**.
11. aequora **F** aequore **NLDV**.

---

on the ground, instead of running
away.

1–10: 'I must get out of sight
of Cynthia; and away from the
tortures she inflicts on me. 11–
30: I will sail away to Athens and
engross myself in new studies and
other interests; 31–34: thus I
shall be cured of my passion, or
die an honorable death.'

1. **doctas**: cf. 1, 6, 13, n. —
cogor: an intense expression frequent in Propertius; cf. 1, 1, 8; 1,
16, 13, etc.; Intr. § 35.

3. **crescit . . . spectando**: cf.
Cat. 51, 6: *nam simul te, Lesbia,
adspexi, nihil est super mi*;
Shakespeare, *Sonnets*, 75: "Some-
time, all full with feasting on your
sight, And by and by clean
starved for a look."— **cura** = *amor*,
as in 2, 12, 4.

5. **mihi**: A. 375. — **quacumque
. . . possit**: the poet's thought
runs faster than his language, so

that he combines the question
of manner of conquering (*qua . . .
possit*) with the resolve to conquer, no matter how (*quacumque
. . . possit . . . fugandus*). Catullus emphasizes the second part
of the thought in 76, 14–16, where
qua = quacumque.

6. **ex omni**: sc. *parte.* Cf. Ovid,
Rem. Am. 358: *ex omni est parte
fugandus amor.* — **premit**: cf. 1,
1, 4; 1, 9, 24; Ovid *Rem. Am.*
530: *saevus Amor sub pede colla
premit.*

7. **admittit**: Propertius takes
it for granted that the reader
knows the subject. Cf. 3, 16, 23, n.

11. **propellite**: 'launch.'

12. **pares**: 'pair by pair,' that
the rowing may be well balanced.
— **sorte**: cf. Verg. *Aen.* 3, 510: *sortiti remos*, upon which Servius
comments: *sortiti, per sortem di-
visi ad officia remigandi, qui esset
proreta, quis pedem teneret.*

iungiteque extremo felicia lintea malo :
iam liquidum nautis aura secundat iter.

15 Romanae turres et vos valeatis amici,
qualiscumque mihi tuque puella vale.

ergo ego nunc rudis Adriaci vehar aequoris hospes,
cogar et undisonos nunc prece adire deos

deinde per Ionium vectus cum fessa Lechaeo

20   sedarit placida vela phaselus aqua,

quod superest, sufferre, pedes, properate laborem,
Isthmos qua terris arcet utrumque mare.

inde ubi Piraei capient me litora portus,
scandam ego Theseae bracchia longa viae.

---

14. secundat: cf. Ovid, *Her.*
13, 136: *blandaque conpositas
aura secundet aquas.*

15. turres: cf. Tib. 1, 7, 19, n.

16. qualiscumque mihi: ' un-
kind as you have been to me '; cf.
3, 1, 30. — **tuque** : on the position
of the conjunction, cf. Intr. § 28.

17. rudis . . . hospes: this is
to be the poet's first voyage on
the Adriatic.

18. undisonos: Propertius here
apparently tried his hand at a
kind of picturesque epithet more
commonly met in Catullus and
Lucretius.

19. fessa: cf. Tib. 2, 5, 45.
— **Lechaeo** : sc. *mari* (and sc.
mare with *Ionium*). Lechaeum
was the port of Corinth on the
Corinthian Gulf, as Cenchreae was
its port on the east side of the
isthmus.

20. phaselus: the term, originally derived from its similarity in
shape to the kidney bean, is used

somewhat loosely by the poets for
any swift-sailing vessel, *e.g.* Cat.
4, 1 ; Hor. *Car.* 3, 2, 29.

21. quod superest refers to the
remainder of the trip, which the
poet in imagination is now, at
Lechaeum, eager to accomplish.
But while he starts across the
isthmus on foot, it is only to take
ship on the Saronic Gulf for
Athens.

22. terris: abl. of inst.

24. Theseae . . . viae: *i.e.* the
road that the poet thinks of as
trodden by Theseus of old up to
Athens, the city of which he is
the mythical hero. — **bracchia
longa**: the 'long walls' extending
from Athens to the Piraeus, here
called ' arms,' after the Roman
military terminology, were called
' legs ' (σκέλη) by the Athenians.
Within these the *via Thesea*
had become a fine street between four and five miles long,
and this is what Propertius pro-

25   illic vel studiis animum emendare Platonis
       incipiam aut hortis, docte Epicure, tuis,
   persequar aut studium linguae, Demosthenis arma,
       librorumque tuos, docte Menandre, sales.
   aut certe tabulae capient mea lumina pictae,
30   sive ebore exactae seu magis aere manus.
   aut spatia annorum aut longa intervalla profundi
       lenibunt tacito vulnera nostra sinu.
   seu moriar, fato, non turpi fractus amore:
       atque erit illa mihi mortis honesta dies.

poses to climb (*scandam*). But in his time, as a matter of fact, the walls were not only a ruin, but had to a considerable degree been removed.

25. illic: *i.e.* at Athens. — **vel**: instead of a corresponding *vel* we have a series of clauses each introduced by *aut*. The poets abound in instances of similar carelessness, *e.g.* Ovid, *Met.* 15, 601: *vel, si dignus erit, gravibus vincite catenis, aut finite metum fatalis morte tyranni.* — **studiis . . . Platonis**: the Academic philosophy.

26. hortis: Epicurus taught his disciples in a celebrated garden at Athens, and left it to be used by his successors for the same purpose.

27. linguae: *i.e. ars dicendi*, which became most powerful *arma* for Demosthenes.

28. librorum tuos . . . sales: hypallage for *librorum tuorum sales.* — **Menandre**: from the unusual nominative *Menandrus*; the most celebrated writer of the new Attic

comedy, to whom, as compared with his nearest rivals, the epithet *doctus* is not inappropriately applied; for he was a pupil of Theophrastus, and had a philosophical training.

29. aut certe: 'or at any rate'; if he cannot concentrate his thought on intense philosophical study, he can at least divert his attention with the abundant works of art at Athens.

30. manus: 'h a n d i w o r k' (works of art); cf. *Aetna*, 598: *vacca Myronis et iam mille manus.* Similarly χεῖρες in Greek (rarely and late).

31. profundi: sc. *maris*.

32. lenibunt: the only case of the archaic future in the Augustan poets. But the corresponding forms of the imperfect occur in 1, 3, 25, and 3, 13, 35.

33. Propertius has changed his tune since he wrote 2, 13, and 3, 16, 22. Cf. also 2, 26, 58.

34. Cf. 2, 8, 27: *ista mihi mors est inhonesta futura.*

24

Falsa est ista tuae, mulier, fiducia formae,
  olim oculis nimium facta superba meis.
noster amor tales tribuit tibi, Cynthia, laudes:
  versibus insignem te pudet esse meis.
5 mixtam te varia laudavi saepe figura,
  ut quod non esses esse putaret amor:
et color est totiens roseo collatus Eoo,

3, 24

The harshness and bitterness with which, in this and the succeeding poem, Propertius renounces Cynthia differ from anything in the other elegiac poets. Catullus still loves after he has learned to hate. The gentle Tibullus cannot bear to hurt the feelings even of one who has jilted him. Ovid is not to be taken seriously when he undertakes to break with his imaginary Corinna. But Propertius, when he ceases to love, transforms his passion into a burning hatred. Cynthia is by name held up to scorn, and the angry poet can explain his former admiration and love as only pure insanity, while he gloats over the misery in which, he prophesies, she will end her days. This elegy should be carefully compared as a kind of palinode with the opening one of the collection. Cf. also Schiller's *An Minna*.

1–8: 'It was under a delusive fascination that I called you beautiful; 9–20: but what no power could compel me to do, I now do of my own will, acknowledge my madness, and pray for sanity henceforth.'

1. Falsa: 'groundless.' — **mulier**: the term, which is seldom used by the elegists as compared with *femina* and *puella*, and nowhere else in Propertius as an address, is significant of his changed attitude toward his mistress.

2. oculis: *i.e.* the admiration of the observer. — **facta**: vocative.

4. pudet: sc. *me*. For a similar thought cf. Tib. 1, 9, 47: *attonita laudes tibi mente canebam, et me nunc nostri Pieridumque pudet.*

5. mixtam . . . varia . . . figura: 'as combining' various types of beauty, or 'beautiful features,' especially in the early poems of the first two books.

6. By such repeated flattery Propertius had actually fooled himself into believing it true.

7. roseo . . . Eoo: cf. Homer's 'rosy-fingered morn.'

cum tibi quaesitus candor in ore foret.
quod mihi non patrii poterant avertere amici,
10   eluere aut vasto Thessala saga mari.
haec ego, non ferro non igne coactus, et ipsa
    naufragus Aegaea verba fatebor aqua.
correptus saevo Veneris torrebar aheno,
    vinctus eram versas in mea terga manus.
15 ecce coronatae portum tetigere carinae,
    traiectae Syrtes, ancora iacta mihist.

---

24. 12. verba O vera *Passerat.*

---

8. quaesitus: 'procured by artifice.' The contrast suggested in the two verses could only arise in the case of one completely blinded by love.

9. quod: the infatuation described in the previous eight verses. The various possible agencies for relief from it following here, — the persuasion of friends, witchcraft, steel, fire, travel over the seas, — are the same that are enumerated in I, I, 19–30.

10. saga mari: Medea, wife of the Thessalian Jason, was the typical witch. The sea is the great purifier in nature. Cf. Schoemann, *Gr. Alt.* 2, 374; De Jong, *Antike Mysterienwesen*, 136; Conybeare and Howson, *St. Paul*, I, 294.

11. haec, although referring to some general idea, such as *quod* (v. 9), has its form determined by the *verba* in v. 12. — **non . . . coactus**: *i.e.* without being obliged to resort to the heroic treatment of I, I, 27, he is now free to tell the simple truth about Cynthia, voluntarily.

12. Even if life were at stake in the journey he has already (3, 21) projected, he is confident he would still stick to the truth, viz. that all his previous raptures were 'empty words' (*verba*). Perhaps he also recalls I, 17, with its far different state of mind.

13. The poet's obsession is here illustrated from the picture of a victim dragged to the witches' caldron for torture. Cf. I, 3, 13: *duplici correptum ardore*; 3, 6, 39: *consimili in positum torquerier.* — **torrebar**: of a habitual condition.

14. Cf. Ovid, *Ex P.* 3, 2, 72: *evincti geminas ad sua terga manus.*

15. coronatae: cf. Verg. *Georg.* I, 303: *ceu pressae cum iam portum tetigere carinae puppibus et laeti nautae inposuere coronas.*

16. Syrtes: among the most familiar and most dreaded perils of ancient navigators.

323

nunc demum vasto fessi resipiscimus aestu,
　　vulneraque ad sanum nunc coiere mea.
Mens Bona, siqua dea es, tua me in sacraria dono.
20　　　exciderant surdo tot mea vota Iovi.

25

Risus eram positis inter convivia mensis,
　　et de me poterat quilibet esse loquax.
quinque tibi potui servire fideliter annos:
　　ungue meam morso saepe querere fidem.

17. resipiscimus: a word peculiarly appropriate for recovery from amorous *mal de mer*, in view of the thought to which it leads in v. 19.

18. ad sanum . . . coiere: *i.e.* 'heal' (*sanum = sanitatem*); cf. Ovid, *Trist.* 4, 4, 41: *neve retractando nondum coeuntia rumpe vulnera.*

19. A temple was indeed dedicated to *Mens* on the Capitoline, in accordance with a vow of T. Otacilius made after the battle of Lake Trasimenus, and the festival of this personified quality was held on June 8th. *Mens Bona* as such we do not hear of elsewhere.

20. exciderant: the poet had wasted many prayers on Jove before he successfully tried the appeal to *Mens Bona*.

3, 25

The dénouement. See 3, 24, Intr.

1–10: 'For years I was foolishly faithful. You will recall it with regret, but no arts can win me back. You are to blame. Farewell. 11–18: As you grow old, may your lot be that of the ugly hag, and may you know yourself how it felt to be disdained! This is my curse.'

1. Risus: 'laughing-stock.' For a similar use of this noun cf. Ovid, *Fast.* 1, 438: *omnibus ad lunae lumina risus erat.* Propertius uses *iocus* in the same way in 2, 24, 16: *me . . . pudet esse iocum.* — **positis . . . mensis**: cf. Plaut. *Most.* 308: *appone hic mensulam:* Verg. *Aen.* 1, 216: *exempta fames epulis mensaeque remotae.* Cf. also the expressions *mensa prima*, and *mensa secunda*, which originally had a literal signification.

3. Cf. Intr. § 33.

4. ungue . . . morso: cf. 2, 4, 3: *saepe inmeritos corrumpas dentibus ungues.* — **querere**: 'lament the loss of.'

5   nil moveor lacrimis : ista sum captus ab arte.
     semper ab insidiis, Cynthia, flere soles.
   flebo ego discedens, sed fletum iniuria vincit :
     tu bene conveniens non sinis ire iugum.
   limina iam nostris valeant lacrimantia verbis,
10   nec tamen irata ianua fracta manu.
   at te celatis aetas gravis urgeat annis,
     et veniat formae ruga sinistra tuae.
   vellere tum cupias albos a stirpe capillos
     ah speculo rugas increpitante tibi,
15   exclusa inque vicem fastus patiare superbos,
     et quae fecisti facta queraris anus.
   has tibi fatalis cecinit mea pagina diras.
     eventum formae disce timere tuae.

25. 7. vincit O vincet ω.

5. ab arte : cf. 2, 27, 11, n.

6. ab insidiis : adverbial, like Tib. 1, 5, 4 : *adsueta versat ab arte puer.*

7. Cf. Cat. 76, 14; 85. *Ego* is emphatic : 'I shall weep as well as you.'

8. tu : 'but it is you who.' — **conveniens . . . iugum :** 'the well-matched span'; cf. 1, 5, 2 ; *sine nos cursu, quo sumus, ire pares.* — **ire :** *i.e.* to trot in " near- " matrimonial harness.

9. lacrimantia : cf. 1, 16, 13, where the door represents itself as driven to tears by the pitiful complaints of a lover : *gravibus cogor deflere querellis.*

10. nec tamen : *i.e.* in spite of the fact that the hand was that of an angry man. This verse is a reminiscence probably of 2, 5, 22 :

nec mea praeclusas fregerit ira fores.

11. celatis : 'which you have tried to conceal.' — **annis :** to be taken with *gravis.*

13. Ovid, *A. A.* 2, 117 ; *tibi iam venerit cani, formose, capilli, iam venient rugae, quae tibi corpus arent.* — **stirpe :** cf. Tib. 1, 8, 45 : *tollere tum cura est albos a stirpe capillos.*

15. fastus : the shoe is to be on the other foot, as compared with 1, 18, 5.

16. quae fecisti facta : *i.e.* complain, when they are done to you, of the very things you have done to others.

17. fatalis : best taken with *diras,* which is here a substantive (as in Tib. 2, 6, 53) = 'curses.' — **pagina :** used five times by Prop.

LIBER QVARTVS

I

Hoc, quodcumque vides, hospes, qua maxima
    Romast,
ante Phrygem Aenean collis et herba fuit:

1. 1. qua *Scioppius* quam O.

4, 1

Propertius had been often urged to give his attention to a more serious type of poetry, and had several times (*e.g.* 2, 1 ; 3, 1 ; 3, 3) pleaded his inability to do so, yet with various hints that he would really like to try his hand on something else. In this elegy he dallies with the temptation longer than usual, and thus practically makes it a fitting introduction for this last book of his poems. For the first part of the elegy dwells at length on the earlier history and character of the city of Rome, and Nos. 2, 4, 6, 9, and 10 in this book likewise deal with the origins of legends or worships connected with particular localities in Rome. It is evident that Propertius was ambitious to imitate the Αἴτια of his great model Callimachus, and planned to treat in topographical manner the various noteworthy places in Rome, as Ovid in his *Fasti* afterwards explained in chronological order the religious customs of the Roman year. In the first half of this elegy, the poet starts to act as guide to a stranger who wants to know Rome, and expresses aspiration to write what will serve a similar purpose for all men; in the second half the stranger reveals himself as a Chaldaean astrologer, who, after magnifying his office and incidentally giving a history of the poet's life thus far, prophesies that Propertius will always be a slave to one woman and fit only to write amatory elegies. The date of this elegy seems thus to have been earlier than that of the other aetiological elegies of this book, before the final break with Cynthia occurred. Cf. Dieterich in *Rh. Mus.* 55 (1900), 191–221.

1–56: 'Humble were the beginnings from which came all the wonders of Rome, the new Troy, according to prophecy. 57–70: It is of this Rome that I would sing and thus win glory as the Callimachus of Rome. 71–102: Hold! rash poet, the gods favor not your project, say I, Babylonian Horos, an infallible seer,

atque ubi navali stant sacra Palatia Phoebo,
    Euandri profugae concubuere boves.
5 fictilibus crevere deis haec aurea templa,
    nec fuit opprobrio facta sine arte casa,
Tarpeiusque pater nuda de rupe tonabat,
    et Tiberis nostris advena bubus erat.
qua gradibus domus ista Remi se sustulit, olim
10 unus erat fratrum maxima regna focus.
curia, praetexto quae nunc nitet alta senatu,

as I can prove by many instances of my skill, *e.g.* the cases of Arria and Cinara. 103–118: All other prophecy is fallible; even Calchas failed. 119–134: Now then I will prophesy for yourself your own destiny, for I know, you see, the whole story of your life. 135–150: Only the elegy inspired by just one girl must be your theme, and you shall be her slave. But beware the Crab!'

1. quodcumque vides : the imaginary position of the speaker might have been on the Palatine, the Capitoline, the Janiculan, or any other such height commanding all the city. — **hospes :** apparently identical with the seer Horos of the second part of the poem.

2. Cf. 4, 4, 3–14; Tib. 2, 5, 25–34.

3. navali . . . Phoebo : the reference is to the great naval victory at Actium and the naval defeat of Sextus Pompey. Cf. 2, 31, Intr. ; 4, 6, Intr. — **Palatia :** cf. Tib. 2, 5, 25, and 87, n.

4. profugae : Euander was represented in myth as an exile from

Arcadia. Cf. Verg. *Aen.* 8, 333–336.

5. Cf. 2, 31, 1 ; Tib. 1, 10, 20, n. Augustus said he found Rome a city of brick and left it a city of marble.

7. Tarpeiusque pater : Juppiter Capitolinus. — **nuda :** the bare rock without temple or building (C. S.).

8. advena : 'a visitor': for cattle only, rather than for a city full of people, and a passing visitor rather than a procession as now (C. S.). The Tiber came from Etruria ; cf. Ovid, *Fast.* 3, 524 : *haud procul a ripis, advena Thybri, tuis.*

9. gradibus : the *Scalae Caci,* which led up the side of the Palatine to the *domus.* — **domus . . . Remi :** the *Casa Romuli,* or traditional home of the twin founders of Rome, which was long an object of veneration. Cf. Platner, p. 128.

11. curia : cf. Ovid, *A. A.* 3, 117 : *curia consilio nunc est dignissima tanto: de stipula Tatio regna tenente fuit.* The new Curia Julia was dedicated by Au-

pellitos habuit rustica corda patres.
bucina cogebat priscos ad verba Quirites:
centum illi in prato saepe senatus erat.
15 nec sinuosa cavo pendebant vela theatro,
pulpita sollemnis non oluere crocos.
nulli cura fuit externos quaerere divos,
cum tremeret patrio pendula turba sacro,
annuaque accenso celebrare Parilia faeno,
20 qualia nunc curto lustra novantur equo.
Vesta coronatis pauper gaudebat asellis,
ducebant macrae vilia sacra boves.

---

19. annuaque **O** annua at *Lachmann.* celebrare **NFLV** celebrate **D** cele-brante *Housman (cf. B. O. Foster in Class. Phil. 2, 217).*

gustus, 29 B.C. — **praetexto . . . senatu**: a large number of the senators had held curule magis-tracies, and being thus entitled to wear the *toga praetexta*, gave a distinctive tone in garb to the whole assembly.

12. pellitos: the primitive method of clothing is contrasted with the modern; the rural with the urban; cf. Theognis, 55.

13. ad verba: 'to their delibera-tions' (C. S.).

14. centum illi: the traditional original senate as created by Rom-ulus. Cf. Livy, 1, 8, 7: *centum creat senatores.*

15. cavo . . . theatro = *cavea theatri.* — **vela**: such as those spoken of in 3, 18, 13, n.

16. sollemnis: 'now custo-mary'; cf. Lucr. 2, 416: *cum scena croco Cilici perfusa recens est.*

17. externos . . . divos: their

name was legion in imperial times at Rome.

18. pendula: 'on tiptoe of emo-tion' (Phillimore).

19. celebrare: sc. *cuique cura fuit*; cf. Hor. *Sat.* 1, 1, 1: *Qui fit, Maecenas, ut nemo . . . contentus vivat, laudet diversa sequentis?* — **Parilia faeno**: cf. Tib. 2, 5, 90, n.

20. curto . . . equo: the 'Oc-tober horse,' annually sacrificed to Mars on the Ides of October. The blood which fell where its tail was cut off was used for *suffimen.* Cf. H. & T. § 205.

21. At the feast of Vesta, on June 9th, garlands of leaves were strung on asses. Cf. Ovid, *Fast.* 6, 311: *ecce coronatis panis de-pendet asellis.*

22. ducebant: 'drew.' — **sacra**: whatever was used in performing the sacrifice. Cf. 2 Sam. 6, 3, and 6.

parva saginati lustrabant compita porci,
pastor et ad calamos exta litabat ovis.
25 verbera pellitus saetosa movebat arator,
unde licens Fabius sacra lupercus habet.
nec rudis infestis miles radiabat in armis :
miscebant usta proelia nuda sude.
prima galeritus posuit praetoria Lycmon,
30 magnaque pars Tatio rerum erat inter oves.
hinc Titiens Ramnesque viri Luceresque Soloni,

31. Soloni **N** coloni **FLDV.**

23. lustrabant compita : at the Compitalia thus humbly celebrated in early days. Cf. Fowler, *Rom. Fest.*, pp. 279–280.

24. ad calamos : 'to the sound of reed pipes.'

25. verbera pellitus : at the feast of Lupercalia, on Feb. 15th, the Luperci, clothed only with a girdle of goatskin, ran about striking with strips of goatskin the women they met. For the rites and their very early origin, cf. Fowler, *Rom. Fest.*, pp. 310 sqq.

26. Fabius : there were two collegia of the Luperci, the Fabii and the Quintilii.

28. miscebant with *proelia* is poetic, and perhaps an imitation of Callinus, 11. — **nuda :** *i.e.* without the protecting armor of later times. — **sude :** cf. Verg. *Aen.* 11, 894 : *stipitibus ferrum sudibusque imitantur obustis ;* 12, 298 sqq.

29. galeritus : 'in wolf-skin helmet' (C. S.) ; cf. Verg. *Aen.* 7, 688 : *fulvosque lupi de pelle galeros.* — **Lycmon :** a Greek form of the Etruscan Lucumo, who according to tradition helped Romulus in battle against Titus Tatius and his Sabine warriors.

30. But Titus Tatius is represented differently in 4, 4, 19–21.

31. hinc : *i.e.* from such humble origins as are indicated in the preceding verses. — **Titiens :** used here substantively and collectively in the singular to give variety. The Titienses represented the Sabine element in Roman citizenship, the followers of Titus Tatius. — **Ramnesque viri :** the followers of Romulus, the Latin element. — **Luceresque Soloni :** the Etruscan element, who followed Lucumo, and crossed the Tiber to settle in Latium. These three groups formed the original *tribus* at Rome. The adjective *Soloni* refers to the city of Solonium from which Lucumo is said by Dionysius Hal. (2, 37, 2) to have come ; cf. Dieterich in *Rh. Mus.*, Vol. 55 (1900), pp. 201 sq.

quattuor hinc albos Romulus egit equos.

quippe suburbanae parva minus urbe Bovillae,

et, qui nunc nulli, maxima turba Gabi,

35   et stetit Alba potens, albae suis omine nata,

hac, ubi Fidenas longe erat ire vias.

nil patrium nisi nomen habet Romanus alumnus :

sanguinis altricem non pudet esse lupam.

huc melius profugos misisti, Troia, penates.

40   o quali vecta est Dardana puppis ave !

36. longe O longa ω. ire FLDV isse N. vias O via ω. 38. pudet ω putet O.

32. albos . . . equos : the poet
ascribes to Romulus the privilege
which had grown up by the time
of the empire, of using white horses
to draw the triumphal car ; cf.
Tib. 1, 7, 8.   Tradition said that
Romulus had enjoyed three
triumphs.

33. suburbanae . . . minus : *i.e.*
farther from Rome itself when the
city had not extended from its
center. — parva . . . urbe : abl.
abs. — Bovillae : the first of a series
here named of four Latin towns
which had by the time of Propertius become practically non-ex-
istent, though flourishing in the
early days of Rome.   It was
situated about nine miles from
Rome on the Via Appia.

34. nulli = *non stant.* — Gabi
= *Gabii* ; cf. Verg. *Aen.* 7, 682 :
arva Gabinae Iunon.s ; it was on
the Via Praenestina.

35. stetit : the verb does duty
for vv. 33-35. — Alba : the head
of the Latin League until destroyed

by Tullus Hostilius. — albae suis :
cf. Verg. *Aen.* 3, 390 ; 8, 43-86.

36. The various arbitrary text
alterations of different editors have
given little relief to this verse. —
hac : sc. *via.* — Fidenas : apparently used here as an adjective agreeing with *vias* after the
Propertian manner ; cf. 1, 1, 13.
Fidenae was five miles from Rome
on the Via Salaria, in the opposite
direction from Alba. — ire vias :
cf. 1, 20, 18 : *egressam longe Pha-
sidos isse viam.*

37. nil patrium nisi nomen :
i.e. their name as derived from
Romulus had been retained, rather
than the simple life of his day. —
Romanus alumnus : the composite
population, native and foreign, of
the imperial city of Rome.

38. The Romans are not
ashamed of the wolf's blood, for it
made them warlike (C.S), whence
came their glorious history.

39. melius : *i.e.* for a better
career than in their Trojan home.

iam bene spondebant tunc omina, quod nihil illam
    laeserat abiegni venter apertus equi,
cum pater in gnati trepidus cervice pependit
    et verita est umeros urere flamma pios.
45 tunc animi venere Deci Brutique secures,
    vexit et ipsa sui Caesaris arma Venus,
arma resurgentis portans victricia Troiae.
    felix terra tuos cepit, Iule, deos,
si modo Avernalis tremulae cortina Sibyllae
50   dixit Aventino rura pianda Remo,
aut si Pergameae sero rata carmina vatis
    longaevum ad Priami vera fuere caput,
  'vertite equum, Danai! male vincitis: Ilia tellus
    vivet et huic cineri Iuppiter arma dabit.'
55 optima nutricum nostris lupa Martia rebus,

41. illam = *puppim Dardanam.*

42. venter apertus: *i.e.* 'the opening of,' etc.

44. umeros . . . pios: *umeros pii Aeneae.*

45. animi . . . Deci: cf. 3, 11, 62, n. — Brutique secures: the patriotic sternness of Brutus against his own sons when they conspired to restore the Tarquins (C. S.).

46. vexit . . . ipsa . . . Venus: *i.e.* by guarding the fleet of Aeneas through all perils to Italy. Cf. Verg. *Aen., passim.*

48. tuos . . . Iule, deos: Propertius, of course, wishes to emphasize the thought that the dominant Julian family is largely responsible for the imperial greatness of Rome.

49. si modo: the protasis here

and in v. 51 implies the actuality of the assumption. Cf. *PAPA.*, Vol. 36 (1905), p. xlii, 1 (*a*). — Avernalis = *Cumaeae* — cortina: an embellishment added to the description given in Verg. *Aen.* 6. The poet is thinking of the oracle of Apollo; cf. Verg. *Aen.* 3, 92.

50. dixit: Propertius probably invented this statement. — Aventino: 'on the Aventine.' The usual place ascribed to Remus in the famous augury of the brothers (cf. Livy, 1, 6, 4); but Enn. *Ann.* 1, 81, gives this hill to Romulus. — rura pianda: merely as a preliminary to the augury.

51. vatis: Cassandra.

53. This prophecy in essence is found in Lycophron, 1226 sqq.

55. Martia: the she-wolf, sacred to Mars, was nurse of his

qualia creverunt moenia lacte tuo !

moenia namque pio coner disponere versu :

    hei mihi quod nostro est parvus in ore sonus !

sed tamen exiguo quodcumque e pectore rivi

60   fluxerit, hoc patriae serviet omne meae.

Ennius hirsuta cingat sua dicta corona :

    mi folia ex hedera porrige, Bacche, tua,

ut nostris tumefacta superbiat Umbria libris,

    Umbria Romani patria Callimachi.

65   scandentes quisquis cernit de vallibus arces,

    ingenio muros aestimet ille meo.

Roma, fave, tibi surgit opus : date candida cives

    omina, et inceptis dextera cantet avis.

sacra diesque canam et cognomina prisca locorum :

70   has meus ad metas sudet oportet equus. —

65. cernit **NLDV** cernet **F**.

twin sons, the founders of Rome ; cf. H. & T. § 205.

57. moenia : the theme now definitely proposed, after these preliminaries. — **namque** : for the position cf. Uhlmann, p. 71. — **pio** : cf. v. 60. — **disponere** = *describere*.

58. 'Ah, me ! that the strain should be so feeble in my mouth ' (C. S.).

61. The spasm of modesty past, Propertius proceeds to emulate the 'father of Roman poetry' and his own great Alexandrian model, Callimachus. — **hirsuta** : cf. Ovid, *Trist.* 2, 259 : *sumpserit Annales,—nihil est hirsutius illis* ; *Am.* I, 15, 19, n. But cf. Prop. 3, 3, 6.

64. Umbria . . . patria : cf. Intr. § 31. — **Romani . . . Callimachi** : cf. 3, 1, 1.

65. Cf. v. 125.

66. muros : like *moenia* in v. 57 ; Propertius includes all that the walls inclose. For the idea cf. Ovid, *Am.* 3, 15, 11.

67. surgit : the poem is compared to a structure.

69. The enthusiasm of the poet leads him to expand his scheme boldly, and announce a theme not unlike that actually treated by Ovid in the *Fasti*.

70. Cf. Verg. *Georg.* 3, 202 : *ad Elei metas et maxima campi sudabit spatia* ; Hor. *Car.* I, 15, 9 : *heu, heu, quantus equis, quantus adest viris sudor !*

'quo ruis inprudens, vage, dicere fata, Properti?
  non sunt a dextro condita fila colo.
accersis lacrimas cantans, aversus Apollo:
  poscis ab invita verba pigenda lyra.
75 certa feram certis auctoribus, aut ego vates
  nescius aerata signa movere pila.
me creat Archytae suboles Babylonius Horops
  Horon, et a proavo ducta Conone domus.
di mihi sunt testes non degenerasse propinquos,
80 inque meis libris nil prius esse fide.
nunc pretium fecere deos, et fallitur auro
  Iuppiter. obliquae signa iterata rotae

---

73. cantans *Baehrens* cantas **O**.   75. aut **O** haud **ω**.   77. Horops **ω**
Horos **N** *m. rec.* Orops **O**.

71. The *hospes*, unmasking himself, rudely interrupts the imaginative flight of the poet.

73. accersis: sc. *tibi*. — aversus: sc. *est*.

75. certa feram . . . aut . . . nescius: *i.e.* I will stake my reputation as an astrologer on the accuracy of my statements to you.

76. pila: such a planetarium, or machine for indicating the movements of the planets, as is described in Cic. *De Re Pub.* I, 22; *sphaerae genus, in quo solis et lunae motus inessent et earum quinque stellarum . . . inventum Archimedi*, etc.

77. creat: for the tense cf. v. 121. — Archytae: the celebrated astronomer of Tarentum; cf. Hor. *Car.* I, 28, 2. — Babylonius, like *Chaldaeus*, refers rather to the astrological skill of the man than to his nationality. — Horops: cf. ὡροσκόπος.

78. Horon: the name is intended to be self-explanatory, as that of a professional astrologer, who casts one's nativity.— Conone: another distinguished Greek astronomer, from Samos; cf. Verg. *Ec.* 3, 40: *Conon et — quis fuit alter, descripsit radio . . . orbem.*

79. degenerasse: transitive. Cf. Ovid, *Ex P.* 3, 1, 45: *hanc cave degeneres.*

81. nunc: 'in these days.' — pretium: 'a means of gain.' — fecere: subject indef. — fallitur: 'is made a mockery of.'

82. The list of subjects that Horos can wisely discuss and interpret depends upon *dicam* (v. 87). — obliquae . . . rotae: *i.e.* the ecliptic. — signa: of the zodiac. — iterata: *i.e.* as the years pass.

felicesque Iovis stellas Martisque rapacis
  et grave Saturni sidus in omne caput,
85 quid moveant pisces animosaque signa leonis
  lotus et Hesperia quid capricornus aqua,
 dicam : Troia cades, et Troica Roma resurges;
  et maris et terrae longa sepulcra canam.
 dixi ego, cum geminos produceret Arria natos,
90 (illa dabat natis arma vetante deo)
 non posse ad patrios sua pila referre penates :
  nempe meam firmant nunc duo busta fidem.
 quippe Lupercus, equi dum saucia protegit ora,
  heu sibi prolapso non bene cavit equo :
95 Gallus at, in castris dum credita signa tuetur,
  concidit ante aquilae rostra cruenta suae.
 fatales pueri, duo funera matris avarae !

83. Of the planets, Juppiter was called lucky, Mars deadly, Saturn disastrous ; cf. Cic. *De Div.* 1, 85 : *cur stella Iovis aut Veneris coniuncta cum Luna ad ortus puerorum salutaris sit, Saturni Martisve contraria.*

86. lotus : 'when it dips'; cf. Hor. *Car.* 2, 17, 19 : *tyrannus Hesperiae Capricornus undae.*

87. Troia cades, etc. : an apodosis to the protasis implied in *dicam* ; *i.e.* if I speak such words of prophecy and wise interpretation as have just been enumerated, they will all infallibly come true, even to the falling and rising again of Troy.

88. longa : 'distant.' From Protesilaus onward through the long years of wanderings as told in the *Iliad, Odyssey,* and *Aeneid.*

89. dixi : proof of the justice of his claims by actual success in the past is cited through two instances, which are not otherwise known to fame. — produceret : *i.e.* in the train of the general departing for war.

90. deo : *which* deity is left indeterminate.

91. The hope of the mother was doomed to be disappointed, prophesied Horos.

92. nempe : 'as a matter of fact.'

93. The pathetic details of the death of the two sons seem to be descriptive of some actual events known to Propertius.

97. matris : the case implies the responsibility of the real author of their fate, in that she persisted against due warning. — avarae : a

vera, sed invito contigit ista fides.

idem ego, cum Cinarae traheret Lucina dolores

100   et facerent uteri pondera lenta moram,

" Iunonis facito votum inpetrabile " dixi :

illa parit, libris est data palma meis.

hoc neque arenosum Libyae Iovis explicat antrum,

aut sibi commissos fibra locuta deos,

105 aut siquis motas cornicis senserit alas,

umbrave quae magicis mortua prodit aquis :

adspicienda via est caeli verusque per astra

---

101. facito votum *Lachmann* facite votum O votum facite ω.

---

common motive, but vague in its application here, unless we could know more of the circumstances. Perhaps Propertius knew her motive ; perhaps he only ascribes a general one.

98. fides : 'prophecy.'

99. Cinarae : a typical name of a Greek *hetaera.* — traheret : 'prolonged.'

100. facerent . . . moram : 'lingered.'

101. Iunonis : sc. *Lucinae.* The case implies that the goddess can claim such worship as a right. Cf. Bursian's *J. B.*, Vol. 140, 3, 26.

103. Iovis . . . antrum : the famous oracle of Juppiter Ammon in the Libyan Desert. By this time, however, its authority had been already much reduced ; cf. Strabo, 17, 813 ; yet Juvenal (6, 553–555) speaks of it as still held in reverence.

104. fibra : the entrails inspected by the Etruscan *haruspices.* — deos : *i.e.* the secrets of the gods. Cf. Tib. 1, 8, 3 : *conscia fibra deorum* ; 2, 1, 26 ; Tac. *Ger.* 10 : *deorum illos [equos] conscios putant.* Cf. the Stoic idea of the immanence of God.

105. Old-fashioned Roman augury. The *cornix* was one of the special divining birds, the *oscines* ; cf. Hor. *Car.* 3, 27, 11 : *oscinem corvum prece suscitabo.*

106. umbrave . . . mortua : 'ghost.' — magicis . . . aquis : a favorite resort for the practice of necromancy. One such well-known spot was the lake of Avernus ; cf. Cic. *Tusc. Disp.* 1, 37 : *in vicinia nostra Averni lacus,* " *unde animae excitantur obscura umbra opertae ex ostio altae Acheruntis.*"

107. per astra trames : cf. *signa,* v. 82, n.

trames, et ab zonis quinque petenda fides.

exemplum grave erit Calchas: namque Aulide **solvit**

110 ille bene haerentes ad pia saxa rates,

idem Agamemnoniae ferrum cervice puellae

tinxit, et Atrides vela cruenta dedit:

nec rediere tamen Danai.   tu diruta fletum

supprime et Euboicos respice, Troia, sinus.

115 Nauplius ultores sub noctem porrigit ignes,

et natat exuviis Graecia pressa suis.

victor Oiliade, rape nunc et dilige vatem

quam vetat avelli veste Minerva sua.

hactenus historiae: nunc ad tua devehar astra:

120 incipe tu lacrimis aequus adesse novis.

108. zonis quinque: the five zones in the heavens supposed to correspond to, and to condition, those on our earth, are described in Verg. *Georg.* 1, 233 sqq.; Cic. *Som. Scip.* 13; etc.

109. Calchas: a well-known case of a mistaken prophet, adapted to serve as a 'horrible example' to all that fail to resort to astrology. — **Aulide**: where the Greeks assembled for the expedition against Troy. — **solvit**: by proxy, of course, in prophesying success and announcing a favorable moment for embarking.

110. pia: 'loyal'; even the rocks would fain have saved their countrymen from the dire disasters that were to come before they reached home again.

111. Agamemnoniae . . . puellae: Iphigenia; the adjective serves as a patronymic. — **ferrum**: the sacrificial knife.

113. fletum supprime: even in her hour of ruin Troy is represented as ceasing for a time her mourning, to gloat over the destruction of the Greek fleet on the rocks of Caphareus; cf. 3, 7, 39, n.

115. Nauplius: who set the false signal fires on the Euboean shore and led the returning Greeks to shipwreck.

116. Graecia: cf. 3, 7, 40, n.

117. vatem: Cassandra, whom Ajax Oileus ravished in the temple of Minerva where she sought protection, clinging to the robe of the goddess.

120. lacrimis: *i.e.* a cause for tears, a new tale of woe. — **aequus adesse**: *i.e.* 'to listen calmly.' Propertius is an adept in discovering substitutes for the adverb, and with Vergil leads in avoiding the adverb in *ē*. See H. Priess: *Usum adverbii quatenus fugerint poetae Latini*, etc.

Umbria te notis antiqua penatibus edit
(mentior ? an patriae tangitur ora tuae ?),
qua nebulosa cavo rorat Mevania campo
et lacus aestivis intepet Umber aquis
125 scandentisque Asisi consurgit vertice murus,
murus ab ingenio notior ille tuo.
ossaque legisti non illa aetate legenda
patris, et in tenues cogeris ipse lares :
nam tua cum multi versarent rura iuvenci,
130 abstulit excultas pertica tristis opes.
mox ubi bulla rudi dimissa est aurea collo,

---

123. qua ω quam O. 125. Asisi *Lachmann* asis **NFL** axis **DV**.

---

121. For the birthplace of Propertius cf. Intr. § 31. — **Umbria**: cf. 1, 22, 9, n. — **antiqua**: cf. Pliny, *N.H.* 3, 112: *Umbrorum gens antiquissima Italiae existimatur.* — **penatibus**: *i.e.* family; cf. 1, 21, 1, n. — **edit**: cf. *creat*, v. 77.

123. **Mevania**: modern Bevagna, on low-lying land full of springs, was formerly a more important place than at present.

124. **lacus . . . Umber**: if the poet means anything more than the spreading waters of the Clitumnus here, he must refer to a lake long since drained, a proceeding of which there are famous examples in Italy. Important operations of this kind were undertaken in this region according to Cassiodorus, *Var.* 2, 21, 2. Cf. *Class. Rev.*, Vol. 22 (1908), p. 245, where H. E. Butler refers to a local

tradition of such a former lake near Assisi. — **intepet**: found only here and in Statius, *Theb.* 2, 377.

125. Cf. v. 65. — **vertice**: may be taken as instrument, referring to the wall, or locative, referring to the high location of the city, but not necessarily = *summo*.

126. Cf. v. 66. — For the preposition cf. 2, 27, 11, n.

127. **ossaque legisti**: cf. Tib. 3, 2, 17. — **illa**: 'at such an' [early]. — **legenda**: *i.e.* he ought not to have been bereaved so early; to be taken, of course, with *ossa*.

128. **tenues . . . lares**: *i.e.* humble circumstances.

130. **abstulit . . . pertica**: *i.e.* his lands were confiscated for distribution to others. Cf. 3, 5, 5.

131. **bulla . . . dimissa**: as was customary at the assumption of the *toga virilis*.

matris et ante deos libera sumpta toga,

tum tibi pauca suo de carmine dictat Apollo

et vetat insano verba tonare foro.

135   at tu finge elegos, fallax opus, (haec tua castra)

scribat ut exemplo cetera turba tuo.

militiam Veneris blandis patiere sub armis

et Veneris pueris utilis hostis eris.

nam tibi victrices, quascumque labore parasti,

140   eludet palmas una puella tuas :

et bene cum fixum mento discusseris uncum,

nil erit hoc, rostro te premet ansa suo.

illius arbitrio noctem lucemque videbis,

gutta quoque ex oculis non nisi iussa cadet.

145   nec mille excubiae nec te signata iuvabunt

---

140. eludet ω eludit O.   141. cum fixum *Memmianus* confixum O. discusseris ω discusserit O decusseris *Broukhusius*.   142. premet ω premat **NLDV** premit **F**.

---

132. matris: now acting as head of the family after the death of his father. — **deos**: the Lares.— **libera**: of a free citizen.

134. Apollo, by inspiring him to poetry, interrupted the normal course of his life as a young nobleman trained to the law. Cf. Ovid, *Trist.* 4, 10, 15–30.

135. fallax: 'unsatisfying,' as the poet's own experience had proved. — **haec tua castra**: cf. 2, 10, 19, n.; Tib. 1, 1, 75.

137. Cf. 1, 6, 29–30.

138. pueris utilis: *i.e.* for them to aim at, a susceptible young man. Propertius is following here the later conception of a plurality of Cupids. Note the succession of words ending in *is*.

140. eludet: 'shall mock.' — **palmas**: a type of successful achievement.

141. bene cum: cf. Tib. 2, 6, 14. — **uncum**: probably the hook with which corpses were dragged from the place of execution; cf. Ovid, *Ibis* 164: *indeploratum proicere caput ; carnificisque manu, populo plaudente, traheris, infixusque tuis ossibus uncus erit* ; Juv. 10, 66; *Seianus ducitur unco.*

142. rostro: the point or barb of the hook which grips like a 'beak.' — **ansa**: 'the handle.'

143. illius = *puellae.*

145. excubiae: 'watchers.' — **signata . . . limina**: 'sealing the doors.' Cf. the legend of Pyramus and Thisbe.

limina : persuasae fallere rima sat est.
nunc tua vel mediis puppis luctetur in undis,
     vel licet armatis hostis inermis eas,
vel tremefacta cavo tellus diducat hiatum :
150   octipedis cancri terga sinistra time.'

3

Haec Arethusa suo mittit mandata Lycotae,
     cum totiens absis, si potes esse meus.

146. persuasae: ' when once she has made up her mind.' This transitive use of the verb belongs to the *sermo cottidianus*. Cf. Uhlmann, p. 24.

147. nunc, used as here to bring the argument to a close, reminds of the modern use of ' now then,' for which the ordinary classical equivalent is *igitur*.

148. armatis: cf. 3, 1, 26, n.

149. cavo: used substantively : ' open in a yawning gulf.'

150. None of the perils enumerated in the preceding verses need terrify him, so long as he avoids the constellation which the astrologer names as his *bête noir*. The ulterior meaning of this absurdity to which the poem here is reduced is obscure.

4, 3

A love letter from a Roman lady to her husband now long absent from her in the wars. Whether or not the names Arethusa and Lycotas represent any

particular persons known to the poet cannot be decided. Some have believed these names stand for the Aelia Galla and Postumus of 3, 12. Rothstein suggests that Lycotas represents the Lupercus of 4, 1, 93. Similarly the attempt to fix the date of the elegy and to connect it positively with a particular campaign (*e g.* that against the Parthians in 20 B.C.) can hardly be successful. The absent warrior has served on many a field, " from the rising of the sun to the going down of the same," and the various references to the Parthian country are not convincing proof that he is actually there at the present time. But wherever he is, waiting for a fair wind to bring him back, or for the summer sun to melt the icy bonds that prevent his return, this letter, which the lovelorn lady would not have known whither to send, must appeal to every reader as one of the most delightful specimens of the poet's art. It reveals a re

siqua tamen tibi lecturo pars oblita derit,
  haec erit e lacrimis facta litura meis :
5 aut siqua incerto fallet te littera tractu,
    signa meae dextrae iam morientis erunt.
  te modo viderunt iteratos Bactra per ortus,
    te modo munito Neuricus hostis equo,

3. 8. Neuricus *Jacob* hericus **NFL** hernicus **D** henricus **V** Sericus *Beroaldus.*

markable acquaintance with the
workings of the feminine mind,
and a sympathetic knowledge of
woman's heart. Though a model
for the *Heroides* of Ovid, it stands
above them all in simplicity, subtle
analysis, and genuine feeling.

1–6: 'I can scarcely write intel-
ligibly, for my grief, 7–10 : to
one who is so constantly a wan-
derer from me. 11–18 : Was this
the meaning of our marriage vows ?
19–22 : Perish the man that taught
the art of war ! 23–28 : Do you
suffer? I hope a little of the
suffering is because you miss me.
29–42 : How is it with me? I
caress your very weapons, pass
sleepless, lonely nights ; weave
garments for you to wear in camp,
and study eagerly about the distant regions where you tarry.
Only sister and nursie are with
me, with vain comforts. 43–48 :
Would that I might follow you to
the ends of the earth ! 49–62 :
Greatest of all is the love of a
wedded wife ; without her husband she has nothing to live for ;
every event of life is turned to his
account. 63–72 : Take care of

yourself, but be true, and when
you come I will praise the gods.'

2. cum . . . absis : the clause
is subordinate to the following
protasis. — **meus** : corresponding
to *suo* in v. 1.

3. derit = *deerit*.

4. Ovid made good use of this
idea ; cf. *Her.* 3, 3 : *quascumque
aspicies, lacrimae fecere lituras* ;
11, 1 ; *Trist.* 1, 1, 13, etc.

6. iam morientis : the hyperbole is to be taken rather more
seriously than the familiar and
thoughtless, "I'm just dying to see
you," of to-day.

7. iteratos . . . per ortus : ' repeated risings,' referring to sunrise,
seems to imply that he had been
in Parthia now on two separate
expeditions. — **Bactra** : a chief city
of Bactria, representing to Rome
the Far East.

8. munito . . . equo : when, in
cavalry, horse and man both were
mailed, they were called *cataphracti* ; cf. 3, 12, 12 : *ferreus aurato
neu cataphractus equo.* — **Neuricus** :
perhaps the Sarmatian tribe which
Tacitus describes as *cataphracti*
(*Hist.* 1, 79). But the word

hibernique Getae, pictoque Britannia curru,
10   ustus et eoa discolor Indus aqua.
     haecne marita fides, hae sunt pactae mihi noctes,
          cum rudis urgenti bracchia victa dedi ?
     quae mihi deductae fax omen praetulit, illa
          traxit ab everso lumina nigra rogo,

11. hae sunt pactae mihi **DV** et pacatae mihi **FL** et parce avia **N** et pactae in gaudia *Rothstein* (in savia *Haupt*). noctes **O** et primae praemia noctis *Housman* et pactae praemia noctis *Foster, alii alia.*

occurs nowhere else, though *Neuri* or *Neuroe* are mentioned among these obscure tribes.

9. **Getae** : just north of the Danube. — **pictoque . . . curru** : Caesar (*B. G.* 4, 24, and 33) does not refer to the adornment of the characteristic chariots of the Britons.

10. **ustus** : ' swarthy ' because of the hot climate. — **eoa . . . aqua** : may be taken of the great southern sea as a whole, extending from Ethiopia to the Far East. It may be considered either an instrumental ablative or locative with *discolor*. Propertius probably neither knew nor cared which. Cf. Ovid, *A. A.* 3, 130 : *quos legit in viridi decolor Indus aqua.* — **discolor** : the peculiar character of the water of the Indian Ocean, as well as of the Red Sea (*e.g.* its effect on a pearl diver), was an article of the geographical creed of the Roman poets ; cf. Tib. 2, 2, 16, n. ; 4, 2, 19. — **Indus** : this may refer to the Ethiopians (cf. Verg. *Georg.* 4, 293), against whom a Roman campaign was conducted by C.

Petronius in 22 B.C. ; but in consideration of the state of geographical knowledge then, it is dangerous to be dogmatic. Cf. Ovid, *Trist.* 5, 3, 23 : *Persidaque et lato spatiantem flumine Gangen, et quascumque bibit decolor Indus aquas.* Cf. Tac. *Agr.* 10, where ignorance of Europe is exploited ; much less did Propertius have any clear conception of the great Southeast.

11. Cf. Ovid, *Her.* 6, 41 : *heu! ubi pacta fides? ubi conubialia iura ?*

13. **deductae fax** : the torches carried in the wedding procession when the bride was conducted to the bridegroom's house. Cf. Cat. 61, 77.

14. **everso . . . rogo** : *i.e.* from fire discovered in poking open the ashes of a funeral pyre after it had burnt out. — **lumina nigra** : cf. Hor. *Sat.* 1, 9, 72 : *huncine solem tam nigrum surrexe mihi!* Ovid, *Fast.* 2, 561 : *conde tuas, Hymenaee, facis et ab ignibus atris aufer ! habent alias maesta sepulcra faces.*

15   et Stygio sum sparsa lacu, nec recta capillis
       vitta data est, nupsi non comitante deo.
     omnibus heu portis pendent mea noxia vota:
       texitur haec castris quarta lacerna tuis.
     occidat, inmerita qui carpsit ab arbore vallum
20   et struxit querulas rauca per ossa tubas,
     dignior obliquo funem qui torqueat Ocno

15. sparsa: as a bride she should rather have been sprinkled with water from a running stream or a spring. Cf. Servius on *Aen.* 4, 167: *aqua petita de puro fonte . . . interest nuptiis.* — recta: Festus (p. 286) refers to an old superstition whereby certain articles of apparel worn on formal occasions must be woven vertically according to an ancient custom, rather than horizontally.

16. deo: Hymen.

17. portis pendent: Cf. *CIL.* 3, 1422: *Fortunae reduci, Lari viali, Romae aeternae.* Altars with such inscriptions might well have stood at the city gates, where vows and offerings were made to ensure the safe return of absent friends (cf. v. 71). A temple to Fortuna Redux and a triumphal arch were erected outside the Porta Triumphalis before the return of Domitian from the Sarmatian campaign; cf. Mart. 8, 65. — noxia: *i.e.* they seem to do more harm than good.

18. quarta: apparently Lycotas had already been absent on several different campaigns. — lacerna:

Lucretia was similarly engaged when Tarquinius came to her house. Cf. Ovid. *Fast.* 2, 745: *mittenda est domino — nunc, nunc properate, puellae! — quamprimum nostra facta lacerna manu.*

19. vallum: carried by every Roman warrior, and accordingly a type of war. The poet makes Arethusa curse the inventor of war; cf. Tib. 1, 10, 1.

20. rauca: proleptic. — per ossa: cf. 3, 9, 26, n.; "make out of bone" is the English idiom.

21. obliquo: Propertius evidently has a picture in mind, perhaps that of Socrates mentioned by Pliny (*N. H.* 35, 137), or its more celebrated prototype by Polygnotus (Paus. 10, 29, 1), where Ocnus is sitting slantwise at his work, spending his strength endlessly in twisting a grass rope which a donkey behind him devours as fast as it is made, — here, a type of the warrior, whose work is vain and endless, and especially of the inventor of weapons, etc. Cf. Tib. 1, 10, 1; Bachofen, *Gräbersymbolik*, pp. 301 sqq. 314, 338 sq., 349 sqq.

aeternusque tuam pascat, aselle, famem.

dic mihi, num teneros urit lorica lacertos?

num gravis inbelles atterit hasta manus?

25 haec noceant potius quam dentibus ulla puella

det mihi plorandas per tua colla notas.

diceris et macie vultum tenuasse: sed opto,

e desiderio sit color iste meo.

at mihi cum noctes induxit Vesper amaras,

30 siqua relicta iacent, osculor arma tua.

tum queror in toto non sidere pallia lecto,

lucis et auctores non dare carmen aves.

noctibus hibernis castrensia pensa laboro

et Tyria in radios vellera secta suos.

35 et disco qua parte fluat vincendus Araxes,

quot sine aqua Parthus milia currat equus.

cogor et e tabula pictos ediscere mundos,

---

34. radios ω gladios O clavos *Mss. of Passerat* (?).   suos O suo *Rossberg.*

---

23. num: Arethusa hopes for a negative answer for her comfort.

24. inbelles: she thinks of him as a bridegroom, not as a hardened soldier.

26. Cf. Hor. *Car.* I, 13, 11 : *sive puer furens inpressit memorem dente labris notam.*

27. diceris: perhaps by some sympathetic fellow-soldier whose letters have reached home.

28. color: by implication from *macie*; cf. also 1, 1, 22, n. — **meo**: objective; cf. 1, 8, 1, n.

29. noctes induxit Vesper: cf. Cat. 62, 7, *Oetaeos ostendit Noctifer ignes*; Verg. *Georg.* 4, 552; *suos Aurora induxerat ortus.*

31. Cf. Ovid, *Am.* 1, 2, 2; *neque in lecto pallia nostra sedent.*

32. auctores: 'heralds' (Butler).

33. castrensia pensa: the spinning for the *lacerna* of v. 18.

34. radios: 'shuttles,' with which the stuff will be woven from the wool now dyed with the costly Tyrian purple.

36. An important question for the use of cavalry in the desert, which the Parthians must often traverse.

37. tabula: 'a map.' — **mundos**: in the same sense as we commonly quote Alexander's phrase, 'new worlds to conquer.'

qualis et haec docti sit positura dei,
quae tellus sit lenta gelu, quae putris ab aestu,
40   ventus in Italiam qui bene vela ferat.
adsidet una soror, curis et pallida nutrix
peierat hiberni temporis esse moras.
felix Hippolyte!   nuda tulit arma papilla
et texit galea barbara molle caput.
45   Romanis utinam patuissent castra puellis!
essem militiae sarcina fida tuae,
nec me tardarent Scythiae iuga, cum pater altas
adstricto in glaciem frigore nectit aquas.
omnis amor magnus, sed aperto in coniuge maior:
50   hanc Venus, ut vivat, ventilat ipsa facem.

---

38. docti . . . dei **O** educti . . . Dai *Ellis* Arctoi . . . soli *Fonteinius.*
47. altas **O** Atlas *Itali.*   48. adstricto *Rothstein* Affricus **NFL** aeris *Rossberg*
Aeolus *Fonteinius* Arctoo *Lachmann* acrius *Postgate.*

---

38. haec . . . positura: 'the arrangement of this earth.'—**docti
. . . dei**: subj. gen. The epithet
sounds strangely modern and may
perhaps be rendered, 'in his wise
providence.'

39. ab aestu: cf. 3, 2, 25, n.

41. curis: the explanation of
pallida.

42. peierat . . . esse moras: a
remarkable construction. The
reference is to delay in the return
of Lycotas.

43. Hippolyte: a queen of the
Amazons, conquered by Theseus,
and taken to be his wife, who
according to one form of the
legend accompanied her husband to
war; cf. Statius, *Theb.* 12, 534 sqq.

44. molle: the poet cannot forget her sex, and gives her the
attributes of an ordinary woman.

46. sarcina: 'even though a
burden'; cf. Ovid, *Her.* 3, 68:
*non ego sum classi sarcina magna
tuae.*

47. pater = *Iuppiter.*

48. adstricto . . . frigore: cf.
2, 26, 36, n.; Ovid, *Trist.* 2, 196:
maris adstricto quae coit unda gelu.
But cf. J. E. Church, Jr., in *Univ.
of Nevada Bulletin*, Vol. 2 (1908),
No. 4, pp. 92–98.

49. aperto: *i.e.* acknowledge as
legitimate; cf. Ovid, *Her.* 13, 30.

50. vivat: *i.e.* burn; cf. 4, 11,
54.—**ventilat**: cf. 3, 16, 16; Ovid,
Am. 1, 1, 8.   The alliteration may
be regarded as onomatopoetic, im-
itating the sound of rushing air.

nam mihi quo ?   Poenis tibi purpura fulgeat ostris
 crystallusque meas ornet aquosa manus.
omnia surda tacent, rarisque adsueta kalendis
 vix aperit clausos una puella lares.
55 Glaucidos et catulae vox est mihi grata querentis :
 illa tui partem vindicat una toro.
flore sacella tego, verbenis compita velo,
 et crepat ad veteres herba Sabina focos.

---

51. tibi **O** te **N** nunc *Housman.*   52. meas **N** tuas **O.**   55. Glaucidos
Puccius Craugidos *Buecheler* Graucidos **NL** Grancidos **AFDV.**

---

51. nam = *etenim.* — **mihi** : emphatic. — **quo** : ' to what end,' sc. *aliquid faciam.* — **tibi** : contrasted emphatically with *mihi.* — **purpura** : a festal garment such as would be appropriate for the home-coming of her husband.

52. crystallusque . . . aquosa : a ring made of, or set with, a white transparent stone. Such stones were supposed to have been derived from ice. Cf. Sen. *Q.N.* 3, 25, 12 ; Pliny, *N.H.* 37, 23. The attractions of personal adornment mentioned in this passage correspond to those named by Catullus (69, 3) : *si illam rarae labefactes munere vestis aut perluciduli deliciis lapidis.*

53. omnia surda : the stupid stillness of her home at present is contrasted with the glad celebration hinted at in the previous distich. — **rarisque** : *i.e.* as compared with the many other occasions when it would happen if the household were in a normal state, on the Nones, the Ides, and holidays. — **adsueta** : one long acquainted with the routine forms of the ceremony. All such matters were turned over to her, as a matter of course, now, and were an empty form.

54. clausos : in the *lararium.* Cf. Mau-Kelsey, *Pompeii,* pp. 252 sqq.

55. Glaucidos : the Greek name of the lap-dog appropriately refers to its color. — **et** : ' even.' — **querentis** : ' whining.'

56. tui partem : ' a part of thy place.'

57. flore . . . verbenis : any *herba sacra* ; cf. Servius on *Aen* 12, 120. Propertius does not hesitate to use the sing. collective in one word, and the plur. in the other. — **compita** : *i.e.* the shrines of the Lares Compitales at the *compita.*

58. crepat : cf. Tib. 2, 5, 81, n. — **herba Sabina** : savin or juniper, commonly used for incense ; cf. Ovid, *Fast.* 1, 343 : *ara dabat fumos herbis contenta Sabinis, et non exiguo laurus adusta sono.*

sive in finitimo gemuit stans noctua tigno,
60   seu voluit tangi parca lucerna mero,
illa dies hornis caedem denuntiat agnis,
    succinctique calent ad nova lucra popae.
ne, precor, adscensis tanti sit gloria Bactris,
    raptave odorato carbasa lina duci,
65   plumbea cum tortae sparguntur pondera fundae,
    subdolus et versis increpat arcus equis.
sed, tua sic domitis Parthae telluris alumnis
    pura triumphantis hasta sequatur equos,
incorrupta mei conserva foedera lecti:
70   hac ego te sola lege redisse velim.
armaque cum tulero portae votiva Capenae,
    subscribam ' salvo grata puella viro.'

59. noctua: cf. 2, 28, 38, n.

60. tangi . . . mero: the regular method of meeting the omen of a sputtering lamp, which was a "sign" of "company," while *merum* was a token of hospitality; cf. Ovid, *Her*. 19, 151 : *sternuit et lumen . . . et nobis prospera signa dedit. ecce, merum nutrix faustos instillat in ignes. 'cras-'que 'erimus plures' inquit et ipsa bibit.* — **parca**: 'scantily fed.'

61. caedem: *i.e.* for sacrifice in honor of the hoped-for return of her lord.

62. succinctique . . . popae: the assistants of the priests at sacrifice were clad in a short garment suitable for their office; cf. Suet. *Cal.* 32 : *succinctus poparum habitu.* — **ad nova lucra**: this was their time to "make hay while the sun shines."

63. adscensis: 'of scaling the walls of.'

64. odorato: a conception of eastern princes as tenacious in modern times as in Roman. — **carbasa lina**: a typical spoil from this region. *Carbasa* signified linen of an especially fine quality, and so has practically adjectival force here with *lina*.

65. plumbea . . . pondera: for an illustration cf. Baum. *Denk.* Vol. 3, p. 2077. — **sparguntur** 'are flying.'

66. versis . . . equis: cf. 3, 4, 17, n.

67. sic: cf. Tib. 2, 5, 63, n. — **alumnis**: 'inhabitants.'

68. pura . . . hasta: the headless spear customarily awarded for deeds of unusual bravery. Cf. Verg. *Aen.* 6, 760 : *pura iuvenis qui nititur hasta.*

4

Tarpeium nemus et Tarpeiae turpe sepulcrum
fabor et antiqui limina capta Iovis.

71. The proper place to dedicate the arms of the returning victorious warrior would be a temple of Mars. The temple most natural and convenient would be that about a mile outside the Porta Capena, near the Appian Way, along which the army would probably return from the east; cf. Ovid, *Fast.* 6, 191 : *lux eadem Marti festa est, quem prospicit extra appositum Tectae porta Capena viae.* — **portae** : poetic dat. of place to which.

72. Cf. 2, 28, 44. — **salvo** = *servato* (abl.).

4, 4

A typical aetiological elegy on the subject of the Tarpeia myth, with characteristic emphasis upon the erotic element. For the development of this myth, and its protean forms and later literary reminiscences cf. H. A. Sanders in *Rom. Hist. Sources and Institutions* (Univ. of Mich. Studies), I, 1–47; and O. Rossbach in *BPW.*, Vol. 25 (1905), Sp. 1563. Its origin is to be sought far back in Greek literature, and its first introduction into Roman legend probably was in connection with the sack of Rome by the Gauls,

instead of the wars with the Sabines. Tarpeia's motive in Livy (1, 11) and Plutarch (Romulus) is avarice; but in making her motive, rather, love, Propertius has doubtless reverted to the original form of the myth as seen in Parthenius, Simylus, and others.

1–2: The theme; 3–6: the scene; 7–20: the circumstances: the Sabine camp near the spring; Tarpeia's duties as a Vestal take her to the spring; she beholds Tatius below engaged in military exercises; 21–30: she conceives a violent passion for the handsome warrior, which becomes all-absorbing; 31–66: her soliloquy, in which she acknowledges that her love overrides all other considerations, plans to betray the city into the hands of her adored one, and dreams of wedding the Sabine King; 67–88: she sleeps, wakes on the festal day of Rome's birth, compacts with Tatius to deliver the city into his hand, accomplishes the betrayal. 89–94: Her reward.

1. Tarpeium nemus : while we need not credit Varro's statement (*L. L.* 5, 41) that the Capitoline hill was originally called Mons Tarpeius, that designation doubtless was often used even in

lucus erat felix hederoso conditus antro,
　　multaque nativis obstrepit arbor aquis,
5　Silvani ramosa domus, quo dulcis ab aestu
　　fistula poturas ire iubebat oves.
hunc Tatius fontem vallo praecingit acerno,
　　fidaque suggesta castra coronat humo.
quid tum Roma fuit, tubicen vicina Curetis
10　cum quateret lento murmure saxa Iovis,
atque ubi nunc terris dicuntur iura subactis,
　　stabant Romano pila Sabina foro?

4. 3. conditus O consitus ω.

the time of Propertius, and whatever remnants of a sacred *lucus*
were still left on the summit could
be easily designated by the phrase
with which this elegy opens. Cf.
Verg. *Aen.* 8, 347: *hinc ad
Tarpeiam sedem et Capitolia
ducit.*— **Tarpeiae . . . sepulcrum:**
her real or supposed tomb on the
Capitol, still pointed out when
Propertius wrote. Cf. 3, 11, 45.

2. The first temple of Juppiter
Capitolinus was built under the
kings. The second temple, built
by Sulla and Catulus, had been
elegantly restored by Augustus in
Propertius's own time.

3. lucus . . . felix: 'a grove
of noble trees,' such as were connected with religious purposes and
associations. — **conditus:** 'se-
cluded.'— **antro:** cf. 1, 1, 11, n.
Propertius is thinking, not of any
one grotto, but of the curving
slope of the hill on the side
towards the Forum, where the

rocks offered many a lurking-
place. The abl. is locative.
With the description cf. Ovid,
Am. 3, 1, 3: *fons sacer in medio
speluncaque pumice pendens.*

4. nativis: *i.e.* of springs. —
obstrepit: the rustling of the trees
vies with the murmur of the waters.

5. Silvani . . . . domus: any
such grove might be considered
sacred to the forest-god.

6. poturas: instead of the
more usual supine.

7. The Sabine leader was
Titus Tatius, acc. to Livy, 1, 10.—
praecingit: *i.e.* he runs the line of
his fortification close to the spring,
without including it.

8. fidaque belongs to the
predicate. — **coronat:** 'encircles';
cf. Ovid, *Met.* 9, 334: *est lacus
. . . summum myrteta coronant.*

9. Curetis: adj. from Cures,
the chief town of the Sabines.

10. lento: 'long-reverberat-
ing.'— **saxa Iovis:** the Capitol.

murus erant montes : ubi nunc est curia saepta,
   bellicus ex illo fonte bibebat equus.
15 hinc Tarpeia deae fontem libavit : at illi
   urgebat medium fictilis urna caput.
et satis una malae potuit mors esse puellae,
   quae voluit flammas fallere, Vesta, tuas?
vidit arenosis Tatium proludere campis,
20   pictaque per flavas arma levare iubas.
obstupuit regis facie et regalibus armis,
   interque oblitas excidit urna manus.

13. montes: they alone surrounded the Forum valley like a wall, whatever the extent of the legendary wall of Romulus. — **curia**: the senate house on the north side of the Forum. — **saepta**: *i.e.* by temples and other public buildings.

14. illo fonte: there was a well-known spring in the Tullianum, near the *Curia*.

15. hinc may possibly refer to *Roma* (v. 9), but seems naturally to refer to v. 14. But the spring in v. 15 must be identical with that in v. 7, which would seem necessarily far removed from that just mentioned in v. 14. Either Propertius is ambiguous here, or his topography must be declared as vague as the notorious geography of these poets. — **deae**: cf. v. 18: the dramatic force of the myth is enhanced in the form which Propertius adopts, whereby Tarpeia is a Vestal, vowed to perpetual virginity. Water for the service of the goddess must be drawn from a running, open

stream; cf. Preller³, Vol. 2, p. 167. — **at**: cf. Tib. 1, 3, 63, n.

16. fictilis: cf. Tib. 1, 1, 38, n.; and the picture of Silvia Vestalis going after water in Ovid, *Fast*. 3, 14: *ponitur e summa fictilis urna coma*.

17. et: used often to introduce an exclamatory question; cf. 2, 8, 2: *et tu me lacrimas fundere, amice, vetas!* Cat. 29, 6; Friedrich, p. 173. — **una . . . mors**: cf. Hor. *Car*. 3, 27, 37: *levis una mors et virginum culpae*.

20. picta . . . arma: the Sabine *scutum* became ultimately the characteristic legionary shield of the Romans. From early times it was painted and carried distinctive designs. — **iubas**: the flowing mane of the horse on which Tatius rode. Cf., however, 4, 1, 30, n.

21. obstupuit: regularly used of love at first sight; cf. Ovid, *Met*. 2, 726: *obstipuit forma Iove natus*.

22. interque: temporal; as her hands forgot to maintain their grip, the pitcher fell. — **excidit**:

saepe illa inmeritae causata est omina lunae
   et sibi tinguendas dixit in amne comas :
25   saepe tulit blandis argentea lilia nymphis,
   Romula ne faciem laederet hasta Tati.
dumque subit primo Capitolia nubila fumo,
   rettulit hirsutis bracchia secta rubis,
et sua Tarpeia residens ita flevit ab arce
30   vulnera, vicino non patienda Iovi :
'ignes castrorum et Tatiae praetoria turmae
   et formosa oculis arma Sabina meis,
o utinam ad vestros sedeam captiva penates,
   dum captiva mei conspicer ora Tati.
35   Romani montes et montibus addita Roma
   et valeat probro Vesta pudenda meo.
ille equus, ille meos in castra reportet amores,

32. formosa **DV** famosa **NFL.**   34. ora *Gronovius* arma **V₂** esse **O.**   37.
reportet **ω** reponet **O.**

cf. Tib. 4, 2, 4 ; Ovid, *Met.* 3, 39 :
effluxere urnae manibus.

23. saepe . . . causata est :
Tarpeia sought excuses to revisit
the spring and perhaps catch
sight of her hero. Cf. Tib. 1, 3,
17.

24. tinguendas . . . in amne :
for purification in the morning. —
amne = *fonte.*

25. blandis : 'gracious.'

26. Romula : cf. 3, 11, 52, n.

27. primo . . . nubila fumo :
i.e. the top of the hill is beclouded
with smoke of the fires kindled in
preparation for the evening meal ;
cf. Verg. *Ec.* 1, 83 : *et iam summa
procul villarum culmina fumant,
maioresque cadunt altis de montibus umbrae.*

28. In her absorption she hardly
noticed the brambles as she hurried
home.

29. Tarpeia : a proleptic use.

30. vulnera . . . non patienda :
such dereliction to her vows would
be intolerable in the eyes of Jove.
The wounds are those inflicted by
Cupid's dart.

31. ignes castrorum : the evening shadows have fallen when
Tarpeia begins her soliloquy. —
praetoria seems inconsistent with
4, 1, 29.

34. captiva : 'even as a cap-
tive.' — **conspicer :** 'catch sight of.'

36. pudenda : 'who will be
shocked.'

37. meos . . . amores = *me
amantem* ; cf. 2, 28, 39, n.

cui Tatius dextras collocat ipse iubas.
quid mirum in patrios Scyllam saevisse capillos,
40   candidaque in saevos inguina versa canes ?
prodita quid mirum fraterni cornua monstri,
    cum patuit lecto stamine torta via?
quantum ego sum Ausoniis crimen factura puellis,
    inproba virgineo lecta ministra foco !
45   Pallados extinctos siquis mirabitur ignes,
    ignoscat: lacrimis spargitur ara meis.
cras, ut rumor ait, tota pugnabitur urbe:

---

47. pugnabitur **O** purgabitur *Huleatt* pigrabitur *Housman* potabitur *Rossberg* cessabitur *Palmer*.

---

38. Tarpeia is already jealous of the caress given by Tatius to his horse when arranging the mane on the right side of his neck.

39. Tarpeia seeks for justification, or at least comfort, from examples of other maidens who had proved disloyal to family or country, for the sake of love. Other parallels are cited by Sanders (*l.c.* above). — **Scylla**: daughter of Nisus, king of Megara. She fell in love with the besieging king Minos, and cut from her father's head the purple (or golden) lock upon which his life, and therefore the safety of the city, depended. But Minos despised her treachery, and caused her death, as Tarpeia's was caused by Tatius.

40. Propertius wrongly identifies the Scylla of verse 39 with the notorious sea monster in the straits of Messina.   But there are several other examples of the same mistake, *e.g.* Verg. *Ec.* 6, 74; and Ovid, *Fast.* 4, 500 and *A. A.* 1, 331.

41. **monstri**: the Minotaur, half-brother of Ariadne, who for her love to Theseus assisted in the scheme for killing the monster by arranging the thread which served as a guide in the Cretan labyrinth.

42. **lecto**: 'by gathering up.'

43. **ego**: emphatic contrast. Tarpeia is to correspond in infamy among the Latins to Scylla and Ariadne among the Greeks.

45. **Pallados**: not only was it supposed that the sacred fire of Vesta had been brought to Rome from Troy, the city of Pallas (cf. Verg. *Aen* 2, 297), but also an image of Pallas, also believed to have been brought from Troy, was kept in the temple of Vesta; cf. Ovid, *Fast.* 6. 421–436.

46. Cf. 4, 3, 4.

351

> tu cape spinosi rorida terga iugi.
> lubrica tota via est et perfida: quippe tacentes
> 50   fallaci celat limite semper aquas.
> o utinam magicae nossem cantamina musae!
> haec quoque formoso lingua tulisset opem.
> te toga picta decet, non quem sine matris honore
> nutrit inhumanae dura papilla lupae.
> 55   sic, hospes, pariamne tua regina sub aula?
> dos tibi non humilis prodita Roma venit.
> si minus, at raptae ne sint inpune Sabinae:
> me rape et alterna lege repende vices.
> commissas acies ego possum solvere: nuptae,
> 60   vos medium palla foedus inite mea.
> adde Hymenaee modos, tubicen fera murmura conde:

48. cape **O** cave **F₂**.

---

48. tu: Tatius, whom Tarpeia's affection longs to save from the dangers of battle and direct by the secret path to the capture of the citadel in a bloodless victory.

49. perfida: 'treacherous.'

50. limite: 'track.' — **semper** modifies *fallaci*.

52. haec quoque ... lingua: as well as Medea's, *e.g.* — **formoso**: Tatius, cf. the original signification of " beau."

53. toga picta: the regulation robe of a triumphing Roman imperator. — **non quem**: Romulus, contrasted with *te*.

54. Cf. 2, 6, 20: *nutritus duro, Romule, lacte lupae.*

55. sic: 'if so,' *i.e.* if I help you to become King of Rome.

56. venit: more emphatic than the expected *veniet* of this apodosis.

57. Cf. Cat. 64, 158 sqq.; *si tibi non cordi fuerant conubia nostra ... tibi iucundo famularer serva labore.*

58. alterna lege: 'by the rule of retaliation.'

59. ego: *i.e.* I, as well as the Sabine women, who rush into the thick of the combat to stop it. Tarpeia's plan depends on prevention.

60. medium ... foedus: 'a compact between the combatants.' — **palla**: as a wedding garment, here used by metonomy for marriage.

61. tubicen: in apposition with *Hymenaee*. Hymen as trumpeter

credite, vestra meus molliet arma torus.

et iam quarta canit venturam bucina lucem

  ipsaque in Oceanum sidera lapsa cadunt.

65 experiar somnum, de te mihi somnia quaeram :

  fac venias oculis umbra benigna meis.'

dixit, et incerto permisit bracchia somno,

  nescia vae furiis accubuisse novis.

nam Vesta, Iliacae felix tutela favillae,

70 culpam alit et plures condit in ossa faces.

illa ruit, qualis celerem prope Thermodonta

  Strymonis abscisso fertur aperta sinu.

---

68. vae furiis *Jacob* se furiis *Livineius* nefariis **O**.   72. abscisso **DV**
absciso **NFL** abscissus . . . sinus *Broukhusius*.   fertur **O** pectus *Hertzberg*.

---

will sound a very different note
from that usually heard in camp.

63. quarta . . . bucina : the
signal for the beginning of the
last quarter of the night ; cf. Eng.
"eight bells," etc. The *bucina*
belongs to the simple manners of
the early age here described : cf.
4, 1, 13.

64. Cf. Verg. *Aen.* 2, 9 : *sua-
dentque cadentia sidera somnos.*

65. te : Tatius.

69. Cf. verse 45, n ; Ovid, *Fast.*
6, 365 : *vidimus Iliacae transferri
pignora Vestae sede;* 258 : *cum
flammae custos aede recepta dea
est.*

70. alit : Vesta regards Tarpeia's case as hopeless, and pun-
ishes her by hurrying her on to
certain ruin. — **faces** : cf. 4, 3, 50.

71. Thermodonta : a river in
Cappadocia, commonly regarded
as the home of the Amazons ; but
Propertius is thinking less of the

geography than of the scene.
Vergil confuses the geography
similarly in *Aen.* 11, 659 : *quales
Threiciae cum flumina Thermo-
dontis pulsant et pictis bellantur
Amazones armis.*

72. Strymonis : a Thracian
woman, here regarded less as a
typical Amazon (like Penthesilea,
who came from Thrace to her
eastern home), than as a Maenad in
Thrace itself, reveling in passionate
frenzy. — **abscisso . . . aperta sinu** :
'exposed by the tearing away of
her garment'; *sinu* is best considered an abl. abs.   The picture
is that shown in the left-hand figure
of illust. No. 929 in Baum. *Denk.*
If we read *absciso,* the picture becomes that of an Amazon whose
characteristic mutilation is exposed
as she rushes into battle.   But
this interpretation is less in harmony with the mood of Tarpeia. —
fertur : 'is hurried along.'

urbi festus erat, dixere Parilia patres:
　　hic primus coepit moenibus esse dies,
75　annua pastorum convivia, lusus in urbe,
　　cum pagana madent fercula divitiis
　　cumque super raros faeni flammantis acervos
　　traicit inmundos ebria turba pedes.
　　Romulus excubias decrevit in otia solvi
80　atque intermissa castra silere tuba.
　　hoc Tarpeia suum tempus rata convenit hostem:
　　pacta ligat, pactis ipsa futura comes.
　　mons erat adscensu dubius, festoque remissus:
　　nec mora, vocales occupat ense canes.
85　omnia praebebant somnos: sed Iuppiter unus
　　decrevit poenis invigilare tuis.
　　prodiderat portaeque fidem patriamque iacentem,
　　nubendique petit, quem velit ipsa, diem.

76. divitiis O delitiis V₂ deliciis ω.　86. tuis O suis ω.　88. ipsa O ipse V₂.

---

73. festus: sc. *dies* from v. 74.
— **Parilia**: April 21st, the birthday
of Rome; cf. Tib. 2, 5, 87, n.

76. divitiis: 'rich viands.'

77. raros: 'here and there';
cf. Tib. 2, 5, 89, n.

78. inmundos: because bare,
and of course increasingly black
and smoky as the leaping pro-
gresses.

81. suum: 'favorable to her
plans.'

82. pactis ipsa . . . comes:
Tarpeia expects to be a voluntary
part of the booty; cf. the remark
of Scylla in Ovid, *Met.* 8, 48: *me
comitem, me pacis pignus haberet.*

83. adscensu: with such an adjective as *dubius* (which suggests

difficilis) this may well be regarded
as a dat., and it would be proper
to class it as a supine. — **festoque**:
the enclitic is pregnant in meaning here: 'and accordingly, it being a holiday.'

84. occupat: sc. Tarpeia; she
anticipates the alarm they would
give.

85. Everything and everybody
was wrapped in slumber. — **Iuppiter**: to whom especially this
hill was sacred.

86. tuis: Tarpeia's.

87. portaeque fidem = *portam-
que fidam.*

88. ipsa: asking that the wedding day should be set according
to her own choice was assuming

at Tatius (neque enim sceleri dedit hostis honorem)
90　　'nube' ait 'et regni scande cubile mei.'
dixit, et ingestis comitum super obruit armis.
　　haec, virgo, officiis dos erat apta tuis.
a duce Tarpeia mons est cognomen adeptus;
　　o vigil, iniuste praemia sortis habes.

6

Sacra facit vates: sint ora faventia sacris
　　et cadat ante meos icta iuvenca focos.

---

93. Tarpeia ω Tarpeio O Tarpeius *Kossberg* Tarpeium *Palmer.*　94. iniuste
AFLDV iniustae **N.**

the queenship which she coveted
rather than an inferior station.

90. nube: ironical indeed! for
the covering she is to have is the
deadly one of the shields, as she
sinks to a bed of death.

91. obruit armis: cf. Livy, I,
11, 7: *accepti obrutam armis
necavere.* But though Propertius
follows the regular account of her
death, the motive of avarice which
was supposed to determine its
method is lacking.

93. duce: their guide up the
citadel.

94. vigil: she alone was awake
keeping guard, but as an official
vigil she was hardly a success, and
the expression is ironical. —
iniuste: *i.e.* Tarpeia did not deserve the everlasting glory of
having the hill called after her
name.

4, 6

The third in the series of aetiological elegies in this Book (cf.
4, 1, Intr.), dealing this time with
the temple of Apollo on the Palatine hill, which was completed in
28 B.C.; cf. 2, 31, Intr ; Hor. *Car.*
I, 31. At the time of the dedication of the temple, Augustus also
established *ludi quinquennales* in
honor of Apollo, under whose
patronage the victory at Actium
had been won. As the submission
of the Sycambri (v. 77) took place
in 16 B.C., it appears probable
that Propertius timed this poem to
be a part of the fourth celebration
of these games. The general correspondence of the scene of the
battle of Actium here with that
described by Vergil as represented
on the shield of Aeneas (*Aen* 8,

cera Philitaeis certet Romana corymbis
et Cyrenaeas urna ministret aquas.
5   costum molle date et blandi mihi turis honores,
terque focum circa laneus orbis eat.
spargite me lymphis, carmenque recentibus aris
tibia Mygdoniis libet eburna cadis.
ite procul fraudes, alio sint aere noxae:

6. 3. cera O ara *Haupt* serta *Scaliger*.

675 sqq.) has led to the presumption that both may be traced to an official picture of the battle, perhaps one carried in the triumphal procession of Augustus.

1–14: As priest of Apollo and the Muses the poet brings his offering of song in honor of the Actian Apollo. 15–26: The scene of the battle. 27–36: Apollo appears equipped for war; 37–54: his address to Augustus. 55–68: the victory of Phoebus and Augustus—not a victory over one woman! 69–86: its ideal celebration.

1. vates: cf. 3, 1, 3; Hor. *Car.* 3, 1, 3: *Musarum sacerdos . . . canto;* 1, 31, 1: *quid dedicatum poscit Apollinem vates? —* sint . . . faventia = *faveant:* cf. Tib. 2, 1, 1, n.

3. cera: the tablets upon which the poet writes, standing for the thing written. — Philitaeis . . . corymbis: 'the ivy-crowned Philitas,' *i.e.* vie with Philitas for laurels in writing. Cf. 4, 1, 61–62; Intr. § 7, n. 1. For the syntax cf. 1, 7, 3, n.

4. Cyrenaeas: Callimachus came from Cyrene. The order of 3, 1, 1 is reversed.

5. costum: a costly oriental perfumed ointment. — date: addressed to the imaginary ministrants at the altar. — blandi: 'grateful,' *i.e.* to the gods; cf. Tib. 3, 3, 2. — turis honores: cf. Tib. 1, 7, 53.

6. laneus orbis: the white fillet of wool; cf. Verg. *Ec.* 8, 64: *effer aquam et molli cinge haec altaria vitta.*

7. spargite: cf. Ovid, *Fast.* 5, 677: *lauro sparguntur ab uda omnia. —* recentibus: *i.e.* made for this occasion, probably of turf; cf. Hor. *Car.* 1, 19, 13: *vivum mihi caespitem . . . ponite.*

8. tibia: cf. Tib. 2, 1, 86. — Mygdoniis = *Phrygiis,* referring to the birthplace of the flute. — libet: so we speak of a bird as 'pouring forth' music from its throat; taken with *cadis* standing for the flute itself, this is a highly figurative verse.

9. procul: Verg. *Aen.* 6, 258: *procul o procul este, profani. —* alio

10   pura novum vati laurea mollit iter.
       musa, Palatini referemus Apollinis aedem:
         res est, Calliope, digna favore tuo.
       Caesaris in nomen ducuntur carmina: Caesar
         dum canitur, quaeso, Iuppiter ipse vaces.
15   est Phoebi fugiens Athamana ad litora portus,
         qua sinus Ioniae murmura condit aquae,
       Actia Iuleae pelagus monumenta carinae,
         nautarum votis non operosa via.
       huc mundi coiere manus: stetit aequore moles
20   pinea: nec remis aequa favebat avis.
       altera classis erat Teucro damnata Quirino,

. . . **aere:** *i.e.* under another sky.

10. novum: a type of poetry new at Rome, though tried by Callimachus. — **laurea:** as dear to Apollo. — **mollit:** for the figure cf. the biblical story of Palm Sunday.

11. After this highly poetic introduction we have here the simple announcement of the real theme of the elegy.

12. Calliope: her function is not restricted in Propertius to any particular field, any more than in Horace; cf. 3, 2, 16.

13. in nomen: 'in praise of'; purpose acc. — **ducuntur carmina:** 'the thread of my song is spun.'

14. vaces: 'keep holiday' (from ruling the universe), *i.e.* have leisure to listen.

15. Phoebi . . . portus: the Ambracian gulf, at whose entrance on the promontory of Actium was a temple of Apollo. — **fugiens:**

'stretching back.' — **Athamana:** the Athamanes were a people in Epirus, northeast of the gulf.

16. condit: 'quiets.'

17. Iuleae: *i.e.* of his descendant, Augustus. — **pelagus:** 'veritable sea'; in apposition with *portus*, as is also *monumenta* ('made memorable by'). A glance at the map will justify the exclamatory addition of *pelagus* to the description.

18. non operosa (*i.e.* of access): this was hardly true till Augustus himself made improvements at Nicopolis after the battle of Actium; cf. Verg. *Aen.* 3, 275: *formidatus nautis aperitur Apollo.* — **via:** 'roadstead.'

19. moles pinea: referring to the two fleets.

20. nec: with adversative force: L. 1445 (d). — **avis:** 'omen.'

21. Teucro: the followers of Aeneas, destined to found Rome, are constantly called Teucri by

357

pilaque feminea turpiter acta manu:
hinc Augusta ratis plenis Iovis omine velis
signaque iam patriae vincere docta suae.

25   tandem aciem geminos Nereus lunarat in arcus,
    armorum et radiis picta tremebat aqua,
cum Phoebus linquens stantem se vindice Delon
    (nam tulit iratos mobilis una notos)
adstitit Augusti puppim super et nova flamma

30   luxit in obliquam ter sinuata facem.
non ille attulerat crines in colla solutos
    aut testudineae carmen inerme lyrae,
sed quali adspexit Pelopeum Agamemnona vultu

25. aciem **O** acies **ω**.

Vergil; the use of the term here emphasizes the decree of fate. — **damnata**: 'doomed to submit.' — **Quirino**: by yielding to Octavian, the enemy really gave new glory to the deified founder of Rome.

22. turpiter: the disgrace lay in being pitted against a woman, whose soldiers were using the national weapon of the Romans.

23. hinc: corresponding to *altera*. — **Augusta**: by anticipation; the title was not given to Octavian till 27 B.C. — **Iovis**: as god of the sky.

24. iam: this battle was only the culmination of a series of victories won by Octavian. — **patriae**: the victor is represented as entirely unselfish, and fighting to save the State.

25. geminos . . . arcus: Octavian's fleet being in concave (inclosing), and Antony's in convex

form. — **Nereus**: as the lord of the sea.

26. picta: by reflection.

27. linquens . . . Delon: Vergil's description of the shield of Aeneas (*Aen*. 8, 704) represents Apollo as present in his own temple at Actium. — **stantem**: Delos was in early times a floating island according to myth, afterwards anchored by Apollo, whose birth took place there. — **vindice**: 'protector.'

28. una: sc. *insula*.

29. nova: 'strange.'

30. luxit . . . ter: thus was the omen most perfect. Cf. Tib. 1, 3, 11. — **facem**: the curve seems to have been like that described by a meteor, for which *fax* is the regular word.

31. Not like the peaceful Apollo, *e.g.* described in Tib. 2, 5, 2–10.

33. Pelopeum: the curse upon the descendants of the crafty

egessitque avidis Dorica castra rogis,
35   aut qualis flexos solvit Pythona per orbes
serpentem, inbelles quem timuere lyrae.
mox ait ' o longa mundi servator ab Alba,
Auguste, Hectoreis cognite maior avis,
vince mari : iam terra tua est.   tibi militat arcus
40   et favet ex umeris hoc onus omne meis.
solve metu patriam, quae nunc te vindice freta
inposuit prorae publica vota tuae.
quam nisi defendes, murorum Romulus augur
ire Palatinas non bene vidit aves.
45   et nimium remis audent prope.   turpe Latinos
principe te fluctus regia vela pati.
nec te, quod classis centenis remiget alis,

45. Latinos *Markland* Latinis O.

Pelops appeared, among other instances, when Agamemnon was punished by Apollo for carrying off the daughter of Chryses.

34. egessitque: *i.e.* on funeral biers. — **castra:** poetic hyperbole. — **rogis:** dative.

35. solvit: 'relaxed' (the tense and sinuous form of Python). — **Pythona:** the fabled dragon that Apollo slew near Delphi.

36. lyrae = *lyristae; i.e.* the Muses.

37. ab Alba: *i.e.* from Iulus, the founder of Alba Longa. For the construction cf. Ovid, *Am.* 2, 6, 1.

38. Hectoreis: 'like Hector,' as a typical Trojan, and so progenitor of Augustus.

39. terra tua est: relatively true ; sufficiently so for a poet.

40. onus: the quiver and its contents.

43. Romulus augur: according to the familiar story in Livy, 1, 6, 4.

44. Palatinas : 'from the Palatine'; cf. Ovid, *Fast.* 5, 152: *prima, Palatinae, signa dedistis, aves.* Remus observed from the Aventine.

45. nimium ... prope: *i.e.* too near to Rome. — **audent:** sc. *hostes.*

46. principe : it was in 28 B.C., however, that Octavian was officially recognized as *princeps senatus.*

47. remiget alis : Propertius's use of this figure here is ambiguous. Most of the commentators, disregarding the warning of Hertzberg, interpret *alis* as = *remis,*

terreat : invito labitur illa mari.

quodque vehunt prorae Centaurica saxa minantis,
50   tigna cava et pictos experiere metus.

frangit et attollit vires in milite causa ;
quae nisi iusta subest, excutit arma pudor.

tempus adest, committe rates : ego temporis auctor
ducam laurigera Iulia rostra manu.'

55   dixerat, et pharetrae pondus consumit in arcus :
proxima post arcus Caesaris hasta fuit.

vincit Roma fide Phoebi : dat femina poenas :
sceptra per Ionias fracta vehuntur aquas.

at pater Idalio miratur Caesar ab astro :

and quote as a parallel Hom. *Od.*
11, 125 : οὐδ᾽ εὖηρε᾽ ἐρετμά, τά τε
πτερὰ νηυσὶ πέλονται; but there
is no sufficient reason why we
should not consider *alis = velis*
after the usual metaphor as seen
so often, *e.g.* Verg. *Aen.* 1, 301 :
remigio alarum ; Ovid, *A. A.* 2,
45 : *remigium volucrum disponit in
ordine pennas* ; Lucr. 6, 743 : *remigi
oblitae pennarum vela remittunt.*

48. invito : cf. 1, 16, 14. As a
matter of fact the heavy weather
on the sea did much to interfere
with the success of the Egyptian
fleet ; cf. Flor. 4, 11, 5 : *non sine
gemitu maris et labore ventorum
ferebantur.*

49. Centaurica saxa minantis :
' forms threatening to cast rocks
like those of the Centaurs.' The
Centaurs in combat were a favorite
subject of artistic representation,
and made a good figurehead for
the bulky ships of the ancients ;
minantis is acc.

50. Cf. Hor. *Car.* 1, 14, 14 :
*nil pictis timidus navita puppibus
fidit.*

53. committe rates = *committe
proelium navale.*

54. laurigera : cf. Ovid, *A. A.*
3, 389 ; *laurigero sacrata Palatia
Phoebo.*

55. pharetrae pondus : cf. *hoc
onus omne* (verse 40). — **consumit** :
' spent.'

56. proxima : cf. Hor. *Car.* 1,
12, 18 : *nec viget quicquam simile
aut secundum, proximos illi tamen
occupavit Pallas honores.*

57. femina : Propertius declines
to mention the name of Cleopatra
as he had declined before, in 3, 11.

58. sceptra : a common emblem
of royal power, here used of the
fleet, another such emblem. —
per Ionias . . . aquas : cf. Hor.
Epod. 9, 29–32.

59. Idalio . . . astro : as Venus
was especially worshiped at
Cretan Idalium, this expression

60   'sum deus: est nostri sanguinis ista fides.'
     prosequitur cantu Triton, omnesque marinae
          plauserunt circa libera signa deae.
     illa petit Nilum cymba male nixa fugaci,
          hoc unum, iusso non moritura die.
65   di melius! quantus mulier foret una triumphus,
          ductus erat per quas ante Iugurtha vias!
     Actius hinc traxit Phoebus monumenta, quod eius
          una decem vicit missa sagitta rates.
     bella satis cecini: citharam iam poscit Apollo
70   victor et ad placidos exuit arma choros.
     candida nunc molli subeant convivia luco,

would most naturally refer to her
own star. But as Julius Caesar
had a star of his own, the comet
which appeared at the games given
in his honor by Octavian (cf. Suet.
Iul. 88; Hor. *Car.* 1, 12, 46:
micat inter omnes Iulium sidus),
Propertius ought to be referring
to that; if so, he is indulging his
penchant for ambiguity. — **miratur**: 'looks on admiringly.'

60. nostri sanguinis ista fides:
'that prowess of yours is proof
enough that you belong to my
family,' *i.e.* are an heir to divinity.
Of course Octavian was really
only an adopted son.

61. Triton: it is appropriate
that the marine divinities lead in
proclaiming the triumph of Rome
on the sea.

62. libera signa: 'standards of
a free state.'

63. illa: cf. v. 57, n. — **cymba**:
hyperbole; Cleopatra's returning

fleet consisted of sixty ships.

64. hoc unum: obj. of the purpose idea in *moritura*, so that the
main idea of the verb becomes an
appositive to this phrase; a
unique construction: 'with this
one thing in view, namely not to
die on the appointed day' (*i.e.*
that of a Roman triumph).

65. melius: sc. *consuluerunt*,
referring to the idea of the previous
phrase. — **quantus**: ironical.

67. The poet hastens to add
that it was not for a triumph over
one woman that Apollo derived
his glory on this occasion, but for
his divine archery in overcoming
the hostile fleet.

71. candida: referring to the
participants, who would be clad in
fresh white garments; cf. Tib. 1,
10, 27; 2, 1, 13. — **convivia**: cf. Hor.
Car. 1, 37, 1: *Nunc est bibendum*,
opening the ode in celebration of
this same victory.

blanditiaeque fluant per mea colla rosae,
vinaque fundantur praelis elisa Falernis,
    terque lavet nostras spica Cilissa comas.
75 ingenium potis inritet musa poetis :
        Bacche, soles Phoebo fertilis esse tuo.
    ille paludosos memoret servire Sycambros,
        Cepheam hic Meroen fuscaque regna canat,
    hic referat sero confessum foedere Parthum,
80   'reddat signa Remi : mox dabit ipse sua.
    sive aliquid pharetris Augustus parcet eois,

74. terque V₂ perque O.   75. potis DV positis NFL.

72. rosae : collective ; gen.

73. Falernis : of the various favorite wines Propertius singles this variety out for mention by name twice (the other passage is 2, 33, 39), but nowhere mentions Caecuban, Massic, Chian, or the vintage of Cales, apparently not being such a connoisseur of wines as Horace.

74. spica Cilissa : Cilician saffron (cf. spikenard), which was especially choice when it came from Mt. Corycus (Plin. *N.H.* 21, 31) ; cf. Ovid, *Fast.* 1, 76 : *sonet accensis spica Cilissa focis.*

75. Cf. Enn. *Sat.* 64 : *numquam poetor nisi si podager* ; Ovid, *Met.* 7, 432 : *carmina vino ingenium faciente canunt.*

76. Cf. 3, 2, 9 ; Tib. 3, 4, 43 : *casto nam rite poetae Phoebusque et Bacchus Pieridesque favent.*

77. ille corresponds to *hic . . . hic* below, thus dividing among different poets the gigantic task of celebrating all the victories of Au-

gustus. — Sycambros : a powerful German tribe, north of the Rhine, who are said to have been subdued in 16 B.C.

78. Cepheam . . . Meroen : Meroë was a famous Ethiopian island on the Nile. Cepheus, father of Andromeda, was king of Ethiopia. For the campaign of Petronius there in 22 B.C. cf. 4, 3, 10, n. — fusca : of the inhabitants.

79. referat : 'let him represent as . . . and say.' — confessum : 'acknowledging submission' ; for this absolute use cf. Ovid, *Met.* 5, 215 : *confessasque manus obliquaque bracchia tendens 'vincis,' ait.* The Parthians had surrendered the standards of Crassus in 20 B.C., but Propertius, like other Romans, was anticipating a more complete subjugation.

80. Remi = *Romuli* ; cf. 4, 1, 9.

82. in : 'for'; purpose. — pueros : Gaius and Lucius Caesar, grandsons of Augustus, whom he had adopted in 17 B.C. Gaius

differat in pueros ista tropaea suos.
gaude, Crasse, nigras siquid sapis inter arenas :
ire per Euphraten ad tua busta licet.'
85 sic noctem patera, sic ducam carmine, donec
     iniciat radios in mea vina dies.

I I

Desine, Paulle, meum lacrimis urgere sepulcrum :
panditur ad nullas ianua nigra preces.

did actually lead an expedition against the Parthians in 2 A.D.

83. nigras : cf. 3, 7, 56.— **sapis** : cf. 2, 13, 42.

84. per : 'across' to Carrhae, where Crassus was slain.

4, 11

This last and finest of the elegies of Propertius, long known as *regina elegiarum*, was intended as a consolation to L. Aemilius Paullus Lepidus (consul suffectus 34 B.C.) nephew of the triumvir Lepidus. The occasion was the untimely death in 16 B.C. of his wife Cornelia, daughter of P. Cornelius Scipio (said to have been of consular rank) and Scribonia, the second wife of Augustus. This connection with the imperial family is doubtless responsible for the elegy. It is spoken by the deceased Cornelia herself at her tomb, and may have been intended as a sepulchral inscription. The reference in verses 65 and 66 to her brother P. Cornelius Scipio, who was consul in 16 B.C., fixes the date. In dignity, nobility of tone, and genuine pathos this elegy is unequaled.

1–14 : ' Paullus, burden not my tomb with idle lamentations ; the grave knows neither sentiment nor reason. 15–28 : Ye powers below, listen to my *apologia!* 29–66 : I have never been unworthy of my noble family and honored kin. 67–72 : Daughter, follow thy mother's example, and win the most glorious reward possible for a woman. 73–84 : To you, Paullus, I commend our children ; be to them henceforth both mother and father. Bear thy sorrow bravely, yet tenderly. 85–98 : And, my children, if your father bring you home a new mother, be kind and tactful ; but if I remain his only mate, keep him from a lonely old age ; and may the years I have been denied be added to your lives ; that you all are spared is my consolation. 99-102 : I rest my case.'

cum semel infernas intrarunt funera leges,
    non exorato stant adamante viae.
5   te licet ornantem fuscae deus audiat aulae:
    nempe tuas lacrimas litora surda bibent.
vota movent superos: ubi portitor aera recepit,
    obserat herbosos lurida porta rogos.
sic maestae cecinere tubae, cum subdita nostrum

1. **urgere**: cf. Tib. 1, 1, 67, n.
— **sepulcrum**: *i.e.* the spirit that
dwells there. Cf. Cat. 96, 1;
PAPA., Vol. 30 (1899), p. xxx, 3.

3. **funera**: cf. 1, 17, 8, n. Body
and soul are not distinguished
here better than in our own common parlance; cf., on the distinction between natural and philosophical expression, W. A. Heidel
in *A. J. P.*, Vol. 33 (1912), p. 94.
— **leges**: 'jurisdiction.'

4. **non exorato**: 'never known
to yield,' and so presumably *in-
exorabili*. — **stant**: cf. Tib. 1, 1,
64. — **adamante viae**: the poet
is thinking particularly of the
gates of the entrance to the
world below, gates which never
open outwards; cf. Verg. *Aen.* 6,
552: *porta adversa ingens soli-
doque adamante columnae vis ut
nulla . . . exscindere*, etc.

5. **licet . . . audiat**: a supposition merely for the sake of argument. — **deus**: Pluto. — **aulae**: cf.
Hor. *Car.* 2, 18, 30: *rapacis Orci
. . . aula.*

6. **bibent**: cf. Cat. 66, 85.

7. **portitor**: Charon. — **aera**:
the coin placed in the mouth of
the deceased according to Greek
custom, to pay the ferryman of the
Styx.

8. **herbosos**: Propertius mixes
his metaphors: here he is thinking of the grass-covered mound
of the tomb: 'beneath the sod.' —
lurida porta: cf. verse 4, n.; the
adjective is a favorite epithet for
places and things connected with
death; cf. Tib. 3, 3, 38. — **rogos**:
'ashes' (from the pyre where they
are produced); cf. English "Peace
to his ashes." It is only another
of the poet's euphemisms for 'the
dead,' and we must not be literal in
trying to conceive what he means
when he says that the gates of the
lower world (which for the living
mourners are practically identical
with the door of the tomb) bar
the ashes under the sod from returning to living friends.

9. **sic**: 'this was the story.'
— **cecinere**: cf. Tib. 1, 7, 47. —
tubae: used in various ways in
connection with funeral ceremonies; here represented as joining in the loud wailing customarily
raised when the torch was applied
to the bier.

10   detraheret lecto fax inimica caput.

       quid mihi coniugium Paulli, quid currus avorum

         profuit aut famae pignora tanta meae?

       num minus inmites habui Cornelia parcas?

         en sum quod digitis quinque levatur onus.

15   damnatae noctes, et vos vada lenta paludes,

         et quaecumque meos inplicat unda pedes,

       inmatura licet, tamen huc non noxia veni:

         det pater hic umbrae mollia iura meae.

       aut siquis posita iudex sedet Aeacus urna,

20   in mea sortita vindicet ossa pila:

       adsideant fratres iuxta, Minoia sella, et

---

11. 13. num **FL** nun **V** non **ND.** habui *Itali* habuit **O.** 21. iuxta **O** iuxta et *Itali.* Minoia **O** Minoida **ω.** sella et **Vω** sella **FLD** sellam **ω.**

---

10. **lecto**: sc. *funebri.* — **caput**: 'my dear self'; cf. Hor. *Car.* 1, 24, 2: *tam cari capitis;* Cat. 68, 120.

11. **quid . . . profuit**: cf. 3, 18, 11; Ovid, *Her.* 11, 17: *quid iuvat admotam per avorum nomina,* etc. — **currus**: *i.e.* triumphs.

12. **pignora**: Cornelia's three children.

13. **Cornelia**: 'for being a Cornelia.' The succession of questions in the first person is most emphatic.

14. Cf. 2, 9, 14: *in parva sustulit ossa manu;* Ovid, *Am.* 3, 9, 40.

15. **damnatae** = *damnatorum;* cf. Tib. 1, 3, 67, n. — **paludes**: cf. Verg. *Georg.* 4, 478: *limus niger et deformis harundo Cocyti tardaque palus inamabilis unda alligat.*

17. **inmatura**: the same im-plication that an early death was commonly considered a judgment for wrong-doing is seen in Tib. 1, 3, 51.

18. **pater**: Dis, *i.e.* Pluto.; cf. Tac. *Hist.* 4, 84: *plurimi Ditem patrem.* — **hic**: in Hades. — **umbrae . . . meae**: = *mihi*: so *mea . . . ossa* in v. 20. Cf. v. 3, n.

19. **siquis . . . Aeacus**: Cornelia speaks thus indefinitely as one who has yet learned practically nothing of the order of things infernal. It was from the time of Plato that the prevalent idea of this bench of triple judgment in the lower world dated.

20. **sortita**: passive. — **vindicet**: 'pass judgment.' — **pila**: instrumental in force: 'in the use of the [white or black] ball.'

21. **fratres**: Minos and Rhadamanthus, who were joint judges

Eumenidum intento turba severa foro.

Sisyphe, mole vaces, taceant Ixionis orbes,

    fallax Tantaleus corripiare liquor,

25 Cerberus et nullas hodie petat inprobus umbras,

    et iaceat tacita lapsa catena sera.

ipsa loquar pro me. si fallo, poena sororum

    infelix umeros urgeat urna meos.

sicui fama fuit per avita tropaea decori,

30   Afra Numantinos regna loquuntur avos,

altera maternos exaequat turba Libones,

---

24. Tantaleus ω Tantaleo O.   corripiare O corripere ore *Auratus*.

---

with Aeacus in the lower world;
the first two, sons of Europa, the
last, of Aegina, and all sons of
Zeus. — **Minoia**: singled out for
convenience, instead of a repetition
of two or three names. — **sella**:
'bench'; in apposition with *fratres*.

22. Eumenidum: who executed
punishment. — **intento . . . foro**:
used for the crowd of spectators
('shades') eagerly watching the
verdict. — **turba**: sc. *adsint* or
adstent, as *adsideant* would hardly
be in keeping with the conception
here.

23–26. Cf. Tib. 1, 3, 71–78, and
nn. The thought is that such a
trial will be of absorbing interest
to all in the lower world. Cf.
Verg. *Georg.* 4, 481: *quin ipsae
stupuere domus . . . Tartara . . .
Eumenides, tenuitque . . . Cerberus ora, atque Ixionii . . . rota
constitit orbis.*

25. Cerberus: cf. 3, 18, 23, n.

26. lapsa: because of Cerberus's

inactivity. — **sera**: the bolt will
not make any noise because the
door will stand open, or because
it may be shut continuously during
the absorbing trial of Cornelia.

27. si fallo: the historic formula
in oaths was, *si sciens fallo*: cf.
Cic. *Ad Fam.* 7, 1, 2. — **sororum**:
the Danaides.

28. infelix . . . urna: cf, 2, 31,
4, n.

29. fama . . . per . . . tropaea:
a Propertian liberty of construction.

30. Afra . . . regna: *i.e.* the
kingdom of Carthage, which included Numantia. — **Numantinos
. . . avos**: P. Cornelius Scipio
Africanus, the younger, took Numantia, 133 B.C.

31. altera: 'on the other side
of the house.' — **Libones**: L. Scri-
bonius Libo, her uncle, was not
an unusually distinguished person,
probably she is hinting rather at
Scribonia's fame for having married into the imperial family.

et domus est titulis utraque fulta suis.

mox, ubi iam facibus cessit praetexta maritis,

    vinxit et acceptas altera vitta comas,

35 iungor, Paulle, tuo sic discessura cubili:

    in lapide hoc uni nupta fuisse legar.

testor maiorum cineres tibi, Roma, colendos,

    sub quorum titulis, Africa, tunsa iaces,

te, Perseu, proavi simulantem pectus Achilli,

40   quique tuas proavo fregit Achille domos,

me neque censurae legem mollisse nec ulla

---

37. colendos **O** verendos **ω**. 38. tunsa **O** tonsa **ω**. 39. te *Santen* et **O**. Perseu *Santen* Persen **LF₂** pseu **F** Persem **NDV**. simulantem **ω** stimulantem **O**. Achilli **O** Achillis **V₂** Achille *Lipsius*. 40. tuas **O** tumens *Postgate* et tumidas *Heyne*.

32. titulis: strictly, the inscriptions placed beneath the masks of the family ancestors, which were kept in the atrium; here used for the famous ancestors themselves as an illustrious line.

33. praetexta: the purple-bordered garment of childhood, which girls laid aside at marriage.

34. altera vitta: *i.e.* the dressing of the hair in the mode of the *sex crines* according to the custom of Roman matrons.

35. sic discessura: cf. the formula, "till death us do part."

36. lapide hoc suggests the use of this elegy as a sepulchral inscription. — **uni nupta**: regarded as a special glory to a woman: cf. *CIL.* 6, 14404, 8: *diceris coniunxs una fuisse viri.*

38. sub . . . titulis . . . iaces: perhaps the poet is thinking of some artistic representation of the humiliation of Carthage, with suitable inscriptions; but *titulis* may be used here much as in verse 32.

39. te . . . quique . . . fregit = *eum qui te . . . et . . . fregit.* Cornelia is appealing to another illustrious member of her family, Aemilius Paullus, who was conqueror of Perseus, and the father of the Scipio Numantinus of verse 30, who came into the Cornelian family by adoption. — **proavi**: Perseus traced his descent through Pyrrhus to Achilles. — **simulantem pectus**: 'making a bluff at the spirit.' — **Achilli**: one of the several variant forms for this gen.

40. proavo . . Achille: scornfully concessive.

41. censurae legem: 'the strictness of the Censor's ideal.' Her husband, Paullus, was one of the Censors in 22 B.C., but disagreed with his colleague L. Munatius;

labe mea vestros erubuisse focos.

non fuit exuviis tantis Cornelia damnum,

quin erat et magnae pars imitanda domus.

45 nec mea mutata est aetas, sine crimine totast :

viximus insignes inter utramque facem.

mi natura dedit leges a sanguine ductas,

ne possem melior iudicis esse metu.

quaelibet austeras de me ferat urna tabellas :

50 turpior adsessu non erit ulla meo,

vel tu, quae tardam movisti fune Cybeben,

Claudia, turritae rara ministra deae,

vel cuius, sacros cum Vesta reposceret ignes,

---

48. ne possem ω ne possim **V₂** ne possis **O** nec *Scaliger*.   51. Cybeben *Lachmann* Cybellem **NDV** Cibelem **FL**.   53. cuius sacros *Rothstein* cuius rasos **O** cui commissos ω cui iuratos *Phillimore*.

---

cf. Vell. Pat. 2, 95, 3. — **mollisse**: 'gave occasion to tone down.'

43. exuviis: *i.e.* 'glory.' — **Cornelia**: 'a Cornelia.'

44. et = *etiam*: 'even.'

45. aetas: cf. 1, 6, 21, n.

46. utramque facem: the torch of the wedding procession and that with which the funeral pyre was kindled. Cf. Ovid, *Fast.* 2, 561 : *conde tuas, Hymenaee, faces et ab ignibus atris aufer! habent alias maesta sepulcra faces.*

49. quaelibet . . . urna: *i.e.* whatever court, no matter how strict. — **tabellas**: the votes of the judges (jury) : these would be marked either C (*condemno*), A (*absolvo*), or N L (*non liquet*).

50. It was the custom for friends to sit beside the accused at trials.

51. tu : Claudia Quinta, a vestal virgin accused of unchastity, who, when the image of Cybele was being brought to Rome, was able, after praying to the goddess, to move the boat, which had grounded in the Tiber, and was thus vindicated ; cf. Suet. *Tib.* 2. — **tardam** : referring to the boat carrying the sacred images and mysteries of the goddess.

52. turritae : referring to the mural crown worn by the goddess as guardian of cities.

53. cuius : sc. *illa*. Aemilia, a *virgo vestalis maxima*, who allowed the sacred fire to go out, was vindicated when her linen garment, which she had thrown upon the hearth sprang into flame. Cf. Val. Max. 1, 1, 7.

exhibuit vivos carbasus alba focos.
55 nec te, dulce caput, mater Scribonia, laesi:
in me mutatum quid nisi fata velis?
maternis laudor lacrimis urbisque querellis,
defensa et gemitu Caesaris ossa mea.
ille sua nata dignam vixisse sororem
60   increpat, et lacrimas vidimus ire deo.
et tamen emerui generosos vestis honores,
nec mea de sterili facta rapina domo.
tu, Lepide, et tu, Paulle, meum post fata levamen:
condita sunt vestro lumina nostra sinu.
65 vidimus et fratrem sellam geminasse curulem;
consul quo factus tempore, rapta soror.

66. consul quo factus *Lachmann* consule quo facto **O** festo *Koppiers.*

54. alba: the prescribed dress of the vestals was white. — focos = *ignes.*

55. caput: here = 'heart'; cf. verse 10, n.—Scribonia: she had been divorced from Augustus since 39 B.C.

56. A common phrase in sepulchral inscriptions is: *de qua vir nil doluit nisi mortem.*

58. ossa: cf. verse 20.

59. nata: Julia, the daughter of Augustus by Scribonia. The poet carefully ignores the scandalous looseness of Julia's character, which was no credit to Cornelia. — sororem: Cornelia, half-sister, daughter of Cornelius and Scribonia.

60. increpat: 'complains'; followed by the inf. also in 3, 10, 10. — deo: cf. 3, 4, 1, n.

61. emerui . . . honores: *i.e.* as the mother of their children, 'I have earned the right to wear the *stola* of honor' (supposed to be awarded to those mothers who thus had fulfilled the condition of the *ius trium liberorum*). — generosos: by hypallage for *generosae.*

63. Lepide . . . Paulle: the sons who were to perpetuate the family name. The former, who was the younger, was consul in 6 A.D. The latter, consul in 1 A.D., married Julia, the daughter of Agrippa.

64. condita: 'closed.'

65. fratrem: P.Cornelius Scipio. — geminasse: 'occupy a second time.' He was consul in 16 B.C. and had presumably been praetor already, as it was no longer necessary to precede the major offices with the curule aedileship.

filia, tu specimen censurae nata paternae,
    fac teneas unum nos imitata virum,
et serie fulcite genus : mihi cymba volenti
70   solvitur aucturis tot mea fata meis.
haec est feminei merces extrema triumphi,
    laudat ubi emeritum libera fama rogum.
nunc tibi commendo communia pignora natos :
    hac cura et cineri spirat inusta meo.
75   fungere maternis vicibus, pater : illa meorum
    omnis erit collo turba ferenda tuo.
oscula cum dederis tua flentibus, adice matris :
    tota domus coepit nunc onus esse tuum.
et siquid doliturus eris, sine testibus illis :

70. aucturis ω uncturis **LDV** nupturis **F.**

67. filia: Lepida was probably born in the year of her father's censorship, 22 B.C. — **specimen**: how much Cornelia meant by this expression it is difficult to tell. The daughter's birth at that time, her likeness to her parents as an indication that her father and mother practiced what they preached, and a model life to follow — all these at least may have been in her mother's mind.

69. serie: *i.e.* of descendants. — **fulcite**: Cornelia is now speaking to all three of her children ; cf. Sen. Rhetor, *Contr.* 2, 1, 7: *non tibi per multos fulta liberos domus est.* Cf. English "pillar of the church." — **cymba**: Charon's.

70. aucturis . . . mea fata: 'destined to add luster to my fame'; the abl. abs. is causal.

71. feminei . . . triumphi: the only triumphal procession a woman could have was that of a funeral like Cornelia's.

72. emeritum . . . rogum: cf. verse 8, n. — **libera fama**: 'repute freely expressed.'

73. tibi: she turns to her husband.

74. spirat: 'lives on.' — **inusta**: cf. Cic. *Ver.* 2, 1, 113: *cur hunc dolorem cineri eius atque ossibus inussisti?* Butler cites Gray's *Elegy*: "Ev'n in our ashes live their wonted fires."

75. Cf. Eurip. *Alc.* 377 : σὺ νῦν γενοῦ τοῖσδ᾽ ἀντ᾽ ἐμοῦ μήτηρ τέκνοις.

76. turba: cf. verses 31 and 98.

79. sine testibus illis: sc. *dole.*

80   cum venient, siccis oscula falle genis.

sat tibi sint noctes quas de me, Paulle, fatiges,

     somniaque in faciem credita saepe meam:

atque ubi secreto nostra ad simulacra loqueris,

     ut responsurae singula verba tace.

85   seu tamen adversum mutarit ianua lectum,

     sederit et nostro cauta noverca toro,

coniugium, pueri, laudate et ferte paternum:

     capta dabit vestris moribus illa manus.

nec matrem laudate nimis: conlata priori

84. tace O iace ω.

80. oscula = *eos osculantes.* Paullus is to maintain cheerfulness for his children's sake.

81. quas . . . fatiges: 'to pass in sleepless weariness.' By day he must take up life's burdens.

82. 'And the visions in which you believe you see my face.'

83. simulacra: likenesses of wax or marble, in lieu of the modern photograph. Cf. Ovid, *Her.* 13, 157.

84. ut responsurae: 'as if you expected me to reply.'— **singula verba tace**: he is to make it like a conversation rather than an address.

85. seu corresponds to the *seu* in verse 91. — **tamen**: *i.e.* in spite of such matrimonial love as now exists between us, Paullus and Cornelia. — **adversum . . . lectum**: the marriage bed (*lectus genialis*) at times of weddings stood in the back part of the atrium directly opposite the front door. Long

before this period this bed (which in more primitive times probably also served as a sofa in the daytime) was usually removed to a *cubiculum* after the wedding ceremonies were entirely completed, and in its place stood the sofa which was the special seat of honor of the *materfamilias* (*lectus adversus*); cf. Ascon. *Mil.* (K. and S.) p. 38: *imagines . . . maiorum deiecerunt et lectulum adversum uxoris eius Corneliae . . . fregerunt*; Laberius, *Compitalia: materfamilias tua in lecto adverso sedet.* — **mutarit ianua**: with poetic license Propertius makes the door responsible for the changes involved in arranging the furniture for a new marriage and admitting a new bride.

87. pueri: 'children.'

88. dabit . . . manus: the imagery is military: 'will surrender' (*i.e.* her heart).

89. conlata: hypothetical.

90   vertet in offensas libera verba suas.

      seu memor ille mea contentus manserit umbra
          et tanti cineres duxerit esse meos,
      discite venturam iam nunc sentire senectam,
          caelibis ad curas nec vacet ulla via.

95   quod mihi detractum est, vestros accedat ad annos:
          prole mea Paullum sic iuvet esse senem.
      et bene habet: numquam mater lugubria sumpsi:
          venit in exequias tota caterva meas.
      causa perorata est.   flentes me surgite, testes,

100   dum pretium vitae grata rependit humus.
      moribus et caelum patuit: sim digna merendo,
          cuius honoratis ossa vehantur aquis.

---

93. sentire O lenire *Schrader*.   102. aquis **NFLV**₂ equis **DV** avis *Heinsius*.

90. **vertet in**: 'will interpret them to imply.'

93. **nunc**: with *sentire*. — **sentire**: 'to realize'; cf. Ovid, *A. A.* 3, 59: *venturae memores iam nunc estote senectae.*

94. **nec vacet ulla via**: 'and leave him no access.'

95. **quod**: sc. *tempus.* Cf. Tib. I, 6, 63: *proprios ego tecum, sit modo fas, annos contribuisse velim.*

96. **prole mea**: a Propertian abl. The idea is essentially causal, however the grammar is to be explained. — **sic**: *i.e.* if you are so spared to comfort him.

97. **bene habet**: 'I am content.' — **lugubria sumpsi**: 'put on mourning.'

99. **flentes ... testes**: Cornelia seems at least to include her family with those previously cited.

100. **dum**: 'while'; she assumes a favorable verdict. — **humus**: *i.e.* the lower world.

101. **moribus** = *bene moratis.* — **et**: 'even.'

102. **honoratis . . . vehantur aquis**: 'to ride in triumph over the dark waters'; *i.e.* to the Elysian fields rather than to a place of punishment.   Cf. 4, 7, 55 sqq.: *nam gemina est sedes turpem sortita per amnem, turbaque diversa remigat omnis aqua. una Clytaemnestrae stuprum vehit . . . ecce coronato pars altera vecta phaselo, mulcet ubi Elysias aura beata rosas,* etc.

OVID MSS. SIGNS

For the
Amores
$\begin{cases}
\textbf{P} = \text{Codex Puteanus.} \\
\textbf{R} = \text{Codex Regius.} \\
\textbf{S} = \text{Codex Sangallensis.} \\
\textbf{O} = \text{Consensus of } \textbf{PRS.} \\
\boldsymbol{\omega} = \text{late or inferior Mss., or corrections.}
\end{cases}$

For the
Heroides
$\begin{cases}
\textbf{P} = \text{Codex Puteanus.} \\
\textbf{G} = \text{Codex Guelferbytanus.} \\
\textbf{V} = \text{Schedae Vindobonenses.} \\
\boldsymbol{\omega} = \text{late or inferior Mss., or corrections.}
\end{cases}$

For the
Tristia
$\begin{cases}
\textbf{A} = \text{Codex Marcianus Politiani.} \\
\textbf{L} = \text{Codex Laurentianus.} \\
\textbf{G} = \text{Codex Guelferbytanus.} \\
\textbf{H} = \text{Codex Holkhamicus.} \\
\textbf{P} = \text{Codex Palatinus.} \\
\textbf{V} = \text{Codex Vaticanus.} \\
\boldsymbol{\omega} = \text{late or inferior Mss., or corrections.}
\end{cases}$

P. OVIDI NASONIS

AMORVM

LIBER PRIMVS

EPIGRAMMA IPSIVS

Qui modo Nasonis fueramus quinque libelli,
   tres sumus : hoc illi praetulit auctor opus ;
ut iam nulla tibi nos sit legisse voluptas,
   at levior demptis poena duobus erit.

I

Arma gravi numero violentaque bella parabam
   edere, materia conveniente modis ;

AMORES

Epigramma Ipsius : there is no reason to doubt the genuineness of this epigram thus prefixed to the first book of the *Amores*. — **Nasonis** : Ovid is fond of calling himself by his cognomen ; cf. *Am.* 2, 1, 2 ; *Trist.* 5, 13, 1 ; etc. — **quinque** : an earlier edition of the *Amores* was published in five books. Ovid later withdrew some of his more youthful efforts from circulation and published the existing edition in three books. Cf. Cicero's change of plan in the *Academica*. — **libelli** : a term of modesty. — **hoc** illi : ' the present to the earlier.' — **ut** : ' even if.' —

legisse : cf. Tib. 1, 1, 29, **n.**

I, I

1–4 : ' I essayed heroic strains, but Cupid drove me to elegy. 5–20 : "Who gave you the right to interfere?" I complained, "let every cobbler stick to his last." 21–26 : But he drew his unerring bow at me, and now love rules my heart ; 27–30 : so elegy is my province.' Cf. 2, 1, 11 sqq. ; Prop. 3, 3.

1. gravi numero : the hexameter ; cf. *modis* (v. 2) (of the melody) and *inferior versus* (v. 3) (*i.e.* the second of a couplet) for a variety of expression of the general idea.

2. edere : ' to produce.'

par erat inferior versus : risisse Cupido
    dicitur atque unum surripuisse pedem.
5 'quis tibi, saeve puer, dedit hoc in carmina iuris?
    Pieridum vates, non tua turba sumus.
quid, si praeripiat flavae Venus arma Minervae,
    ventilet accensas flava Minerva faces?
quis probet in silvis Cererem regnare iugosis,
10   lege pharetratae virginis arva coli?
crinibus insignem quis acuta cuspide Phoebum
    instruat, Aoniam Marte movente lyram?
sunt tibi magna, puer, nimiumque potentia regna :
    cur opus adfectas, ambitiose, novum?
15 an, quod ubique, tuum est? tua sunt Heliconia Tempe?
    vix etiam Phoebo iam lyra tuta suast?
cum bene surrexit versu nova pagina primo,
    attenuat nervos proximus ille meos;

---

4. **unum . . . pedem**: *i.e.* the two half feet which the pentameter lacks, as compared with the hexameter. — **surripuisse**: the poet was taken unawares, like Apollo when Hermes stole his cattle.

5. **saeve**: a common epithet for Cupid in the elegiac writers; cf. Tib. 3, 4, 65. — **in carmina**: this construction with *ius* is not infrequent in the poets.

6. **vates**: cf. *Am.* 3, 9, 17.

7. **flavae**: so Minerva is described, *e.g.* in *Fast.* 6, 652; *Trist.* I, 10, 1.

8. **ventilet . . . faces**: cf. Prop. 4, 3, 50, n.

9. **in silvis . . . regnare**: *i.e.* attempt the task of Diana.

11. **crinibus**: cf. Tib. 2, 5, 8; Prop. 3, 13, 52: *intonsi Pythia regna dei.* — **cuspide**: the spear (of Mars); the term is common in the poets.

12. **Aoniam**: cf. Prop. I, 2, 28, n.

13. **nimiumque potentia**: 'and all too powerful.'

15. 'Do you "want the earth"?' — **Heliconia Tempe**: the beautiful Thessalian valley through which ran the Peneios here becomes typical, and the poet means the beautiful regions where dwell the Muses, who were commonly located on Helicon.

17. **surrexit**: *i.e.* 'started off.' — **pagina**: sc. *mea*.

18. **ille**: Cupid.

nec mihi materia est numeris levioribus apta,
20   aut puer, aut longas compta puella comas.'
questus eram, pharetra cum protinus ille soluta
    legit in exitium spicula facta meum
lunavitque genu sinuosum fortiter arcum,
    'quod' que 'canas, vates, accipe' dixit 'opus!'
25   me miserum! certas habuit puer ille sagittas:
    uror, et in vacuo pectore regnat Amor.
sex mihi surgat opus numeris, in quinque residat:
    ferrea cum vestris bella valete modis!
cingere litorea flaventia tempora myrto,
30   Musa per undenos emodulanda pedes!

3

Iusta precor.   quae me nuper praedata puellast,
    aut amet, aut faciat cur ego semper amem!

19. nec: adversative; the negative force is carried over to the correlatives *aut* in the following verse. — **numeris levioribus**: elegy.

20. longas: cf. *Am* 3, 3, 3: *quam longos habuit nondum periura capillos.*

22. in exitium: purpose acc.

25. Cf. Prop. 2, 12, 9–12 ; 13, 2.

26. vacuo: 'hitherto fancy-free'; cf. Hor. *Car.* 1, 6, 19: *cantamus, vacui, sive quid urimur.*

27. Cf. Schiller's couplet:
*Im Hexameter steigt des Spring-
    quells flüssige Säule,
Im Pentameter drauf fällt sie
    melodisch herab*;
and Coleridge's English version:

" In the hexameter rises the fountain's silvery column,
In the pentameter aye falling in melody back."

29. cingere: the imperative used reflexively. — **litorea**: cf. Mart. 4, 13, 6: *litora myrtus amat:* for the myrtle as sacred to Venus cf. *A. A.* 3, 53: *dixit et e myrto (myrto nam vincta capillos constiterat) folium granaque pauca dedit.*

I, 3

A model love letter of an ardent, though still somewhat shy lover, who does not even mention the name of his flame.

1–4: 'May Venus favor my suit! 4–10: Accept me, lady, as

ah, nimium volui! tantum patiatur amari:
audierit nostras tot Cytherea preces!
5   accipe, per longos tibi qui deserviat annos,
accipe, qui pura norit amare fide!
si me non veterum commendant magna parentum
nomina, si nostri sanguinis auctor eques,
nec meus innumeris renovatur campus aratris,
10   temperat et sumptus parcus uterque parens:
at Phoebus comitesque novem vitisque repertor
hinc faciunt at, me qui tibi donat, Amor,
at nulli cessura fides, sine crimine mores
nudaque simplicitas purpureusque pudor.

3. 12. hinc *Merkel* haec **PS** hac *Palmer.* at me *Merkel* ut me **P** et me **S**.
13. at *Ehwald* et **O**.

your lover, though I bring you
neither nobility, nor wealth;
11-16: but I have the favor of the
gods, fidelity and constancy.
17-26: Love me, live with me;
and I will make your name as well
known throughout the world as
the names of the heroines of old.'

1. **praedata ... est**: 'has captivated me'; cf. *Am.* 1, 2, 19:
tua sum nova praeda, Cupido.

2. **amet**: his petition to Venus
is in the third person, appropriately, in an address to his lady love.

3. **tantum**: 'simply.'

4. **Cytherea**: cf. *Am.* 2, 17, 4.

5. **accipe**: the poet addresses
the unknown lady, whose shadowy
personality receives the name Corinna first in 1, 5, 9.

7. With this passage cf. Prop.
3, 2, 11 sqq.

8. **eques**: Ovid was proud that

his equestrian rank was not of the
parvenu type; cf. *Am.* 3, 15, 5;
and *Trist.* 4, 10, 7, to which he
adds: *non modo fortunae munere
factus eques.*

9. **renovatur**: cf. Tib. 3, 3, 5, n;
Prop. 3, 5, 5.

10. But the poet's biography in
Trist. 4, 10, and the manner of his
life at Rome do not indicate
straitened circumstances. Cf. Tib.
1, 1, 5, n.

11. **comitesque novem**: the
Muses. — **vitisque repertor**: Bacchus, who also inspired poetry and
song; cf. Tib. 1, 7, 29, n.; Prop.
4, 1, 62.

12. **hinc faciunt**: 'are on my
side'; cf. Cic. *Ad Att.* 7, 3, 5:
dignos illinc facere.

14. **purpureusque pudor**: *i.e.*
modesty such as would cause a
'rosy blush'; cf. *Am.* 2, 5, 34:

15 non mihi mille placent, non sum desultor amoris :
   tu mihi, siqua fides, cura perennis eris.
  tecum, quos dederint annos mihi fila sororum,
   vivere contingat, teque dolente mori ;
  te mihi materiem felicem in carmina praebe :
20   provenient causa carmina digna sua.
  carmine nomen habent exterrita cornibus Io
   et quam fluminea lusit adulter ave
  quaeque super pontum simulato vecta iuvenco
   virginea tenuit cornua vara manu :
25 nos quoque per totum pariter cantabimur orbem,
   iunctaque semper erunt nomina nostra tuis.

15

Quid mihi, Livor edax, ignavos obicis annos
 ingeniique vocas carmen inertis opus ;

conscia purpureus venit in ora pudor.

15. **desultor** : the figure is from the circus rider who leaped from one horse to another ; cf. Prop. 4, 2, 36 : *traicit alterno qui leve pondus equo.*

16. **cura** : cf. 3, 3, 32, n.

17. **fila sororum** : cf. Hor. *Car.* 2, 3, 15 : *dum res et aetas et sororum fila trium patiuntur atra.*

19. **in carmina** : purpose acc.

20. **causa** = *materie :* cf. Prop. 2, 1, 12 : *invenio causas mille poeta novas.*

21. **cornibus Io** : cf. Prop. 2, 28, 17, n.

22. **quam** : Leda, wooed by Juppiter (*adulter*) in the form of a swan (*fluminea . . . ave*).

23. **quaeque** : Europa ; cf. Prop. 2, 28, 52, n.

25. Cf. *Am.* 1, 15, 8.

I, 15

The poet justifies his profession.
1–6 : ' Envy says, I am wasting my time in poetry, which has no practical value. 7–30 : Nay! my work will be immortal, like that of my great Greek and Roman predecessors. 31–34 : Then let all bow before poetry. 35–42 : The rabble may be wedded to their idols, but if Apollo fosters my art, I shall have undying fame after envious tongues have ceased to wag.' With the thought as a whole cf. Prop. 3, 1.

non me more patrum, dum strenua sustinet aetas,
   praemia militiae pulverulenta sequi,
5 nec me verbosas leges ediscere, nec me
   ingrato vocem prostituisse foro ?
mortale est, quod quaeris, opus ; mihi fama perennis
   quaeritur, in toto semper ut orbe canar.
vivet Maeonides, Tenedos dum stabit et Ide,
10   dum rapidas Simois in mare volvet aquas.
vivet et Ascraeus, dum mustis uva tumebit,
   dum cadet incurva falce resecta Ceres.
Battiades semper toto cantabitur orbe :
   quamvis ingenio non valet, arte valet.
15 nulla Sophocleo veniet iactura cothurno.
   cum sole et luna semper Aratus erit.
   dum fallax servus, durus pater, inproba lena

---

1. **Livor edax:** cf. Prop. 1, 8,
29. — **ignavos . . . annos:** cf.
Prop. 1, 12, 1.

5. **verbosas . . . ediscere:** a regular exercise for incipient Roman
citizens, and recognized as a necessary part of their education.

6. Cf. Prop. 4, 1, 134. — **prostituisse** probably implies not merely
public use, but also venality.

8. Cf. 1, 3, 25.

9. **Maeonides:** Homer ; cf. Prop.
2, 28, 29. — **Tenedos:** it is on
the Roman side of the legend
that Tenedos becomes especially
famous; cf. Verg. *Aen.* 2, 21
sqq.

10. **Simois:** cf. Prop. 3, 1, 27.

11. **Ascraeus:** Hesiod ; cf. Prop.
2, 10, 25, n. — **uva tumebit:** one
of the favorite themes in the *Works
and Days* of Hesiod.

12. **Ceres** = *arista.*

13. **Battiades** = Callimachus ;
cf. Cat. 65, 16, n.

14. A most acute characteriza-
tion of the weakness of Callimachus and the other Alexandrians ;
cf. Intr. § 7.

15. **Sophocleo:** Sophocles, chronologically the middle one of the
great group of authors of Greek
tragedy, may well typify this remarkable branch of Greek literature. — **cothurno** : *i.e.* tragedy.

16. **Aratus:** an astronomical
poet from Soli in Cilicia, who
flourished in the third century B.C.,
and wrote Φαινόμενα καὶ Διοσημεῖα,
a work much used by Roman
authors, *e.g.* by Cicero, fragments
of whose *Aratea* still survive.

17. **fallax servus:** with this
group of representative characters

vivent et meretrix blanda, Menandros erit.
Ennius arte carens animosique Accius oris
20 casurum nullo tempore nomen habent.
Varronem primamque ratem quae nesciet aetas
     aureaque Aesonio terga petita duci?
carmina sublimis tunc sunt peritura Lucreti,
     exitio terras cum dabit una dies.
25 Tityrus et segetes Aeneiaque arma legentur,
     Roma triumphati dum caput orbis erit.
donec erunt ignes arcusque Cupidinis arma,

---

15. 19. Accius **S** Actius **P.**   25. segetes (*restored by Bentley*) ω fruges **PS.**

from the New Attic Comedy, described in the apt series of individual epithets, cf. the more complete list of stock characters found in Quint. 11, 3, 74 and 178; Apul. *Flor.* 3, 16.

18. **Menandros**: the most celebrated of the writers of the New Comedy.

19. **Ennius**: the 'father of Roman poetry' properly heads this part of the list of poets; cf. Prop. 3, 3, 6. — **arte carens**: Ovid repeats this judgment in *Trist.* 2, 424: *Ennius ingenio maximus, arte rudis;* cf. Hor. *A. P.* 259: *Enni . . . magno cum pondere versus aut operae celeris nimium curaque carentis aut ignoratae . . . artis;* Prop. 4, 1, 61. — animosique **Accius oris**: Accius was the last and probably the most finished of the great Roman writers of tragedy; with this reference to his sublime manner cf. Hor. *Ep.* 2,

1, 55: *aufert Pacuvius docti famam senis, Accius alti.*

21. **Varronem**: Varro Atacinus, whose works included an imitation of a Greek epic on the Argonautic expedition; cf. Intr. § 12.

22. **Aesonio**: here used as a patronymic.

24. **dabit una dies**: the words of Lucretius himself in 5, 95. Cf. Ovid, *Trist.* 2, 426: *casurumque triplex vaticinatur opus;* Prop. 3, 5, 31, n.

25. **Tityrus**: the opening word of the *Eclogues* of Vergil. — **segetes**: *i.e.* the *Georgics*, treating of this and similar themes. — **arma**: the first word of the *Aeneid*.

26. **triumphati**: *i.e. victi*, as commonly. — **dum caput . . . erit**: cf. Hor. *Car.* 3, 30, 8: *dum Capitolium scandet cum tacita virgine pontifex, dicar.*

27. **ignes** = *faces.* — **arcus**: cf. Prop. 2, 12, 9.

discentur numeri, culte Tibulle, tui.

Gallus et Hesperiis et Gallus notus Eois,

30   et sua cum Gallo nota Lycoris erit.

ergo cum silices, cum dens patientis aratri

depereant aevo, carmina morte carent.

cedant carminibus reges regumque triumphi,

cedat et auriferi ripa benigna Tagi.

35   vilia miretur vulgus; mihi flavus Apollo

pocula Castalia plena ministret aqua,

sustineamque coma metuentem frigora myrtum

atque ita sollicito multus amante legar.

pascitur in vivis Livor, post fata quiescit,

40   cum suus ex merito quemque tuetur honos.

ergo etiam cum me supremus adederit ignis,

vivam, parsque mei multa superstes erit.

38. atque O aque *Mueller.*

29. Gallus: cf. Intr. § 12. — **notus**: cf. Ovid, *A. A.* 3, 537: *Vesper et Eoae novere Lycorida terrae.*

30. Lycoris: cf. Intr. § 12.

31. cum: concessive. — **silices . . . aratri**: cf. Lucr. 1, 313: *stilicidi casus lapidem cavat, uncus aratri ferreus . . . decrescit vomer.*

32. Cf. Prop. 3, 2, 26.

34. auriferi . . . Tagi: the gold-bearing stream of the West, in Spain, corresponding to the Pactolus in the East; cf. Prop. 1, 14, 11; Cat. 29, 19: *amnis aurifer Tagus.*

35. vilia . . . vulgus: cf. Tib. 3, 3, 19-20. — **flavus**: cf. *Am.* 1, 1, 7, n.

36. Castalia: cf. Prop. 3, 3, 13.

37. myrtum: cf. *Am.* 1, 1, 28, n.

38. multus: we should expect the adverb. Cf. *plurimus* in *Trist.* 4, 10, 128. With the whole idea cf. also *Am.* 1, 3, 25; 2, 1, 5: *me legat in sponsi facie non frigida virgo et rudis ignoto tactus amore puer; atque . . . conposuit casus iste poeta meos;* Prop. 3, 3, 19.

39. fata: cf. Prop. 1, 17, 11.

40. Cf. Prop. 3, 1, 22.

41. supremus . . . ignis: *i.e.* on the funeral pyre.

42. parsque mei multa: cf. Hor. *Car.* 3, 30, 6: *non omnis moriar multaque pars mei vitabit Libitinam.*

LIBER SECVNDVS

6

Psittacus, eois imitatrix ales ab Indis,
  occidit: exequias ite frequenter, aves.
ite, piae volucres, et plangite pectora pinnis,
  et rigido teneras ungue notate genas.
5   horrida pro maestis lanietur pluma capillis,
  pro longa resonent carmina vestra tuba.
quod scelus Ismarii quereris, Philomela, tyranni,

2, 6

The death of Corinna's parrot.
The rhetorical wealth of elaboration employed by Ovid on this
somewhat trifling theme furnishes
an excellent commentary on his
mind and art when the elegy is
compared with the familiar little
poem of Catullus on the death of
Lesbia's pet sparrow. Ovid must
have had Catullus in mind; but
the heartfelt simplicity of mourning in the earlier poet was beyond
the reach of his imitator. (Yet
cf. Martinengo, p. 165; Mart. 1,
7; Statius, *Silv.* 2, 4.)
  1-6: 'Come, all ye birds to
mourn Corinna's parrot; 7-10:
Philomela, never mind your old
complaint; 11-16: all come! but
especially you, turtledove, the
parrot's dearest friend. 17-24:
What gifts and graces you had,
parrot! 25-42: It must have been

envy that caused your death, — a
bird so superior to others; but
death is always claiming the best.
43-48: So he died, amid Corinna's
grief; 49-58: he has entered the
bird's paradise; 59-62: and his
tomb has a suitable inscription.'
  1. **imitatrix**: cf. v. 37. —
Indis: cf. Pliny, *N. H.* 10, 117:
India hanc avem mittit, etc.
  2. **exequias**: cf. Prop. 2, 13,
24, n.
  3. **plangite pectora pinnis**: note
the onomatopoetic alliteration.
  4. Cf. Tib. 1, 1, 68.
  5. **capillis**: tearing the hair
was a common expression of
human mourning.
  7. **Ismarii . . . tyranni**: the
Thracian king Tereus, husband
of Philomela and father of Itys.
He betrayed Procne, his wife's
sister, and in revenge Philomela
killed Itys. When Tereus pursued the fleeing sisters, all three

383

     expleta est annis ista querella suis ;
     alitis in rarae miserum devertere funus :
10   magna, set antiqua est causa doloris Itys.
     omnes, quae liquido libratis in aere cursus,
       tu tamen ante alios, turtur amice, dole.
     plena fuit vobis omni concordia vita,
       et stetit ad finem longa tenaxque fides.
15   quod fuit Argolico iuvenis Phoceus Orestae,
       hoc tibi, dum licuit, psittace, turtur erat.
     quid tamen ista fides, quid rari forma coloris,
       quid vox mutandis ingeniosa sonis,
     quid iuvat, ut datus es, nostrae placuisse puellae ?
20   infelix, avium gloria, nempe iaces !
     tu poteras fragiles pinnis hebetare zmaragdos,
       tincta gerens rubro Punica rostra croco.
     non fuit in terris vocum simulantior ales :
       reddebas blaeso tam bene verba sono !
25   raptus es invidia : non tu fera bella movebas ;
       garrulus et placidae pacis amator eras.
     ecce, coturnices inter sua proelia vivunt,

---

6. 9. devertere *Heinsius* devertite **PR** divertite **S** devertito *Mueller.*

were metamorphosed into birds ;
cf. Cat. 65, 14, n.

  11. libratis . . . cursus : 'poise
yourselves'; cf. Verg. *Georg.* 4,
196 : *sese per inania nubila
librant.*

  12. turtur amice : cf. Pliny,
N. H. 10, 207 : *amici pavones et
columbae, turtures et psittaci.*

  15. iuvenis Phoceus : Pylades,
whose friendship with Orestes was
as celebrated as that of Damon
and Pythias.

  17 sqq. : a typical *consolatio* ;
cf. Prop. 3, 18, 11 sqq. — **fides** : *i.e.*
to Corinna.

  19. ut datus es : 'from the
moment you became hers.'

  21. hebetare : by contrast.

  22. Punica : cf. Prop. 3, 3,
32, n.

  23. Cf. v. I.

  26. garrulus : *i.e.* a mere talker,
as contrasted with a fighter.

  27. coturnices : notoriously quar
relsome birds.

forsitan et fiant inde frequenter anus.

plenus eras minimo, nec prae sermonis amore
30   in multos poteras ora vacare cibos.

nux erat esca tibi causaque papavera somni,
pellebatque sitim simplicis umor aquae.

vivit edax voltur ducensque per aera gyros
miluus et pluviae graculus auctor aquae ;

35   vivit et armiferae cornix invisa Minervae,
illa quidem saeclis vix moritura novem :

occidit illa loquax humanae vocis imago,
psittacus, extremo munus ab orbe datum.

optima prima fere manibus rapiuntur avaris :
40   inplentur numeris deteriora suis.

tristia Phylacidae Thersites funera vidit :
iamque cinis, vivis fratribus, Hector erat.

quid referam timidae pro te pia vota puellae,
vota procelloso per mare rapta noto ?

45   septima lux venit, non exhibitura sequentem,

---

28. fiant: the subjunctive of modesty adds a sly thrust to the irony. — **inde**: 'for that very reason.'

29. minimo: sc. *cibo*. The parrot would rather talk than eat.

31. causaque papavera somni: cf. Verg. *Georg.* I, 78: *Lethaeo perfusa papavera somno.*

34. graculus auctor aquae: cf. Prop. 4, 3, 32; but the crow is more common as a messenger of rain; cf. Hor. *Car.* 3, 17, 12: *aquae nisi fallit augur annosa cornix.*

35. invisa Minervae: the crow talked too much, and besides was at enmity with Minerva's favorite, the owl; cf. *Met.* 2, 535 sqq.

36. Cf. v. 34, n.

39. A familiar sentiment; cf. Cat. 3, 13: *malae tenebrae Orci, quae omnia bella devoratis.*

41. Phylacidae: Protesilaus; cf. *Her.* 13; Cat. 68, 74, n. — **Thersites**: the hateful figure of Hom. *Il.* 2, 212 sqq.

42. fratribus: including the cowardly Paris, who brought on all the trouble of the Trojan War.

43. vota: offered during the illness of her parrot.

45. septima: believed by the ancients to be a critical day in certain diseases; Cic. *Ad Fam.* 16, 9, 3 : *ne in quartam hebdomada incideres.*

et stabat vacuo iam tibi Parca colo,

nec tamen ignavo stupuerunt verba palato:

clamavit moriens lingua 'Corinna, vale!'

colle sub Elysio nigra nemus ilice frondet,

50   udaque perpetuo gramine terra viret.

siqua fides dubiis, volucrum locus ille piarum

dicitur, obscenae quo prohibentur aves.

illic innocui late pascuntur olores,

et vivax phoenix, unica semper avis.

55 explicat ipsa suas ales Iunonia pinnas,

oscula dat cupido blanda columba mari.

psittacus has inter nemorali sede receptus

convertit volucres in sua verba pias.

ossa tegit tumulus, tumulus pro corpore magnus,

60   quo lapis exiguus par sibi carmen habet:

'colligor ex ipso dominae placuisse sepulcro;

ora fuere mihi plus ave docta loqui.'

---

46. Parca: Clotho, the emptiness of whose spindle signifies that the thread of life has run out.

49 sqq.: an ideal scene in bird paradise. The poet's imagination is helped by the memory of his boyhood home; cf. 2, 16, 5 sqq.

51. siqua fides dubiis: sc. *est*. For the thought cf. Cat. 96, 1, n.

52. obscenae: 'ill-boding'; cf. Verg. *Aen.* 12, 875: *ne me terrete timentem, obscenae volucres*.

53. olores: poetic for *cygni*.

54. vivax phoenix: which, according to mythology, rose again from its own ashes; cf. the poems on this subject by Claudian and Lactantius.

55. ales Iunonia: the peacock; cf. *A. A.* 1, 627: *laudatas ostendit avis Iunonia pinnas*. Pausanias (2, 17, 6) tells of the golden peacock in the Hera temple at Mycenae.

56. Cf. Cat. 68, 125–127; Prop. 2, 15, 27: *exemplo iunctae tibi sint in amore columbae*.

59. pro corpore magnus: 'correspondingly small.'

60. Cf. Prop. 2, 1, 72: *breve in exiguo marmore nomen ero*.

61. colligor: 'it may be inferred.' — **ex ipso . . . sepulcro**: *i.e.* the very existence of a tomb is a mark of unusual affection.

62. plus ave: *i.e.* like human beings.

I I

Prima malas docuit, mirantibus aequoris undis,
   Peliaco pinus vertice caesa vias,
quae concurrentis inter temeraria cautes
   conspicuam fulvo vellere vexit ovem.
5   o utinam, ne quis remo freta longa moveret,
   Argo funestas pressa bibisset aquas!
ecce, fugit notumque torum sociosque penates,
   fallacisque vias ire Corinna parat.
quid tibi (me miserum!) Zephyros Eurosque timebo
10   et gelidum Borean egelidumque Notum?
non illic urbes, non tu mirabere silvas:
   una est iniusti caerula forma maris.
nec medius tenuis conchas pictosque lapillos

2, 11

Ovid would fain dissuade Corinna from her contemplated journey by sea; but, if she is resolved to go, wishes her *bon voyage*, in the form of a propempticon.

1–8: 'Would that no Argo had ever taught the way of the sea! For now Corinna plans to sail away. 9–32: Dear me! How anxious I shall be! Why do you go? There is nothing on the sea to interest a girl; the land is safe. Let others tell you of the perils of the deep; when once you have embarked, 'tis too late to regret. 33–42: But if you are resolved to go, may the gods protect you, and may you yourself long to return! 43–56: I will be on the watch to

welcome you royally: and you shall tell me of your adventures. Hasten the glad day!'

1. **Prima . . . pinus**: the Argo; cf. Cat. 64, 1: *Peliaco quondam prognatae vertice pinus.* — **mirantibus . . . undis**: cf. Cat. 64, 14–15; *e gurgite vultus aequoreae monstrum Nereides admirantes.*

3. **concurrentis . . . cautes**: the Symplegades; cf. Prop. 2, 26, 39, n.

9. **quid** nearly = *quantum* or *quantopere.*

10. The tradition is that this verse was one of three which Ovid and his friends agreed upon as too artificial.

12. **iniusti**: cf. Prop. 3, 7, 18; 1, 15, 12: *sederat iniusto . . . salo.*

    pontus habet : bibuli litoris illa morast.
15 litora marmoreis pedibus signate, puellae :
    hactenus est tutum, cetera caeca viast.
    et vobis alii ventorum proelia narrent,
        quas Scylla infestet quasve Charybdis aquas,
    et quibus emineant violenta Ceraunia saxis,
20   quo lateant Syrtes magna minorque sinu.
    haec alii referant ; at vos quod quisque loquetur
        credite : quaerenti nulla procella nocet.
    sero respicitur tellus, ubi fune soluto
        currit in inmensum panda carina salum.
25 navita sollicitus quin ventos horret iniquos,
        et prope tam letum quam prope cernit aquam !
    quod si concussas Triton exasperet undas,
        quam tibi sit toto nullus in ore color !
    tum generosa voces fecundae sidera Ledae
30   et 'felix,' dicas 'quem sua terra tenet !'

---

11. 21. at *vulg.* ad **PS.**   22. quaerenti **P** credenti *vulg.*   25. quin
Riese quia **P** qua *Heinsius.*

14. Cf. Prop. 1, 2, 13 ; Lucr. 2,
374–376 : *concharumque genus
. . . qua mollibus undis litoris
incurvi bibulam pavit aequor
harenam.* — mora : *i.e.* cause for
mora.
15. marmoreis pedibus : cf. Cat.
68, 71 ; Verg. *Georg.* 4, 523 : *marmorea caput a cervice revulsum.*
18. Cf. *Am.* 2, 16, 25.
19. Ceraunia : cf. Hor. *Car.* 1,
3, 20 : *infamis scopulos, Acroceraunia.* Particularly dangerous
because near the most natural track
of navigation from Italy to the
east, and *vice versa.*

20. Syrtes : cf. 2, 16, 21 ; Tib.
3, 4, 91 : *horrendave Syrtis.*
These dangerous shoals were
dreaded as much, and were probably quite as destructive of vessels,
in the long run, as the cliffs of
verse 19.
22. quaerenti : *i.e.* inquiring of
others about their adventures.
23. respicitur : the "longing,
lingering look behind."
27. Triton's power over the
waves is described in *Met.* 1, 330
sqq.
29. sidera Ledae : cf. Prop. 1,
17, 18, n.

tutius est fovisse torum, legisse libellos,
  Threiciam digitis increpuisse lyram.
at si vana ferunt volucres mea dicta procellae,
  aequa tamen puppi sit Galatea tuae!
35 vestrum crimen erit talis iactura puellae,
  Nereidesque deae Nereidumque pater.
vade memor nostri vento reditura secundo,
  inpleat illa tuos fortior aura sinus!
tum mare in haec magnus proclinet litora Nereus,
40 huc venti spirent, huc agat aestus aquas!
ipsa roges, Zephyri veniant in lintea soli,
  ipsa tua moveas turgida vela manu.
primus ego adspiciam notam de litore puppim
  et dicam 'nostros advehit illa deos'
45 excipiamque umeris et multa sine ordine carpam
  oscula: pro reditu victima vota cadet,
inque tori formam molles sternentur harenae,
  et tumulus mensae quilibet instar erit.
illic adposito narrabis multa Lyaeo:
50 paene sit ut mediis obruta navis aquis,
  dumque ad me properas, neque iniquae tempora noctis

---

40. aestus *Merkel* (*from old Mss.*) eurus **PS.**   41. soli *vulg.* pleni **PS.**
48. instar erit *vulg.* esse potest **PS.**

31. Cf. Tib. 1, 1, 43-48; the idea of this verse is repeated in *Her.* 3, 117-118.

32. **Threiciam**: because Orpheus was from Thrace.

34. **Galatea**: cf. Prop. 1, 8, 18, n.

35. Cf. Prop. 2, 28, 2.

38. **illa . . . aura**: the *vento . . . secundo* of verse 37.

41. **Zephyri . . . soli**: *i.e.* in their capacity as fair winds, regard-

less of direction. But cf. also v. 9.

45. **excipiamque**: sc. *te.* — **umeris**: the landing is made through the surf; many harbors in Italy and the east are still without facilities for landing voyagers on a pier. — **multa sine ordine**: cf. Cat. 5, 7-13.

49. **Lyaeo** = *vino*, by metonymy.

51. **properas**: note the mood.

　　nec te praecipites extimuisse Notos.
　　omnia pro veris credam, sint ficta licebit:
　　cur ego non votis blandiar ipse meis?
55　haec mihi quam primum caelo nitidissimus alto
　　Lucifer admisso tempora portet equo!

16

　　Pars me Sulmo tenet Paeligni tertia ruris,
　　　parva, sed inriguis ora salubris aquis,
　　sol licet admoto tellurem sidere findat,
　　　et micet Icarii stella proterva canis:
5　arva pererrantur Paeligna liquentibus undis,
　　　et viret in tenero fertilis herba solo.
　　terra ferax Cereris multoque feracior uvis,
　　　dat quoque baciferam Pallada rarus ager,

---

55. Cf. Tib. 1, 3, 93.
56. Cf. Prop. 3, 1, 13.

2, 16

1–10: 'I am in lovely, well-watered Sulmo; 11–14: but without you, my love, I should be discontented in the skies. 15–32: Bad luck to those who invented journeys!—unless, indeed, lovers could ever accompany their lasses; then I would not fear to brave every peril known to travelers, and if shipwreck should come, I would save us both, swimming as Leander did for his Hero. 33–40: Away from you, even fair Sulmo seems a very Caucasus. 41–46: Why must I be without my mate? You swore to stay: why trust a woman's words? 47–52: Yet, if

you care for me, come quickly, and may all obstacles to your progress vanish as you approach!'

1. Sulmo: the birthplace of the poet, in the fertile valley among the mountains of the Paelignian country. Cf. *Trist.* 4, 10, 3.—**tertia**: the two other districts were Corfinium and Superaequium; cf. Pliny, *N. H.* 3, 106.

2. parva: cf. 3, 15, 12 sqq.—**salubris aquis**: cf. 2, 1, 1: *Paelignis natus aquosis.*

3–4. Cf. Tib. 1, 7, 21.—**Icarii . . . canis**: the faithful dog that discovered his master's corpse, and was metamorphosed by Dionysus into the star Sirius.

8. Pallada: by metonymy for the olive, which Pallas gave to the Athenians.

perque resurgentes rivis labentibus herbas
10   gramineus madidam caespes obumbrat humum.
at meus ignis abest: verbo peccavimus uno!
    quae movet ardores, est procul; ardor adest.
non ego, si medius Polluce et Castore ponar,
    in caeli sine te parte fuisse velim.
15 solliciti iaceant terraque premantur iniqua,
    in longas orbem qui secuere vias;
aut iuvenum comites iussissent ire puellas,
    si fuit in longas terra secanda vias!
tum mihi, si premerem ventosas horridus **Alpes,**
20   dummodo cum domina, molle fuisset iter.
cum domina Libycas ausim perrumpere Syrtes
    et dare non aequis vela ferenda Notis.
non quae virgineo portenta sub inguine latrant,
    nec timeam vestros, curva Malea, sinus:
25 non quas submersis ratibus saturata Charybdis
    fundit et effusas ore receptat aquas.
quod si Neptuni ventosa potentia vincit,
    et subventuros auferet unda deos,

16. 25. quas *Postgate from old ed.* qua **P** quae **S.**

10. **obumbrat**: *i.e.* because of
its luxuriance.

11. **ignis**: a familiar metaphor
in the poets; cf. 3, 9, 56.

13. **medius . . . ponar**: *i.e.*
translated, like Castor and Pollux,
to the skies; cf. 2, 11, 29, n.

15. **terraque premantur**: the
curse is the opposite of the customary wish, *sit tibi terra levis*; cf.
Tib. 2, 6, 30.

16. Cf. Tib. 1, 3, 35–36.

17. The form of the wish implies an unfulfilled obligation.

19. There is no sign in Roman
literature of any appreciation
of the beauty and grandeur
of the Alps, in the modern
manner.

23. **virgineo**: *i.e.* of Scylla.

24. **Malea**: the promontory had
a bad name for the stormy weather
that was prevalent there. Cf.
Prop. 3, 19, 8: *saeva Malea*; and
Cape Hatteras to-day.

28. **subventuros**: 'who might be
expected to come to the rescue.'
—**deos**: perhaps the poet is think-

　　tu nostris niveos umeris inpone lacertos:
30　　corpore nos facili dulce feremus onus.
　　saepe petens Heron iuvenis transnaverat undas:
　　　tum quoque transnasset, sed via caeca fuit.
　　at sine te, quamvis operosi vitibus agri
　　　me teneant, quamvis amnibus arva natent
35　　et vocet in rivos currentem rusticus undam,
　　　frigidaque arboreas mulceat aura comas,
　　non ego Paelignos videor celebrare salubres,
　　　non ego natalem, rura paterna, locum,
　　sed Scythiam Cilicasque feros viridesque Britannos,
40　　quaeque Prometheo saxa cruore rubent.
　　ulmus amat vitem, vitis non deserit ulmum:
　　　separor a domina cur ego saepe mea?
　　at mihi te comitem iuraras usque futuram
　　　per me perque oculos, sidera nostra, tuos.

---

ing of the images of the gods carried on the afterpart of the ship.

31. iuvenis: Leander, who, according to the familiar story, swam the Hellespont every night to visit his beloved Hero; cf. *Her.* 17 and 18.

32. tum: on the fatal night when the storm extinguished his guiding light and he perished in the waves.

35. vocet . . . rusticus: the practice of artificial irrigation is no modern invention.

36. mulceat: 'caress'; cf. Cat. 62, 41 : [*flos*] *quem mulcent aurae;* Prop. 4, 7, 60 : *mulcet ubi Elysias aura beata rosas.*

39. A series of the most forbid-

ding places, to Roman thought, in the cold and barren north.

40. saxa: *i.e.* the Caucasus Mountains; cf. Hor. *Car.* 1, 22, 6: *inhospitalem Caucasum.*

41. ulmus amat vitem: the elm was the favorite tree for a vine-prop; the vine was said to be wedded to any tree so used, and other trees to be unwedded; cf. Hor. *Epod.* 2, 9-10 : *adulta vitium propagine altas maritat populos;* *Car.* 2, 15, 4 : *platanusque caelebs;* Cat. 62, 49 sqq. : *ut vidua . . . vitis . . . si forte eadem est ulmo coniuncta marito.*

44. oculos, sidera nostra, tuos: cf. Tib. 4, 2, 5-6; Prop. 2, 3, 14 : *non oculi, geminae, sidera nostra, faces.*

45 verba puellarum, foliis leviora caducis,

  inrita, qua visum est, ventus et unda ferunt.

siqua mei tamen est in te pia cura relicti,

  incipe pollicitis addere facta tuis,

parvaque quam primum rapientibus esseda mannis

50   ipsa per admissas concute lora iubas.

at vos, qua veniet, tumidi subsidite montes,

  et faciles curvis vallibus este viae!

17

Siquis erit, qui turpe putet servire puellae,

  illo convincar iudice turpis ego.

sim licet infamis, dum me moderatius urat,

  quae Paphon et fluctu pulsa Cythera tenet.

5 atque utinam dominae miti quoque praeda fuissem,

---

45. foliis leviora: cf. *Her.* 5, 109: *tu levior foliis.*

46. ventus et unda: cf. Cat. 70, 4.

47. Cf. Tib. 4, 11, 1.

49. rapientibus esseda mannis: a rig suitable for a stylish young lady. Cf. Prop. 2, 32, 5: *cur tua te Herculeum deportant esseda Tibur?* Hor. *Epod.* 4.

2, 17

1–10: 'I will gladly be known as Corinna's slave; but I wish she were not so hard a mistress! Her beauty makes her overweening in pride. 11–22: You need not despise me. Calypso, Thetis, Egeria, loved mortal men; and even lovely Venus gave herself to ugly Vulcan. Even my verse illustrates the happy union of greater and less. 23–34: So take me, darling; and you need not be ashamed of me; my verse offers you an enviable glory, and you alone will I sing.'

1. Cf. Prop. 3, 11, 1.

3. urat: cf. 1, 1, 26.

4. Paphon: Paphos, on the island of Cyprus, was a famous center of Aphrodite worship; cf. Hor. *Car.* 1, 30, 1: *Venus, regina Cnidi Paphique.* — **Cythera**: this island, south of the promontory of Malea, was another celebrated home of Aphrodite, and according to one tradition she was born there from the waves of the sea.

5. Cf. Prop. 1, 7, 5–8.

formosae quoniam praeda futurus eram!

dat facies animos: facie violenta Corinnast.

me miserum! cur est tam bene nota sibi?

scilicet a speculi sumuntur imagine fastus:

10   nec nisi conpositam se prius illa videt.

non tibi si facies nimium dat in omnia regni,—

o facies oculos nata tenere meos!—

collatum idcirco tibi me contemnere debes:

aptari magnis inferiora licet.

15   traditur et nymphe mortalis amore Calypso

capta recusantem detinuisse virum.

creditur aequoream Phthio Nereida regi,

Egeriam iusto concubuisse Numae:

Volcano Venerem, quamvis incude relicta

20   turpiter obliquo claudicet ille pede.

carminis hoc ipsum genus inpar: sed tamen apte

---

17. 11. nimium *vulg.* animum P(?)S. in omnia *vulg.* nomina PS et omina *Owen.*

7. **facies**: 'beauty'; cf. v. 11; Prop. 1, 2, 21; etc. — **violenta**: 'presuming.'

9. **speculi . . . imagine**: *i.e.* from admiring one's self in the mirror. — **fastus**: 'proud disdain'; cf. Prop. 1, 1, 3.

10. **conpositam**: 'when adorned.' Corinna, like Cynthia (cf. Prop. 1, 2, *passim*), believed much finery essential to the success of her charms.

11. **in omnia regni**: cf. 1, 1, 13.

12. **tenere**: poetic purpose infinitive with *nata.*

15. **mortalis**: Odysseus.

16. **recusantem**: because he longed to return to his home and his faithful Penelope.

17. **Phthio . . . regi**: Peleus; cf. Cat. 64. — **Nereida**: Thetis.

18. **Egeriam**: the nymph whose shrine was outside the Roman Porta Capena, where she used to give counsel and love to Numa, the early Roman lawgiver.

20. Homer explains the lameness of Vulcan as caused by his fall when thrown out of heaven down to Lemnos; cf. Hom. *Il.* 1, 560 sqq.; later writers represented Venus as making fun of the physical defects of her divine spouse.

21. Cf. 1, 1, 3 sq. — **inpar**: sc. *est.*

iungitur herous cum breviore modo.

tu quoque me, mea lux, in quaslibet accipe leges:
te deceat medio iura dedisse foro.

25 non tibi crimen ero, nec quo laetere remoto:
non erit hic nobis infitiandus amor.

sunt mihi pro magno felicia carmina censu,
et multae per me nomen habere volunt.

novi aliquam, quae se circumferat esse Corinnam:

30 ut fiat, quid non illa dedisse velit?

sed neque diversi ripa labuntur eadem
frigidus Eurotas populiferque Padus,

nec, nisi tu, nostris cantabitur ulla libellis:
ingenio causas tu dabis una meo.

LIBER TERTIVS

9

Memnona si mater, mater ploravit Achillem,
et tangunt magnas tristia fata deas,
flebilis indignos, Elegeia, solve capillos!

22. herous: sc. *modus*; the hexameter was recognized as the regular vehicle of heroic poetical narration; cf. I, I, 2.

23. lux: cf. Cat. 68, 132.

24. deceat: concessive. — **iura dedisse:** *i.e.* as my superior.

25. crimen: 'cause for reproach.'

27. Cf. Prop. I, 8, 39-40.

29. circumferat: 'tells it around'

34. Cf. Prop. I, 12, 20.

3, 9

On the death of Tibullus, 19 B.C. In this beautiful elegy Ovid, whose acquaintance with Tibullus was all too short (cf. Intr. § 38; *Trist.* 4, 10, 51), drops the conventional formality of most of the *Amores*, and we seem to see the genuine sorrow of a sympathetic soul. Moreover, when death touches the poets' guild, Ovid too is touched, and aroused to claim

ah, nimis ex vero nunc tibi nomen erit!
5 ille tui vates operis, tua fama, Tibullus
ardet in extructo, corpus inane, rogo.
ecce, puer Veneris fert eversamque pharetram
et fractos arcus et sine luce facem.
adspice, demissis ut eat miserabilis alis
10 pectoraque infesta tundat aperta manu!
excipiunt lacrimas sparsi per colla capilli,
oraque singultu concutiente sonant.
fratris in Aeneae sic illum funere dicunt

immortality for his work. As a *consolatio* it may be compared with 2, 6, and Prop. 3, 7; 18; 4, 11.

1–6: 'Mourn, Elegy! for thy chief exemplar is no more. 7–16: Venus and Cupid are in tears. 17–32: What a mockery to suppose that poets bear charmed lives! think of Orpheus, Linus, Homer! Nay, 'tis their work that is immortal. 33–46: What availed thee all thy piety? the gods, if gods there be, heed not. 47–58: Yet, how much worse it might have been! Thy mother and sister, Delia and Nemesis too, were by thy bedside, Tibullus. 59–66: If there be an Elysium, Tibullus will be there with Calvus, Catullus, and Gallus. 67–68: Peace to thine ashes!'

1. **Memnona**: son of Tithonus and Eos, king of the Ethiopians. He went to the assistance of the Trojans after the death of Hector, and was killed by Achilles. Cf. *Met.* 13, 621 sqq. — **mater . . . Achillem**: Thetis in turn had to

bewail her wonderful son, who so narrowly escaped immortality.

3. **flebilis**: *i.e.* elegy of the threnetic type. — **indignos**: that have deserved no such bereavement as the early death of Tibullus. — **Elegeia**: here personified, to address.

4. **ex vero . . . nomen**: cf. Intr. §2.

6. **corpus inane**: cf. Prop. 3, 18, 32.

7–8. Cupid's regular attributes are so disordered as to indicate mourning.

8. Cf. Tib. 2, 6, 15–16.

9. **alis**: cf. Prop. 2, 12, 5, n.

10. One of the signs of mourning; cf. 2, 6, 3; 3, 6, 57: *quid fles et madidos lacrimis corrumpis ocellos pectoraque insana plangis aperta manu?*

11. For disheveled hair as a sign of mourning cf. Tib. 3, 2, 11.

12. **concutiente**: 'convulsive.'

13. **fratris**: Aeneas, like Cupid, was a son of Venus. Cf. Verg. *Aen.* 1, 667: *frater ut Aeneas.*

egressum tectis, pulcher Iule, tuis.
15   nec minus est confusa Venus moriente Tibullo,
        quam iuveni rupit cum ferus inguen aper.
   .   at sacri vates et divum cura vocamur!
        sunt etiam, qui nos numen habere putent!
        scilicet omne sacrum mors inportuna profanat,
20   omnibus obscuras inicit illa manus.
        quid pater Ismario, quid mater profuit, Orpheo?
        carmine quid victas obstipuisse feras?
        et Linon in silvis idem pater 'aelinon!' altis
        dicitur invita concinuisse lyra.
25   adice Maeoniden, a quo, ceu fonte perenni,

---

9. 23.   et Linon **P** aelinon . . . aelinon *vulg.*

---

14. pulcher Iule: cf. Verg. *Aen.*
I, 709: *mirantur Iulum flagran-
tesque dei vultus.*

15. est confusa Venus: because
Tibullus was a poet of love.

16. iuveni: Adonis, beloved of
Venus, but mortally wounded in
the hunt by a wild boar.

17. at . . . vocamur: ironical:
'yet they say that we are.' — **vates**:
cf. I, I, 6; Tib. 3, 4, 43: '*salve,
cura deum: casto nam rite poetae
Phoebusque et Bacchus Pieridesque
favent.*'

18. numen: cf. our expression,
"divine afflatus."

19. scilicet : not ironical, but
here with conviction. — **profanat**:
death made ceremonially unclean
the place and the persons immediately concerned. The cypress
at the door was the sign of the

presence of this uncleanness; cf.
the ancient Hebrew law.

20. obscuras: cf. Tib. I, 3, 4.

21. pater: Apollo, who was
also father of Linus (v. 23). —
Ismario: *i.e.* Thracian, from Mt.
Ismarus. — **mater**: Calliope. — **Or-
pheo**: note the synizesis.

22. victas: 'captivated.'

23. Linon: son of Psamathe
and Apollo. — **aelinon** = αἴλινον:
'Ah! Linus!' cf. the origin of
the word *elegeia*, Intr. -§ 2. It
is a second accusative with *concinuisse* and *Linon* in a double
accusative construction.

25. Maeoniden: cf. I, 15, 9;
Trist. 4, 10, 22; Prop. 2, 28, 29. —
fonte perenni: the debt of all
the poets to Homer was recognized more and more in Roman
times.

vatum Pieriis ora rigantur aquis :
hunc quoque summa dies nigro submersit Averno :
    defugiunt avidos carmina sola rogos.
durat opus vatum, Troiani fama laboris,
30   tardaque nocturno tela retexta dolo.
sic Nemesis longum, sic Delia nomen habebunt,
    altera cura recens, altera primus amor.
quid vos sacra iuvant ? quid nunc Aegyptia prosunt
    sistra ? quid in vacuo secubuisse toro ?
35   cum rapiunt mala fata bonos, — ignoscite fasso ! —
    sollicitor nullos esse putare deos.
vive pius : moriere pius. cole sacra : colentem
    mors gravis a templis in cava busta trahet.
carminibus confide bonis : iacet ecce Tibullus ;
40   vix manet e toto, parva quod urna capit.
tene, sacer vates, flammae rapuere rogales
    pectoribus pasci nec timuere tuis ?
aurea sanctorum potuissent templa deorum

28. defugiunt *J . C. Jahn from* 2 *Mss.*

26. Pieriis . . . aquis: the inspiring springs of the Muses, Aganippe, Hippocrene, Castalia.

27. Averno: the term is typical for the entrance to the lower world.

28. Cf. 1, 15, 32 ; Prop. 3, 2, 25–26.

29. Troiani fama laboris: the *Iliad*.

30. The *Odyssey*, represented by Penelope's well-known trick to put off the suitors.

31. The first book of Tibullus may be called a Delia book, though not with so good ground as the *Cynthia Monobiblos* of Propertius is so named. The second book,

likewise, may be designated the Nemesis book.

32. cura = *amor* = *amata* ; cf. Prop. 1, 1, 36, n.

33. Cf. Tib. 1, 3, 23–24.

35. Cf. 2, 6, 39 ; Tib. 1, 3, 52 ; Prop. 3, 7, 18.

37. The imperatives have concessive force.

40. Cf. *Met.* 12, 610 sq.: *iam cinis est ; et de tam magno restat Achille nescio quid, parvam quod non bene conpleat urnam.*

41. tene: the question is exclamatory, expressing surprised incredulity.

43. potuissent: sc. *flammae.*

    urere, quae tantum sustinuere nefas.

45   avertit vultus, Erycis quae possidet arces:

       sunt quoque, qui lacrimas continuisse negant.

    sed tamen hoc melius, quam si Phaeacia tellus

       ignotum vili supposuisset humo.

    hinc certe madidos fugientis pressit ocellos

50   mater et in cineres ultima dona tulit;

    hinc soror in partem misera cum matre doloris

       venit inornatas dilaniata comas,

    cumque tuis sua iunxerunt Nemesisque priorque

       oscula nec solos destituere rogos.

55   Delia descendens 'felicius' inquit 'amata

       sum tibi: vixisti, dum tuus ignis eram.'

    cui Nemesis 'quid' ait 'tibi sunt mea damna dolori?

       me tenuit moriens deficiente manu.'

    si tamen e nobis aliquid nisi nomen et umbra

60   restat, in Elysia valle Tibullus erit:

    obvius huic venias hedera iuvenalia cinctus

       tempora cum Calvo, docte Catulle, tuo;

44. sustinuere: *i.e.* ventured.

45. quae: Venus Erycina, whose temple was on the heights of Mt. Eryx.

46. continuisse: sc. *te*; cf. Tib. I, 3, 27.

47. Cf. Tib. I, 3.

49. hinc ... hinc: 'on one side ... on the other.' — fugientis: 'as his spirit fled.' — pressit: 'closed.'

52. inornatas dilaniata comas: cf. v. 11, n.

53. tuis: sc. *propinquis.* — priorque: Delia; cf. Tib. I, I, 61, for the poetic prophecy of which this was the fulfillment.

55. descendens: from the funeral pyre.

56. vixisti: cf. Cat. 68, 34, n. — ignis: cf. 2, 16, 11, n.

58. Thus Nemesis claims for herself the fulfillment of what Tibullus in I, I, 60, had wished might be the function of Delia.

59. Cf. *Trist.* 4, 10, 85; Cat. 96, I, n.; Prop. 2, 34, 53: *si post Stygias aliquid restabimus undas.*

61. hedera ... cinctus: the ivy of Bacchus, inspirer of poetry, was appropriate for poets' wreaths.

62. Calvo: cf. Intr. § 12. — docte: cf. Intr. § 16.

tu quoque, si falsum est temerati crimen amici,
  sanguinis atque animae prodige Galle tuae.
65 his comes umbra tua est; siqua est modo corporis
      umbra,
  auxisti numeros, culte Tibulle, pios.
ossa quieta, precor, tuta requiescite in urna,
  et sit humus cineri non onerosa tuo!

15

Quaere novum vatem, tenerorum mater Amorum:
  raditur hic elegis ultima meta meis;
quos ego conposui, Paeligni ruris alumnus
  (nec me deliciae dedecuere meae),
5 siquid id est, usque a proavis vetus ordinis heres,

63. **amici**: Augustus; cf. Intr. § 12. — The form of the hypothesis implies the belief of Ovid, which was probably well grounded, that the particular accusation which drove Gallus to suicide was false.

65. Cf. v. 59, n.

67. Cf. Buecheler, *Car. Epig. passim.*

68. = S·T·T·L. Cf. Tib. 2, 6, 30, n.

3, 15

In saying farewell to erotic elegy the poet takes occasion also to speak of his origin and to claim great fame for his work; cf. Hor. *Car.* 3, 30; Prop. 1, 22.

1–2: 'Venus, search for a new bard! 3–16: Sulmo shall henceforth be known as the birthplace of Ovid, the poet of love; 17–20: but now Bacchus calls me on to broader fields.'

1. **mater**: Venus.

2. **raditur . . . meta**: this kind of poetic composition has run its course, and according to the figure of circus racing is now for the last time rounding the *meta*. In the race the driver's skill was shown by avoiding the *meta* as narrowly as possible.

3. **alumnus**: the relation of a native to his country.

4. **deliciae**: erotic poetry; cf. Cat. 68, 26. — **dedecuere**: Ovid was more inclined to speak apologetically in after years, however.

5. The same verse occurs in *Trist.* 4, 10, 7; Ovid was proud that he was no *parvenu* knight,

non modo militiae turbine factus eques.
Mantua Vergilio gaudet, Verona Catullo :
     Paelignae dicar gloria gentis ego,
quam sua libertas ad honesta coegerat arma,
10   cum timuit socias anxia Roma manus.
atque aliquis spectans hospes Sulmonis aquosi
     moenia, quae campi iugera pauca tenent,
' quae tantum ' dicat ' potuistis ferre poetam,
     quantulacumque estis, vos ego magna voco.'
15 culte puer, puerique parens Amathusia culti,
     aurea de campo vellite signa meo.
corniger increpuit thyrso graviore Lyaeus :
     pulsanda est magnis area maior equis.
inbelles elegi, genialis Musa, valete,
20   post mea mansurum fata superstes opus!

but belonged to an old equestrian line ; cf. Intr. § 38.

6. As a slave was whirled around when formally freed, so the whirligig of military life often suddenly made an equestrian out of a man of ignoble birth.

7. Cf. Mart. 14, 195 : *Tantum magna suo debet Verona Catullo, quantum parva suo Mantua Vergilio.*

8. gloria : ' pride.'

9. libertas : ' longing after freedom.'

10. socias : the Paeligni were leaders in the *bellum sociale.*

11. Cf. Prop. 4, 1, 65–66. — **aquosi** : cf. *Trist.* 4, 10, 3.

15. Amathusia : like Cytheris, Cypria, Erycina, and other similar proper adjectives, referring to a

favorite seat of the worship of Venus, here Amathus in Cyprus.

16. Decamp! your campaign is finished.

17. corniger : cf. Tib. 2, 1, 3, n. — **thyrso graviore** : an inspiration to more serious writing. Bacchus was responsible for tragedy as well as for comedy, and was looked upon as a patron of all poetry. Cf. Prop. 3, 2, 9, n.

18. area maior : the figure of verse 2 is repeated in another form ; cf. 3, 1, 26 : "*haec animo*" dices "*area facta meost*" ; Prop. 2, 10, 2.

19. genialis : in the modern sense of the word ; cf. 2, 13, 7 : *genialiaque arva Canopi.*

20. fata : cf. Prop. 1, 19, 1–2, n.

EPISTVLARVM HEROIDVM LIBER

13

LAODAMIA PROTESILAO

Mittit et optat amans, quo mittitur, ire salutem
  Haemonis Haemonio Laodamia viro.
Aulide te fama est vento retinente morari:
  ah, me cum fugeres, hic ubi ventus erat?
5 tum freta debuerant vestris obsistere remis,
  illud erat saevis utile tempus aquis.
oscula plura viro mandataque plura dedissem:

HEROIDES, 13.

For the *Heroides* cf. Intr. § 39;
Prop. 4, 3, Intr. For the story of
Laodamia cf. Cat. 68, 73, n; Hom.
Il. 2, 698–702; Lucian, *Dial. Mort.*
23. The tradition that Protesilaus, allowed to return to earth to
visit his wife, found her embracing
his image, is here utilized by Ovid
in another form (vv. 151–158).

1–2: 'Loving greetings! 3–10:
Why did you sail, against unwilling winds? 11–28: I said, "Good-
bye," watched you out of sight, and
swooned away; why did I not die?
29–42: Since then I mourn; 43–64:
Paris, Menelaos, ye gods, spare
my husband! How I dread those
Trojan places and men! 65–92:
Be careful! you have no need to
risk your life; and the omens were
unpropitious on your departure;

93–106: And that dreadful oracle!
see that you don't fulfill it! but
hurry back to comfort me. 107–
122: Why in my visions are you
sad? When shall I see you in
very truth, and embrace you as I
listen to the story of your deeds?
123–136: Troy! gloomy thought!
why should the Greeks hurry
thither for such a cause? 137–150:
How I envy the women of Troy
and their happy husbands, who
can cheer each other before and
after battle! 151–158: I can only
comfort myself with your image.
159–164: I will follow you in life
or death. 165–166: Again I say,
be careful!'

2. **Haemonis** = *Thessala*; cf.
Prop. 2, 10, 2.

6. **saevis**: *i.e. esse saevis* ('for-
bidding').

7. **dedissem**: sc. *si freta obsti-
tissent.*

et sunt quae volui dicere multa tibi.
raptus es hinc praeceps, et qui tua vela vocaret,
10   quem cuperent nautae, non ego, ventus erat.
ventus erat nautis aptus, non aptus amanti:
    solvor ab amplexu, Protesilae, tuo,
linguaque mandantis verba inperfecta reliquit:
    vix illud potui dicere triste ' vale.'
15   incubuit Boreas abreptaque vela tetendit,
    iamque meus longe Protesilaus erat.
dum potui spectare virum, spectare iuvabat,
    sumque tuos oculos usque secuta meis.
ut te non poteram, poteram tua vela videre,
20   vela diu vultus detinuere meos.
at postquam nec te, nec vela fugacia vidi,
    et quod spectarem, nil nisi pontus erat,
lux quoque tecum abiit, tenebrisque exanguis obortis
    succiduo dicor procubuisse genu.
25   vix socer Iphiclus, vix me grandaevus Acastus,
    vix mater gelida maesta refecit aqua.
officium fecere pium, sed inutile nobis:
    indignor, miserae non licuisse mori!
ut rediit animus, pariter rediere dolores.
30   pectora legitimus casta momordit amor.
nec mihi pectendos cura est praebere capillos,
    nec libet aurata corpora veste tegi.
ut, quas pampinea tetigisse Bicorniger hasta,

13. **mandantis**: sc. *mei* (*mea*).
16. **erat** = *aberat*.
23. **obortis**: sc. *mihi* (= *meis oculis*).
25. **Iphiclus**: king of Phylace; cf. v. 35. — **Acastus**: Laodamia's father; according to one tradition, one of the Argonauts.

28. **indignor**: 'I feel abused.'
29. **rediit**: it is in compounds of *eo* in Ovid that the long quantity is often found.
30. Cf. Prop. 4, 3, 49.
33. **quas**: the Bacchantes. — **pampinea . . . Bicorniger hasta**: the thyrsus; cf. *Am*. 3, 15, 17.

creditur, huc illuc, qua furor egit, eo.
35   conveniunt matres Phylaceides et mihi clamant
        'indue regales, Laodamia, sinus!'
     scilicet ipsa geram saturatas murice lanas,
        bella sub Iliacis moenibus ille gerat?
     ipsa comas pectar, galea caput ille prematur:
40   ipsa novas vestes, dura vir arma ferat?
     qua possum, squalore tuos imitata labores
        dicar et haec belli tempora tristis agam.
     Dyspari Priamide, damno formose tuorum,
        tam sis hostis iners, quam malus hospes eras!
45   aut te Taenariae faciem culpasse maritae,
        aut illi vellem displicuisse tuam.
     tu, qui pro rapta nimium, Menelae, laboras,
        ei mihi, quam multis flebilis ultor eris!
     di, precor, a nobis omen removete sinistrum,
50   et sua det reduci vir meus arma Iovi.
     sed timeo, quotiens subiit miserabile bellum:
        more nivis lacrimae sole madentis eunt.
     Ilion et Tenedos Simoisque et Xanthus et Ide
        nomina sunt ipso paene timenda sono.

---

13. 37–40 *are mostly lost from* **P.**   37. lanas **ω** vestes *vulg.*   38. gerat
vulg. geret **Gω**.   40. ferat *vulg.* feret **GV**.   41. qua *vulg.* quo **ω**.

35. Phylaceides: Laodamia is
naturally in her husband's home
at Phylace.

37. scilicet: ironical.

38. ille: Protesilaus; cf. Prop.
I, 8, 28, n. on *illa*.

41. qua = *quoquo modo*.

43. Dyspari: 'Paris, ill-omened
son of Priam'; cf. Hom. *Il.* 3, 39;
Δύσπαρι εἶδος ἄριστε, γυναιμανὲς
ἠπεροπευτά.

45. Taenariae . . . maritae:
Helen. Taenarum is the dreaded
cape at the southern extremity of
Laconia.

46. vellem: of a vain wish.

48. flebilis: 'to cause tears ';
cf. Hor. *Car.* I, 24, 9: *multis ille
bonis flebilis occidit.*

50. reduci . . . Iovi: Juppiter
as the author of safe return.

51. subiit: sc. *animo.*

55 nec rapere ausurus, nisi se defendere posset,
        hospes erat: vires noverat ille suas.
    venerat, ut fama est, multo spectabilis auro,
        quique suo Phrygias corpore ferret opes,
    classe virisque potens, per quae fera bella geruntur:
60   et sequitur regni pars quota quemque sui?
    his ego te victam, consors Ledaea gemellis,
        suspicor: haec Danais posse nocere puto.
    Hectora nescio quem timeo: Paris Hectora dixit
        ferrea sanguinea bella movere manu.
65 Hectora, quisquis is est, si sum tibi cara, caveto:
        signatum memori pectore nomen habe.
    hunc ubi vitaris, alios vitare memento
        et multos illic Hectoras esse puta
    et facito, ut dicas, quotiens pugnare parabis:
70   'parcere me iussit Laodamia sibi.'
    si cadere Argolico fas est sub milite Troiam,
        te quoque non ullum vulnus habente cadat!
    pugnet et adversos tendat Menelaus in hostis:
        [ut rapiat Paridi, quae Paris ipsa sibi!
75 inruat et causa quem vicit, vincat et armis:]
        hostibus e mediis nupta petenda virost.
    causa tua est dispar: tu tantum vivere pugna
        inque pios dominae posse redire sinus!

59. **quae** refers to an antecedent including *classe virisque*.

60. **quota**: 'how small'; *i.e.* in proportion to the vast wealth kept in reserve at home.

61. **his**: *i e. opibus.* — **consors Ledaea**: Helen, daughter of Leda, and sister of the twins, Castor and Pollux. For a similar use of *con-*

sors cf. *Met.* 8, 444: *consorti sanguine.*

63. Laodamia has apparently heard only a rumor of what Paris said to Helen, and knows but vaguely of Hector.

71. **fas est**: 'is decreed.'

77. **vivere**: poetic infinitive of purpose.

parcite, Dardanidae, de tot, precor, hostibus uni,
80   ne meus ex illo corpore sanguis eat!
    non est, quem deceat nudo concurrere ferro
        saevaque in oppositos pectora ferre viros;
    fortius ille potest multo, quam pugnat, amare:
        bella gerant alii, Protesilaus amet!
85 nunc fateor: volui revocare, animusque ferebat;
        substitit auspicii lingua timore mali.
    cum foribus velles ad Troiam exire paternis,
        pes tuus offenso limine signa dedit;
    ut vidi, ingemui tacitoque in pectore dixi:
90   'signa reversuri sint, precor, ista viri!'
    haec tibi nunc refero, ne sis animosus in armis:
        fac, meus in ventos hic timor omnis eat!
    sors quoque nescio quem fato designat iniquo,
        qui primus Danaum Troada tangat humum:
95 infelix, quae prima virum lugebit ademptum!
        di faciant, ne tu strenuus esse velis!
    inter mille rates tua sit millensima puppis
        iamque fatigatas ultima verset aquas!
    hoc quoque praemoneo: de nave novissimus exi!
100   non est, quo properes, terra paterna tibi.
    cum venies, remoque move veloque carinam
        inque tuo celerem litore siste gradum!
    sive latet Phoebus seu terris altior exstat,
        tu mihi luce dolor, tu mihi nocte venis,

---

81. est: sc. *Protesilaus*.

86. Laodamia hesitated to speak, for fear she might add some ill-omened word.

88. Cf. Tib. 1, 3, 19–20.

90. Laodamia tried to interpret the omen as favorable.

93. sors: 'an oracular response.'

The word is used loosely, as if one sort of divination was essentially the same as another.

97. mille: 1186 in Homer; cf. Prop. 2, 26, 38, n.

104. dolor: almost the same as *cura*, *i.e.* a cause for worry. — **venis** = *es*.

105 nocte tamen quam luce magis : nox grata puellis,
      quarum suppositus colla lacertus habet.
    aucupor in lecto mendaces caelibe somnos :
      dum careo veris, gaudia falsa iuvant.
    sed tua cur nobis pallens occurrit imago ?
110   cur venit a verbis multa querella tuis ?
    excutior somno simulacraque noctis adoro,
      nulla caret fumo Thessalis ara meo :
    tura damus lacrimamque super, qua sparsa relucet,
      ut solet adfuso surgere flamma mero.
115 quando ego, te reducem cupidis amplexa lacertis,
      languida laetitia solvar ab ipsa mea ?
    quando erit, ut lecto mecum bene iunctus in uno
      militiae referas splendida facta tuae ?
    quae mihi dum referes, quamvis audire iuvabit,
120   multa tamen rapies oscula, multa dabis.
    semper in his apte narrantia verba resistunt :
      promptior est dulci lingua referre mora.
    sed cum Troia subit, subeunt ventique fretumque,
      spes bona sollicito victa timore cadit.
125 hoc quoque, quod venti prohibent exire carinas,
      me movet : invitis ire paratis aquis.

124. sollicito *Merkel* sollicitae *Riese* solliciti **P.**

107. **mendaces** : because in slumber she sees *mendacia somnia*, apparently bringing Protesilaus to her side.

111. **adoro** : *i.e.* to ward off any untoward effect ; cf. Pers. 2, 15 : *Tiberino in gurgite mergis mane caput bis terque, et noctem flumine purgas.*

114. Cf. Prop. 4, 3, 60.

116. **languida laetitia . . . ab . . .** **mea** : 'fainting for very joy.' — **solvar**: 'sink.' — **ipsa** : for a similar position of *ipsa*, cf. *Her.* 12, 18 : *et caderet cultu cultor ab ipse suo.*

121. **his** : *i.e.* osculis. — **apte** : to be taken with *resistunt.*

123. **subit, subeunt** : cf. v. 51, n.

125. **exire** : *i.e.* from Aulis.

126. **invitis . . . aquis** : concessive. — **paratis**, like *prohibent* (v. 125) and *datis* (v. 128), and

quis velit in patriam vento prohibente reverti?
    a patria pelago vela vetante datis!
ipse suam non praebet iter Neptunus ad urbem.
130   quo ruitis? vestras quisque redite domos!
quo ruitis, Danai? ventos audite vetantis!
    non subiti casus, numinis ista morast.
quid petitur tanto nisi turpis adultera bello?
    dum licet, Inachiae vertite vela rates!
135 sed quid ago? revoco? revocaminis omen abesto,
    blandaque conpositas aura secundet aquas.
Troasin invideo, quae sic lacrimosa suorum
    funera conspicient, nec procul hostis erit:
ipsa suis manibus forti nova nupta marito
140 inponet galeam barbaraque arma dabit.
arma dabit, dumque arma dabit, simul oscula sumet —
    hoc genus officii dulce duobus erit —
producetque virum, dabit et mandata reverti,
    et dicet 'referas ista fac arma Iovi!'
145 ille ferens dominae mandata recentia secum
    pugnabit caute respicietque domum.
exuet haec reduci clipeum galeamque resolvet

137. Troasin *Salmasius* Troas **P** Troadas **GV**. quae sic *vulg.* quae si *Heinsius* (**P** ?) qui sic **V** (**P** ?) quamvis *Lehrs*.

the other present tenses in this passage, pictures Laodamia for the moment imagining herself back at the time of the starting of the expedition.

129. suam ... urbem: Neptune and Apollo, according to tradition, built the walls of Troy.

134. Inachiae: Argive, Greek; from Inachus, the traditional first king of Argos.

135. She comes to herself, and fears she may have uttered some ill-omened words in so speaking.

137. Troasin: Greek dative plural of *Troas*. — quae sic: 'even though, as it is, they.' — suorum: whether lovers or husbands.

144. Iovi: cf. v. 50. Ovid makes the Greek Laodamia represent the Trojan wife as thinking in terms of the Roman religion!

excipietque suo corpora lassa sinu.
nos sumus incertae ; nos anxius omnia cogit,
150   quae possunt fieri, facta putare timor.
dum tamen arma geres diverso miles in orbe,
    quae referat vultus est mihi cera tuos.
illi blanditias, illi tibi debita verba
    dicimus, amplexus accipit illa meos.
155 crede mihi, plus est, quam quod videatur, imago :
    adde sonum cerae — Protesilaus erit.
hanc specto teneoque sinu pro coniuge vero,
    ut, tamquam possit verba referre, queror.
per reditus corpusque tuum, mea numina, iuro
160   perque pares animi coniugiique faces
perque, quod ut videam canis albere capillis,
    quod tecum possis ipse referre, caput,
me tibi venturam comitem, quocumque vocaris,
    sive — quod heu ! timeo, sive superstes eris.
165 ultima mandato claudetur epistula parvo :
    si tibi cura mei, sit tibi cura tui !

161-162. *bracketed by Postgate.*   162. quod tecum *vulg.* mox tutum *Riese.*

152. **cera** : wax likenesses of lovers are referred to in *Rem. Am.* 723 : *si potes, et ceras remove.*

158. Cf. Prop. 4, 11, 83.

159. **numina** : *i.e. reditus corpusque tuum* ; cf. *Fast.* 2, 842 : *perque tuos Manes, qui mihi numen erunt.*

161. **perque** : to be taken with *caput.* — **ut videam** : optative.

162. **ipse** : 'in person,' rather than have his ashes brought home by some kind friend.

164. **sive —** : Laodamia avoids speaking the ill-omened word referring to death.

TRISTIVM

LIBER PRIMVS

3

Cum subit illius tristissima noctis imago,
  qua mihi supremum tempus in urbe fuit,
cum repeto noctem, qua tot mihi cara reliqui,
  labitur ex oculis nunc quoque gutta meis.
5 iam prope lux aderat, qua me discedere Caesar

TRISTIA, I, 3

Ovid's last night in Rome. Cf. Intr. § 38. This is one of the most pathetic pictures Ovid has left us, designed, indeed, to move Augustus to relent, yet true to life in its details.

1–4: 'The thought of that night moves me to tears. 5–12: Though the time had arrived, I was too dazed to act or plan. 13–26: At length, trying to collect myself, I spoke farewells; it seemed like a funeral, or the fall of Troy. 27–46: As it grew late, I addressed the gods; my wife, too, with sobs and disheveled locks, offered many vain petitions. 47–68: Night hastened. Often I essayed to go, yet multiplied excuses for delay. Why hurry from Rome to Scythia? Every moment with my dear ones is precious. 69–76: But amid my tears and goodbyes up rose the daystar, and I

tore myself away. 77–90: Loud was the wailing of my loved ones. My wife would fain have accompanied me; but I went like one going alone to his own obsequies. 91–102: They say she swooned, then reviving cried unto the gods and mourned as for the dead. She longed to die; but may she rather live for me!'

1. subit: the thought is commonly completed by *animum* or a similar word; cf. *Met.* 7, 170: *animum subiit Aeeta relictus*.

2. in urbe: from 'the city' no Roman could bear long to be separated; cf. Intr. § 38; Cic. *Ad Att.* 5, 11, 1: *non dici potest quam flagrem desiderio urbis*.

4. Cf. Prop. 4, 1, 144. — nunc quoque: this elegy, as well as the rest of Book 1, was written on the journey to Tomi.

5. lux = *dies*. Ovid's description of the last night seems to include that of at least part of the preceding day.

finibus extremae iusserat Ausoniae.
nec spatium fuerat, nec mens satis apta parandi :
    torpuerant longa pectora nostra mora.
non mihi servorum, comites non cura legendi,
10   non aptae profugo vestis opisve fuit.
non aliter stupui, quam qui Iovis ignibus ictus
    vivit et est vitae nescius ipse suae.
ut tamen hanc animi nubem dolor ipse removit,
    ut tandem sensus convaluere mei,
15   adloquor extremum maestos abiturus amicos,
    qui modo de multis unus et alter erant.
uxor amans flentem flens acrius ipsa tenebat,
    imbre per indignas usque cadente genas.
nata procul Libycis aberat diversa sub oris :
20   non poterat fati certior esse mei.
quocumque adspiceres, luctus gemitusque sonabant,

---

6. **finibus extremae . . . Ausoniae** = *finibus extremis Ausoniae.* Residence at Tomi would remove the poet entirely from 'the western land' of promise.

7. **parandi** depends upon **spatium.**

8. **longa . . . mora** : not to be taken absolutely, of course (cf. v. 7) ; but from the time the news of the decree of banishment reached him on the island of Elba till the day of his actual departure from Rome there had been little enough time for actual preparations, but all too much opportunity for brooding over his fate.

9. Note the careless inconsistency of construction, in harmony with the mood of the writer at the time. As the sentence against Ovid was only *relegatio*, he might take with him what or whom he pleased.

13. **animi nubem** : *i.e.* the torpor of v. 8.

15. **extremum** : 'for the last time.'

16. **modo** belongs with **multis** ; cf. Hor. *Car.* 1, 35, 26 : *diffugiunt cadis cum faece siccatis amici, ferre iugum pariter dolosi.*

17. **uxor** : cf. 4, 10, 73, n.

18. **imbre** : cf. Cat. 68, 56, n.

19. **nata** : cf. 4, 10, 75, n. This daughter's second husband was Cornelius Fidus, who was at this time proconsul in Africa.

21. **adspiceres** : cf. H. 602, 3 and 4.

formaque non taciti funeris intus erat.

femina virque meo, pueri quoque, funere maerent:

inque domo lacrimas angulus omnis habet.

25 si licet exemplis in parvo grandibus uti:

haec facies Troiae, cum caperetur, erat.

iamque quiescebant voces hominumque canumque,

Lunaque nocturnos alta regebat equos.

hanc ego suspiciens et ad hanc Capitolia cernens,

30 quae nostro frustra iuncta fuere lari,

'numina vicinis habitantia sedibus,' inquam,

'iamque oculis numquam templa videnda meis,

dique relinquendi, quos urbs habet alta Quirini,

este salutati tempus in omne mihi!

35 et quamquam sero clipeum post vulnera sumo,

attamen hanc odiis exonerate fugam

caelestique viro, quis me deceperit error,

dicite, pro culpa ne scelus esse putet,

ut quod vos scitis, poenae quoque sentiat auctor:

40 placato possum non miser esse deo.'

---

3. 25. parvo **A** parvis **GHPV**.   29. ad hanc **AGHPV** ab hac **ω**.

22. non taciti funeris: cf. Hor. *Sat.* 1, 6, 42: *hic, si plostra ducenta concurrantque foro tria funera magna, sonabit cornua quod vincatque tubas.*

26. Cf. Verg. *Aen.* 2, 486 sqq.: *at domus interior gemitu miseroque tumultu miscetur*, etc.

27. iamque quiescebant: *i.e.* it was bedtime in Rome.

28. equos: Luna drove a *biga*; cf. Preller⁸, Vol. 1, p. 328.

29. ad hanc: 'by her light.' Cf. Verg. *Aen.* 4, 513: *ad lunam quaeruntur . . . herbae.* — **Capi-**

tolia: poetic plural. The poet lived near by.

30. frustra: *i.e.* since their proximity had not saved him from this disaster. — **lari** = *domo*.

33. urbs . . . alta: cf. Verg. *Aen.* 1, 7: *altae moenia Romae.*

35. The proverb means much the same as to "lock the stable door after the horse has been stolen."

37. caelestique viro: an interesting variation on the more familiar *divo Augusto*; cf. v. 40. — **error**: cf. Intr. § 38.

hac prece adoravi superos ego : pluribus uxor,
 singultu medios impediente sonos.
illa etiam ante lares passis adstrata capillis
 contigit extinctos ore tremente focos,
45 multaque in adversos effudit verba penates
 pro deplorato non valitura viro.
iamque morae spatium nox praecipitata negabat,
 versaque ab axe suo Parrhasis Arctos erat.
quid facerem ? blando patriae retinebar amore :
50 ultima sed iussae nox erat illa fugae.
ah ! quotiens aliquo dixi properante 'quid urges ?
 vel quo festinas ire, vel unde, vide ! '
ah ! quotiens certam me sum mentitus habere
 horam, propositae quae foret apta viae.
55 ter limen tetigi, ter sum revocatus, et ipse
 indulgens animo pes mihi tardus erat.
saepe 'vale' dicto rursus sum plura locutus,
 et quasi discedens oscula multa dedi.
saepe eadem mandata dedi meque ipse fefelli,
60 respiciens oculis pignora cara meis.

43. adstrata G attracta HP attacta V intracta A prostrata ω.

42. sonos = *verba*.

44 extinctos . . . focos : a sign
ct mourn᾽ng over the desperate
condition of the family ; cf. Tib.
I, I, 6, n.

45. adversos : 'before her.'

48. Arctos = *Callisto :* cf. Cat.
66, 66, n. The revolution of the
Great Bear is a nightly phenomenon.

51. urges : sc. *me.*

52. quo : *i.e.* Tomi. — festinas :
the subjunctive is more usual in
this form of question ; but vide

may best be considered paratactic.
— unde : *i.e.* Rome ; cf. vv. 61–62.

53. Cf. Tib. I, 3, 16 sqq. —
certam : probably one supposed to
be especially propitious, from astrology or other divination.

55. ter : cf. Tib. I, 3, 11.

56. pes . . . tardus : cf. Tib. I,
3, 20.

59. meque ipse fefelli : 'lost
my self-control.'

60. pignora here seems to include other friends besides his
immediate family.

denique 'quid propero? Scythia est, quo mittimur,'
    inquam :
'Roma relinquenda est. utraque iusta morast.
uxor in aeternum vivo mihi viva negatur,
    et domus et fidae dulcia membra domus,
65 quosque ego dilexi fraterno more sodales,
    o mihi Thesea pectora iuncta fide !
dum licet, amplectar — numquam fortasse licebit
    amplius : in lucro est, quae datur hora mihi.'
nec mora, sermonis verba inperfecta relinquo,
70   conplectens animo proxima quaeque meo.
dum loquor et flemus, caelo nitidissimus alto,
    stella gravis nobis, Lucifer ortus erat.
dividor haud aliter, quam si mea membra relinquam,
    et pars abrumpi corpore visa suost.
75 sic doluit Mettus tunc, cum in contraria versos
    ultores habuit proditionis equos.
tunc vero exoritur clamor gemitusque meorum,
    et feriunt maestae pectora nuda manus.
tunc vero coniunx, umeris abeuntis inhaerens,
80   miscuit haec lacrimis tristia verba suis :
'non potes avelli : simul hinc, simul ibimus' inquit :
    'te sequar et coniunx exulis exul ero.
et mihi facta via est : et me capit ultima terra :
    accedam profugae sarcina parva rati.
85 te iubet a patria discedere Caesaris ira,
    me pietas : pietas haec mihi Caesar erit.'
talia temptabat, sicut temptaverat ante,

62. **mora** : 'cause for delay.'

66. **Thesea . . . fide** : the pro-verbial friendship between Theseus and Pirithous.

68. **in lucro** : 'clear gain.'

75. **Mettus** : Mettius Fufetius, who, for treachery against his Roman allies, was condemned to be torn asunder by two *quadrigae* driven in opposite directions.

vixque dedit victas utilitate manus.
egredior — sive illud erat sine funere ferri —
90   squalidus, inmissis hirta per ora comis.
illa dolore amens tenebris narratur obortis
    semianimis media procubuisse domo:
utque resurrexit foedatis pulvere turpi
    crinibus et gelida membra levavit humo,
95   se modo, desertos modo conplorasse Penates,
    nomen et erepti saepe vocasse viri,
nec gemuisse minus, quam si nataeque meumque
    vidisset structos corpus habere rogos,
et voluisse mori, moriendo ponere sensus,
100   respectuque tamen non voluisse mei.
vivat! et absentem — quoniam sic fata tulerunt —
    vivat ut auxilio sublevet usque suo.

LIBER QVARTVS

10

Ille ego qui fuerim, tenerorum lusor amorum,
    quem legis, ut noris, accipe posteritas.

97. meumque **A** virique **GHV**.

88. **dedit . . . manus**: 'gave in'; a gladiatorial expression; cf. Cic. *De Am.* 99: *ad extremum det manus vincique se patiatur.*

89. **sine funere ferri**: 'my funeral without my corpse,' and of course largely, if not entirely, lacking in mourners.

90. 'In mourning garments, with unkempt hair and unshaven face'; all signs of mourning.

97. **nataeque**: her daughter by a former marriage (cf. 4, 10, 73, n.);

wife of P. Suillius Rufus, a man of good rank and various honors, who subsequently himself suffered banishment.

99. **ponere sensus**: *i.e.* to drown her sorrows.

101. **tulerunt**: 'have decreed.'
102. Cf. 4, 10, 73, n.

4, 10

Autobiography of Ovid. The custom of the Augustan poets was

Sulmo mihi patria est, gelidis uberrimus undis,
    milia qui novies distat ab urbe decem.

5   editus hinc ego sum ; nec non ut tempora noris,
    cum cecidit fato consul uterque pari.

siquid id est, usque a proavis vetus ordinis heres,
    non modo fortunae munere factus eques.

nec stirps prima fui.   genito sum fratre creatus,

10   qui tribus ante quater mensibus ortus erat.

Lucifer amborum natalibus adfuit idem :
    una celebrata est per duo liba dies.

haec est armiferae festis de quinque Minervae,
    quae fieri pugna prima cruenta solet.

15   protinus excolimur teneri, curaque parentis
    imus ad insignes urbis ab arte viros.

---

10. 7. siquid id *vulg.* si quis et *Postgate.*   8. modo *vulg.* sum *Riese.*

to put such poems at the close of some work (cf. *Am.* 3, 15, Intr.). Here Ovid at the end of Bk. 4 of his *Tristia* gives the most complete account of his life, though it is supplemented by many other passages in other *Tristia* and other groups of poems. Written in the spring of the year 11 A.D. at Tomi.

1. **Ille ego**: 'the well-known writer that I am.' — **qui**(= *qualis*) **fuerim**: indirect question. — **tenerorum . . . amorum**: probably intended to include the *Heroides* as well as the three books of the *Amores.* — **lusor**: cf. Cat. 68, 17.

3. **Sulmo**: cf. *Am.* 2, 16, 1, n. — **gelidis . . . undis**: cf. 3, 15, 11.

6. Cf. Tib. 3, 5, 18, n.

7. Cf. *Am.* 3, 15, 5. For a description of the opposite type of equestrian nobility, referred to in verse 8, cf. Hor. *Epod.* 4.

10. Ovid's older brother, Lucius, was exactly a year older than he. He died at the age of twenty (cf. v. 31).

12. **liba**: for the offerings on birthdays cf. Tib. 2, 2, 7-8.

13. **festis de quinque**: sc *diebus.* The festival of Quinquatrus or Quinquatria was sacred to Minerva, and was originally celebrated on the fifth day after the Ides of March. After 168 B.C., however, the original significance of the name being forgotten, the festival was extended to include five days. Ovid was born on the second of these, March 20.

16. Cf. Intr. § 38.

frater ad eloquium viridi tendebat ab aevo,
　　fortia verbosi natus ad arma fori.
at mihi iam puero caelestia sacra placebant,
20　　inque suum furtim Musa trahebat opus.
saepe pater dixit 'studium quid inutile temptas?
　　Maeonides nullas ipse reliquit opes.'
motus eram dictis totoque Helicone relicto
　　scribere conabar verba soluta modis:
25　sponte sua carmen numeros veniebat ad aptos;
　　et quod temptabam dicere, versus erat.
interea tacito passu labentibus annis
　　liberior fratri sumpta mihique togast;
induiturque umeris cum lato purpura clavo:
30　　et studium nobis, quod fuit ante, manet.
iamque decem frater vitae geminaverat annos,
　　cum perit, et coepi parte carere mei.
cepimus et tenerae primos aetatis honores,
　　eque viris quondam pars tribus una fui.

34. eque *vulg.* deque **A.**

17. **eloquium** = *eloquentia*, a variation common after this time.

18. Cf. Prop. 4, 1, 134.

19. **caelestia sacra**: *i.e.* the poetic art.

21. **studium . . . inutile**: poetry was not "practical," as the saying goes to-day of similar pursuits.

22. **Maeonides**: cf. *Am.* 3, 6, 25, n.

23. **Helicone**: the Boeotian mountain recognized as the abode of the Muses.

24. **verba soluta modis**: 'prose.'

27. **labentibus annis**: the date for the assumption of the *toga virilis* was not definitely fixed,

but usually came on the Liberalia (March 17), and not often later than the boy's seventeenth year.

28. **liberior**: since it indicated a greater degree of freedom for the young man.

29. **lato . . . clavo**: instead of the usual *tunica angusticlavia* of the knight. Sons of senators and of noble knights often in the Augustan epoch assumed the *tunica laticlavia* as a token that they were planning a higher official career.

32. Cf. Cat. 68, 22.

34. **viris . . . tribus**: either the *tresviri capitales*, who punished

35   curia restabat : clavi mensura coactast :
        maius erat nostris viribus illud onus.
      nec patiens corpus, nec mens fuit apta labori,
        sollicitaeque fugax ambitionis eram,
      et petere Aoniae suadebant tuta sorores
40   otia, iudicio semper amata meo.
      temporis illius colui fovique poetas,
        quotque aderant vates, rebar adesse deos.
      saepe suas volucres legit mihi grandior aevo,
        quaeque nocet serpens, quae iuvat herba, Macer.
45   saepe suos solitus recitare Propertius ignes,
        iure sodalicii quo mihi iunctus erat.
      Ponticus heroo, Bassus quoque clarus iambis
        dulcia convictus membra fuere mei ;
      et tenuit nostras numerosus Horatius aures,
50   dum ferit Ausonia carmina culta lyra.
      Vergilium vidi tantum ; nec amara Tibullo
        tempus amicitiae fata dedere meae.

44. iuvat *vulg.* iuvet **AH.**   46. quo *vulg.* qui **A.**   51. amara **ω** avara *vulg.*

slaves and criminals of low rank ; or the *tresviri monetales*, who had charge of the coinage. Ovid was also a member of the *decemviri stlitibus iudicandis*, and of the centumviral court ; but he never really entered on the regular senatorial offices, which properly began with the quaestorship.

35. curia : the senate house, to which he would have naturally looked forward, had he chosen to follow the senatorial career. — **clavi mensura coactast** : *i.e.* he was obliged, on giving up the senatorial career, to relinquish also

the senatorial dress (cf. v. 29, n.).

39. Aoniae : Boeotian ; cf. v. 23, n.

43. volucres : the *Ornithogonia* of Aemilius Macer.

44. Other works of Macer were the *Theriaca* (on poisonous creatures) and a poem *De Herbis*.

47. Ponticus heroo : for the epic *Thebais* of Ponticus, cf. Prop. I, 7. — **Bassus** : . . . **iambis** : probably the Bassus referred to in Prop. I, 4.

49. numerosus : 'tuneful.'

51. vidi tantum : Vergil lived at Naples, the latter part of his life.

successor fuit hic tibi, Galle : Propertius illi :
   quartus ab his serie temporis ipse fui.
55 utque ego maiores, sic me coluere minores,
   notaque non tarde facta Thalia meast.
carmina cum primum populo iuvenalia legi,
   barba resecta mihi bisve semelve fuit.
moverat ingenium totam cantata per urbem
60   nomine non vero dicta Corinna mihi.
multa quidem scripsi : sed quae vitiosa putavi,
   emendaturis ignibus ipse dedi.
tunc quoque, cum fugerem, quaedam placitura
     cremavi,
   iratus studio carminibusque meis.
65 molle Cupidineis nec inexpugnabile telis
   cor mihi, quodque levis causa moveret, erat.
cum tamen hic essem minimoque accenderer igni,
   nomine sub nostro fabula nulla fuit.

53. Galle: cf. Intr. § 12.

56. Thalia : 'Muse,' in general ; here for the product of the Muse.

57. The custom of holding readings (*recitationes*) of one's own works before publication, in the presence of a select company of invited guests, was introduced by Asinius Pollio.

58. The first cutting of the youthful beard was a festal occasion ; and the cuttings were offered to divinities (the *depositio barbae*).

60. nomine non vero : her real name is not known, if indeed there was any real person involved. The name may have been easily derived from the Greek name for girl,

κόρη. There was also a Boeotian poetess of the same name.

63. fugerem : of going into banishment ; cf. Tac. *Ann.* 3, 24. — **placitura** : 'which would probably have proved popular.' — **cremavi**: cf. Intr. § 39 ; *Trist.* 1. 7, 15 sqq.

64. iratus : 'grieving for.'

68. fabula : 'gossip.' Ovid's life, he maintains steadfastly, was pure, in spite of the impurity of some of his writings. Cf. *Trist.* 2, 353–354 : *crede mihi, distant mores a carmine nostro : vita verecunda est, musa iocosa mea.* Other Roman writers, *e.g.* Catullus, Martial, and even Pliny the younger, argued similarly.

paene mihi puero nec digna nec utilis uxor
70   est data, quae tempus per breve nupta fuit.

illi successit quamvis sine crimine coniunx,
non tamen in nostro firma futura toro.

ultima, quae mecum seros permansit in annos,
sustinuit coniunx exulis esse viri.

75   filia me mea bis prima fecunda iuventa,
sed non ex uno coniuge, fecit avum.

et iam conplerat genitor sua fata novemque
addiderat lustris altera lustra novem;

non aliter flevi, quam me fleturus ademptum
80   ille fuit.   matri proxima iusta tuli.

felices ambo tempestiveque sepulti,
ante diem poenae quod periere meae!

me quoque felicem, quod non viventibus illis
sum miser, et de me quod doluere nihil!

85   si tamen extinctis aliquid nisi nomina restat,
et gracilis structos effugit umbra rogos:

85. restat *vulg.* restant **AV**.

69. **paene mihi puero**: 'when I
was hardly more than a boy.'   A
Roman boy might marry as early
as the age of fourteen, and a girl
at twelve; but a greater age was
more usual. — **uxor**: one of Ovid's
first two wives came from Falerii,
as we learn from *Am.* 3, 13, 1.
Both were divorced from him.

73. Ovid's third wife proved
faithful and devoted through the
long years of his banishment, and
survived him. She belonged to
the noble family of the Fabii, and
was a widow with one daughter
when married to the poet. He
preferred to have her remain in
Rome, in the hope that she might
exert influence to secure his recall.

75. **filia . . . mea**: by his first
or his second wife. The daughter
was herself twice married.

77. **conplerat . . . sua fata**:
cf. Hom. *Il.* 4, 170: αἴ κε θάνῃς
καὶ πότμον ἀναπλήσῃς βιότοιο

78. Ovid's father died at the
age of ninety.

80. **iusta tuli**: 'paid the last
honors,' like *iusta solvere* and
iusta dare.

82. **poenae**: *i.e.* his *relegatio*.

85. Cf. *Am.* 3, 9, 59, n.

86. **gracilis**: 'substanceless';
cf. Tib. 3, 2, 9.

fama, parentales, si vos mea contigit, umbrae,
    et sunt in Stygio crimina nostra foro :
scite, precor, causam — nec vos mihi fallere fas est —
90   errorem iussae, non scelus, esse fugae.
manibus hoc satis est.   ad vos, studiosa, revertor,
    pectora, qui vitae quaeritis acta meae.
iam mihi canities pulsis melioribus annis
    venerat, antiquas miscueratque comas,
95   postque meos ortus Pisaea vinctus oliva
    abstulerat decies praemia victor equus,
cum maris Euxini positos ad laeva Tomitas
    quaerere me laesi principis ira iubet.
causa meae cunctis nimium quoque nota ruinae
100   indicio non est testificanda meo.
quid referam comitumque nefas famulosque nocentes ?
    ipsa multa tuli non leviora fuga.

96. equus *Bentley* eques *Mss.* equis *Strachan.*

88. Cf. Prop. 4, 11, 19.

90. Cf. Intr. § 38 ; *Trist.* I, 3, 37-38 : *quis me deceperit error, dicite, pro culpa ne scelus esse putet.*

91. studiosa ... pectora : ' eager souls.'

94. antiquas : ' of old age.' — miscueratque : sc. some word for ' with that of youth.' For the position of the enclitic, cf. Tib. 2, 5, 72, n.

95. Pisaea : the Olympic games were celebrated near Pisa in Elis. — vinctus oliva : the victors were crowned with wreaths of olive.

96 The Olympic games were held every four years, *i.e.* after four years ; so Ovid calls it every

fifth year. The *lustrum* was a common five-year period in reckoning, which fostered the confusion. Cf. *Met.* 14, 324-325 : *per annos quinquennem ;* Tac. *Ann.* 14, 20 : *quinquennale certamen.* Ovid was past fifty when banished.

97. positos ad laeva Tomitas : Tomi was on the left side of the Euxine as one passed through the Bosporus.

99. nimium quoque : ' only too well.'

100. Ovid consistently preserves this judicious silence.

101. Cf. *Trist.* I, 5, 63 sqq. ; Hor. *Car.* I, 35, 25.

102. fuga : cf. v. 63.

indignata malis mens est succumbere seque
   praestitit invictam viribus usa suis.
105 oblitusque mei ductaeque per otia vitae
   insolita cepi temporis arma manu
totque tuli casus pelagoque terraque, quot inter
   occultum stellae conspicuumque polum.
tacta mihi tandem longis erroribus acto
110 iuncta pharetratis Sarmatis ora Getis.
hic ego finitimis quamvis circumsoner armis,
   tristia, quo possum, carmine fata levo.
quod quamvis nemo est cuius referatur ad aures,
   sic tamen absumo decipioque diem.
115 ergo quod vivo durisque laboribus obsto,
   nec me sollicitae taedia lucis habent,
gratia, Musa, tibi! nam tu solacia praebes,
   tu curae requies, tu medicina venis.
tu dux et comes es, tu nos abducis ab Histro
120 in medioque mihi das Helicone locum.
tu mihi, quod rarum est, vivo sublime dedisti
   nomen, ab exequiis quod dare fama solet.

106. **temporis arma**: *i.e.* patience and hope.

107. Both sorts of experiences are detailed for the reader here and there in the *Tristia*; cf. 1, 1, 42 sqq.; 1, 2, etc.

108. **occultum . . . conspicuumque**: the north polar star and its neighbors are visible to those dwelling in the northern hemisphere, while those stars near the south pole are invisible; cf. Hyginus, the astronomer, 1, 6: *quod stellae inter polum septentrionalem, qui conspicuus nobis est et meridionalem, qui semper sub horizontem est.*

110. The *Sarmatae* and *Getae*, who dwelt near the Danube, used the bow and arrow as their special weapons in war.

112. For Ovid's achievements at Tomi cf. Intr. § 39.

113. **referatur ad aures**: no *recitationes* of Latin poetry were in vogue at Tomi, and Ovid could only guess what reception his complaints had in Rome.

122. **ab exequiis**: 'only after death'; cf. Prop. 3, 1, 24.

nec qui detrectat praesentia, Livor, iniquo
ullum de nostris dente momordit opus.
125 nam tulerint magnos cum saecula nostra poetas,
non fuit ingenio fama maligna meo,
cumque ego praeponam mihi multos, non minor illis
dicor et in toto plurimus orbe legor.
siquid habent igitur vatum praesagia veri,
130 protinus ut moriar, non ero, terra, tuus.
sive favore tuli, sive hanc ego carmine famam,
iure tibi grates, candide lector, ago.

125. **cum** : concessive.

128. **plurimus** : used adverbially.

130. **ut** : concessive. With the thought of the verse cf. Hor. *Car.* 3, 30, 6 sq.: *non omnis moriar, multaque pars mei vitabit Libitinam.*

131. **carmine** : *i.e.* meritorious poetic achievement as contrasted with mere *favore.*

132. **iure**: *i.e.* I owe them.

INDEX OF FIRST LINES

425

INDEX OF FIRST LINES

GENERAL INDEX

A

ab insidiis, adverbial, Prop. 3, 25, 6

ablative, causal, with *in*, Prop. 3, 2, 2

ablatives, vague, Prop. 3, 1, 34; 3, 18, 9; 4, 11, 96

abstract nouns, plural, Tib. 1, 1, 4

Acastus, Ovid, *Her.* 13, 25

Accius, Ovid, *Am.* 1, 15, 19

accusative, cognate, Prop. 1, 7, 16; 3, 11, 47

of purpose in Propertius, Prop. 1, 7, 6

Achaemenes, Prop. 2, 13, 1

Achaia, Prop. 2, 28, 53

Achilles, Prop. 2, 13, 38; 3, 1, 26; Ovid, *Am.* 3, 9, 1

Acroceraunia, Prop. 1, 8, 19; Ovid, *Am.* 2, 11, 19

acroterium, Prop. 2, 31, 11

Actium, Prop. 4, 6, 15

battle of, Prop. 3, 11, 29 and 67 sqq.; 4, 1, 3; 4, 6, Intr. and 48

ad = apud, Cat. 68, 69

adiuro with accusative, Cat. 66, 40

adjectives in active sense, Tib. 1, 3, 16; 2, 1, 44 and 46

Adonis, Prop. 2, 13, 53

Adriatic, Prop. 3, 21, 17

adverbs, substitutes for, Prop. 4, 1, 120

used adjectivally, Tib. 1, 3, 50; Prop. 1, 1, 2; 1, 22, 2

Aeacus, Prop. 4, 11, 19

Aegean, Prop. 3, 7, 57; 3, 24, 12

Aemilia, a *vestalis maxima*, Prop. 4, 11, 53

Aemilius Paulus, victor at Pydna, Prop. 3, 3, 8

Aeneas, Tib. 2, 5, 19 and 39; Prop. 4, 1, 2 and 44; Ovid, *Am.* 3, 9, 13

shield of, Prop. 4, 6, 27

uetas = senectus, Tib. 1, 1, 71

Aethiopis, Cat. 66, 52

aetiological elegy, Prop. 4, 1, Intr.; 4, 4, Intr.; 4, 6, Intr.

aetiological series planned, Prop. 4, 1, Intr. and 69

Aetna, Cat. 68, 53; Prop. 3, 2, 7

Agamemnon, Prop. 3, 7, 21 sqq.; 4, 6, 33

Aganippe, Prop. 2, 10, 25

Aitia of Callimachus, p. 19

a model for Propertius, p. 20

Ajax Oileus, Prop. 4, 1, 117

Alba Longa, Tib. 1, 7, 57 sq.; 2, 5, 49; Prop. 4, 1, 35; 4, 6, 37

Albunea, Tib. 2, 5, 69 sq.

albus an ater, Cat. 93, 2

Alcinous, Prop. 1, 14, 24; 3, 2, 13

Alcmaeon, Prop. 3, 5, 41

Alexander the Aetolian, p. 20

Alexandria, Prop. 3, 11, 33

Alexandrian elegy, pp. 18 sqq.

aliquis = quisquam, Cat. 73, 2

alliteration, Cat. 76, 20; Tib. 1, 10, 2; Prop. 4, 3, 50

Alps, Ovid, *Am.* 2, 16, 19

Amalthēā, Tib. 2, 5, 67

Amathus, Cat. 68, 51

Amathusia, Ovid, *Am.* 3, 15, 15

Amazons, Prop. 3, 11, 14; 4, 4, 72

Ambarvalia, Tib. 1, 1, 20 and 21; 2, 1, Intr.

ambiguity, Prop. 1, 9, 4 and 13; 3, 4, 7; 3, 11, 37 and 51; 3, 18, 30; 4, 6, 47 and 59

Amor, Tib. 2, 1, 80; Prop. 1, 1, 4; 1, 2, 8; 2, 12, 1

Amores, revision of the, Ovid, *Am. Ep. Ips.*

Amphion, Prop. 1, 9, 10

Amphitryoniades, Cat. 68, 112

Amymone, Prop. 2, 26, 47

Anchises, Tib. 2, 5, 39

Andromede, Prop. 2, 28, 21

429

GENERAL INDEX

animi, pleonastic, Cat. 102, 2

Anio, Prop. 3, 16, 3 sq.

ante . . . donec, Prop. 1, 9, 29

Antilochus, Prop. 2, 13, 49

Antimachus, Cat. 95, 10

Antimachus of Colophon, p. 18
  author of the epic *Thebais*, p. 18
  prototype of Alexandrian elegy, p. 18

Antioch, Prop. 2, 13, 30

Antony, p. 24; Prop. 3, 11, 31

antrum, Prop. 1, 1, 11; 4, 4, 3

Anubis, Prop. 3, 11, 41

Apama, Cat. 66, 27

Apelles, Prop. 1, 2, 22; 3, 9, 11

Aphrodite Anadyomene, Prop. 1, 2, 22

Apis, Tib. 1, 7, 28

Apollo, Tib. 2, 5, 1; Prop. 1, 8b, 41; 2, 31, 5 and 13; 3, 9, 39; 4, 6, 67; Ovid, *Am.* 1, 15, 35; 3, 9, 21
  Citharoedus, Prop. 2, 31, 15; 4, 6, 69
  Leucadian temple of, Prop. 3, 11, 69
  Lycian, Prop. 3, 1, 38
  Palatine temple of, Prop. 2, 31, Intr.

Appendix Vergiliana, p. 28

Aqua Marcia, Prop. 3, 2, 14

Aquarius, Cat. 66, 94

Aquilo, Prop. 3, 7, 13 and 71

Aquitanian campaign of Tibullus, p. 34, n. 1; Tib. 1, 7, Intr.

Arabes, Tib. 3, 2, 24

Arabia, Prop. 2, 10, 16

Arabs, Tib. 4, 2, 18

Arar, Tib. 1, 7, 11

Aratus, Ovid, *Am.* 1, 15, 16

Araxes, Prop. 4, 3, 35

archaisms, Cat. 84, 9

archers, the typical, Tib. 2, 5, 105

Archilochus, p. 16

Archytas, Prop. 4, 1, 77

Arctos (Callisto), Ovid, *Trist.* 1, 3, 48

Arellius Fuscus, p. 55

Arethusa, Prop. 4, 3, Intr.

Arethusa and Lycotas, p. 57

Argo, Prop. 2, 26, 39; Ovid, *Am.* 2, 11, 1

Argynnus, Prop. 3, 7, 22

Ariadne, Cat. 66, 60; Prop. 4, 4, 41

Arion, Prop. 2, 26, 18

Aristaeus, p. 24

Aristotle, p. 18

Armeniae tigres, Prop. 1, 9, 19

Arrius, p. 25; Cat. 84, *passim*

Arsinoë, Cat. 66, 54

Ascanius, Tib. 2, 5, 49

Ascra, Prop. 2, 10, 25

Asinius Pollio, Tib. 1, 1, 53; Ovid, *Trist.* 4, 10, 57

aspirate in Latin, Cat. 84, Intr.

Assisi, Prop. 1, 22, 9; 4, 1, 124 sq.

assonance, Tib. 1, 10, 2

Assyria, Tib. 3, 2, 24

Assyrius = Syrius, Cat. 66, 12; Tib. 1, 3, 7

astrology, Prop. 1, 6, 36; 2, 27, 3; 4, 1, 83

at, Tib. 1, 3, 63

at = ac, Tib. 1, 3, 87

Atalanta of Arcadia, Prop. 1, 1, 10

Atax, Tib. 1, 7, 4

Athamanes, Prop. 4, 6, 15

Athena's eyes, Prop. 2, 28, 12

Athens, Prop. 1, 6, 13; 3, 21, 1

Athos, Cat. 66, 43

atque, adversative, Prop. 1, 9, 8; 2, 13, 43

Atrax, Prop. 1, 8, 25

Atrides, Prop. 3, 18, 30

Attalus, Prop. 2, 13, 22

attitude in prayer, Cat. 66, 10

audit = dicitur, Cat. 68, 112

augury, Roman, Tib. 2, 5, 11

Augustus, Prop. 2, 10, 15 and 17; 2, 31. 2; 4, 6, 23
  diplomacy of, Prop. 3, 4, 1
  Princeps, Prop. 3, 11, 55
  worship of, Prop. 3, 4, 1

Aulis, Prop. 4, 1, 109

Aurora, Tib. 1, 3, 93

autobiographies of the poets, Prop. 1, 22, Intr.; Ovid, *Trist.* 4, 10, Intr.

Aventine, Prop. 4, 1, 50

Avernus, Prop. 3, 18, 1; Ovid, *Am.* 3, 9, 27

"Ayenbite of Inwyt," Prop. 3, 3, 4

B

Babylon, walls of, Prop. 3, 11, 23

Bacchus, Tib. 2, 1, Intr.; 2, 1, 3 and 55; Ovid, *Am.* 1, 3, 11
  effeminate garb of, Tib. 1, 7, 46
  festival processions of, Tib. 1, 7, 48

Mors, Tib. 1, 1, 70; 1, 3, 4
Moschus, Prop. 2, 12, Intr. and 6
mourning, tokens of, Ovid, *Trist.* 1, 3, 90
mulier, Cat. 70, 1; Prop. 3, 24, 1
Muses, Prop. 3, 1, 17 and 19; Ovid, *Am.*
    1, 3, 11
    unrestricted functions of the, Prop. 3, 2,
    16; 4, 6, 12
Myron, Prop. 2, 31, 7
Myrrha, Cat. 95, 1
Mys, Prop. 3, 9, 14
Mystes, p. 23

N

nam = etenim, Prop. 4, 3, 51
nam elliptical, Tib. 1, 1, 11
namque elliptical, Cat. 99, 3
Nanno, p. 17
    model for Propertius, p. 17
Naso, Ovid, *Am. Ep. Ips.*
    L. Ovidius, brother of Publius, Ovid,
    Trist. 4, 10, 10
Natalis, Tib. 2, 2, 1
nature, Roman lack of appreciation of,
    Ovid, *Am.* 2, 16, 19
Nauplius, Prop. 4, 1, 115
navigation, beginnings of, Prop. 1, 17, 14
Neaera, p. 36; Tib. 3, 2, 12
Nemesis, mistress of Tibullus, p. 35;
    Tib. 2, 5, 109 sqq.; Ovid, *Am.* 3,
    9, 31 and 53
    the sister of, Tib. 2, 6, Intr.
Nemesis (*Rhamnusia virgo*), Cat. 66, 71
Neptune, Prop. 2, 26, 9 and 46; 3, 7, 15
    and 62; 3, 9, 39; Ovid, *Her.* 13,
    129
Nereids, Prop. 1, 17, 25; 3, 7, 67; Ovid,
    Am. 2, 11, 35 sq.
Nereus, Ovid, *Am.* 2, 11, 36 and 39
Nesaee, Prop. 2, 26, 16
Nestor, Prop. 2, 13, 46
Neuricus, Prop. 4, 3, 8
New Year's in Rome, Tib. 4, 2, Intr.
Nicopolis, Prop. 4, 6, 18
Nike of Samothrace, Tib. 2, 5, 45
Nile, Tib. 1, 7, 22 sqq.; Prop. 2, 28, 18;
    3, 11, 42
Ninus, Prop. 3, 11, 26
Nireus, Prop. 3, 18, 27
non . . . aut, Prop. 2, 13, 50

Nonnus, Prop. 3, 2, 8
non . . . utriusque = neutriusque, Cat. 68,
    39
novissima verba, Cat. 101, 10
Nox, Tib. 2, 1, 87
Numa, Ovid, *Am.* 2, 17, 18
Numantia, Prop. 4, 11, 30
Numicius, Tib. 2, 5, 43
Numidian marble, Prop. 2, 31, 1
nunc = νῦν δέ, Cat. 66, 79
Nux, p. 58

O

Oarion, Cat. 66, 94
oaths, formula in, Prop. 4, 11, 27
oblitus (pass.), Prop. 1, 19, 6
Oceanus, Tib. 2, 5, 60
Ocnus, Prop. 4, 3, 21
Octavia, Prop. 3, 18, 12
Octavian as *princeps*, Prop. 4, 6, 46
'October horse,' Prop. 4, 1, 20
odorifer, Prop. 2, 13, 23
Odysseus, Ovid, *Am.* 2, 17, 15
Odyssey, Ovid, *Am.* 3, 9, 30
Oeta, Cat. 68, 54; Prop. 3, 1, 32
Olympia, Zeus statue at, Prop. 3, 9, 15
Olympic games, Prop. 3, 9, 17; Ovid,
    Trist. 4, 10, 95
omens, Prop. 4, 3, 60
    triple, most perfect, Prop. 4, 6, 30
Omphălē, Prop. 3, 11, 17
onomatopoeia, Tib. 2, 5, 94
onyx, Cat. 66, 82
Orcus, Tib. 3, 3, 38
Orestes, Ovid, *Am.* 2, 6, 15
Oricum, Prop. 1, 8, 20; 3, 7, 49
Orion, Prop. 2, 26, 56
Orithyia, Prop. 2, 26, 51; 3, 7, 13
Ormes, Prop. 3, 11, 26
Oromedon, Prop. 3, 9, 48
Orontes, Prop. 1, 2, 3
Orpheus, Prop. 2, 13, 8; 3, 2, 3; Ovid,
    Am. 2, 11, 32; 3, 9, 21
Ortalus, Cat. 65, Intr.
Ortygia, Prop. 2, 31, 10
Osiris, Tib. 1, 7, 27 sqq.
ossilegium, Tib. 1, 3, 6; 3, 2, 9 sqq.
Ostia, Prop. 1, 8, 11
Ovid, pp. 55 sqq.
    Amores, pp. 56, 58

439

GENERAL INDEX

Persians, Prop. 3, 11, 21
personal pronouns, liberal use of, in Tib., Tib. 1, 1, 5
Perusina . . . sepulcra, Prop. 1, 22, 3
Petronius in Ethiopia, Prop. 4, 6, 78
Phaeacia, Tib. 1, 3, 3
Phanocles, p. 19
Pharos, Tib. 1, 3, 32; Prop. 3, 7, 5
Pheneus, Cat. 68, 109
Phidias, Prop. 3, 9, 15
Philetas, p. 19; Prop. 3, 1, 1; 3, 9, 44; 4, 6, 3
Philip of Macedon, Prop. 3, 11, 40
Philitas (?), p. 19, n. 1; Prop. 4, 6, 3
Philomela, Cat. 65, 14; Ovid, *Am.* 2, 6, 7
Phlegraean plains, Prop. 3, 9, 48; 3, 11, 37; 3, 18, 5
Phocylides, p. 17
Phoebe, Prop. 1, 2, 15
Phoebus, Tib. 4, 2, 22; 4, 4, 2; 4, 4, 3 and 19; Prop. 4, 6, 27; Ovid, *Am.* 1, 1, 11
Phoenix, Ovid, *Am.* 2, 6, 54
Phraates, Prop. 3, 4, 1
Phylace, Ovid, *Her.* 13, 35
Phylacides, Prop. 1, 19, 7
Phyto, Tib. 2, 5, 68
Pieria, Prop. 2, 13, 5
Pierian springs, Ovid, *Am.* 3, 9, 26
Pierides, Tib. 4, 2, 21; Ovid, *Am.* 1, 1, 6
Pindus, Prop. 3, 5, 33
Piraeus, Prop. 3, 21, 23 sq.
Pirithous, Ovid, *Trist.* 1, 3, 66
Pisa, Ovid, *Trist.* 4, 10, 95
"pitcher kiss," Tib. 2, 5, 92
Pitys, Prop. 1, 18, 20
planetarium, Prop. 4, 1, 76
Plato, p. 18; Prop. 3, 21, 25
Pleiades, Prop. 1, 8, 10; 3, 5, 36
Pliny as an elegist, pp. 18, 22
plow, Tib. 2, 1, 6
  invention of, Tib. 1, 7, 29
pluperfect for imperfect, Prop. 2, 13, 38
Pluto, Prop. 2, 28, 47; 4, 11, 5 and 18
poetic geography, Cat. 66, 36
poetic plural, Tib. 1, 3, 13
Pollio, Asinius, p. 24
Pollux, Cat. 68, 65
Polydamas, Prop. 3, 1, 29
Polygnotus, Prop. 4, 3, 21
Polynices, Prop. 1, 7, 2

Polyphemus, Prop. 3, 2, 7
polysyllabic endings in the hexameter p. 63
Polyxena, Prop. 2, 13, 38
Pomona, Tib. 1, 1, 14
Pompey, Prop. 3, 11, 35, 38 and 68
pomum = pomus, Tib. 1, 1, 8
Ponticus, pp. 45, 55; Prop. 1, 7, 1; Ovid, *Trist.* 4, 10, 47
popae, garments of the, Prop. 4, 3, 62
Porcius Latro, p. 55
Porcius Licinus, p. 22
Porticus Octaviae, Prop. 3, 18, 14
Poseidippus, p. 20
postilla, Cat. 84, 9
post modo, original meaning of, Tib. 2, 5, 102
pote, Prop. 3, 7, 10
potis est, Cat. 72, 7
praetexta of childhood, Prop. 4, 11, 33
Praxiteles, Prop. 3, 9, 16
precor with inf., Tib. 2, 5, 3
Priam, Prop. 2, 28, 54
Priapea by Tibullus (?), p. 38
Priapus, Tib. 1, 1, 17 sq.
Procne, Cat. 65, 14
Prometheus, Prop. 1, 12, 10; 3, 5, 7 sq.; Ovid, *Am.* 2, 16, 40
propempticon, Ovid, *Am.* 2, 11, Intr.
proper names, short forms of, Prop. 3, 3, 7
Propertius, p. 43 sqq.; Prop. 1, 22; 3, 3, 17; Ovid, *Trist.* 4, 10, 45
  abruptness in, Prop. 3, 7, 1 and 43
  adulation in, Prop. 3, 9, 55
  birth and early life, p. 43 sq.
  character, p. 49
  chronology of the poems, p. 49
  connected elegies in, Prop. 3, 5, Intr.
  debt to Callimachus, p. 20
  division of the elegies into books, p 48
  editions, p. 54
  estrangement for a year from Cynthia, Prop. 3, 16, 9
  friends, p. 45
  Horace and, p. 45
  Maecenas and, p. 45
  manuscripts of, p. 52
  spontaneous sympathy in, Prop. 3, 7, Intr.

440